BOOKS BY ELIZABETH DREW

Washington Journal: The Events of 1973–1974

American Journal: The Events of 1976

AMERICAN JOURNAL

AMERICAN JOURNAL

The Events of 1976

ELIZABETH DREW

RANDOM HOUSE   NEW YORK

Library of Congress Cataloging in Publication Data
Drew, Elizabeth.
American journal.
"Most of the material . . . appeared originally in
the New Yorker."
1. Presidents—United States—Election—1976.
2. United States—Politics and government—1974–
1977.   I. Title.
E868.D73   329'.023'730925   77-5983
ISBN 0-394-40867-5

Most of the material in this book appeared originally in *The New Yorker,*
in slightly different form.

Manufactured in the United States of America

9 8 7 6 5 4 3 2

First Edition

For William Shawn

CONTENTS

INTRODUCTION

In 1976, I was assigned by *The New Yorker* to keep a journal of the events of the year. The assumption on which William Shawn, the editor, and I proceeded was that the period would be a significant one for a number of reasons. Among these was that the country would be electing a President against the background of a particularly large number of great questions, national and international, that were unresolved. It was almost as if every important question was up in the air, and, as if the country was, in its Bicentennial Year, at some momentous turning point. Beyond this, there were questions about the very way we go about choosing our President, about the strange and brutal process that we put our potential leaders through. It is a process from which few human beings could emerge whole—and some do not. I wanted to learn more about *Homo candidatus*—about what happens to the people who run for our highest office. I wanted to describe how it looked and felt as the year's events took place, to watch closely the many people involved, to try to understand the process—the grand strategies, the tactics, the fumbling and confusions, the absurd details that people struggling for the ultimate power feel they must attend to, the various ambitions that fuel a campaign and the various calculations that must be made.

In addition to travelling and talking with the candidates and their staffs, I tried to place the campaign in the context of the other large questions that were before us. From time to time, I would simply talk with someone who I thought was particularly wise about those questions and about the period we were going through. Inevitably, as the election itself neared, such questions tended to recede further and further from our consciousness. What was right in front of us became reality, and the difficult matters that would confront the next leader seemed to fade. It was as if the world stopped while we went through the process of choosing a President.

In my journal, I recorded as many of these things as I could. Essentially, what I set down was my impressions of the events of 1976.

April 1, 1977   —E. D.

WINTER

1

A NUMBER OF THINGS set this year apart from any other year in our history. It is our Bicentennial Year, and we don't seem to know how to celebrate it. There is a vague feeling that the merchandisers have already made off with the occasion, and that the orators will bore us to death with it. The celebration is so diffuse, so all around us, that it seems not to be there at all. And there is also an uneasiness about celebrating. Our history began so grandly, and it doesn't seem so grand anymore. We seem to have been more confident two hundred years ago. The world was newly minted then. Now it is older, and complex almost beyond comprehension.

This is the year of our first Presidential election after Vietnam, our most shattering failure in foreign affairs. Ever since the nation began, we had thought we had a mission: first as an example, the "city upon a hill"; then as the vessel of Manifest Destiny; then to "make the world safe for democracy"; and, since Pearl Harbor, to "keep the peace," protect "the free world," halt aggressors. Vietnam left us without any sense of what our role in the world should be.

This is the year of our first Presidential election since Watergate, which shook our confidence. We had had a kind of faith that we would never elect a really bad man as President—an incompetent or a fraud, perhaps, but not a man who would preside over criminal activities and seek to take away our liberties. We had a deep, unexamined confidence in the electoral system. The system was messy, but we had come to depend on it to keep us well within the range of safety. And then it didn't.

This is a time when, as someone here put it recently, "nothing important is resolved." It's a period of waiting—for what, no one knows. In the background are big and perplexing questions. Among the important things that are unresolved are: our future role in the world; the historic stirring of the developing nations; how to deal with new forms of international power as well as with the spread of nuclear weapons; the nuclear predicament that the

United States and the Soviet Union find themselves in; the sale of arms to the smaller nations; the world's burgeoning population; the threat of widespread food shortages; the continuing energy problem; the threatening scarcity of other natural resources; the federal government's proper role and its effectiveness in carrying out that role; the proper relationship between the executive and the legislative branches of the government; the inflationary-recessionary economy; the excesses, at home and abroad, of our secret intelligence-gathering agencies; the continuing social and economic plight of the country's black people; the crisis of the cities; the increasing number of ecological problems. In the foreground, campaigning in a style and with words that mostly seem disconnected from the big questions, and engaged in a process that itself raises a number of questions, are the candidates for the Presidency of the United States. As a reporter based in Washington, I plan to keep a journal in order to record something of what happens in this unusual political year.

Last night, the crowds gathered once more in Times Square—this time in a chilly rain—to cheer in the New Year. At the Waldorf-Astoria, shortly after 1976 began, Guy Lombardo led merrymakers in singing "Happy Birthday, America." In Philadelphia, some forty thousand people gathered to watch the Liberty Bell being moved, at midnight, from Independence Hall to a large building nearby where it could be viewed by expected crowds of Bicentennial tourists. An "official" Bicentennial celebration took place today: the Rose Bowl parade, with Kate Smith as the grand marshal.

JANUARY 2

Today, in what seemed like the beginning of a Monopoly game, eleven candidates for the Presidency were given checks from the United States Treasury for federal funds—matching private contributions—for their campaigns. These were the first federal contributions to Presidential campaigns in the history of the country. They came about as a result of the campaign-reform law passed in 1974, which is now under review by the Supreme Court.

The Democratic Presidential candidates who received matching money today were Senator Birch Bayh, of Indiana, who made a brief race for the Presidency in the 1972 campaign; Senator Lloyd Bentsen, the conservative from Texas; Jimmy Carter, the former governor of Georgia; Fred Harris, the former senator from Oklahoma, who also made a brief race four years ago; Senator Henry Jackson, from Washington, who ran poorly in 1972; Terry Sanford, the former governor of North Carolina, who also ran in 1972; Sargent Shriver, the brother-in-law of the Kennedys, who wound up as George McGovern's running mate in 1972; Morris Udall, the representative from Arizona; and George Wallace, the governor of Alabama. Milton Shapp, the governor of Pennsylvania, was the only announced Democratic candidate not to qualify yet for matching funds. The Republican candidates—President Ford and Ronald Reagan, the former governor of California—also received federal checks for their campaigns.

JANUARY 11

Sunday. Seven of the eleven declared Democratic candidates are in Iowa, where the first precinct caucuses will take place a week from tomorrow. The Iowa precinct caucuses—the first selection process of the year—have become the new New Hampshire. Caucuses have received increasing attention from politicians and the press ever since Barry Goldwater, in 1964, used caucuses to sneak up on the Republican Party (and the press). In 1972, George McGovern used them to help him get his nomination. Moreover, that year a new set of Democratic reform rules opened the Party caucuses to all Democrats who cared to take the trouble to participate. In May, forty-seven of the Democratic National Convention's three thousand and eight delegates will be chosen by the Iowa Democratic state convention. The precinct caucuses are the first step toward that end. Only about thirty-five thousand Democrats are expected to vote in the Iowa caucuses next week, but, as with New Hampshire, politicians and the press have already given what happens in Iowa a great deal of importance. And, in the symbiosis that will link the candidates and the press throughout this election year, many representatives of each are out in Iowa. For the candidates, a win in Iowa, or even a strong showing, will provide the increased press coverage that those now dwelling in crowded obscurity need. It will provide what is commonly referred to as momentum. The candidate who looks like a "winner" will get more money and other forms of help.

One's "winnerness" may be more important in this process than what one stands for. And, as usual, there will be a consensus on who's ahead. The electoral process does not seem to permit an absence of consensus. People have to be told what is going on, even if nobody knows. The consensus today—that is, the prevailing opinion among politicians and members of the press, who constantly talk to one another—is that Jimmy Carter is doing especially well in Iowa, and that either he or Birch Bayh will win there. (Carter has been organizing there for almost a year.) A story by R. W. Apple, Jr., in the *Times* last October saying that Carter was doing well in Iowa was itself a political event, prompting other newspaper stories that Carter was doing well in Iowa, and then more news-magazine and television coverage for Carter than might otherwise have been his share. This consensus helps Carter do even better—not only in Iowa but in other states, too. Perhaps he is qualified for the Presidency, but as of now there is no way of knowing. His ability to organize in Iowa and his attractive looks do not tell us that.

Today, in freezing weather, several of the Democratic candidates travelled all around Iowa—from Des Moines, where some of them appeared on *Meet the Press,* to Sioux City, to Dubuque. On *Meet the Press,* the candidates (Bayh, Carter, Harris, and Shapp) came off as answer men. They had answers to questions, or if they did not they improvised, all the while projecting images of likableness and sincerity. There was no way to detect how much thought lay behind the answers. It was perhaps revealing that the first two respondents, Bayh and Carter, when they were asked how they felt they differed from Hubert Humphrey, cast the answer not in terms of philosophical or policy differences but in terms of how they felt they were doing as against how Humphrey was doing in the race for the nomination.

This week, the television news showed Reagan throwing snowballs in New Hampshire. We also saw President Ford visiting his campaign headquarters in Washington, where he pledged that he would work "twenty-four hours a day to have a program that you can go out and sell."

JANUARY 15

It has been announced that Secretary of State Henry Kissinger will go to Moscow next week to seek further agreement to limit nuclear weapons. There is some question whether the two nations can reach a new SALT (Strategic Arms Limitation Talks) agreement—or, in the case of the United States, want to do so. Any agreement is destined for the crossfire of election-year politics.

Kissinger's announced trip is itself being criticized by some people for coming at a time when the United States and the Soviet Union—in a disturbing revival of the action-reaction phenomenon —are backing opposite factions in Angola. Oddly, some of the criticism is being voiced by those who do not think we should be involved in Angola, but most of it is being voiced by those in the Republican Party who, along with Senator Henry Jackson, are openly skeptical of détente. Kissinger argues that issues like Angola must not interfere with the pursuit of détente—generally described as a relaxation of tensions between the two great powers. The debate over arms limitations and détente misses a larger point. The old, familiar, bipolar Cold War rivalry has given way to something infinitely more complicated and dangerous. But our politics and our policymaking have not yet caught up with that.

The New York *Times* reports today that both the United States and the Soviet Union are employing new methods in trying to discover a source of unlimited energy in a nuclear-fusion process similar to that which powers the sun.

JANUARY 16

Gerald Parsky, an Assistant Secretary of the Treasury, speaking in San Francisco yesterday, announced that the United States would not sign an international agreement to support world prices of cocoa. The speech was part of a running dispute between Kissinger, who has recently begun to espouse such agreements as a method of propitiating the interests of the increasingly restive—and increasingly powerful—developing nations, and Treasury Secretary William Simon, who objects to interference in matters involving free-market principles. While there had been a concurrence within the government not to sign the agreement in question, Parsky annoyed people in the State Department by enunciating a general policy. Parsky said that the United States must not "sacrifice economic principles for the sake of political gains." The bureaucratic contretemps was symptomatic of a deep confusion about how to construct a foreign policy—including a foreign economic policy— for a rapidly changing world. The success of the Organization of Petroleum Exporting Countries in taking collective action to use a commodity as an economic and political weapon encouraged other nations to turn their natural resources to their own greater advantage. (Meanwhile, our dependence on OPEC for oil has been increasing.) Power politics had moved into the economic arena, and been transformed. To have bauxite is to have power; to be a nation of dark-skinned people who share grievances with other nations of non-whites against nations of whites is to have power. To be one of the most powerfully armed nations on the globe is not necessarily to have power. The most powerful weapons cannot be used without unacceptable risk. Moreover, several other nations now have nuclear weapons, or the potential to make them. Helping the developing nations has become a matter not just of morality but also of exigency. In a speech delivered to the United Nations last September by Ambassador Daniel Patrick Moynihan, Kissinger proposed a number of steps to bolster the economic security of developing nations. A fundamental question surrounds these and other international issues: To what degree can any nation be expected to subordinate what is thought to be its short-term self-interest to longer-range balance, or even harmony? This is not a new question.

JANUARY 19

Monday. Congress reconvenes today, and tonight the President will deliver his State of the Union Address. Also, the Iowa precinct caucuses will be held today. This morning, in Room 3302 of the Dirksen Senate Office Building, David Lilienthal is testifying before the Senate Government Operations Committee, which is holding hearings on nuclear proliferation. John Glenn, the former astronaut, who is now the junior senator from Ohio, is in the chair. Glenn, wearing glasses rimmed in gold wire, looks like a slightly mod businessman. The committee has before it a bill to reorganize the procedures whereby the government approves the sale by private firms of nuclear reactors to foreign countries. Interest in greater control over the sale of nuclear reactors grew after President Nixon went to the Middle East in the summer of 1974 and, as souvenirs of his visit, offered to sell Egypt and Israel nuclear reactors and fuel. At the time, Kissinger said that the reactors would be sold under what he termed "agreed safeguards," to prevent them from being converted to military uses. But there is some question whether ultimate "safeguards" exist. Concern over proliferation continued to grow with the increasing incidence, and sophistication, of international terrorism. There was concern not only about the possibility of terrorists' stealing the makings of a nuclear weapon—however complicated and difficult to detonate—but also about the fact that some terrorist movements have connections with governments that have the capability for developing a nuclear bomb. As of now, five countries—France, Great Britain, China, the U.S.S.R., and the United States—have nuclear weapons, and a sixth, India, has already detonated a nuclear device. According to government experts, other countries have the capability for developing a nuclear bomb: Argentina, Australia, Austria, Belgium, Canada, Czechoslovakia, Denmark, Finland, East Germany, West Germany, Israel, Italy, Japan, Mexico, the Netherlands, New Zealand, Norway, Pakistan, Portugal, South Africa, Spain, Sweden, Switzerland, Turkey, and Venezuela. They add that South Korea and Brazil will have a nuclear capability soon, and there may be others that we don't know about. Compared to the present, there was a kind of stability, unpleasant as the situation was, when the United States and the Soviet Union maintained hegemony over most of the globe. Then there were two scorpions in the bottle. Now there are many scorpions.

Within the United States, pressure for the overseas sale of nuclear reactors grew as the market for them within the United States failed to reach expectations—because of opposition to nuclear power plants. Nuclear energy was neither as technically attractive nor as politically acceptable as had once been hoped. Yet large American companies, including General Electric and Westinghouse, had made large investments in the nuclear-reactor business. Major oil companies were in the business of fabricating nuclear fuel. Within the United States government, the Energy Research and Development Administration, established in 1975, took up where the Atomic Energy Commission, which it replaced, left off in promoting the development of the domestic nuclear industry. The worldwide nuclear industry is estimated to be on the scale of about one hundred billion dollars—and the grim reality is that no one knows how to call the whole thing off.

Lilienthal, a gray-haired, grandfatherly-looking man, who was the chairman of the Tennessee Valley Authority and then, under President Harry Truman, the first chairman of the Atomic Energy Commission, reads a prepared statement to the committee. "The tragic fact is," he says, "that the atomic-arms race is today proceeding at a more furious and a more insane pace than ever." He goes on, "Proliferation of capabilities to produce nuclear weapons of mass destruction is reaching terrifying proportions.' And he tells the committee, "I have not abandoned hope that truly effective international nuclear control and development will one day come to pass." Then he suggests that the committee call upon the President and the Congress "to order a complete stop to the export of all nuclear devices and all nuclear material, that it be done now, and done unilaterally." He continues, "Further, unilaterally, the United States should without delay proceed by lawful means to revoke existing American licenses and put an end to the future or pending licensing to foreign firms and governments of American know-how and facilities paid for and created by American taxpayers' funds and American brains." While a unilateral cessation of the export of nuclear reactors will not put an end to proliferation, Lilienthal says, "The fact is that we, the United States, our public agencies and our private manufacturers, have been and are the world's major proliferators." Lilienthal goes on to say, "What we do on our own others may not follow. They will criticize us, but they will not lightly disregard American leadership. . . . I suggest we should not be overly impressed by the morally indefensible doctrine that if our manufacturers do not continue to sell these potentially deadly materials and this technology, the manufacturers of other foreign countries will do so. I think most private citizens of this country would be shocked and indignant if they realized the extent to which the United States has been putting into the hands of our own commercial interests and of foreign countries quantities of bomb material."

Shortly after eleven, in the lobby of the East Front of the Capitol, there is a celebration of the opening of the Congress in the Bicentennial Year. Under the sponsorship of the Joint Committee on Arrangements for Commemoration of the Bicentennial, Carl Albert, the Speaker of the House, is to open a safe that has been sitting around the Capitol since 1877. The safe, according to a press release issued by the Joint Committee, is there because "one hundred years ago, an enterprising and forward-looking New York publisher, Mrs. Charles F. Deihm, had an idea: to create a depository of materials gathered at the time of the United States Centennial celebration that could be unveiled 100 years later." Visitors to the Centennial Exposition in Philadelphia autographed albums that are contained in the safe. Also, according to the release, Mrs. Deihm "toured the country to gather photographs and autographs of distinguished political and business leaders, orators, clergymen, and poets," and "these were placed inside the safe along with, among other items, the 'Blue Book' containing 800,000 names of government employees; a book on temperance; a photograph of Mrs. Deihm; and a silver inkstand lined in gold with two pens of gold and pearl used to autograph the books."

Members of the Joint Committee stand on a platform at one end of the lobby. Nearby is a souvenir stand, where silver replicas of Richard Nixon's 1968 Inaugural Medal are on sale for a hundred and twenty-five dollars apiece. Representative Lindy Boggs, chairman of the Joint Committee, opens the ceremonies, saying, "Happy birthday, America." The Senate and House chaplains say prayers. A few onlookers are here, including some members of Congress. John Warner, the administrator of the American Revolution Bicentennial Administration, presents Bicentennial flags to Senator Mark Hatfield, who is representing Vice-President Nelson Rockefeller, the President of the Senate, and to Carl Albert. Warner says that some eight thousand Bicentennial flags are flying throughout the country. "I can believe that," says a member of the House who is standing behind me. "I've been handing them out right and left." Albert, who is a bit hoarse, makes a speech. "We meet today under very inspiring circumstances," he says. He quotes George Washington. Finally, the safe—a big black-lacquered iron box with two large doors—is opened. Inside one of the doors of the safe there is printed in gilt paint "It is the wish of Mrs. Deihm that this safe may remain closed until July 4, 1976." So the interior will not be opened until then.

This afternoon, I met David Lilienthal in the Senators' Dining Room in the Capitol. Over coffee, Lilienthal said that he has decided to devote much of his time to working against nuclear proliferation, and explained why. "We are entering a whole new era of life," he said. "We had all these theoretical physicists who didn't know what the hell they were doing when they were tampering with God. And now it's back to the politicians, who have to answer to the people. The question is how people can take the strain of having the whole world pointing atomic weapons at each other. That's the long and the short of the situation we're in. Several years ago, when I spoke out against this goddam thing, you had Glenn Seaborg"—a former chairman of the A.E.C.—"saying that if we didn't push these reactors someone else would. That was the thinnest moral line you could take. It's an extreme case, but a classic case, of the conflict surrounding all technology—since the Luddites and the mowing machine. There are two sides of technological knowledge—good and evil. I'm concerned about the extraordinary power of these weapons and the strain that they impose on humanity. I've been lying low for some time about this, figuring that people who know the most about it would come forward and lay out the facts. They haven't. They've covered it with a lot of goo. The technology people seem tired. I've given up on that hope. So I figured it's time for a private citizen with nothing to lose to speak out. The only people who can clarify the situation and take it to their home towns are the politicians. They were elected. There's a mystical relationship. They weren't appointed, and they aren't there by contract. When it comes to this deadly technology, we follow people who are mad, because people who are sane and understand the democratic process haven't taken charge."

I asked Lilienthal who has been propelling the spread of nuclear technology.

"There has been a commendable, praiseworthy feeling among scientists that since science is universal and at some point all things become known to all people, we should extend our knowledge to all countries, and they to us," he replied. "Then some public-relations character came up with a slogan that Dwight Eisenhower and Lewis Strauss"—another former chairman of the A.E.C.—"grabbed in 1953: 'Atoms for Peace.' The first part of the 'Atoms for Peace' was great. Scientists met at Geneva, and it was very stimulating. But right afterward the troubles began. At first, there was an exchange of information about the medical use of isotopes, the agricultural use of tracers, the physical properties of matter. All these things I worship: the extension of the mind into new realms—Newton, Magellan. Then they started sending things—devices, fuels—instead of ideas, and these became a major export."

I asked Lilienthal how he assessed the danger resulting from the spread of nuclear technology.

He replied, "We have the danger of a world where these weapons are ideally, from a military point of view, suited for surprise, and have the capability of maximum destruction without any warning. They are weapons against which there is no defense. When I first met this monster, in 1945, the idea of surprise attack was inherited from standard military concepts. If you have the potential of surprise attack from twenty sources, as a result of the replication—that's a better word than 'proliferation'—it's a nightmare. The heartache I have about this comes from trying to put myself in the position of my three grandsons. There they are, looking forward, with that wonderful fresh look. And then five years from now, if we don't make some headway on this, we're going to have a terrible period. What I'm proposing is tough stuff, but there's too much at stake. Suppose you have a little old country that needs to do something prominent, and the people in power feel they are threatened. The present methods of safeguarding can do nothing in a situation of that kind. Multiply that by the situations of economic and political instability . . ." He did not finish the sentence.

With Congress opening, with a political year upon us, and with the President about to attempt to set the agenda in his State of the Union and Budget Messages, I decided to talk today with some Democrats, to see what they thought about the state of the country and of politics.

I talked with Senator Walter Mondale, Democrat of Minnesota, in his office in the Russell Senate Office Building.

"I think maybe the Democrats can get back on the offensive on the issues of the economy and government," Mondale said. "We may win the political argument for several reasons. Congress often wins the fight by retail rather than wholesale methods. The President opens it on nationwide television, and then Congress goes home and talks to unions and Rotary Clubs and, drip by drip, things change. Look at the issue of aid to New York City. When Ford started out, there was tremendous antagonism against New York. Then it turned around and his position collapsed. You have to distinguish between the opening round and the final rounds—he always starts out ahead, because he defines the issue. The second thing that's happening is we're reaching the point where the economic issue is no longer going to be theory—waste, inflation, cutting federal programs. There are millions depending on these programs, and when it's discovered how he defines 'waste' there may be some different attitudes. I grant that Ford is winning the argument about federal programs and inflation, but I think the longer the argument goes on, the more he may lose. There is waste and unresponsiveness in federal programs, and there is work we can do and have begun to do. The more the people see us digging in, the more they may be with us."

I asked Mondale if he did not think that Ford had liberals on the defensive.

"We should be on the defensive about some of these things," he replied. "If you take the position that we have no waste, you have a dizzy position. That's not the position I take. It seems to me that a progressive Democrat ought to be angrier than Ford about waste— because that's money that could go to better purposes, and it undermines respect for social justice. Ford's handling the politics of waste very shrewdly, but not the mechanisms. You have to get at the programs and see what they are doing and what else could be done with the money."

Talking with me in his office down the hall, Senator Adlai Stevenson, Democrat of Illinois, was not sanguine.

"I think we're going to celebrate the Bicentennial by marking time," Stevenson said. "The stalemate on policy between Congress and the White House will continue. Both sides are preoccupied with politics—waiting for the outcome of the elections. The sides are too far apart. Congress can't initiate policy, so now it's an army without a general. In foreign policy, the consequences are tragic. What the nation really requires is a policy it can support, but there is no policy, so Congress is adrift and is exercising the only power it has, which is a negative power. The institutions of free enterprise aren't equal to the realities of the new era: cartels, fixed prices, commodity shortages. The political complexion in Europe may be changing ominously. And the United States isn't putting its own house in order. I don't see any leadership coming from the United States until after the elections, if then. We don't seem to have the capacity now for developing the appropriate instruments of trade, for coping with the questions of international security, the tremendous problem of nuclear proliferation. We're not coping with the national or international economy. The transportation industry is failing. We're not dealing with the food and fuel problems. But there's not a chance of a new idea's taking root in this soil. To make it worse, the failures of government are causing a reaction against government. The politicians are running against the very idea of politicians. For the first time, the Presidential candidates are running against the very idea of government. The issue is big government instead of sound government."

After a question or two, Stevenson continued, "I fault the press as much as I do the politicians." It is hardly uncommon to hear politicians complain about the press—which never, as far as they are concerned, gives them enough coverage—but Stevenson's point was a different and important one. He said, "Henry Stimson said that cynicism is deadly. The public is cynical, and it's cynical because it's uninformed and misinformed and confronted on all sides with evidence of obscenity and trivia and failure, and scarcely ever with a note of hope, a prophetic idea. And it isn't because nobody speaks any sense. There's precious little, but it's not nonexistent. Yet there's a preoccupation with sensationalism and trivia. The public wasn't warned of the dangers of the energy and fuel shortages and nuclear proliferation, because the press didn't listen. It wasn't that no one understood."

In various conversations on Capitol Hill today, there was evident a sudden, and reluctant, taking notice of Jimmy Carter. Although nothing has happened yet, "the word"—that ephemeral set of assumptions which circulates and becomes, at least temporarily, the accepted truth in Washington—is that Carter is doing well and should be watched. Carter seems to cause an uneasiness among politicians here, because they do not know him, and because he is running an ostensibly anti-political campaign. Politicians here are troubled by the substance of what he is saying. They are also bothered by the fact that, a loner, he does not seem to need them.

"The Carter phenomenon is spreading," said one Democratic House member today. "It worries me. He's running against all institutions. But the problem of a politician criticizing him is that you build up his anti-politician role. I'm for Udall, and I suppose I should be helping him, but I don't know . . ."

Candidates often have people ready to help them after they have done well.

The State of the Union Address is, of course, aimed at the public, with the members of Congress assembled in the chamber of the House of Representatives as props for the President's television show. Many have already drafted their "reaction" remarks, to be phoned in to the local press after the President finishes. The announcer tells us that the President worked fifty hours on this speech. President Ford stands at the rostrum where he was sworn in as Vice-President, next to a hovering Richard Nixon. Carl Albert and Nelson Rockefeller are behind him. We had almost forgotten about Rockefeller, who last fall removed himself—before he could be removed—from consideration for Ford's 1976 ticket. "As we begin our Bicentennial . . ." the President says. At one point, the cameras show us Edward Kennedy, playing his role, applauding. Kennedy is, as of now, sitting out this political year, but he still gets attention. The President speaks against federal programs. He says, "In our rush to accomplish great deeds quickly, we trampled on sound principles of restraint and endangered the rights of individuals." He calls "for a fundamentally different approach—for a new realism." He quotes Thomas Paine about "the times that try men's souls," about "summer soldiers and sunshine patriots," and he frequently uses the term "common sense." One begins to wonder whether our Revolutionary heroes are going to make it through the year. The speech is an odd combination of Calvin Coolidge and Franklin Roosevelt. For all the talk about cutting back government, Ford goes in for his share of interest-group politics: offering something for the elderly (insurance coverage for catastrophic illnesses), something for farmers and small businessmen (tax relief for inherited small farms and businesses), and a tax cut. He is appealing, essentially, to the middle class. He quotes Dwight Eisenhower and Abraham Lincoln. He invokes "the silent image of George Washington kneeling in prayer at Valley Forge."

JANUARY 20

Even though more of the votes cast at the Iowa precinct caucuses yesterday were for "Uncommitted" than for any candidate, the press attention is on Jimmy Carter, who did better than the other Democrats. This morning, Carter, who managed to get to New York in time, was interviewed on the *CBS Morning News. The Today Show* and ABC's *Good Morning America,* also ran segments on Carter. On the *CBS Evening News,* Walter Cronkite said that the Iowa voters have spoken, "and for the Democrats what they said was 'Jimmy Carter.' "

Carter, Bayh, and Harris had the backing of some unions in Iowa. Labor, for the most part, did not do well in the delegate-selection process in 1972, because the reform rules were unfamiliar. The result was that, by its lights, it was under-represented at the 1972 Convention. It does not want that to happen again, and its interest is heightened by predictions that this year's will be a brokered Convention. Nine unions representing the more liberal forces within the union movement—the United Auto Workers; the American Federation of State, County and Municipal Employees; the Communications Workers of America; the Graphic Arts International Union; the International Association of Machinists and Aerospace Workers; the International Union of Electrical, Radio & Machine Workers; the National Education Assocation; the Oil, Chemical and Atomic Workers International Union; and the United Mine Workers—have formed what is called the Labor Coalition Clearing House to work to get their members elected as delegates. Therefore, its members will support certain candidates in certain states not necessarily because they are enamored of those candidates but because they see them as vehicles for getting seats at the Convention. This is an example of what might be called the "back-yard principle" that runs all through our politics: the positions that various people and forces take have to do not so much with great questions such as who should lead our nation as with how best to protect their own back yard. Six of the nine belong to the A.F.L.–C.I.O., whose official position is neutrality.

Tonight, Carter, in New Hampshire, was shown on the television news smiling and saying, "To lose, even if you make a respectable showing, is not as good as winning."

2

SOME TIME AGO, Jimmy Carter agreed to appear before a meeting
of the board of the Urban Coalition to be held today, and now he is
here, in the Lincoln Ballroom of the Washington Hilton—the victor, to be taken more seriously and to be questioned more carefully
than he might have been before this week. As he is introduced, he
sits at the head of a large table, grinning broadly at nothing in particular. It seems to be not a natural smile but more like a mouth
exercise—possibly reflexive—in which the lips are stretched to the
side, revealing the already well-known rows of large, healthy teeth.
As he entered the room, he shook hands with everyone in sight. The
members of the Urban Coalition board sit around the table. They
are business, labor, religious, black, ethnic, and community leaders,
about half of them black or Hispanic—an influential and skeptical
lot, having seen a good deal. Taking the rostrum, Carter makes
some opening remarks. His style of speaking is Southern soft. The
sandy hair is not as bushy as the pictures of him indicate, but he
looks far more like John Kennedy than I had imagined. The resemblance—the shape of the eyes and nose—is almost unnerving. It is
hard enough to judge these politicians on their own, without the
further confusion of irrelevant memories.

Carter tells the group, "This year is going to be very special in
my life, and I think in your life." He continues, "I don't think any
human being has travelled more than I have, met more people,
answered more questions, gotten more free advice—and I've
thoroughly enjoyed it." He is trying to make a virtue of his dogged
campaigning. He says that he feels better about the country than he
did when he first started campaigning. He says there is not the
hatred in the country there used to be, and he talks about our
approaching our future "with a quiet hurt and a quiet searching."
He refers to "the question which you address so well—which is
what we can do about deprived people," and then says, "I don't
have any easy answers." He says, "I'm in the process of searching,"

and adds, "as are you." He seems to have almost perfect pitch with this group. He says that people who receive the services of federal programs should have more opportunity to shape them, and that most of the time the programs are drawn up "by people who haven't suffered."

Striking one of his major themes, Carter says, "I tell people, 'Don't vote for me unless you want to see the federal bureaucracy totally reorganized.' " (He has been saying that he will reduce the number of federal agencies from about nineteen hundred to two hundred.) The bureaucracy does need reorganization, but that is not the heart of the problem of making government more effective and responsive. He tells how in Georgia "any citizen in my state today can pick up the telephone and dial a number"—which has been distributed with welfare checks and broadcast on the radio—and bring up a complaint with the appropriate government official. He gives as an example that someone may buy a chicken at the market and then get it home and find that it is underweight. That person, Carter explains, can dial the number and be connected with the official in the state agriculture department who is responsible for scale weight. "Try to do that with the federal government," says Carter. "It's impossible. But it can be done."

He talks about popular issues, but not bloodlessly. He talks about public employees who began their work with "their hearts full of love"; he talks about people on welfare and says that "most people want to work." He affects great confidence, saying, "I intend to be elected." But is it really affectation? Presidential candidates must exude confidence, and inwardly most do begin to believe they might succeed. They have to believe it in order to go through what they do. But Carter's assertion seems rooted in some combination of confidence and steely determination—the steeliness masked somewhat by the gentling Southern accent—as if he has been at it a long time and is going to keep at it until he has convinced everyone of what he already knows. It does not seem to be entirely an act. His mother has been quoted as describing him as "a beautiful cat with sharp claws." Besides, the more he convinces others that his victory might come about, the more it is likely to. The Washington *Post* reported recently that not long ago Carter bought some land around his home in the small town of Plains, Georgia, where he runs a peanut farm and a peanut-warehousing business, and plans a zoning code to control commercial developers and souvenir shops there "when I am President." He talks to this group of the search in our society "for truth and honesty and decency." He is a gifted speaker; the pauses are well placed. He refers to Lincoln and Franklin Roosevelt and Martin Luther King.

The first question is on abortion. Stories are coming out of Iowa that he switched positions there—leading some Catholic officials to believe that he would back a Constitutional amendment against abortion and then, when it became known that he would not, indicating that he would back some sort of national statute against it. This morning, an Evans and Novak column was devoted to the subject of Carter's allegedly misleading statement on the issue. Asked if he will clarify his position on abortion, Carter replies without hesitation; he is ready for this. His answer is quick and concise, and he manages to come out as well as one can on both sides of the issue—but not quite. "I think abortion is wrong," he says, apparently appealing to those who would like it outlawed. "I do not favor a Constitutional amendment," he says, thus closing that door. "I do not favor a law totally abolishing abortion," he adds, closing that one, too—if such a law should prove to be Constitutional, which is doubtful. Then he says that he favors government action to prevent abortion through offering help with family planning, contraceptives, and the like—and so he ends with, in effect, a liberal position couched in conservative rhetoric. "I don't favor mandatory busing if an alternative can be worked out," he tells the group, and he adds that his daughter goes to a public, integrated school. He says Presidents should be accessible.

Watching Carter, one realizes that he might be President, might be a major part of our lives, and then again he might disappear, ending up a minor footnote in our history, a fleeting image.

After Carter's appearance, I speak with a man from Georgia who does not oppose Carter but who has misgivings. "Look at what he is, as against what he says," this man says. "He talks about working in harmony with the Congress, but he did just the opposite with the state legislature. He was not a coalition builder, he was a loner. He comes on as man of sweet reasonableness; in reality, he is headstrong, opinionated, inflexible. He's terribly effective, but what he has been effective at is not all that great." Others have remarked on the fact that Carter does not seem to have peers with whom he works. Then, there are the reports about his campaign for the governorship against the liberal former governor Carl Sanders, in which, while he did not mention race, he appeared to align himself with George Wallace and Lester Maddox. And then when he was elected he announced at his inauguration, "The time for racial discrimination is over."

JANUARY 29

Thursday. George Wallace won the Mississippi precinct caucuses on Saturday, defeating Carter by about three to one. ("Uncommitted" came in second.)

Terry Sanford, president of Duke University and former governor of North Carolina, withdrew from the Democratic Presidential race on Friday. "The ordeal of running a political campaign from a nonpolitical position is tougher than I anticipated," Sanford said. Sanford, who had made an unsuccessful attempt at the nomination in 1972, had not been taken seriously, or paid much attention, this time. Sanford is a thoughtful, "issue-oriented" man, and an unexciting campaigner by conventional standards. He was, according to several people who observed him, an unexciting candidate for governor of North Carolina. But he was an exceptionally good governor.

The House has voted, by 323 to 99, to prevent the Administration from spending any of the money in the defense-appropriations bill for military support for forces fighting in Angola. The Senate had approved the same ban before the Congress adjourned last year. The Administration proposed to use about thirty million dollars. In a letter to Speaker Albert, the President wrote, "The failure of the U.S. to take a stand will inevitably lead our friends and supporters to conclusions about our steadfastness and resolve." A large segment of the Congress has a different world view, and, still hurting from Vietnam and the disclosures of C.I.A. excesses, it is rebelling against our involvement, undertaken in secrecy, in Angola—one more country in which our interests are unclear. These actions, and the secrecy that surrounded them, grew out of assumptions that developed after the Second World War—Cold War assumptions that are now being questioned in Congress. This is what has caused the strains between the Congress and the executive over both foreign policy and some of the methods used in conducting that policy.

The Supreme Court's ruling yesterday on the campaign reform law has the ring of a compromise. The Court upheld the limits on the amounts that can be contributed (for individuals, a thousand dollars to any Presidential or congressional candidate, and for political-action committees five thousand dollars per candidate), the requirement that campaign contributions be disclosed, and the provision for public financing of Presidential campaigns. On the other hand, it struck down the overall limits on campaign spending as impermissible limits on free speech, but it said that the spending limits could be imposed on Presidential candidates who accepted public financing. The Court also struck down the limits on spending one's own money for one's campaign, except for Presidential candidates who receive federal financing, and permitted unlimited "independent expenditures" on behalf of a candidate, as long as it was done without consulting the candidate. Finally, the Court ruled that the way the Federal Elections Commission had been established, with four of its six members appointed by the Congress, violated the principle of separation of powers, and that the Commission therefore could not issue rulings or distribute funds unless Congress rewrote the law. This set off an immediate scramble in the Congress to revise the law, and in the process to get in a few changes some congressmen and interest groups desired. Nonetheless, the provision limiting campaign contributions has already had profound effects on our politics—but not entirely the effects expected. It has reduced the power of the wealthy contributor, which was the major goal. But while some wealthy contributors have been ruled out of the game, others—those who have a lot of contacts, which is most of them—have not, because they can gather the thousand-dollar contributors a candidate needs. For this reason, and for reasons of habit—it will take a while to adjust to the new law—many of the old money-raisers are still called upon by the candidates. Still, individual voices are muted. Bothersome big donors don't have to be coddled, their opinions taken seriously. And because money must be raised in small sums, the new law, if anything, seems to require that the candidate spend more time than before raising money. But now no one can buy an election, or a candidate, even if the candidate wishes to be bought.

Jimmy Carter ran strongly in Maine municipal caucuses yesterday, and said that this would help in "resolving a doubt that someone from the South can be acceptable to the rest of the nation." As in the case of Iowa, Carter saw psychological importance in doing well early, and in this case in a state next door to New Hampshire. Carter spent more time in Maine than did the other candidates, and his wife and sons campaigned there, and his Aunt Sissy (Emily Dolvin) moved to Maine for most of the last month.

Daniel Patrick Moynihan, increasingly at odds with the Administration over his defiant style, resigned today as Ambassador to the United Nations. Henry Jackson has issued a statement saying that Moynihan's resignation is "a sad day for America."

Three engineers from the General Electric division that builds nuclear reactors resigned today, saying they believed that nuclear energy presents a profound threat to man.

Today, Nelson Rockefeller told reporters that he would not rule out running for the Presidency if President Ford was defeated in the primaries.

This afternoon, I dropped by to talk with John Gardner, to see what he was thinking about. I talked with him in his Common Cause office, at Twenty-first and M Streets. As usual, Gardner viewed what is happening on levels that few other people here do.

"I can't help thinking," he began, "that one of the toughest problems we face is creating some new modes of organization. Our vaunted pluralism has hardened into a multiplicity of rigid vested interests, and it's becoming paralyzing to both our politics and our government. The question is: How can anyone mobilize power to get things done?"

I asked Gardner if this was really a new problem.

"Its character has changed," he replied. "Clear back to Colonial days, there were pretty strong vested interests, representing shippers and traders and landowners. Then in this century labor and farmers proved they could play the same game. But now even the symphony orchestras have organized. The change has to do with the growth in government. Each special interest has to protect itself against the intrusions of government, or bring about intrusions favorable to it, or simply fight for its share of the pie. So the number of special interests is greater; their professionalism is greater; the degree to which they organize for the narrow and short-term self-interest is greater. Government is powerful, and has a lot it can give, so you're going to get these consequences. Today, you have public-interest groups that take a longer and broader view, but they are issue-oriented and not power mobilizers. Until now, the power-mobilizing elements in the political system have been the parties. They have always reached across special interests—and they should. They should be the putters-together of the splinters. But the parties themselves are affected by the rising power and professionalism of the special interests. They are captured by multiple masters. The Democratic Party still has the strong voice of Texas oil, minorities, blue-collar workers—each organized, tough, skilled in getting its way, and resistant to mobilization in a coalition. That's also why the parties aren't instruments of power that are useful to the Presidents whom they've elected. And that's why Presidents have so much trouble governing."

I asked Gardner, who had seen government at first hand as Secretary of Health, Education, and Welfare in the Johnson Administration and has been watching it closely ever since, to describe the way he saw the nature of the trouble Presidents have in governing.

Gardner replied, "There is a myth that says there is a powerful entity called the Federal Government, which lords it over something quite separate called the Private Sector. But in reality the federal government is to a considerable degree a collection of disconnected pieces, each under the virtual control of some private-sector interests. What we really have is the Special Interest State, in which every well-organized interest owns a piece of the executive branch, and has its well-disciplined allies in Congress to boot. The mythology says Congress and the executive are wholly separate branches that fight like cat and dog. It's true at the top, but the middle-level bureaucrat locks arms with the members of Congress, and they both lock arms with the powerful private-sector interests that are calling the tune. It's a great old barn dance, but there are a dozen different people calling different steps."

"And that's what causes the paralysis?"

"That's right," Gardner replied. "There are so many special interests they cancel each other out. Each has a veto, and no one has the power to make the whole thing work. The fragments of our government have no effective way of working together or thinking together. The government is an organism without a cerebral cortex. We cannot think as a nation. No President in recent history has been able to govern domestically. That is why every recent President has retreated eventually to foreign policy. When the next President enters office, in 1977, we'll see a charade we've seen many times before. After a few weeks, he will discover that the buttons on his desk aren't wired to anything. They're just there to make him feel good. He'll conclude that he is being thwarted by the Big Bad Bureaucracy—all those big agencies, all those little people in green eyeshades. So he will appoint a distinguished Commission on Executive Reorganization, and they'll tell him pretty much what previous commissions have told previous Presidents—how to reorganize the bureaucracy. But when he tries, he'll confront the constituencies that made him a viable candidate. At that point, he'll quietly drop the whole subject, and that's the last we'll hear about executive reorganization until the next President arrives. But even if he changed the organization chart, he'd run into the same conflicting constituencies whenever he attempted significant policy changes. And our paralysis on domestic policy will continue. That's one of the dilemmas we don't know how to face. People walk away from the subject, because they don't know how to deal with it."

3

SATURDAY. The Manchester, New Hampshire, airport, shortly before noon. It is a bright, cold day. Only about a thousand people are here to greet President Ford, who will arrive shortly, in pursuit of his party's nomination. Leaflets were distributed this morning urging people to come to the airport to see their President and his wife, and for good measure Air Force One, the President's plane. But still the turnout is modest. It seems that the President, with his large entourage of officials and reporters, his paraphernalia and equipment, might sink this tiny state. Estimates of what this primary is worth, commercially, to New Hampshire—which has made sure that its primary continues to be the first one—vary from five million dollars to ten million; it is one of the state's largest industries. In a little over two weeks from now, New Hampshire's one hundred and sixty-four thousand registered Republicans, one hundred and sixteen thousand registered Democrats, and one hundred and forty thousand independents will make their statement, its meaning to be interpreted by the press and what is referred to as "the political community." Even a victory here is not necessarily a "victory"—as Lyndon Johnson, who defeated Eugene McCarthy in the 1968 primary, and Edmund Muskie, who won this primary in 1972, learned. The New Hampshire primary has become an important and potentially decisive test, because that is the way it is interpreted, and many of the candidates have accepted it as such. Including the President. Gerald Ford has never submitted to an electoral test outside his former congressional district of Grand Rapids, Michigan, and now he is facing an aggressive opponent. The President's campaign apparatus is in shaky condition. The opinion polls, to the extent that they are known, indicate that the race between the President and his challenger is very close, with a substantial "undecided" vote. Ronald Reagan is said to have the more effective organization, as the candidates with the more zealous backing often do. Reagan is the ideological and sentimental favorite of the Republican conservative wing, which in recent years has worked harder within the Party than the moderate and liberal wings and therefore has been heavily represented, or perhaps over-represented, at the Conventions.

The President swoops down the field in the great, sleek blue-and-white plane with "United States of America" printed on its side. It is Plane No. 27000—the same one that Richard Nixon named "Spirit of '76." This year, there appears on its tail, just below the American flag, the emblem of the Bicentennial.

Nixon is the Banquo's ghost of this election. Yesterday, it was announced that he would visit China, at the invitation of the Chinese government—the trip to begin on February 20th, four days before the New Hampshire primary. Ford, like the country, simply cannot shake Nixon. Ford the President is of Nixon's creation. Ford's sudden pardoning of Nixon, on a September Sunday morning, may be an invisible issue—one of those issues that people don't talk about much but that are there, below the surface, bothering them. Politicians often miscalculate about such issues, figuring that if people aren't talking about them they aren't there. Ford figured when he pardoned Nixon that the public outrage would "blow over." It did, but then it went underground. People can shout for only so long, and politicians often mistake silence for contentment. People don't talk much about Watergate—or Vietnam, either—anymore, but it is commonly accepted that both have deeply affected attitudes toward government and politics.

A high-school band, dressed in blue and white, swings into "Hail to the Chief" as the President's plane taxis to a stop and its door opens. Other candidates, of course, aren't greeted with "Hail to the Chief," but this is a President-candidate, which is different. The President; his wife, Betty; and his daughter, Susan, all look terribly healthy. Politicians' families are, of course, part of the props; their smiling appearance alongside the candidate may have nothing to do with how they feel about being there, or about him. But the Fords do seem to be a family with real bonds, the President a man with human connections. We have learned to watch for this in our public figures.

The cafeteria of the Rundlett Junior High School, Concord, New Hampshire, at lunchtime. Local officials and members of the state legislature are seated in rows of metal folding chairs. A disembodied voice announces, "The President of the United States." The President comes out and stands behind a rostrum to which the

Presidential seal—the travelling Presidential seal—has been affixed. The President is going to hold a briefing on his budget, apparently to show his command of his own programs. One he held in Washington last month when his Budget Message was released was considered such a success that now he has taken the performance on the road. On either side of the President are the American flag and the Presidential flag, and large charts on easels covered with blue cloth. Behind him is a blue curtain. A number of Presidential assistants and an official of the Office of Management and Budget are here. The President, dressed in a navy-blue pinstriped suit and a blue shirt, begins by referring to the "good news" announced yesterday by the Labor Department that unemployment has dropped to 7.8 percent from 8.3 percent. He shows the audience two of the charts, which indicate how much the state, counties, municipalities, and townships of New Hampshire will receive under his new revenue-sharing proposal. "This is federal money . . . with no strings attached," he tells them. He is the President, bringing them their boodle. The situation lacks majesty. More is at stake in this election than how much Concord, New Hampshire, will get from revenue sharing.

The interesting thing about the questions that are put to the President is how many of them show an eagerness to get more, not less, from the federal government: more for the treatment of alcoholism, more for schools, more for mass transit. The President is a plain, unassuming man, not unlike the people he is talking to. But with all that equipment and all that blue he looks Presidential. (In an effort to dispel the hapless-nice-guy image, his campaign photographs for posters and leaflets have the President looking stern.) He offers, without having been asked, the information that he will not close the Portsmouth Naval Shipyard. He has been well briefed on local issues. Asked about a controversial proposal, now pending before the Nuclear Regulatory Commission, to build a nuclear reactor at Seabrook (the questioner is for the project, which is expected to provide three thousand jobs), the President says that he cannot speak about issues that are before a regulatory commission but "I strongly believe in a nuclear-power program."

Saturday evening. The gymnasium of the Nashua Senior High School. The President is here, attending the fiftieth annual dinner of the Nashua Chamber of Commerce. This is a good occasion for the President, since the audience is heavily Republican. At least a half-dozen White House assistants, plus officials of the President Ford Committee, considered the many questions surrounding the President's trip here, including the very important one of whether or not he should ski this weekend. The President's extensive travelling about the country last fall—attracting two apparent assassination attempts—brought forth widespread criticism. He was dissipating his one major advantage—the Presidency—and doing the one thing that politicians, in this cycle of our politics, are not supposed to do. He was "acting like a politician." His occasional displays of physical awkwardness had become a national joke. It was at that point that the opinion polls showed the President's popularity beginning to sink. Shortly after Reagan announced that he would be a candidate for the Presidency, on November 20th, the polls briefly showed Reagan to be ahead. No one was sure whether this was a reflection of the widespread coverage that Reagan was receiving, of the President's lack of popularity, or both. Last week, I talked with Stuart Spencer, deputy chairman of the President Ford Committee. Spencer has, in effect, been in charge. A former California political manager—his firm, Spencer-Roberts, managed Reagan's campaigns for governor in 1966 and 1970—he is considered very able, and a good catch for Ford. "We've made the gut decision that the best strategy for the President is to be President," Spencer told me. "So we're walking a thin line: he'll go to some of the states and get as much press out of it as possible. You'll notice he's going weekends." This complicated further the question of whether he should ski. I was told at the White House that the President Ford Committee wanted the President to ski this weekend but that White House assistants did not think he should. People at the President Ford Committee did not concede that they had taken such a position, and, indeed, one person there listed the negative considerations: it would take a lot of time; there were logistical difficulties in getting the President and his large entourage to and from a ski area; a Presidential ski outing might displace a large number of other skiers and thus hurt the area more than it would help, and might even hurt the President politically. And so, after careful deliberations, high policymakers in our government concluded that the President should not ski this weekend.

After the President of the United States has sat for what seems like a long time on the red-white-and-blue-draped dais this evening, making polite conversation, listening attentively to the preliminary speeches, he is invited to participate in the presentation of the

"Citizen of the Year" award to Sam Tamposi, who is the treasurer of the Reagan campaign. President Ford has a prepared address for the occasion. The Presidential seal is on the rostrum where he speaks. He congratulates Sam Tamposi. He points out that the first warship to fly the American flag—a ship commanded by John Paul Jones—was built at the Portsmouth Shipyard, and he departs from the prepared text to remark that he will not close the shipyard. Ford tells the audience, "The patriots who built America understood that poverty is abolished by economic growth, not by government-imposed redistribution of money." The President seems to be trying to infuse more drama into his delivery than usual. Instead of the customary monotone, he raises his voice for emphasis and then lowers it almost to a whisper. The style seems unnatural, forced. Noting that a brewery was opened in New Hampshire in 1970, he says, "I don't think the United States government could make beer for less than fifty dollars a six-pack." He gets big applause for this. (Last week, he said in Dearborn that he didn't think the government could build a Model T for less than fifty thousand dollars.) He defends his revenue-sharing program and tells the members of the Chamber of Commerce how much Nashua will receive. He tells them that the citizens of Nashua, who have made such progress, have defied the nation's pessimists, "as exemplified in the fable about Chicken Little," and he tells of how Chicken Little, having been hit by an acorn, said the sky was falling. He continues, "The fact is that America has been hit on the head by some very heavy acorns in recent years—recessionary acorns, inflationary acorns, unemployment acorns, energy acorns. . . ."

FEBRUARY 8

A conference of Third World nations ended in Manila yesterday, with the participants agreeing to put pressure on the industrialized nations for a "new international economic order." They expressed their "firm conviction to make full use of the bargaining power of the developing countries, through joint . . . action" to receive better terms for their commodities.

It is Sunday. I have been designated one of two pool reporters to accompany the Fords to church this morning. There is always a press pool—to fly on Air Force One, to ride in the motorcade closer to the President's car than the press bus does, and to attend events too small to accommodate the entire press corps. The pool reporters then file a report for the rest of the press. Somehow, I drew the church duty. It is a clear, sunny morning as we set out to watch the Fords emerge from the private house in which they have been staying in Nashua. There are three carloads of cameramen and photographers—they sometimes seem to be what this is all about—and one car for the writing press: a wire-service representative and the other pool reporter and me. Our car is equipped with a telephone and has been provided by the telephone company, which is a service offered for Presidential trips (but not for those of other candidates). We watch carefully, take notes and pictures as the President and Mrs. Ford and their son Mike and his wife, Gayle, emerge from an attractive red brick house at No. 3 Swart Street. They smile and wave and greet some of the neighbors who have come out to see them, and we record the President's words: "Good morning. Nice to see you." On our way to church, the wire-service man phones in his report, which he has managed to develop into a fairly long story.

The church is some distance away, in Bedford, a bedroom community of Manchester. The President is an Episcopalian, but this morning he is attending a picturesque white New England-style Presbyterian church. After the service, the President and his wife pose for pictures on the church steps and then greet people, gathered behind a rope, who have come to see them. The President is natural and friendly; he has an appealing, open laugh. We dutifully note that Mrs. Ford pats a dog. My fellow pool reporter interviews Mike Ford on his views about abortion.

The University of New Hampshire, Durham. The gym is packed for the President's appearance tonight. Politicians and advance men love gyms for political appearances, because the sounds resonate and make an enthusiastic crowd seem all the more enthusiastic. In the audience tonight are representatives of the People's Bicentennial Commission, a group of young people from around the country who are trying—in a project that they call the Common Sense Campaign for a Democratic Economy—to insert questions about the economic structure of America into the Presidential contest. Their tactics are often rude. Tonight, they shout catcalls while the President tries to speak. In response, the other students give the President especially enthusiastic cheers. Ford handles the situation well, moving on with his remarks without becoming visibly tense or angry, and he maintains his equanimity as he takes questions, some of them hostile. It is hard to imagine Lyndon Johnson or Richard Nixon handling this situation with as much calm, or perhaps even being here at all. Many of Ford's answers indicate that he and the students—not just his P.B.C. questioners—are living in different worlds, proceeding on different sets of assumptions. No one is persuading anybody, but it is good that the President is there, taking questions and offering his answers. And as he does so, his wooden, "Presidential" manner slips away and he becomes the natural "nice guy." It is his most appealing performance of the weekend.

4

THE SOVIET-BACKED and Cuban-backed forces in Angola have captured Huambo, the capital of the forces backed by the United States.

It is Monday. The major Democrats in the race here in New Hampshire are Bayh, Carter, Harris, Shriver, and Udall. Jackson is not taking part in the popularity contest, but he has entered a slate of delegates. New Hampshire residents like to be courted by the candidates—expect it—but some are getting a little tired of answering the telephone. Canvassers for the candidates try to determine which voters favor the caller's candidate and the degree of fervor with which they do so. Those who might be persuaded to favor that candidate are called again, and then efforts are made to get all those who favor that candidate to the polls. This process is most adaptable to a state as small as New Hampshire, and is difficult to duplicate elsewhere. It is as if each voter here were wired. Proposals to shorten the duration of campaigns, or ideas that the more aloof, thoughtful candidate might be more appealing, must come to terms with this: that there will be candidates who will simply go out and work and campaign and organize and conduct a sort of relentless guerrilla war on the election—as Jimmy Carter is doing. Probably a candidate without appeal could not get very far on a mechanistic organization alone—in fact, could not attract the support to mount such an organization. The ability to attract such support may even be a credential for the Presidency, since a President should have the ability to rally. But rally whom? And for what? An organization is a neutral thing.

Another dilemma: The number of Democratic candidates has become the subject of jokes, and these increase the cynicism and lack of dignity with which this election is surrounded as of now. Candidates enter for a variety of reasons. There are more flukes connected with who is in and who is out—the process is far more irrational—than we would like to think. Some candidates run because they really want to be President, some to get better known for a future race, some to secure their situation in their own state, some because they do not have anything more interesting to do. But it is not any candidate's fault that there are so many others. And who is to say who should or should not be in the race? In previous elections, the complaint has often been that there was so little choice.

Monday evening. Berlin (pronounced *Burr*-lin), New Hampshire, a dreary mill town in the northern tip of the state, not far from the Canadian border, and about a three-hour drive from Manchester. Berlin, with a population of fifteen thousand, contains three and a half percent of the state's Democrats, and, according to some estimates, the highest density of Democrats of any municipality in the state. It is a bit of a shock to come upon Berlin, with its spewing smokestacks, narrow streets, and cramped, cheerless houses, after driving through the spectacular White Mountains, their slopes and evergreens covered with snow. It is as if some perverse force had placed this Dickensian throwback here to show what man can create in the midst of such beauty. Along Main Street, there are headquarters for Sargent Shriver, Birch Bayh, Fred Harris, and Jimmy Carter. Carter got the best spot, on the corner next to City Hall. Some signs along the street advertise a ninety-nine-cent ham-and-bean dinner for Fred Harris on Wednesday night.

The Riverside Motor Inn, an old, dank hotel, is tucked away hard by the Brown Company, which manufactures paper products and sends a most unpleasant odor into the night air. In the bar, shortly before six, two musicians who are part of a band called McWendy and the Midnight Specials are rehearsing. When a blond waitress idling by the dining-room doorway is asked her opinion of the candidates, she replies, "None of them is good enough to run the country." Downstairs, the Women's Bowling League—about thirty-two women, dressed in slacks—has assembled for candlepin bowling, popular in New England. The room, with a low ceiling, green paint peeling off the walls, and a damp, gymnasium smell, is noisy with the crashing of pins and the shouting of the women.

Shortly after six, Birch Bayh, dressed in a navy pin-striped suit and a blue shirt, his hands in his pockets, strolls into the bowling alley. Bayh is following the sort of frantic schedule that all candidates do these days. He began the day at 6:30 A.M. at a plant gate here, gave a newspaper interview in Groteton, and attended a coffee hour and toured a paper plant there, toured in Lancaster, walked down a street in Gorham, and then returned to Berlin, where he gave a newspaper interview and two radio interviews, stood at a plant gate again, and visited a hospital. And now he has come to this bowling alley, where thirty-two women are bowling, in quest of votes. Bayh, as usual, has the look of an alert squirrel; his blue eyes dart about, the dimples showing in his cheeks even when his face is in repose. The women are largely uninterested in his presence, so Bayh makes his way along the two rows of benches, sticking out his hand and saying, "Can I say hello? I'm Senator Birch Bayh. How's the game going?" From time to time, he stops to watch one of the women bowl, and cheers if she hits a few pins. The women shake his hand and return to their bowling. With Bayh are an aide, two officials of Local 75 of the United Paperworkers International Union, who have endorsed him, and a young woman carrying a yellow legal pad, who says that she is checking the candidates' positions on the issues for some wealthy California contributors. Bayh's campaign is said to be in trouble, because, among other things, he has had difficulty raising sufficient money. As of today, he has raised a little over half a million dollars, less than nearly all the others. The new law tends to reward those who start early and work long at raising money, and Bayh did not announce his candidacy until last October (though his fund-raising began before that). Jackson raised over a million dollars in 1974, before the new law took effect. Bayh spots a young man working behind the bowling pins and walks down the long gutter to the end of an alley to talk with him. As he leaves the bowling alley, one of the women tells him that the men's league will be here later. "Is that right?" Bayh says. "Maybe we ought to come back." In the lobby, he buys a Tab from a vending machine. I ask him if he is having fun. "You might as well," he replies. "It's either that or cry."

As Bayh arrives at City Hall, where people have been rounded up to meet him, a campaign film of his is running in a darkened room. In the film, a car is driving down a dusty road, and bluegrass music is playing in the background. Then we see Birch Bayh, looking straight into the camera, very sincere, saying, "I've worked all my life," and "That's what America's all about." The film shows us Bayh's baby pictures, and Bayh's voice says, "I always laugh when I see those." Bayh's Aunt Kay (his mother died when he was young) talks about him, and we see pictures of his wife, Marvella. Bayh looks into the camera and tells us that "Marvella's the best thing that ever happened to me." He says, "I come off a farm in a little place called Shirkieville," and the film shows Bayh walking in a field and picking up a lump of dirt. "My dad's the finest human being I ever met," says Bayh, and then we see his father, who says that Bayh "will be honest and clean and he'll work his head off." We see clips of John Kennedy and Robert Kennedy. We see Bayh answering a question about how to deal with crime. A voice on the soundtrack says, "The thing that separates Bayh from the rest of those guys is, I think, he's written more of our Constitution than anyone since James Madison." We see shots of Bayh holding a child, Bayh with his shirtsleeves rolled up to mid-biceps, Bayh squatting on the floor answering questions about energy. The film ends with the sun setting over a cornfield, and then Birch Bayh standing in front of the gold-domed statehouse at Concord saying, "That's why I'd like to be President."

The film, which lasts eighteen minutes, is a campaign novelty. No one would sit through an eighteen-minute speech about a candidate. As the film nears its conclusion, Bayh comes into the hall and stands at the back, like a performer ready to go onstage. The film enables him to launch right into answering questions. As he talks, he strolls about the room holding a microphone, like a standup comic. He tells the audience—about a hundred people, seated with paper coffee cups in front of them at long tables—that he is concerned about people who think they are "being swept along individually and collectively as a nation by forces and interests—the multinationals, the oil giants—they can't control." He cites his record ("the record of fighting some tough battles they said couldn't be won") and refers to his leadership of the successful fights to deny Senate confirmation of Clement Haynsworth's and G. Harrold Carswell's appointments to the Supreme Court, and to his authorship of the Twenty-fifth Amendment, providing for Presidential succession, and the Twenty-sixth Amendment, giving eighteen-year-olds the right to vote. He advocates tax reform, breaking up the oil companies, and giving people jobs. He gets worked up when he talks, and waves his arms. He is asked about Angola. There is a long pause; he looks down, as if he is really troubled by this subject, and then he says, in a low voice, "Look. I don't know why it is we never learn." He says that in many places the United States has been "on the wrong side." He talks about the necessity of reducing the nuclear weapons held by the United States and the Soviet Union. He says that we need better planning, that solar energy is more promising than nuclear ("I think that's going to be very disappointing"). Several of his answers are intelligent, or have a grain of intelligence. But his delivery is so slick—the folksiness cutting the dignity—that much of what he says does not sound thought through, even if it has been. He says that he doesn't think anyone has all the qualities to be President, and, referring to himself as "Birch Bayh," says that he wants to restore confidence and believability, to be honest and forthright, to establish goals and meet them, to set standards of excellence. Then he leaves to fly to Buffalo.

FEBRUARY 10

Tuesday. Robert Pollard, a project manager for the Nuclear Regulatory Commission, resigned yesterday, protesting what he said were insufficient safety precautions in the design and construction of nuclear power plants.

Noon. Sargent Shriver is at the Elderly Nutrition Center in Manchester, where, through a federally funded program, people over sixty can come and receive a free lunch. New Hampshire has a high proportion of elderly people, so nutrition centers are considered good places for candidates to go. There are no income ceilings for receiving the benefits of the Elderly Nutrition Program, and while some of the people here—there are about a hundred—seem to need the program, some seem not to. Those who wish can leave a contribution for their meal. Shriver circulates among the dozen or so long tables, where the people are eating a lunch of meat loaf with gravy, rice, and squash. An aide follows him with a plastic bag containing Shriver buttons, which the candidate distributes. Shriver is dressed in beige corduroy trousers and jacket. As always, he is ebullient and friendly; he jokes cheerfully with the people here. This seems to be natural for him, and he seems to enjoy it. Today, Shriver has already shaken hands at the gate of Pandora Industries (two shifts), spoken at Memorial High School, and toured a plant and a bank. After he leaves here, he will tour a life-insurance company, visit a nursing-care center, and then go to Salem, where he will tape a radio interview and attend a coffee. A tall man who says that his name is Big Jim and that he will be Uncle Sam in the Fourth of July parade asks Shriver, "Sargent, what do you think about raising the Social Security tax?" Big Jim asks him a number of other questions, always calling him "Sargent." Afterward, Big Jim says he is for Reagan. "Nice food here," he says, helping himself to seconds. One woman says, "I like Reagan. I changed parties so I could vote for him." Eating her free lunch, the woman says, "The government is too big—let's face it."

After a while, Shriver sits down to eat a meal. This is a premium "photo opportunity," and CBS and NBC videotape it, and several photographers take pictures. Someone suggests that a woman move into an empty seat next to Shriver, because that will look better in the pictures. Shriver's reputation is that he is "lightweight"—an assessment that seems to have to do with his breezy, salesmanlike style. He is as thoughtful as some of the other candidates, or more thoughtful. Watching Shriver, one thinks that he is a nice man, who would not do bad things. One used not to have to consider such a question. Shriver's campaign is strapped for money and is not expected to last. Political wisdom has it that he must do very well in Massachusetts, the home of the Kennedys, in order to stay in at all. A woman seated across from Shriver as he eats his lunch turns to a woman next to her and asks, "Is he a Manchester fellow?"

The Kalivas Apartments, 175 Chestnut Street, Manchester—a high-rise housing project for the elderly. Jimmy Carter, who arrived in New Hampshire a short while ago from Florida, via Boston, is due here shortly after 6:30 P.M. About a hundred people, all of them elderly, are gathered in a meeting room. They stare straight ahead, unperturbed, as they are filmed by Danish television. NBC arrives. One woman tells me that Shriver has been here and Reagan is coming. She and a friend sitting next to her say that they haven't made up their minds yet whom to support. I ask her how they will decide. "When we see them," she replies. I ask her if she feels that she has to see the candidates. "It's best if we do," she replies firmly. One begins to sense that the large undecided vote among the Democrats—said to be forty percent, and in some areas sixty—may be caused in part by the New Hampshire citizens' reluctance to say whom they are for. They seem to enjoy holding out, heightening the mystery, getting more attention. Sometimes it seems that this is not so much an election as a quadrennial play, starring the village butcher.

Several members of the national press are here. There is a bustle about a Carter appearance which there is not about appearances by the other Democratic candidates. Carter enters the room, smiling, with one arm raised in a wave. It is the entrance of a conquerer. Several people in the room cheer. Carter kisses Lucille Kelley, a prominent Manchester Democrat who sided with him early, and then he moves about the room shaking hands. He is neatly dressed in a navy-blue suit. He moves deliberately, not too eagerly. Carter, as a friend of mine in show business puts it, "lights up a room." Perhaps it is his extraordinary self-possession, perhaps the invisible aura of a winner. The mind plays tricks on us: as politicians do better, they look better, more in command. Their own growing confidence helps to create the change. Carter stations himself at the front of the room and begins a little speech. "This is a heartwarming experience," Carter tells the group, in his soft drawl. He says that he has just come from Florida, "but this is just as warm a place." He tells them he understands the problems of having to live on a fixed income. He says the same thing he did at the Urban Coalition about nobody's having travelled around the country, and so on, more than he has. "We've still got the best system of government on earth," he says. He talks about the need "to bind our people together to work in harmony and love one another." He says, "Let us have, in the future, hope, pleasure, security, and a mutual respect for one another." He says, "It's a very fine country. We've got a couple of problems." He says that "our federal government is not well organized"—which seems to be his main issue. "We've got a bureaucracy in Washington that's very confused," he says, and he says that we have to see to it that government is "decent and honest and truthful and fair—that it represents what the American people are." He tells the assembled elderly people that "all of you have led lives of great service and a lot of love" and that they have "added to this country immeasurably." He tells them, "When I get in the White House, I don't want you to leave me there all by myself." He tells them, as he tells other audiences, to come visit him in the White House, "and I'll be there at the front door waiting for you."

Referring to the forthcoming primary, Carter tells his listeners, "The eyes of the whole nation are going to be focussed on you." He goes on, "I don't intend to lose the election." He tells them that there have been four elections so far, in Iowa, Mississippi, Maine, and Oklahoma, and that "in one state I came in second and in three states I came in first"—which is stretching matters a little, but the group is impressed and applauds. "I've got a good family," he says, and he adds, "I hope that you'll be part of my family." Carter then says, "We all love our country," and adds, "I intend to be the next President of it."

In response to questions, Carter says that "one of the top priorities of my administration" is to establish a "nationwide comprehensive, mandatory health-insurance program" and says that he will cut government agencies to two hundred. "I don't want anybody to vote for me in this room unless they want to see the executive branch of government completely reorganized," he says. The man comes across forcefully—regardless of what he is saying. He talks as if he has no doubts that he can "completely reorganize" the government. He is at ease standing there selling himself. He does it with the poise of someone who knows he is charming and can take from that another wave of confidence and be still more charming. He is a taut, compact package, doesn't seem to be a needy man, or vulnerable. He does not convey warmth. What is it about him that makes him come across? The confidence, perhaps. Or his toughness. Toughness wrapped in a soothing message. It may be something physical, chemical. After the questions and answers, Carter spends time talking with some of the group. He looks one woman directly in the eye, and listens intently. The photographers take pictures: it is another good scene. Afterward, I ask the woman whom she is for. She says that she is for Carter, because "I think he's one of the best speakers I've ever heard—he's articulate."

Carter tells reporters that he came in first in Oklahoma, that most of the uncommitted delegates will come to him, that he will be helped in the later stages in Iowa by victories in other states, and that he defeated Harris in Harris's home town. "I'm not saying this in criticism of Fred," he says. Carter uses his sharp claws subtly. (In the Oklahoma caucuses this weekend, "Uncommitted" came in first and Carter and Harris were closely tied for second.) There are more questions about him. He has left a trail of enemies. He has come a long way on sheer doggedness and charm. His success says something about the process. Certainly there are others in politics who are as able, many who are abler, who seem to know more about the country and about governing. But Carter seems to have the ability to self-start and self-propel—to have the almost unnatural belief in self that the process requires. Some start out with it, some seem to develop it along the way, and some never quite acquire it—and its absence shows. At this point, Carter seems to have a higher quotient of that belief-in-self than the other candidates, and it is helping his cause. What is one to make of his obsessiveness? He seems to be a sort of automatic candidate—automatic answers, automatic lines, automatic smiles—and one wonders what gets through to him. We really don't know very much about who he is or what he cares about. We do know that he has been planning this race for a long time. No one seems sure of his politics. Some think he is more liberal than he appears, some think more conservative. It may simply be that his politics defy categorization—perhaps intentionally. One Washington man (who has been courted by Carter) said this about the Carter puzzle: "I don't know if he's Franklin Roosevelt or Richard Nixon."

A coffee at the modest home of John and Janet Windhausen, in Manchester. The first of two coffees Carter will attend this evening. As he moves from place to place, he has a larger caravan than would be expected at this point in the process. People smell a winner. Carter understood the public-relations value of "victories" in the earliest states, which used not to receive much attention.

Carter is standing in the living room telling an attentive audience of about a hundred that he will run in all the states: "I'll be in all of them, meeting anybody who's there, head on." He adds, "I don't criticize the other candidates." He is asked about foreign policy. He says that the American people have been too excluded from the making of that policy; that in Vietnam, Cambodia, and Angola we abandoned our natural allies and friends; and that we do not pay enough attention to the Third World. He says that he has been in eleven countries in the past four years, and "I wouldn't defer to any candidate in my knowledge of foreign affairs." He refers to "my friend Mr. Rabin," the Prime Minister of Israel, and says that he has been a guest of Golda Meir, says that he has been to Germany and has met Chancellor Helmut Schmidt. He says that as President he would "establish personal relationships on an individual basis with the small, weak yellow or black nations." He goes on to say, "We have overemphasized the so-called advantages of détente. I hope we've learned we ought to never again get involved in the internal affairs of other countries unless our security is involved." About jobs, he says he agrees with President Ford that jobs should be provided through the private sector. He talks about jobs that could be provided in solar energy, pollution control, railroads, day-care centers. He says that he would provide jobs in general through the federal government only as a last resort but that he would provide jobs right away for young people. He praises Lloyd Bentsen, who dropped out of the race today. He talks about the importance of predictability in federal policy. He sounds knowledgeable, and he holds the attention of the group. What he doesn't know he glides over, but there is no question that he is smart, and a learner. He is puffing his foreign experience, but then most Presidential candidates, including senators, do, having little to offer except their travels. He stands up straight and keeps talking, and it doesn't seem hard for him. He seems to have the energy. In fact, energy doesn't seem to be a question. He doesn't seem to be exerting himself, as Bayh and Shriver do. He just stands there coolly, talking. The blue eyes are cold. It is hard to tell whether he is a likable man.

Some of the people at this house are upset about the number of members of the press who are present, and at the photographers who push their way through for one more picture of the candidate. At the rate things are going, these traditional homey New Hampshire coffees are not going to be feasible much longer. "I promise that when I'm President I'm going to work out a complete revision of the tax code of this nation," Carter says. "If I can't do it, nobody can." His certainty is persuasive: I'm going to win and you'd better believe it and go along; this train is leaving the station and you'd best be aboard. A number of people in national politics who have been holding back do believe him and are getting aboard. There is something in everyone that wants to get aboard history. And Carter might be a vehicle to power. If Carter can magnetize people, get all kinds of people to think that he is with them, that he is their instrument, is that bad? Isn't that something that Presidents have to do in order to get things done? When Franklin Roosevelt campaigned for the Presidency, many liberals considered him a snake-oil salesman. And he was in fact a shameless seller of snake oil when there were things that had to be done. But he got them done. Carter is essentially progressive. And Carter's intelligence and his shrewdness may offer a kind of safety. He closes with what has become a standard little speech, which he seems to deliver with the same pauses and the same catches in his voice each time: "I've tried to answer your questions. I don't know all the answers. . . . Many of you can be as good or better a leader. . . . I think I'm going to be your next President. As the returns come in, you're going to see me gaining strength. I think I've got the best, most organized campaign that this country has ever seen. I'd like you to be part of that campaign. I won't be any better President than I am a candidate. . . . I don't want to do anything to disappoint you. I'll never tell a lie. I'll never make a misleading statement. I'll never betray your trust or avoid a controversial issue. If I ever do any of these things, then I don't deserve your support." And then, in a low, quiet voice, he says, "I want to have a government as good and honest and decent and compassionate and filled with love as are the American people." Carter smiles and reaches down to help to their feet some young women who have been sitting on the floor.

FEBRUARY 11

Wednesday evening. Morris Udall is at radio station WSMN in Nashua, answering questions that are called in by listeners. Udall will spend all of February in New Hampshire and Massachusetts. Today, he has greeted workers at the gate of the GTE Sylvania plant in Manchester at 6 A.M., spoken at Manchester's Memorial High School, given interviews to newspapers in Derry and Goffs-town, toured the Goffstown Town Hall, lunched at the Elderly Nutrition Center, where Shriver lunched yesterday, and where Udall encountered Jimmy Carter's Aunt Sissy, campaigning. After his appearance here at the radio station, Udall will go to a meeting in Amherst, New Hampshire, and then, later this evening, he will fly to Berlin, arriving in time to greet the midnight shift at the plant gate of the Cascade Mill. Tomorrow, he will greet the 6:45 A.M. shift at the Burgess plant. Udall has staked a great deal on New Hampshire, having started here early and put together an organization, consisting mainly of people who worked here for McGovern or Muskie in 1972, that is generally considered to be the best in the state. The idea, of course, was to win in the first primary, thus putting Udall on the map. But Jimmy Carter stole a march on him. Moreover, even if Udall does do well here, despite the money, attention, and support that such a victory brings it is hard to see how he could repeat this sort of extensive effort elsewhere. Udall is a thoughtful man and is fairly popular with the press—because of that thoughtfulness, and because of his sense of humor, his capacity for seeing absurdity. He seems to be a whole man, humane and vulnerable. As Udall answers questions, reporters and photographers watch him through a glass partition. *Newsweek* is getting pictures of him and the other candidates for possible use on its cover—depending on who wins in New Hampshire. Udall has received the endorsement of Archibald Cox, and the endorsement of the special prosecutor whom Nixon fired is said to be helpful here.

As listeners call in, Udall answers questions about Angola ("President Ford and Secretary Kissinger want another Vietnam in Angola. . . . Kissinger's great failing is that he lost the trust of the Congress"), about national health insurance (he is for it), about Nixon's trip to China. A little girl calls in and says, "I have lost a cat." Udall smiles, and replies, "I promise to solve all the people's problems. Maybe I can find a lost cat."

In the City Hall of Amherst, New Hampshire, a lovely New England town, Udall is addressing a meeting of the town Democratic Committee. About a hundred and fifty people are here. He tells this group, as he told the radio audience, that this primary may be "the last shot" for New Hampshire, because there is some sentiment in the Congress for establishing regional primaries. He talks of the need to "make some fundamental changes" as we face our third century. He says, "We're simply going to have to break up these big corporate monopolies that dominate our lives." He says that people should be encouraged to own stock in the companies they work for. "Give the people some leaders they can trust—that's the unspoken issue of the year," he says. He is applauded warmly, and then invites questions. The woman with the yellow legal pad who was following Bayh the other night is here. Udall answers questions about nuclear power plants (he says that the original justification for nuclear power was that it would be inexpensive, but it isn't, so why go ahead with it), about OPEC, about where he would find the money to create jobs (he cites the budgetary cost of unemployment and also mentions tax reform and cutting the defense budget), about monetary policy, about amnesty, about crime, about revenue sharing. And then a man says, "I am impressed by your glib responses to such a wide variety of questions, for which you have so many answers. But I must say that in the areas I know something about I found your answers to be very empty, and unsatisfactory." Udall replies, "You obviously don't agree with a number of my answers. . . . You don't think they have enough depth. . . . I don't know what you do in a thirty-minute public meeting to solve inflation and unemployment, the Cold War, the Middle East, and everything else." He continues, "You ought to have at least a half an hour on full employment, and I had about three or four minutes. I don't know what else to do but try to answer people's questions, and if you take all of the evening for the first one on full employment you have no time for nuclear power. . . . That's part of the process." Udall is on edge during the exchange. The man has clearly struck a nerve. Udall seems to know that he has been giving superficial answers, and that the pressures in a campaign are bound to cause a candidate to do that. He was, in fact, recently advised by his media consultants to avoid talking about the issues, because people don't really want to hear about them. Issues, he was told, interest only the press.

There may be more to that than we care to think. On occasion, of course, campaigns bring important ideas to the forefront. But, despite ourselves, we know that there is little connection between what candidates say about issues and governing. We know that candidates—even this year's, when it is out of fashion to over-promise—select what they will say about many issues according to the pressures of the moment. We know—and they know—that, of all the things they say, there is only a fraction that they can do; that Presidents are limited in what they can do by such factors as the opposition of interest groups, loss of momentum, the passage of time, unexpected events, and, finally, dissipation of power. More-over, we know that while candidates are pressed to spell out exactly what they would do about this or that—and the more specific they are willing to be, the more they are pressed—there is much about the details and maneuverings of governing that cannot be spelled out in advance. It is like standing on land and trying to tell some-one how to sail a boat. We know these things, but we don't talk about them much, because it seems only proper and responsible to be interested in issues, and because we don't know what to do about what we know. There are ways of finding out more about these people—about their characters, about how their minds work—than we can learn by asking their opinions on absolutely everything, but what we don't do, and don't seem to know much about how to do, is to find out how these people would be at governing. Governing, as it happens, is not a subject that is even given much thought in this process. It disappears in the excitement of the campaign. Gov-erning is the big question; it is, or should be, what the election is about. Yet it largely disappears from our thinking while we focus on such things as a candidate's smile and his affability and how he is doing in Illinois.

FEBRUARY 12

Earlier this week, the United States Commission on Civil Rights issued a statement in which it said that equality of opportunity in the United States "is still too much an unrealized dream."

The Manchester *Union Leader* has a front-page editorial about Nixon's forthcoming trip to China. The headline is "LET THE RED CHINESE KEEP HIM."

Thursday Morning. Outside the Star Market, 1111 South Willow Street, Manchester, in a shopping center. It is a cold morning, with a biting wind. Fred Harris, in a scarf and a navy-blue overcoat, is staging an event. He holds up a loaf of Wonder bread, which, he points out, is a product of a company owned by I.T.T. Harris, whose campaign motto is "The Issue Is Privilege," is campaigning against big business and big money. His is the most uninhibited campaign, a kind of lark. No one expects Harris to win, and that gives him the liberty to say what he thinks. He doesn't really have anything else to do, so he is having a good time running for President. In the process, he has attracted a following of dedicated believers and is doing better than anyone expected. But Harris, too, is running out of money. Harris's just might be a prophetic campaign. Five loaves of white bread cost a dollar in 1969, says Harris, and each loaf costs forty-nine cents today. A dozen navel oranges cost fifty-nine cents in 1969, he says, and cost a dollar seventy-eight today. On he goes, holding up each grocery item—Nestlé's cocoa, Del Monte fruit cocktail, Pillsbury flour. A few members of the press and some cameramen and photographers are here. In fact, they are just about the only people who are here. Hardly a citizen of New Hampshire in sight. The photographers take a lot of pictures. That is what this is about. It is all that this is about.

The Sheraton-Wayfarer Motor Inn. Now Harris is addressing a meeting of the New England Directors of the Community Action Program. The woman with the yellow legal pad is here. Harris is a portly, jowly man with a loud voice. The way he parts his hair down the middle gives him the air of an old-fashioned evangelist. He is an intelligent man, with a sense of humor, and he talks quickly, with a heavy Oklahoma accent. The trouble with the war on poverty, he says, was that there was not sufficient recognition "that you can't really do something about poverty unless you're going to do something about the distribution of wealth and income and power." He says there is a notion in America "that if you just give poor people enough advice they'll quit it." Punching the air with a finger for emphasis, he shouts, "Too few people have all the money and power!" Citing Rousseau, he says that the only way to have a just society is to have "a kind of implied social contract based on our mutual self-interest." As Harris is in full flight, a camera crew, its equipment clanging, makes its way around and behind the table where he is standing. "We're making a movie here," Harris jokes. "You all think this is a campaign, but it's a movie." And then he returns to his condemnation of wealth and power in America.

5

RONALD REAGAN'S campaign plane—a chartered United 727. I joined the retinue of Ronald Reagan at the airport in Manchester, New Hampshire, at six o'clock this evening, to travel with him over the next two days, in Illinois and Florida. Reagan has been in New Hampshire four days this week and will return at the end of next week. In all, he expects to have spent nineteen days in New Hampshire by the time the primary is held. His last two days in New Hampshire were long and grueling, one of them ending with a flight to New York and back, so that he could address a dinner on Staten Island. Both Reagan and his staff are aware of the pressures to adopt punishing schedules, to fill in the white space on the calendar, and Reagan has complained to his staff that he is being over-scheduled.

Reagan is out to topple a President, and Florida and Illinois hold the next two important primaries after New Hampshire. Two days ago, in New Hampshire, Reagan attacked Ford's foreign policy, criticizing détente; all it had gained us, he said, was "the right to sell Pepsi-Cola in Siberia." The press on the plane is down to the hard core that will follow him anywhere—representatives of the New York *Times,* the Los Angeles *Times, Time, Newsweek,* ABC, NBC, and CBS—but he also travels with a substantial personal entourage. His top assistants are Michael Deaver and Peter Hannaford, both of them low-keyed, friendly men who were on Reagan's staff when he was governor of California. Deaver had worked for the Republican State Central Committee, and then was Reagan's number-two staff man during his eight years as governor. Hannaford was a public-relations man who joined the Reagan administration during its last year. When Reagan's term of office was over, these two men formed a Los Angeles–based public-relations firm—Deaver & Hannaford, Inc.—of which Ronald Reagan was a major client. They arranged the speaking engagements, radio commentary, and column-writing by which Reagan supported himself and kept himself in the public eye in 1975 before he entered the race for the Presidency, last November. They wrote a substantial portion of his columns and radio scripts. And so one wonders where the firm of Deaver & Hannaford ends and Ronald Reagan begins. For all that he has been on the national scene, or been a force in our politics—and he certainly is one now—Reagan is a dim figure. There is much that we don't know about him. What is he doing with these public-relations people as his key advisers? How does his own mind work? Is he a contrived figure? One cannot shake the idea that this is Ronald Reagan the movie actor, and while that should not be held against him, it does make it somewhat difficult to take him seriously. But he is a serious force—the current vehicle of conservative Republicans' dreams and a determiner of some Presidential policies now. There are many people—including some who opposed him—who say that he was a reasonably competent governor of California and that his administration was more progressive than his political rhetoric would suggest.

Other members of the Reagan travelling staff are Martin Anderson, a conservative economist and former Nixon assistant; Lyn Nofziger, Reagan's rumpled, unbuttoned press aide; Matt Lawson, an assistant to Nofziger who worries about our schedules and our baggage while Nofziger entertains us and tells us what he wants us to hear; another assistant to Nofziger; an assistant to Hannaford; Dennis LeBlanc, an advance man; Kurt Wurzberger, who handles our baggage; and Dana Rohrbacher, who tapes all of Reagan's statements and then offers "actualities"—excerpts from the candidate's remarks—to local stations in cities where the candidate appears. Rohrbacher is a mustachioed young man who plays a kazoo and a guitar (simultaneously) on the plane. Except for him, and the loose Nofziger, it is a fairly buttoned-up entourage, pleasant but cheerless. In size it seems almost Presidential. The candidate—whom they all refer to as "the Governor"—sits in a forward compartment, remote, like an exotic bird that is being protected.

FEBRUARY 13

The grand ballroom of the Holiday Inn, just outside Kankakee, Illinois. About six hundred people have turned out for a "ranch breakfast" with Reagan. The audience is mostly middle-aged and completely white. Reagan, at the head table, looks just right in a blue Western shirt and brown Western pants. Jo Anne Bailey, who starred in *Gypsy* in the Kankakee Valley Theatre, belts out, to the tune of "Everything's Coming Up Roses," a song called "Everything's Coming Up Reagan" ("Hear us shout! Hello, Dutch! / You have—that magic touch. . . . You can do it . . . Kankakee's gonna see to it"). Signs and banners are hung about the room, and the crowd is enthusiastic. Campaign workers in straw boaters pass out sign-up sheets to get people to work for Reagan. For a dollar and twenty-five cents, one can buy a paperback entitled "Sincerely, Ronald Reagan," in which Reagan's secretary has collected his correspondence.

Reagan begins by telling a couple of jokes, which the accompanying reporters inform me he tells all the time. They have no particular point, but they are audience warmers. Reagan looks good at the rostrum: a tall figure with ruddy cheeks, his reddish-brown hair swept back in a slight pompadour. He speaks with a somewhat husky Midwestern voice. He tells the group of a poll "that made me angry" because it showed that people thought the Democrats were more capable of solving the nation's economic problems, and he says that the Democrats have brought the nation to "the brink of economic ruin" with their "wild spending ideas." He talks of Americans' capacity for self-reliance, and says, "I happen to believe that there was a divine plan in the setting of this land between the oceans." He excoriates "a little band of intellectual élites on the banks of the Potomac" who think they know better than the people what's good for them. He talks of the need to "give back to the people of this country the right to run their own country and determine their own destiny—and that has been taken away from us by the central government in Washington, D.C." Being in Illinois, he attacks the embargo on the sale of grain to the Soviet Union. Like other politicians, he is speaking to people's grievances.

He invites questions from the audience.

A man asks how long it will be before the budget can be balanced.

Reagan replies that "deficit spending is responsible for all the economic problems confronting us today." He works up a sense of astonishment at what they do in Washington, those foreigners. He does not mention Ford. The enemy is "Washington," whose mists surround the bureaucracy, the Congress, and, of course, the incumbent Administration. He campaigns against "the buddy system in Washington." He says, "Government is the problem." Reagan tells this audience, "Many of us are going to have to give up some programs that are pets of ours." One looks forward to his examples, because politicians do not often tell people that they should learn to live without programs they have come to enjoy. Reagan offers as examples what he describes as two grants made by the National Endowment for the Arts—one of seven hundred and fifty dollars for a one-word misspelled poem, "lighght," and one for a nude play that ends in a sexual orgy. (Actually, the latter was not funded by the government.) "Don't tell me the country would go to rack and ruin" if we got rid of programs like that, Reagan says. He explains his own proposal—the ninety-billion-dollar plan—to transfer programs to the states. The idea has been considerably refined since Reagan first launched it, in a speech in Chicago last September. In that speech, Reagan proposed the "transfer of authority in whole or part" in at least six areas—welfare, education, housing, food stamps, Medicaid, and community and regional development—which he said "would reduce the outlay of the federal government by more than ninety billion dollars." Under his proposal, he said, local governments, which are closer to the people, would decide which programs would be continued. (When Reagan was asked earlier this year what would be done about states that did not pick up some of the responsibilities, such as welfare, he suggested migration, saying, "You can vote with your feet in this country.") As the program came under attack from the Ford Administration—which argued in New Hampshire, where there is neither a state income nor sales tax, that state taxes would have to be raised to pay for programs Reagan would cut—and under close questioning by the press, Reagan and his staff made a series of adjustments. The ninety-billion figure was dropped. ("A mistake," Reagan explained.) The staff emphasized the point that the idea was for a *transfer* of programs, not their elimination, and a program of financing them at the state level, by earmarking certain federal taxes for the states, was worked out. The states would have the option of not continuing the programs. Reagan says that his proposal would reduce the overhead on the programs and would provide for an "orderly transfer." He talks about it as if it were just a matter of the press and his opponents getting the thing all confused and one should wonder what all the questions were about.

Asked about Angola, he says that we don't know which side to take, because "no one in our government has told us whether Angola has any strategic importance." Asked about welfare, he talks about abuses and gives an example, as he has often done in his campaign, of a woman in Chicago who, he says, has eighty names, thirty addresses, and fifteen telephone numbers, and is collecting veterans' benefits on four dead husbands who never lived—for a total estimated income of a hundred and fifty thousand dollars a year. The audience laughs. (There are some questions about this example. The woman, in actuality, is being prosecuted on charges of using four aliases and fraudulently collecting eight thousand dollars.) He comes across as a pleasant man who understands why people are angry.

Shortly after the breakfast in the ballroom, Reagan holds a press conference. He has changed into a brown suit. He wears an American-flag pin in his lapel. Up close, he looks surprisingly older than he did at a distance. The face is pale and creased; the voice is weaker. He seems somehow shrunken. He begins by making a correction in something he had said about how his tax-transfer plan would work. Pressed by a reporter about what he would do to balance the budget, he says that he may be able to be more specific later, and adds, testily, "What you would like to do is pick at it and keep picking at it." He also becomes annoyed when he is asked for details of his program-transfer plan. He says that he would not have gone to Helsinki, as the President did at the end of July, 1975, or signed the Helsinki agreement, which ratified Europe's postwar borders; that he would not have signed the energy legislation (which held down the price of oil); that he would not have approved "the sixty-billion-dollar deficit which turned out to be a seventy-six-billion-dollar deficit." This man wants to be President. He seems to have grasped a few issues, or parts of issues, and to be clinging to them. There is a slight atmosphere of masquerade about all this. He talks to people's grievances, but he doesn't seem mean. He doesn't even seem very fired up about what he is saying. And he doesn't seem very well informed. He projects a kind of earnestness, and when he says that something makes him mad it is a respectable mad, a decent American fedupness. He expresses not so much anger as indignation—nineteenth-hole indignation—at welfare chisellers and bureaucrats and taxes. It is the same list that George Wallace and Spiro Agnew attacked. But Reagan comes across as doing it in a much nicer way.

At the Condesa del Mar, in Alsip, a town in the southern part of suburban Cook County, Reagan addresses an enthusiastic crowd of about twelve hundred. He begins by telling the same jokes he told this morning, and adds a third—a barnyard story, which he also tells frequently. As he talks, he tilts his head slightly to one side; his eyes crinkle. He comes on as a regular guy. He delivers essentially the same speech he gave this morning, and he delivers it forcefully. He is accomplished at this; he has been in the business for years. He once called himself a liberal, and some attribute his transformation from a liberal into a conservative to the period in the early fifties when, his movie career on the slide, he became the host of *General Electric Theatre* and a travelling spokesman for General Electric. (Reagan had been president of the Screen Actors Guild and had coöperated with the anti-Communist investigations of the film industry—a position that cost him many of his liberal connections and made him a subject of bitter controversy.) Some attribute the change to his second marriage—to Nancy Davis, an actress and a neurosurgeon's daughter, who is said to be highly conservative. Reagan and his wife, a strong woman, are very close. In any event, Reagan has for years now been travelling the banquet circuit telling jokes and making speeches about the horrors of big government. His jokes are the toastmaster's jokes, neither very clever nor really pertinent. His "speeches" are actually sets of four-by-six-inch cards on which he has written paragraphs and anecdotes with a felt-tipped pen, and which he shuffles to give slight variations. His fund of knowledge seems to be made up largely of clippings—stories and polls he has come across that will make good material. Sometimes his syntax gets a little confused and it is not clear what point he is trying to make. Today, for example, one thing that makes him mad is that "a housewife can't buy a box of breakfast cereal without being cheated unless there's a government agency there to protect her."

Again he takes questions from the audience. The questions are friendly. He says that he would like to go to Washington, and that he is not "part of that family, that Establishment in Washington, and therefore not a part of that buddy system that goes on." The audience—mainly middle-aged and older—applauds and whistles. Reagan looks ruddy again, not the way he looked at the press conference. He is very good at being "on." He says that détente "has deteriorated into a one-way street." He says, "Inflation is caused by the government spending more than the government takes in." On arms, he says, "In a few years, if we do not reverse the course, the Soviet Union is going to be able to deliver an ultimatum." He tells again about the woman in Chicago who he says is receiving one hundred and fifty thousand dollars in welfare benefits.

I spent some time talking with people around Reagan, and then with Reagan himself, to see if I could understand why he is running, and how he reached the decision to run. To many, Reagan seemed to be the sentimental favorite at the Republican Convention in 1968, but Nixon was nominated, because many Republicans remembered what had happened in 1964. Reagan and his men deny that Reagan was seeking the nomination in 1968. Reagan told me that as soon as he was elected governor of California in 1966, people began to ask him if he would run for President, and that when it appeared that the 1968 race would be between Robert Kennedy and Nixon the requests that he run increased. "I never once lifted my finger," Reagan said as I talked with him late this evening on the plane on the way to Orlando, Florida. He continued, "At the Convention, they asked would I speak to the delegates. I never made a pitch that 'O.K., now I'm a candidate.' Confusion arose because the California delegation made a statement that they considered me a candidate. That's how much I ran in '68."

But the idea had been planted. Moreover, Reagan had become the conservative spokesman. In the summer of 1974—while he was still governor and Nixon was still President—some of Reagan's aides and advisers began to meet on the question of a race for the Presidency. Among those at the early meetings were Deaver, Hannaford, Nofziger, John Sears (a former political aide to Nixon who worked briefly in the White House and is now Reagan's campaign director), Richard Wirthlin (a pollster for Reagan), M. Stanton Evans (a writer and radio commentator), William Rusher (publisher of the *National Review*), and Robert Gray (of the public-relations firm Hill and Knowlton). Reagan remained noncommittal, his aides say, but the group did urge him, as one put it, "to keep his options open." One aide explained, "When we began, we thought a liberal like Percy"—Illinois Senator Charles Percy—"would be the candidate. But I've always been convinced that the liberals in our party fool themselves. The conservatives are not a minority of a minority, they are a majority of a minority, and we were convinced that any liberal who ran, we would wax him. Then Nixon dropped out, and we had to reassess and see how Ford was doing. It became obvious to us by the first of last year that Ford was not setting the country on fire, and then we looked at all the other drawbacks he had, such as not having a national constituency, the people with whom he surrounded himself—ex-congressmen and congressional staff. We saw him making the mistake all Republican Presidents make—trying to be all things to all people, getting a consensus. In the process, the people who can enthusiastically support him fall by the wayside. The surveys we took showed us behind but within striking distance of getting the nomination and within striking distance of election." The Republican right, then, in a strong resemblance to the Democratic left, cannot accept compromises even by someone who is essentially sympathetic. Gerald Ford may be as conservative a President as the Republican right is likely to get, but he does not ultimately satisfy it. And so, like other politicians who have tried to reach across some divisions in order to get elected, or to govern, Gerald Ford is being keelhauled.

In late 1974 and early 1975, as the group continued to meet—sometimes with Reagan present, sometimes not—Deaver and Hannaford put together their public-relations firm and set up a system by which Reagan could earn a substantial income and remain a visible spokesman. He spent from twelve to fourteen days a month on the road; through his radio program, he reached ten or fifteen million people a day; his column appeared in about a hundred and eighty newspapers. In July of 1975, with Reagan's assent, a committee was formed to raise money, begin organizing, and survey the potentialities of a Reagan race. An aide tells me that the Reagan strategy was very carefully arrived at. He says, "We weren't running against Gerald Ford. We weren't running against the Congress. We weren't running against Democrats as such. We were running against evil incarnate as embodied in the buddy system in Washington." In December of 1974, according to Reagan's associates, Ford phoned Reagan and said that he wanted him to be part of his government, mentioned that there would be some openings in the Cabinet, including the Transportation Department, and said that he would like Reagan to take one of the jobs. A few days later, Reagan called Ford back and said that he did not think he would enjoy being a Cabinet officer after being governor of the largest state. In the spring of 1975, when Reagan was in Washington for a meeting of the Rockefeller Commission on the C.I.A., of which he had agreed to be a member, Donald Rumsfeld met with him and offered him the job of Secretary of Commerce. Again Reagan said no. "So," says a Reagan aide, "when they saw they couldn't coöpt him they set out to embarrass him, by getting some of the Governor's friends and political allies to support Ford for reëlection." And then the aide cut to what is probably the heart of the matter of why Reagan is running: "He didn't really have any choice. If he was going to have anything to say to this country, if he was to be a spokesman for any segment, he had to go. With all those people saying, 'Ron, you've got to lead us,' he had to go or be seen as a bag of hot air, and they would have turned to someone else as their spokesman." Reagan had to run for the Presidency or forfeit his role as the conservative spokesman, which had become his career. The explanations that are given—that it was Ford's signing the tax bill, and the like—seem to be justifications after the fact. Even if he loses, his position is secure. He will have fought the noble fight.

In our conversation, on the plane to Florida, Reagan assigns an important role to his wealthy friends Justin Dart, head of Dart Industries, and Holmes Tuttle, a wealthy California friend of Reagan's who is said to be the largest Ford car dealer in the world and who did not want him to run. "More and more people came and said, 'You've got to do this,'" he tells me, and he continues, "They still said no. Finally, it just kept growing to the point where they said yes." But Reagan portrays himself as the reluctant candidate. The organization Citizens for Reagan was formed. "Finally," Reagan says, "in fairness to them, I gave them a date by which I would become a candidate—November 20th." Reagan says that he felt he had to run because "the Administration did not follow the path where it would not be necessary to do this—meeting the problems of inflation, the budget deficit." He goes on, "I deplore the Helsinki agreement. I think too much was given away at Vladivostok. And also there was the whole segment of people who did not accept Ford as a leader. I just felt that, win, lose, or draw, there were things that needed to be said, a debate needed to take place. When you're not a professional politician—I guess there was almost a sense of unreality about it, for both Nancy and myself. It was a little bit like the drunk hanging on to the lamppost, and the moon was reflected in the gutter, in the water of the gutter, and a fellow going by, and he grabbed him and said to the man, 'What's that down there?' And the fellow looked at him and he said, 'It's the moon.' And the drunk says, 'What the hell am I doing way up here?'"

He should probably be taken at his word: he is propelled by a combination of intoxication and a sense of responsibility. How does one separate those, in any event? What is it that persuades someone that he must offer himself to the people? Particularly when, for all the effort you must make, what you must do is not altogether unattractive: ride in limousines, travel with entourages (never having to worry about your suitcase), listen to crowds cheering, to people telling you that you're needed, that you're the only one who can set things straight. Reagan is accustomed to living in a kind of cocoon: his conservative advisers huddle around him; his friends are wealthy California businessmen. And his life's work has been receiving adulation.

FEBRUARY 14

Orlando. We arrived at our motel at about one-thirty this morning. Ford was here yesterday, and the paper is filled with stories about his visit. The paper, the Orlando *Sentinel Star,* which is for Ford, is an important force here in central Florida. The President announced that the International Chamber of Commerce would hold its 1978 convention at Disney World, near here, which he said could generate more than a million dollars for the economy of central Florida. The federal connection was that the United States Travel Service, in the Commerce Department, was instrumental in attracting the convention. Ford also said that people shouldn't "nit-pick" foreign policy and that we must "keep cool" in foreign policy and "keep our powder dry." Jerry Thomas, the 1974 Republican candidate for governor of Florida and a conservative leader, announced his support of Ford earlier this week. He has been offered an important job, rumored to be Under-Secretary of the Treasury. George Wallace, Jimmy Carter, and Henry Jackson are also in the state this weekend.

The Ford-Reagan contest in Florida is being carried on against a background of swamp politics, of fights among local politicians for control of the Party in each congressional district—each is a sort of separate barony—and in the state. The Presidential candidates become somewhat incidental as the local politicians figure what is at stake for themselves if they take one or another side. This is another example of the "back-yard principle." It was this intramural warfare in Florida that was causing severe organizational problems for the Ford campaign until a few weeks ago, when Stuart Spencer called in William Roberts, his former partner in the California public-relations firm that created the politician Ronald Reagan. The Ford campaign here is said to be taking shape. L. E. (Tommy) Thomas, a big, beefy man who is Reagan's campaign chairman in Florida, has become more subdued. The Florida delegation at the 1968 Convention almost went for Reagan "I have said all along it would be two to one for Reagan here," Thomas said today, "but now I'm not sure."

Reagan's itinerary today took him to small communities of retirees and citrus farmers, to a Citizens for Reagan barbecue in Eustis, in Lake County, and to a Republican Club rally in De Bary, in Volusia County. Many of the citizens of these towns came there from the Midwest and the Northeast. Our bus travelled long distances through land that was marked by citrus groves, lakes, and trees covered with Spanish moss. Reagan told the same jokes he had been telling yesterday, made many of the same remarks, and answered questions. Asked about energy, he said that the way to get more oil and gas is "for the government to get out of the way of the private sector." Referring to an issue he has begun to use against Ford in Florida, he criticized the negotiations to revise the treaty between the United States and Panama granting the United States sovereign control over the Panama Canal "in perpetuity." He said that the Canal is sovereign United States territory in the same way Alaska is, and that the leader of Panama is "a Marxist military dictator." Reagan said, "I think we should tell him to shut up— 'We're keeping the Canal.' " For which he received loud cheers and applause.

Tomorrow, before returning to California for some rest, Reagan will participate in Bicentennial ceremonies in Winter Park.

6

SUNDAY. Richard Nixon is in China (his picture is on the front pages of the papers). Gerald Ford and Ronald Reagan have been campaigning in New Hampshire. On Tuesday evening, the President held a televised news conference, ostensibly to announce his own plans for reorganization of the C.I.A. and other foreign-intelligence agencies (thus getting the jump on Congress), and took advantage of his free prime time to get in some jabs at Reagan. The President said that Reagan had suggested from time to time that the Social Security system be voluntary (a position that Reagan once supported but has since repudiated), and that its funds be invested in the stock market (which Reagan mentioned that other people had mentioned, and which he then dropped). One begins to wonder what candidates would do without Social Security—to promise to increase the benefits of, or to accuse each other of wanting to do in. Asked about his statement in an interview with Walter Cronkite that there was no philosophical difference between himself and Reagan, the President explained that there was a distinction between "philosophical" and "pragmatic" differences.

Today, I had lunch with Carl Holman, the president of the Urban Coalition. That is his formal title; informally, and quite apart from his particular form of employment, Holman is one of the most important blacks in America. He has lines out to and in from practically all segments of black communities. He is a friend and adviser of many black leaders; he is one of the leaders most trusted by those blacks who are not leaders. His protégés are scattered throughout America in influential positions. He also has lines out to and in from various segments of the white world. Holman is widely consulted, because of his wisdom and his experience. Now fifty-six, he has had a remarkable life, beginning in Minter City, Mississippi. The recipient of a Whitney fellowship at Yale, Holman was an established poet and playwright by the late nineteen-forties, when he began teaching English at Clark College, in Atlanta. He was a strategist for the student sit-ins (from which several of his protégés came), and he edited a black weekly paper. He advised Martin Luther King, Jr., and he bailed students out of jail. He came to Washington in the nineteen-sixties to work for the Civil Rights Commission, and then moved to the Urban Coalition. All the way, he devoted himself—often to the detriment of his health—to improving the condition of blacks and the relations between blacks and whites. He is a tall, slim, gentle man who speaks slowly, sometimes circularly, and often with humor. I have talked with him frequently over recent years. I was surprised by the intensity and despair of his remarks today.

I began by asking Holman why issues relating to blacks seem to have slipped from the public agenda.

"A white reporter came up to me recently," he replied, "and said, 'Isn't it true people don't care about the cities?' I said yes—that that's because in the sixties, when there were the riots, cities became a metaphor for blacks. That's firmly fixed in people's minds. Cities are out. They're out of style—despite all the noise about New York. Some urban experts suggest that the blacks who were salvageable were swept up and out into the suburbs—into decent jobs, and all that. And they were acceptable, because they do not frighten people with their differentness. So the ones who are left behind are locked in a life style that the rest of America finds repugnant, and they are considered unsalvageable, you see, and it is considered a waste to spend time and money on them and worry about them. As the cities of the Northeast have become more and more the preserves of the blacks and Latinos, they have come to be seen as expendable."

Holman went on, "What's clear about the reaction of many blacks to the President and the way many Democrats and Republicans dealt with New York City was to say in any private gathering that New York City would never have been dealt with like that if it had been seen as a city of Wasps. Vernon Jordan"—executive director of the Urban League—"talks all the time about how difficult it is to get people to see that because there are so many more whites in the country, there are more whites on welfare than blacks. People have been going over these great landmarks for blacks, and nobody's looking at the rifts that began to appear. You could see the growing view that there would not be a larger sharing of the pie but a sharing of the same slice. So if jobs were to be open to blacks they would have to be in the public sector. And then, in the school system, you ran into the administrators and the teachers. And then came the DeFunis case." In that case, a white applicant to the University of Washington Law School sued on the ground that he had been denied acceptance in favor of minority students with lower test scores. He won the case in a lower court. "You began to see people splitting up," Holman said. "Busing is a trap for blacks. We've given up a broad terrain on which we might have fought, and have retreated to a kind of Dunkirk, with the sea to our backs. There is so much hostility and tension. There are three options: busing, compensatory education, career education. What's happening? We're losing all three options and ending up with zilch. The truth is people are not happy with the status quo. There is a great move to the status quo ante. People are talking about how much better it would have been if 'we' had not brought 'them' over, or thinking about how much better it was before the sixties."

I asked if this was really true.

He replied, "One member of the Coalition says we have to distinguish between the paranoia that's unhealthy and that which is necessary. That quip that if you're not paranoid you don't understand the situation has some validity for blacks. We used to say, 'Oh, no, Nixon would never appoint a Carswell.' Look at the nostalgia craze. E. L. Doctorow, in *Ragtime,* talks about these white ladies going out to see the fleet, and he says there were no Negroes, there were no Jews. In the early part of this century, everyone knew his place. It's no accident that that book is a best-seller."

Holman went on, "I think it's a mistake, if one looks at race in this country, to look at legislation or the so-called big issues, because most blacks aren't involved in those. I see happening in the country what happened in Atlanta when white people asked me why it was that the older black leaders who had contact with the white world did not warn them that the student movement was coming. I said, 'One, because they were your message-bearers who did not want to bring you a message you did not want to hear; two, they were not trusted; three, they were to serve as apologists for you, and couldn't have any victories.' Now blacks see their leaders ignored by the executive branch of the government, ignored by the legislature, ignored by the media, and they bring no victories. You talk about black mayors and they say, 'Yeah, what can they do?' What's happening now is a great cynicism not only among black

leaders but also among young blacks as regards their leaders. I don't
see a lot of young blacks aspiring to leadership, because they figure
it's a losing game. You see a kind of dangerous cynicism and
anomie among young blacks—the kind of despair where you don't
care whether you live or die. What can we say? We can't keep
going back and saying, 'Look at our civil-rights victories.' "

Then Holman said, "Even white people think politicians don't
care about them. Then what the hell do you think blacks think?
What Watergate meant to a lot of blacks was 'This was what we
always thought they were like.' There's a great feeling of being out
of it—outsiders in your own country—which was a feeling they
began to lose in the sixties. And it's come back double-barrelled
now. Some of the blacks feel, as Paul put it in the Bible, that they
are 'aliens from the commonwealth.' Everything operates to make
them think that. Meanwhile, strong crosscurrents develop that are
rarely detected, like Moynihan's saying that it was no accident that
Amin—and I'm no fan of his—was chairing the Organization of
African Unity, when it was his turn. It's beyond such things as the
percentage of blacks that are unemployed. It's the basic non-caring
for those who don't make it—the 'Too bad about them. I've got
mine, Jack.' Everyone knows that proportionately more blacks are
out of jobs than whites. The President knows that national figures
for joblessness are all but meaningless when it comes to blacks.
You'll have seven percent nationally and forty-five percent in a
whole segment in Chicago. The government stopped making those
breakdowns and brought in someone else to deal with labor statistics. Bernard Anderson, a young black economist at the Wharton
School, has been saying that we are coming up with a generation of
young blacks who have never had any job experience. They have
been jobless and they are going to stay jobless and can't even col-
lect unemployment benefits. The President knows what it means
when he says we have to wait three or four years to reduce unemployment by any significant amount. And he knows another
thing—he knows he's not going to be contested by liberal whites, as
he might have been before, because it is less and less popular to
defend blacks, and because blacks in the know have become more
and more disaffected and vote less and less. We are in that kind of
Arctic Zone now, and I think most blacks feel that an ice age has
come, and it slows and it chills and you don't get a reaction."

"Then what might happen?" I asked him.

"In terms of young blacks and blacks who are out of work, they don't feel any of those old allegiances—to liberals, to labor," Holman replied. "I see a kind of opacity—you can't get through. The kind of subterranean and sporadic violence we're getting now is worse than it was before. My son said that he knows a lot of young black folks who say, 'What's the use of living? We might as well be back in slavery, because then we'd get a meal.' I was kind of surprised at this; it was so different from the kind of militant statement you'd get a few years ago. Young people feeling defeated is unusual. They usually think in terms of options; old people feel defeated. You get to the point of asking what the options in this country are if you want to get up and out. The options for blacks are shrinking. They'll show you a black who has a fancy job in a computer firm, but the cold, cold fact is that the income gap between blacks and whites in the last fifteen, twenty years has not altered to any significant degree. The gap between most blacks and most whites has widened. What has altered is that there is a thin layer of blacks who are getting ahead. And that's a grim, grim reality. Nobody knows what the final straw will be."

FEBRUARY 25

The results of the New Hampshire primary yesterday suggest an optical illusion. In the Republican race, President Ford defeated Ronald Reagan by only about thirteen hundred votes, and his victory is being seen as more of a victory than it was because it was a victory at all. (That is something of an advance: in previous New Hampshire primaries a loser who had such a substantial percentage would have been called the winner.) It is interesting to consider how different it would be if some six hundred and fifty people had voted the other way. The blow to the President would have been devastating.

The Democratic race is being subjected to overinterpretation. Jimmy Carter won with twenty-nine percent; Morris Udall received twenty-four percent; Birch Bayh sixteen percent; Fred Harris eleven percent; Sargent Shriver nine percent. It is being said that Carter won the Democratic primary because he won the "conservative" votes and the others divided the "liberal" vote. Yet the results also show that Carter received a substantial portion of the "liberal" votes. It is possible that the results had very little to do with ideology—that Jimmy Carter received more votes than the others because he simply was more appealing to more people. Ideological considerations did not seem apparent as I watched the candidates in New Hampshire. It is doubtful whether many votes were cast on the basis of Carter's saying he would prefer to create jobs through the private sector, while the other Democrats talk about creating them through the public sector. The voting seems influenced much less by issues, and much more by subjective reactions, than that. It is said that the results show that an "anti-Washington" mood is dominant, but by that measurement the majority of those who voted in the Democratic primary were "pro-Washington."

FEBRUARY 29

The President, campaigning in Florida this weekend, called Fidel Castro an "international outlaw." He also told an audience of Cuban refugees that he has ordered a speedup in the process by which they can become United States citizens. There are more than half a million Cuban refugees in Florida. In Boston, Jimmy Carter told an audience in Faneuil Hall that recent criticism of him by his opponents "won't hurt me, but I'm afraid it might hurt the country."

MARCH 1

A study prepared for the Arms Control Association, the Institute for World Order, and the Members of Congress for Peace Through Law Education Fund says that the world's spending for military purposes has risen to almost three hundred billion dollars a year, with the most rapid increase taking place in the developing nations.

In South Carolina precinct caucuses last night, the highest percentage of the votes—forty-seven percent—was for "Uncommitted." Among the votes for specific candidates, George Wallace came out slightly ahead of Jimmy Carter.

MARCH 2

In an interview for a Miami television station yesterday, President Ford said, " 'Détente' is only a word that was coined," and he added, "I don't think it is applicable anymore." The President said, "I think what we ought to say is that the United States will meet with the superpowers—the Soviet Union and with China and others—and seek to relax tensions so that we can continue a policy of peace through strength."

Today, I had lunch with Fred Dutton, a Washington lawyer who is a graduate of the Presidential campaigns of Adlai Stevenson and of John and Robert Kennedy and George McGovern. Dutton is an unconventional man and usually has something original to say about what is going on. I was particularly eager to talk with Dutton, because when I talked with him last fall he had made a convincing case for a new approach to seeking the nomination. His argument then was that not only was all the frenetic running around by candidates degrading but a more philosophical, aloof approach would be more successful. In the light of what has been happening—the race seeming to go to the most dogged campaigner of them all—I wanted to see what Dutton had to say now.

"This is a traditional election," Dutton said, and he continued, "We're letting go of the bar of one trapeze and we haven't yet got hold of the next one. As a nation, we're giving up old premises and moving to new ones. What we need in our politics—what we're looking for—is somebody to reinstill a sense of character in the country, to make sense of the eclecticism. It takes a personality to do that. The process of diffusion that is going on is not something that can be handled politically very easily. Our elections are always a little behind what's happening. Look at it historically. In the nineteen-twenties, the immigrant wave was rising to power and we elected Herbert Hoover. We all know about the 'cultural lag.' The political lag is even behind the cultural lag. The nineteen-thirties dealt with the mess of the nineteen-twenties. Now we're moving out of the turbulence of the sixties. We're moving away from the New Deal–Roosevelt-Truman collective action. We're going back to individualism, eclecticism. What the current anti-government theme is really about is the search for the proper relationship between the individual and government. Hubert Humphrey and Thomas Jefferson are at war with each other in this election."

I asked him what had become of his idea of the philosopher-candidate.

He replied, "The philosopher has to have flair, drama—to interest the media. I can't see why a Socrates or a Hobbes can't interest the media of his day as well as anyone else. Carter is not just a product of organization. He is a natural for the early primaries, and he's doing what my philosopher would do—making good news copy. Jefferson was a man of flair as well as of sub-stance. Carter is filling a vacuum. He hasn't got where he's got by organization. He is a product of the media's saying he is really out there moving around, shaking hands. As for issues, the public doesn't want programmatic details. It has a short attention span, conditioned by television. People want to hear about individualism, basic values. I think the public out there is talking more about basic values than has ever before been the case in my lifetime. I don't think it's desultory. Jimmy Carter is responding to that."

But, I asked him, how would his aloof, cool philosopher survive against a candidate such as Jimmy Carter, who was out there, everywhere, working the people?

"What Carter has done has generally been misinterpreted," he replied. "He has been pictured as running around, but his has been a fairly plodding, deliberate thing. It's a sustained approach. You have to take a deliberate approach. That can consist of steady campaigning, which is what Carter has done, or it can be aloof, like the philosopher king. The guys who fall between stools are Jackson and Udall. You don't know what they are. The question is how, as a practical matter, you get across to the voters. How many people has Carter actually seen? Probably one-hundredth of one percent. All the rest of it is imagery—newspaper stories, shadows on the cave walls. If you are able to get through in the media with your force of personality, your image, your quotability, your timeliness, your interestingness, then you can get across. And if you reach the people through the media, you are going to reach just as many people as the man in all the motorcades. It's not Jimmy Carter's running around that's getting across; it's his style and image and message. A lot of the candidates' running around is to meet the needs of the media, and is what the media have become accustomed to. The philosopher can't just be in love with ideas. He would have to be in touch with people. That can be done."

March 3

Henry Jackson won yesterday's primary in Massachusetts, and his victory has upset calculations and sent people scrambling—participants, would-be participants, observers, journalists. All these primaries have to be seen in terms of their impact as well as in terms of the literal result of delegates amassed. Jackson, who did poorly in 1972—he never came in higher than third in any primary—had been dismissed by observers. He stressed jobs, in a state with high unemployment, and his opposition to busing, in a state where emotion on the issue runs high. (He took out newspaper ads that said, "I am against busing.") Daniel Patrick Moynihan, who had endorsed him, campaigned by his side. Last week's truism was that the anti-Washington stand was carrying the day. This week, in Massachusetts, the most votes were cast for the candidate who has the longest record of service in Washington and who unashamedly espouses a number of federal programs. Jackson, usually a fairly solemn man, has been all over the papers and television beaming, announcing, in the tradition of politicians who seek to invest their victories, however narrow, with great significance, that he has revived the "grand coalition" of the Democratic Party and has won the "lunch bucket" vote—a phrase that seems patronizing. Jackson, with the strong support of unions—primarily the construction unions—was by far the best organized of the candidates. Labor supplied about twenty-five hundred workers for Jackson. They canvassed and—in the driving snow—got their voters to the polls. Actually, the "grand coalition" did not exactly fling itself at Jackson as if he were the new Franklin Roosevelt. Jackson shared the blue-collar vote with Wallace and the black vote with Carter (for whom Representative Andrew Young, a black from Georgia, campaigned in Massachusetts and the Reverend Martin Luther King, Sr., made a radio ad that was used in the state) and, essentially, surrendered the intellectuals to Udall. Jackson won, which is what matters, but, as in New Hampshire, the number of candidates picking over the same voters tended to throw things off. Jackson received twenty-three percent of the vote; Udall came in second, with eighteen percent; Wallace third, with seventeen; Carter fourth, with fourteen; then Harris with eight, Shriver with seven, Bayh with five, Ellen McCormack with four, Shapp with three. (Mrs. McCormack, a Long Island housewife, is the candidate of the Pro-Life Action Committee, an anti-abortion group, and qualified for federal matching campaign funds last week. Shapp also has qualified.)

The Bayh strategy, which seemed so sound on the drawing boards, was to build a candidacy on a collection of blocs, including labor (traditional and liberal), farmers, blacks, women, and Jews. The strategy so impressed Party professionals that in January some were predicting Bayh's nomination. But it collapsed utterly at the hands of the voters. Carter, the invincible candidate, has been shown to be vincible, and Carter's protestations that he did not make a major effort in Massachusetts, concentrating instead on Florida, are not helping him much. He had counted on "momentum"—one of the most overused words of the year—from his New Hampshire victory. He had reason to: this week, his picture is on the covers of *Time* and *Newsweek*. Udall claimed that the Massachusetts primary established him as the leader of the "progressives," but that left the question of what this means and what he can do with it. It was a question on many minds today—of people who had to do some quick calculating about what it meant for themselves, and just maybe the Democratic Party. Jackson, on the one hand, is very upsetting to liberals and, on the other, has some support—by traditional unions—that Hubert Humphrey, waiting on the sidelines, would inherit if the Jackson candidacy collapsed. "We're back to Square One," said one liberal activist today. This man, like many of his colleagues from the McCarthy and McGovern campaigns, is not quite in politics and not quite out of it. These people keep in touch with one another and with the press, and while they do not have tangible power, they can affect others' decisions about whom to back and can affect the press's view of what's going on. They supply some of the atmospherics that influence events and fill the air of an election. They are spending a lot of time on the phone today.

This afternoon, I went to see Hubert Humphrey. The Humphrey phenomenon—the thought that, after all, "old Hubert" deserves and should have the nomination—seems to be a product of some combination of political calculation, sentiment, guilt, fear of the unknown, and self-interest. A great many people in and around politics, of course, examine the candidates in terms not of what the candidates would do for the country but of what the candidates would do for them—the back-yard principle. And there is a predilection for the familiar. A Humphrey candidacy is looked upon favorably by many of Humphrey's Senate colleagues and by several governors and congressmen as well as by lawyers and lobbyists in Washington. A Humphrey candidacy is very important for a number of investors in power. "If Humphrey were nominated," a friend of mine remarked recently, "most of the people at the Federal City Club wouldn't have to change a name on their Rolodexes." Some people want Humphrey because they want Humphrey, and some people want Humphrey because they don't want anybody else— especially Jimmy Carter. "Carter can't be President," an important journalist remarked the other night. "He doesn't know his way around this city." In a conversation today, I asked one Senate Democrat, "Why Humphrey?" He said, "Both because his colleagues like him and because they think his candidacy will help them. Everybody figures that if Humphrey is President the tent flaps will be up and everybody can come in. He's an open, happy man. He doesn't have the others' problems—Muskie's 'breakdown' in '72, Kennedy's Chappaquiddick. There is some guilt feeling—feeling that people were too tough on him when he ran against Nixon in '68. He has done well since he came back to the Senate. With the exception of John Kennedy's election in 1960, we have gone back to familiar faces, to something comfortable."

Former candidates, convinced that they would have been nominated but for this or that, usually want to try again to be nominated. They almost have to convince themselves that their failure was caused by the stars. Encouraged by their aides and associates, they begin to see how it would all be different the next time. So Muskie, too, is known to still covet the Presidential nomination. But he, like Humphrey, has no stomach for seeking it through the primaries (which were so painful to him in 1972), and, moreover, must seek reëlection to his Maine Senate seat this year. Those around Muskie used to say that he was a terrible Presidential candidate but would be a fine President. There is evidence that Muskie shares at least the latter part of that view. The series of events that could lead to a Muskie nomination this year, according to some people close to the Senator, is that no one who is now running could win the nomination, and that the Convention would find Humphrey wanting, because of old scars; then the Convention would turn to Muskie. Muskie is said to believe that this might happen.

There are, predictably, two schools of thought concerning the effect on the Humphrey candidacy of the Jackson victory in Massachusetts. One is that it hurt Humphrey, because labor support that would otherwise have moved to Humphrey will stick with Jackson; the other is that it helped Humphrey, because it makes it less likely that any of the candidates can reach the Convention with enough votes to win. I talked with Humphrey this afternoon in his office in the Old Senate Office Building. Humphrey's office is as busy as any on Capitol Hill, and busier than most; it is as if he were a head of state rather than a senator. He looks better than at any other time I remember: his complexion ruddy, his eyes clear, his face and figure clear of flab. His hair, no longer dyed, shows gray at the temples. During his Vice-Presidency and his Presidential candidacies, his natural good humor was often dampened by the anguish of his situation. Now he is unmistakably a happy man. His position is that he will not enter the primaries but will accept the nomination if it is offered. What he has built by standing aside might well be destroyed if he began to campaign. The big question about Humphrey is whether his personal transformation could translate into a political transformation. He wows them at union conventions and at political dinners; he still ranks high in the opinion polls, which could be a reflection of continuing well-knownness compared to the other candidates. But no one can be sure what would happen if there was extended public exposure to Humphrey: whether he would talk too much; whether he would again come across with a certain weakness, too eager to please, impressionable; what memories (of the Johnson Administration and Humphrey's defense of the war) would be aroused; what questions would rise to the surface (one former member of Humphrey's staff pleaded guilty to charges of illegally aiding and abetting the donation of corporate campaign funds and another has been convicted of accepting illegal funds from milk producers); whether he would come across as an unreconstructed proponent of federal programs.

I began by asking Humphrey what, in the light of the Massachusetts primary yesterday, was going on.

"Less is going on today than went on a week ago," he replied, a bit uneasily. He continued, "After the New Hampshire primary, when Carter won, a number of my Democratic friends were worried. There was a lot of pressure on me to get in and make a statement saying I would be a candidate. I turned it aside. The governors were meeting in Washington at the time." A number of the governors had made statements critical of Carter who is quite unpopular among them. "They are highly political, and a number of them came to see me. There was lot of pressure on me to pick up the mantle."

I asked him which governors had been to see him, and he listed Calvin Rampton, of Utah; Wendell Anderson, of Minnesota; Hugh Carey, of New York; Brendan Byrne, of New Jersey; and Philip Noel, of Rhode Island. "A number of my colleagues in the Senate talked to me," Humphrey went on. "And I had labor people call me as well. Over the weekend, I appeared in New Jersey, New York,

Pennsylvania. I had an incredible number of people come up to me and say that I should run." He named a number of New Jersey state Democratic officials; Humphrey knows these people. "I spoke at a COPE dinner in Philadelphia," he continued. COPE is the A.F.L.–C.I.O.'s Committee on Political Education. "That's where I saw my labor friends. I think it's no exaggeration to say those people are always with me." He mentioned other people who had called or visited him today.

Humphrey went on, "You see, Jackson has many of the Humphrey-Muskie-type people with him. They were down in the dumps before yesterday; today they're up. So more people were calling me when it looked as if Jackson would come in third in Massachusetts. Politics is very volatile. Jackson has some people traditionally identified with me—in the labor movement, the Jewish community, the Coalition for a Democratic Majority." This is a "centrist" group. "Those are my people. What you have now is much less pressure on me than a week ago. It's sort of like a pendulum swinging back and forth. One week it hits you, one week it misses you." Humphrey laughed. "To put it bluntly," he said, "I never had so many people ask me to do something I don't want to do. In the past, I'd have been jumping through fiery hoops at the chance to run. As the primaries go along, I think you'll find the supporters of these candidates becoming more hardened supporters. So I feel the chances of being nominated at the Convention without being a primary contestant are quite remote."

Perhaps Humphrey believes that, perhaps not; perhaps he himself does not know, and is poised between permitting himself to be hopeful and forcing himself to be realistic. Humphrey has had his share of disappointment and pain, and that fact comes through when he talks about why he does not want to enter the race for the nomination. "I've been through all that," he said. "I don't want to do it. I just don't want to do it—physically, emotionally, financially. I have a big job to do in the Senate. I'm not anxious to be a candidate. My life does not require that I be President in order that I be satisfied. At one point in my life, it did. I'm much more at peace with myself now. I think I'm at my peak as a senator now."

I asked Humphrey if he would like to be a Presidential candidate.

He replied without hesitation, "Yes, I'd like to do it. I'd do it well. But there's a difference between scrambling and clawing for the job and being somewhat more reserved about it. You have to decide what you want to do, and you have to decide what price you're willing to pay for what you want to do."

I asked him if his posture of standing aside was not in fact the more effective one for him anyway.

"Yes," he replied, and he continued, "But if you want to be President you're limiting your options if you stand back. I have terribly mixed emotions—particularly when I go through a week when so many people want me to run, especially people who didn't back me before. But then I take another look . . ."

I asked Humphrey if he was resigned, then, to the idea that the nomination might pass him by.

"Not completely," he replied. "I'd be the biggest liar in the country if I told you I didn't want to be President. It would be the crowning achievement of my life. But I'm not younger than I was four years ago. I feel better, and people say I look better. But I also think this is a time to enjoy life. My wife and I talk about it. Muriel said, 'We're both healthy. Why don't we enjoy life?' She's not anxious for me to run, but there's no veto. There is an understanding that if I do it I won't ask her to do what she did before. I would never put her through what I did before."

And then Humphrey said something that seemed to come from deep inside him, and to explain both his good spirits now and his dread of running for the nomination.

"It's so wonderful that for the first time in my life I don't have to ask anybody for anything," he said. "You have no idea how good that feels. Since 1960, I have been in every national campaign. In 1960, '64, '68, '72, Hubert Humphrey was out asking people to help him. In 1976, I don't want to ask anyone to help me."

When I inquired whether running for the Presidency, as opposed to running for the nomination, would not put him back in that position, he replied quickly, "That's different. That's different because that's the ultimate test. It's not like spring training. Every competitor likes to get into the Super Bowl or the World Series."

Did he think, then, I asked, that a race for the Presidency would be different for him this time?

"Greatly," he replied. "Greatly. What hurt me so in '68 and '72 was the loss of some of my natural constituents. I was really a casualty of that war. I sense a great deal of affection in the country for me, and I have a great feeling for people. I never have a day now when people aren't kind to me. People bring their children to see me. People say, 'I wasn't for you before, and now I am.' You can't imagine how good that feels."

Late afternoon. The House of Representatives is debating the annual military-assistance bill. In recent years, the amount of money this country spends for economic assistance to foreign nations has been going down and military assistance and sales have been rising. At the same time, the Third World has learned that passivity is not the only course open to it in dealing with major powers. And also at the same time, worldwide arms sales are increasing. It is considered quite an achievement that the military-assistance bill that the House is debating sets an annual ceiling of nine billion dollars on the amount of military equipment and services that the United States may export. Current exports are valued at about eleven billion dollars. The restriction, however, may be, as many congressional restrictions may be, waived by the President. The bill also contains provisions—some of them approved by the Senate earlier this year—tightening control over nongovernmental commercial arms transactions and giving Congress the right to veto certain such transactions. But no one is sure now how, or whether, these provisions will work. (A provision enacted in 1974 gave Congress a voice in certain government-to-government arms transactions.) Yet congressional responses do not always fit neat action-reaction patterns, offering specific solutions for specific situations. They often arise from mood, from an accumulation of events, and in their effect are as much psychological as they are practical. Even if they don't make any real difference in policy, they can make Congress feel better. And there is always a chance the Administration will think Congress is serious, and take it seriously. Today, a Senate staff man said, "There may not be dramatic turnarounds, but at least this might inhibit the process of selling arms. Angola wasn't totally germane, but the thought that that could go on—that fifty million dollars could find its way there without being passed upon by the Congress—contributed to the feeling that we've got to get a handle on things. Whether it's the right handle or not, I don't know. It was an outgrowth of the C.I.A. thing, an updating of the idea of checks and balances. It's all part of the same theme and mood and awareness."

Interestingly, the Administration did not put up much of a fight against the provision to give Congress more voice in arms sales, apparently assuming that the game was lost. One House Republican said that the Administration "poked around to find someone to lead the fight for them, and gave up." He added, "The days when Kissinger could come up here and importune to get his way are over."

Donald Fraser, a Democratic representative from Minnesota and a member of the House International Relations Committee, a reflective man, came off the House floor to talk with me for a while during the debate on the military-assistance bill this afternoon. "The bill isn't one that anybody feels particularly proud of," Fraser said. "The subject is an uncomfortable one. The choices aren't particularly attractive. There are no restrictions on aid to Korea, but there is a provision calling for study by the Administration of phased withdrawal from Korea. We're continuing to aid authoritarian regimes—the Philippines, Latin-American countries. There are attempts to get a congressional role. I don't think anybody has any confidence in them. They are very tentative moves in dealing with an awkward problem. The provisions for congressional review are a big change in position, but whether they will have any effect remains to be seen. This bill comes up a few days after they released that study showing that three hundred billion dollars is being spent in the world for military purposes. Well, there's a kind of sense of impotence that we're not able to find ways to channel those enormous amounts spent for military purposes into more productive activities."

Fraser's comments reminded me of something that a businessman friend said to me earlier this year. He said that if one looked behind the normal measurements of the economy one would find a sick economy—one that contained too many dying or stagnant industries, and did not provide for change. Lockheed, Chrysler, the railroads were only the beginning, he said. And he said that only the arms business kept more industries from going under. I do not believe that I have heard any Presidential candidate talk about reconversion.

I asked Fraser if the Congress had in fact begun to carve out a new role for itself in foreign policy. It had denied the Administration's final request for assistance to a collapsing South Vietnam, had voted to enforce the law against the use of military assistance for aggression in the case of Turkey, and had denied funds for activities in Angola.

"The fundamental problem is that there is a lack of consensus between the executive and the Congress on what our foreign policy ought to be," Fraser said. "If we got a Democrat in the White House, I don't think we would interfere as much as we have been doing lately." Then he added, "I don't think we want to."

MARCH 4

Morris Udall, back in his office in the Longworth House Office Building, is unusually tense. Birch Bayh, as had been expected, dropped out of the race this morning (Bayh said he was "suspending" his campaign), and Udall must move quickly to persuade members of the liberal wing of the Party to, as he puts it, "coalesce" around him as the leader of the, as he puts it, "progressive" wing of the Party. He carefully avoids using the word "liberal." Jackson is unacceptable to many liberals, because he supported the Vietnam war for so long, because he supports high military expenditures, and because he has had bitter fights with the liberal wing of the Party in recent years. The objections go beyond ideology and include questions of style and of alliances, and end up in the back yard. There is suspicion about those who would have power if Jackson won—big business, the military, George Meany. Said a liberal labor leader today, "Can you imagine George Meany being President of the United States?" George Wallace is out of the question, and there are still many questions about Carter. Sargent Shriver and Fred Harris are finished, even if they stay in the race a while longer. (Neither of them has anything more interesting to do.)

Yesterday, Udall spoke with Edward Kennedy, with Birch Bayh, with Governor Jerry Brown of California, with Humphrey. On Tuesday, the day of the Massachusetts primary, he called Frank Church, the Democratic senator from Idaho, who is planning to enter the Presidential race soon, to try, as Udall explained, "to head him off." Today, Udall will meet with the Congressional Black Caucus; as a Westerner, a non-urban politician, Udall has not yet really connected with blacks. He will also meet today with the New York Democratic congressional delegation. He plans to set up meetings with Democratic representatives from Wisconsin, Michigan, Indiana, Ohio, and California. He hopes to see George Meany or Alexander Barkan, the A.F.L.–C.I.O.'s political director, and he has been trying to reach Leonard Woodcock for two days.

Woodcock, the president of the United Auto Workers, is in Florida, campaigning for Jimmy Carter. Woodcock's effort is for the purpose not of electing Carter but of defeating Wallace—reducing Wallace as a threat in Indiana and Michigan. (As one U.A.W. official explained to me, "We'd rather deal with the bastard in Florida than have to meet him on our own turf.") Some members of the coalition of liberal labor unions are working for Carter in Florida: the U.A.W. is organizing its communit.es of retirees there; the Machinists are organizing their large bloc of airline and space workers; the American Federation of State, County, and Municipal Employees is organizing its workers in Miami and Jacksonville; the Communications Workers are organizing their Florida members. These unions have printed pamphlets and set up phone banks. As we talked, Udall finally located Woodcock, in a Miami hotel. Udall says that Woodcock was "noncommittal" and said he would have to talk with his people.

Udall's problem is that he does not fit well into the particular format of a campaign for the nomination—a point that goes beyond Udall's particular problems, and illustrates one of the most important factors in contemporary politics. Other candidates, or people who become discouraged from being candidates, also confront it. He does not "project." He is thoughtful and informed and knowing, but the campaign format requires that a candidate project something easily and quickly recognizable. Ford—the President. Reagan—the conservative challenger. Jackson—for labor and for a strong defense and being tough with the Russians. Carter—love, compassion, honesty, and being outside Washington. Udall? It doesn't come in a few words. Carter comes across on television, and Udall does not. Udall's style does not meet what seem to be the current requirements for coming across on television. Political television is not very compatible with thought, hesitancy, complexities. Udall has tried to run on the theme of integrity, but even there his most effective pitch was made by somebody else (Archibald Cox). His detachment can come over to the voters as standoffishness, and it raises the question whether he badly wants the Presidency. His wit raises the question whether he is serious. And so now Udall's main rallying point is that he is, as he says, the leader of the "progressives." Since this is a contest not of issues but of style, however, that is not enough.

Udall may find himself increasingly pulled to the left. I asked him today if that was a problem.

"I have obviously got to broaden out," he replied. "We have to reach out and emphasize labor support. I'm spending a week here to try to get in touch with mayors and governors and labor leaders. This is a period of pause. What happens in Michigan and California is a hell of a lot more important than charging from airport to airport."

I asked Udall if he found that some politicians were hanging back, waiting to see if Humphrey gets into the race.

He replied, "There's a little bit of that." He looked pained as he said it.

An official of the A.F.L.–C.I.O. said in a telephone conversation this afternoon, "Our people are divided between Humphrey and Jackson, but they would prefer either one of them to any of the others. The unions that were for Jackson in Massachusetts are encouraged. They might have gone to Humphrey; now they'll stick with Jackson. A lot of our people don't see Udall as a liberal. He voted wrong on the key labor vote." In 1965, Udall voted against repeal of that section of the Taft-Hartley Act (14b) which permits states to prohibit union shops. The labor official continued, "We still identify liberalism as 'friendly to labor.' By our standards, Udall is more conservative than Jackson." And then he got to what might be an even more basic point: "His is the kind of liberalism that flourishes in more exotic quarters; it's the suburbanites'. If Udall calls Meany, the response will be 'Thank you for calling, Mr. Congressman.' " Labor can be as unforgiving as the liberal left that it despises.

A liberal labor-union man said this afternoon, "We're suddenly faced with a narrowed field. We no longer have the luxury of wandering around among the various candidates. So we say, 'Holy mackerel, how do we handle this?' We're constantly up against deadlines in different states. Each week, as we get the primary results, there have been enough surprises to cause changes in strategies; then we have to adapt those to the logistical situations. Take Indiana. We thought we had a candidate there in Bayh. Now our people there want to know what to do. I think we should stay cautious, work with various strategies—some go with Udall, some stay uncommitted, and some even deal with Jackson, on the ground that he needs us because we represent the progressive element. Several of the liberal labor unions are divided. A lot of our people

are very disturbed about Jackson. The unions with the largest political-action staffs and the largest cadres of workers are in the liberal
coalition. Timing is crucial. Some of them came out early for
Muskie in '72 and got burned. On the other hand, you can wait too
long."

Much of the Democratic Party's constituent groups' activity in
selecting the nominee is a search less for the ideal nominee than for
power within the Party. Forming the liberal coalition has given the
members increased power. An official of one of the coalition's
unions said to me, "The complexity of the Party's rules is so
enormous that if we had not started this a year ago, we would have
been completely out of it. And now we have been helped by the
A.F.L.–C.I.O.'s policy of neutrality on the candidates. So we will
have an impact." The purposes of these unions extend beyond having power at the Convention, which in itself strengthens one's hand
in the writing of the platform and the rules for the next Convention
as well as in the choosing of the Presidential candidate. These
people are experienced practitioners of back-yard politics. To have
power is to have power. Much more than Party business is at stake
in Party business. For example, the American Federation of State,
County, and Municipal Employees—which is rapidly growing in
membership, in voice in the management of cities and states, and in
importance to our civil order—sees power in the Party as an instrument of power at the bargaining table. One A.F.S.C.M.E. official
explained, "This union is negotiating with governors, mayors, all
over the country, in a business relationship. So not only is it important that we have stature as an employee union but, since our
employers are politicians, it is even more important that we have
political standing. We got about four hundred people elected in the
Minnesota precincts to the county conventions. We can't help but
get some payoff from that."

A Democratic strategist this afternoon said, "There is no left
left."

In Florida today, Reagan made his strongest attack yet on President Ford's foreign and military policy, saying, "All I can see is
what other nations the world over see: collapse of the American
will and the retreat of American power." Reagan continued,
"There is little doubt in my mind that the Soviet Union will not stop
taking advantage of détente until it sees that the American people

have elected a new President and appointed a new Secretary of State."

At 12:04 P.M. today, the Senate press galleries received Mike Mansfield's announcement that he would not seek reëlection, and thus the position of Senate Majority Leader was opened. The statement of Mansfield's second-in-command, Majority Whip Robert Byrd, on how sorry he was Mansfield was retiring arrived at the press galleries at 12:09 P.M. Mansfield's retirement announcement set off a scramble that includes Humphrey, Muskie, Byrd, and Ernest F. Hollings, of South Carolina. That makes two positions of power that Humphrey and Muskie either are or are not angling for, depending on how you look at it.

This morning, Henry Kissinger, appearing before the House International Relations Committee, warned Cuba that it should act "with great circumspection" in southern Africa. Yesterday, Mozambique closed its border with Rhodesia, which is ruled by a white minority, and so brought increased economic pressure on that nation. Kissinger did not say what the United States would do if Cuba ventured into southern Africa.

MARCH 5

Friday. "As we speak," a liberal-coalition labor official said to me this afternoon, "there are efforts to get Humphrey into the race—now. Some of us think that this weekend, in New York, is the point to launch a draft-Hubert movement, to get the Bayh slates for him, on the ground that Udall can't make it." Some New York Bayh delegates—who had backed Bayh because they thought that was the "pragmatic" thing to do—were now looking for somewhere to go for tickets to the Democratic Convention, and were afraid that Udall would not get them to the Convention. Hence the idea for a draft-Humphrey movement. Some people thought that it might appear self-serving if such a movement should be originated by those who are looking for a way to the Convention. So the idea arose that this weekend Senator Mondale, Minnesota's other senator and Humphrey's protégé, should go to New York and announce that he was starting a draft-Humphrey movement. A lot of people are very much excited and are making a lot of telephone calls—to Mondale, to Mondale's administrative assistant, to other senators who have backed Humphrey, to each other. Now Humphrey is getting more calls, including several from New York politicians. They figure that Carter is not organized to take on Jackson in New York or Pennsylvania. "We are worried about a campaign for the nomination which keeps shifting to the right," said one member of the liberal labor coalition. And so Hubert Humphrey, who began as the great hope of the Party traditionalists, is at the end of the week the vessel for the dreams and ambitions and anxieties of the liberals. Politics does summon forth flexibility.

MARCH 6

President Ford opened his Illinois campaign yesterday on the front steps of Abraham Lincoln's home in Springfield. As he left for the trip, he called the unemployment rate for February—down to 7.6, and at its lowest level in more than a year—"extremely encouraging." Afterward, at a farm forum, he spelled out his plan, which he had previously mentioned in his State of the Union Message, to ease estate taxes on family farms and businesses; said that a repetition of last year's embargo on grain sales to the Soviet Union was highly unlikely; and announced that a new Cabinet committee dealing with the nation's food policies, including international issues, would be headed by Agriculture Secretary Earl Butz. This would replace policy committees that have been run by the State and Treasury Departments, and would be very pleasing to farmers. International food policy has three competing claimants: foreign policy, consumers, and farmers. Architects of foreign policy see food as an instrument—the withholding of food, or of food sales, can be used to attempt to bring about a desired policy. The people who provide them with their "agri-power"—farmers—don't want them to use it, because it can reduce markets. Consumers are for the use of "agri-power," because that increases supplies and lowers prices in the United States. Government officials spend considerable time negotiating among these competing claims. Everyone knew what it meant when the President—on the eve of the Illinois primary—put Earl Butz in charge.

The United Nations predicted yesterday that the world's population would reach eight billion by the year 2010 if the most recent annual growth rate is maintained, nearly doubling the population as of mid-1974.

MARCH 7

Sunday. Senator Mondale did not go to New York. Humphrey did not give the nod.

MARCH 9

Tuesday. Jimmy Carter won the Florida primary today, with, as of the moment—the numbers have been changing all evening—thirty-five percent of the vote. George Wallace got thirty-two percent, and Jackson twenty-two percent. President Ford defeated Ronald Reagan, fifty-three percent to forty-seven percent.

At the State Department, talking with Henry Kissinger's closest aides, once the studied casualness ("The word 'détente' may have been dropped but not the policy," "Henry himself has suggested that we stop using the word") has been passed, one encounters despair. The President's suggestion that he found the word infelicitous was in its literal terms not of major moment, but in terms of the signals by which Washington conducts its affairs it was. The signal was unmistakable—as clear as a line in a James Reston column. And Henry Kissinger is an expert in signals. He has become an election issue. The struggle now is to retain as much of his dignity and his policy—the two are intertwined—as he can. Kissinger's aides attribute the President's statement to the President's aides, whom they see as reacting shortsightedly to election pressures. "Booting détente in the primaries would be a tragedy," said one of Kissinger's aides, and he continued, "It would be a good issue for the G.O.P. in November." Another aide said, "Ford has reacted more because of Reagan than because of anything else. They clearly anticipated that Ford could not get the nomination, and ran scared."

And all three Kissinger aides with whom I spoke this afternoon made one point about the President, suggesting strongly that it was a thought shared by Kissinger: that a lot of Kissinger's trouble stems from the fact that the President is "unelected." "I've just begun to realize the monumental problem of having a President who is unelected," said one. "That's at the heart of Henry's problem."

I asked him why.

He replied, "Because it so weakens the political base. When

Watergate was going on, people with a sense of responsibility weren't going to tackle Henry. After Nixon was gone, the barriers were down; and Henry is a residue of Nixon."

"I won't deny that détente was oversold," said another of Kissinger's aides, "in the sense that people got the impression that the Soviets had changed—or would change—their spots, and vestiges of the Cold War would be removed. It created expectations that could not be fulfilled. It works less well when you get away from head-to-head confrontation—from Berlin as opposed to Angola."

I asked him for an official definition of "détente."

He replied, "It's a process. Everyone makes a terrible mistake who thinks it is more than that. The process is one of establishing those areas where the United States and the Soviet Union have, or can have, a community of interests, and then doing what you can to expand those areas. One area, obviously, is that of curbing the arms race. Détente did work in the Middle East: the Soviets did put limits on their involvement. The problem with defending détente is you have to talk about things that did not happen. Détente was not our invention, though there was a time when we wanted people to think it was. There was the Spirit of Camp David the Spirit of Glassboro. And the word—meaning relaxation of tensions—has been around a long time. It just got currency in this Administration."

Kissinger's aides see that things are coming apart for Kissinger, and attribute that to a variety of factors. "The secret of Henry Kissinger has been his ability to control events, and he's losing that," said one. "It's a fact. It's a fact Henry sees. When you're forced into an entirely reactive policy, you're in trouble. In the last year, the last time Henry put it all together was in the Sinai agreement—and he was playing on the edges when he did that. Now he has to hold things together. The tragedy of Henry is that, after seven years, conservation won't be looked at as an achievement—though holding things together without major strains on the system right now is a major achievement. Look at what he is doing: working toward a SALT agreement, even if there is not one, which I doubt there can be, given this election year; convincing Europe that we have not lost our minds; convincing the Soviets that if they move in a serious way we will react; convincing the Chinese that we are worth maintaining an alliance of sorts with; convincing others that we have not lost our rudder—that if we can't move things forward, at least we won't move back. If Henry left, the Egyptians might conclude that movement toward a settlement in the Middle East was over. Historians will look back and see he was playing with mirrors: in the middle of Watergate he was able to maintain confrontation with the Soviet Union; he was able to put together shuttle diplomacy on the basis of the fact that he represented the United States, which was coming apart at the seams. That's beginning to catch up with him. The emperor has no clothes. He's down to his underwear in terms of what he has in backing." SALT is expected to be one specific casualty of this election; some people at the State Department think the negotiations on the Panama Canal may be another. "It's the endemic weakness of the structure," this man continued, reciting the sources of Kissinger's troubles. "An unelected President coming out of Watergate, coming out of Vietnam. A Congress that can't control itself. A country with no sense of purpose. The funny thing is that Henry Kissinger, who is as deeply conservative as any man I know, is under attack from the right. It's too ironic."

Kissinger's main political problem used to be with foreign-policy liberals, who saw him as too strongly inclined toward the Cold War tradition, too enamored of big weaponry, too willing to employ force. He continued the war in Southeast Asia longer than almost any of them considered necessary. And he was too sly, too secretive, too tricky. Traits that were tolerable—that even brought him praise when matters were going well for him—were the very ones that hastened his decline. The very people who were charmed and amused by his dinner-party, out-of-school comments on Richard Nixon later came to think of him as two-faced. He suffered the consequences that others do of having ridden so high.

One of Kissinger's aides sees the problem as broader than that of the election year, and, of course, he is correct. He said, "This is a time of inflation and recession, which limits your resources for carrying out foreign policy. It leads to protectionism, and raises new issues, such as food and energy. So economic issues provide a new situation for debate." And then he used a phrase that was reminiscent of Kissinger. He referred to "this poisonous atmosphere" in Washington, and he said that Kissinger, who has been travelling the country, making speeches, is more popular in the rest of the country than he is in Washington. Moreover, the "turbulence," he said, was being caused by the fact that our foreign policy is now caught between the Munich generation and the Vietnam generation. The revelations that our government was involved in foreign assassinations, our intelligence agencies in a variety of illegal and excessive acts, our corporations in widespread bribery in order to get foreign contracts have added to the disturbance, he said. "The reason we're in trouble is that the conservatives, with the help of their allies in the Pentagon, are attacking arms control, while the liberals are trying to keep us from stopping Soviet expansion, as in Angola—whether or not you think that is the right place," he said. "So both the sticks and the carrots are being withheld. We're getting it from both sides."

7

WEDNESDAY, 11:30 A.M. O'Hare Airport, Chicago. Jimmy Carter, holding a press conference upon his arrival here from Orlando, Florida, looks exhausted. I have come here to meet the Carter entourage and follow the candidate for the next couple of days. It is time for a close look at him. The difference in his appearance today and the way he looked when I saw him a few weeks ago in Washington and in New Hampshire is startling. He looks tired, drawn; there seem to be more lines in his face. He has a cough—the residue of a cold. He has been on the road for eleven days, with just one full day off. Monday evening, he zipped up from Florida to North Carolina, where a primary is to be held in two weeks, and then he returned to Florida Tuesday evening to watch the primary returns. This morning, when he saw the schedule for his two days in Illinois, he blew up at his staff. Carter is encountering some of the classic problems of *Homo candidatus:* being overscheduled by a staff that assumes that the candidate's energies are limitless (even when it knows they aren't) and assumes that each stop, each event, each television taping will make a difference. Whatever protectiveness, whatever resistance to overscheduling, there is on the part of the candidate's staff is eroded by the state staff, which has its chance at the candidate—its most important asset—for only a brief period and wants to make the most of it. The members of the state staff want to do well in the primary, of course, because their political futures are on the line, and the candidate is their most effective instrument for doing well. And so the candidate—any candidate—becomes a thing, a totem to be paraded about. The fact that he is a human being, with limits to his energy and resources—and even Jimmy Carter has limits—is forgotten. The chairman in one state is not particularly concerned about the problems of the chairman in another state. He just wants to produce his candidate and produce for him. The problem is that the candidate becomes both the vessel and the vehicle of so many people's ambitions. Not to mention his own. And so, fuelled by these converging ambitions, he keeps going.

It is only March, and the campaign is beginning to tell on Carter. And his schedule for the next two days is brutal. Today, he will fly, on a chartered 727, from Chicago to Rockford to Peoria to Champaign to Marion to Springfield and back to Chicago. He will speak to a United Auto Workers gathering, hold three press conferences, do a television taping, and give three talks: to supporters in Marion, at the southern end of the state; to students at the University of Illinois in Champaign; and at a fund-raiser in Springfield. Tomorrow, he is scheduled for sixteen events in Chicago, which include early-morning appearances at two commuter railway stations and six television or radio tapings. The Carter state chairman, James Wall, remarked anxiously to some of us as we awaited Carter's arrival, "We only have one day with him in Chicago." For the candidate, the tapings, of course, are seen as a valuable way of obtaining free television and radio time. For the local stations, which have to fill their inexhaustible talk-show time, a Presidential candidate is at least as promising a guest as the bowling champions, race-car drivers, and authors of books who also come through town in search of "exposure." And so this mutually convenient arrangement sends the candidate racing from studio to studio, having to appear fresh, alert, and gracious for each performance. (Tomorrow's schedule, spelled out in unusual detail by the Illinois staff, informs us that when Carter goes to the Dill Pickle Delicatessen Sandwich Shop for lunch he "will order own sandwich from counter made by Ira Omens.") On Friday, to the consternation of the Illinois staff, Carter will fly to California, to raise money at a reception and a dinner—but other events, including a press conference and a speech at the University of California in Los Angeles, have been tossed into the schedule—and then he will fly all night to Georgia, with a change of planes at 5:30 A.M. in Dallas. On Sunday, he will fly to Washington to appear on "Face the Nation," and on Monday he will return to Chicago, to give what is billed as "a major foreign-policy address." Carter's strategy of entering every state primary is producing enormous demands for staff, money, and the candidate's time, all of which are now in short supply. Hence the foray to California. Hence the collision between drive and human flesh. Hence the clear signs of fatigue in the face of this supposedly indefatigable man. Even his triumph of last night cannot mask it.

Carter stands behind the rostrum that has been set up in the Friendship Lounge at the airport, but he does not smile as much as usual. But that may be because this is a press conference rather than a meeting with voters. He says that he is in Illinois "to test my ability to get support in a large, metropolitan state." Chicago's Mayor Richard Daley, he says, "has told me he has no intention of getting involved with any Presidential candidate." There are actually two Presidential races on the ballot in Illinois. One is a popularity contest, in which only Carter, George Wallace, Fred Harris, and Sargent Shriver are entered, and which Carter is expected to win. Carter had the wit to see the benefit of headlines declaring him the winner in Illinois; he makes efforts in states others do not, not just in order to get a significant number of delegates but because he understands the public-relations value of being declared, wherever possible, a victor. The other is a contest for a hundred and fifty-five of the state's delegates—the remaining fourteen are to be chosen later—in which there are delegate slates pledged to Senator Adlai Stevenson, most of them, in fact, backed by Mayor Daley, and delegates pledged to Governor Daniel Walker. Harris, Wallace, and Shriver have also entered delegate slates. Carter has entered eighty-five delegates, and he and his aides talk about a modest goal of one-fourth of them winning. Even so, Carter suggested to reporters in Florida this morning that they were not paying enough attention to the delegate contest. Yet Carter did not enter slates in Chicago, because the Daley machine is virtually unbeatable there and also, presumably, because he did not wish to offend the Mayor. No one seems quite sure what is on Mayor Daley's mind. He is believed to favor the candidacy of Edward Kennedy and, failing that, perhaps Humphrey. Mainly, it is thought that Daley wants someone who can win—perhaps even Carter. Beyond that, it would make sense that Mayor Daley simply wants to be a power at the 1976 Convention. So do others, but Daley, now seventy-three—who sat amidst the turmoil of the Chicago Convention in 1968 and was ejected from the 1972 Convention for not having adhered to the Party's reform rules—has special reasons. His attention for the moment is on the gubernatorial primary, in which he is trying to oust the independent incumbent, Dan Walker. The sample ballots distributed by the Daley organization leave the Presidential-preference boxes blank. Carter phoned Daley upon his arrival here this morning.

Carter has become more modest in his claims. At the airport, he says a victory in Illinois is "no guarantee I would be the nominee." But then—continuing to exaggerate somewhat his success—he points out that he has entered twelve state contests and has come in first in six of them and second in three of them. Carter frequently speaks of what he is about in terms of mechanics and numbers, giving the impression that that is how he thinks of it. "I've got substantial labor support," he says. "I've got substantial liberal support." This is the moment, then, when the Carter campaign, with the early and long-planned victories behind, really goes national, and is subjected to new tests. Carter is no longer an interesting surprise; he is a serious and determined candidate for the Democratic Party's nomination for the Presidency. No matter that it is the consensus now that no one will reach the Convention with sufficient votes to win the nomination on the first ballot. Carter has never paid attention to consensus. He says that a sorting out of candidates is taking place, and that there will be a nomination on the first ballot. Carter, who understands what moves people in politics, says that he will "pick up the support of people for whom the chance to win is very important." A reporter asks Carter when he thinks he has to show that he can beat Senator Henry Jackson. "Yesterday," Carter replies evenly and very slowly, with a slight edge in his voice, "in Florida [pause], I beat Henry Jackson."

On the plane to Rockford, I mention to Carter the brutal schedule that has been arranged for him for the next two days, and about which he complained vehemently to his staff this morning.

"We try to make the best of every day," he replies, smiling.

The purpose of this swing is to give Carter media exposure throughout the state, and also to get exposure for those who are running as Carter delegates. At the United Auto Workers' union hall in Rockford, Carter delegates are introduced, and sample ballots have been given out showing how to vote for them. Carter looked pale and exhausted when he arrived at O'Hare Airport this morning, but, as he talks here, Carter, who has sat through several introductions and a speech about unemployment, seems to get some color back in his face. He speaks of "my intimate relationship with the working people of this country," of his labor support in Iowa, and of Leonard Woodcock's ("whose picture is behind me") support in the Florida primary. He misses nothing. "I know what it means to work for a living," he tells the audience, and he offers himself as someone who can relate to "liberals, moderates, conservatives, blacks, whites, rural, and urban," and as "someone who can actually manage the affairs of government, for a change." He says,

"We've lost our vision of what this country can be," and he talks of his support for providing jobs (through the private sector to whatever extent is possible, and then through the federal government, this being a more moderate position than that of most of the other Democratic candidates), for a "comprehensive nationwide, mandatory health-insurance program," for a day-care program, and for "the aggressive sale of American products overseas." Carter is, in effect, a programmatic liberal. The difference between him and the others is one of degree, of the emphasis each chooses to place on what. Talking about the same things, they can sound quite different. In addition to those he has mentioned, he is for tax reform (he calls the present tax system "a disgrace to the human race"), welfare reform, aid to transportation, housing programs. But he treads lightly, and manages to wrap his espousal of these programs in words about dissatisfaction with government. He does not say he will reduce government; he says he will reorganize it. (His reorganization of the Georgia government was accompanied by increases in its size and in what it did.) But the suggestion is that he will reduce it, because he says he will reduce the number of government agencies. One must listen to him carefully. He has spoken previously of many of the things he is speaking of today, but in front of this labor audience he rearranges the pieces and puts together a package that is particularly appealing to labor. That is what a good politician does. And, like a good politician, he makes the group feel that he understands it. "I think we need somebody who understands what it means to work," he says. "Government has held working people at arm's length." Later, he says, "I feel like an outsider"— and presumably so do they. And he has another message: he tells them, referring to the delegate slates committed to Stevenson and Walker, to "express your own preference about who will be your President," and to not "vote for people who are not running for President." Then he says, "I don't want to make anybody angry" (skirting a clash with Daley), but he doesn't want them to vote for someone who isn't running. As he talks, his aides bustle about with briefcases, green-and-white "Carter" stickers, and high hopes. Carter closes with what is becoming his standard closing, delivered in his soft, Southern voice: "I don't claim to know all the answers. I'm just like you, a regular human being." And then he tells them that he wants a government "as good and honest and decent and truthful and fair and competent and idealistic and compassionate and as filled with love as are the American people."

Leaving Rockford, we are eight minutes behind schedule, and James Wall, who has arranged this itinerary, is tense. Other campaigns get behind schedule—sometimes hours behind schedule—but not the Carter campaign. Carter, for all his surface pleasantness, gets testy when he is tired and when his campaign is running late, and both are now the case. The staff is being especially protective of him this afternoon. Only once does Carter leave his front seat in the chartered 727 and wander back in the plane to talk to reporters. Reporters say that he is more inaccessible than most candidates. One of them said, "Even when he is accessible, he is inaccessible." They say he never lets his hair down, and they don't get beyond the smile. He is pleasant enough but not particularly funny; he enjoys—or appears to enjoy—the reporters' banter, but he does not offer much himself. On the plane, Carter talks with the state chairman and with his sister, Ruth Stapleton, the evangelist and faith healer. Mrs. Stapleton is an attractive woman, who looks much like her brother. When one asks her about Carter, out come the stories—some of them by now familiar, some seeming new—about Jimmy's determination. About how hard he worked to get into Annapolis—as difficult for a boy from Plains, Georgia, to do, she says, as it is for an ex-governor to become President. (No member of the Carter family before him had gone beyond high school.) About how, when their father died, she and Jimmy, who was twenty-eight then and a Navy officer working for Admiral Hyman Rickover on the development of atomic-powered submarines, went around to tell the farmers, and then that evening Jimmy cried and said, "If I die, what will I have done?" And when he then decided to leave the Navy and return to Plains to take over the family business, Mrs. Stapleton recalls, he studied agricultural encyclopedias—"just like he studied up for this campaign." About how he went around Plains with a petition to get all the people in the town to paint their house and plant five shrubs—and they did. About how he wrote to every graduate of the local high school to raise money to build a community swimming pool. "Jimmy was always driven," she says.

At Peoria, the stop is only long enough for a press conference and a taped television interview at the airport. Carter lopes from the plane, head thrust forward, as usual. He smiles the wide smile, as usual. But there are puffs beneath his eyes, and he draws a deep breath before he begins. Carter is an uncommonly disciplined man. At the press conference, he is asked about détente, and gives an answer that manages to come down on both sides: he thinks that détente is a good idea, but "every time we have had a tough negotiation with the Soviet Union we have lost or come in second-best." He lists the first wheat agreement, the Helsinki agreement ("We ratified the Russian takeover of Eastern Europe"), the Vladivostok agreement ("We lost again"), and the joint American-Soviet space flight ("We got very little in return—again, I think we lost"). He says that he "would be very much tougher in the future in our negotiations with the Soviet Union." He offers a widely shared criticism of Kissinger's style. "The American people have been excluded from the process," he says. In the television taping, he says that as President he would keep "an intimacy with the people" through frequent press conferences, restoring Franklin Roosevelt's fireside chats, and restoring "the proper relationship" between the President and the Congress. There is little reason to doubt that Carter would be an active and assertive President, confident of his ability to relate to the people, and willing to use that as a weapon against his opponents. Some troubling questions have to do with his certainty about himself: too much self-doubt can be paralyzing, but just a little can be healthy. Unrelieved purposefulness can wall out capacity for self-criticism, perspective. Would he admit to a mistake and change course? Would people be able to get through to him? He has certain traits that raise the question whether he would be able to engage in the political give-and-take that is essential to governing: his faith in himself; his sense of his own righteousness; his thin skin (as is evidenced by his reaction to criticism from opponents and to questions he does not like); his apparent lack of humor; his stubbornness; his loner political style. These are more important questions than that of his positions on the issues. "I haven't been part of the Washington scene," Carter tells his interviewer.

At the University of Illinois in Champaign, Carter tells a student audience, "I intend to be a successful candidate," and "I don't intend to lose. I don't belong to anybody." The not-belonging-to-anybody could be invaluable to him as President—assuming he maintains it throughout his campaign—if he uses it right. Working from outside the party, he has a greater chance than those who do not of maintaining some independence from its constituent special interests. Political independence is, of course, valuable, and Carter's independence could be one of his greatest assets as President. But politics, by definition, and governing also require the forging of alliances, the ability to deal with colleagues, peers, rivals. This is something other than simply being "one of the boys." But Carter is a loner, with a striking number of enemies. That some of his former fellow-governors dislike him may be understandable among a group of ambitious men; that most of them dislike him merits attention. To the students here he talks of strength and idealism and religious faith and love of country. He says that the country has "lost its basic competence" and, with a catch in his voice, says, "We feel there is a wall of government between us and them." Like the workers, he was an outsider; like the students, he is an outsider. And he says, "The American people are competent. Why shouldn't the government be competent?" He goes on to say, "The people tell the truth. Why should our government lie? If we could just have a government as good as our people are."

Answering questions, he says that the C.I.A. cannot be supervised by a committee of the Congress but only by the President. "If the C.I.A. ever makes a mistake, I will call a press conference and tell the people," he says. "If it ever happens again, I will be responsible." (He seems to have missed the point of the recent concern about the President's unchecked control of the intelligence agencies.) After a few questions, he says that he will take just one more. Other candidates let the questions go on, as if to show what good guys they are, but not Carter. Carter likes to stay on schedule.

Carter's message about government—unlike that of other candidates who are casting their campaigns against government—is delivered without a sneer. He takes the same theme, and attaches himself to people who feel "left out," but he wraps it in uplifting sentences about how good we really are and how good government can therefore be. He talks quickly, and when he has finished it is not always clear what he has said. He combines an anti-government message—for those who want to hear it that way—with a message of hope. Carter touches anxieties without stirring them up; his style is understanding and soothing. The message sounds plausible, because of the style in which it has been delivered. Perhaps he means that the American people are good and filled with love—he says that the government should be as good as the people, which could be taken another way—but he must know that, like any collection of human beings, they are both good and not so good. He does not explain how a good people produced a bad government, and, in fact, does say at times that the government is still good—that Watergate did not hurt it, Vietnam did not hurt it. Our system of government is "still pure and decent," he says. We haven't been very proud of ourselves in recent years, and Carter tells us we're good. Nor is he quite clear about how he will produce a good government—if it is not already good—except through him, the embodiment of goodness and truth and love and trust. Government would presumably respond to the example and the blandishments and the reorganization efforts of the President. Carter must know better, of course, but he shows a shrewd understanding of the possibilities of style. And while his words sound mushy when they are committed to paper, they do not when he says them. Perhaps because there is nothing slovenly about Jimmy Carter. He talks of love and compassion, but his style is reserved and cool. Perhaps because behind his words there is the faint rattle of steel.

Carter is increasingly upset about the schedule. The size of his entourage makes it impossible to keep to it—it was made with the recollection of simpler and less successful times. Last year, it was often just Jimmy Carter and Jody Powell, his press secretary, flying all over the country. He does not like to race in and out of a city; he really does like to take the time to shake hands. At the Champaign airport, in the rain, though he was late, he paused to shake hands with the few people lined against a fence. Several stops are being removed from tomorrow's schedule.

On the stage of the Civic Center in Marion, a farming and mining community in southern Illinois, Carter is introduced to the audience by the Reverend Frank Trotter, pastor of the Third Baptist Church here and an old friend of Carter's, as someone who "is fast becoming a man of the people throughout these United States," as "one of the most sought-after lay speakers of all the Baptist speakers in America." Carter is a lay speaker for the church and worked as a missionary in New England. He has told reporters that every night he reads the Bible in Spanish. The Reverend Trotter also describes Carter—as Carter has described himself—as a "born again" believer. When Carter talks to this group, he speaks of his "boyhood days on the farm," and he says, "I'm a farmer, businessman, engineer, scientist, a father (of four children), a husband (almost thirty years), a Christian, a politician." He says he sees no reason to be less Christian on Monday than when he teaches Sunday school on Sunday, less loving of the poor than he is of his eight-year-old daughter. In Marion, we are farther south than the borders of several Border States. He talks like a lay speaker here, weaving the spiritual through what he says. Other politicians have manipulated religion and have affected piety, but there is no reason to doubt that Carter believes. Yet he talks about it before only certain audiences. He tells them that "one of the reasons I work as a campaigner six days a week from six in the morning to eleven at night is so that when I get in the White House I can send Earl Butz back where he came from." (Of course he would. All the incumbent Cabinet officers would go. One recalls Richard Nixon, in 1968, saying that he would fire Attorney General Ramsey Clark.) And then Carter tells the audience something that may lie at the heart of what he tries to do. He says that he has established "a close and intimate relationship with the voters," and he adds, "That's been the secret of my campaign."

At a fund-raising reception in Springfield, he carries the theme further. He tells of his three sons and his eight-year-old daughter, Amy. He makes a little joke—which I heard him tell in New Hampshire—about why the daughter is so much younger than the sons. "My wife and I had an argument for fourteen years," he says, and he adds, "And I finally won." The audience always laughs appreciatively. It is the only joke I have heard Carter make. Then he goes on, telling the audience, "I'd like you to be part of our family. I'd like to form an intimate relationship with the people of this country. And when I'm President, the country will be ours again." Carter woos the voters, in the old-fashioned sense of that word. He doesn't want to just restore the government to the people, he wants to establish an *intimate*—the word is underlined when he says it—relationship with them. He tells them he wants them to be part of his family. (He seems to have stopped inviting them to the White House. Perhaps he can invite New Hampshire to the White House but not Illinois.) He has positions on issues—on welfare and détente and nuclear energy and jobs, and even abortion and amnesty—but that is not what this election is about. It's about style, which is no more superficial or irrelevant than many of the "issues" that come to dominate political campaigns. It's about spirit, mood, how we feel. It's about whether we can believe again. Carter understands that well. It's about character, and that is why so much time is spent puzzling over Carter, the enigmatic and hidden man. He is asking us to take a very big gamble. It is with good reason that we pay close attention to style and character, and try to glimpse what is hidden. He may be accomplished, at binding voters to him, but then what, when he has to govern? To what purposes would he put his ability to bind people to him? We don't have any idea how he would respond to a difficult challenge, not to mention a crisis. He does not have the foundation of knowledge that many people longer in public life have—those who have dealt longer with national questions. He drops names of advisers, sometimes exaggerating their role. He does seem to have less specific positions on issues than some of the other candidates. But he is a serious man, with a sharp, agile mind—a learner—and campaign positions have a way of dissipating when they collide with reality. His ideas, like most of the ideas in this campaign, do not seem very striking or original, or part of a systematic body of thought. When he is pressed about his apparent lack of position on the issues, he says that he answers every question he is asked. He does. He has answers. Like those of many candidates, they are composed of experiences and things he has read and been told and matters that are already in the air. Some of his ideas—like the one of making the Justice Department independent of the Cabinet—seem wrongheaded. They are, like most of the ideas in this campaign, largely conventional and slightly shopworn. He talks about "the poor and the ignorant"—in the United States and in the world—and he appears to mean it. But there are some paradoxes. His soft words about love and compassion are in striking contrast to what one sees as his tough-minded, and even hard, nature. He says, "I will never lie to you, will never mislead you," and yet he must know that politicians, like other human beings, have to engage in at least a little lying and fibbing and misleading—for however good reasons—in order to function. (The degree to which Carter may be misleading at least about his second race for the governorship of Georgia and his record as governor is one of the questions about him.) He says that he will never avoid a controversial issue, but he does. Most politicians do to the extent they can. So why does he keep saying these things? He has a certain toughness and even ruthlessness, but Presidents may need to be tough and even ruthless. The question, as always, is one of limits.

Carter has been coughing a fair amount today, and at the last event he acknowledged that he was hoarse. Shortly after he boards the plane in Springfield, to return at last to O'Hare, he sits alone in the front seat, puts his head on a pillow, and goes to sleep.

Thursday afternoon. Carter has greeted voters at a commuter stop (one such event was cut from today's schedule, but this one, at which a Daley ally, Lieutenant Governor Neil Hartigan, was to campaign with him, was retained); has breakfasted at a delicatessen (where he was presented with a salami); has done some tapings; has spoken at the Chicago campus of the University of Illinois (where he told the students that they offered hope, because "you're basically idealistic, you're basically mobile, you're not wedded to the status quo, you're not bogged down being subservient to a boss or trying to please a senior partner"); has lunched at the Dill Pickle Delicatessen Sandwich Shop (where he was presented with another salami); and now is at the Merchandise Mart, holding a press conference. Every once in a while, Carter says something that seems quite candid, straight, and revealing about himself and his intentions. He may be presenting more of himself to us than is generally recognized. When he said last night that his ability to establish intimacy with the voters was the secret of his successful campaign, he probably thought, and meant, exactly that. Similarly, there is no reason not to take him at his word when he says today, "I'm not running against Mayor Daley, I'm running for President. I don't have any inclination to defer to anyone." He points out that Udall "has written off the entire South" and hasn't won a single primary, and that Jackson is concentrating on one state—New York. His jabs at opponents are quick and sharp and fairly frequent—and one recalls that his mother called him a beautiful cat with sharp claws. When he talks about arms control today, he confuses the first and second SALT agreements. Asked to explain a recent modification of his suggestion that mortgage deductions be eliminated as part of a total tax reduction—a suggestion that Jackson made much of in Florida, perhaps reinforcing Carter's reluctance to go into such specific details—Carter says, "I don't really have the capability or the inclination at this point to elaborate or describe the specifics," and "I don't have time to study it." He is in a bad mood, testy. The smiles are gone. Carter does not seem to enjoy—one is tempted to say "like"—the press. He does not seem to take kindly to close questioning, to being challenged, though the questioning today is not notably unfriendly. In his fatigue, he is unable to cover his feelings. Carter does not have a particularly good relationship with much of the press that covers him regularly—which is unusual, and is therefore worth some attention. Candidates, particularly winning candidates, usually do. But much of the press is suspicious of his style and put off by his evasions and worried about his self-righteousness. It seems odd that Carter has not taken more pains to soothe it. Moreover, handling the press is part of the process of campaigning and of governing. It may ask annoying or repetitive questions, but that is part of the deal. The press can be a pain, but so can a lot of people one comes across in public life—or life. The able politician learns to roll with it. Carter says that he is at present "looking as best I can at the next four states," and that it is "hard for me to project my own inclinations down to the eighth or tenth or twelfth state down the list." He also says that "we've adhered to our original strategy so far without deviation."

Following the press conference, I am permitted to ride with Carter in his car to the next stop, in order to talk with him. Carter had told a staff member that he wanted me to read his book before we talked—a very unusual request for a public figure to make. A staff member has been trying, unsuccessfully, to obtain for me a copy of the book—a campaign autobiography called *Why Not the Best?*, published by Broadman Press, in Nashville.

I begin by asking Carter where his campaign stands in relation to the plan that was drawn up three years ago, which he referred to in his press conference. I am interested in hearing him describe how he conceived this most ambitious of plans.

"We're much further along," he replies. "We had three states targeted that we thought we wanted to do well in—Iowa, New Hampshire, and Florida. We thought we would be at ten to fifteen percent in the public-opinion polls; we expect the next one to show me ahead of Humphrey. We had a goal in 1975 of raising five hundred thousand dollars; we've raised about a million. We have had an explosion of volunteers."

Striking the more modest note that occasionally creeps into his public statements, he says, "It's still too early to have any feeling of equanimity or assurance. There are too many imponderables. I thought one of the liberal candidates would emerge from New Hampshire and Massachusetts. That none did is one of the most unpredictable things that have happened. No clear challenger to me has been identified. We'll have to wait to see about that for the next six or seven states. Meantime, we'll be winning and accumulating delegates."

I then ask Carter to tell me something about the drawing up of the plan. I want to hear him tell how—in defiance of convention—he decided to run for President and how this most determined campaign was drawn up. A unique man is making history and leaving his stamp on our politics, and I want to hear how he talks about it.

"It's in the book," Carter says. "How I decided to run for the Presidency, and the plan are in the book. There's no point in our talking about these things when they're in the book."

A campaign book is a campaign book, so I tell Carter that I still want to hear him talk about these things, and I assure him I will read the book and tell him that his staff has been trying to get a copy for me.

"It's in the stores," he says, incorrectly. Carter's voice and eyes are cold and hard. No smiles, no warmth.

To ease the situation, get past this moment, I ask Carter a couple of fairly routine questions, and he gives fairly rote answers.

When we arrive at the next stop, for a television taping, Carter, without a word, gets out of the car and strides into the building. A few minutes later, he is on the television monitor, smiling broadly.

The strain shows as Carter talks on television. Asked why he thinks he has become a target of criticism about his failure to take positions on the issues, he replies that it is because "the Washington political figures, including news-media persons" are upset "that someone unknown to them could be a success without their knowing it." The press, on the whole, has been kind to Carter and has played an important part in his buildup. It was inevitable that there would be articles examining his statements and record. It seems early for Carter to be showing one of the classic symptoms of *Homo candidatus*—paranoia about the press. It is also early for him to be showing other symptoms, but he is showing them. He is exhausted. He pulls himself together for his public appearances, but one gets the impression that he is just barely making it through them. His campaign at this moment seems to be on thin ice in terms of the candidate's physical, emotional, and intellectual resources. He smiles, but he is on the edge.

The TV interviewer, who is aware of Carter's mood of the past couple of days, asks him what it has done to him to have started from nowhere and become the front-runner, whether it has made him testy.

Carter smiles, and replies, "It hasn't really been a surprise to us. We were confident two, three years ago I would be elected. I feel as good now as I did when I began to campaign."

At a fund-raiser (two hundred and fifty dollars a person for cocktails, followed by a dinner, for a thousand dollars a person) at the Metropolitan Club in the Sears Tower, Carter stands on a chair and tells the gathering of a hundred-odd contributors, "I want to have the kind of relationship with you as key and strong supporters on a personal plane." He tells them to call him at his headquarters in Atlanta, from which his staff will reach him, and he will return the call that evening—"or right away, if you want." He continues, "I'd like you to feel toward me that same way I feel toward you. I feel close to you. I want you to be part of my family. When I get in the White House, I want to stay close to you." The contributors, holding their cocktails, listening attentively, are obviously charmed.

The Monument of Faith Evangelistic Church, a large black church—actually a converted synagogue—on the South Side of Chicago. The church is only about half full, and the program is running more than an hour late—bad advance work. Carter, annoyed, has been using the time backstage to make phone calls. And then he is brought onstage to sit through more songs and speeches. But seldom has a candidate received such an introduction. A hundred-voice chorus, The Voices of Monument, has stirred the crowd with handclapping, foot-stamping gospel singing. Five professional athletes—four of them from the Atlanta Falcons football team—are introduced. A young woman reads a poem, called "Bi-Century and Bicentennial" ("They said then, 'Jesus Who?' or 'Who is Jesus?' . . . A John the Baptist, Jimmy Carter"). Three little girls present him with roses. A black woman from Georgia praises Carter's compassion and concern for all people. A minister gets quite worked up introducing Carter. "This is a Christian when we need Christians in key positions," he says. As the minister talks, an organist plays frenzied chords. "He's heading for Pennsylvania Avenue in Washington, D.C.," the minister says, and the organ music swells and the crowd cheers. He shouts, "LET THE TRUMPETS BLARE!" and they cheer. "LET THE TROMBONES SLIDE!" And shortly the slim, fair white man who is running for the Presidency is standing in the pulpit, looking as ruddy and well as ever. It is a rare human being who could fail to respond to such worship.

67074

Carter speaks softly now. He talks of growing up with blacks. He says, "We worked in the same fields, we fished in the same creek bed, went swimming in the same swimming hole, played with the same steel rails, homemade toys." He continues, "When we got on the train, me and my black playmates, we didn't sit together. My playmates—I couldn't understand why—went to the back." He speaks slowly, rhythmically, with frequent pauses, like a preacher. The vast church is dead silent except for the sound of his soft voice. He tells of unveiling the portrait of Martin Luther King, Jr., at the State Capitol when he was governor, of how Coretta King and Daddy King and Andrew Young were there, "and we sang together 'We Shall Overcome.'" He quotes Reinhold Niebuhr (as he does in his book), saying that the purpose of politics "is to establish justice in a sinful world." It appears to be the one line from Reinhold Niebuhr he quotes. "You don't see any rich people in prison," he tells them. He talks about John Kennedy, about government. Again he has perfect pitch for his audience. "We all feel like we're outsiders," he says. He talks of his defeat of George Wallace and says, "In Massachusetts, I didn't come in first. But in Roxbury [pause], where the black people live [pause], I came in first." Carter has an undeniable ability to relate to blacks; he is the Southerner who grew up with them in a small town and did play with them and understands them. And his record in Georgia on race also commends him to them. The southern part of Georgia where he grew up was particularly racist. His father was a segregationist, but Carter supported the integration of his church. Despite his racist-tinged campaign for the governorship, he did do things for the blacks as governor, and took symbolic steps to place himself against racism. Perhaps it served his political purposes, but he did it. People like Andrew Young support him because he is, as Young puts it, "white trash made good." And many blacks will trust a Southern white who sides with them over a Northern one who does so, judging, from experience, that Northerners are hypocrites. And so the word about Carter is spreading in black communities—helped along by a radio ad for Carter by Daddy King—and Carter knows how to talk to them. Carter again talks a lot about compassion for "the poor and the ignorant," and there is no reason to doubt his sincerity. "I don't see any conflict between religion and politics," he tells the crowd tonight. "The purposes are the same—to establish justice in a sinful world." Speaking about his campaign for the Presidency, he says another one of those candid things. He says, "I've never been more determined in my life to win anything." There is no reason to doubt that. Carter seems to want to be President more than anyone else around. He adds, "Not because I just want to be President but because I honestly believe in the bottom of my soul that I can accurately represent what our people are and what we want to be and what we can be." And he concludes, "I believe we've got a bright prospect ahead of us in this country. I feel good about it. We've made a lot of progress, got a long way to go, but I believe that we as free people under God, working together, can accomplish great things." He talks of a future with "our strength enhanced in a country where we can prove that people of all kinds can take whatever talents or ability God might have given us and use it to the utmost in God's kingdom and for our fellow-man."

MARCH 12

President Ford returned to Illinois yesterday, and tomorrow he will go to North Carolina, which will hold its primary a week from Tuesday. The President's campaign style is more confident and vigorous than it was when he started out in New Hampshire. The Administration announced today that a stretch of the New River in North Carolina will be made part of the nation's scenic-rivers system. State officials had requested the scenic-river designation in the hope of barring the construction of power dams on the river. The plans of the Appalachian Power Company to build two dams on it have been the subject of considerable controversy in the state.

Milton Shapp, the governor of Pennsylvania, dropped out of the Democratic race today, and Governor Jerry Brown of California said that he would enter it. Carter, in California, said he would enter the race in every state, no matter who else was in it.

MARCH 16

This morning, in Washington, I have an appointment with Jimmy Carter. Carter is in town to mend fences and build bridges and do whatever other labor he can to construct a victory. Carter may disparage the "in crowd" in Washington, as he has done, but he has sense enough to know that there are people here with power—through their professional roles, their contacts, their access to various networks of other people with power and influence—whose support or benign attitude, or even neutrality, can help.

Last night, he went to a dinner attended by, among others, Clark Clifford, Katharine Graham, Senator Gaylord Nelson, of Wisconsin (an active backer of Humphrey), and John Gardner. This morning, he met with Andrew Young, and later in the morning he is to go to see Jerry Wurf, the president of the American Federation of State, County, and Municipal Employees. Then he is to lunch with the Washington *Post's* editorial board, meet with the Congressional Black Caucus, attend a fund-raiser, and fly to New York. There he will be within easy reach of the media, to react to the results of the Illinois primary, which takes place today. In Washington, Carter is staying in a town house that belongs to a friend of his. The Secret Service is outside the house and in a room on the ground floor.

Upstairs, Carter sits in the living room, receiving visitors. He still looks very tired. His skin is pasty and blotched. He coughs frequently, and when I remark on the cough he says, "I think it's permanent." But he seems relaxed—far more relaxed than I have ever seen him before. In fact, despite the campaign-brochure pictures of a relaxed Jimmy Carter, I had begun to wonder whether he ever could be relaxed. His meeting with Andrew Young ran late—later than Carter permits his campaign appearances to run, if he can help it. He begins our interview by waving his hand casually and saying, "The time is yours," as if he had all day, and he is undoubtedly making amends, as his staff told me he would, for our last encounter. I begin by saying lightly that I have read his book, and he understands the point and grins. I had not known that Jimmy Carter grinned. It is not that stretched smile—sometimes natural, sometimes not—of his public appearances but seems to be a real grin. As we talk, Carter, in shirtsleeves, slumps on a couch, with an arm slung behind his head.

Since it is clear he is going to be coöperative, I ask him again to tell me how he came to his decision to run for the Presidency.

"I was inaugurated as governor in January, 1971," he replies, and he continues, "And during the election year of 1972, with Atlanta being a crossroads, a lot of the Presidential candidates came through there, and I would invite them to stay at the mansion. They'd bring their wives, and we'd talk for four, five hours—about foreign policy, everything. It wasn't a blinding flash of light; it was just a growing realization that they were human beings. I lost my awe of Presidents. I had never seen one except Truman, when he came to the submarine base in New London, Connecticut, in 1952. I got to know Nixon, I got to know Agnew."

I ask him, not entirely seriously, if those two acquaintances helped him lose his awe of Presidents.

He is even in his response. "Them, and the Democratic candidates," he replies.

Carter continues, "I never thought about running for the Presidency during the spring of 1972. It wasn't until after the Convention that anyone first mentioned running for the Presidency. Dr. Peter Bourne wrote me an eight-, ten-page letter about it." Dr. Peter Bourne is a thirty-six-year-old psychiatrist who ran a drug-rehabilitation program for Carter when Carter was governor and has become a close friend. In 1972, Bourne moved to Washington to establish the Carter front here. "That was the first anyone put it in writing. My wife and I discussed it privately. Then I talked about it with my staff, and then we started meeting, examining my strengths and weaknesses. I thought my opponents would be Kennedy and Wallace, so we started on that basis."

Did they later, I ask, change strategies?

Carter has been talking softly and easily, as if he really wanted to be helpful. But at this question he flashes, for just a moment, that sharp, hard look that he does when he gets a question he does not like. He knows that I am referring to a story in the Washington *Post* that the original campaign was to have made a more direct appeal to the Wallace vote.

He says, "We had mixed emotions when Kennedy withdrew. It changed the prospect from one new fresh face against Kennedy and Wallace to an indeterminate group of candidates. But we didn't change strategy, no. The strategy remained the same: the time allotted to each state, the determination to go in all the states. I haven't gone back and read those early papers in a long time."

There is reason to speculate that what Carter had in mind at the outset was not the Presidency but the Vice-Presidency. As a Southerner, he would be a good running mate for Kennedy, and as a Southerner who beat Wallace in Florida and ran well in other primaries he would have to be considered.

I ask him when the decision to run was made.

"In September, '72," he replies. "The first person we told outside the inner group was Senator Talmadge"—Herman Talmadge, the senior senator from Georgia. "That was because there was all this speculation I was going to run against him in '74."

Carter breaks off to take a telephone call, in another room, from Hamilton Jordan, his thirty-one-year-old campaign director. When he returns to the room, I ask him what he thought were his special advantages in running for the Presidency. Almost every candidate, in working up a rationale for running, figures out not only why he is qualified but why he is uniquely qualified.

Carter replies, "I've always felt at ease in approaching voters directly. I've never felt any constraint. Also, I had two or three things that I knew about. One was a full, solid year of intense campaigning for the governorship." In his book, Carter says that he and his wife shook the hands of six hundred thousand Georgians in the 1970 campaign—he had lost the Democratic nomination in 1966. He tells of how, in an earlier campaign for the State Senate, on election night he "went to bed sick and exhausted." He continues now, "And a full commitment to go all the way with a certain degree of tenacity." When Carter says that, I give him a look— a tenacity-understates-the-case-and-you-know-it look—and again he grins. It seems to be a natural grin by someone who might, after all, have a sense of humor about himself. It is odd to spend time considering whether a grin just might be natural. To conclude that someone may be grinning naturally and may have a sense of humor about himself should not, of course, be an event, but in the case of Carter it is.

Carter continues his list of his particular assets for a Presidential campaign. "Second," he says, "a superb staff, able to work together. Third, a knowledge of government, of the ineffectiveness of federal programs assessed by my people and by me as governor." And then he refers to factors listed in the book. "I am a farmer," he wrote, and he pointed out that that is a political advantage because "being a farmer makes one willing to face apparently insuperable difficulties and still take a chance even though the future . . . may seem just one big gamble." Also, he went on, "I can claim with credentials to be an engineer, a planner, a nuclear physicist, a businessman, and a professional naval officer. So, for those who might have an aversion to farmers, for whatever reason, there are some alternative ways of looking at what my candidacy has to offer."

Continuing our conversation, Carter says, "Those gave us a degree of confidence. We couldn't know and don't know now whether we can be sure of winning"—a changed tone from the one he strikes before audiences—"but we've never lacked confidence." Not so changed a tone. He then says, "Also, the sequence of the primary elections would seem to play in my favor. We could see three years ago that the first crucial election would be when I met Wallace in Florida." This would play in Carter's favor, as he puts it, because of Florida's proximity to Georgia, easing the problems of organizing and campaigning there, and giving Carter a good chance to compete against Wallace in northern Florida, and because of the drama that a race against Wallace in Florida would hold.

In his book, Carter says that "four or five of the major opinion pollsters worked closely with me, and helped to delineate the most important issues among the American electorate as the elections approached." I am interested in how he arrived at the theme he is using in his campaign—the combination of trust, love, integrity, open government, and anti-government that is working so well for him, and so I ask him what the pollsters told him.

He replies, "All Democratic candidates—congressional, governors—have available to us polls showing broad thematic studies. The polls showed us the post-Vietnam feeling, the feeling of exclusion, the embarrassment at lower ethical standards, at Watergate. Those were available."

Carter continues, "My relationship with wide-ranging groups of voters has always given me a sense of assurance about my feeling for their aspirations and hopes. I feel at ease with farmers; I feel at ease with blacks; I feel at ease with workers; I feel at ease with businessmen; I feel at ease with environmental, conservation groups. This is a *very* important political attribute."

Does he, then, I ask, base his campaign in large part—as it seems he does—on his ability to relate to groups he is speaking to?

"It's not something I think about," he replies. "It's not something I contrive. When I go to a college campus, I never feel ill at ease. I feel like one of them. It's just there. It is a very important attribute."

I then ask Carter about the increasing charges that he is vague on the issues. Wanting to move on from his standard answers—that he answers any question he is asked, that he cannot work out in advance a detailed plan for reorganizing the federal bureaucracy— I tell him that I understand the latter point and agree that some proposals can be worked out only after a President is in office.

Given all this, I ask, how much responsibility does he feel for spelling out his positions during the campaign?

"I don't have the time to work it all out," he replies, and he continues, "And I don't know the answers to some of those complicated questions. I don't feel under any constraints to spell out everything. I spell out what I know." But Carter is taking steps to try to meet the criticism. "Take the speech on foreign policy I gave in Chicago yesterday"—a thoughtful, if general, speech to the Chicago Council on Foreign Relations. "I read books and books and books and articles and talked to several advisers. In April, I'm going to give a speech on health. In May, I'm going to address a U.N. group about nuclear proliferation. But the demands on candidates for specificity at this particular stage of the campaign are much more advanced than they were in earlier campaigns. It's hard for candidates who work full time to get off and work on these things."

I ask Carter if he may, then, change the balance in how he spends his time.

"Inevitably," he replies. "I'm going to cut down the travel in the next few weeks to five days"—Carter grins again, seeming to recognize that to suggest that this is a leisurely schedule is absurd—"and spend a day and a half at home with my advisers." He continues, "But I don't feel intimidated. I won't be pressured into making rash statements." That's the point. He intends to be careful, and would prefer to be criticized for saying little than say something that might offend a group to which he does not wish to give offense, or that he would have to spend the rest of his campaign days defending and explaining. He knows what happened to McGovern in 1972. (In his book, Carter says that "in order to avoid mistakes" he "studied the campaign platforms of all the unsuccessful candidates for President since our electoral process began.") "Originally, I would spend a day and a half at home," Carter continues, referring to a period earlier in the campaign, "and I found that that time's vulnerable. Everyone looks on it as fair game: one more speech to be made, one more cover story with long interviews and photographs. My staff is very enthusiastic—but then they work as hard as I do. I was going to take last weekend off. I needed it badly. Then *Face the Nation* came up, so I flew back here for that. This weekend, I still have two days intact—and I need them."

I bring up the problem of how competing interests can prevent change, and ask him how he thinks he can deal with this.

He replies, "There, again, the campaign experience, and the wide-ranging affinity I have with those groups—blacks, unions, farmers, businessmen. I think I know very clearly and certainly, or will when the campaign is over, the order of priority of their concerns. It will be up to me as President to determine the priorities among groups. I don't have any fear about my ability to do that."

This gets to the question of governing—as opposed to the candidates' stated positions on this and that issue—and a question that is even harder to gauge them on, but a crucial one. Carter seems to understand the point behind the question, and, from his answer and from other things we know about him, seems to have the sense of power that is necessary to deal with the problem. In fact, if one takes him at his word, he has no doubts about his ability and authority to arbitrate among competing interests. What some see as a "chameleon" quality—of identifying with whatever group he is before—can also be seen as not just politicking but accumulating power to govern. A candidate who can win the support of a variety of segments of the public has a chance, once in office, to use that support to bring about real change. Whether a politician will use the affirmation of the groups whose support he solicits to get things done, or will be paralyzed by it, we don't know until he is in office. But we can watch and listen and see if he seems to understand the difference. And Carter is equally confident of his ability to rally the public. If Carter is elected and does some of the things he says he will, this would amount to strenuous use of power. Power is out of style now; it is considered not nice to talk about it or seem to covet it. Thus, so many of the candidates strike a humble pose and talk about serving the people, returning government to the people. If they want to do even these things, they will have to exercise power, for they will have to wrest levers from the grip of the interest groups. If they want to make changes, if they do not intend a passive Presidency, they will have to exercise power. So that even if Carter understands this—and it seems that he does—there are certain things that he, or any candidate, cannot say in the midst of a campaign for the nomination. He cannot talk about his intention to assert more control over the domestic side of government (which is different from reorganizing it); he cannot say that he will not permit George Meany to get in the way. And so even the candidate who understands something of the nature of the paralysis the country has been suffering from cannot let on that he does. The question is whether he has the courage and the wit to take this problem on after he is elected President, or whether his hopes and promises will sink in the same bog where those of so many of his predecessors lie buried.

"A lot of members of Congress are ready for change," Carter continues. "There are many fine people in Congress. Congress as a body is in very low esteem, because of its inability to act in harmony either with the President or, very much, on its own. I think Congress is looking for strong leadership in the White House, and I'm willing to give Congress credit for everything that it does that is beneficial to the public." Carter did not get on at all well with the Georgia legislature. And since Carter's stubbornness is rather well known—Carter talks about it in his book, quoting someone who called him "as stubborn as a South Georgia turtle"—I give him a skeptical look, and he grins again.

"It's not an impossible hope that the conflicting special interests' desires can be correlated," Carter says. "If there is disclosure of what they are trying to do and expression by the President to the public of what is involved, then I think you can accomplish a lot."

Aides bustle about to signal an end to the interview, and I ask if I can raise one more question, and I tell Carter that it is about his religious beliefs. He nods, knowing that this is a matter of increasing attention. I ask him to tell me what he meant when he said, as he has been quoted as saying, that he was "twice born."

"I never do raise the question myself," Carter begins. "Sometimes it comes up. I know I was quoted as saying I was 'twice born,' but the expression I use is 'born again.' We believe that the first time we're born as children, it's human life given to us; and when we accept Jesus as our Saviour it's a new life. That's what 'born again' means. I was baptized when I was eleven years old. I never did have a personal feeling of intimacy with Christ until, I'd say, ten, twelve years ago, and then I began to see much more clearly the significance of Christ in my life, and it changed my attitudes dramatically."

I ask him how.

He replies, "I became much more deeply committed to study and using my example to explain to other people about Christ. I did a lot of missionary work."

I ask Carter in what way his religious beliefs might guide his political career.

He says, "It has no particular political significance. It's something that's with me every day."

President Ford easily won the Illinois primary yesterday, with fifty-nine percent of the vote to Reagan's forty percent. Among the Democrats, Carter won. Carter's victory in the popularity contest was not a surprise, but his success at winning delegates—somewhere between fifty and sixty—was. In the popularity contest, Carter won forty-eight percent of the vote, Wallace won twenty-six percent, Shriver won eighteen percent, and Harris won eight percent. Even allowing for the deliberate understating of their objectives by candidates and their aides, Carter's delegate collection (he had predicted about twenty-one) was a surprise—and therefore will have an impact. It may be that once voters vote for a candidate, they do not then vote for someone else's delegate slate. Why should they? In any event, the results may suggest that favorite-son slates do not do well against real—and especially against popular—candidates.

8

IN FOLLOWING THE EVENTS of this year, I make a point of trying to step back from the swirl and talk with people who have cool, clear minds, and an ability to make sense of what is going on around us. There are such people, even in chatter-filled Washington, and they are of particular value at a time when politics tends to crowd out reason and perspective and any sense of what the real questions before us are. Today, I talked with Paul Warnke, who was an official in the Defense Department in the Johnson Administration and is now a Washington lawyer. As Assistant Secretary for International Security Affairs, Warnke was instrumental in changing the attitude of Johnson's Defense Secretary, Clark Clifford, from one of support of the Vietnam war to opposition. Clifford, in turn, became one of those who were most instrumental in persuading Johnson that his policy must change. Warnke is now Clifford's law partner. A cheerful man, with a ruddy complexion and straight gray hair, Warnke is consulted by all sorts of people on international questions, and remains a man of some influence.

I asked him what he thought were the most important international questions we were, or should be, facing. I was somewhat surprised by where he began his answer.

"I think maybe the number-one issue is how you go about restoring your alliances," he said.

I asked him whether he meant alliances based on the old Cold War assumptions.

"No," he replied. "Based on some old and some new considerations." He continued, "Economically, there is a great deal of interdependence between us and Western Europe, and between us and Japan. And there is still a risk of the Soviet Union's trying to gain some of what the Chinese call 'hegemony' in Europe. I don't think either the Nixon or the Ford Administration has appreciated the importance of our allies, and the difference between their attitude toward us and our attitude toward them. They are much more concerned about us than we are about them. I don't think Kissinger or Nixon or Ford has done enough to keep the alliances repaired. Remember the 'Year of Europe'—in 1973. Why did there have to be a year of Europe, and what happened in it? Not very much. If you think, as I do, that there is going to be a hard time bringing about a new economic order, you need the kinds of relationships that make it possible for those on whose coöperation you count to have an understanding of what you're doing. We've done a very poor job of it. The Third World thinks it's going to be easy. It isn't. They want equality—meaning that they come up close to the existing level of wealth in the world or we come down. The question is: How do you adjust the system to bring a better return for those who have been outside the system?"

I asked Warnke if he thought that our government was giving enough recognition to the needs, or demands, of the Third World.

"No," he replied. "And you can't resolve the questions until you get the proper relationships with the countries that have to be involved. It's a major problem, if you look at the possibility of mischief—you can't have a constant condition of stress with the bulk of the human race. The industrialized world has never been able to live without the unindustrialized world. They used to rely on it economically through colonization. If you can't do it through exploiting their raw materials and people, you have to have some kind of economic interchange. What kind of economic interchange can you have with a pauper? Besides, if you assume, as I do, that the proliferation, if not of nuclear weapons, then of nuclear-weapons material is inevitable, the cheeky little bastards, if they get sufficiently annoyed, may blow us up."

But can we ever satisfy them, I asked Warnke.

He replied, "I'm not sure. The population problem may mean that we're always behind the power curve."

Where does one draw the line, I asked him, since there are those who think that the Third World is profligate with our aid and insatiable in its demands?

"It's really an instance of how do you know until you try," Warnke said. "Kissinger, testifying before the Senate Finance Committee, asked how you can deal with these people when they're behaving badly and not in our interests. Maybe you turn that around and ask how they can deal with us when we don't act in their interests. The answer to the argument about profligacy is that that's not the way to give them aid. You should work through international institutions. You don't give them money; you give them trading preferences, commodity-stabilization agreements, so that you get them to do something useful. The Administration says it won't go ahead with the good ideas Kissinger proposed along these lines in his U.N. speech until they start behaving better at the U.N. Christ, that's a non sequitur. As long as they're in a parlous economic situation, they aren't going to behave better at the U.N."

I asked Warnke about our present military budget.

"That's another problem," Warnke said. "What the hell do you do with the military budget at this point?" He had been consistently critical of the size of the military budget, but now he was saying something slightly different. "Anyone who is realistic feels that you have to be concerned at the amount the Soviets are putting into theirs," he said. "Much as you'd like to, you can't make drastic cuts. But I still think we ought to see who is driving whom—how much of what they're doing is in reaction to what we're doing. You have to hope for genuine, effective arms control, and you have to decide what it's best to spend your money on. The two efforts ought to be going on simultaneously."

I asked him if they were.

"I don't think the Administration's trying hard enough on arms control," he replied. "I think we are spending too much time on the non-military side of arms control. Kissinger is overly concerned about the domestic implications—instead of taking on the military, he's assuming he can't get a certain degree of control, because he can't get domestic support. And that is buttressed by our approach to SALT: we say if you don't do *x,* we'll build anti-ballistic and cruise missiles, and we go ahead and build them. The impetus for the cruise missile came out of the first SALT agreement, in 1972, when the Soviets were allowed one thousand six hundred and eighteen intercontinental ballistic missiles to our one thousand fifty-four. One of the ways the agreement was sold to the military was to leave them room to speculate about what else they could do. And one of the things announced by Mel Laird"—then Secretary of Defense—"shortly thereafter was that we could build cruise missiles. So there's not that much cutting to be done unless we get serious about arms control and use détente to demilitarize the competition that is going to continue between the Soviet Union and the United States. Maybe neither one of them is possible, but you never know until you try."

Warnke continued, "And that's my fundamental quarrel with our Angola policy. You're going to have a continuing competition between the United States and the Soviet Union, with differing views about the world structure each wants to see. That always comes as a great surprise. People say, 'See? Despite détente, they still want the world to be Communist.' And the Soviets say the same thing about us and capitalism. The world is dynamic, and you have a lot of situations that are fluid—Portugal, Italy, France, Yugoslavia, even Eastern Europe. The driving force on both sides is the feeling that you have to be in a position to affect the decision by the use of arms. So our two budgets are not based just on defense. We both continue to equip ourselves to influence political decisions on a worldwide basis. You have to assume, when you get an Angola, or a situation in Latin America where those in power decide they are tired of urban guerrillas and a wealthy north, that they will make decisions on both internal and external policy that we won't like. I think we ought to use détente to work out with the Soviet Union an understanding that neither of us is going to try to affect a political decision in an emerging or changing nation by the use, or the threat of use, of military power. People say that such an understanding won't work, but you never know until you try. Neither side has tried it. Why not, for example, try to work out some agreement with respect to bases in the Indian Ocean?"

I asked Warnke if he thought that Angola was symptomatic of what we were doing in relation to a number of larger questions, and he said that it was. I asked him what he would have done differently.

He replied, "I never would have put myself in a position where I was contributing arms in a civil war. I think I would have to start out with the proposition that if Angola is Marxist, I can live with that, and support by other means the forces for good. I should avoid blotting my copybook by supporting the Portuguese there. And I strongly suspect we encouraged South Africa to intervene. Wouldn't we have been a hell of a lot better off if we had tried to convince the Soviet Union that we should both keep hands off?"

But, I asked him, what if it wouldn't agree to such an arrangement?

"You have to decide that on a case-by-case basis," he replied. "On Angola, I'd have let it go, because we'd clearly have been coming in on the losing side. I'd feel the opposite in Portugal—if as Gonçalves went down the drain the Soviets came gunboating into the harbor, I'd respond. It seems to me it's our obvious willingness to use the military route that makes it impossible for us to marshal opinion against the Soviet Union when it does. Take Angola. It's an egregious thing to have Cubans there, but our objections get nowhere when the other side can say, 'For Christ's sake, the United States brought in South Africa." The point is, I think we've got to take the chance that people will opt against us, and we ought to start doing some of the non-military things that may lead them to opt with us. The alternative is that the Soviet Union will continue to build up its military force and we will have to match it."

I remarked that over the past few years Warnke had been saying our strategic military arsenal was insanely overbuilt, and now he did not sound the same way.

"I still believe it," he replied. "That gets you down to specific weapons systems. If you proceed on the assumption that the Soviets may intervene anywhere, you have to go on with a massive military structure to act as a deterrent. But why proceed on this assumption? I don't think you can get anywhere with the argument 'Look at them—they're building up this enormous force for intervention.' But we're doing the same thing. If we try to get them to stop, even if we fail, we put the onus on them. More people might like us. And it would help the domestic debate—carping critics like me would have to keep quiet if we tried. But you have to make one decision. Are you willing to allow some countries to go sour on their own? So far, for our government, the answer is no."

We turned to the subject of arms transfers, by sales or by credits, to other countries. Military sales had been under Warnke's jurisdiction when he was in the Pentagon, and the subject has disturbed him.

"What we're doing is to expand our arms transfers very substantially," Warnke said. "Since 1968, when I was the chief 'merchant of death,' arms sales have gone up more than ten times. There you have to start with deciding what it is you want to transfer arms to foreign countries for. I suppose the answer is 'common defense.' But the reasons involved in that can be very different. Another reason we do it is the balance of payments. A third one is to preserve influence and prevent others from getting influence. Fourth, it's a form of rent for the use of foreign bases. In the first instance, you have to decide what will contribute to the common defense. Perhaps the standardization of equipment—our buying European equipment—would lead to the strongest NATO. Some of the transferring of arms goes into setting up a regional power—filling a vacuum because the British have left. That's lousy. Why should we sit down and decide who should be the regional superpower? That's going to aggrieve the ones who weren't chosen and the ones who don't want a new suzerain. And you have to assume that whoever it is you give arms to will last and be a permanent friend of the United States. What if the Shah wanted to use them to take over Bahrein or Abu Dhabi? Even if you have some strings on him, you don't know who will be in control in ten years. You could end up with a Colonel Qaddafi as commander-in-chief of all these American weapons. The influence argument hasn't proved to be worth a damn. Cyprus is the classic example. We couldn't exert influence even though we were the principal suppliers of both the Greeks and the Turks. The result is that Greece is no longer a participant in the military functions of NATO. Part of the problem is that by building up this tremendous business in arms for foreign countries you build up a tremendous interest in our own country to keep it going—and tremendous pressures. It's the same reason you're not going to get a serious review of weapons programs, especially in a recession. If you called for an end to the Trident submarine, you'd see some liberal senators rise in opposition, because it involves too many jobs in Connecticut and Rhode Island. You get too many decisions that are militarily irrelevant. The influence argument doesn't strike me as a particularly valid one. And on the rental argument—you ought to buy them off with money. I think if you did that, you might decide that some of the bases weren't that essential to the national defense. In other words, in order to cut the defense budget you have to make some policy decisions. If you don't, you're not going to get very far. You have to try arms control, try some agreement with the Soviet Union about the uses of arms. I'm afraid that proliferation is inevitable. Can't you see the slogans of the nineteen-nineties? 'If you outlaw nuclear weapons, only the outlaws will have nuclear weapons.' It'll be the gun lobby all over again. That's why it infuriates me when Kissinger loses one with Congress or Congress cuts the budget by a few million and he says this shows the erosion of our will. Some people in other countries will begin to believe Ford and Kissinger when they say this. It's a lie. We have eighty-five hundred nuclear warheads to the Soviets' twenty-six hundred. We have fourteen large carriers; they've got two mini-carriers. We're ahead as far as tactical air capability is concerned. Granted the Russians in uniform outnumber our forces by more than two to one, but, given their common border with China, their military problem is at least twice as great as ours. Where there are imbalances that ought to be corrected—for instance, in tanks—that can be done without massive additions to our defense budget. That should be done, without poor-mouthing our overall defense capability. Yet I read a German publication saying that the Soviet Union is superior and Europe had better develop a nuclear deterrent of its own. Our whole policy for twenty years has been to prevent Germany from becoming a nuclear power. We have to try non-military ways of making it a more compatible world—convince the emerging nations that we're on their side. Continuing to shriek at them at the U.N. and giving them the back of our hand economically is not very compelling behavior. I don't think you could do better than Kissinger's September 1st speech to the U.N., but not much has been done to put his recommendations into effect. From the security standpoint, an investment of a few billion in that direction instead of in military hardware would probably advance the cause. Since proliferation is inevitable, having a lot of people dissatisfied and desperate is going to be more risky in the future than it has been in the past."

MARCH 19

Senator Frank Church, Democrat of Idaho, entered the Presidential race yesterday. Church's entry had been delayed, pending completion of the work by the committee he heads on the C.I.A. and the F.B.I. But the committee's work has dragged on—there is much negotiating among the members over what the final report will say and recommend—and so Church, who has been toying with the idea for a long time, has entered anyway. His strategy is based on faltering by other liberals and on his winning some of the later primaries in the West. Church may or may not think this will come to pass. What seems to have happened is that he considered the race for some time, built a staff and raised money and considered his unique qualifications, and then could not turn it off. A lot of people enter Presidential politics that way.

Ronald Reagan, campaigning in North Carolina (with Jimmy Stewart at his side), responded with exasperation to questions about whether he would quit the race soon. Ford aides and allies have been suggesting that he do so. Referring to the President, Reagan said, "Tell him to quit." The problem with suggestions that Reagan quit is that they overlook the fact that to quit would leave him without a role. Moreover, it is in the interests of conservatives—as long as they can afford it—to keep Reagan in the race, so as to keep pressure on Ford. Not that, without Reagan, the President would become an unrestrained liberal, but there is no question that Reagan's presence acts as a conservative pull. Reagan's candidacy has always served a dual purpose. The President will return to North Carolina tomorrow. I am going there to see George Wallace.

SPRING

9

THE GREENSBORO, North Carolina, Coliseum Auditorium. Saturday night. George Wallace will hold a rally here tonight. Wallace is expected to lose the North Carolina primary to Carter on Tuesday —a defeat that will finish Wallace's role as a political force. It seems hard to believe, since he has been with us so long—running for the Presidency, and frightening politicians in both parties, since 1964. Wallace was widely seen as a dark force, a demagogue who stirred anger and hatred. But, like an effective demagogue, he was on to what bothered people, and good at articulating their grievances. This gave him his power, causing more "respectable" politicians to echo much of what he said, and giving him a constituency with which he could upset the calculations of both major parties. Wallace would never be President, but he was a major force. Now another Southerner has set out to finish him off as a force, and appears to be succeeding, and, in the process, may secure a place for himself on the Democratic Party ticket. Wallace and Carter: the one dark, ugly, country, a fomenter; the other blond, well turned out, modern, cool. Carter is what "the new South" likes to think it is. As a friend of mine from North Carolina put it, "We don't want to think of ourselves as breaking into Rebel yells and driving pickup trucks anymore." And so Wallace and Carter are meeting here, amid the mountains and red clay hills and coastal plains of North Carolina. Wallace carried North Carolina in 1972: former Governor Terry Sanford entered the race against him late here that year, and could never quite shake Wallace's charge that he was a stand-in for Hubert Humphrey. Many people used to vote for Wallace in the confidence that he would never be President; he was the vehicle whereby they could, as Wallace put it, "send 'em a message." Now they can send the message through Carter, and, better still, Carter might actually be President—a point that Carter underscores by telling people not to waste their vote. Wallace has retaliated by saying he is a serious Presidential candidate, but that argument hasn't taken hold—especially now that he is confined to a wheelchair. Carter has absorbed much of the Wallace appeal, from the anti-bureaucracy position to the fundamentalism. Carter has beaten Wallace in Florida and Illinois. The political careers of these two men have been strangely intertwined over the years, and Carter's precise relationship with Wallace, and what Carter says about it, has been one of the issues trailing Carter. The polls show Carter far ahead of Wallace, and the confidence seems to have gone out of Wallace's campaign. His crowds have been thin, his speeches have been dispirited, events have been cancelled. Members of his staff are openly criticizing each other. Organizers and Alabama state officials have been brought into North Carolina at the last minute. And, as I learned from talking with him this afternoon, George Wallace is upset.

I talked with Wallace in his room at the Howard Johnson's Motor Lodge in High Point, a short distance from Greensboro. Wallace had just attended a reception of the Veterans of Foreign Wars Ladies' Auxiliary. He was dressed in a navy-blue suit; a carnation from the reception was in his lapel. He looked surprisingly well: tanned and rested—not the pallid, ghostly Wallace who made that dramatic appearance at the 1972 Democratic Convention. But the flat, broad face was familiar, as were the wisp of dark hair that fell on his forehead, the wide mouth, the tongue smile. Accustomed as we have become to the fact that Wallace gets about in a wheelchair, I couldn't help being startled by the wheelchair and thinking of what life had become for him since he was nearly fatally shot by Arthur Bremer in a Maryland shopping center in May, 1972— what it must be like for this vital man to be paralyzed, and physically dependent on others. And of the grit it took to pull himself— after the shooting and several subsequent operations—back to this point. And now Jimmy Carter was threatening to wreck it all.

I began by asking Wallace how he felt about his campaign at that point.

Wallace does not always speak in sentences—particularly when he is distracted, which he clearly was now. He replied, "I feel good about the campaign. I did so well in 1972 before I was taken out." That is how Wallace refers to the shooting. "There has been quite a bit of organized effort against me this time." He was referring to the support for Carter against Wallace in Florida, and the reports that others were urged to stay out of the race there. "Of course, my wheelchair. The polls showed in Florida two out of five who wanted to vote for me voted against me. I never thought about that matter, because I get around. I operate functional. Governor's office full time, travel to Europe, travel around. I have delegates—in Mississippi, Massachusetts, Florida. In Illinois, I didn't have any organization; didn't expect anything in Illinois. I shouldn't have been in Illinois without organizing. Pretty soon, the people of this country will have learned about— Learned about many of the candidates. They'll learn about those who talk one way here and one way yonder and you can't put your finger on 'em. Maybe they ought to take polls back in the states from whence they come."

Wallace had avoided mentioning Carter by name, but finally his distress over him could no longer stay hidden. For this evening's rally, his staff had assembled newspaper clippings and telegrams, including one from the former Mississippi governor Ross Barnett, to show that in June, 1972, Carter had attended a fund-raiser for Wallace in Red Level, Alabama, and said that Wallace was a great American and would be a good President and that he would try to keep the Georgia delegation in the Wallace column as long as possible. (Carter's staff has said that when Carter spoke to the group in Red Level he "explicitly stated his appearance was in no way an endorsement of Wallace and that his visit was solely for the purpose of joining with them in wishing Wallace a speedy recovery from the assassination attempt only six weeks before.") Wallace picked up the documents and some newspaper clippings from the bed next to his wheelchair and waved them. He referred to an article in the Atlanta *Journal* which quoted Carter as saying, in June, 1972, before the Democratic Convention, that a Humphrey-Wallace ticket would be acceptable and would run well in the South. "This kind of stuff," he said. "Now he's saying he vaguely remembers." Wallace read to me from the clippings, and then he said, "And now he says, 'I never supported Wallace and never would.' " Wallace's contempt and despair were clear. He started speaking with more vehemence, talking about a now familiar part of Carter's second, and successful, campaign for the Georgia governorship, in 1970, when he ran against the former governor Carl Sanders, a liberal. Sanders, during his governorship, had blocked Wallace from speaking before the Georgia legislature, and Carter said that when he was governor he would invite Wallace to speak in Georgia. Wallace said, "He went all over Georgia saying, 'I'll invite Wallace to speak in this state.' Do you know that? He made a big issue of it. If you go around and use a man's name in an emphatic fashion—'I'll *invite* him to come to this state'—Now, if you're not for him when you say that, you're *misleading* people, aren't you?" He made "mislead-ing" into a very long word. *Misleeeeeeeding*. He paused, waiting for me to agree, and I just looked at him, waiting for him to go on. "Aren't you?" Another pause. "Well, sure you are." Wallace, quite worked up now, continued, referring this time to a news story that on Thursday, in Winston-Salem, Carter, talking about his deep re-ligious beliefs, said, "I spent more time on my knees the four years I was governor in the seclusion of a little private room off the gover-nor's office than I did in all the rest of my life put together, because I felt so heavily on my shoulders that the decisions I made might very well affect many, many people." Wallace said, "That little room where he said he spent all that time on his knees—that's where he made that little agreement with me that I wouldn't run delegates against his precinct delegates in Georgia, and he said he would support me provided I got three hundred or more delegates, and we shook hands. I had no reason to doubt it—he had been so friendly, and used my name running for governor. I went there with four hundred. We asked him to nominate us, and he said, 'I'm sorry, I'm an old friend of Scoop Jackson's.' Maybe someday he'd like to take a polygraph test on that." The Carter staff denies that such an agreement was made.

Trying to change the subject, I asked Wallace what effect he thought he had had on our politics. My impression, I told him, was that it had been a profound one.

He replied, "Already the Democratic Party's moved back toward the center. Every one of them is talking about the things I talked about in '72, aren't they? I was talking about welfare; I was talking about foreign aid; I was talking about national defense; I was talk-ing about tax reform. Even Scoop Jackson's talking about busing."

But his mind could not stay off the subject of Carter. He seemed at times nearly distraught. At one point, he fell silent and buried his head in his hands, and I did not think he was acting. "He says he's not going to campaign in Alabama, because, according to the papers, he says he doesn't want to rub my nose in it." One must hear how Wallace says it to get the full effect: he doesn't say "nose," he says *"noooooooohse,"* and he says it with deep sarcasm. And then he said slowly, working in a menacing tone for emphasis, "Well, I'm going to run against him in Georgia." Wallace con-tinued, "The other candidates didn't come to power in their states using my organization, my mailing list, and my name. I was very popular in Georgia. They don't owe me anything." He pointed his finger at me and spoke slowly. "But a man who rides your coattails, uses your organization . . . He stayed with me as long as I was popular." Wallace seemed to be getting to what really hurt. "They thought I was dying, that I was through with politics, that I'd be a vegetable the rest of my life, or I'd die. You wouldn't have bet that I'd be in a primary four years later, would you, honey? I wouldn't feel the way I do if he said, 'Yes, I supported Governor Wallace in those days. I didn't support everything he was for, but we were friends. But he understands I'm running for the Presidency.' He has a right to run if he'd still be my friend. He has a right. I'm not the only one that can run for the Presidency; I'm not the only one in my region. I'm the reason some of them are running—because I proved they could do well in other parts of the country."

Trying to change the subject again, I asked Wallace why he had made his races for the Presidency.

"One of the first motivations in the early days was, I believe, people were tired of big government," he replied, and he continued, "I did so well. It wasn't running for President. I wanted to show that people were beginning to tire of government. I also wanted to prove that the people of my region were in the mainstream of American political thought. I was a little tired of the national politicians kicking us around. That was the beginning, and then we did so well in 1968. Many people who didn't feel I had a chance to win wanted to vote for me. I also wanted to help shift the Democratic Party back to becoming the party of Jackson and Jefferson and the great middle class. Not that we should forget those who are unable to look after themselves, but remember explicitly those who are producing, paying the taxes, fighting the wars, holding the country together, and stop paying all the attention to the exotic noisemakers of the left—like they ended up doing at the '72 Convention. I like doing it, because I get a satisfaction out of feeling we did some good. For me to go in Massachusetts in '76 and win the second-largest number of delegates in the citadel of Eastern liberalism . . . I carried the city of Boston. Did you know that? You wouldn't have bet a dime on that four years ago, would you—that Wallace would ever carry Boston?"

I asked him if the recent losses had been tough for him.

His voice was soft as he replied. "Oh, no, honey," he said. "Nothing's that tough. After you've been shot five times and suffered the loss of walking, what's a loss?" He paused, and then he continued, "Not being able to walk. But I'm living. I thought I was going to die as soon as I was hit. So losing a campaign—my goodness, that's not your life. That's not the right to look at the sky, the trees, your wife and your family, enjoy your friends. Of course I would like to win, but I've lost some pretty tough battles. You don't win every time, but the election is not over yet. This is the first quarter."

Wallace kept talking, returning again and again to the subject of Carter. For a while, his wife, Cornelia, who is a handsome and vibrant woman, was in the room, but then she went out for a walk. Twice, he asked me to get him a glass of water. He apologized for asking for my help. He went on talking about Carter, the fair-haired Southerner who had capitalized on him and made him an instrument of his own success. The acceptable Southerner. Wallace was not acceptable, and he knew it, and now, filled with bitterness and resentment, he sat in this Howard Johnson's motel room facing his ultimate defeat at Carter's hands, not wanting to be left alone. He did imitations of Carter: "I will never lie to you; I will never *misleeeeeed* you." He talked about Carter's saying in Massachusetts that he was for cutting defense spending and saying in Florida that he was for strong defense. He talked about being in the wheelchair. "He can go out and shake hands and get on television," he said. "I can't do that. He was my friend when I was popular. He said he was for me when he thought I'd die. I don't mind the other ones, because they say what they think. Udall's a true liberal, and he's honest about it. Those other fellows criticize me, but they didn't use me. He talks about spending all that time on his *kneeeeees*. Well, I'm going to church tomorrow, but I don't go around talking about my religion. I might not get such a big crowd tonight. Saturday night. Not a good night for crowds. I've always said what I believed. You might not have agreed with me, but you knew where I stood, didn't you? When I said I was against integration, I believed that. That's how I was brought up. Even when I stood in the schoolhouse door, that was because we were mad at the federal government forcing it on us. But it would have happened in a few years. Anyway, that's over now. And I made sure those little black children were protected. Did you see, one of them said to Dan Rather on *Sixty Minutes* recently that they would support me? Anyway, that's all over now."

A half-hour Wallace ad came on the television screen as we were talking. "Fix the color on that, will you, honey?" he asked. "I want to see how I look. Do I look healthy?" Then: "He says he's a *gooooood* Southerner."

After a while, Mrs. Wallace returned to the room and told him that his dinner was coming, so I said good-bye and started to leave. He called after me, "He *yuuuused* me when I was popular." And then he said, "Look out for phonies, honey."

Other politicians make speeches to groups that have been assembled for this or that purpose. George Wallace's rallies are road shows, put on by the candidate and his travelling troupe. Steve Sammons travels with him for the purpose of acting as m.c. Sammons, a stocky man in his late twenties, used to do voice-overs for television commercials, and now produces commercials—one of his clients was Colonel Sanders' Kentucky Fried Chicken—in Montgomery. Steve Sammons' job is to warm up the crowds. Then Billy Grammer, a Grand Ole Opry singer, accompanied by a three-piece band—all of whom also travel with Wallace—performs. The routine seldom varies: Grammer and his group play "Under the Double Eagle," "Gotta Travel On," and "Detroit City"—a song about a country boy who is lonesome in the big city. This week, Wallace and his troupe have already played for rallies in Raleigh, Asheville, Charlotte, and Rocky Mount, and on Monday night, election eve, will play in Fayetteville, in the south-central part of the state—Wallace country. The Wallace road show also has its own set. As Billy Grammer plays, one's attention is caught by the low podium—about three feet high, with about another foot of bulletproof glass on its three sides—that sits, empty, at center stage. The podium is on a metal ramp. After the rally, the set will be struck and moved to the next town, for the next performance. Steve Sammons and Billy Grammer get the crowd relaxed, clapping along with the thrumming music. Tonight, Billy Grammer adds an embellishment: in the middle of "Detroit City," he gets the crowd to sing, "We're sending Jimmy Carter home." And then, as Steve Sammons introduces Wallace, Billy Grammer's group breaks into "Alabama Jubilee," and Wallace—as the crowd cheers and claps and screams —is wheeled onstage and up the ramp and placed behind the podium. He sits there, smiling and waving, while the crowd cheers and cheers.

One hand resting atop the bulletproof glass, the other waving in the air, Wallace tells the crowd, "They're well organized against George Wallace this time." He announces, "I'm well. Franklin Roosevelt was elected President of the United States four times in a wheelchair. Maybe you've forgotten that." Wallace says, "I'm tired of all this hypocrisy"—pronounced *"high*-pocrisy"—and he adds that people are "cynical about people who run for office being everything to everybody." And shortly he swings into a denunciation of Jimmy Carter. "These newsmen down there," Wallace says, sweeping his hand toward the press table that has been erected in front of the auditorium, the journalists being one of his props, "whether they like me or not, they know I mean what I say. You can't tell what Mr. Carter means." At that, the crowd stands and cheers and applauds. The auditorium is only about two-thirds full, but the cheering of the crowd—enthusiastic, with him, cheering— fills it. Wallace is clearly pleased. He becomes more fiery than he has been in a long time, he and the crowd feeding each other's enthusiasm, egging each other on. Watching Wallace, one wonders what would have happened if he had been given a handsome face, or even a face in which the hatred did not show. And he goes down his litany of complaints against Carter. "He went all over the state," Wallace says. "He used my name. Did he really mean that he was not for me in his heart but he used it politically? I was very strong in Georgia in those days. . . . Was he misleading people when he said, 'I will invite George Wallace to come and speak in this state'?"

Wallace apologizes, saying he is sorry to have to do this—that he does not like to make personal attacks on his opponents, which is apparently true. Wallace is seldom personal in his attacks. But Jimmy Carter is unlike any other opponent Wallace has ever had. His face twisted in anger, his voice ringing with contempt, Wallace says, "I'm not one who says, 'I'm a Southerner but I'm a *different kind* of Southerner.' What kind of Southerner does he *mean?* I think all Southerners are good." This is not the feigned anger of a speechmaker. As Wallace goes through his list of issues, one is struck with how they have been picked up by other candidates and made a standard part of our politics: big government; regressive taxes; the bureaucracy ("Everybody's talking about it now"). He was a prophet, a populist, and an authentic spokesman for people's grievances. He goes a little further than the others: the bureaucrats (pronounced "beuuurowcrats"), he says, come out of some "upper-repute college"; they're "totin' briefcases around and writin' things for one another." He talks about the "rip-off artists on welfare"— another fixture in our politics. The startling thing is that Wallace has almost nothing fresh to say now. They've all stolen his lines. So he sits there in his wheelchair, his campaign all but over, saying them anyway, because what else can he do? And Wallace is the best orator of them all—his timing and delivery expert, his applause lines perfectly designed. "The judges in the federal system pay more attention to those who shoot you than those of you who get shot," he says. "What we ought to have returned to the United States is the good old electric chair." He talks of "pointed-head" bureaucrats; it would have been as disappointing if he hadn't as it would have been if Jack Benny hadn't gone to the vault. You expect certain things of George Wallace, and he does not disappoint you. He is the effective demagogue, and, like many effective demagogues (the Longs of Louisiana come to mind), Wallace is funny. He has a sense of the absurd, the comic, and he has the timing. And, like other funny performers (again the Longs, or Will Rogers), he uses his accent to advantage. "The New York *Times*," he says, "called Fidel Castro 'the Robin*hooood* of the Caribbean.' I said, 'He looks like a Communist.' I looked at pictures of him in those Cuban hills, and I said, 'Anything that looks like a duck and walks like a duck and quacks like a duck—is a duck.'"

And then he swings into his peroration—about Paul Revere riding through towns telling them "The British are coming." He says, "You give me a good vote here in North Carolina and I'll ride to Washington"—George Wallace, now in a wheelchair, will ride to Washington—"and tell them, 'The people are coming.'" The people in the audience are on their feet, applauding and cheering and whistling and shouting. He is still their hero, their spokesman—their message-bearer. Billy Grammer and his group swing into "Alabama Jubilee." George Wallace waves both his fists in time to the music. And then, as the music plays and the crowd cheers, he is pulled away in his wheelchair, waving.

MARCH 22

Sargent Shriver withdrew today from the Presidential race.

In a speech in Dallas, Henry Kissinger said that the United States "cannot acquiesce indefinitely in the presence of Cuban expeditionary forces in distant lands for the purpose of pressure and to determine the political evolution by force of arms." While the United States will not support the white-minority government of Rhodesia, Kissinger's statement also put the United States in the position of opposing any Cuban involvement in bringing that government down.

Tuesday. Ronald Reagan, surprising nearly everyone, defeated President Ford in North Carolina today. Reagan received fifty-two percent of the vote to Ford's forty-six. So much for prognostication. Jimmy Carter trounced Wallace, with fifty-four percent of the vote to Wallace's thirty-five. Wallace has said he will go on, but, strapped for money, he has dismissed Steve Sammons and Billy Grammer.

10

NEW YORK. The Roosevelt Hotel. Henry Jackson is here to address the annual dinner of the Social Democrats, U.S.A., the successor of the old Socialist Party. Surrounding Jackson at two long tables that form the dais are many of the people who, officially and unofficially, are the basis of his support in New York. Jackson expects to do well in New York, with strong support from traditional labor, which likes his big-program domestic policy and his hard-line foreign policy, and from Jews, who appreciate his support of Israel and his efforts to increase the emigration of Soviet Jews. An argument can be made that Jackson's foreign-policy approach is not really helpful to Israel, because it does not encourage Arab-Israeli negotiations and could undermine the more flexible forces within Israel. In addition, his amendment making the extension of trade benefits to the Soviet Union contingent upon an increase in the emigration of Jews was followed by a Soviet rejection of the trade agreement and a decrease in such emigration. Jackson puts the blame for this on a number of other factors, but still this was the one instance in which his approach to dealing with the Russians was put into effect, and it did not work. His support by the old-crowd labor leaders is motivated in part by the fact that they like his policies and in part by their rivalry with the more liberal labor unions. These bedroom quarrels run all through our politics. The unions that are strong for Jackson here in New York are the building trades, the United Federation of Teachers, the Steelworkers, the International Ladies' Garment Workers, the Paperworkers, the Maritime Union (Jackson, from the state of Washington, has a record very favorable to the maritime industry), and the Longshoremen (who especially like Jackson's foreign-policy ideology). And while no one knows to what extent union leaders' political preferences can be transferred to the members, there is much that the unions can deliver—as the unions in Massachusetts did. For one thing, these unions, combined, have about two million members, according to Robert Keefe, Jackson's campaign director, and, he says, "Communication with their members is the first thing we're stressing." Some of the union leaders do it through mailings; some do it at the work sites. And then the unions can provide the organization and the manpower to get Jackson supporters to the polls. (These are the kinds of contributions that unions can make to campaigns without having them counted as contributions.)

At one point, Jackson was predicting that he would win New York by a landslide—a prediction that he may regret. Anything less than that, in the way political results are interpreted, would be considered a failure. And any sort of respectable showing by Carter or Udall, or both, would be considered a triumph. Neither is making much of an effort here, and both are playing down what efforts they are making. (Fred Harris's New York telephones have been cut off.) Udall has now been endorsed by Robert Abrams, Bronx borough president and a leader of the New Democratic Coalition, and by Victor Gotbaum, the head of the American Federation of State, County, and Municipal Employees in New York, and has received the endorsement of the New Democratic Coalition, which last December, in the interest of being "pragmatic," gave most of its support to Birch Bayh. Now several of the Bayh delegates have signed on for Udall.

This gathering tonight is, like the candidate who is appearing before it, both of history and of the moment. Seated at the head tables are Daniel Patrick Moynihan (who received more applause than Jackson when the two men were introduced), Albert Shanker (president of the United Federation of Teachers), David Dubinsky, Sol Chaikin (president of the International Ladies' Garment Workers' Union), Robert Georgine (president of the Building and Construction Trades Department of the A.F.L.–C.I.O.), Norman Podhoretz (the editor of *Commentary*), A. Philip Randolph, and Bayard Rustin. (The A.F.L.–C.I.O. provides more than half of the funds for the A. Philip Randolph Institute, which Rustin, national chairman of the Social Democrats, heads. Rustin has argued for years that blacks should not fight the unions, even if the unions are not very accommodating to blacks. His argument is that only if the unions achieve their own goal of full employment can blacks be helped. During the New York teachers' strike of 1968, Rustin was the only prominent black leader who would show up at the side of Albert Shanker.) The group here tonight is the Old Old Left, representing a generation of social reformers. But they are well fed now, and the world around them has changed. It is no longer fashionable to be so rigidly anti-Soviet as they became in their fights against Communist infiltration of the union movement and in their maturation during the Cold War, and as they remain. This group has absorbed many shocks in the past decade: the New Left, the Vietnam war, the new militance of the blacks, and the violent reaction of George Meany and many of his allies to all this. Jews who had reason to see themselves as exemplars of the liberal tradition suddenly found themselves hostile to blacks—a feeling that stemmed from the anti-Semitism of some blacks and from the feeling of New York's Jewish teachers that they were being pushed around by the blacks, with their demands for quotas. Moynihan, the liberal who has to be the maverick, the dissenter, found that his road to power was through the Nixon Administration, and so he made adjustments, uttered interesting phrases, and awaited another wave to ride. The United Nations was a wave waiting for Moynihan. The blacks and the younger liberals will never forgive him. The union leaders who fought for social progress find their achievements belittled and themselves reviled by the next generation.

This gathering is symbolic of the intellectual and political confusion currently surrounding the idea of liberalism. The people in this room are bound together by old ties and new reactions—old fights for social justice and new reactions against the events of the sixties, culminating in the Democratic Party's nomination of George McGovern in 1972. They are reacting (in different ways) to what they see as the liberal excesses of the sixties. They are bound together by reactions against what they see (in different ways) as too much government intervention, too many demands by blacks, too little appreciation of the battles they have fought, too little militance against Communism. They are reacting against social and political changes symbolized by "the kids" and their sympathizers of the late sixties, against practitioners of the "new politics," who push, as they see it, exotic political notions and issues, and who also changed the rules and, of all things—at least temporarily—took over the Democratic Party. And so ex-radicals, ex-Socialists, old liberals, new conservatives, exemplified by the group in this room tonight, have banded together in search of new and common ground. At times they find common ground, at times they are separated by great gulfs. They are on common ground in their anti-Communism: the intellectuals in their writing and the labor leaders in their political action are for strong defense policies and for anti-Soviet policies. (It was unions led by some of the people in this room tonight who beat up "the kids" on Wall Street who were demonstrating against the war in 1970.) They are on common ground against what they see as the spoiled children and their indulgent elders of the late sixties and early seventies—against exoticism. They are on common ground in their shared belief that blacks have gone too far. And they are on common ground in their shared feeling of having been kicked in the teeth. But while the intellectuals set about building a body of literature about the supposed failures of the Great Society social programs and the dangers of big government, the labor unions push for more social programs and big government (as long as the programs do not help blacks and the poor at the expense of the middle class). George Meany probably favors the sort of government regulations that would drive Irving Kristol into a frenzy on the editorial page of the *Wall Street Journal*. This reactive politics doesn't get you very far, doesn't say very much about what to do next, and may not form the basis for a political movement at all. But many of these are "old politics" people, accustomed to gathering together the blocs of power. Ben Wattenberg, a theoretician and adviser to Henry Jackson, has tried to tell them how to do it through a kind of politics aimed at the blue-collar worker. And into the middle of all this comes the old-politics liberal—the Presidential candidate Henry Jackson. Jackson is trying to reconstruct a coalition that will not coalesce. He is not Franklin Roosevelt, and the year is not 1932. Labor is fractured. Labor and blacks have serious differences. Other Democratic intellectuals have moved on to a different politics and are not attracted to Jackson.

In his speech tonight, Jackson makes a brave attempt to make sense of the whole thing. "Isn't it interesting," he tells the gathering, "that I am the only Presidential candidate who is willing to call myself a liberal?" (Udall uses the term "progressive," and Carter has avoided using any term at all.) Referring to the fact that he supports higher defense budgets than most other Democrats do, and to his criticisms of détente, he says, "Some people have criticized me and criticized the labor movement and said we weren't liberals, just because we believed in a strong America." And now, he adds, they have "stopped calling themselves liberals."

The unions, like Jackson, support new weapons systems. The labor support is based in part on ideology and in part on the fact that new weapons mean new contracts. Like Meany, Jackson was one of the last supporters of the war in Southeast Asia. Jackson's foreign-policy views are fairly consistent, and appear to proceed from a set of beliefs. But yesterday he told a television interviewer, "If you want to get people to their feet in a hurry, you just talk about 'we do all the giving and they do all the taking.' " Last night, at the Bossert Hotel, in Brooklyn, at a gathering to meet him and his local delegates, he said, "What we have is a kind of phony détente, which is a coverup for one series of events after another where we end up on the short end of the stick." Now he continues, "I'm still a liberal, and I still believe, my friends, in a 'human' détente." He says that those who are anti-Washington are echoing the sentiments of those who have opposed the civil-rights movement, the labor movement. He makes a good, strong speech, reaffirming things that they hold—and probably he holds—dear.

It is sometimes hard to tell with Jackson, a man of both deeply held and acquired beliefs. Politics, by definition, involves a certain degree of exploitation, of attempting to convince a certain group that one is with it, so as to gain its support. All politics is a compact of sorts—a compact between the politician and his supporters that in exchange for their support he will do things they want done. The line between the compact and exploitation, as is true of many things about government and human relations, is impossible to define. But, as is also true of many things about government and human relations, one can sense when a certain line has been crossed. And there are times when one senses that Henry Jackson has crossed the line. He had been a stolid, serious, hardworking representative and senator, an unassuming, undramatic, pleasant enough man. And he had, by dint of his seniority, his seriousness, and his hard work, become a power in the Senate. And then something happened to him. He began running for the Presidency. He was one of the numerous people "mentioned" for the Vice-Presidency in 1960, but instead John Kennedy made him chairman of the Democratic National Committee. In 1970, he was reëlected to the Senate from Washington with eighty-four percent of the vote—a higher percentage than any other Northern Democrat—and at once it was said in the press that this made Jackson a Presidential contender. Jackson believed it. He did poorly in the 1972 primaries but, as most candidates do, he went through the "but for"s and decided to try again. Along the way, people began to notice some things about

Jackson: his attacks on opponents often went further than other politicians' (it was Jackson who, in 1972, labelled George McGovern the candidate of "amnesty, acid, and abortion"); he had a certain way of reaching for publicity uncommon even among politicians (he chose to make a point against the oil companies by calling in their senior executives, en masse, to testify, placing them under oath, and then proceeding to castigate them before the television cameras). In 1972 in Florida, where the busing issue was especially sensitive, he talked not just against busing but about a Constitutional amendment against busing. Perhaps he only seems to wear a yarmulke more than other candidates. Perhaps he has been a longtime admirer of Daniel Patrick Moynihan. Jackson is an overdoer. In substance and in style. He does not just defend the liberal programs and suggest that there is more to be done but promises all kinds of big new programs—far more than there are resources to pay for in the foreseeable future. Last night in Brooklyn, Jackson promised federalization of the welfare program (he said that someone can move to New York in the morning and be on welfare that afternoon, which is not true), a national health-insurance program, more hospitals, a "massive program of public works," a fifteen-billion-dollar program of increased federal aid to education, more subsidized housing, a big jobs program. His explanation that all this will be paid for by lowering unemployment does not suffice. "I'm going to lay it on the line," he told the group last night, shouting. He shouts a fair amount. "One of the candidates goes around talking about a lesser America," he said—he was referring to Udall's talk of the necessity of adjusting to the idea that natural resources are not unlimited—and as he said it he clasped his arms to his body and shrank backward. Referring to Carter's pledge to reduce the number of government agencies, Jackson said, "He wants to abolish all the things, I guess, that help people here." And then he dropped his voice and added, offhandedly, "I suppose Social Security." Sometime since the last election, aware that his speaking style was considered dull—the dullness had become a joke—Jackson got coaching in how to speak forcefully. (In 1975, he also had surgery performed on a drooping eyelid.) Now he gesticulates, using gestures that politicians seldom use anymore, and here, too, he doesn't seem to know when to stop. As he makes a point, an arm shoots out, index finger thrust forward, and stays there until well after the point has been made. It's just out there, doing nothing, until Jackson seems to remember that it is there and draws it back. Shortly, the other arm shoots forward, and remains for a similar period. Sometimes he sends both arms at once out to the side and waves them up and down, as if he were imitating a bird. Jackson is a throwback, in his politics and in his style, and he appeals to those for whom the old ways are comfortable. It is still good to be for these things, he tells them, and they feel better. He tells them that they are still liberals, and that that is good.

APRIL 4

The première tonight of *All the President's Men,* at the Kennedy Center, provided an almost confusing blend of journalism and Hollywood. It was like watching a movie within a movie. In the movie, about Bob Woodward and Carl Bernstein's work on the Watergate case, Washington celebrity became movie celebrity, real people with whom we were familiar—from reporters and editors to Richard Nixon—became characters in a movie. Most of us drove by the Watergate, and the Howard Johnson's across the way—the lookout spot for the Watergate burglars—on our way to the Kennedy Center, which is next to the Watergate. Figures portrayed in the movie were in the audience. Suddenly Washington was show business. There was a ferocious scramble for tickets to the première, with various people having their various reasons for wanting to be there. Robert Strauss, now the chairman of the Democratic National Committee, with hard work obtained eight tickets. "After all," he said, "they spent a lot of time filming my office." Senators Edmund Muskie and George McGovern were there, being reminded of what they were up against in 1972. Some members of the House Judiciary Committee were there, and so were staff members of the Ervin committee, and so were others who had become, and remained, Watergate addicts. For many, the première had become a major social occasion, a scene at which it was smart to be seen. And it was a political event.

APRIL 6

Milwaukee. Wisconsin and New York hold their primaries today. The attention is on Wisconsin, because Carter hopes to defeat Udall here, thereby paring down the effective entrants in the race to himself and Jackson. The polls are predicting a Carter victory, but Udall's polls show the race is getting close. With Udall out of the picture, the theory has it, the liberals will turn to Carter as the man to defeat Jackson. If Carter then goes on to defeat Jackson in Pennsylvania in late April, according to this theory, he cannot be deprived of the nomination; Humphrey will have let his chance go by.

Udall has put more time and effort into the Wisconsin primary than Carter has, Udall having long ago marked Wisconsin—generally a liberal state—as one of the most important in his campaign. But the Udall organization supposedly established here a year ago (it is one of the few campaign organizations ever listed in a local telephone directory) was until about three weeks ago largely phantom. The Udall campaign has therefore suffered somewhat from its own public relations, which have long stressed that Udall had a strong organization in Wisconsin, in an effort to persuade people that Udall would do well. A classic problem for candidates is how to inflate their prospects in order to attract allies and followers without creating a standard against which they can be measured unfavorably. Udall is being backed by the liberal labor unions in seven Wisconsin congressional districts, and Carter in two. Local U.A.W. leaders wanted to go all out for Udall, but Washington union officials were concerned that this would be seen as a decision to back him nationwide. Meanwhile, the liberal unions are bringing pressure on Carter to be more specific on issues of concern to their members, such as budget allocations and economic stimuli. This was strongly pointed out to Carter when he was in Washington recently, and in a subsequent meeting of union officials with Hamilton Jordan, his campaign director. The union officials have to have something to deliver to their members. One union official said, "They don't seem to grasp the fact that there is not only an electoral constituency—they are playing to it well—but an institutional constituency that will weigh in at the Convention, perhaps more strongly than it should. We have to have justifications for what happens. They don't seem to have come to grips with this." Carter is now confronting the interest-group politics of the Democratic Party. He is coming under increasing pressure to back the Kennedy-Corman health plan and the Humphrey-Hawkins jobs bill—the liberal touchstones. (The Humphrey-Hawkins bill was recently modified by its sponsors to set a less ambitious target of full employment—three-percent adult unemployment in four years, instead of three-percent unemployment in eighteen months, thus

making it more realistic and less inflationary.) The unions' decisions about whom to back where can get complicated. Carter is
being backed in districts in which the unions were afraid Wallace
would run well, and the unions were reluctant to back Carter in
any of the six districts whose congressmen have endorsed Udall.
Udall's campaign is showing signs of trouble, however. There is
discord among the staff members (there may soon be a third
change in its management), a seeming lack of direction, poor
scheduling of the candidate's time. Last Tuesday, Udall flew all the
way here from Pittsburgh in order to go to a small home in south-
west Milwaukee to stage an event in which he protested high property taxes, and then he flew to Buffalo. (The event did, however,
get on the local evening news.)

Udall's advantages in time and money spent here may well be
more than offset by the national publicity that Carter has been
receiving. Carter has become a phenomenon now—the phenomenon of this year's election—and he is receiving the most attention.
Now he is recognized at plant gates. Carter was the spokesman for
the Democrats at the Gridiron Club dinner in Washington on Saturday—where important journalists and their publishers and other
public figures gathered. And Carter took the opportunity of his visit
to Washington to be photographed in front of the White House with
his wife and eight-year-old daughter, Amy. Monday's papers carried the picture, the captions quoting Carter as saying, "I look
forward to living there." Carter has had some minor setbacks in
recent days, but they have not received much attention. In Virginia's caucuses on Saturday, where he hoped to do well, he got
only thirty percent of the vote. Sixty-two percent was for "Uncommitted"—most of these apparently Humphrey delegates. In state
conventions in Oklahoma and South Carolina, uncommitted delegates remained uncommitted in the face of Carter efforts to win
them over. (In Oklahoma, the governor had come out for Carter.)

Carter has been displaying a certain mean streak in his campaigning in Wisconsin. Responding to a comment made by Humphrey to reporters in Washington that there was some "racism"
behind the criticism of federal programs—an observation that
seems valid, and from which Humphrey specifically excluded Carter—Carter said that Humphrey was a "loser," and "too old" to be
President. He brought up the fact that Humphrey's 1970 senatorial
campaign manager had been convicted for accepting an illegal

campaign contribution (the case is on appeal), that Humphrey was alleged (by a former aide to Howard Hughes) to have accepted an unreported cash contribution from Hughes in 1972. Carter also said—and this was the point—"I think the American people would react adversely to the Convention awarding the nomination of our party to someone who had not gone to the people." Carter is running against Humphrey now, and showing Humphrey that if he tries to get the nomination things could get rough. Carter uses his daughter, Amy, as a weapon. He tells audiences what a nice, grandfatherly man Humphrey is, and of how when Humphrey came to the governor's mansion in Atlanta, Amy crawled on his lap and smeared a brownie on his face. Or of how Edmund Muskie tried to play with Amy, pick her up, but Amy would not let him, was not drawn to him. He does not say where Amy stands on public-service jobs.

When Carter is asked about the fact that Julian Bond, the black Georgia legislator who was nominated for Vice-President at the 1968 Convention, came to Wisconsin to campaign for Udall, he says that that was because Bond wanted to be Vice-President and knew that he could not run on Carter's ticket. Humphrey himself made an appearance in Wisconsin, as if he couldn't quite stay away from the primaries. Jackson, concentrating on New York, was here for only one day, and Wallace was here for five days. Gerald Ford and Ronald Reagan have been here. Ford promised to establish a Cabinet-level committee to investigate the overseas bribes made by American corporations seeking contracts. Reagan broke off his campaigning here two weeks ago to devote his time and dwindling resources (his campaign was in debt, and he had to give up his chartered jet) to a half-hour speech, carried on NBC, in which he reeled off his various complaints against Ford and the Congress and then concentrated his attack on Henry Kissinger and foreign and defense policy. The speech has brought in about four hundred thousand dollars.

Wisconsin enjoys a special place in our political history: Kennedy's victory here was a turning point in 1960, and so was McGovern's in 1972. (In 1968, Lyndon Johnson pulled out before the Wisconsin primary.) And so the candidates have been here, making their obligatory pilgrimages to dairy farms to pose with cows. About two hundred Georgians have flown here at their own expense, as they did to New Hampshire and to Florida, to canvass and pass out leaflets for Carter. The fact that they would do this is believed to impress the voters. The Georgians are staying at the Marc Plaza Hotel, Morris Udall's campaign headquarters.

Today, the weather is beautiful—clear and about sixty degrees— which is said to be "Carter weather." Bad weather gives the edge to the candidate with the better organization. Udall's staff had been praying for bad weather.

Jimmy Carter's campaign organization has prepared a memorandum on how to go about selecting Carter's Vice-Presidential running mate. An announcement about it is planned soon. This is characteristic of the combination of tactical and psychological warfare and foresight which has marked the Carter campaign. Today, I had an opportunity to talk with Carter's top campaign aides— Hamilton Jordan, the campaign director; Jody Powell, the press secretary; and Jerry Rafshoon, an Atlanta advertising man, who is the media director—as they were waiting for tonight's results. They had done their work. Their candidate was in Indiana and would arrive here this evening, so they had several hours this afternoon to sit around and talk. They are young and attractive, and give an appearance of openness and friendliness. They seem almost loose when they talk, and they have a sense of humor that is not apparent in their candidate. But they seem, too, to be people who could be tough if necessary. After talking with them and with a few others, one has a much clearer understanding of the Carter campaign.

No one—perhaps not even Carter—seems to know exactly when the idea of seeking the Presidency came to his mind. But in 1972, when he had been governor of Georgia for only about a year and a half, he did, contrary to his denials, seek the Vice-Presidency. "He's ambitious, you know," said one aide. After McGovern was nominated, Carter, who had placed Jackson's name in nomination, sent emissaries to the McGovern camp. Hamilton Jordan and Jerry Rafshoon and Peter Bourne were in Miami Beach then, trying to obtain the Vice-Presidential nomination for Carter. At one point— and they now recall the story with amusement—they went to the Doral Hotel and tried to get a junior McGovern aide to arrange an appointment with Patrick Caddell, McGovern's then twenty-two-year-old pollster. Allowed in Caddell's presence for what now seems to them to have been less than a minute, they showed him an admittedly questionable poll to document the less than compelling argument that Carter would be McGovern's strongest running mate in Georgia. An aide recalled, "We left the Convention and thought how stupid we had been, and we thought, Why hustle around the Convention seeing if we can get the Vice-Presidential nomination? Why not run for the Presidency?"

In late September of 1972, Rafshoon, Bourne, Jordan, and Landon Butler, an Atlanta businessman, went to the governor's mansion to talk with Carter about making the race. "We told him he should think about it," one aide recalled, and he continued, "It came as no surprise to us that he was already thinking about it." Carter was dressed in bluejeans and a T-shirt, and was barefoot. He and his aides and friends talked for several hours about making a race for the Presidency. They talked about how his having been a governor and how his being from the South could be turned to his advantage. Carter asked Hamilton Jordan to put on paper a plan of action, and at Thanksgiving time Jordan gave Carter a memorandum of about ninety pages. This was the beginning of what has come to be thought of as a master plan, but it now seems that the plan was less a single, comprehensive strategy than some recent descriptions— and even Carter's remarks—have suggested. It was a set of strategies, which kept evolving as the political situation did. There were things that Carter and his staff knew they could control, and things they knew they could not. One aide said, "On the things we could control, we did a good job. On the things we could not, we were fortunate." Among the things that could be controlled was Carter's approach, his themes. Among the things that could not were external events, and in the case of one external event—Watergate— Carter was fortunate. As one aide put it, "Watergate made it an advantage for the first time in the history of the country not to be an incumbent." So Carter stresses that he was once a governor, and that that shows he is competent—the Carter campaign group thinks that competence is a big point—and also the fact that he is no longer a governor sets him apart from "the politicians."

The big question that Carter and his staff had to consider was how a former Southern governor who wants to run for President advances himself without letting people know what his purpose is, without appearing too ambitious, and, at the same time, how he gets better known. Various possibilities were studied for 1975, when Carter, who, under Georgia law, could not run for reëlection, would be out of office: a university presidency, a position with a foundation. As it turned out, Carter spent 1975 running for President. Carter's appointment, during the last year of his term as governor, by Robert Strauss to head the Democratic Party's 1974 election campaign was extremely fortunate, and not accidental. Carter was one of the governors who had helped put Strauss into the chairmanship, and several of the other governors were running for office in 1974; Carter, who did not dare challenge Senator Herman Talmadge for his Senate seat, had the time, and saw an opportunity, and so he volunteered for the job. "I have more than once wondered what would have happened without that assignment," one aide said. The assignment gave Carter and Jordan, who moved to an office in Washington, excuses to visit about thirty states and make useful contacts all over America. There is some question how much good their efforts—conferences and position papers and the like—did those who were running for office that year. Carter's efforts did not result in support by members of Congress for his campaign for the nomination. On being asked about this, one aide explained, "I told Jimmy we'd get more help from people who lost," and he named a few contacts. But the assignment, whatever it did for those who were running for office in 1974, served Jimmy Carter's purposes very well.

Meanwhile, the members of Carter's staff read every book they could find on the 1972 campaign, and made their plans. At Christmas of 1974, Jimmy Carter sent Christmas cards to everyone who had written him when he was governor—some seventeen thousand people. The fact that the staff had worked together for several years, and worked out the relationships of each with Carter and with each other, also gave Carter a great advantage. The staff of just about every other candidate is faction-ridden, as candidates' staffs usually are. Hamilton Jordan went to New Hampshire to find out how George McGovern had managed such a strong showing against Edmund Muskie there in 1972. Early successes and surprise were key elements in Carter's plan. The assumption then being that the other candidates would be Kennedy and Wallace, the idea was to astonish everyone by doing very well against Kennedy in New Hampshire and against Wallace in Florida. Later, it was decided that McGovern could have done better in Iowa, whose precinct caucuses would be the first contest of the year, so that was the place to score the first great surprise. The basic idea was to show early that the Southerner could do well in the North and could beat

Wallace in the South. Carter and his staff were not sure that Wallace would run, but if he did, the idea was to beat him without offending his constituency. A great deal of work would be done in 1974, when no one was looking. Organizing for 1976 was begun in some of the states. At that point, the local papers were more important than the national ones, and local TV stations more important than the networks. It was cultivation time. Carter developed the practice—which he still continues—of staying in people's homes, rather than hotels, and thus forming friendships that would be useful. It was also time to work up the themes and the image. During 1974, Carter gave Jerry Rafshoon a list of words and phrases to work with, including "not from Washington," "competence," "integrity," "non-royalist." "Politicians don't create issues," explained one of Carter's aides. "The issues exist in the minds of voters, to be discerned or misunderstood. After Watergate, you found people looking beyond the issues for qualities and competence. They were looking for integrity. Voters can't understand the complexities of energy policy and the Middle East." As the Carter group saw it, the voters were looking for people who could handle the issues, and the qualities that the voters were looking for were the qualities that Jimmy Carter projected. The themes of "outsider" and "executive," they thought, were actually sub-themes, which would reinforce the themes of "integrity" and "competence." The themes were tested as Carter travelled around the country in 1974.

Some themes were almost inevitable. When Carter ran for the gubernatorial nomination in 1966, he ran—although he was a member of the state legislature—as an "outsider" against "the establishment." The theme of love, an aide explained, was never really decided upon—it was simply "vintage Carter." Some aides, however, worried about it—were concerned about how it would sound outside Georgia. "We're dealing with a cultural difference," one said. Some were worried about his bringing religion into the campaign. The theme of competence grew out of hunch, one aide explained—a gut feeling, reinforced by a poll taken in June, 1975, which found that people felt that a governor would make a better President than a member of Congress would. The changing mood of the country both helped shape and coincided with the themes that Jimmy Carter would stress in his Presidential campaign. "When he was elected governor of Georgia, in 1970, he could not have done what he is doing today," said an aide. "The mood of the country wasn't right."

The small-town, rural image was debated long and hard. The prevailing feeling was that although most people did not have anything similar in their own lives, it had appealing overtones of roots, stability—things to which even people in cities would be drawn. The decision to situate the Carter campaign headquarters in Atlanta instead of Washington, another much debated one, was based not just on logistics—the fact that Carter and his staff lived in Atlanta, the availability of volunteers—but also on image. While some aides saw advantages in being in Washington, near centers of power and people of influence, the image of being not-of-Washington prevailed. Even the role of the peanut was discussed. Some argued that it should be played down, because it might seem a little corny. But then it was found that the peanut had a sort of humble quality to it, and this became convenient to a campaign in which, as an aide put it, smiling, "humility was not our long suit."

When Kennedy did not make the race for the Presidency, the plan was only jiggled, not disrupted. Now there would be more candidates to compete against, but the goal remained the same: to do well early, taking the country by surprise. Carter's people say that they have never thought there would be a brokered Convention, perhaps in part because they could not allow themselves to think there would be one, because they knew Carter would never be the choice of one. He was "the outsider" only partly by design; he was also a man with strikingly few political allies. So Carter had to do everything through the voters, and this led to the strategy of campaigning everywhere. While the strategy is sometimes painted as a great nationwide communion with the people, Carter and his strategists thought it was also the only way he could get enough delegates to be nominated. As a full-time candidate and an effective one, they figured, he could go into places like Maine, which others wrote off. The prevailing wisdom that trying to campaign in every state is disastrous they saw as a misreading of what happened in 1972. They explained that while some political people say that Muskie's mistake was trying to run in too many states in 1972, the fact is that Muskie's campaign was in effect finished after New Hampshire. They said they figured, moreover, that by running in a primary or a caucus almost every week Carter would get a disproportionate amount of attention from the media. Running everywhere—if it didn't kill the candidate—was a psychological and tactical strategy. Hamilton Jordan drew a chart for me to demonstrate the strategy. It showed the approximate number of delegates that were obtainable in three periods: January through March; April; and May and June. The chart looked like this:

$$J/F/M \quad 700$$
$$A \quad 700$$
$$M/J \quad 1600$$

"We felt that most of the big confrontations would take place in the first few months, when few delegates were at stake," he explained, "and that if we could survive them and eliminate a lot of competitors, we could pick up enough delegates later."

Room 630, part of the Udall suite at the Marc Plaza Hotel, shortly before 7 P.M. The beginning of an evening of watching the Wisconsin primary returns. Udall has just given a press interview, saying, "I think we're very much alive with a strong second here. I think a result of forty-one to thirty-nine would be a great victory for us." The polls have all shown him losing to Carter—some by substantial amounts. He talked about how the press built up Carter victories in places like Vermont and Maine, and he pointed out that Carter had been in only two industrial-state primaries thus far— Massachusetts, "where he came in fourth," and Illinois, "where he had no real opposition." As soon as the reporter has left, Udall and a staff aide express annoyance at press reports that the Udall campaign tonight is, as Udall puts it, "in its death throes." Udall plans to stay in the race even if he loses tonight. For one thing, he may have to, in order to receive the federal matching money that is due his campaign, which is now in debt. For another, he is not yet inclined to drop out. Candidates give a number of reasons for staying in, but they are seldom inclined to drop out until they have no choice. Although much has already happened in this election, it is still early. There are still questions about Carter—about what he is really like and how he will hold up as a campaigner. Perhaps he will continue undeterred in his march to the nomination, but some politicians feel that it pays to stick around and be ready in case he does not. They have not been able to head him off yet, but one must always take into account the possibility that something will happen. Udall's daughter Bambi, a tall, long-haired twenty-one-year-old who has been campaigning in Wisconsin for three weeks, comes into the room. Udall tells her that CBS and NBC are reporting that it's forty to forty. Bambi jumps up and down and says, "We're going to win!" Udall, smiling but saying nothing, puts his arm around her.

Udall was up at five this morning, to make one last visit to shake hands at a plant gate. His wife, Ella, a spirited woman, went with him. Now they are finishing dressing for tonight—they will have to appear on television, whatever happens—and are waiting for the returns. Udall tells me that one of the things he did today was "write a speech on why we didn't win—which I'm now getting ready to discard." He adds, "I thought I ought to have one ready. If I win tonight, I think I'll use that quote 'I've been rich and I've been poor, and, believe me, rich is better.' " He smiles; he likes the line. "Any damn fool can make an acceptance speech." Udall is now beginning to entertain the thought that he will win the Wisconsin primary. "I'm now going on the assumption it's there," he says. "Either a win or a narrow loss. I figure that, with Carter's publicity avalanche, a strong second would not be written off. After tonight, I could end up with more delegates than Mayor Daley."

David Obey, the thirty-seven-year-old Democratic representative from Wausau, Wisconsin, comes into the suite. Obey, along with Henry Reuss, the Democratic representative from Milwaukee, was among the first members of the House to urge Udall to make the Presidential race. Udall tells Obey, "I think we have the makings of a win here." Slowly, the suite starts to fill—with staff members, other people who worked hard for him in Wisconsin (his state chairman and a labor leader, among them). Stewart Udall, the candidate's brother and campaign director, and his wife arrive. It is such people who go through election-night vigils. An aide tells Udall that CBS will project a winner at eight-thirty, and that it looks "terrifically good." CBS has told Udall's people that they will be informed fifteen minutes before Udall is "projected" as a winner, so that he can get ready to be interviewed by Walter Cronkite. These days, one wins elections when the networks say one wins. It is hard to remember the time when it was otherwise, and one wonders how else it could have worked.

"A victory?" Udall asks.

The aide waves his hand noncommittally.

Stewart Udall stands rocking back and forth tensely.

David Obey says, "My stomach hurts."

Morris Udall says, "The story tonight, if we win here, is that people began to be troubled by Carter. They think he's too cute and plays both sides."

Udall begins to make one little joke after another—a sign of tension. Then Udall and I talk for a few minutes.

I ask him if he is surprised by what Carter has been able to do.

"Just staggered by it," he replies. "It's incredible. There's no precedent in American political life for someone coming from nowhere and just sweeping it. For a Southern ex-governor, it's amazing. I got to the point last week of thinking there was no stopping him. My intellect told me the gloss would wear off. The figures tonight may show that. This may be his Gettysburg—as far north as he can penetrate."

I ask Udall how he thinks the Carter phenomenon happened.

"Relentless, indefatigable, intense campaigning," he replies. "Skillful organization. He not only wove a hypnotic spell with the voters—his people followed up the next day. He's been masterly at getting Leonard Woodcock to endorse him 'just for Florida'; labor people in Iowa 'just for Iowa.' There weren't other good horses; they were old and tired, like Jackson, or untried, like me."

I ask Udall if he is troubled by Carter. There have been reports that he is.

"Yes," he replies. "If the CBS polls are right, my faith in the American people will be vindicated. I couldn't believe the American people wouldn't turn on somebody who tries to be all things to all people." Tonight's CBS news reported that in its polls of Wisconsin voters high proportions of those questioned said Carter was "too fuzzy" on the issues, and that "the honesty issue" was going to Udall. An argument can be made that the elaborate polls the networks are conducting over-refine the questions, and find more than is there—that people are far less rational and more instinctual in their voting than can be reflected by this sort of polling.

I ask Udall how he feels.

"Good," he replies. "We thought we'd win New Hampshire. We thought we'd win Massachusetts. I thought we'd get beaten here bad. Now here tonight all the dreams may come true. All the hard work may pay off. I always thought if I got well enough known I'd get momentum. Now that may be happening. If we win, we'd get what I've been waiting months to get: the liberals to coalesce, people coming out of their shells and supporting me. This puts us on the threshold of a whole new chapter."

Not likely, but not out of the question. Political history tells us that candidates who look very strong can suddenly look very weak—that the way they are seen, as attractive and strong and capable and all together (winning) or as fumbling and weak and a little pathetic (losing), can change quickly and dramatically. Suddenly Muskie was down, a loser, a fumbler, and suddenly McGovern was up, strong, a winner. Even a candidate's physical appearance seems to change in the eyes of the public. How this happens is one of the mysteries of American politics, but it happens. John Kennedy *looked* different after he was nominated and began to do well in his Presidential campaign. George McGovern *looked* different as he neared his party's nomination—and then he looked different again when he began to make mistakes. Richard Nixon *looked* different when he finally became President. There was a time when Spiro Agnew looked sleek and strong. It probably has something to do with their success and growing confidence and with our reaction to their success and confidence—which reinforce each other, as they do in other human transactions. So it is not out of the question that tomorrow Udall will acquire some of the attributes of a winner and Carter some of those of a loser, that new weaknesses in Carter and new strengths in Udall will suddenly be seen.

At eight-fifteen, people start to drift toward the television set. There is a good bit of hugging in anticipation of the glorious announcement, and people are getting very tense.

"Christ, I want this one," David Obey says.

Stanley Kurz, Udall's fund-raiser, who refuses to get elated, says to me, "We've been here before. We really expected to win New Hampshire. We really expected to win Massachusetts."

"This is it," says Bambi Udall.

It is. It is a moment in and of itself. The people here, enclosed in what is happening right now, are isolated from the realities of what-happens-even-if-he-wins. Right now, either he wins—with whatever consequences that carries—or he loses and he is through, even if he doesn't get out. If he wins, it's also a vindication, a triumph over all those who wrote Udall off. That's why the people in this room are more excited than other victors, in other suites, have been. At eight-twenty, Udall tells Bambi in a soft voice, "CBS believes they are going to predict a win." Then he sits quietly. A labor organizer comes in with champagne. Udall seems to be trying not to smile—to be reluctant to allow himself to be too happy just yet. A staff member comes in and says that CBS says it will not call a winner until nine-fifteen. "I might as well take my coat off," says Udall. "It may be a long night." A staff member bringing in results gathered from a "boiler room" down the hall announces that in one bell-wether precinct it's Udall 38.7, Carter 31.6. Cheers.

At eight-thirty-five, CBS says that, with one percent of the vote counted, it's Udall forty percent, Carter thirty-four percent. But CBS does not project. An aide says that CBS has said that it will project Udall. Bambi hugs Udall. Ella Udall kisses him. An aide announces that Udall is beating Carter in the tenth ward of Racine, which Carter was expected to carry. Cheers and applause.

At eight-forty, ABC projects that Udall wins.

David Obey says, "I can't react."

The returns from Kenosha, and even the South Side of Milwau-kee—an ethnic neighborhood—as relayed by staff members, look good for Udall.

Just before nine o'clock, Udall himself announces to the group that, with twelve percent of the vote in, it's Udall thirty-eight, Car-ter thirty-five, Jackson eight, Wallace twelve.

David Obey tells me, "We should be ahead early. Then the small towns, which use paper ballots, come in, and they will be for Car-ter."

At nine, Udall says, "I wish Walter Cronkite would come around."

A few moments later, Walter Cronkite announces that, with nineteen percent of the vote counted, Udall is "holding on to a very narrow lead." It's Udall thirty-eight, Carter thirty-five.

Udall, talking to a few of us, says, "There are going to be a lot of red faces tomorrow—all those people who thought he was invinci-ble and wanted to get ahead. How can they back someone who's against the Humphrey-Hawkins jobs bill and the Kennedy-Corman health-insurance bill? How can they be for someone who says he's just for voluntary busing? They say they will go with him because that way they can influence him. Translation: They're thinking about positions of power in the future."

And then he says, "Come on, Walter Cronkite."

The interesting thing is how much difference there is between a victory and a loss. Ronald Reagan found that out with his narrow loss to Ford in New Hampshire. Udall insists that he would have won New Hampshire if Harris hadn't been in the race. Perhaps. Perhaps it would have been different if there had been fewer candi-dates. It is hard to see how Udall could have capitalized sufficiently on such a victory. There is a cruel arbitrariness to the numbers—

either you win or you lose. This year, there are no moral victories. Just victories. So while the "but for"s may be consoling, they are also irrelevant.

At nine-twenty-six, a staff member says that NBC has projected Udall. Bambi says that NBC says the Udall campaign now "has momentum."

The people in the room are overjoyed.

"Jimmy Carter is in trouble," a jubilant staff man tells me. "We'll be able to raise money now. I see the vault door opening. Jimmy Carter is in trouble. The wind has been taken out of his sails."

David Obey says, "We got every ward in Wausau. That's incredible."

More precincts come in for Udall.

At ten o'clock, Walter Cronkite announces that, with forty-five percent of the vote in, it's Udall thirty-nine, Carter thirty-five. The returns from New York show that Udall is doing better at getting delegates there than was expected, and might come in second.

"I've seen elections turn around at the last round of voters," Udall says.

Shortly after ten, the question comes up whether Udall should go down to the ballroom and claim victory. The decision is that he will claim victory at ten-fifteen. A staff aide explains that this is because it is now eleven-fifteen in New York, and they want their time on the networks before everyone goes to bed. The thought that it might turn around has been dismissed. Two networks have projected Udall. The feeling is that Walter Cronkite is just being stubborn.

As Udall's party makes its way down the hall and down a back stairway to the floor below, I ask David Obey if he is letting himself believe it now.

"Yes," he replies jubilantly.

"Happy Days Are Here Again" may be a cliché, but it is a buoyant tune and makes a happy crowd even happier. Its title becomes literal. Like "Hail to the Chief" or "Here Comes the Bride," it is an announcement as well as a song. And tonight it is being played to a very happy crowd, and the drums and the horns and the cheers fill the vast ballroom. This is no routine victory. It is a vindication. And it wasn't expected. And so the crowd cheers—"GO, MO! GO, MO!"—and Morris Udall, on the platform, happy, his face ruddy, beams.

"Oh, how sweet it is," Udall tells the crowd, and they break into a prolonged cheer, and he smiles some more. I have never seen him look so happy. He has won, and the band is playing, and the crowd—as devoted a crowd as a person can get—is cheering for him. Politicians work and work for this moment—a moment when yesterday's fatigue and disappointment and tomorrow's realities and responsibilities are swept away in one brief spell of pure joy.

Udall tells the crowd, "I've been rich and I've been poor, and, believe me, rich is better." He continues, "I've been second and I've been first, and, believe me, first is better." And, to more cheers, he finishes his brief speech, thanks those who helped him win, and then proceeds to give victory interviews to ABC and NBC.

Shortly before eleven o'clock, Carter, on CBS, explains that he could not give Wisconsin the necessary time, because he was busy campaigning in Illinois and North Carolina (where Udall did not campaign). Walter Cronkite says, "It's far too close to call yet." Back in Udall's suite, Henry Reuss, smiling broadly, says that he will return to Washington tomorrow and line up members of the House from Pennsylvania for Udall. "I think I can deliver a package by tomorrow night," he says. And then the suite is largely cleared. Udall must get up at 5 A.M. to fly to Detroit, where he will meet with U.A.W. officials, and then to Pittsburgh, where the state A.F.L.–C.I.O. is holding a convention. Carter and Jackson will be in Pennsylvania tomorrow, too. Everyone agrees that Pennsylvania is the next big test.

John Gabusi and Terry Bracy, two top Udall staff members, and I are talking alone in the living room of the suite. Gabusi, who will take over management of the campaign shortly, explains to me why Udall has done so well in New York—Jackson is getting less than a majority of the delegates, Udall is a strong second, "Uncommitted" (much of it for Humphrey) is third, and Carter is a surprisingly poor fourth—and goes into the intricacies of the delegate-selection system in New York and Pennsylvania.

At eleven-forty-five, Udall comes into the room, holding a beer. He fiddles with the dials on the television set, listens to Gabusi, and, when his aide finishes, says softly, "We've got bad news."

We all know what he means as soon as he says that, but still one of the aides asks.

"CBS is going to project Carter," Udall says. "It's down to thirty-seven, thirty-six."

Gabusi swears quietly.

Terry Bracy says after a few moments, "It's still a victory, Mo."

Udall turns up the television set. A local news broadcaster announces enthusiastically, "Wisconsin tonight handed Morris Udall his first real Democratic victory."

Udall, sitting in a stiff-backed chair, holding his beer, watches and smiles slightly as he sees himself, on a tape replay, saying, "I've been rich and I've been poor, and, believe me, rich is better."

11

THE SHERATON HOTEL, Philadelphia. Tuesday afternoon. Jimmy Carter has just flown in from Atlanta. He looks positively relaxed. One would never guess from his appearance that he is believed to be in the worst trouble so far in his long campaign. He apologized last week for having said that federal housing programs should not break up the "ethnic purity" of neighborhoods, but the stir he caused has not abated, nor have the suspicions about him that the incident raised. He returned home to Georgia, exhausted, late on Saturday (he has not been able to keep to his intended schedule of taking Saturdays and Sundays off), and this morning he held a rally in Atlanta, where several blacks including the Reverend Dr. Martin Luther King, Sr., embraced him. For good measure, Carter has flown in some blacks from Atlanta to stand here at this press conference with him and, along with some Pennsylvania blacks, attest to his *bona fides.*

It had begun to seem that Jimmy Carter would not make a big mistake, and then, on the eve of last week's Wisconsin and New York primaries, he did. He told an interviewer for the New York *News,* "I see nothing wrong with ethnic purity being maintained" in a neighborhood, and, under questioning in subsequent press conferences, defended his remarks by saying that there should not be "intrusion of alien groups" into neighborhoods. Whether Carter understood the full import of the code terms he used, and intended to use them, cannot be known, so the incident raised questions about his understanding, his judgment, and his character. Moreover, when it happened, it seemed to some—perhaps because they wished it to—that this might be one of those statements catastrophic to Presidential aspirants, like George Romney's statement about "brainwashing." Part of the reaction stemmed from the fact that there is so much suspicion of Carter, so much uneasiness about him, that the statement reverberated. Because so many people had been waiting for Carter to make a mistake, because it just might be a historic event, it became magnified. Furthermore, the next two important primaries for Carter are in Pennsylvania and Indiana, states with large "ethnic" populations, and the question had been raised of whether Carter could do well in a Northern industrial state; Pennsylvania, in two weeks, is the test. From his record as governor, it is clear that he is not a racist. From his comments, it appears that he may have been dipping into the literature of Michael Novak and others who celebrate ethnicity and try to fan it into a political movement. (Carter has talked with Novak.) The honoring of ethnic identity and diversity is fine until it ventures into unreality—suggesting an America that can never be again—and into exploitation by the politicians. Politicians who play around with it do so at their peril. Either way, there is a problem with what Carter said: If he did not understand the implications of the terms he used, that is a problem; if he did, that's a problem, too. His political opponents—with the exception of Frank Church—naturally leaped on what he said, even though their policies do not differ much from Carter's. The Congressional Black Caucus, and even Carter's important black supporter Andrew Young, criticized him for his remarks. The United Auto Workers withheld a planned endorsement of him for the Michigan primary. Liberals who had been wavering also held back their support. A number of his own backers were given pause. Finally, after repeating his remarks a few times and suggesting testily that the press was persisting in making too much of the matter, Carter, in a press conference in Philadelphia, apologized for using the word "purity." He also threw in support of the Humphrey-Hawkins jobs bill, saying that now that the bill had been modified he could back it. But, even as he apologized, he said, "I don't think the government ought to go in just arbitrarily requiring people of a different background to live in a community." I can't think of anyone who does. There are federal regulations that are intended to prevent government housing projects from contributing to racial-segregation patterns. The subject is among the sorest ones in our national life, and a bad one for political campaigns.

The gaffe (if that is what it was), plus Carter's eyelash defeat of Udall in Wisconsin last Tuesday and his poor fourth-place showing in New York on the same day and in the Virginia district caucuses the previous weekend, gave heart to the anti-Carter forces in the Democratic Party. The forces behind a Humphrey candidacy felt a new surge of life, and, through strategic leaks, let it be known last weekend that they would establish a Washington office to solicit support for Humphrey from uncommitted delegates. Some of Humphrey's allies began to tell him that he should enter the New Jersey primary—which is one of the last three Democratic primaries, and the only one after Pennsylvania that can still be entered —in order to forestall the charge that his nomination was engineered in a "smoke-filled room." They told him that he could beat Carter in New Jersey. One senator who supports Humphrey said to me recently, "All the candidates have negatives. Carter's negatives are that he is an outsider, his positions are vague, nobody knows who he is. The whole heart of democracy is knowing about a person before you put him in a position of authority. The mayors want to know, poor people, educators—all will want to know about him. His advantage of not having to cast votes on tough issues before Congress which might offend some is offset by the fact that people are bothered by not knowing where he stands." This senator also said that Humphrey's hopes rested on a "fluid" situation at the Convention, and that now it seemed that the situation would be fluid. He explained, "The way he has this planned assumes he's the number-one choice of the Democrats."

Yesterday, I dropped by to see Humphrey. He came off the Senate floor, where a resolution trying to establish a congressionally set budget was under debate. The new budget process, which many think constitutes a revolution, is an attempt to achieve some coherence among the various appropriations bills that Congress adopts. The idea—to use the term everyone seems to use—is to "establish priorities." The process is in its infancy and, up to now, has taken only a few wobbly steps. The hard tests are still to come. Humphrey was acclaimed last week during an appearance at the Pennsylvania state convention of the A.F.L.–C.I.O.—his perfervid backers in 1972. Humphrey has a way of showing up in primary states as their elections near. Yesterday, he seemed tense. Earlier in the year, he was enjoying the clamor for him to run, the indications that he was indeed the most beloved of Democrats. But now he is just about out of time and is facing difficult choices. If he is going to run in New Jersey, he must file by April 29th, two days after the Pennsylvania primary. If he runs in New Jersey and does not win, he risks losing his prestige and his dignity; if he does not run in New Jersey, he risks losing his last chance for the nomination. Yesterday, he told me he was under "tremendous pressure" to run. He seems to relish talking about how much in demand he is. "People say, 'We need you, we expect you to run,' " he said. "The pressure has really built up. But it hasn't caused me distress. It's almost too late to contemplate any primaries. I don't see myself going into New Jersey. It takes money, and we don't have it." That may be a more important point than people think. He continued, "I suppose we could raise money in a hurry. If Pennsylvania should be a draw, there would be no need for me to file in New Jersey. If Henry Jackson is strong, the liberals will be down here practically demanding that I enter. If Carter is strong, I have no question but that the traditional labor people will be here. If I were running for the Presidency—if I were really out after it—I can see that it would be necessary and wise for me to enter New Jersey. But I'm not doing that. If I entered the primaries, it would not be to get known. For me, the primaries would be a test of strength. The best test of strength is with the delegates at the Convention. If it happens, it happens."

Humphrey said that he had been discouraging the formation of uncommitted slates in his name. He said he had told the Erie County (Buffalo) Democratic leader, Joseph Crangle—who subsequently arranged to have delegates in New York who were actually for Humphrey run as an uncommitted slate—that Jackson and Udall would be angry if Humphrey's name was entered in the New York primary, and he had asked Crangle not to enter it. He said he had told people in Pennsylvania the same thing.

I asked Humphrey whether, as some people believed, he had an understanding with at least Jackson that he would stay out of the primaries, give the others their run at the nomination, and then see what happened.

He replied that he had told all the candidates who "visited" him—and all but Carter "visited" him—that he would stay out. "I told them all that I had no intention," he said. "You know, you don't give absolutes. But that's not why I'm staying out."

I asked Humphrey about the view that he should not be given the nomination if he had not run in any state at all.

"That's an argument outside the Convention," he said. "Outside its politics. The Convention will want someone who'll win. The plain rank and file don't care if I enter the primaries. They say, 'You're going to run, aren't you, Mr. Humphrey?' The details don't bother them. Whether I've run in the primaries or not is a detail."

The Pennsylvania Presidential primary is in many ways an extension of Pennsylvania's junglelike politics. As in other states, but to a greater degree, the Presidential candidates become instruments through which local factions vie for power, settle scores. In Pennsylvania, the "back-yard principle" becomes high art. Jackson has the backing of the Philadelphia machine headed by Mayor Frank Rizzo—Philadelphia is believed to have one of the last working machines in America—but the Presidential race is really of secondary concern there. The Philadelphia Democratic organization is more interested in the election of precinct committeemen, who elect the ward leaders, who elect the city chairman, who names the slates of city judges and the register of wills and various court officers, and who handles patronage from Harrisburg. State Senator Henry J. (Buddy) Cianfrani, who is also a Philadelphia ward leader, said to Albert Hunt, of the *Wall Street Journal,* "Anybody that doesn't tell you the first priority is the election of committeemen is crazy." The backing of Rizzo, the heavy-handed former police chief, who is extremely unpopular outside Philadelphia, is not a pure blessing. A local black leader who is a bitter opponent of Rizzo is backing Udall. But Jackson also has the backing of several state labor leaders. Their hearts are really with Humphrey, and they have to convince people that they should vote for Jackson in order to help Humphrey. Yet labor's storied ability to "deliver" is in question.

Carter, as is his wont, is trying to capitalize on what others see as adversity. This afternoon, at the press conference, he holds up a copy of a Philadelphia newspaper which has a front-page story headed STOP-CARTER ALLIANCE IS FORMED. Carter, perhaps only trying to look perturbed, says, "I'm not going to yield anything to the political bosses." He says, without seeming very sorry about it, "Jackson is being used," and he says, "I am letting the voters know that I belong to them, and not to the political bosses." He adds, "I never have predicated my campaign on endorsements." Thus he makes a virtue of necessity—just as he does when he talks about having run practically everywhere. Because he had no base of support in the Party, he had to run practically everywhere in order to accumulate enough delegates to win the nomination. A political loner, unlikely to get endorsements, he had to predicate his campaign on not getting endorsements. As it happens, he does have the endorsement of Pittsburgh's mayor, Peter Flaherty, and he is obviously delighted to have the support of Andrew Young. But still he says these things. He smiles as he is asked a question about "ethnic purity"—it seems to be that reflexive, almost nervous smile, which does not seem quite real. He replies that his "only mistake" was to use "the word 'purity.' " He says that he stands behind the thought.

On Friday, President Gerald Ford opened his campaign for the May 1st Texas primary in front of the Alamo, where he said, "All of our courage, all of our skill in battle will profit us very, very little if we fail to maintain the unsurpassed military strength which this dangerous world demands of us." Reagan, campaigning in Texas, continued his criticism of Henry Kissinger and of the Administration's defense policy. Reagan's attacks on our defense policy may be without foundation, but in an election year that doesn't necessarily matter. So Gerald Ford, whose devotion to heavy defense spending has never been in question, must now prove that he is not soft on defense. Part of his response has been to threaten (at a ceremony at the Pentagon) to veto a defense-spending bill if he found that it "shortchanges the future safety of the American people." Congress, however, has thus far also shown itself loath to become subject to the charge that it is shortchanging our future safety. The House and Senate Budget Committees have rejected all but token cuts in the defense budget that the President submitted to Congress.

The Pennsylvania primary—indeed, the nominating process—is being distorted by the failure of Congress to enact a new campaign-spending law. A simple revision—changing the way the members of the Federal Election Commission are appointed—was called for by the Supreme Court in January, but the lawmakers could not resist trying to incorporate other changes, which would, first, make the law more amenable to the Democratic majority and, second, curb the power of the Federal Election Commission. Meanwhile, federal funds to match private contributions, on which there are limits, have ceased to be distributed. This affects the candidates unequally. President Ford is better financed than Reagan at the moment and also has his incumbency to draw upon. Carter, being the front-running Democrat, is better able to raise money than the others. And so money, which was supposed to be irrelevant this time, is affecting the process after all.

Fred Harris withdrew from the Presidential race last week. His "people's" campaign had been fuelled more by the commitment of his followers, who were excited by his main issue—how wealth and power in America are distributed—than by funds, but the funds became too scarce even for that. Harris was one of the few candidates in this election with a sense of humor, and the other day, speaking of how he did in the early primaries, he told a press conference, "You couldn't call it victory, because we didn't run that well. But we ran well enough to keep going, so it really wasn't defeat. We didn't know what to call it, and we just decided to call it quits."

APRIL 19

Clearly, one of the great questions before our country, and one that is constantly talked about by our politicians, is the economy. No one seems to know quite what to do about it, as we are in a situation that we have never been in before, and one that defies classic economic theory—simultaneous high unemployment and inflation. In essence, the Democratic candidates say that we must produce more jobs, and suggest that the government must play a larger role in providing them—all the Democratic candidates endorse the Humphrey-Hawkins bill—and President Ford insists that to do much more about unemployment would set off unacceptable inflation. I decided to try to find out what the real problem is, and to see how close the politicians' talk comes to the real problem. As often happens, I found that the distance between reality and what gets talked about in the political atmosphere is considerable. Unemployment is going down, but it is still at a rate—seven and a half percent now—that used to be considered unacceptable. I wanted to understand whether the only alternative actually is unacceptable inflation, and, if so, whether there is a way out of the dilemma. I talked today with Charles Schultze, an economist now with the Brookings Institution, who headed the Bureau of the Budget during the Johnson Administration. Schultze has one of the clearest minds around, and he keeps rethinking old questions. Unlike many other members of his trade, he does not seem intent on promoting a particular point of view, and does seem receptive to new ideas. Schultze is a good-humored man; he looks something like a middleweight boxer, and he has a gravel voice that makes him sound like a dead-end kid.

I began by asking him to explain just what the main economic problem is.

"The central problem is that no Western country, including the United States, has learned to have a satisfactorily high level of economy without setting off what to the public—and probably in reality—is an unacceptably high rate of inflation," he replied. "A corollary to this is that by far the most important thing for us in the longer pull—for integrating the ten to twenty percent of our population that is worst off into a productive social life, for dealing with the problem of the central cities—is a tight labor market, where employers are scrambling for workers. I'll trade a government jobs program for that. If we could get three and a half million businessmen, in their own interest, scrambling for labor, you'd find the unemployable employable, the uneducable educated. We saw it during the Second World War. I don't think we can afford to give up that goal."

"How can we get there?" I asked.

"A lot of different ways," Schultze replied. "I'll put it in its most general form. Society is going to have to learn to intervene with a light hand to influence wage levels and, to a lesser extent, price increases. It can't be left to the market. Otherwise, we stay trapped in the wage-price spiral. I stress 'with a light hand'—not with a huge bureaucracy making every decision. We know how to get to full employment. That's not the problem. We know how to do it with the old, standard, tried-and-true techniques: tax cuts, easy money, putting more money into certain government programs. But when we do that we set off the inflation. That's not the only problem, either. And it's not just *our* problem. Almost all other Western countries are facing the same problem. So many other things follow from it. If you ask what is the greatest single thing we can do for the developing countries, it's to run a high-level, fairly rapidly growing economy in the West. That would give them an expanding market for their exports, and without exports they're dead. That's the cutting edge of growth for them."

I asked Schultze to explain exactly why taking the sorts of actions he enumerated causes inflation.

"There are a lot of things that cause inflation," he said. "But the toughest, most pervasive problems are twofold. First, imagine an economy at what I call the threshold of inflation, where unemployment is lower than it is now but higher than we want it to be—say, at five and a half percent. And let's look at the labor market when you're at that threshold. It's more or less experienced adult male workers in blue-collar and white-collar jobs, with very low employment rates and a lot of vacancies for them. So wage rates go up as employers compete for that group. This sets off a new round of wage inflation and then price inflation. At the same time, there is a large pool of unemployment—ten to fifteen percent for teen-agers, eight to nine percent for young adults. Those unemployed teen-agers and young adults are not mainly long-term unemployed. Many of them bounce from one cruddy job to another. So the question is, why don't employers, instead of bidding up wage rates, hire those unemployed? Yes, they pass along the costs of employing the workers who get higher pay, but that's not really the answer. If one guy could get a competitive jump on the others, he'd go that route. One way to reduce unemployment among teenagers and young adults and also reduce inflation is to make the unemployed employable—through training, through placement services. I'm all for doing that—keep pushing, keep trying—but the experience of the past is that this is not going to be the major answer. The problem is non-substitutability. In a complicated, modern industrial economy, it costs employers more and more to hire and fire. Experience counts. When you look around for people to hire, you pay a lot of attention to prior work experience. With the existence of the minimum-wage laws, you're not willing to take as much of a chance. That's where the anti-liberal argument does have a certain amount of weight. The manpower-training programs have had some successes, but they're something like the successes in education: You can always point to the school in East Oshkosh and its Grade 3-D, where it was observed that the application of Technique X in teaching reading led to a twenty-point increase in a year, and everyone says, 'By God, let's have a grant program to apply it nationwide.' Whereas it was probably a particular teacher, who could have done it with a McGuffey's Reader. The same thing happens with manpower training. Don't get me wrong—you don't put all your chips on it, but you don't give up, either. So the first problem is that when you get the economy over that threshold, inflation takes off. The second problem is that once it takes off, it tends to perpetuate itself for a hell of a long time, even if the economy goes into a recession. And that's the part we're living with right now. Big unions and big firms contribute to it. To exaggerate the problem: Once the inflation takes off, no one wants to give an inch; labor pushes for bigger wages, and companies pass them on, and on it goes. Therefore, you have to move to an incomes policy, which I have to describe as a second-best world. And you have to do it with a light hand: be willing to tolerate deviations, be fairly relaxed, not try to tie down every detail. It may also mean using the tax system to bribe people to accept it. You might, for example, set up guidelines and tell labor that if it behaves prices will behave, but that if for some reason prices still go up, you'll give labor a tax cut. You would guarantee—preënact—it, so that you could tell labor it can't lose. There are devices for buying coöperation."

I asked Schultze about the political problems that these ideas encounter.

"There are two things," he replied. "Labor, on one side, and conservatives, on the other, both of whom think this is the first step toward full-blown price control and a full-blown regulated economy. I'd have to, in all honesty, say that the chances this would be successful are far from certain, although better than fifty-fifty. But it's a little bit like not throwing someone a life preserver because it's not certain that it'll save him. There are a whole host of other things you could do, but this is the central one. The others would be to establish international agreements governing grain and some other commodities, to reduce fluctuations in their prices. There is the good old standby of reducing or removing government regulations, such as in transportation, that keep prices up. And we ought to modify—but we'll never get it, because of the opposition of the union—the Davis-Bacon Act provisions that call for the prevailing wage rates to be paid on any government-aided construction project. We ought to avoid like the plague restricting imports—if we do avoid it, that may do more than the anti-trust laws to promote competition. And, finally, I think there is some usefulness to the idea of public-service employment—but just to fill in the cracks, and on a much more limited basis than the Humphrey-Hawkins bill visualizes. Humphrey-Hawkins does not take realistic account of its inflationary effects. Its idea of having the government serve as the employer of last resort is unrealistic: If the pay were high enough to make the jobs attractive, it would draw a lot of workers out of private industry and so be inflationary. On the other hand, if the pay were low enough to avoid this danger, it wouldn't be a very attractive program for most people, except in periods of high unemployment. So I would have a broad-scale public-service employment program just for periods of recession, and I think we should try a government wage subsidy for employers who hire and train disadvantaged kids for permanent jobs. Humphrey-Hawkins is too rigid in setting a goal of three percent adult unemployment no matter what the cost or the circumstances. And it simply doesn't address the question of an incomes policy. Humphrey-Hawkins places the right emphasis on the importance of high employment, but it isn't fully thought through."

Tuesday. Today is the day of the Pennsylvania primary. It is being watched closely not just for the direct results but for the implications for Hubert Humphrey, who has until Thursday to decide whether to enter the New Jersey primary—his last chance to run in any primary this year. A lot of people assume that the A.F.L.–C.I.O. is holding out for Humphrey. Today, I phoned one of its top officials. Here is what he said: "If Jackson falls flat in Pennsylvania, he's in trouble. I'm not particularly interested in stopping anybody. If Carter makes it on the strength of his ability to capture the imagination of the public and the press, then I'm prepared to discover virtues in him his mother hasn't." Carter is getting by far the most coverage in the press of any of the Democratic candidates. The A.F.L.–C.I.O. official continued, giving further instruction in some nuances of political science, "Carter's not our preference. There have been people on staffs of our affiliates who are plugging other candidates. But we're assuming that the probability is that whoever makes it to the Democratic nomination, we'll support. It's not particularly constructive to start attacking someone you might end up embracing." There is another consideration. "We want it to be a good Democratic year," this man said. The unions are always interested in electing to Congress as many sympathetic candidates as possible. He continued, "So why get in a bruising battle?" Still another consideration is that the Democratic nominee might end up in the White House, and it might not be so good to have opposed him. Said the union official, "Why impair relations? And why denigrate him when later we might be telling our people to support him?"

One interesting thing that is happening is that people are not talking very much about Senator Edward Kennedy. Of course, things have a way of changing, but this year might go down as the one that marked the end of the idea of the Kennedy legacy—at least, for Edward Kennedy's generation. For sixteen years, the Kennedys have had a grip on people's imagination, and for most of that time have been widely granted a claim on the Presidency. People waited for Robert Kennedy to run and, from the time he was shot, for the youngest brother. In 1968 and in 1972, the Party hung on the question of whether "Teddy" would run. Edward Kennedy did not mind the attention and speculation, and even encouraged it somewhat. When he took himself out of the current race in September of 1974, many weren't sure he meant it. But now he seems largely overlooked. His troubles piled up to the point where increasing numbers of people assumed his ineligibility. There was always the danger that if he ran he would be the target of an assassin. Then, there was Chappaquiddick, and widely publicized rumors that he had marital problems. At the same time, some of the gloss began to come off John Kennedy's reputation: there were increasing doubts about his Presidency, and there were the reports earlier this year about his extramarital affairs. All this damaged Edward Kennedy's national political prospects, even though he may still be the Democrat who stirs the most excitement.

By ten o'clock this evening, the news reports were saying that Jimmy Carter had won an "overwhelming" victory in Pennsylvania. President Ford, as predicted, is carrying the state, in which Reagan did not contest him. Polls taken today jointly by the New York *Times* and CBS said that Carter was leading among union voters despite their leaders' efforts for Jackson. On television later this evening, Carter attributed his victory to what he has been calling the secret of his campaign. "It was the candidate-voter intimate personal relationship that has been our style," he said. And then, in that manner in which he sometimes makes strange use of long words ("I have no inclination to answer that," he will say), he said tonight, "There's no other candidate . . . who has a presumption of success." True enough. Of Humphrey, he said, "If he runs, he'll just have to beat me." In Pennsylvania, Carter is getting more than twice the number of delegates Jackson is. "Ethnic purity" did not do Carter in, after all. Udall is coming in third. Frank Rizzo delivered Philadelphia for Henry Jackson, but that was not enough. Tonight, Jackson, obviously disappointed, announced that there would be "a dramatic change" in his campaign, which would eliminate "a lot of gimmickry and press-the-flesh campaigning." Earlier this week, we saw pictures of Jackson showing his young son the Liberty Bell. Gimmickry and press-the-flesh campaigning can be a problem, but they were not Jackson's problem. It became clear in the closing days of the campaign that although labor leaders endorsed Jackson, their organizations did not make very strenuous efforts on his behalf. There was back-yard politics within back-yard politics—sandbox politics. The Steelworkers, who were to provide the foundation of the Jackson labor support, were caught up in their own squabbles over who is to succeed I. W. Abel, their retiring president. Factions fighting over the succession did not want to risk themselves by becoming heavily involved and having too much at stake in the Pennsylvania primary. Moreover, some labor people here say that the unions' decision to back Jackson in Pennsylvania came too late. Said one union man, "In this game this year, if you're not ready and organizing two or three months ahead, you're out of it." Sometime before today, a point was reached— such was the buildup—where the Pennsylvania primary started being treated almost as if it were the election itself. As Buddy Cianfrani made his rounds of the Philadelphia wards today, he was followed by crews from NBC and CBS and by a number of newspaper reporters. It is as if everything were being magnified this year, beginning with the Iowa caucuses in January. This disproportionate attention to certain kinds of events—the winning or losing of a primary or a caucus—affects the political process itself.

Carter, understanding the stakes in Pennsylvania, changed his schedule so as to spend ten days there instead of three. His weekend rest at home in Plains, Georgia, was abandoned. He borrowed money in order to increase his advertising in Pennsylvania, spending a total of about a hundred and forty-six thousand dollars on it. In addition, his ads were revised to announce that they would show "Jimmy Carter on the issues," though what followed was essentially the same messages he had been using before. Because his aides were concerned about polls showing that people considered him "fuzzy" on the issues, he also issued a statement on his economic views and gave a speech on national health insurance. His health-insurance speech, like his recent embrace of the Humphrey-Hawkins bill, brought him into the orbit of the Democratic Party's interest-group politics. The speech was worked out in negotiations with the United Auto Workers and others who have formed a lobby to push national health insurance. Carter did not satisfy them completely, since he remained silent on the critical question of whether his plan would be carried out through public institutions (as the health lobby wants) or private ones (which Carter does not want to rule out). Such is Carter's capacity for attracting publicity that his speech on national health insurance rated coverage on the network news programs and on the front pages of newspapers, despite the fact that he had been saying since before New Hampshire that he was for a comprehensive, compulsory health-insurance program. Other candidates also talk about national health insurance, but I can recall no similar coverage of what they say. Carter, in his economic program, still placed more emphasis than the other Democratic candidates do on creating jobs through the private sector, but he was vague about how this would be done. He was noncommittal about his tax proposals, too. He is now saying that he will have to be in office for a year before he can come up with his proposals for reforming the tax code and reorganizing the federal government. In 1975, he said he would have a tax plan by the end of that year; early this year, he said he would have one for the election, or perhaps by the Convention. Obviously, these are complicated fields, and the kinds of sweeping proposals that Carter talks about would have to be drawn with care. And there are obvious reasons a candidate would not want to air such proposals, which, if there is anything to them, would upset many interest groups and some segments of the public. Nor would he want to spend a lot of time in a campaign explaining and defending. The memory of George McGovern's problems in 1972 has not died. This is not, it seems, a situation similar to the campaign of Richard Nixon, who said he had a plan but didn't. And it is probable that Carter, a determined and even stubborn man, will make his proposals in due course if he is elected. But he talks about grand schemes without indicating the difficulties they would incur—difficulties that his steady retreat from proposing these schemes nevertheless suggests.

As the result of the Pennsylvania primary, it appears that Carter's opposition has collapsed. There is no clear challenger to him left. The only one that now stands between him and the nomination is Hubert Humphrey.

12

Washington's cross-pollinators were busy today, buzzing around with news, rumors, speculation about what Hubert Humphrey is going to do. He has until tomorrow to decide whether to enter the New Jersey primary. For a number of those in Washington, of course, the question of what Humphrey will do goes beyond interest in the political drama, beyond keeping up with what is going on, which so many people in Washington spend so much time doing. (The subject can be what "Hubert" is going to do or what "Teddy" is thinking or how long "Henry" will stay in his job or whether the latest veto will be overridden or whether the latest Middle East settlement will hold. The curiosity is nondiscriminatory and one-dimensional and rather unengaged.) On Humphrey's decision rest the prospects for power and influence of a large flotilla of lawyers, lobbyists, and hangers-on from previous Administrations. For a generation of them, it's the last chance. Humphrey's collection of followers is so extensive because of the length of his own career and because there are so many who have worked long in the Democratic Party who have nowhere else to go. Today, one man said, "He has the '48 people, the '52 people, the '56 people, the '60 people, the '64 people, the '68 people, the '72 people. A lot of these people see power slipping through their fingers." And this is undoubtedly Humphrey's last chance, too. So Humphrey phoned a lot of people today, and a lot of people phoned Humphrey.

The collapse of the Jackson effort in Pennsylvania meant the collapse of the strategy of using surrogates to keep Carter from getting the nomination. Today, people told Humphrey he had to either enter New Jersey or effectively concede the nomination to Carter. Still, there are a number of reasons for him to hesitate. As he mentioned to me a couple of weeks ago, he doesn't have the money. Moreover, as one liberal labor man said to me today, "the labor and Party machines in New Jersey are about as good as those Jackson had in Pennsylvania." He said that in 1968 New Jersey's

Democratic governor and labor officials had told Humphrey they could "deliver" New Jersey for him. But they didn't. And for Humphrey to run in New Jersey would be to risk his most prized political asset—his standing. Now he is acknowledged to be the most popular figure in the Party. "If he should lose New Jersey," said the labor man, "no one would touch him." And one Party official told Humphrey today that, just as there were many people clamoring for him to get in the race, there were many, especially in the press, who would cry "Stassen" (after the oft-candidate Harold Stassen) if he did. Finally, there were a number of people about Washington today, particularly in the labor movement, who were beginning to consider that, while their hearts were with Humphrey, he might not do as well against Ford as Carter would—in fact, he might lose to him. In the face of such considerations, sentiment has its limits. It was realized that Humphrey, as the labor man put it, "has substantial negatives that Carter does not have." This man had in mind, among other things, the charges that would be brought up if Humphrey became a candidate. Jimmy Carter has made it clear that such unpleasant business would come up.

This morning, nevertheless, Humphrey instructed James Dugan, the New Jersey Democratic state chairman, to gather the necessary one thousand signatures for a petition to file for the race. The petition would have to be filed tomorrow. Humphrey was advised by a Democratic National Committee official that he had at least an even chance of winning the nomination. Alexander Barkan, the director of the A.F.L.–C.I.O's Committee on Political Education, urged him to get in, and so did a number of senators and governors. A number of Party liberals, worried about Carter, urged Humphrey to get in. Senator Thomas Eagleton, of Missouri, sent word that he did not know how long he could keep the Missouri uncommitted delegates uncommitted if Humphrey did not enter the race. A poll taken in New Jersey shows Humphrey leading Carter sixty-two to sixteen.

At five o'clock, Humphrey met with a number of advisers, the corridors outside his office a mob scene. At the end of the meeting, which went on for two and a half hours, Humphrey was still undecided. He will announce his decision tomorrow. One of his friends, who attended the meeting, said, "This is a traumatic moment for him. He's wanted to be President his whole life, and this is his last chance."

* * *

It was announced that Henry Jackson will not begin campaigning in the Indiana primary today, as he had planned, and it appears that his campaign is over. Much of his campaign staff is being let go. His idea for a new kind of campaign, via something he called an "open-mike system"—it appeared to mean getting on the radio as much as possible—went by the board before it ever started. Jackson's campaign, which began as one of the best-financed, has run out of money and is in debt. Money and organization helped him win in Massachusetts and New York, but his heavy campaign style finally sank him. His efforts to change that style by becoming more theatrical only made things worse. His efforts to piece together the old Roosevelt coalition met with inevitable failure. His efforts to appeal to different groups by offering big programs, big weapons, tough talk with the Russians, and an anti-busing position were not enough to overcome misgivings about him. In fact, they increased them.

APRIL 29

At a one-thirty press conference today, Humphrey shut the door on his Presidential ambitions. Or almost. Not quite able to let go, he said of the nomination, "I shall not seek it; I shall not compete for it; I shall not search for it; I shall not scramble for it. But I'm around." He named some of the reasons for his decision not to enter the New Jersey primary. He said that it would be difficult to organize a campaign in such a short time. He told the press, "One thing I don't need at my stage of life is to be ridiculous." Some of the press laughed, but for Humphrey it was not a funny point. Until late last night, it seemed he would enter. Bruce Solomonson, his son-in-law, made past-midnight calls saying he would. There were those close to him who until noon today thought he would. The misgivings of his family, particularly his wife, had been overcome. A friend of his told me later today, "He wanted it bad. He had to lock the door on the White House for himself today, and that was hard. He said, 'I don't want to go down in history as a Harold Stassen.' He thought he'd run a chance of being humiliated and lose the comfort of the years that remained. He knew that some of the old junk would be brought up, that he might get the nomination but risk his dignity." Humphrey, then, got Carter's message. He could look back on a career of enough disappointments to have sunk a less ebullient nature: his bruising battle with the Kennedys for the nomination in 1960; the narrow defeat in 1968 and all its lingering "what if"'s; his failure to win the nomination in 1972, when many of those now urging him to run were his bitter opponents. But now, at last, he had dignity. Two of the things he has wanted most are the Presidency and dignity. Hubert Humphrey's problem was that he could not run for the one without risking the other.

In Beaumont, Texas, Jimmy Carter said today, "Without seeming to be arrogant, my wife and I decided we would prefer that Senator Humphrey had run in New Jersey. Not because we underestimated his popularity and strength, but it would have given us an opportunity to focus our attention on a direct, personal confrontation with Senator Humphrey among the voters of that state. I believe that his withdrawal is actually better for me, as far as the ultimate nomination is concerned. But as for myself, individually, I was a little bit disappointed that he decided not to run. . . . I believe I would have won in New Jersey had he run."

Today, at a press conference in Houston, Texas, Gerald Ford called Jimmy Carter a challenger "who has not dealt with the hard decisions in the Oval Office."

MAY 1

The annual black-tie dinner of the White House Correspondents' Association at the Washington Hilton. The President, the Vice-President, and the Cabinet—except for Kissinger, who is in Africa—are here. This event began in Roosevelt's day as a way for the President and the reporters covering him to get together for an informal evening, but now about fourteen hundred people are here in the vast ballroom. Some god of irony seems to hover over these dinners. In 1973, it was held on the weekend in mid-April when the Watergate case was breaking, and we watched the Nixon Cabinet sit frozen-faced on the dais while Bob Woodward and Carl Bernstein were given awards. It was arranged for President Nixon to arrive late, so he would be absent during the presentation. Last year, the dinner was held the weekend after Saigon fell. Tonight, as the President speaks, the returns are coming in from Texas, and they signal a disaster for Mr. Ford. The President proceeds with the jokes his speechwriters have assembled for him. "I have a great many friends in Texas," he says, "but we won't know exactly how many for an hour." He says there were two things he learned in Texas: "Never underestimate your opponent" and "Always shuck the tamale." (While campaigning in Texas, he had bitten into a tamale without removing the husks.) And then, after saying "I totally agree with Governor Reagan about the Panama," the President of the United States puts on a panama hat and says, echoing Reagan's litany about the Panama Canal, "I bought it, I paid for it, I own it, and I'm going to keep it."

MAY 4

Walter Cronkite has made it official. As a result of Reagan's victory in the Indiana primary today, Cronkite said, "Ronald Reagan as of tonight looms as a serious threat." A couple of weeks ago, Reagan didn't seem to loom as anything, but then his overwhelming victory in Texas—he won all ninety-six delegates—and today's victory over Ford in Indiana have altered the picture. Reagan won both his victories with the help of "cross-over" votes by conservative Democrats for whom there was no longer any point in voting for George Wallace, but even so it is clear that the President is in trouble within his own party. Ford has been on the defensive, forced to answer questions everywhere about détente, defense, and the Panama Canal. After he had said that the United States "will never give up" its rights to the Canal, it was learned—through a leak by a member of Congress friendly to Reagan—that the Panama Canal Subcommittee of the House Merchant Marine and Fisheries Committee had been told by Ambassador Ellsworth Bunker, who is negotiating a new Canal treaty, that his directive from the President was to yield the Canal Zone "after a period of time" and the Canal itself "over a longer period of time." Now the Panama Canal negotiations, which were to be concluded this year, are not to be concluded until sometime next year.

The Panama Canal story and that of Henry Kissinger's present visit to Africa, in an incredibly belated recognition of the currents that are running through that continent and of the fact that we have been dug in against them, are almost classic examples of what happens to us in election years. Reason goes out the window, and we are left with slogans and charges that the other side has trouble replying to, because they are based on emotion. (The "missile gap" of 1960 which turned up missing after the election was another example.) Those who want to believe the charge believe the charge.

And so hedging is done and policies are trimmed in order to head off the opposition. The President has charged that Reagan is "demagogic" on the defense issue, and has said that Reagan's position on the Panama Canal invites "bloodshed," but these statements have not helped him. Neither, apparently, has his warm embrace of the new B-1 bomber, the costliest weapons system ever and also a very controversial one (its necessity and its utility are both in serious doubt), or his request to Congress, made just before he embarked on a campaign trip to Texas, for almost one-third of a billion dollars' additional funds to continue production of the land-based Minuteman missiles. (In January, the Defense Department explained that a decision to stop production of the Minuteman missiles had been reached, because officials thought that to continue to build them made no sense. White House spokesmen explained that the change of policy was a routine decision to proceed with an option that the Administration had been reserving for itself.) And neither has his defense by Senator Barry Goldwater, who said last Sunday, "I have to support Ford's position" on the Panama Canal.

Jimmy Carter won the Indiana primary easily, as he won the Texas primary on Saturday, and the general assumption now is that he will be the nominee. There have been a couple of blips on the screen—perhaps only that, perhaps more. It is hard to tell in the middle of a campaign. Yet we have to keep looking for signs of what the candidates are really like—especially one still as hidden as Jimmy Carter. The fact that people are looking for signs, and for incidents that might document whatever misgivings they have, explains why much has been made in the last day or two of the resignation of a speechwriter, Robert Shrum, who had been with Carter for only nine days. Shrum, a thirty-two-year-old man, who had written speeches for Edmund Muskie and George McGovern when they were running for President, knows a lot of people, and has friends who know a lot of people, including reporters, so his story spread fast. The story was fanned by some who do not wish Carter well, but it also attracted notice because of the particular nature of his complaint against Carter: that Carter took positions that varied in public and in private on issues such as defense and whether funds from the highway program should be diverted to the construction of mass-transit systems. There was no way to tell whether Shrum was giving an accurate picture, but his contentions lent credibility to suspicions that Carter's flexibility on issues verged on calculated manipulation. To make matters worse, Carter at first issued misleading statements about the Shrum episode. And then there was the matter of political endorsements. Carter has made a big point of saying that he does not seek them. Yesterday, in Indiana, he was endorsed by Birch Bayh, who said that Carter had phoned last week and asked for his help. The following day, Carter said that he had "never gone to anyone yet and asked them to endorse me." Questioned about this apparent contradiction yesterday, he explained, "My point was that I have never depended on endorsements to put me in office," and added that while he had asked for Senator Bayh's help, he had not asked for an endorsement. Carter is now saying that he will reduce his campaign schedule and spend more time talking with Party leaders and uncommitted Convention delegates.

MAY 6

The Washington *Post* reported today that in the last fifteen years the United States has exported enough plutonium to make more than two hundred atomic bombs. The recipient countries have been Japan, Germany, Italy, France, Australia, Norway, Sweden, Belgium, Switzerland, and Great Britain. The Energy Research and Development Administration says that most of the plutonium is being used in experimental fast-breeder reactors, which manufacture more plutonium. Of the six countries (the United States, the Soviet Union, Great Britain, France, China, and India) that have tested nuclear weapons, all but one (China) made their first devices out of plutonium.

MAY 10

Today, Mayor Daley, who knows something about giving signals, said that he was not ready to endorse Carter but that he thought that Carter and Senator Stevenson, in whose name Daley holds eighty-six uncommitted delegates, would make an "outstanding" ticket. Daley, of course, could have told Carter this on the telephone, and perhaps he did. But Daley knew that everyone would understand what it meant when he said it publicly. It told politicians around the country that Daley was getting ready to move. Daley, the last of the old bosses, the disgrace of the Party in 1968, still mattered—to prove it, he got himself a herd of delegates—and he was making sure that everyone understood that.

Frank Church won the Nebraska primary today, and tonight on television Jimmy Carter, in black tie for the annual Democratic congressional fund-raising dinner in Washington, smiled what seemed to be a forced smile and said, "I can't win them all." Perhaps even more significant is the fact that Carter just barely defeated Morris Udall in Connecticut today. Udall has acknowledged that he left Nebraska to Church and put pressure on Church to stay out of Connecticut. Senator Robert Byrd, the favorite son, won in today's third primary, in West Virginia—a primary that Carter did not contest. That Church, not considered one of the more colorful campaigners around, could beat Carter will fuel the hopes of those who still want him stopped. Senator Humphrey, for example, has of late been praising his new-found friend Jerry Brown, who is campaigning in Maryland, and the independent young Californian has the support of Maryland's antique Democratic machine. Maryland's governor, Marvin Mandel, dislikes Carter, as do several of Carter's other gubernatorial colleagues. Not only is Brown capturing attention but he is succeeding in ridiculing Carter, which no other candidate this year has done—few have even tried. Brown is suggesting that Carter is evasive on the issues ("Where is the real Jimmy Carter? There's the smile, but what's the person behind that?"), and he makes fun of Carter's suggestions for reorganizing the executive branch and proceeding on zero-based budgeting— requiring each agency to defend its budget from scratch, rather than its increments—as solutions to the problems of government. Carter, in turn, says of Brown, "My opponent says, 'It's the focus of government that means something . . . it's the direction you're going that counts.' Well, I don't know what that means, and neither do you."

In Nebraska, Ronald Reagan defeated President Ford—his fifth victory over the President in the last eleven days. (The President defeated Reagan in West Virginia, but the attention is on Nebraska.) This came on top of efforts to give the President a "new" campaign style. In this one, the President was to be more "Presidential," stressing peace and prosperity (after all, it worked for Eisenhower), and he was to throw in "trust," by which everyone was to understand how different he is from Richard Nixon, and he was to try to move the campaign away from Ronald Reagan's agenda. In a further effort to make that move, the President will now avoid question-and-answer sessions at his campaign appearances, during which he has been faced with questions about Reagan's issues. The President's advisers are taking potshots at each other through the press—a classic sign that a campaign is in trouble.

Carter came to Washington this time as the conqueror at the gates, and he and Washington are tentatively exploring the possibilities of arranging some sort of truce. It is perhaps symbolic that he attended the congressional dinner tonight, redolent as it is of the old congressional-lobbyist-money arrangements by which so much here has proceeded. The dinner is not one of Washington's most refreshing occasions. This is the week when Carter presses for endorsements—in Washington, in New York, around the country. The message going forth from the Carter camp is that this is the time to get aboard—that it will be important to have come aboard when needed. Politicians and others are now faced with delicate questions of timing. On Friday, Carter will see George Meany. Today, Carter met with a number of House Democratic freshmen, and received the endorsement of eighteen of them. I talked with one of the freshman Democrats. Because of complications in his own political situation, he did not endorse Carter, but he was impressed. What he said is revealing about Carter's approach and his gathering support. "What impresses me is he's as bright as I've heard," this man said. "He's very much a coalitionist. McGovern put together enough delegates to win the Convention, but in the process he made some forty-five percent of the Democrats mad. Carter does not cause the same problems. He has a broad base. It's going to be the most united Party since I don't know when. He told the freshmen that as he went around the country he was impressed by how well regarded they were in their districts. He said he especially wanted the support of the freshmen, because they were not marked by the problems of the senior members, who were caught in the old ways. He said he'll do better than any other Democrat in November." Spelling out what is on the minds of many members of Congress—and especially the freshmen, a large number of whom won in 1974 in normally Republican districts—this man continued, "The members of Congress who are facing strong challenges are concerned only with who will do them the most good at the head of the ticket. In 1972, some were worried about McGovern. This time, people who have marginal seats are very pleased about Carter, saying 'I wasn't for him, but . . .' His style is very appealing to people in politics. The complete politician is someone who can be his own man and still have everybody like him. That's the epitome of the politician. Carter appears to be his own man and still have all kinds of groups liking him. It's a model of what people running for office ought to do."

President Ford is delaying the signing of a treaty with the Soviet Union on underground nuclear explosions for peaceful purposes. The treaty limits the size of such nuclear explosions to one hundred and fifty kilotons for a single device and permits, for the first time, on-site inspection of certain explosions. The President's aides say that his delay in signing the agreement doesn't have anything to do with the forthcoming primary in Michigan, which has been designated all around as "crucial," but, of course, few believe this. The President has been affected by that strange process by which people seem to change physically with changes in their fortunes. The physical changes undoubtedly have to do with their own rising and falling confidence, with what they are going through. Now the President looks different—worried, shrunken, weaker.

Senator Eagleton gave way to the tide today and announced, along with other Missouri political leaders, that he would support Carter. Missouri has seventy-one delegates. In New York, Mayor Abraham Beame, a Jackson supporter, is reported to have decided to endorse Carter.

In New York today, Carter made a speech about nuclear proliferation. He is the only Presidential candidate who has done this so far.

MAY 19

Wednesday. Jimmy Carter has been wounded, and people are moving in. Jerry Brown beat him badly in Maryland yesterday—the vote was forty-nine percent to thirty-seven percent—and Carter just barely defeated Morris Udall in Michigan. Once more, a number of people, including candidates, journalists, investors in power, and others who play a role in the election, are taking a new view of what is going on in the Democratic race. Before yesterday, the common assumption was that Carter would be nominated easily and was the odds-on favorite to defeat Ford—or, of course, Reagan —in November. Today, the phone lines of Paul Simon, a Democratic representative from Illinois who wants a Humphrey candidacy, were busy, and on Capitol Hill it seemed to some that there was a new spring to Hubert Humphrey's step. Simon and Joe Crangle have decided to launch a draft-Humphrey committee tomorrow, rather than wait until June 9th, the day after the last primaries. More calls than usual came into the office of Edward Kennedy; there are those who will not believe until someone else has been nominated that Kennedy will not run. A Democratic member of the House told me today that his colleagues, meeting over coffee this morning, had taken notice of Carter's irritability in Michigan, where he refused to disavow an attack that Coleman Young, Detroit's black mayor, had made on Udall for having belonged to the Mormon Church, which discriminates against blacks. (Udall has been inactive in the Mormon Church for more than thirty years.) Moreover, Carter said that he himself had been attacked by Udall "on religious grounds" in New Hampshire—a charge that the Carter staff was unable to document. "He seems to be getting a little testy," the Democratic member of the House said of Carter. "Most of my colleagues weren't for Carter, but we will be with him if he proves himself in the market-place. We've seen polls that show that we would do better ourselves in November with him at the head of the ticket than with any other candidate. His credibility and integrity were his broadest appeals but also his thinnest appeals."

The Udall and Church camps are in touch with each other, trying to carve up the remaining states so that Carter will have only one opponent in each of the remaining primaries; they are having trouble getting coöperation from the Brown camp. A trend may be indicated by the fact that polls taken a couple of weeks before the primaries in Wisconsin, Connecticut, Maryland, and Michigan all showed Carter leading by a wide margin, whereas the actual results showed him just squeaking through or losing. It is possible that the early leads were based on the publicity, and that Carter is not wearing well. But this trend, if that is what it is, is showing up almost too late for the others to stop Carter. On television last night, Carter said that Governor Brown "is identified quite closely with me." Carter continued, "I'm not taking away from the Governor's winning the popular vote in Maryland [pause, smile] but we got the delegates."

Carter's virtual dead heat with Udall in Michigan seems even more telling than his loss to Brown in Maryland. In Michigan, Carter, who says that he scorns organization support and endorsements, won the endorsements and backing of Leonard Woodcock, of Henry Ford II, and of Mayor Coleman Young. The turnout in Michigan was quite low—it has been low almost everywhere all year, and that may tell us something else—but even up to the end the general expectation was that Carter would be an easy victor. So now "the word" is that Carter "must" win the Oregon primary, where he will face Jerry Brown and Frank Church. I'm going to go to Oregon.

Before yesterday, the President looked weak, on the ropes, beleaguered. Today, he is the victor, successful, in charge. He not only won in Michigan but won well. Last weekend, he went on an expensive and—given the current requirements of Presidential communication and protection—unwieldy whistle-stop tour of the state. But there are still questions about the strength of his candidacy, the nature of the race he has run, and the prospects for the Republican Party. Today, I talked with Senator Robert Dole, Republican of Kansas, who was once chairman of the Republican National Committee. Dole, who is moderate to conservative, is a fairly blunt man and he usually has a pretty good feel for what is happening.

"It changes so quickly," Dole began. "I'd have said something different yesterday from today."

I asked Dole what he thought was happening to the Republican Party.

"I said early on that the Reagan-Ford thing was not bad, because Reagan was attracting new people and the Party would at least have a shot at them," he replied. "Ford was the first Republican candidate in a long time to appeal to younger voters. So there were little things that showed maybe the Republican Party might finally be getting off the dime and up from the twenty-one-percent thing." According to various polls, only somewhere between eighteen and twenty-two percent of the country's eligible voters identify themselves as Republicans, while between forty and forty-six percent call themselves Democrats and the rest describe themselves as independents. "Ford is proud of his Republicanism, and doesn't try to hide it," Dole continued. "Nixon tried to hide it, building his New American Majority, or whatever he was building. Ford went around and spoke and raised money, and still we are where we were. I always thought the Republican Party would be built by a Republican President managing things, but we're in the unfortunate position of having a President vetoing bills and getting on the wrong side of 'people' issues. You don't broaden the base of the Party by saying no. I don't think you should say yes all the time, but pick out some areas and have a reasonable position. He's vetoed the education bill, the jobs bill—you name it. We get accused by business of being more anti-business than the Democrats when we're in power. You could rationalize it by saying there is a divided government between the executive and the Congress now, with different parties in charge, but the point is we haven't moved beyond the twenty-yard line. There are people out there who have a fairly reasonable philosophy as far as spending is concerned, but so often they don't see any results, and it always appears that we're *against* people's interests. Republicans have failed to come up with a program. Strong defense—that's fine, but you don't build a party with that platform, and that's been Ford's biggest thrust in the past year. Deregulation of oil and natural-gas prices has sort of spattered—his energy program was not very attractive for getting people involved in a party. We're still going to be the minority party after the election. A more imaginative program should be put together. If we're against jobs in the public sector, then we should put together a program of jobs in the private sector. I think Ford's been preoccupied with holding back, cutting back, reducing spending. I don't think we'll become a majority party doing that."

"Fiscal responsibility does not bring people to their feet?" I asked.

"No," Dole replied. "You can always make a speech and point out some ridiculous example of waste, if you know your audience. But if you talk about something they like, they're not going to react very well." This brought to mind Ford's first campaign trip to New Hampshire, when he briefed local officials on his budget, and most of the questions they asked had to do with wanting more, not less, from the federal government. Similarly, Reagan got into trouble with his proposal to reduce the federal budget by ninety billion dollars. He later tried to make it clear that he would just shift responsibility for these programs to the state level. Somehow, the

Ford campaign let the issue of Reagan's ninety-billion-dollar plan die, but Governor William Milliken, of Michigan, a Republican, who worked hard for Ford in the Michigan primary, revived it in that state, with apparent success.

I asked Dole what he felt the problems were with the campaign Ford had conducted.

"Reagan has been running both campaigns," Dole replied. "His and Ford's. He lays out the issues, and Ford responds."

Wednesday afternoon. The Senate is debating Senate Resolution 400, "to establish a Standing Committee of the Senate on Intelligence Activities," and Senator John Stennis, Democrat of Mississippi, has the floor. The bill, the result of the work of the Senate Select Committee to Study Governmental Operations with Respect to Intelligence Activities—the Church committee—barely made it to the floor in its present form, and now Senator Stennis and some of his allies are engaged in one last attempt to weaken it. The new committee would take the place of the Church committee, which was established temporarily to investigate allegations of abuses by the intelligence agencies and to make recommendations. While the establishment of a successor committee may not sound like a very significant departure, the new committee would alter the institutional arrangements by which the intelligence agencies had conducted their activities almost unchecked. Only a few senior members of Congress, Stennis among them—men who could be counted upon to agree with what the agencies were doing, and to keep secrets—had known what was going on, and apparently none of them had known all of it. Under this arrangement, the agencies had proceeded without any real interference, and their congressional confidants had enhanced their own power. That is why Stennis is fighting this afternoon. The new committee would have one of the most important forms of power that can be allocated on Capitol Hill—the power to authorize funds for all the intelligence agencies. Using this power carefully, the members of the committee would have at least a chance to find out what was going on. A secondary power would be the power to disclose its findings, if necessary, to the Senate as a whole in a closed session. And the new committee would be empowered to propose new legislation embodying guidelines, statutes, charters for the intelligence agencies. Depending on how this is carried out—the proviso that attaches to any federal enterprise—what is being debated on the Senate floor today could represent the beginning of fundamental changes. At bottom, the difficulties have been that the agencies had no clear instructions on what they were or were not to do, from either the executive branch or Congress; that Constitutional procedures for making important decisions in the area of intelligence operations did not exist; and that all the processes involved—the making of policy, the decisions about activities, the supposed supervision—were warped by secrecy. The peculiar role of secrecy is subtle, and its importance is often hard to grasp. This was reflected in remarks made to me by one man who was involved in the Senate investigation of the intelligence agencies. He said that the experience had brought home to him the impact of dealing with secret matters. He said, "The more you know, the more you become drawn in, the more aware of the cost of talking." And then he made an even more interesting point. He said, "You lose any sense of the worth of what you know, because it's secret, and you can't talk to people who might use it in ways it is not supposed to be used. So one of the paradoxes of the work of the intelligence agencies is that it's contrary to the rational process, because it limits the process of intelligent analysis. The more sensitive it is, the less analysis is involved. It becomes a thing in itself, not to be confronted by anything else."

As usual, the interest on the part of Congress in the subject was brought about by outside pressures. It is another example of the fact that Congress is essentially a reactive branch, but sometimes it does react. Although there was ample evidence that the C.I.A. and the F.B.I. had been exceeding what might have been expected to be their charters (there were no effective ground rules or charters), that they had been impinging on the liberties of American citizens, and that the C.I.A. had been involved in questionable and embarrassing activities abroad, sometimes luring us into the equivalent of war without war's ever being declared, Congress was not aroused to move until late 1974, in response to a series of stories by Seymour Hersh in the New York *Times.* The abuses laid bare by Watergate had been all but forgotten. Hersh wrote that files were maintained on at least ten thousand Americans, and that activities conducted against them included break-ins, wiretapping, physical surveillance, infiltration, and the opening of mail. It was in almost reflexive response to these revelations that the President appointed a commission, headed by Vice-President Rockefeller, and the Senate and, subsequently, the House appointed committees to investigate the charges. For the first time, a fairly broad spectrum of politicians, who were powerful but were not part of the inner group, realized what was going on—how the President and the heads of sensitive executive agencies had operated for the last thirty or forty years. The politicians were forced by new, widespread press interest and public outrage to examine things they had long left unexamined. They had to look at these things for their own survival, if not for the country's. In the course of their looking at them, old relationships were broken down. Senator Stennis must have seen that they would be, and he therefore opposed the Senate investigation from the outset. When he failed to head it off, he tried to head it. But he failed at that, too. Slowly, the senators who examined it came to see that tens of billions of dollars, tens of thousands of lives, and our national reputation were being handled in a way that was not in accord with Constitutional processes. So they had to invent a Constitutional process, and that is what they are doing now. Whether they want to or not, they are heading toward a situation wherein the decisions that are made will have to be made jointly and a broad group of senators will have to decide if, when they see something that disturbs them, they will act. Thus, they will share authority and responsibility—a role in which they are not entirely comfortable. It was easier to leave things to the likes of Senator Stennis and to see no evil.

But the investigations turned up enough to make inaction impossible. Even the Rockefeller Commission, a number of whose members, including its chairman, shared the general Cold War assumptions on which the agencies proceeded, confirmed much of what Hersh had written, and it found that some of the activities were illegal and some governed by laws that were unclear. The Rockefeller Commission and the Church committee brought to light operations with names that sounded as if they had been taken from our adversaries—COINTELPRO and CHAOS—to disrupt domestic black, student, and antiwar groups. Both operations began as counterintelligence against domestic subversives, and spread. The Senate committee found that, in the midst of the Cold War, F.B.I. Director J. Edgar Hoover supplied the White House under Truman and Eisenhower with what amounted to precursors of the "enemies lists" compiled during the Nixon Administration. The Senate committee said in its report that "intelligence agencies have served the political and personal objectives of Presidents and other high officials." It said that "unsavory and vicious tactics have been employed—including anonymous attempts to break up marriages, disrupt meetings, ostracize persons from the r professions, and provoke target groups into rivalries that might result in deaths." It found that the C.I.A. was opening the mail of Americans, including—unfortunately for it—a letter from Senator Church to his mother-in-law. It found that the National Security Agency was intercepting the overseas cables of Americans. The senators learned that the F.B.I. was keeping files on them—some read them—and on other Americans who had never broken any law. They learned that the Fourth Amendment to the Constitution had been violated by secret acts of the executive branch. And they learned that many of these things had been going on for forty years. The Senate committee concluded that "the Constitution has been violated in secret and the power of the executive branch has gone unchecked, unchallenged."

So the bill now on the floor is the first step toward broadened supervision of the intelligence agencies and the drawing up of charters for them. Stennis is offering an amendment that would keep the jurisdiction over the Defense Department's intelligence agencies in the Armed Services Committee (which Stennis heads) rather than transfer it to the new committee. Stennis is making his last stand. His power is about to be cut, and—perhaps more important—the way he has carried out his role as an "overseer" of the C.I.A. and the military intelligence agencies is about to be repudiated. This is a man who has seldom been defied. The fight that is taking place on the Senate floor is nominally a fight over the Stennis amendment but is really a fight over power, over a style of operating, and over philosophy. Those who are siding with Stennis this afternoon—Barry Goldwater, John Tower—have a different view of the world from those on the other side. To them, the world is no less dangerous than it was a quarter of a century ago, and the military must be given its head, and its friends must protect it. To them, spreading the responsibility for what these agencies are doing is dangerous. Stennis, speaking in his deep, boll-weevil voice—he is almost a caricature of what we used to think senators should be like—says of the military intelligence activity, "We could hardly do a worse thing than to subject all of it to the ordinary legislative process of this congressional body. That is just a matter of common sense." Stennis doesn't speak—he orates.

So does Frank Church, who follows him. "The Armed Services Committee," Church says, "speaking through its distinguished chairman"—and he sweeps an arm toward Stennis's seat, which is empty (Stennis has left the floor)—"opposed sharing any legislative authority" over the military intelligence agencies. Then, stretching his arms out in front of him to form a circle, he explains, "For years, the problem has been that there has been no committee in Congress that could reach out and embrace the entire intelligence community. Now we have one, if this substitute resolution is adopted. But if the Stennis amendment is approved, we are right back to where we started from. The net, that seamless web, has been broken, and we are back to piecemeal jurisdiction distributed among several committees of Congress, no one of which can do the job." Church yields the floor to Senator Mondale, a member of the Church committee who devoted a great deal of effort to the investigation of the violations of citizens' rights, and Mondale holds up a copy of the report and talks about the "abuse of human rights and legal rights by these agencies." The implied question: Where was Stennis when this was going on?

And then Senator Tower makes a valid point: "If there has been any dereliction, then the entire U.S. Senate and the House of Representatives must bear the responsibility." The agencies, he argues, were following the standards of the time. Then Stennis concludes, arguing, "We're not trying to keep the information away from the senators or from the American people." What he is worried about is "disclosures to our adversaries, those that are pitted against us, that are planning against us," he says. He continues, "And we're trying to keep it from our adversaries," and adds that what is needed is better intelligence: "Better alternative methods will bring better and more valuable results." Stennis has gone off in an entirely different direction. And when the roll is called on his amendment, he loses—perhaps to a degree that John Stennis has never lost before. His amendment is defeated sixty-three to thirty-one. Then the Senate votes, seventy-two to twenty-two, to establish the new oversight committee.

Afterward, I ask Senator Charles Mathias, Jr., Republican of Maryland, who was a member of the Church committee and one of the catalysts behind its establishment (Mathias was among the first senators in recent years to speak out about the dangers to our liberties of actions taken in the name of national security), how effective he thinks the new committee will be. He replies, "If the executive sets out to defeat it and undercut it, I have no doubt that it has a high degree of capacity to do so. The second question is whether the committee will have guts. Anyone standing on the brink of a moment in history can have courage, but the courage that matters is the courage to stand alone and blow the whistle day by day. Third, the members of the Senate have to have common sense about where to bear down and where to be flexible—more sense than the select committee sometimes showed. But I think the new committee will make a difference. I think the people downtown—and that includes the C.I.A. headquarters, in Langley, Virginia—will stop and think before they take either pen or gun in hand. H. L. Mencken said, 'Conscience is the inner voice which warns us that someone may be looking.' That's what's going to be different—they may have all the opportunities and desires they had before. And I haven't lost faith that people will obey the law if they know what the law is. We'll see."

13

Portland, Oregon. Jimmy Carter is addressing a luncheon of the City Club, a civic organization, at the Benson Hotel. Carter had planned to be here today and to return tomorrow to Plains for three days of rest. But yesterday, as he had done before in this campaign, he cancelled the time off, and he will devote most of the weekend to campaigning in Oregon. Carter used to talk about taking more time off to think and plan for the fall campaign for the Presidency, but, in the tradition of *Homo candidatus,* he has yielded to the impulse to keep campaigning for the nomination—make more of an effort. When Jody Powell, Carter's press secretary, told the accompanying press last evening that Carter would campaign through the weekend, one of the major questions that arose was how the reporters would cope with the logistical problem of getting clean laundry. (The problem has not yet been solved.) George McGovern once told me that candidates reach a point where they don't want to stop —find the sudden cessation of the flow of adrenalin too painful— and don't want to think. In Oregon, Carter has a difficulty and an opportunity. The difficulty is that he has lost two important primaries in a row, and his "winnerness" is wearing off. The opportunity is that here he is faced with two opponents—Church and Brown—instead of one. Moreover, the Oregon primary has its own mystique and a disproportionate importance, which Carter recognizes. Only thirty-four delegates are at stake in the Democratic race, but this primary usually gets more attention than several primaries in which a greater number of delegates are involved. The Oregon primary has a disproportionate importance partly because it always has had; it has become a tradition, like New Hampshire. And it gets the attention it does partly because so many members of the national press are drawn to Oregon—to its natural beauty and its fresh salmon and its generally attractive people. Oregonians take their politics seriously, and, on the whole, Oregon elects politicians of a high calibre. Oregonians like to think of themselves as independent, and as playing an important part in Presidential elections. They like to think of Oregon as New Hampshire at the other end of the line. They like to point out that in the last fifty years no one has been elected President who lost the Oregon primary. It is a relatively untroubled state—no race issues (few blacks), no urban crises. Oregon is not tense. Oregonians worry about "nice" issues, like disposable bottles. (They passed a law banning them.) In other states, politicians have to demonstrate their concern about shoe imports or naval bases; when they come to Oregon, they must address themselves to questions about the environment. For members of the press and others, the Oregon primary is a social occasion, just as the New Hampshire primary is. All these factors affect our politics more than people might think.

Last night, in Los Angeles, Carter met with representatives of the Jewish community, many of whom remain skeptical about him, because, among other things, he goes about saying that he is a Christian—an assertion that offends certain sensibilities. Some are also troubled by the degree to which he stresses his Baptist faith—worried about anti-Semitism among Southern Baptists. Carter has Jewish associates, but he has not been able to place himself beyond suspicion. In addition, his cool political style and his failure to embrace positions that liberal Democrats consider important have played a part in creating a certain resistance to him among Jews, many of whom are liberal Democrats. After the meeting with the Jewish leaders, Carter attended a fund-raising dinner—about twelve hundred people, at a hundred and twenty-five dollars each—in the large ballroom of the Beverly Hilton Hotel, which was called the "kickoff dinner" for the California primary, to be held June 8th. Jerry Brown is favored to win the California primary, but Carter is making an effort there, and said last night of Brown that "every delegate he gets, he's going to have to fight me for." In response to the criticisms that Carter is "fuzzy" on the issues, Carter has in recent days begun to mention four issues—government reorganization, welfare, tax reform, and nuclear proliferation—and talk about them briefly in the course of what has become his standard speech. But he hasn't seemed comfortable with them, and so last night, after saying "I share with you and with others deep commitments about some of the major issues," he said, "There are two levels of the campaign. One level is the tangible issues: unemployment, inflation, environmental quality, agriculture, education, welfare, health, taxation, and many, many others. And the other level of the campaign is the intangibles." More comfortable with the

"intangible issues," such as "competence" and "compassion," he
stuck with those. Carter likes lists—particularly lists of adjectives—
and last night he spoke of the "horrible, bloated, confused, over-
lapping, wasteful, inefficient, ineffective, insensitive, unmanageable
bureaucratic mess." And then he said, as he has said all year, that
he did not want anyone to vote for him if that person did not want
the executive branch of the government "completely reorganized."
He makes it seem like a very daring thing to say. He still talks of
reducing the number of government agencies from nineteen hundred (no one, even in the Carter camp, can document that there
are this many) to two hundred—about which one wonders if he is
serious. Some consolidation of government agencies is obviously
desirable, but the result of what Carter proposes would be ungainly
superagencies—such as he is charged with having established in
Georgia—and the achievement would be questionable. "I consider
myself to be a tough, competent manager," he says. There is some
variation in Carter's speech as he has delivered it throughout the
year, but the astonishing thing is how little variation there is. Whole
segments are delivered—word for word, pause for pause, catch in
the voice for catch in the voice—just as they have been delivered
all year. The audience at any given time does not know this, and
therefore responds as an audience hearing it for the first time. The
audience is not in a position to know how this repetition diminishes
the appearance of sincerity. But in the case of Carter's speech it is
not just the repetition that raises questions. It is hard to say what it
is: the message itself, perhaps—all that idealism coming forth from
such a steely, and even somewhat ruthless, man—or perhaps the
obvious packaging of the message to strike certain chords. Not just
repetition but perfect, unerring repetition. It becomes hard not to
be dubious when one hears him say, just exactly as one has heard
him say so many times before, "What we want in this country is a
government, once again, that's as good [pause] and honest
[pause] and decent [pause] and truthful [and the pauses con-
tinue] and fair, and competent, as idealistic, and compassionate
[and then, dropping his voice and placing his hand, palm out, in
front of him exactly the way he does it every other time he says
this], and as filled with love [pause] as are the American people."
The cadence and the pauses, the raising and dropping of the voice
are crucial to the effect that Carter's speech creates. In his speech
last night in Los Angeles, he said that the other candidates decided
"not to run for the office itself" but to run in a few states and go "to

the Convention to get in some back room and horse-trade." Carter chose to run in almost all the states, because, his aides explained to me earlier this spring, they felt he had to, in order to get the requisite publicity and delegates. They felt that Carter, not particularly popular in the Party, would not have a chance of winning the nomination if he did not come to the Convention with just about enough delegates to win. Here, again, Carter makes a virtue of necessity, and he told his Los Angeles audience how many delegates he claims and how many he expects to get on the next Tuesdays, and he recited how many candidates he has retired along the way.

"When I ran in the state of Iowa," he said, repeating the distinction he has created between running for President and running against an opponent, "I didn't run against Senator Birch Bayh, I ran for President [pause] and I won." He continued, "When I went to New Hampshire, I didn't run against Congressman Udall, who was a favorite there, I ran for President [pause] and I won." He said the same of George Wallace in Florida, and even of Sargent Shriver, who was not exactly a formidable opponent, in Illinois. He then listed the things that have happened in the past which trouble Americans: "We didn't decide as a people to start a war in Vietnam and Cambodia and see hundreds of thousands of women and children killed and lose fifty thousand young American lives and spend one hundred and fifty billion dollars, but our nation did, our government did—my government [pause] and your government. We gave Richard Nixon an overwhelming vote, and later we didn't decide to wrap the White House in secrecy, to cause a prostitution of the office of Attorney General, to damage the professional reputation of the F.B.I., to bring disgrace on our whole nation in the eyes of the world with Watergate. It happened in our government, in my government [pause] and your government. And we didn't decide to plot assassinations and murder against leaders of nations with whom we were not at war—I wouldn't plot murder and neither would you—but our government did it. We didn't make the decision, but it happened, in my and your government. Those things need not be, and through the process of politics they can be changed. A lot of people say, well, we don't need to set a higher level, a standard of ethics and morality and excellence in politics— you've heard this a great many times, but that's just talk, yes it is, it's ours [pause] and yours [pause], my nation [pause] and yours, my country and yours, my life [long pause] and yours. The sordidness need not be, the insensitivity need not be, the callousness need not be, the dishonesty need not be, and the lies need not be." He said, "Not so long ago, I was standing at the Liberty Bell the day before the Pennsylvania primary. . . . I thought about George Washington and Thomas Jefferson and Benjamin Franklin and Patrick Henry and Thomas Paine and John Jay and John Adams and John Hancock." And he told an utterly still room, "We have within us the same strength, the same courage, the same will, the same intelligence, patriotism, love of our land, religious faith, concern about our children, compassion, and love. . . . It's a reservoir waiting to be tapped." And he told the people in the vast room—as he has been telling people all across the nation all year—that he considered them part of his family, that "the friendships that we've formed will be permanent," and that "I want that same intimacy to carry on into the White House." He said, "I want you to be proud of me, because I'm proud of you." (He told a group of elderly citizens in New Hampshire, whom he had presumably never laid eyes on before, that "all of you have lived lives of great service.") He went on to tell the people in the Beverly Hilton about the injustices he has seen in America, about how the affluent do better at the hands of government than the poor do. But Carter cloaks his liberalism in expressions of conservative values—home, family, land, religion, patriotism. The presumption is that any politician who invokes these values cannot be dangerous. They aren't really conservative values, they are simply values, but in recent years the liberals have permitted conservatives to appropriate them. And Carter ended by saying, "We still live in the greatest nation on earth."

Carter may be in some trouble, but he doesn't appear so before audiences. He is a rebounder. He gets a knock, but he keeps going—seeming, most of the time, imperturbable. He has stumbled over ethnic purity, and in Nebraska and Michigan and Maryland, but he keeps going, appearing imperturbable and confident. He smiles, but it is a gritted-teeth sort of smile, and—like the beautiful cat with sharp claws that his mother once called him—he scratches. His targets are those who oppose him—political leaders, the press, anyone who gets in the way of his determined march to the White House. There are by now a number of people across America who know the feel of those claws. Today's New York *News* ran a story saying that Edward Kennedy would accept a draft at the Democratic Convention, and would also be agreeable to running as Hubert Humphrey's Vice-Presidential nominee. Kennedy said that the story was "pure speculation," but there was reason to suspect that Kennedy was once more doing his quadrennial dance of the seven veils. Even a hint that Kennedy might run can cause some people in the Party to withhold their support from anyone else. Moreover, Kennedy has been cool to Carter, as Carter undoubtedly knows. The *News* said that one reason Kennedy had changed his mind was "his growing concern that the sweeping legislation that he and other Senate liberals have worked on for the last seven years . . . would not get full support from Carter." If Carter is elected, Kennedy would, because of his continuing political standing and his ability to draw attention, be one Democrat who could cause him trouble. And Kennedy seems to be reminding Carter—and the world—that perhaps Carter is doing so well because Kennedy did not choose to run. This morning, in a press conference in his chartered plane, flying here from Los Angeles, Carter said he thought that the "immediate impact" of the Kennedy story would be to increase Kennedy's vote in Oregon. Kennedy's name is on the Oregon ballot, even though he has not entered the race. Carter undoubtedly knows that Kennedy is not likely to get many votes, but Carter's saying that Kennedy should now get a fair number of votes sets a standard against which Kennedy might be judged.

Carter now has a more sizable entourage than he had earlier in the year: more staff, more press, more of the sort of people who travel along with a candidate and say that they are working on "issues" or drafting statements that the candidate may or may not use. Other campaigns frequently pass out press releases, statements, but not the Carter campaign. Carter pretty much sticks to his speech. Today, his campaign did prepare a statement—for him to read at a mock Convention of Oregon high-school students—in which Carter pledged, as candidates in elections past have pledged, to limit the power of the White House staff and to have a strong, independent Cabinet. ("There will be no all-powerful 'palace guard' or 'shadow' Cabinet in my White House. There will be no anonymous aides, unelected, unknown to the public, and unconfirmed by the Senate, wielding vast power from the White House basement. . . . Part of the problem has been the tendency of Presidents to select Cabinet members on the basis of political considerations. . . . I will pick my Cabinet on the basis of merit, not politics, and I will restore my Cabinet to its proper role as the President's first circle of advisers.") But at the mock Convention Carter, as if he were uncomfortable with the idea of reading a statement, merely made a brief reference to what it said. (The Convention was in its second ballot; Carter got the most votes on the first ballot, but not enough for the nomination.) Then he told the students that other candidates were "horse-trading for the highest elected office of the world—I've not done that." He mentioned the need to "first control and then reduce and then eliminate completely all nuclear weapons in all nations on this earth." He talked of the need for tough, aggressive determination to protect the outdoors, and he told the young Oregonians, "I'm a canoeist—I've spent a lot of time on a kayak."

At the Civic Club luncheon here at the Benson Hotel, he adds to his familiar list of qualifications—that he is a farmer, an engineer, a businessman—that he has "substantial timber holdings." Timber is a major industry in Oregon. He tells his listeners that he favors Oregon's proposition—on the ballot this November—to place limits on the construction of nuclear power plants over the stricter proposition that will be on the California ballot. Oregon is said to be an "issue-oriented" state, and he touches on some issues—on government reorganization, zero-based budgeting, long-range planning, health care, welfare reform, tax reform, environmental quality—and says that he has a position paper on every conceivable issue. If they want to know his position on any subject, he says, they should write to Atlanta, to Box 1976—"That's this year."

The big headline on today's Los Angeles *Times* is S. AFRICA MAY GET REACTORS. The story says that the State Department is leaning toward approval of an application, submitted by General Electric, for licenses to export two nuclear reactors to South Africa.

14

SUNDAY. The coffee shop of the Portland airport. Jerry Brown is sitting on a bench at the end of a long table, reading a newspaper. On the campaign bus on the way to the airport, he had asked me if he could borrow the paper, saying, "I want to see what the dialogue is." Several reporters and Brown aides are at the table, having coffee and awaiting a plane that is to take us around the state of Oregon for the next two days. Brown, like Carter, changed his schedule at the last minute to add time in Oregon. Brown's campaign here is only ten days old. Since his name is not on the Oregon ballot, he is attempting to get people to write his name in. Ordinarily, this is a difficult process, but Oregon is a highly literate state, and Brown has come in on a wave of excitement. In the coffee shop, an elderly woman spots Brown and comes over to talk with him, telling him that she supports him. Suddenly, she looks up and sees the candidate's entourage. Somewhat startled, she says, "Are all these people with you?" Brown sweeps an arm in our direction and says, "They're not really with me. They're kind of *around* me." The woman says, "Oh, I thought you were alone." Brown replies, quietly, "I am kind of alone."

Bend, Oregon. Brown stands on the steps of the Deschutes County Courthouse, a greenish sandstone building. A sizable crowd has been waiting for over an hour. Bend, a hundred and twenty miles southeast of Portland, is a lovely town of sixteen thousand people, with snowy mountains in the background. Spotting the crowd as we approached, Brown said, "That's a *crowd!*" As his comment on being alone suggests, as well as much of what he says and does, Brown approaches the campaign with a combination of reality and artifice. He does seem to be a lonely figure, but he seemed aware of the effect of what he said and how he said it. Yesterday afternoon, in the lobby of the Benson Hotel, he foisted upon a puzzled reporter a scholarly paper on "appropriate technology"—the search for technology that is appropriate in scale to its purpose and setting—and urged him to read it. What the reporter was interested in was how many delegates Brown thought he might get in Rhode Island. After journalists called upon Brown in recent years, their copy as often as not included references to the book of Aristotle on the coffee table and the meal in the health-food restaurant. This afternoon, Brown referred with some satisfaction to having taken one sophisticated journalist to a health-food restaurant. He is different—though not very different—and he capitalizes on his differentness. He savors getting off a good line. At the coffee shop, he referred to charges that he was not sufficiently specific on the issues. "Specificity is a rhetoric all its own," he said. And then he did an imitation of John Kennedy in 1960 giving figures—infant-mortality rates, figures about children who could not read—and saying "We've got to do better." Brown went on, "Then they appoint more examiners, and then the examiners redefine reality. There's a lot of that—redefining reality." Effective. And even the fact that the Brown campaign is chronically falling behind schedule seems a result of reality—the campaign is disorganized, and the candidate, even though he is not a very relaxed man, does not get upset at being late—and of some consciousness of effect. It is attractive for a candidate to tell reporters, as Brown told us this afternoon in the coffee shop, to order some food if they like—the plane will wait—and it is useful for a candidate to be able to show that crowds will wait for him, as in Brown's case they do. He doesn't just ask to borrow a newspaper—he remarks that he wants to see what the dialogue is. On the plane, a rickety twenty-eight-seat DC-3 in which we flew here from Portland, Brown came back to where some reporters were sitting and said, "Want some coffee? There isn't any." A few days ago, in a meeting with the editorial staff of a Eugene, Oregon, newspaper, he was asked how he thought he differed fundamentally from Jimmy Carter and he replied, "Fundamentally? How about superficially? Or existentially?"

In Bend, Brown tells the crowd, "A write-in is unusual—it's a little unorthodox. But so is my campaign." He poses as unorthodox, yet in Maryland he made common cause with the most orthodox of politicians. The Bend crowd applauds. It is white, not particularly young or mod. He deals with the fact that there is substantial resentment in Oregon against California, its rival for resources;

Oregonians tend to think that California is a hype, and they are particularly disturbed that so many Californians have been fleeing the increasing crowdedness of their state and moving to Oregon, thus threatening Oregon with sudden leaps in population. Brown tells the crowd, "One thing I'm doing for California, I'm making it so nice that people won't come here to Bend," and the crowd laughs and applauds. Brown jokes with his audiences, plays with them. And he takes steps to confront his critics. For all his famous popularity in California, there is also criticism—criticism of a sort that might catch up with him. The criticism is that he is indecisive, waffles on important issues, does not get very much done—that he does not display much taste for the hard work of governing. He even seems a bit bored with the job, some of his critics say, and so he is running for President. In the last few days, he has taken steps to meet some of the criticism and, in the process, to enhance his position with the Oregon voters, to whom environmental questions are important. He tells the people of Bend that he has signed a bill (he did it two days ago) to provide a ten-percent tax deduction to homeowners who install solar-heating. For which he is applauded. And then he tells them that he has signed a measure to lower the amount of water that toilets must use from seven gallons to three and a half gallons per flush. He always pauses before the "per flush," and the audience always laughs and applauds. He tells the people here that he will sign bills next week—he talks of signing bills in a way that suggests that he sponsored them, even if he did not—that provide stricter safety standards for the construction of nuclear power plants, "similar to the nuclear initiative that you're going to have in November." For which, again, he is applauded. He has avoided taking a position on Proposition 15, which is on the California ballot and would impose strict limits on the construction of nuclear energy plants.

The voice is youthful, and Brown comes across younger than his thirty-eight years. Perhaps it is the youthful voice, but there also seems to be an unsettledness about him. I know men younger than he who seem much more settled. It is said that there is an electricity about him, and there is. It seems to be the slight, taut body; the dark, ferretlike eyes, which dart about (except when he locks them into almost disconcertingly long eye contact) under thick, dark brows; the sense of leashed energy, of tension; and the youthful voice. Brown is not a still man, and he does not produce stillness in his audience. The features are sharp: a thin, angular face; a hooked nose. From time to time, he brushes back a lock of his straight, dark hair which falls over his forehead. And he offers his audiences a mixture of seriousness and humor, of idealism and cool, of conventional and unconventional politics, as he stands there in the sunshine, talking into the microphone. He does not, like most other politicians, speech at his audiences, nor does he, like Jimmy Carter, weave a spell. Carter could make the same speech to an empty room. But Jerry Brown, like a California entertainer, works his audiences. Though he fosters the image of an unconventional and anti-program politician, he tells his audience here that he favors the Humphrey-Hawkins jobs bill, which is about as conventional and programmatic as one can get. (His espousal of Humphrey-Hawkins came shortly before he entered the Presidential race.) Then he says, "I can go to Washington unencumbered with the baggage and the alliances of the last twenty years." He says, "We have fiscal limits, we have ecological limits, we even have human limits." He is dealing in realities and is also exploiting people's concerns. He talks often of how there has been "too much overpromising, too much overselling." His television and radio ads have him telling us that a President "comes in the morning, leaves at night," and saying, "He is just a human being, like everybody else. There's no magic, there's no genius to it." He is an effective debunker. And he talks about real issues. He talks of "the Faustian bargain" according to which we buy forty-five percent of our oil abroad and pay for it by selling twelve billion dollars' worth of arms. He talks of the necessity of slowing down the arms race, and says that "the human species is not going to make it unless we can figure out a different way." He talks of overpopulation. He asks, "How long is it going to take before we blow this whole planet up?" He is the only candidate who talks this way. He talks of the necessity of a foreign policy that will protect the environment, and of the need for coming to grips with the interdependence of nations. Appropriating Buckminster Fuller's evocative image, he says, "We're on a very small Spaceship Earth, and we've got to respect the limits, the resources. They're not endless, the air and the water, the soil and the oil; we have to use them wisely. Now, I don't know that the President can give any guarantees. He's just one person, but he can provide for leadership, he can set a tone, and a direction, and I think the emphasis has to be on the interdependence of countries, on our own strength, and I think that starts with honesty, with full employment, and with a recognition that the rules of the road are changing as we have more people and we have to be more cautious and not be consuming things in our energy. . . . There are a lot of things we can do; I'd like to try to bring that same openness and energy to Washington as I've tried to in California. To do that I need your help." And he concludes, "As Bend goes, maybe so goes Oregon and so goes the country." He is not entirely serious when he says this. He is saying it, and at the same time he is mocking political rhetoric. Just as he is a deadly serious, ambitious politician who gets pleasure and applause out of mocking politics.

In a question-and-answer session, Brown is asked what he would do about the military budget. He replies, "That's a part of the budget that I'd like to take a look at"—an unexceptionable response, as is his further observation that "you have to have a strong defense, but you have got to make choices." He says, "I'd want to take a very hard look at the B-1 bomber," which on Thursday the Senate voted to postpone a decision on. (The B-1 bomber would be assembled by Rockwell International, in Palmdale, Los Angeles County, California, which is the prime contractor for the new plane. Thousands of other contractors in California are already making money on the B-1 prototypes and stand to win even more business if the bomber goes into production.) He says that he cut the California highway department from sixteen thousand employees to thirteen thousand five hundred. He never says that he would cut the defense budget. When several people in the audience start to talk at once, he remarks, "Maybe we ought to just open this up for general discussion." He says, "I would come to Washington with a different perspective." He says, "I came into politics later," and says that he came in through the civil-rights movement, the antiwar movement, the McCarthy campaign. (He puffs up his role in these movements.) He offers, he says, "a difference of generations." He comes across as fresh, new, different, with-it. He is not the first politician of his generation—there are many in the Congress. He is the first politician of his generation to get national attention. He is the first politician of his generation to get national attention by being hip. He is hip—California hip—and he knows how to use it to political effect: health food, Zen, appropriate technology, quoting E. F. Schumacher's "Small Is Beautiful." He makes his with-itness into a kind of revolutionary politics, even though his politics are hardly revolutionary. He is a mixture of a conventional politician and a modern, with-it young man. He has made anti-rhetoric into (to paraphrase him) a rhetoric all its own. He is a master of style, a skillful manipulator of symbols. His refusal to move into the new governor's mansion built by Ronald Reagan for a million three hundred thousand dollars—choosing instead a two-bedroom apartment in Sacramento—put him on the map. He always gets laughter and applause when he refers to "the house that Ronnie built." When he describes the place—"seventeen rooms, nine bedrooms, six or seven bathrooms"—it sounds like a preposterous place for anyone, not to mention a bachelor, to live, and he also points out the practical consideration that Reagan failed to furnish it. And it does not seem to matter that, in addition to his apartment in Sacramento, Brown maintains a three-bedroom house in Laurel Canyon, in Los Angeles. He wears expensive-looking, conservative suits (usually gray pin-stripe), initialled shirts, and ties from Giorgio, a plush Beverly Hills shop, and he has enjoyed dinner parties at Malibu, but by the simple expedient of turning down Reagan's mansion he has got across the idea that he is "ascetic." He is often described that way. Asceticism is an old trick, which has been employed by some masterly moral and political leaders. Socrates. Gandhi. Henry David Thoreau wrote a whole book about how he had abandoned worldly pursuits and withdrawn to Walden Pond, but he made it into Concord—less than two miles away—every day or two. What would happen if Ralph Nader moved out of his rooming house and into a house in Georgetown?

Like Nader, Brown has a well-developed sense of theatre. Brown tells this audience, as he has told almost all his audiences lately, about the people he has appointed to office in California. His appointments, again, make use of symbols, but then it must be said that symbolism is an important part of governing. And, in this case, behind the symbolism could also lie substance. He tells of how he appointed to the Medical Quality Assurance Board a nurse, a pediatrician, a director of a free clinic, and an acupuncturist. He has appointed more women, he tells them—as Secretary of Agriculture and Services, Secretary of Resources, on the men's parole board, on the Fish and Game Commission, as Director of the California Department of Transportation, as Director of Veterans' Affairs. He has also appointed blacks and Mexican-Americans to important jobs. When he talks of appointing a woman to the parole board, he pauses, then says, "I figured she'd know when to let them out." The point is not clear, but the audience always laughs. Closing, he says, "I once drove through Bend on my way to Idaho." He says, "I remember Bend," and then, after a pause, he adds, ' I don't know why I remember Bend." He keeps going, and appears to finish three more times. He seems intoxicated by the group, by its response, by the clear, cool air. They like him and it's a nice afternoon and he's in good form. He likes the name Bend. In a variation on an old joke, he asks, "What has Jimmy Carter done for Bend?" The audience does not seem to notice that he is mocking.

Flying from Bend to Roseburg, Oregon, I have a conversation with Brown.

Since he talks of himself as representing the future and is often depicted as the candidate of change, I ask him how he would like to see the country change.

"I think there is a long way to go before there is sufficient unity or integration of this country," he replies. "There are still barriers to people. There is a divisiveness that is always part of a pluralistic society. But the divisions seem to be increasing. It's the task of public policy to promote harmony. One way to do that is through jobs—opening up careers that are rigid and stratified, and doing that within ecological limits. I think there's a level of unpredictability and confusion in public policy that undermines people's confidence—it undermines private investment. Keeping in mind that a lot of people can't work at the level of their talent, making that more possible in the context of economic growth takes leadership that enjoys a lot of confidence."

"That's a pretty conventional answer for someone who is supposed to be an unconventional politician," I remark to Brown.

"That's right," he replies. " 'Change' is just a word." he goes on. "We need continuity just as we need change. Just to stay where we are may take some pretty profound changes."

I ask him what he means.

"Well, just to keep New York where it is will take some changes," Brown explains. "We've tried redevelopment, welfare, Social Security."

I say that much of his rhetoric seems to be anti-federal-program, which raises questions about what he is for, and then point out that the Humphrey-Hawkins bill is highly programmatic.

"It's a commitment to a process that will have to be filled in,"

Brown says. "I think we're at a transitional point. The Chief Executive would have to raise questions and scrutinize things to find new programs. I'm not critical to be negative. I'm critical to learn. You can't just choose up sides and run the country. There are too many sides."

I tell Brown that I was recently in the office of a liberal Democratic senator who was reading an interview with Brown in which Brown talked about the necessity of thinking smaller, of cutting back on what government tries to do. The senator, I tell him, said, "Fine, but what does that do for an illiterate Indian child?"

"That's a non sequitur," Brown replies. "I'd like to see some of these senators. Have they ever been to an Indian village?"

I tell him that this one had.

"What does he mean?" Brown continues. "That the Senate is going to solve all the problems—a program for everything? That's a pretty dismal prospect." And then he shifts his line of argument. "California has more programs than anyplace else," he says. "Sometimes I raised the budget for them. Is there something unpermitted about questioning?"

The question about it, I say, is, what is the positive side?

"The positive side is that California is doing more than any other state in the country," he replies. "The education people think there is a theological imperative to educate. The health people think there is a theological imperative to provide health. Well, there are limits. The totalistic statist view is ultimately totalitarian in its thrust. What is the logical extension of all this? Total government involvement in everything. Do you think a senator in Washington can teach a kid in Bend, Oregon? Be serious."

I ask Brown if he is for federal education programs, and he says that he is, but that he feels—as just about everyone does—that the current programs give out the money in too many categories that carry too many special regulations. "Take manpower-training programs," he says. "The trainers get the jobs, the trainees get the certificates. I think that's an insight that's worth holding out to people. Everything that government does is good—educating people, defending the country, cleaning up the environment. The question is, how do you sort out among good things? You have to take each program and look at it. After all the federal aid, have we made schools any better? And is there a way in Washington to find out? A lot of the evaluating is itself an institution that wants to grow. It's a process that is never complete. We used to rely on the local school board. Now we have the Princeton testing service. My attitude is that you want to liberate people to find themselves and find space to live and explore life. How do you do that? I accept that government has to have a strong role. I'm working at it. I'm trying to come up with things. I've got a lot of ideas. There are a lot of things I want to look at."

He is a jumble of thoughts, themes, moods. They don't seem to be ideas thought through as much as vibrations he has absorbed: glimpses. He has an active, playful mind. "I don't have answers," he likes to say. "I have questions." A clever position, but what does it lead to?

One does not hold a conversation with Brown—one holds a symposium with him. Brown plays with you in conversation; he debates, turns questions back on you. He has a debater's turn of mind. He says that he won awards in debating and extemporaneous speaking at St. Ignatius College Preparatory School in San Francisco but that he preferred debating. He is a counterpuncher. Brown does not radiate warmth; it sometimes seems that he does not know how to. When his face is in repose, the corners of his mouth are down at the sides, giving him a petulant look. Much is made of the fact that he is publicly cold to his father—Edmund G. (Pat) Brown, the former Governor of California—who is a genial man, and comparisons are often drawn between the father's warmth and the son's coldness. But one must consider that it may not have been easy to be a politician's son.

Jerry Brown can be good-humored and very funny. He can be kindly in small ways. On the plane, as he inquires into one's comfort, there are what seem to be normal human exchanges. He can be cold and remote, but there seems to be a part of him that reaches out for normal human exchanges. In conversation, Brown veers between the straight and the smart-aleck, between the serious and the point-making. A lot of what he says is conventional, and even the questions he asks are not unusual. Many people in Washington ask the same questions. But he wraps his conventional approaches, ideas, thoughts in unconventional rhetoric, in aphorisms, in shots at bureaucrats and evaluators. He is Humphrey-Hawkins and health food.

Brown knows what he is doing. Talking about his race for the Presidency, he says, "What makes so many people in California like me? An ability to identify with young people and people who aren't a part of what's been going on, and at the same time be seen as conservative about government. It's just a possibility. We'll find out. And anyway there was nothing to lose. I think it's a process I had to go through."

In Roseburg, another lovely town, with a population of seventeen thousand, people wearing sweaters and jackets have been waiting on the lawn of the Douglas County Courthouse for Brown for two hours. He tells them some of the same stories he has told before, and he tells them to write his name in on the ballot on Tuesday. He tells them that there is a blank space on the ballot. He says, "That doesn't represent my mind—it's not blank. But it's open." He says, "Being President is not the same as just sitting there in the Senate reading the *Congressional Record.*" He talks of running the most populous state in the country. He tells them that "there are limits to the ecology, there are limits to the economy, and there are limits even to what a President can do." He, like other candidates, has a set talk, but he delivers it with more variety and spontaneity than most. He seems to be having fun. Why shouldn't he? As he said, he has nothing to lose. "Some people think I'm a little tight on the budget," he says. "But it's not because I'm conservative—it's because I'm cheap." A good line, and it gets laughs. "Everybody who comes to government tries to press their advantage probably a little further than they ought to go," he says, and the people in Roseburg cheer when he tells of reducing the amount of water that toilets must use—"per flush." Oregon is hunting country, so when he tells the audience that he is against the mandatory registration of guns or the confiscating of all guns (he does not say who does advocate that), the audience cheers. He says that he offers "an open spirit, a new generation of leadership." And then he talks of "Spaceship Earth," saying, "There's only so much air and water and soil. In another twenty-five years, the ocean's going to be dead if we don't protect the sea life, if we don't protect the air, the ozone layer. And I think that if we could project to the other countries of the world a planetary realism that dealt with all the issues—economic, environmental, as well as military—we could recapture the spirit that we had in this country when Jack Kennedy was President, when we were on the upbeat. I don't think we have to concede anything to other countries. This is a very young country. Look at the kind of business changes we have, or the changes in technology, culture, and music. This is a very new and vital country. It's a revolutionary country, and I think that that kind of energy is what we need to bring to Washington—honest, open, that's ready to try a few things. There's no one easy answer." As he talks, he is standing on a grassy bank, the leaves of a large elm tree grazing his head. The sun is going down. He looks very small. "We've got a limited number of cookies in the jar," he says. "The greatest priority is rebuilding this country domestically"—fixing up the cities, he explains, and cleaning up the environment, and providing jobs. It becomes harder and harder to tell what he would do, or whether he knows; at this point in his speech he sounds like a programmatic liberal. But he is probably candid in his answer to a question about what took him so long to get into the Presidential race. After pausing a few moments, he says, "Well, I looked at the thing and didn't think any of the candidates were catching on. I knew I was popular in California. I figured, 'Well, why not?'"

Back on the plane, Brown shows me a printed sheet titled "Selected Highlights of Governor Brown's First 16 Months in Office" and listing thirty things that Brown did—bills he proposed, bills he supported, bills he signed. "That's my thirty-point program," Brown says, and he indicates items covering child-care programs, low-cost vaccines for senior citizens, health services for American Indians, meals for needy students. "Show that to your senator," he says.

"But you don't talk about these things before audiences," I remark.

"That's not part of my process," he replies, and he fumbles for words for a few moments and then says, "No, I don't talk about those things. Someday, someone will figure that out."

From time to time, Brown has mentioned the necessity of long-range planning, which seems somewhat out of character. I ask him how he would do it.

"I have a lot of skepticism about the planning process that I've seen," he replies. "You have to think ahead and get a sense of where the country's going and make judgments. Economic planning is necessary, but I think it's very difficult, because you can't know the consequences of what you're doing. We've got to plan more, but we can't fine-tune it. That's a paradox. We have to plan more because we can't leave things to the vagaries of the economy and the environment. The government has to assert a greater role in matters like clean air, the regulation of automobiles, energy policy. In energy, the whole price structure has encouraged growth and overconsumption. The government has to bring pressure on the use of automobiles, to get more people on trains. It has to get more investment in solar heating, in coal. There should be different membership on the Federal Power Commission. I'm trying to get the idea over that we are in an era of limits. I don't think there are a lot of mysteries in all these issues. The ideas are out there."

I then ask him how his belief in Zen, which stresses the moment, fits in with the idea of governing and of planning for the long run.

"I don't know if it does," Brown replies. "It just fits into everything I've learned, the way I do things. I pick things up from a variety of sources. Zen stresses living in the moment. So do the Jesuits, so does monastic living—living in the present moment, don't worry about tomorrow, Divine Providence will take care of it. Be in the present moment. *Age quod agis*—that's a Jesuit motto. Do whatever you're doing. That could be Zen as well as Jesuit."

"How does it square with governing?" I ask.

"Many possibilities can be in your mind," Brown replies. "You try to think ahead, but you recognize the multiplicity of possibilities. You can't control events and you can't predict them. That's not really a contradiction, because you can do only what's before you. As governor, I just get into what I'm doing. It's like the Supreme Court. The Supreme Court doesn't decide issues unless they're before it. If you try to decide things before they're before you, you get into trouble. A lot of action has adverse consequences that people didn't expect." He goes on for a while, listing programs, such as urban renewal and the highway program, that have had such consequences. He talks about the importance of "creative nonaction."

I say that I understand what he is getting at, but couldn't it lead to a paralyzing philosophy?

"That's a point," Brown says. "A lot of what goes on in political dialogue is sloganeering—people jousting back and forth without knowing what they want. Like defense. 'We want a strong defense,' 'We want to cut the military budget.' They become symbolic jousts. A lot of the advocacy groups are talking about positions, not specifics. So you have to find a workable path. That's what governing is. A lot of the things at the top of the agenda are bad ideas. There are so many ideas that are already proposed that just to sort them out is full-time work. How much you do is not the essential part of leadership. The important thing is the clarity of mind in laying out alternatives. The ideas of what is to be done—these appear in the Congress and the interest groups. All that the President can do is emphasize his values and give a sense of direction to the whole process."

At Coos Bay, a large crowd has been waiting at the airport. Brown stands on a luggage dolly and tells them, "We got delayed a little in Bend." This time, when he mentions the blank space on the ballot he says, "That's a certain amount of Zen emptiness." In his appearances, he picks up things he has been talking about on the plane. He remarks to the crowd, "After a while, you make so many speeches you don't know where to tune in." Then, selecting a popular target, he tells them that "the pundits and the Pooh-Bahs of the Potomac almost had Carter nominated last week" but that "Maryland changed that." He tells them, "I haven't spent a lot of money, because I've found that the programs aren't as spelled out as they should be." But then he lists things he has backed—child care, scholarships, and so on. He says, "I think there is a real question as to whether the human species is going to survive."

It is a cool night in Coos Bay, and the crowd is paying close attention to this young man who tells it that the world may blow up. Just when one begins to wonder whether he is serious, he lands on an utterly serious point. "We have to realize that the Third World is out there," he says, "and that the distribution of resources is unequal." He also says, "If we have cities falling apart, we're not going to offer much of a vision to the rest of the world." And then, asked what he would do about foreign policy, he gives an answer he has given elsewhere. "What's Brezhnev going to do with me? I don't think he's ever dealt with anyone like that." It's late at night, and he keeps going, answering questions from the crowd. "I give you A for your questions," he jokes. "Are we going to stay here all night?" he asks good-humoredly. "Aren't you getting cold?" The crowd loves it.

MAY 24

Monday morning. The North Bend, Oregon, airport, just outside Coos Bay. Brown has already spoken with some fishermen near Coos Bay, which provided good scenes for tonight's television news. Now the network correspondents are asking Brown how he thinks he will do in the Oregon primary, what percentage of the vote he would consider a victory, whom he considers his most formidable opponent. Brown talks earnestly, with assurance, the way politicians talk into TV newsmen's microphones. "I wouldn't be surprised if I won," he says. "They're equally formidable adversaries. I'm not in the game of predicting. The Oregon people have the same independence and fiscal frugality that I have." He says he also wouldn't be surprised if he lost. Then, seeming to tire of playing it straight, he says, "I don't understand why you always want to write the story of tomorrow today and then the day after tomorrow write what happened. I think that's a bit of a journalistic redundancy, but I haven't been able to convince anyone." And then he jokes, "There's a heavy dateline: From North Bend—neither surprised nor unsurprised." He goes back to talking about the sense of limits he has tried to convey, the importance of creating jobs, rebuilding the cities, stabilizing the economy. One television reporter tells him that four minutes elapsed between the time he said that he wouldn't be surprised if he won and the time he said that he wouldn't be surprised if he lost, and therefore both statements can't be used. As the reporters rush to the phones to call in their stories, Brown wonders aloud why both statements can't be used. "Does that not conform to the Columbia School of Journalism?" he asks, now really warming to the possibilities of mocking journalism. Brown doesn't smile or laugh much; the amusement shows in his intense eyes. He starts on the idea of paragraphs. "Have paragraph, will phone," he says. And then, when it is time for us to board the plane, he says—apparently delighted with the thought—"Pick up your paragraphs and move out."

On the plane, Brown tells me that the training in the Jesuit seminary—where he spent three and a half years, one of them in almost total silence—was "that the world is an absurd situation." Brown does have a strong sense of absurdity, which is amusing, and which also feeds his impulse to cut through pomposity—an attractive political attitude. The Jesuits, he tells me, teach you to ignore questions of long life, of health, of wealth, of how you are regarded. This may have given Brown, as he suggests, a kind of detachment from this world, yet he has also embarked on one of man's most ambitious courses.

I tell him that I have read that one of his models was Gandhi, and that he himself wanted to change the life styles of America radically.

"That's a view," he replies. "There can be only so many views. After a while, you can just write 'op. cit.' "

This afternoon, Brown speaks to two university crowds—at Southern Oregon College, in Ashland, and at Oregon State University, in Corvallis. At both stops, the crowds are large and enthusiastic. Brown does well with college crowds, and he knows it. "I've tried to carve out a new path in politics," he tells the crowd in Ashland. "I've tried to get beyond the stereotypes and divisions that are tearing us apart. I think that I have a sense of what we are in this country and what we can become." He knows what people are looking for. People, in politics as in life, want to have a sense that there is another chance, that we can begin afresh, and talking to this impulse is a traditional political approach. With a slight Wallace-like populist touch, he says, "I'm very skeptical of the experts, the people who come down with their special pedigrees"—and the audience laughs—"and give us the answer." He says, "What I'd like to do as President is to scale back on the inflated pomposity, the ritual of self-congratulation that has characterized too much of government activity." He talks of setting up a public-service corps, saying, "We've exerted too much negative energy, and when we do that, then the country begins to really go on the downbeat, and I think we've been on the downbeat too long. I think it's time to start moving up, and that's positive energy."

On the plane, flying to Corvallis, Brown tells me of a phone call he made at the last stop. He tells me that he has just called a California state senator to ask him to support a bill that would give state workers—janitors as well as department directors—a flat pay increase, rather than an increase of a percentage of their income. Brown says, "That's something the people really respond to."

Brown does know how to touch things that "the people really respond to," and, as a result, his campaign is the only thing in this year's elections which resembles a movement. Carter staff people passed by the Brown campaign office in Portland and observed it with envy. The place was always filled with intense people, most of them young, several of them Mexican farm workers—followers of Cesar Chavez, and skilled organizers. As often as not, there would be a young woman breast-feeding. On the walls were hand-painted posters quoting Jerry Brown. One read, "The role of the leader is to help shape the discussion of national issues and not help foster unreal thinking." Brown's Oregon campaign director, Llewellyn Werner, is inclined to quote the Zen scholar Shunryu Suzuki's aphorism: "In the mind of the beginner, the possibilities are infinite. In the mind of the expert, they are few." These people believe that they are on to something; they believe in Jerry Brown, the man in the conventional pin-stripe suits and Giorgio ties who talks politics in an unconventional way. They think he will change the face of America.

Brown's ability to manipulate symbols stirs the imagination. Like the ability to organize, it is a neutral thing, which can be turned to good or bad ends. Great leaders stir the imagination; so do dangerous ones. Brown is neither at this point. What we don't know about him is what he will become, if anything, beyond what he is. He is still forming. We don't know what power will do to him, or heightened popularity. When it comes to choosing those who will govern us, we are presented with a dilemma. We want them to have enough support so that they can move, but not so much that we can't hold them down. We are uneasy, or should be, about a politician riding a popular wave—especially a politician about whom we know little, who hasn't been much tested. Brown is new at running for the Presidency—this is only his second state. On the plane to Corvallis, he drops into a seat, rests his face on a hand, closes his eyes, and says wearily, "A lot of interaction out there. People coming up to you. You have to focus."

This afternoon, at Oregon State University, he has his largest crowd of this campaign swing. The crowd seems to give him a new surge of energy. His voice is flat, but there is an energy that comes across in what he says. On the campus, he uses more hip language than he has used in other appearances. He says that the big automobile is a "macho ego symbol." He says that Ronald Reagan, in making the Panama Canal an issue, is "on some kind of a macho trip." Laughter and applause. And, having listed some difficult issues, he tells this crowd, "I'd like to try. That's all I can do is try. That's all." He says that he would come at the questions with "a different ethic, a different approach." Then he says, "That's what this election's about. Are we going forward, or are we going to prop up the things of the past?"

*   *   *

Something is happening that helps explain the Brown phenomenon. Brown's ability to stir the imagination and capture attention and command extensive coverage and, in practically no time after entering national politics, be taken seriously as a possible President has to do with the magnification that goes on in our communications. The speed with which a person, or a fashion, is blown up from a speck into a phenomenon—and, as often as not, burns out afterward—seems to have increased in recent years. The velocity with which we move from inattention to saturation to boredom is almost dizzying. There are some identifiable markers along the way: the covers of the news magazines, television features, *People* magazine. Our capacity for boredom may have increased in direct ratio to the velocity of the magnification process. And it seems to be affecting our politics. The flower children of Haight-Ashbury. Patty Hearst. Henry Kissinger. Secretariat. Twiggy. Burt Reynolds. Within five months, Jimmy Carter was the unknown face, then the face on the magazine covers, then a very familiar face. Jerry Brown is new. And because of the magnification process he is coming across as more different than he is. The magnification process cannot linger long, study nuances, wander around among complexities. It moves fast. It is well suited to such things as a governor who turns down the governor's mansion. (Just as Michael Dukakis, the Governor of Massachusetts, got national attention for riding the subway.) It is not well suited to issues. It can make a man a national force—perhaps even a President—before we have time to find out very much about him.

Portland. At nine o'clock, Frank Church is having his television call-in program. Jimmy Carter had one last night, and Jerry Brown will have one at ten o'clock. In all three cases, the candidates bought the time for the program. Such a program is a relatively inexpensive way for a candidate to reach a wide number of voters, and to appear to submit himself to all questions. Perhaps some of the programs are in fact spontaneous, but an aide to one of the candidates tells me that his campaign makes sure to tie up the lines—phoning in questions that his candidate wants to answer and at the same time preventing the opposition from phoning in embarrassing questions. Church, at fifty-one, has a youthful face. If Jimmy Carter had not already appropriated the symbol, Church's would be his teeth. When Church is not projecting a look of deep earnestness and sincerity, he breaks into a great, wide smile, often accompanied by a deep laugh. Church is a puzzle. He is a serious, thoughtful man with good instincts—he fought early and hard against the war in Vietnam—but he hasn't quite shaken his boy-orator style, which makes him seem to be posturing, and he can't quite avoid exploiting issues, as he did in his investigation of the C.I.A. He is an old-fashioned speaker; on the stump, he waves his arms and speaks in an orotund style. He has campaigned hard in Oregon, his campaign a mixture of serious issues and trite stunts. He talks about the dangers of secret intelligence agencies and of multinational corporations, and he turns up on television and in the newspapers sawing wood, riding a bicycle, throwing a Frisbee. To-night, on the call-in show, Church looks tired. The first question is what he would do about the C.I.A., and he talks about the impor-tance of constraints and oversight (saying "I know the importance of intelligence"). He is asked about the bureaucracy, and he likens it to "an orchestra band that has spilled over the stage," and says that too many programs are centralized in Washington. He keeps referring to the moderator, who reads him the questions, by name—"Ben." As the program approaches its close, Church faces the camera, saying, "Well, Ben, I appreciate the questions you've asked," and then he makes a little speech to the voters. Church is running as a good, safe, traditional Democrat, a responsible sen-ator. He says, "I hope here in Oregon that those Democrats who have supported Jackson and Humphrey and Udall will unite to-gether behind my candidacy." He is running in Oregon as a man from a neighboring state, Idaho, who understands the region's problems, and he says in his closing, "Here in the Northwest, we have a certain quality of life. Our problems are different. I think it is about our turn." He smiles, and looks into the camera. But then Ben says he has another question. He says that he is impressed by "the substantive quality of what you've done," and he in effect paraphrases a Church ad about the difference between rhetoric and reality on the energy question. Then Church does another closing. "I just don't believe that the White House is a proper place for on-the-job training," he says. And he smiles at the camera. But Ben goes on. Clearly, there has been a mix-up: the signal to cut was given while there was still time remaining. Ben asks Church a ques-tion about the fact that "you're a man who is trying to think through the problems," and Church denounces "the simplistic ap-proach" and "the politics of style," and he does still another clos-ing: "I ask the people of Oregon for their support on the basis of a record." And he gives the camera that closing smile again, and at last he says, "Thank you and good night."

Today's papers say that Edward Kennedy says that Jimmy Carter can't be denied the nomination if he comes to the Convention with one thousand three hundred and fifty delegates. (Fifteen hundred and five are needed to win the nomination.) That is an even higher requirement than the one set by Hubert Humphrey, who began by saying that Carter should not be denied the nomination if he had eleven hundred delegates, and then raised the ante to twelve hundred.

Oregon's high-school mock Convention the other day was won by Hubert Humphrey, on the fifth ballot.

MAY 26

The papers reported today that Iran has announced that it has signed contracts to buy two nuclear power plants from France. Iran's Prime Minister, Amir Abbas Hoveyda, said that the agreement "covers the whole gamut of nuclear technologies."

Another inconclusive day of primaries yesterday. Frank Church won the Oregon primary, Carter came in second, and Brown was a close third, with a strong write-in vote. Church won Idaho, his native state, and Brown won Nevada, a neighbor of California. (Campaigning in Idaho, Carter told listeners that he had a deep sense of kinship with them because both he and they raised products that grew underground.) Carter's victories were in the South —in Kentucky, Tennessee, and Arkansas—where he was virtually uncontested. President Ford, as had been expected, won in Oregon, but he lost Nevada and Idaho to Reagan. The President carried Tennessee and Kentucky but lost Arkansas. Reagan caused himself some trouble in Tennessee by saying that selling the T.V.A. to private enterprise "would be something to look at."

Now the consensus is that we must wait until June 8th, when the final primaries take place.

15

FOR THE FIRST TIME, the poll taken by CBS and the New York *Times* shows Jimmy Carter defeating Gerald Ford in November. For people with a finger to the wind, in both parties, this kind of information, whatever it means—it's a long time to November—is important. It helps Carter, who has just suffered two major primary losses, and faces additional serious challenges, and it also helps Ronald Reagan.

Testimony offered yesterday to the African Affairs Subcommittee of the Senate Foreign Relations Committee on an application by General Electric for permission to sell South Africa two nuclear reactors and the fuel required to operate them revealed the kinds of thinking and pressures that lead to the spread of nuclear capability. Myron Kratzer, the chief State Department official concerned with questions relating to the export of nuclear plants and fuel, offered the somewhat dizzying proposition (while not explicitly stating that the State Department favored the sale, which it is said to do) that "among the factors to be considered" was "our long-standing policy for the United States to abide by its existing agreements and remain a reliable supplier of nuclear equipment and fuels under effective controls as a means of furthering our non-proliferation objectives." He explained that "beginning in 1953 South Africa, which possesses large uranium reserves, became an important supplier of uranium to the U.S. for defense purposes," that it continued to play that role until the early nineteen-sixties, and that "it was therefore natural that . . . South Africa should be among the countries with which coöperation in this field would be established." (Since 1961, the United States has shipped South Africa two hundred and twenty-eight pounds of highly enriched uranium—material that can be converted into nuclear bombs.) Under questioning, Kratzer confirmed that three years ago the United States approved the sale of two computers to South Africa without knowing how they would be used, and that they were used in running a secret uranium-enrichment plant. Mr. Kratzer explained that "through our role as a reliable nuclear supplier" we diminish proliferation because "we have played a key part in framing and strengthening the inspection system of the International Atomic Energy Agency in proposing and encouraging widespread adherence to the Non-Proliferation Treaty, and in achieving a substantial measure of conformity in the nuclear-export policies of major suppliers." He also explained that "while South Africa has not adhered to the Non-Proliferation Treaty, its leaders have stressed that the South African nuclear program is exclusively devoted to peaceful purposes, and it is our understanding that South Africa has by no means ruled out the possibility of becoming a party to the treaty"; and that "the opportunity for the U.S. to have an affirmative influence on this decision will be enhanced by continuation of our peaceful nuclear coöperation."

A spokesman for the Export-Import Bank, a government agency that guarantees the loans of other banks and itself lends funds to finance exports of American goods, and that has been asked by South Africa to guarantee loans for the purchase of the two reactors, told the subcommittee that the bank had been informed that "competition for the nuclear power stations has come from French and German suppliers," and that "we have been advised by General Electric that this project would have a significant positive impact upon employment within the United States, since it will involve about three point two million man-hours divided among G.E. and U.S. subcontractor facilities in sixteen states."

The United States and the Soviet Union today signed a treaty governing peaceful underground nuclear explosions. Several disarmament experts oppose the treaty, because of the large-size explosions it permits, because they fear it will encourage such testing, and because, they argue, the provision for "on-site inspection" is not what it seems. Instead of permitting inspection by United States or Soviet inspectors at any time, anywhere, upon receipt of information suggesting that there has been nuclear testing, the treaty simply outlines a complex procedure whereby invited observers can come to a predetermined site to witness a prearranged explosion. This, like the other provisions of the treaty, and like other recent "disarmament" agreements, is not what advocates of arms limitations had in mind.

Jimmy Carter lost the Rhode Island primary yesterday to "Uncommitted" (Jerry Brown, whose name was not on the ballot, had urged Rhode Island voters to vote that way), and Senator Frank Church ran a close third. Carter had been ahead in the polls in Rhode Island, and last weekend he cancelled some time off—as he has repeatedly done on recent weekends—and increased his campaigning in the state. Carter defeated Morris Udall yesterday in South Dakota, where Udall had hoped to at last have his first primary victory. Udall was supported there by the state's two Democratic senators, George McGovern and James Abourezk. I recall that when Carter was campaigning in Oregon reporters were informed that his wife had called from South Dakota and told him he had a chance of carrying that state, so he should come and campaign there during part of the weekend time he had planned to take off, and he did. Over this past weekend, McGovern fired two assistants who were involved in the "stop-Carter" movement, and Carter said he was "grateful." The aides charged, and McGovern denied, that Carter and his supporters had brought pressure on McGovern to fire them.

In the Republican race, Ford defeated Reagan in Rhode Island, and Reagan defeated Ford in South Dakota.

The conference between developing and developed nations which has been going on in Nairobi since the first week in May ended in disagreement last weekend—an indication of the difficulty of reconciling differences not only between the two blocs but among the developed nations, and even within the United States. The major interest of the developing nations is to find a way of protecting their principal export commodities from wild price fluctuations. Having observed the success of the OPEC nations in establishing a common front and raising the price of their product, the other developing nations have begun to try to present a unified position on a number of other commodities—and they have begun to succeed. The subject is of importance beyond matters of economics and prices, for the developing nations are becoming more restive, more nationalistic, more aware of their newfound commodity power, and better armed. Many experts within the United States have assumed that these countries were incapable of agreeing on a common position on commodities—just as they assumed that the OPEC nations were.

In Nairobi, the developing nations were united, and the developed nations were not—neither among nor, in the case of the United States, within themselves. The major proposal made by Kissinger in Nairobi, in early May, was for an International Resources Bank to serve as an intermediary between, on the one hand, suspicious private investors from industrialized nations and, on the other, suspicious developing nations. The idea was to smooth the way for investment, because potential investors had become increasingly wary as a result of political instability and expropriation in several developing nations. The trouble with this approach was that it was not what the developing nations wanted. Their proposal was for the establishment of a common fund available to finance buffer stocks, or stockpiles, of commodities such as bauxite, cocoa, coffee, copper, cotton, jute, rubber, sisal, sugar, tea, and tin, so as to maintain their price levels. The trouble with that proposal was that some—but not all—of the developed nations did not like the idea. Among the nations that did not was the United States. The objections were technical, economic, political, and philosophical, and in essence the position of the United States was that it would, with misgivings, consider arrangements for buffer stocks on a commodity-by-commodity basis. Many of the developing nations were not keen on the idea of greater investment, not only because they were mistrustful of the multinational corporations but also because such investment might increase supplies of products whose prices the countries were already trying to protect. Moreover, they saw Kissinger's bank as a detour around their proposal for a common fund for buffer stocks, which it was. In an attempt to assuage them, Kissinger suggested that the new bank could, if necessary, supply the funding for whatever buffer stocks were agreed upon. But even before Kissinger made that proposal it had been undercut by Gerald Parsky (the Assistant Secretary of the Treasury who had spoken out against the idea of commodity agreements earlier this year) in testimony before Congress. The Treasury Department, run by ideologically militant free-enterprisers, is generally cool to the idea of commodity arrangements; Parsky's speech to that effect early this year put the Treasury Department at odds with the State Department, undercut the State Department's negotiating position with the developing countries, and raised some question in the world as to what our position really is. "The policy difference is not all that great," one man involved in our government's deliberations said to me. "The question about these meetings with the developing nations is whether you go in waving the banner of free enterprise and self-righteousness or say that you have reservations and will discuss their proposals. The big question in these things is what your attitude is." The Nairobi conference ended with neither the developing nor the developed nations accepting the others' position and with the two groups agreeing simply to have another meeting in October to prepare for yet another meeting next March. Yesterday, Kissinger and Treasury Secretary William Simon issued a joint statement criticizing the conference for rejecting the United States position, and saying that the result "does not augur well for the future of the dialogue of the worldwide development effort." Moreover, the Treasury Department emphasized that the United States had not committed itself to a common fund for buffer stocks. And Parsky, who has a habit of trying to make policy by making speeches (so does Kissinger, but Parsky is giving him some competition), said in a speech in Los Angeles that the United States "cannot support any trading system that requires a prior commitment to commodity agreements based on a system of government-administered prices."

JUNE 4

Cleveland. Next Tuesday, both parties hold their final primaries, in California, New Jersey, and Ohio—all populous states, in which both for the Democrats and for the Republicans about one-third of the delegates whose votes are needed to win the nomination will be selected. The Republicans will hold eleven state-convention contests between then and the National Convention, but for the Democrats Tuesday is essentially the end of the pre-Convention contest. As it turns out, in a year that has seen both parties' nominations alternately "sewn up" and unravelled, both parties' last three primaries are critical. Should Jimmy Carter not win the Ohio and New Jersey primaries, which he is now expected to win—as he is expected to lose California to Jerry Brown—the Democratic contest could remain open. Hubert Humphrey, who travelled to New Jersey this week (he said the trip was to fulfill "long-standing commitments"), has once again said he might enter the race if Carter should stumble. He has been waiting quite a while now—as have a number of others—for Carter to stumble. There has been some question about whether the uncommitted slate in New Jersey is for Humphrey or for Brown; now, apparently, it is for both. The Carter camp has been worried that Brown might do very well against

Carter in New Jersey. In Ohio, Carter faces Udall and Church, which from his standpoint is preferable to facing just cne opponent. Both Carter and Ford have virtually conceded California to the obvious front-runners, Governor Brown and former Governor Reagan. (But both are conducting substantial media-advertising campaigns there, and Carter has set up thirty-two California field offices, covering all of the state's forty-three congressional districts.) Reagan has conceded New Jersey to Ford. Therefore, for both parties the Ohio contest has become pivotal. If either Carter or Ford is defeated here, he will be in deep trouble. Reagan, confident of victory in California, has made a last-minute decision to come to Ohio for some campaigning this weekend. Ford will also be here. Carter had cancelled a projected trip to California in order to spend more time in both Ohio and New Jersey. Church and Udall arrive here today. The scheduling and counter-scheduling by the candidates is part of the strategic warfare they wage against one another; candidates try to command not only their own schedules but also those of their opponents. This is the sort of thing they think about as they run for the Presidency of the United States. The Carter camp, for example, has tried to keep Brown campaigning in California, where he is already ahead and the return on an increased investment of time would be marginal, rather than in New Jersey, where he could cause trouble. Therefore, there is reason to question whether Carter had planned to go to California on Monday or had just wanted Brown to think that he planned to do so. "We're faking people out right and left," a Carter aide said to me yesterday. Often the candidates' headquarters don't know what their own candidates' plans are. One must be careful about assuming that the candidates and their staffs know what they are doing. They try one thing and another, never sure what will work. Only the front-runners seem to know what they are doing, and that is largely because they are the front-runners.

When histories of this year are written, there will undoubtedly be a temptation to see more of a pattern in events than there has been. Even contemporary accounts often tend to find more meaning in events than is there—to overconclude. That is happening in the case of this year's elections. It is said that they reflect a search for spirituality, for something to believe in again, a desire to be soothed. There is undoubtedly a certain amount of truth to that, since Americans have been disturbed by recent history and are also showing a greater interest in religion and life-guiding philosophies than in recent years. But there is the danger of overconcluding. The Democratic candidate who pitched his campaign toward the search for spirituality will probably win his party's nomination, but the very same campaign could have failed. His triumph, if it does come, will be fortuitous in many ways. It is altogether possible that if one or two fewer candidates had been in the New Hampshire primary, or, perhaps, if Henry Jackson had chosen to enter that primary, Jimmy Carter would not have won it. His picture would then not have been on the covers of *Time* and *Newsweek*. He would not have received more attention than the other candidates. He would not have had so much "winnerness." Perhaps his relentlessness and his clear talents as a campaigner and his ability to meet public moods would still have won him the nomination, but a number of people look at the year without a Carter victory in New Hampshire and are not so sure. This is not to detract from Carter's achievement; it is to suggest that there may be less meaning and more accident in what has happened than many suppose. Politics, like the rest of life, contains a lot of happenstance.

Still, the year thus far does suggest a triumph of style over substance. There are important issues at stake, and, to some degree, even the successful candidates talk about them, but that does not seem to have much to do with their success. I have yet to come across a single person who says he is for Carter because of Carter's position on nuclear proliferation or health insurance. Ford tries to talk issues, in part because he does not have a style. He is, though President, in a neck-and-neck race with a style candidate who also talks issues of a sort. Reagan has capitalized on the issues of defense and the Panama Canal, but the response seems to be to his style—forceful, a take-charge guy. The President Ford Committee has found through its own polling that Reagan "projects" leadership and is seen as a stronger leader than Ford. A campaign aide to the President said to me a few days ago, "Reagan and Ford believe basically the same things, but they project different styles." He continued, "Issues were much more important than the candidate in 1960, 1964, 1968. But 1972 was more a year of the candidate— style. People are looking for certain things. If you can talk about what their desires are, their emotions, people start identifying with you." This man said that it was harder than ever to get across to the public on the issues, and he suggested that one reason was that the public was tired, battered by news. He also said that it was harder than ever to get the press interested in issues. The people around

President Ford tried to develop a "thematic" campaign. It began with the evocations of Thomas Paine and *Common Sense* in the State of the Union Address. When that didn't work, they tried "We're at peace in the world," and "The economy has turned around," and "He has restored integrity to government," but the President failed to get much mileage out of those, either. I asked the Ford campaign aide why that was so. "I don't know," he replied, and then he added, "Maybe it's because he hasn't been able to develop a style."

Perhaps the attention to issues is diminishing because of television. One's reservation about ascribing this to television is that television gets blamed for just about everything. The explanation may simply be that the problems are very complex and that our national mind is tired. And the triumph of style over substance in our politics mirrors other things that go on in our culture, such as the way we bestow celebrity. But it is true that television plays a large part in the magnification process, and that it rewards style. If a politician has anything to say, it is rare for us to see him say it for more than sixty seconds, if at all. Television has little patience with complexity. If television had already become a force, Adlai Stevenson might never have been nominated for the Presidency. It is doubtful whether this year he would have made it out of New Hampshire. He might not even have run. A lot of thoughtful people do not. For the last year and a half, Jimmy Carter and Ronald Reagan have had nothing else very important to do.

While we tend to say that we want "the issues" discussed in a Presidential campaign, we don't have a very good way of defining "the issues." And the issues that do get discussed often have little relation to real questions, or become issues without having been given much careful thought. Some of them develop into litmus tests: they become symbolically important, carry emotional freight, and gain the backing of powerful constituencies, and it is very difficult for a candidate seeking the support of some of the most powerful constituencies within his party to take a negative stand on these issues, or even to be hesitant about them. They become ends in themselves. This seems to be true, within the Democratic Party, of three liberal issues in this year's election—the Humphrey-Hawkins jobs bill, national-health-insurance legislation, and proposals to require vertical divestiture by the oil companies.

The Humphrey-Hawkins bill, an elaborate plan for reducing adult unemployment to three percent within four years, was sailing along, picking up sponsorship by Democrats in Congress and endorsements by Presidential candidates. (Jimmy Carter's endorsement came reluctantly, and only in the wake of the "ethnic purity" controversy.) And then Charles Schultze and other liberal economists began to point out that the scheme was highly inflationary and, with its emphasis on government employment, would not offer any real long-term solution to the unemployment problem. Moreover, current estimates are that it would cost from fifteen to twenty billion dollars. Some Democrats in Congress thereupon began to edge away from it, but they didn't dare say so out loud.

National-health-insurance proposals also present a number of problems. They assume that the goal of a national health system is not simply to provide health care for the poor or insurance for catastrophic illnesses for the poor and the middle class but to help everyone confront the rising costs of medical care. However, since no one really knows how to control the costs of medical care, national-health-insurance plans would be very expensive. (The Kennedy-Corman national-health-insurance bill makes a stab at the problem of costs, but no one is sure how it would work.) In addition, there is the problem of how to avoid having a health-insurance program pour money into a health system that distributes services inequitably and inefficiently. Some people have ideas about how to approach this problem, but no one knows how to get the medical profession to go along with the kind of reorganization that many think necessary or whether such a reorganization could be achieved without incurring staggering new government controls and regulations. (Some advocates of health-care reform would prefer to begin on a more modest basis, with partial programs, which would provide certain kinds of medical care, such as care for especially expensive illnesses or pre-natal care for mothers and preventive care for children.) And there is also some doubt, which advocates of national health insurance are loath to concede, whether the provision of substantially more medical care will lead to substantially more health. (In the United States, the life expectancy of white males at forty-five has improved by three and a half years since 1900.) It is argued that other factors—such as personal habits, the environment, accidents—are far more important in determining health. As in the case of the Humphrey-Hawkins bill, the climate of a political campaign is not conducive to discussion of these dilemmas and subtleties and trade-offs. Nor is it hospitable to consideration of the risk, for liberals, of enacting programs that might end up making all liberal ventures more vulnerable. And, just as providing jobs and providing medical care for everyone sound like worthy things to do, so does "breaking up the oil companies." The idea is that if each of the major oil companies were no longer permitted to refine, market, and transport oil as well as to produce it, the country would be better off. But there isn't convincing evidence that forcing the companies to divest would either lower prices or produce more oil. Moreover, independent companies have been entering the market, so there is not a classic monopoly problem. And such a move would not solve the real energy problem, which is to find ways of making us less dependent upon oil. Thus, the divestiture issue, too, is a diversion. But all good liberals are under pressure to say that they are for breaking up the oil companies. Again, this is an issue that some Democrats have misgivings about, but, in an election year, they are reluctant to say so.

Someone here whom I talked with about these issues suggested another reason—beyond emotional impact and backing by powerful constituencies—that proposals of this kind, needing more thought, move to the center of political debate: the growing complexity of governing. Some of the real questions are extremely complicated, and even to the extent that we understand them they do not lend themselves to political discussion. In the past ten or fifteen years, the government has become far more ambitious than ever before in what it has tried to do for our citizens. What it should be doing and whether it does those things well become less and less questions of ideology or of good guys versus bad guys. On matters like the environment, energy, even full employment, the difficulty comes, first, in getting general agreement on what the problem is and, second, in figuring out what the best approach is to solving it. The approaches more and more often involve technical answers. That makes it harder and harder to carry on political debate about the important issues. The alternatives to be considered and debated are not of the order or nature of William Jennings Bryan's free silver, or whether or not there should be a social-security system. The energy question does not really get down to a good public versus bad oil companies. The alternatives cannot be posed as simple choices.

The end of the primary season also invites questions about the primary system itself. It has become increasingly brutal, demanding of superhuman energy, and antipathetic to thought. It rewards doggedness and organization and "winnerness." It is filled with quirks. Even the sequence of the primaries has its impact. Voters in one primary are often reacting not just to the candidates and to the questions before them but to what happened in the previous primary. They are not so much making a rational decision as being swept along in a current. There are proposals for reforms, the most commonly approved one being for regional primaries. The idea is that these would cut back on the travel that candidates must endure, and put more coherence into the primary season. But there could be dangers in that system, too: a candidate with at least short-term "winnerness" might sweep a region and then sweep succeeding regions before we had a chance to find out much about him, to ask some questions. The possibility of a one-shot triumph is what makes a national primary, proposed by some, seem a singularly bad idea. It may be that there is no good solution. It may be that what has been opened up cannot be closed. Jimmy Carter read the books and decided that he would outdo George McGovern in starting early. The next candidates may decide that they will outdo Jimmy Carter.

It is somehow fitting that Ohio, a state that is average America, now becomes the focus of the primary contests. Ohio is neither Eastern nor Western—it borders on Pennsylvania, Michigan, Indiana, Kentucky, and West Virginia—and it is industrial, urban, and rural. Ohio is large—about eleven million people live here—and it has more cities of over a hundred thousand than any other state except California and Texas. Ohio is not as liberal as Michigan; it has no strong university-connected liberal community. In the north, from Cleveland west to Toledo—where about a third of the state's population lives—it has absorbed waves of Eastern and Southern European immigration. The south, centering on Cincinnati, is marked more by immigration from Germany and, later, from Appalachia.

Udall and Church are concentrating their Ohio campaigns in the northern tier of the state, where about sixty-three percent of the Democratic vote is concentrated—about forty percent of it in the Cleveland media-market area. They have virtually conceded central and southern Ohio—the more conservative parts of the state—to Carter. The coalition of liberal labor groups which has formed in order to have influence at the Convention, if the race remains undecided, is supporting Udall in nine congressional districts in the north and Carter in ten central and southern districts. But this large state has eight media markets, so the candidates fly about it in search of exposure. When Udall's Ohio campaign got under way in earnest, he moved his campaign headquarters from Columbus to Cleveland, and he begins or ends each day with some event here. An attempt is made to show him doing something "visual" with an interesting group—at Slovenian parades, United Auto Workers rallies, Ukrainian social halls—in the hope that he will be the subject of the lead or the second story on the night's news programs in at least this part of the state. He had come to be identified as the candidate of the suburban liberals, so he is staying out of the suburbs this time. Udall, whose campaign organization has gone through more changes than a campaign organization should, has brought in a special campaign manager for Ohio. Udall's campaign staff is making one last effort to show that its candidate is warm and funny, not aloof—one last effort to get this candidate, who has failed to come across, to do so. What is happening, however, is that Udall is coming across as something he has not been earlier in his political career—negative, and even mean. Udall is not really mean, but his reaction to Carter makes him appear so. Upset by Carter's successful use of a sometimes evasive and contradictory approach to issues, tired, desperate, egged on by his staff, Udall has succumbed, at the end of his campaign for the Presidency, to being something he never was before. His near-success in Michigan (he lost by only two thousand votes out of seven hundred thousand), where he ran television commercials with cartoon faces suggesting that Carter was two-faced on issues, has encouraged his campaign aides to follow a similar formula here. The commercials for Ohio question Carter's positions on the Vietnam war, tax reform, health insurance, and the oil companies. In 1971, Carter called for a withdrawal of troops from Vietnam, on the ground that the United States government was not doing enough to win; in the same year he urged the Democratic governors not to make an issue of Vietnam in the 1972 Presidential election; in 1975 he supported last-minute military assistance to South Vietnam. Udall points out that he himself was against the war all along, and he concludes, "So who is Jimmy Carter? What does he really believe?" (An Associated Press story appearing in today's Cleveland *Plain Dealer* says that only twenty percent of those who back Carter know where he stands on the issues.) The hope is not only to raise doubts about

Carter—whose rating is now between forty and fifty percent in the polls in Ohio—but to get under his skin, try to make him react irritably. This is not—frustrating as it may be to have Carter for an opponent—the noblest of goals.

A fish fry at the Martin de Porres Center, a community center supported by the Catholic Church, in a former church building, for blacks who live in the Glenville section of Cleveland. Udall is to appear here tonight. About three hundred people are gathered in a large basement room. By the time Udall arrives, they have had their dinner, of fried perch and cole slaw. As Udall enters, a small combo plays "Happy Days Are Here Again." The last time I heard that was in Wisconsin, in the ballroom where Udall claimed his victory that later the same night turned into a loss. Udall looks very tired tonight, but there is something about the entrance of a candidate, flooded with television lights, that seems to give snap and importance to any occasion. Today, Udall has been in Newark, Trenton, Dayton, and Akron. He is slightly late in his arrival here, because the sheriff in charge of his motorcade directed it to the wrong church. Therefore, a buildup that he was given by George Forbes, President of the Cleveland City Council and a fiery speaker, has been dissipated. Udall pumps more enthusiasm into his remarks than seems possible under the circumstances. His speech is part talk about how he has fought for equal rights and jobs, and part jabs at Carter. He says that "we were after him for a year and a half" to endorse the Humphrey-Hawkins bill, and "he finally came around last April after we had all this talk about 'ethnic purity.' " And, he goes on, "we haven't had a word from him since." Udall talks about his support of national health insurance and day-care centers. He is talking old-fashioned politics. If Carter were here, he would probably be preaching. Udall talks about the fact that black family income is only sixty percent of what white family income is, and says, "They don't charge you sixty percent at the grocery checkout counter." He quotes Robert Kennedy's saying "I would wish that my country would be a just country."

In Udall's car on the way to a Holiday Inn at which he will stay tonight, I ask Udall how he feels. Mrs. Udall, who says she did fourteen radio interviews, is with us.

"Tired but surviving," he replies. "I'll be glad when this rat race is over. My spirits are good; I think I've kept my cool. It's been a long struggle, but I've had a stability and a philosophical approach to it: you go on and fight the fight. I went through a stage in South Dakota, and then here, where I had three nights of only five hours' sleep. And my legs get cramped riding in cars and airplanes." (Udall is six feet five.) He continues. "I got tough with the staff. They had two other events for me to appear at tonight, and I said no. When I'm this tired, I'm not sharp and I'm not good—and my legs hurt."

I ask Udall how he feels about turning his campaign into an outright anti-Carter campaign.

"Not comfortable," he replies. "I would strongly prefer to run my own kind of campaign. I have traditionally run my own campaign and left the others alone. I confronted this in Michigan. He was running off with the blacks and the anti-blacks, the pro-abortion people and the anti-abortion people, the pro-guns and the anti-guns. So the question was whether you folded your tent or you fought back. I decided I had been lucky in my previous campaigns —I've never had to run against an incumbent. You don't beat an incumbent or a front-runner by saying 'Ladies and gentlemen, he's a good man.' Jimmy Carter *is* fuzzy on the issues. He's not for things that leaders of the Democratic Party should be for. I don't have any misgivings about what I'm doing. He's not going to get beaten unless people understand what he's up to: that he's not for what working people are for—Humphrey-Hawkins, breaking up the oil companies. At first, I was uncomfortable—it's not my style. I'm generally understanding of other people. But it's worked out well. It was burned into my mind after Pennsylvania, when Jackson pulled out and Humphrey decided he didn't want to go, that it would have been all over if I had got out. I felt responsible in two ways: one, I represented millions of people who were for Sargent Shriver and Fred Harris and Birch Bayh and were for the kinds of things Carter wasn't for; two, I remember 1972, when Humphrey cut up McGovern and so weakened him that he couldn't win. I determined that I would proceed with restraint, so people wouldn't look back and say, 'Mo Udall cut up Carter.' "

I ask him if the race for the Presidential nomination turned out to be much more difficult than he had expected.

"I knew it was going to be hard, I knew it was going to be tough," Udall replies. "I've adapted pretty well. God, I get tired of riding in cars and airplanes. It's not like running for Congress, where the next stop is ten minutes away. I got up this morning at seven and will quit at eleven. Of those sixteen hours, eight or nine were in a car or a plane." But it isn't just the discomfort and the fatigue; Udall talks about something else that happens to even the most thoughtful of candidates. "I thought there would be more of an opportunity to deliver thoughtful speeches on a range of subjects," he says. "These last few hectic weeks, you end up mostly just shouting slogans. You work out a three- or four-point hardboiled message. As the pressure grows, all you think about is how to work up a group or get your message across. The last six weeks are really brutal. Every Tuesday, you have new primaries to face and new equations to solve. You don't have time to think about your Administration or how to organize your Cabinet."

Mrs. Udall interpolates that she thinks her husband looks and is especially tired now.

"We've had a running feud with the staff," Udall says, echoing things that survivors of previous campaigns have told me. "I really had to fight to get two good nights of sleep in succession. The schedulers and the managers see that they have four more days, and they don't see that if I go to all the things they want me to I'm going to look haggard. Nobody is going to write a story saying my staff is tired and haggard, but they'll write one saying I am. I had five straight days without a decent night's sleep, and some guy doing an interview with me asked me a question and I just drew a blank."

He continues, "After Pennsylvania, people were going over to Carter. I held the line. I held the line. I came in third in Pennsylvania, and people said, 'Get out.' I held on for Connecticut and Michigan. I gave Church and Brown a chance. I really think my firmness stopped a stampede. I don't get credit for that." And then Udall talks about members of Congress who have endorsed Carter, and his pain and disappointment are clear. It is late at night now, and Udall is extremely tired, but before he goes to bed his Ohio chairman wants some time with him, and so do several staff members. His staff has planned that tomorrow he will go about the state with a map of the United States, a pointer, and an easel, and make a statement charging that Jimmy Carter took varying positions on issues in different parts of the country. Tonight, the staff wants him to clear a statement he will release tomorrow, and it wants him to get up a half hour earlier than he had planned, so that he can rehearse his performance with the map and the pointer. He will perform this act in the morning in Cleveland, and then in Columbus and Cincinnati, hitting three major media markets.

JUNE 5

Saturday evening. The Bicentennial Wagon Train, in Aurora, Ohio, about twenty miles southeast of Cleveland. Frank Church, for reasons that are not clear, is here this evening for an appearance. In California this week, he came down with a strep throat, so he had to cancel his appearances there on Thursday yesterday he flew to Ohio, but this afternoon he was still feeling ill, so he cancelled an appearance at something called the World's Greatest Garage Sale, in Berea. The appearances he will make this evening are too late to be shown on the television news. There is really some question about why they were scheduled at all—these events cannot make very much difference. Of course, there is a candidate's own inclination to keep going, and the pressures from the staff, and there is the possibility that if a candidate chooses to spend an evening doing nothing, the press will think that that is very strange, raise questions about his lack of industry. But the big question is what Church is doing in Ohio at all. No one believes he can win here. The simplest explanation is that Church, like other candidates, is propelled by his own ambitions and the ambitions of those around him. By that reasoning, he is in Ohio because he has been winning primaries in the West and he thinks Ohio offers him a chance to show that he can do well in an industrial state. Church's television commercials here stress his investigations of the multinationals and his concern that they move jobs overseas. There are suspicions, however, that since Church's presence in Ohio is likely to hurt Udall more than Carter (the assumption is that Church and Udall compete for the same voters), Church may have more complex reasons for being here. It is a fact, at least, that members of Carter's staff encouraged members of Church's staff to encourage Church to go into Ohio, and told Church's staff that Church had some potential there. Fortunately for Carter, Church stayed out of California, where the Carter people felt that Church could hurt Carter, perhaps forcing him into third place.

This is a rather strange scene. In the warm setting sun, covered wagons are drawn up in a circle around the parking lot of a shopping center. People in pioneer costumes mingle with people in sports clothes on the pavement and on surrounding grassy slopes while behind them some fairly fatigued-looking horses munch their dinner. A man in Indian dress who says his name is Walking Fox signs autographs. The Bicentennial Wagon Train—a project of the Pennsylvania Bicentennial Commission, supported by the American Revolution Bicentennial Administration, Gulf Oil, Holiday Inns, and the Aero Mayflower Transit Company, among others—is making its way across the country from Blaine, Washington, in the extreme northwest corner of the United States, to Valley Forge, Pennsylvania, which it hopes to reach on July 3rd. The wagon train covers about twenty miles a day—followed by horse trailers, and campers carrying some members of the Penn State Show Troupe— and each night the troupe puts on a show of singing and dancing.

This evening, after the show ends, Frank Church makes a speech. His wife, Bethine, an intelligent and strong woman, who campaigns with him constantly, stands beside him, smiling. "I've been hoping to catch up with the Wagon Train," he says to the crowd. He talks about the importance of wagon trains and says that "the nineteenth century was a great period of expansion, of manifest destiny that stretched this country of ours from sea to sea." The audience does not pay much attention. Church says that the wagons symbolize the family farm, which "has proved to be the most efficient producer of food and fibre that has ever been created anywhere in the world." The children in the audience are restless and noisy, and Church, still suffering the effects of the strep throat and taking antibiotics, is standing there, characteristically waving his arms, making a classic stump speech in the manner of a trained orator, his voice rising and falling within sentences. His wife keeps smiling. Church has a slim body topped by a large head. The face is still youthful, but the hair is graying. He does not look well; there are bulges under his eyes. He has probably assessed the situation to-night correctly: if there is to be any speech at all to these people who have come out on a late-spring evening to see a wagon train, it should be an old-fashioned stump speech about American virtues. When Church mentions that we have "a society in which the people are still free," the audience applauds. It cares about that. He gets back to basics, tying in what he has been working on in the Senate and what he has been talking about in his campaign with the spirit of the Bicentennial Wagon Train. He does not mention Watergate. The Democratic candidates talk about Watergate, but only in a gingerly and fleeting and largely indirect way. It seems that it is considered something we shouldn't talk about—that it is bad manners to bring up such unpleasantness. We are treating our country as if it were a person who has some sort of disease or disfigurement, which it is not polite to mention. Similarly, we set about forgetting Joseph McCarthy, and then in fairly short order we ended up with something even more dangerous, led by a man whose career began with McCarthyism. Church says, "The men and women of 1776 knew that you didn't fight crime with crime, or evil with evil, or delinquency by becoming delinquent. They knew that the only way they could successfully avoid the terrors of a police state was to design a government that would remain subordinate to the law, and that the only way they could escape a closed society was to have the nerve to live in an open one."

Shortly after we board the bus for the next event, we are asked to get off again. Senator Church has an announcement. "I've just received word that a terrible disaster has struck my home state of Idaho," he says quietly. His hands trembling, he says that the Teton Dam, on the Teton River, has broken, producing "a devastating flood," and that "a wall of water fifteen feet high is headed toward Idaho Falls." Fate, in the form of a frightening natural disaster, has thrown itself across the path of Frank Church's Presidential ambitions. He says that he will break off his Ohio campaign to return to his native state. He has no choice, of course. There may not be much he can do in Idaho, but his constituents would never understand it if he were too busy campaigning for the Presidency to come home. Besides, he backed the dam, which was the subject of some controversy.

While Church's staff works out the logistics of a flight to Idaho later in the evening, Church proceeds to the next event—a dinner dance celebrating the ninetieth anniversary of the Carpenters Local 171, at the Mahoning Country Club, in Girard, Ohio, some forty miles southeast of Aurora. He is about an hour behind schedule now, and must fly to Idaho tonight, but he feels he cannot—or he cannot bring himself to—cancel his next appearance. I talk with Church on the bus on the way to the dinner dance. I begin by asking him if there have been any surprises in his campaign. His answer indicates that he has acquired several of the attributes of *Homo candidatus*.

"It's pretty much what I expected," he replies. "I knew the problem would be legitimizing my candidacy, and I anticipated a news blackout—which occurred in the first couple of months. I knew I had to pull off a miracle in Nebraska. I've won four out of five primaries, and I nearly won the fifth, in Rhode Island." He was actually entered in six primaries, but when he talks about how many primaries he has won, he leaves out Nevada, just as when Carter says that he ran in all the states, he leaves out West Virginia. "It's worked out as I had hoped it would," Church continues. "But there have been some complicating factors I didn't foresee. The late, late start was such a high flyer that I thought I'd have it to myself. But then Brown came in. Otherwise, the concluding scenario would have fallen into place. I would have won California. And I've campaigned on a shoestring. My Rhode Island campaign was underfunded. I can't match Udall or Carter in spending on media here, and now I have to return to Idaho. But that's Kismet. It all worked out better than I could have hoped, until"—he breaks into a dry laugh—"we got to the end. And then it all came apart."

I ask Church, a serious man, and more an issue candidate than a style candidate, whether he has found it hard to get people interested in issues.

"That was not a problem in Nebraska and Oregon and the smaller states, where you feel you can reach people personally," he says. "In those situations, I would make a short statement and then have questions and answers. I found out people were very responsive. I was able to address myself to questions that interested people in that locality. I found that people were really hungry to hear the issues discussed, despite what people say. I think that that was part of the reason for the success that I have had." And then he returns to how he has done in his campaign, and how he might have done better—like other candidates, he has become preoccupied with this. "I think if I had been able to get into it earlier the outcome might have been different," Church says. "If Mo had won anywhere along the way, it would have broken the momentum of Carter's campaign. Carter was on the covers of *Time* and *Newsweek* the week of the Nebraska primary. People don't take to a secret police and government agencies pushing people around. People don't like government. The government has earned people's contempt. The very fact that I have been conducting this investigation and exposing these abuses and investigating the multinationals means that I am not seen as part of that establishment—also because I have a reputation for opposing the war. At the same time, I think people think the job is so important that it takes some experience. So there are two moods in the land. There's the anti-Washington mood, which is understandable, because people feel betrayed, and, on the other hand, there is understanding that the Presidency has such potential for good or for ill that there is real doubt that it ought to be entrusted to someone who has had very little experience. So people are groping. I have a feeling that if it had been possible to get in earlier I might well be in Carter's position now. There is one good feature about the late, late strategy—it gives you more time to think. When you're campaigning, you don't have time to think about much besides what you're going to do next and say next, and how to deal with day-to-day crises. But when I was in the Senate I had time to think about what I would do. You can't do that in the course of frantic campaigning. Bethine and I have had one day of rest since the nineteenth of March. But I've no regrets. I've conducted a good campaign. I've won primaries nobody thought I could win. I've come out stronger. I achieved a measure of national recognition that wouldn't have come to me any other way. This will help me in the Senate. When I won in Nebraska, there was hardly a senator who did not come up to me and congratulate me. It was not simply out of courtesy, and it didn't have to do with ideology. There was an institutional pride—you know, one of the boys did well."

As we talk, Church fiddles with a piece of paper bearing statistics he may use at his next appearance. After a while, he decides not to try to learn them. He talks about the press. "The point I found hardest in dealing with the press was the constant dealing in political, technical questions," he says. "You have to deal with the constant put-down questions: 'If you don't win this race, does that mean you have no further chance?' 'How much of the vote do you expect, and if you don't get it is that a failure?' "

JUNE 6

Cincinnati. Sunday afternoon. Oddly, this city, where I grew up, has become a political traffic center at the end of the Presidential primaries. Ronald Reagan is coming here this afternoon, and President Ford will arrive tonight. Tomorrow, Jimmy Carter will show up. Reagan made a last-minute decision to try to get delegates in Ohio. Since the central and southern parts of the state were virtually surrendered to Jimmy Carter by his opponents, his margin here is being counted on to help offset whatever strength his opponents have in the north. Cincinnati is one of the most conservative large cities in America. When I was growing up here, people who backed a Democratic candidate for President were considered a little strange, and perhaps even suspect. Cincinnati is a lovely city—especially as Midwestern cities go—built on hills along the Ohio River. Its conservatism, unusual for such a large city, seems to stem from the original settlement here, of German immigrants, in the early eighteen-hundreds. They were the conservative Germans—Bavarians, Rhinelanders. The Socialist Germans, in a subsequent wave, went to Milwaukee. Cincinnati lies on the borders of Kentucky and Indiana. The city has enjoyed (if that is the term) a kind of stability—at least, compared with other Northern industrial cities. It has fewer Southern and Eastern European immigrants than the industrial cities of the northern part of the state. The blacks in their northward migration tended to skip over Cincinnati, and its population is only twenty-seven percent black, whereas blacks make up almost forty percent of Cleveland's population. The political base of the Tafts—who for a long time owned the city's afternoon paper, and still own a radio station and a television station—Cincinnati has probably been governed by Republicans more of the time than any other large city in the country. Republicans now control all the offices in Hamilton County—Cincinnati's county—except sheriff. Some of the city's black leaders are conservative, and so are many of its blue-collar workers. The city's Jewish population, while influential, is small, and even the Jews are heavily Republican. The city refers to itself, burgher style, as "solid Cincinnati"; and "solid Cincinnati" is behind only Dallas and San Diego in the degree to which it votes Republican. The German culture brought with it strong support for the arts. One grew up on Tafts, baseball (we were excused from school on opening day), the smell of soap emanating from "Ivorydale" (the area in which Procter & Gamble has several plants), pride in the thought that because of its machine-tool plants Cincinnati was important enough that the Luftwaffe might bomb it, and, in the summer, Metropolitan Opera stars performing at the Zoo. The High Victorian fountain of Fountain Square—a dreary bus terminal when I was a child—has been moved down the street and is now surrounded by a European-style plaza. The river has been cleaned up and the riverfront beautified. But some things remain the same. The city is still insane about its baseball team—Cincinnati may be the only city whose airport shops sell not only T-shirts advertising its baseball team but also reproductions of a painting that features a baseball mitt and the team's cap. And Cincinnati remains conservative. It is no accident that Ronald Reagan and Jerry Ford and Jimmy Carter are all giving the city their attention in the next couple of days.

That the race between the President and Ronald Reagan has got to this point is astonishing—yet it really shouldn't be. Gerald Ford may be President, but he was a dim figure, a Republican spear-carrier, in the House of Representatives before Richard Nixon, engulfed by crisis, reached for him. After that, Ford was subjected to the imputation process—the process by which we impute to public figures, especially Presidents, authority and qualities that we want them to have. Moreover, while incumbency carries with it a certain aura and also access to helpful levers, it is not all that it is thought to be. John Kennedy was believed to be facing some reëlection difficulty when he made his fateful trip to Dallas. All of Lyndon Johnson's and Richard Nixon's efforts to manipulate incumbency could not save them. Ford has come across as a nice and decent man—even though his politics often fail to convey compassion—but not *Presidential,* the imputation process notwithstanding. His Presidency has been confused: within months, Administration positions have changed on tax policy and labor policy and antitrust policy; high officials, including his Vice-President, his Secretary of Defense, and his Secretary of State, have been embraced and then literally or figuratively dumped; he said that the word "détente" would be dropped but the policy would not. His Administration has been, to paraphrase Winston Churchill, a pudding without a theme. People have a way of sensing such uncertainty. Ford is conservative, but not conservative enough for the Party's conservative wing, which has had a strong, and possibly dominant, role in the Presidential-nominating process since 1964. A Reagan manager said to me earlier this year, "We are a majority of a minority." Ford ignited neither the conservative nor the moderate wing of his party. While Reagan was igniting a grass-roots movement in his campaign for the Presidency, Ford relied on his Presidentialness, which he had largely squandered, and his base in Congress. Such has been the despair within his own party that a House Republican who supports him said recently, "Ford is so inept that we'd have been better off if Nixon had burned the tapes on the back lawn." Even Ford's apotheosis by the media, which went on as if the Nixon experience had taught us nothing, did not do him enough good. (There was the week in which we were permitted to see pictures of our leader toasting an English muffin.) His first two notable acts once he was in office were the sudden Sunday-morning pardon of Richard Nixon and the WIN program. The pardon, coming without any preparation of the public, made him seem impulsive and also insensitive to a widespread public feeling that Nixon should be brought to at least some kind of justice. Ford thought the outrage would blow over, but such outrage seldom does; it just quiets and goes underground. The WIN program, with its vacant ideas for dealing with the economy, and with its hyperbolic P.R., made the President seem ludicrous. Public figures do not often recover from seeming ludicrous. He has been spared the consequences of some of his own policies. The economy appears to be improving, but more as a result of the Democratic Congress's balking at some of his approaches and the innate rhythms of the business cycle than as a result of anything his Administration did. The economy is still not good, but the direction is, and that may be what matters politically. Ford was thwarted in his efforts to send additional military assistance to a collapsing South Vietnam. As for the Mayaguëz incident, he was fortunate that it did not last longer—that the Cambodians were not in a position to fight back. Then, he does not seem to understand the spread of deadly weapons. Also, he has let nuclear-arms-agreement efforts be overtaken by election-year politics, but then perhaps almost any President in his situation would; elections always take their toll of policy. While some praise Ford for the Eisenhower-like domestic tranquillity, he is toying with the sore busing issue, and, as Carl Holman, the president of the Urban Coalition, pointed out earlier this year, a generation of black youths—who cannot find jobs and for whom there are no unemployment benefits—despairs.

The seesaw nature of the Ford-Reagan struggle suggests that nominating battles, like military ones, do have periods in which one side or the other has momentum (that overused word), morale, strategic advantage. They do not provide clear-cut tests. They are not clinical, or even rational. They are not simply contests in which the candidates present who they are and what they propose to do, and ask the voters to choose. They are more like a large-scale land war, with the contesting sides employing a variety of stratagems, some of which work, some of which do not, and all of which can be second-guessed. They often take place in a psychological atmosphere of what has gone before. Ford's narrow victory in New Hampshire, followed by victories in Florida and Illinois, suggested that Reagan could not mount a serious challenge. A Ford strategist said to me recently, "We had the initiative until North Carolina. Reagan had the initiative after North Carolina. Texas we wrote off as an aberration—they're conservative beyond belief in Texas. Then Reagan began to score on two issues—the Panama Canal and defense, which includes Kissinger. Kissinger is not all that unpopular in the nation, but when you talk about Texas, Nebraska, Indiana, he is. Then we made a comeback in Tennessee and Kentucky. People are getting tired of Reagan's issues." There are several members of the Ford staff who say they have argued that the President should take the "offensive" on the defense issue, whatever that means. He did stand in front of the Alamo and say we're number one, but to no avail. There are also some who have argued that he should use his Presidentialness more. One says, "After we got through with the State of the Union, which we milked until April, we ran out of anything to be Presidential about." They have argued that he, rather than unknown bureaucrats, should have been announcing the monthly improvement in unemployment statistics. "He's not a showboat President," says one. But there is a question as to whether that would have worked. Previous Presidents have made more imaginative use of the trappings of office and it didn't work. President Ford may not have seized every opportunity for Presidential theatre, but he hasn't missed many. He has flown about in Air Force One, and bands have played "Hail to the Chief," and he has summoned local broadcasters and given away boodle in important primary states. The problem lies in the particular personalities of Gerald Ford and Ronald Reagan.

This afternoon, Reagan is holding a rally in the auditorium of the Sycamore High School, on the outskirts of Cincinnati. (Actually, the Reagan forces have failed to qualify a slate of delegates in one of Cincinnati's two congressional districts.) This is one of the more conservative sections of the conservative city, and Reagan has drawn an impressive crowd for a warm, sunny Sunday afternoon. As usual with Reagan events, the auditorium is draped in red, white, and blue. He is the candidate who has appropriated the national colors; Ford's décor usually consists of blue-and-white President Ford banners. A man in the audience, wearing a Reagan button, tells me that he supports Reagan because "I think he's a much more capable administrator—he's more of a leader of the people than Ford." This man says, "I understand that it isn't Ford who is holding defense spending down, it's Congress, but Reagan would do something about it." Reagan, as usual, gets an ovation when he enters—it is the emotional response of fervid followers. The only other candidate I have seen get such responses this year was George Wallace. These days, Reagan travels with a supporting cast. Ken Curtis, a man with a wizened face, who played Festus in "Gunsmoke," tells the crowd that he is here "speaking up for Governor Reagan because I am a concerned American." Then Jimmy Stewart—a retired brigadier general in the Air Force Reserve, he is introduced as "General Jimmy Stewart"—speaks for Reagan. Jimmy Stewart looks old now, and his hair is longish and white. He is wearing a conservative navy-blue pin-stripe suit and a maroon-and-navy tie. He looks like a banker. But the voice is unmistakably Jimmy Stewart. People listen quietly while Jimmy Stewart explains why he is for Ronald Reagan, and how Reagan is able to talk to all sorts of people. Stewart says, "I know in the acting racket this is one of the first things you're supposed to be able to do. . . . There are all sorts of tricks." He stumbles just the way Jimmy Stewart is supposed to as he tells the crowd that Reagan has "great respect and admiration and concern for the welfare and the security of the United States of America."

Reagan looks good. His cheeks are rosier than when I saw him earlier in the year. He is successful now, and it shows in his looks and his demeanor. It is the sort of success that feeds on itself. Two things happened to Reagan in mid-campaign: he got more confident, and he got angry. Mike Deaver, Reagan's chief of staff, tells me that he can pinpoint the day when Reagan, whose determination had seemed uncertain, changed. Deaver says, "The real turning point in his mind was the day the Ford people had the mayors calling him to get out, the governors calling him to get out, and then the President suggested he should get out. That was it for him." That was a week before the March 23rd North Carolina primary. Deaver continues, "He became much more aggressive, more confident." Since Presidential-selection contests are not rational tests, such things matter. Reagan's wife, Nancy, a slim, attractive woman who is clearly her husband's political partner and who has perfected the adoring gaze, is with him this afternoon. Reagan does not tell the same pointless jokes he did earlier this year, but he has a new one—supposed to illustrate a point about communicating—which has to do with changing a baby's diaper. And his speech, formerly a grab bag of anecdotes and random points, has been pulled together into something fairly coherent. He still uses four-by-six cards, but the speech is different. He begins by saying, "I think it is time to point out that there are differences" between him and President Ford. Earlier in the year, he referred to Ford only indirectly. Now he says, "Mr. Ford has spent most of his adult life as a member of the Washington establishment." He objects to a Ford commercial now running in California which says that "Governor Ronald Reagan couldn't start a war, President Ronald Reagan could." The reference is to Reagan's recent suggestion that the United States might have to send troops to Rhodesia to be used as a peacekeeping force—a suggestion the President and his associates pounced on happily. Reagan later said that he had been answering a hypothetical question, and not advocating that American troops be sent to Rhodesia. These days, Reagan talks more about his experience as governor of California than he did in his speeches earlier in the year. His aides say that they learned through polls taken after the New Hampshire and Florida primaries that his strongest point was his record as governor of California. Actually, he was not a bad governor, though he sometimes seemed not very interested in his work. His tenure was less conservative than his rhetoric—perhaps because of his own lack of energy, the countervailing powers in California, and the inertial character of government. But it also seems to be a possibility that Reagan is less conservative than his rhetoric. It is hard to know what he really thinks, or how much he thinks about these things. But now he is trying to portray himself as a man sincerely interested in governing—a point on which, with reason, he has not been taken very seriously. So he talks about how much he did—for education, for medical care—and he sounds almost like a disciple of the Great Society.

Today, as he often does, he talks of his proposal, when he was governor, to turn back a budget surplus to the people. He quotes one government official as saying, "It's never been done," and he continues, "And I said, 'Well, they've never had an actor up here before.'" The line works with his audience; his aides say that it always does. As he did when I saw him earlier in the year, he gives an example of a ridiculous federal project—this one about a government-financed study of "the demography of happiness." He says the government spent two hundred and forty-nine thousand dollars "to find out it's better to be young, rich, and healthy than old, poor, and sick." He always delivers his lines smoothly, as well he might.

He talks about the increasing reliance on foreign sources of energy since Congress passed, and the President signed, the energy bill, and he concludes that the government "does its best for us when it does nothing." The audience applauds and cheers enthusiastically. Up to this point, the audience has been responsive but not very enthusiastic. Now, as he makes his way toward foreign policy and defense, it begins to get worked up. His aides say that their poll also showed that defense was the President's weakest issue, and so a decision was made to emphasize it. "The Canal Zone is sovereign United States territory every bit as much as is the State of Alaska," Reagan says. I remember when he was just beginning to try out the issue in Florida, and he and his aides noticed that it won big applause. Since then, as politicians do, he has worked on it and polished it and made it a staple. Now, strange as it may seem, the Panama Canal is one of the major issues of current American politics. "I don't believe the United States can afford to give up something that belongs to us because we've been threatened with trouble from a dictator," he says. Then he says, "The Soviet Union's Navy now outnumbers our own better than two to one in submarines and surface vessels." And then he says, "Détente has become a one-way street." As he strikes each chord, the audience responds. Referring to Ford's statement that the word "détente" would no longer be used, Reagan says, "He said the policy would remain the same. Well, it never was the word that disturbed us, it was the policy." He still makes the curious point that "housewives are told that they can't go to the market and buy breakfast food without being cheated unless there's a government agency to protect them." The style of his speech is still that of the nice guy, but he has dropped the nice-guy wording in favor of more ringing political rhetoric. "Let's put up a banner," he says, "and let's put some things on it that we believe in, and let's promise that we won't compromise our principles for political expediency." An aide says that if Reagan had made this speech in New Hampshire he would have won there, and he adds that if Reagan had won New Hampshire giving the old speech he would not be a candidate today, because he would not have become more aggressive. This speech was developed about two months ago. Reagan continues down the keyboard of conservative chords. "It's time to give the schools back to the states and to the local school districts, where they belong," he says. And then comes his biggest applause of the afternoon—an aide tells me to get ready, that it always comes at this point—when he says, "And who knows? If we can get Washington out of the classroom, maybe we can get God back in." He manages to strike a nerve about Vietnam. "We committed a great immorality in the last decade," he says. To Reagan, the immorality is not what it is to some people. He says we must vow "that never again will we ask young men to fight and die for their country unless it is for a cause this country intends to win." The line gets the second-biggest applause of the afternoon. Now the Reagan race for the nomination has changed from a sport, from something he almost had to do to maintain his credentials— and livelihood—as the conservative spokesman, to a real challenge to the President. He is not a very serious or a very well-informed man, and he does not seem to be interested in informing himself, nor does his particular following care whether he is well informed. His new speech notwithstanding, his appeal has to do not with competence at governing but with the emotion he evokes. Reagan lets people get out their anger and frustration, their feeling of being misunderstood and mishandled by those who have run our government, their impatience with taxes and with the poor and the weak, their impulse to deal with the world's troublemakers by employing the stratagem of a punch in the nose. Reagan, whether his subject is welfare mothers or the Russians, appeals to the basic human desire to feel superior. This year has taught us not to underestimate him.

JUNE 7

Monday morning. The Convention Center in downtown Cincinnati. About fourteen hundred Hamilton Country Republicans have gathered for a breakfast of juice, hard scrambled eggs, sausage links, bland rolls, and coffee with the President. A minister giving the invocation thanks God for this Bicentennial Year and asks God to "bless our great Republican Party" and grant victory in November. A combo off to one side plays "Sweet Sue" and "Down by the O-Hi-O." It seems a bit early in the morning for that. The President, dressed in a navy-blue suit and vest and a blue shirt, sits on the dais under a blue-and-white banner that says "President Ford '76." Yesterday, he was in New Jersey and then in Cleveland, and he arrived here last night just as the late-evening news was coming on the air. The Cincinnati *Enquirer* endorsed him yesterday for the second time. He is flanked by local and state Party officials, including Governor James Rhodes, Senator Robert Taft, Jr., and local congressmen. Earl Barnes, the county chairman, says that Hamilton County Republicans are "united enthusiastically behind President Ford." This sort of official backing by Party leaders, working from the top down, is what the President has been relying on all year, rather than on popular sentiment rising up to the leaders. In Ohio, he is in pretty good hands, because its Party is one of the few state Republican Parties with machinery in good working order. The officials may well prefer Gerald Ford to Ronald Reagan—they probably do, since he is more their type—but there is also the fact that Reagan's ascension could cost the elected officials their seats and the unelected officials their jobs. Fifteen of the twenty-three members of the House from Ohio are Republicans. The back-yard principle is at work. Barnes sent out a newsletter last month reminding Hamilton County Republicans of the "disastrous" results of the 1964 election and asserting that, even though some people say there are distinctions between 1964 and 1976, "I am firmly convinced that the Republican Party cannot afford the luxury of taking such an awesome risk." Governor Rhodes, in his remarks this morning, says, "This is a meeting of the SOS Club—save our seats." No man for subtlety, Governor Rhodes reminds the audience that President Ford has recently promised the construction in Portsmouth, Ohio, of a plant to provide enriched uranium for nuclear fuel. Ohioans are to see this as a gift. My home area is supposed to be pleased that the President is providing it with a plant that can help blow up the world. The construction of the plant alone, Governor Rhodes says, will provide five thousand jobs. The Governor also points to the construction of the Appalachian Highway—actually a network of highways connecting southern Ohio and various parts of the Appalachian region—and says that when it is finished "they will pour into Cincinnati to spend their money." President Ford, he says, "has given us more money and more latitude in the highway fund than any other President." President Ford likes the highway program, and, even in the midst of trying to hold down spending last year, released money for it. Senator Taft, who is up for reëlection this year, and who lost a race for the Senate in 1964, says that to him President Ford's nomination is "a matter of saving our country."

When Ford leaves here, he will travel by motorcade to Toledo, at the northwest end of the state—a trip of about two hundred and thirty miles, counting side trips, which is scheduled to take ten and a half hours. No one drives from Cincinnati to Toledo if he doesn't have to ("Are you joining up for our death march?" a White House aide asked me last night), but some campaign aides say the President could not afford another whistle-stop train, and his strategists and some congressmen from the area thought it important that he shore up his support in the western part of the state. So the President of the United States will spend a day driving from Cincinnati to Toledo.

In his remarks to the breakfast group, the President commends, "the finest Repulican organization in any part of the country." He says that, being from Michigan, "I'm very, very much in favor of a strong and prosperous automobile industry," and that "in 1976 I don't want to see a reliable Ford turned in for a flashier model." The President seems far more relaxed than when he first began to campaign. He looks tired, but he speaks more forcefully than before. He praises his Administration's record on the economy. He says that public trust and public confidence in the White House have been restored, "because of the candor and frankness and forthrightness of the Ford Administration." He says that his vetoes have saved the taxpayers thirteen billion dollars. He says that "we have the military capability to maintain the peace." He says that "not a single American boy is fighting and dying on foreign soil under this Administration," and he adds, for good measure, that "the Ford Administration is not going to send any troops to southern Africa or to Rhodesia." He is striking the notes that are supposed to work for an incumbent President: peace and prosperity. Also safety. We are safe with him, he tells us. But his grip has been unsteady. He speaks his familiar line about what is happening in the economy: "Everything that is supposed to be going up is going up and everything that is supposed to go down is going down." He refers to "the tragedy of 1964," and says that Senator Taft, like him, remembers the tragedy of 1964. The President says that if he is nominated "we can have a total Republican victory from the White House down to the courthouse." He is pleading, selling himself, telling these people that their fate is wrapped up with his. As a politician, he knows what matters to other politicians. "There is no question in my mind whatsoever that I can be elected," the President says. After he finishes, the combo plays "When You're Smiling."

Before the President leaves on the motorcade, he has some meetings with small groups and grants some television interviews. Over the weekend, he invited Ohio radio broadcasters to the White House to interview him (they applauded him at the end of the interview), and yesterday he appeared on *Face the Nation* (on which he talked about his Administration's current efforts to draw up legislation to limit the scope of court orders on busing, and upheld for private schools that do not receive federal funds the right to discriminate: a position contrary to one that his Justice Department is taking in court, but a position that Carter has also taken).

In a small room at the Cincinnati Convention Center, the President meets with about thirty labor leaders, most of them from the construction unions. They all sit in a circle on metal folding chairs. It is a very democratic scene. The President gives a little talk about his economic policies and says he thinks that unemployment is still too high, particularly in the construction trades. He points out that he has proposed two hundred nuclear power plants, and that it takes "a lot of jobs not only to build them but to operate them." (Actually, his energy program envisions the building of these plants by private companies.) He says that he submitted to Congress a request for one hundred and seventy-eight million dollars for the Portsmouth uranium-enrichment plant. The union leaders complain that the building of nuclear power plants is being held up by bureaucratic red tape, and the President agrees. They tell him they want national health insurance, and he disagrees, telling them that it would end up costing just as much as their private insurance. But the President is successful in talking with these people, because he is a truly unaffected man, and he listens. He agrees that minority hiring should be required of unorganized as well as organized labor —something that would seem to be rather difficult—and asks an aide to make a note of that.

As we go down the hall to the next meeting—the President surrounded by Secret Service agents, advance men, his physician, carrying a black case, and his military aide, also carrying a black case—we come upon a man standing at a microphone holding up a card. As the President reaches the man, the man says into the microphone, reading from the card, getting it just right—and it is piped into the next room—"Ladies and gentlemen, the President of the United States." I had always wondered how that was done. As the man makes his announcement, a band in the room strikes up. Standing around in the room are elected officials, ward chairmen, Party officials, and some business leaders, such as the chairman of the board of Procter & Gamble. There was a certain amount of fuss over who would be invited to this event: people do want to meet the

President—any President. Governor Rhodes says to the President, "When these people say yes, they deliver." A local politician tells me that this is true—that there is still a lot of courthouse patronage in Hamilton County. The President reminds them in some brief remarks, of "the clobbering in 1964," and says, "We can win. I can be elected."

Next, the President tapes three television interviews of about eight minutes each. He used to give a half-hour interview to three interviewers at once, from different stations, but then his advisers noticed that each interviewer would broadcast only a minute or two—when he was asking the President a question. So now the interviews are granted separately for a shorter period, and are considered very successful. "The local stations play hell out of them," says Robert Mead, the President's television adviser, who was formerly a producer for CBS. A mock studio has been set up at the Convention Center, with the usual sofa, coffee table, and two end tables with matching lamps. The President asks his first interviewer, Robert Braun, if he should call him Bob. They make small talk about Hank Aaron. Then the interview begins.

"Mr. President, welcome back to Ohio," Braun begins.

"It's good to see you, Bob," the President replies.

Bob recalls that the President once autographed a baseball for him at the Cincinnati stadium.

The President observes that last year's World Series was a "humdinger," and he praises the Cincinnati Reds for "their competence and their leadership and their ability to come through when the chips were down."

Bob expresses pleasure over the uranium-enrichment plant, and he asks, "How about the Appalachian Highway, Mr. President?"

The President says that he recently signed a bill authorizing two hundred million dollars for highway construction.

The President is then asked what he thinks of those who say that the issues are not important, and he replies, "I have a lot of confidence in the American people, Bob. They know what's right and what is wrong in a legislative way."

Bob observes that the President seems to be "more committed to permanent employment as opposed to stopgap measures or jobs for six months."

The President replies, "Bob, you put it better than I can." The President looks Bob in the eye, as if he were really interested in talking to him. He must be getting tired of these interviews.

Invited to make his own closing, the President says, "I've entered every primary," which sounds startlingly like Jimmy Carter, and then, "We've restored trust and confidence," and then, "We've been able to achieve the peace."

Having learned that he should call the next interviewer Tom, the President calls him Bob. It is understandable that he can't keep all these names straight.

Tom, after observing that "Cincinnati has a vested interest," asks, "Are we going to get the B-1?" The General Electric plant near Cincinnati would make the engines for the B-1.

The President replies, "I certainly hope so. . . . We have to have the B-1." The President of the United States comes to my home town bearing a uranium-enrichment plant, a highway, and the B-1 bomber.

The third interviewer, whom he remembers to call Al (he also has to remember to make his main point in each interview, which is that he is going to win in Ohio and can win in November), asks if it isn't "the sort of doubletalk which has made a lot of people cynical about politics" that he is cutting up Reagan and also saying that Reagan might be his Vice-Presidential choice.

"Not at all, Al," the President responds, and he explains that the Vice-President doesn't make policy decisions, and suggests that "a little experience in Washington might moderate" Reagan's views.

The President tells Al that he enjoyed the interview, which is what interviewees are supposed to say. And then he returns to his hotel room to prepare for his ten-and-a-half-hour motorcade to Toledo.

It is a lovely day—good for a motorcade, if one has the misfortune to have to go on one. Shortly before noon, people are out in Fountain Square, reading and lazing in the sun. A couple from Americus, Georgia, are passing out leaflets for Jimmy Carter. The Carter campaign in Ohio is being directed by Timothy Kraft, who also directed the Carter campaigns in Iowa, Pennsylvania, and Michigan. Kraft, a soft-spoken young man with a Pancho Villa mustache and a crinkly-eyed smile, worked in the 1974 campaign of Governor Jerry Apodaca, of New Mexico, and was among the people Carter made contact with during his travels that year on behalf of Democratic candidates. He is one of the skilled political technicians who have been helping Carter pile up his victories. He arrived in Ohio three weeks ago and called in twenty-five workers.

They were to move in quietly and politely on local chairmen who might not be inclined to be very active. He tells me that the Carter campaign has been blessed with middle-level workers—some of them students, who "intern" at a hundred and twenty-five dollars a month, others people who work for anywhere from fifty to a hundred dollars a week. These workers fan out into the congressional districts. They work with local organizations, obtain lists of Democratic households, operate phone banks to canvass and get out the vote; they get volunteers active in spreading literature about Jimmy Carter. The Carter campaign is canvassing voters in Ohio to ascertain their preferences and the degree of their fervor, and getting supporters of their candidate to the polls—a technique that used to be employed just for smaller states—but the Udall organization is not doing that here. The Udall campaign's emphasis is on winning people away from Carter. The purpose of the local Carter organization is not only to influence voters directly but to create an appearance of activity and enthusiasm for the Carter campaign. The theory is that people are impressed by signs of activity and enthusiasm. One hundred Georgians have also come into the state—as they came into other primary states—spreading the word about Jimmy Carter.

Carter has been in good spirits today. He is human, and tomorrow marks the end of the gruelling primary season. This morning, he said to a worker at a plant gate in Cleveland, "Only one more day, God love you." But he was also sufficiently tired to confuse Ohio with New Jersey at one point. Actually, it is a wonder he knows where he is as much as he does. It has been a long way from New Hampshire to this warm afternoon in Cincinnati. Next, he will attend a rally in Akron and then make some stops in New Jersey, and tomorrow he will fly to Atlanta to await the returns from the final primaries. If he does well enough tomorrow—and it appears that he will—he will have a good chance of being nominated on the first ballot. If he does not win on the first ballot, there are many people who doubt whether he will win at all, on the theory that his reservoir of good will is small within the Party and that recent primary results raise the question of how well he stands up under close scrutiny. His campaign staff has been concerned enough about his image so that it bought five minutes of time last night on all three networks. One reason was that a nationwide telecast proved to be not much more expensive than statewide broadcasts in New Jersey, Ohio, and California. But it was also said that Carter's aides felt he was coming across as too mechanistic, counting up his victories and his delegates, and talking about the mechanics of his campaign instead of about what he stood for, and they blamed television for this. In part, they are right; television has tended to cover the horse-race aspect of the campaign, and, even when the candidate talks about other things, to excerpt the section where, in response to a question, he is telling how he thinks he is doing. In part, however, television shows Carter as having a mechanistic approach to the campaign because Carter has a mechanistic approach to the campaign. He chose to approach it that way, relentlessly moving from state to state, and telling us how well he is doing, and avoiding issues, and giving essentially the same speech over and over. Television won't repeat the same speech—won't even show it once at any length. Carter has moved through the nomination contest making an unusual kind of speech in a distinctive way, and yet people I know, frequent television watchers, have never seen or heard this speech.

When Carter arrived at the Cincinnati airport today, he predicted that he would win on the first ballot. He said the same thing in New Hampshire, but now he has more reason. For all we know, he was just as confident then. When he was asked a joking question about peanuts, he replied, "I think a lot of people have become more aware of the presence of peanuts in this country this year. I think that the image of a peanut, which is a crop that I grow, being kind of small and insignificant but cumulatively being very important to the American people is one that fairly accurately mirrors the kind of campaign that we've run."

The close of Carter's campaign for the nomination leaves us with the same sorts of questions we have had all along. The main question, of course, has to do with how he would be at governing—what he would do with the power he has worked so doggedly to win. The causes for concern are fairly familiar now: the doggedness itself, the humorlessness, the almost unnatural self-assurance. We still do not know whether he has the requisite flexibility to govern. Governing a complicated nation amid a variety of interests that are determined to get their way, are working at cross-purposes, and are willing to play very rough—which is what trying to govern America is like—requires doggedness and self-assurance. The question is how much is enough, and no one can even guess what a man will do until he has been put to a number of tests. Try as we may, we cannot, as we have learned, anticipate a would-be leader's behavior in important situations. We still do not know how he would react to difficult challenges. We have seen that Jimmy Carter does not like challenges, does not take to them very well. He has made it clear that he seeks power and intends to use it. That can be good and that can be bad. On the one hand, if we want change, governing this country requires the tough use of power. On the other hand, the mistakes of an activist President can be greater than the mistakes of a passive President. The manner in which Carter has negotiated his way toward the nomination could be good and it could be bad: it could mean that the support of different groups he has gathered up behind him will be used to get things done; it could mean that he does not stand for anything except winning. It is my own impression, from watching him, that when he talks about the blacks and the poor deserving more justice he means it. It is something that seems not to be lately acquired but to come from deep in his roots. And there is no reason to think that the same determination he brought to winning the nomination would not be applied to the next stages of his political career: to winning the election and to governing. This is not to venture into the "grow-in-office" school, which has proved so disastrously wrong. It is not to suggest that Carter will change. On the contrary, it is to suggest that his ambition will continue to propel him. The question is, toward what? One cannot rule out the possibility that he will want as desperately to be a good and effective President as he wanted to be President. He seems to have an absorbent and agile, if somewhat superficial, mind, more technical than creative. His instincts on the war in Vietnam raise questions. He has not been on the cutting edge of anything except his own ambition. But then there is room in our public life for consolidators, especially when there is so much to consolidate. Perhaps he will use his relative independence from interest groups to move some of the furniture around, or perhaps he will surrender that independence. Perhaps he will squander his time and energy and political support on his misguided idea of combining nineteen hundred government agencies, or however many there are, into two hundred. Some reorganization is in order, but it will solve fewer problems than he thinks and will raise new problems. Carter is cold, and he can be mean, and even vindictive, but so have other people been to whom we have comfortably entrusted power. We have seen that he does not wear particularly well—or, at least, that he hasn't up to now. He has said that he wants to curb nuclear proliferation and to provide more social justice and jobs and health care and to reform the tax code and to revise our relationships with the developing nations and to bring about more open government. It is not out of the question that he means to at least try to do these things. Perhaps he is as serious about them as he was when he said, long ago, that he intended to be President.

This afternoon, Carter is to appear at the Vernon Manor, a residential hotel where, when I was growing up, our family went for dinner once in a while, and where my friends occasionally held little parties. Some proper young things were sent to the Vernon Manor to learn ballroom dancing from Mme. (Fifi) Federova. Now the Vernon Manor looks a bit shabby—genteel shabby—but perhaps it always did and I just didn't notice. In the bar, the television set is tuned to the station at which Jimmy Carter is to be interviewed before he comes here. His interviewer, it turns out, is Bob—the Bob who questioned the President this morning. After Bob holds up a box of Pampers and extols their virtues, he introduces "the front-runner" for the Democratic nomination. Bob invites Carter to tell about how his family campaigned for him, and observes that "it must take a supportive family" to do that. Carter agrees. He does not call him Bob. Bob says that he does not think Carter has been fuzzy on the issues, and invites Carter to speak about that. Carter alludes to Udall, whom he does not name, as running a "negative campaign," and says that people don't take well to that—and he may be correct—and then he uses the opportunity to make some of his points: that he is for zero-based budgeting; that he would never get involved in the internal affairs of another country unless our security was at stake; that he would never give up control of the Panama Canal, though he would renegotiate the treaty. He says that members of his Cabinet would go before joint sessions of Congress to answer questions and that if they ever made a misleading statement he would get rid of them. He has his points down, and he is good at this. Invited to make closing remarks, he says—just as he said way back in New Hampshire— that he "will never tell a lie, never betray a trust."

In the Garden Room of the Vernon Manor, Carter addresses a group of black leaders. Standing behind a low lectern, he tells them, "I could not have chosen a better way to spend the last day of a campaign than to come here and meet with you and other people in Ohio." And he talks, as he has talked so many times before, about his long campaign, which he says began sixteen and a half months ago. Once more, he makes virtues of his necessities: he campaigned almost everywhere, but that was because he had to; he did not plan his campaign "on endorsements of powerful political people," but then he was not in a position to get them. He talks here, as he talked in Los Angeles to campaign contributors, about the advantages that the wealthy and the powerful have. He goes through many of the litanies he went through there, and has gone through countless times, including the litany about the C.I.A. and Watergate and the other things that went wrong, and the "my government and your government" litany. He tells the black leaders, as he has told countless audiences of different kinds across the country, "Most of us feel that there's a kind of wall built around Washington that we can't quite get through." Again, he does not make a speech—he weaves a spell. His gray suit is a bit frayed, and one is struck again by how slight he is. As he has done other times, he rearranges his speech for the audience before him—today invoking the name of John Kennedy, and stressing the support he himself has had from such black leaders as Andrew Young and Martin Luther King, Sr. He says, "I would rather lose the election, I would almost rather lose my life, than to let down someone like Dr. Martin Luther King, Sr." And he is applauded. But he does not preach, as I saw him do earlier this year in a black church in Chicago. This is a sophisticated group, interested in questions of programs and power. When he finished speaking, and before he takes questions, he draws a deep breath. These would have to be long, hard days even if they did not come on top of hundreds of days like them. And only a phase is drawing to an end. Next, there is the Convention, and, if he is successful, there will be the Presidential campaign. His answers to questions are similar to the answers he gave to questions when I first saw him, before the Urban Coalition in Washington in January. He talks with assurance and apparent knowledge about federal programs. He was, after all, a governor. He talks about the way he improved the delivery of health services to poor people in Georgia. (He no longer talks about a government program under which people might call in and complain about short-weight chickens.) And he manages to sound knowledgeable even when it is not clear that he knows what he is talking about; his version of the history of Angola—that the Russians and the Cubans had been there for ten years, that they sent doctors and nurses—seems questionable. He comes out against making Shirley Temple Black an ambassador to a country in Africa. Laughter and applause. He says that he will clear sensitive appointments "with strong spokesmen for the disadvantaged groups," and he tells the audience that tomorrow "you will decide to let other people make the decision for you or whether you will shape your own country, your own nation, your own government, and your own life." He says that he wants to "give us a government"—he pauses, as if deciding whether to go through his most familiar litany and then deciding not to (perhaps he is getting tired of it)—"as good as you are."

16

Tonight's returns present a mixed picture. Carter is winning Ohio by a substantial margin, but he is losing New Jersey to the uncommitted slate, which is either Hubert Humphrey or Jerry Brown—probably heavily Brown, since Brown campaigned there yesterday and drew large and enthusiastic crowds. This invites further consideration of what might have been if Brown had entered the race earlier. There are many what-ifs, but it is too late. Carter, as expected, is losing to Brown in California. Carter had spent some time there last week and had invested two hundred and eighty thousand dollars in advertising in the state, and even so Brown's margin over Carter may be three to one. Carter, on television late tonight, appears unperturbed—as he must—but subdued. He smiles from time to time (that automatic public smile), but still he seems subdued. On being asked what he thinks Senator Humphrey will do— Humphrey said three days ago that he was still considering entering the race and would decide within ten days after the final primaries —he says, "It's hard to predict what Senator Humphrey will do. He's made this announcement every week." Then he says, "I feel good about the prospective results of the first ballot." He says that he spoke with the other candidates today, and he says, "I don't think it will go all the way up to the Convention." He starts to list the number of uncommitted delegates in Hawaii, in Alaska . . .

Udall, who on the last day of the campaign stopped attacking Carter, says on television tonight, "I want to finish up the process with honor and dignity and a sense of humor." He seems to be trying to make a recovery from the damage of a bruising Presidential campaign. And yet, perhaps naturally, he still sees himself as a force, cannot let go. "I want to influence the platform," he says. "I want to influence where my country's going." He also remarks that "the political commentators have a scoreboard mentality." He says that the Carter people are "shrewd" and probably have "some prominent bandwagon jumpers ready to jump tomorrow."

Today, in an exquisite piece of timing, Mayor Daley said that if Carter won Ohio he would be the nominee. The Mayor's statement was issued not so soon that it would antagonize voters—Carter having made such a point of running without the support of the "bosses"—but soon enough for Daley to at least have a hand in anointing Carter. Daley, of course, is tending to his own back yard. He wants the Democrats to carry Illinois so that, among other things, his candidate for governor will win. Of Carter, Daley said, "He started out months ago and entered into every contest in every state and he won 'em and he lost 'em and, by God, you have to admire a guy like that." He also said that he admired Carter for injecting "a religious tone" into the campaign. And he sounded the death knell for Hubert Humphrey's ambitions. (Many of us had forgotten that Daley has nursed a grievance against Humphrey ever since Humphrey criticized him for the handling of the 1968 Democratic Convention.) Today, Daley said of Humphrey, "Who says he . . . should be a man on a white horse? Our Party isn't in bad enough shape to have to go to someone and demand him and draft him."

On television tonight, Frank Church looks exhausted. Ordinarily an articulate man, he talks hesitantly and confuses some of his words. He says he told Carter today that "he had established an entitlement that it would be hard for the Convention to deny." Asked about the Vice-Presidency, Church says, "Yes, I've thought about it," and adds, "It's presumptuous to think about the Vice-Presidency." He says he is not conceding. Neither he nor Udall is quite ready to give up. Nor, clearly, is Jerry Brown. Exhilarated, Brown says, "Every state I've gone into, Jimmy Carter's lost. So I will go forward. . . . The Democratic contest is still on." He says he will go to Louisiana, where there are still nineteen uncommitted delegates (whom Carter has been wooing). He is worked up tonight, and seems very young. He talks excitedly. "The American people have begun to question what Carter is saying, if he's saying anything at all," Brown says. "I recognize it's an uphill battle, it's a long shot." Then he challenges Carter to a debate, and says, "I'm not trying to smile away the profound and difficult economic and ecological problems this country faces."

The Republican returns left everything uncertain. As had been expected, the President carried Ohio and New Jersey, and Reagan carried California, but Reagan didn't do very well in Ohio after all.

He didn't get any delegates in Cincinnati, and got only nine delegates in the state. Now the President of the United States will fight it out, delegate by delegate, in the remaining state conventions and among the uncommitted delegates. This may be a nice time for an uncommitted delegate, but it's not such a nice time for the President of the United States.

JUNE 9

Today, the walls came tumbling down. Politicians fell over each other rushing to Jimmy Carter's side. They may not love him any more than they did earlier in the year, but they scrambled to line up with him before it was too late—if it wasn't already. The reaction was a psychological one, which didn't have much to do with the figures in last night's results—couldn't have, since Carter didn't do so well. He lost to an uncommitted slate in New Jersey, and Brown beat him in California by more than a million votes. But there was no one else who could get the nomination. Mayor Daley had lowered the boom on Hubert Humphrey's hopes, and today Humphrey made a terse statement taking himself out of the race once and for all. "The primaries now are over, and Governor Carter has a commanding lead," said Humphrey, giving recognition to something he had hoped he would never have to recognize. "He is virtually certain to be our party's nominee." And so Humphrey—one would assume, once and for all—put his Presidential ambitions away. Now he can turn, without distraction, to trying to become Majority Leader of the Senate. George Wallace, of all people, led the rush to Carter last night, when he telephoned him to offer his support. Today, in Montgomery, Alabama, Wallace said to the press, "The people want Carter, and he's entitled to the nomination." Wallace, over whose crippled body Carter almost literally strode in his struggle to be nominated, who was embittered by this man who he felt had used and then humiliated him, was clever enough or magnanimous enough, or whatever, to acknowledge the inevitable. Today, Wallace recalled that "in the heat of the campaign" he had called Carter "a liar," but now he said, "We've got to overlook many things. He'll make a fine candidate." Henry Jackson, with whom Carter has recently held several conversations, agreed today to throw his support to Carter. Mayor Daley said, "The ballgame is over." Senator Stevenson, in whose name Daley held eighty-six delegates, released them. Edward Kennedy said, "I expect the nominee will be Mr. Carter." Carter, dressed in denims at a press conference in Plains, said that his nomination was "as certain as it can be under the particular circumstances."

President Ford met with advisers and then went to the White House Rose Garden and told reporters that he is "electable." This Friday, he will fly to Springfield, Missouri, a thousand miles away, where nineteen at-large delegates are to be chosen at a state convention.

Proposition 15, the item on the California ballot which would have sharply limited the development of nuclear energy in the state, was defeated by about two to one. The proposition was opposed by utility companies in California and other states, and also by the Atomic Industrial Forum, an international association of corporations, labor unions, engineers, and researchers in the nuclear-energy field, and by some separate labor groups. Around four million dollars was spent on advertising about the issue, three million of it by opponents. Moreover, the bills recently signed into law by Brown which set less severe restrictions on nuclear-energy development eased the way for the defeat of Proposition 15. But both sides conceded that the fight over the development of nuclear energy in this country would be carried on in the future in a number of other states. The Energy Research and Development Administration, which includes the part of the former Atomic Energy Commission that was to promote the development of nuclear energy, has prepared a pamphlet (it was distributed in California) answering the "myths" that are used as arguments against the development of nuclear power.

JUNE 11

Uttering magnanimous-sounding statements, Democratic politicians continued to race toward the winner. Senator Robert Byrd released thirty-one delegates he had held as West Virginia's favorite son—at one time he apparently pictured himself as a "broker"—saying he did it "in the interest of Party unity." Philadelphia Mayor Frank Rizzo, Carter's Pennsylvania foil, said that to deprive Carter of the nomination "would make a mockery of the Presidential-primary system" and that "I am pleased to be on the Carter team." Senator Lloyd Bentsen, who had already released his six Texas delegates, and who was long ago a Presidential contender, said that Carter offers the Party "its best hope of regaining the White House and giving the nation the type of leadership it deserves." And the Marine Engineers' Beneficial Association announced its support of Carter and released a letter, written a couple of weeks ago, in which Carter promised to develop "a maritime program which will return us to the seapower status we deserve and need." In Louisiana, however, Governor Edwin Edwards gave Jerry Brown the support of eighteen of the state's nineteen uncommitted delegates.

It is odd how our view of things changes. For example, George Wallace's endorsement of Jimmy Carter was not considered the kiss of death. The sting has gone out of the old demagogue, and in his collapse as a national force he has won a kind of respectability. There was a time last year when people were constructing plots in which Wallace might capture the Democratic nomination. As for the Republican race, there is a view that there is something bad about the fact that the President of the United States has to fight for the nomination. But I wonder whether so many people would hold that view if more people were sympathetic to Reagan. We used to despair at the idea that incumbent Presidents were beyond challenge.

Jimmy Carter has shown that there may be no such thing as a Democratic Party. Whatever there was that called itself a party was opposed to his nomination but was powerless before his assault. The week saw the old titans of the Party capitulating in profusion and rushing to his side. First Eugene McCarthy and then George McGovern had led the way in showing the vulnerability of the Party. Their followers had opened up the Party rules. The resistance of the traditional Party powers—political leaders and old-line labor leaders—to the changes in the rules was, from their point of view, well founded. Then the campaign-finance-reform laws turned money into a far less important factor. And so the self-appointed candidate whom no important members of the Party wanted—not elected officials, not Party officials, none of the old Party powers— captured the prize while they looked on helplessly.

JUNE 13

In the Missouri Republican state convention yesterday, Reagan won eighteen of the nineteen at-large delegates. The one Ford delegate was the governor, Christopher Bond—for whom the Reagan forces arranged a place at the Convention, which will be held in his state. Both Ford and Reagan had spoken to the delegates in Springfield.

And yesterday afternoon Jimmy Carter went to Montgomery, Alabama, to pay a call on George Wallace. Carter, in answer to a reporter's question, said, "I don't think there's any doubt" that Wallace gave Southern politicians national acceptability. Wallace, asked if he was bitter, said that he was not. "We have to realize that we can't win all the time," he said. "I lost. The people voted for Carter. . . . That was it."

JUNE 16

The platform that the Democratic Party's Platform Committee finished drafting last night at the Mayflower Hotel in Washington— a day sooner than had been expected—reflects the politics of this year. Like earlier party platforms, it contains a long list of new things to be done, programs to be enacted, and concessions to the party's interest groups, but the tone is cautious and "sensible." Interest groups fight for representation of their purposes in a party's platform because they see the platform as a legitimizer of issues, as moving issues forward on the public agenda. Platforms can be "realistic" or they can be "visionary," and this year's Democratic platform is, relatively speaking, "realistic." It is, on the whole, Jimmy Carter's platform. Carter had asked the Party not to enact a "wish box or Christmas tree" for a platform, and to some extent the Party acceded. But that was mainly because Carter had the votes in the Platform Committee. In line with Carter's coalition politics, compromises were struck with other forces to keep them happy. Still, the platform also reflected the fact that while much of this year's political rhetoric is negative about big federal government and federal programs, as a practical matter programs—more programs—continued to be favored. And so this platform advocates a number of new initiatives, and bows to various interest groups, without, as some had urged, indicating what the priorities are or what the costs will be. It has no focus, offers no sense of some overriding public purpose. Just about everyone could come away saying he had won something. Potential schisms were papered over by the Carter forces through a combination of exercising influence and compromising; and the sweet smell of success—the idea that the Democrats, if they behaved, might actually inhabit the White House once again—mellowed the usually fractious Party.

A report by the staff of the United Nations World Food Council, which is meeting in Rome this week, predicted that there will be a world food disaster by 1985 unless many nations change their policies and more international coöperation is obtained. It said that "food imports of the developing countries have risen alarmingly, their nutritional problems have grown, and their production performance has not improved." The Washington *Post* quotes a United Nations official as saying, "The world food problem is enormously political. Almost everything that governments do in the agricultural area has domestic political repercussions. The result is that the situation is getting worse and there are no political leaders anywhere with a high level of concern."

JUNE 17

Earlier this year, it was considered quite an achievement that Congress, in its annual bill to provide military assistance to foreign nations, had included provisions to limit the amount of that assistance and to give Congress more of a voice in nongovernmental commercial arms transactions. Mild as these provisions were, the President vetoed the bill, and now Congress is working on a new bill, which accedes to his demands. Among the provisions that have been dropped were one that limited to a total of nine billion dollars the amount of military assistance and services that could be transferred by the government or through commercial transactions in one year and one that allowed Congress to veto certain of these transactions. The new bill does include an amendment that represents Congress's first attempt to slow down nuclear proliferation. The amendment, sponsored by Senator Stuart Symington, Democrat of Missouri, would cut off military and economic assistance to any country that delivers nuclear-enrichment or reprocessing equipment to or receives it from any other country. This equipment enables a country to produce a nuclear bomb by enriching uranium or by extracting plutonium from the spent fuel that results from the operations of nuclear reactors. Because the Administration has objected to the provision, Congress, typically, is adding a section that permits the President to waive it under certain conditions. The amendment is aimed at Pakistan, which is buying a reprocessing plant from France, and at Brazil, which is buying one from West Germany. South Korea, yielding to pressure from the United States, earlier this year dropped plans to buy a nuclear-reprocessing plant from France. Partly as a result of protests voiced by members of Congress to General Electric's proposed sale of two nuclear reactors to South Africa, South Africa will purchase reactors from France instead. Yesterday, Albert Wohlstetter, a professor of political science at the University of Chicago who recently did a study for the Arms Control and Disarmament Agency, told a House committee that by 1985 about forty countries will have nuclear-energy programs yielding enough spent fuel to provide them with nuclear bombs. He pointed out that without any violation of international controls any country's spent fuel could in a few days be developed into a bomb.

The military-assistance bill authorizes economic assistance for Zaire and Zambia amounting to about twenty-seven million dollars apiece, and additional funds for other African nations that have been harmed by participating in the economic boycott of Rhodesia. The New York *Times* reported a few days ago that the United States has agreed to discuss plans for military-aid programs for Kenya and Zaire in order to offset what our government sees as a growing Soviet influence in Africa.

JUNE 20

Yesterday, in Iowa, President Ford won nineteen delegates and Ronald Reagan won seventeen. The President's aides indicated that they considered this an achievement, given the President's near wipeout in Missouri a week ago, but they conceded that they had hoped the President would do better. Yesterday, too, Reagan won thirty-one of thirty-eight delegates selected in Washington, all three delegates selected in Colorado's Second Congressional District, and all four of the at-large delegates in Texas. The President won thirteen of seventeen delegates selected in Delaware. Delegate counts now show the President leading Reagan by less than a hundred votes, with several states still to select their delegates. The President cancelled a weekend trip he had planned to make to Iowa, where he would have confronted Reagan for the first time, so as to stay at the White House during a military evacuation of American civilians from Lebanon, which had been decided upon Friday after the

American Ambassador to Lebanon and an economic adviser were murdered by unidentified gunmen. The whole exercise, of course, raised the suspicion that the President was putting on an election-year show—playing Commander-in-Chief—which is a suspicion that has dogged other Presidents. The problem is that it is so difficult to know when a crisis is real that in a real one we may be too suspicious. The White House released photographs over the week-end showing the President and his top aides poring over maps. In all, slightly more than a hundred Americans elected to leave Lebanon, and about fifteen hundred elected to stay.

SUMMER

17

Tuesday. On the House of Representatives' side of the Capitol, just before noon, House Democratic leaders, looking very solemn, are coming from a meeting with some other House Democrats to decide what to do about a recent embarrassment. The embarrassment stemmed from the publication of allegations by Elizabeth Ray, a former employee of Representative Wayne Hays, of Ohio, the powerful, feared, and disliked chairman of the House Administration Committee, that she had been hired, and paid fourteen thousand dollars a year, for the sole purpose of being his mistress. Sex on Capitol Hill had hardly been a secret in Washington, and the situation perhaps differed only in degree from other situations in which men of power were in a position to exploit impressionable or ambitious women. Congress is said to be in this respect a pale imitation of state legislatures. In any event, there are many men in Congress —rather ordinary men—whose families do not live in Washington and who suddenly find themselves considered glamorous by young women impressed by their power. Moreover, members of Congress, with their special elevators, their special perquisites, become accustomed to being paid deference. Capitol Hill has a kind of plantation aura. There is no job protection for the staffs, and most staff members are expected to pay homage; the House dining room is run by underpaid and unprotected workers from whom obsequiousness is expected. Hays was a well-known bully, but he took care of his colleagues, and so most of them shrugged. There are, of course, a great many serious, responsible people in Congress—more than is generally recognized. But the plantation aura is there, and Wayne Hays was one of the masters. Hays' particular power was handed him— heaped upon him—by the House, which is now proceeding to take it away. Under pressure, he has already resigned as chairman of the House Administration Committee, and of the House Democratic National Congressional Committee, which distributes campaign funds. No Democrat now wants Hays' signature on a campaign-fund check. And today the Democrats, working fast, are about to remove from the Administration Committee power that they happily gave it in recent years—power to set House members' perquisites, such as stationery allowances and government-paid trips home, so that the members would not be subject to charges of taking too good care of themselves by voting for these things on the House floor. The proposals for change aren't very important, and have almost nothing to do with the real problems in making Congress an effective institution—problems of leadership and of outmoded committee jurisdictions and of conflicts of interest and of indebtedness to the large contributors.

Nevertheless, embarrassment and worry are powerful motivating forces, and a House of Representatives that has been unable to bring itself to do very much this year about anything that matters is working fast on these "reforms." For some members, the Ray-Hays problem caused extreme cases of there-but-for-the-grace nerves. There was no telling how many other current or former employees would be emboldened to speak out. But guilt or innocence was almost immaterial; in an election year in which so many signs were pointing to voters' annoyance with, or even antipathy to, Washington, the Hays-Ray affair seemed a disaster. Not long after the story broke, a House Democrat said to me, "The tension around the House is not to be believed." Members gathered in the cloakrooms in silence to watch the evening news programs.

Perhaps inevitably, the questions of what and whose reforms to institute have become caught in the intramural struggles for leadership in the House next year. In fact, both the House and the Senate will be choosing new leaders; House Speaker Carl Albert and Senate Majority Leader Mike Mansfield have both announced their retirement, setting off leadership struggles down the line in both chambers. These intramural struggles have received little national attention, but a lot may be at stake, no matter who is President. A President's capacity for governing is linked with the impediments to governing that are thrown up by Congress's current methods of operating. This is not to say that whatever a President wants he should get; the events of recent years should have made that clear. On the contrary, one of the questions that will arise during the leadership fights—particularly in the Senate—is whether Congress will be led by people who will be all too willing to do a Democratic President's bidding, no matter how wrongheaded his ideas. We have learned that there are benefits—even safety—in a balky Congress. The question is, what is the reason for the balkiness. It is one thing for Congress to want to give slow and careful consideration to a President's proposals—to act, as it is supposed to, as a check on his powers. It is another for Congress simply to be unable to function, because it is paralyzed by competing jurisdictions and special-interest access.

"If you were to list the ten worst problems facing the country," said Abner Mikva, a Democratic Representative from Illinois and one of the most thoughtful and respected members of the House, as we talked this noon, "you would find that Congress hasn't done much about any of them, because it hasn't got its act together." Mikva continued, "The problem is both leadership and followership. The leadership is weak, but it isn't standing in the way of action. In tax reform, health care, transportation, welfare reform, there has been a failure to initiate and a failure to follow through. We haven't quite the self-confidence and the belief that the institution is capable of doing these things. There is a history to that. There was forty years of disintegration of the initiative of the institution. Franklin Roosevelt came in with the idea that Congress was in the way: the thing to do was to figure out how to get around it on foreign affairs; the test of a good congressman was whether he voted blindly for whatever Roosevelt wanted. All this went on for forty years—with some exceptions during the Eisenhower years. Then, in the nineteen-seventies, people began to ask whether the pendulum had swung too far. Lately, we've been doing a little better in foreign affairs, but that has been largely by vetoing Presidential actions. In domestic affairs, the President doesn't do anything, so there's nothing to block. We did a little better job on the economy, because the President sent up proposals, in his tax bill, and we modified them. Now we are overreacting to the Hays affair, but most people don't really care about such matters. What the people really want is for us to solve the problems of inflation and energy and education and housing and health. And if we aren't doing that, and we aren't, what these things—peccadilloes—do is confirm suspicions that we are callous and insensitive. Our approval rating is at nine percent in the polls. It wouldn't go from nine percent to ninety if we castrated every member of the House."

As Mikva and I spoke, the House Ways and Means Committee, meeting just off the House floor, was marking up a bill that embodies the President's proposal—made in his State of the Union Address and reiterated shortly before the Illinois primary—to ease the estate and gift taxes for farms and small businesses. From the number of lobbyists who were gathered outside the committee room, one would have thought that the committee was giving away Fort Knox, which in a sense it is. Efforts by some committee members to get certain reforms to tighten taxes on estates were being beaten by trust officers of banks. And the Senate is working on a bill to extend the income-tax cuts for another year as an anti-recession measure, to which have been added all sorts of tax preferences for special interests. The bill—more than fifteen hundred pages long—is ostensibly a tax-reform measure, but the provisions added would lose the Treasury about four billion dollars a year after a few years. It repeals three tax preferences, restricts some, and adds or expands thirty-odd more. Among the special interests to be aided under the bill are oil companies, railroads, shipping companies, and numerous individual firms. The problem is that, while many people are for tax reform in the abstract, a few people care intensely about their own tax-relief provisions and the public is not mobilized to counter them. Moreover, even now that there are limits on the amounts that can be contributed to the campaigns of members of Congress—one thousand dollars by individuals and five thousand by organizations—representatives of the special interests are able to contribute enough to give them a critical mass that gets attention from members of Congress. Access can still be purchased.

Included in the tax bill that is before the Senate are the remains of what was to be a great legislative initiative to deal with what was once recognized as an energy crisis. Since the generally recognized crisis, the nation's dependence on imported oil has risen. Yet efforts to reduce consumption by raising taxes on gasoline have been beaten. All that is left in the energy part of the bill is about fifteen tax preferences—for people who insulate their homes for the coal industry—which will do almost nothing about the energy shortage, and which will cost the Treasury (us) about five hundred million dollars.

Representative Les Aspin, a thirty-seven-year-old Democrat from Wisconsin, who was formerly a Pentagon economist and is now a member of the House Armed Services Committee, said in a conversation we had one day that there are several reasons Congress has made only minor reductions in the military budget this year. He listed the unemployment rate, the Reagan campaign, and the fact that the general attack on "big government" has undercut moves for "new priorities"—that is, social programs in lieu of military spending. As a result, the President's military budget is being approved virtually in its entirety, which represents a fifteen-percent increase in defense spending over last year (a seven-percent increase when allowance is made for inflation). While attention was focussed on the B-1 bomber, because it was a new and expensive and arguably unnecessary new weapon, other weapons systems and military expenditures went through virtually unexamined. In the kind of climate Aspin described, such expenditures do not get examined carefully. Yet Congress has never rejected a major weapons system. (It managed only to scale down the antiballistic missile system in 1970. One ABM site was built, and has been abandoned —leaving a kind of twentieth-century Stonehenge near Grand Forks, North Dakota.) Aspin, who knows, says that three or four percent of any military budget represents what is known as "cut insurance"—on the assumption that Congress will cut it by at least that amount. But Congress hardly touched this year's budget, so now the Pentagon is getting things it did not really want. Aspin says the Pentagon will be coming back to Congress next year with "reprogramming" requests, to adjust for Congress's unanticipated generosity.

I asked one senator how he viewed this year's session of Congress, and he replied, "Long, interminable—and when we get all done we're about where we started." In part, this has to do with the fact that Congress is always distracted in an election year, and particularly in a Presidential-election year. In part, it has to do with the structural and leadership problems. In part, it has to do with the government's being divided between a heavily Democratic Congress and a Republican President. And in part it has to do with the fact that Congress does not seem to know quite what to do. While many members see a mandate for new social programs—at least, health-insurance and job programs—others are not so sure. They have doubts about the proposals that are before them, and are not convinced that the country has spoken.

Moreover, members of Congress this year seem uncommonly fearful of the voters. "The job is no fun," said another senator, who does not even have to stand for reëlection this year. I asked him why. He replied, "Because the people are so angry. They don't say all that much, but their silence is very expressive."

Congress hasn't worked out sensible ways of dividing up its jurisdiction or—and these two things are partly related—handling its work load. Many members are constantly rushing from meeting to meeting, carrying cards with long lists of appointments, but they don't get much done as a result. Members of Congress chronically look harried and feel unappreciated. They are not a very cheerful lot. There are some fine people in Congress, but the system usually keeps them buried (remember our surprise at the quality of so many members of the House Judiciary Committee), and the pressures tend to wear them down. An uncommon number have decided not to seek reëlection—about fifty as of now. If Democrats feel frustrated at not getting an agenda enacted, many Republicans are even more depressed. Earlier this year, I talked with a House Republican over breakfast in the cafeteria of the Longworth House Office Building. I asked him about the unusually large number of members of Congress who were voluntarily retiring.

He replied, "The unusually large number is going to get larger. I'm telling you that as one who thought about getting out himself. I have no real reëlection problems, but I had second thoughts about continuing. I feel we're just milling around—not moving up or down, forward or backward, right or left. Just circular. And enough circular motion and you get dizzy after a while. The debate is so sterile. It all seems so aimless. We're just tracing punches. There is no clearly defined sense of direction—of moving from A to B to C. We are still essentially a reactive body. The collapse of the man Nixon hasn't reduced the whole institution of the Presidency to shards." There are other reasons for the large number of retirements. Incumbency is no longer the comfortable perch it used to be. Many politicians are unhappy about the new laws that are designed to curb the way they raise campaign funds and that tighten the requirements on disclosure of contributions. Many are annoyed by the degree to which they must now account for these things and by the skepticism that now surrounds politics. That skepticism itself makes incumbency a less safe perch; incumbents are no longer as unlikely to be challenged as they once were. Many of them are unaccustomed, and uninterested in becoming accustomed, to the annoyance of a challenge. And even some of the good ones have decided that private life is preferable.

Yesterday, the Nuclear Regulatory Commission, the federal agency that grants export licenses for nuclear facilities and materials, defeated a move by one of its members, Victor Gilinsky, to place tighter controls over the uses of a nuclear reactor that was being sold to Spain by Westinghouse. Gilinsky, a physicist, said in a press conference that the agreement to sell the reactor "contains a vital flaw involving the controls over the plutonium—a nuclear explosive—which will be produced in the operation of the reactor." He had sought a provision to require that the reactor operate with fuel supplied by the United States only, thus giving the United States control over the plutonium that was then produced. He was outvoted three to one. The other commissioners argued that even if Spain purchased fuel from sources other than the United States the plutonium produced would be subject to supervision by the International Atomic Energy Agency, but Gilinsky said its inspection systems were inadequate. The chairman of the N.R.C., Marcus Rowden, said in a separate press conference that the provision Gilinsky sought would offer "only the illusion" of a safeguard, because the United States had already agreed to supply Spain with equipment for eight nuclear reactors that were not subject to such a condition. Gilinsky, at his press conference, quoted a letter in which the State Department said that efforts to obtain assurances from Spain that it would use only United States fuel "would result in protracted negotiations, the outcome of which cannot be predicted."

Yesterday, the Senate approved a new agreement for American bases in Spain.

Yesterday, in the elections in Italy, the Communists made substantial gains; the Christian Democrats won enough votes to remain in power, but whether enough to govern effectively no one was sure. The United States position had been, as set forth by Henry Kissinger, that if the Communists gained seats in the Cabinet, Washington would have to reassess its relations with Italy.

JUNE 24

Thursday morning. The Sheraton Carlton Hotel. Jimmy Carter is here for breakfast with "the Sperling group"—reporters invited by Godfrey Sperling, Jr., the Washington bureau chief of the *Christian Science Monitor,* to have breakfast with various politicians. There are sometimes several of these breakfasts in a week. They offer an opportunity for the journalists to get a story and for the source to make some news or to get known by the reporters. Not being much of a "morning person" (I managed to get through the primaries without ever accompanying a candidate on a dawn visit to a plant gate), I don't make it to a breakfast very often, but I thought it would be interesting to see Jimmy Carter at this point in his effort to become President of the United States.

In the view of the Carter campaign staff, the current phase is next in importance to the one in which he won the nomination— and more important, perhaps, than the traditional election campaign in the fall. One of his aides says, "The theory is that because he's the nominee way ahead of the time of the Convention and because he's way ahead of Ford and Reagan in the polls, he will be more and more seen as a possible President. That will happen very rapidly. A lot depends on how he conducts himself in the next couple of months—before the Convention, at the Convention, in his choice of a Vice-Presidential running mate. People will be thinking now about Jimmy as President and seeing if it fits. Most of them will have made up their minds by Labor Day. So now we put him in situations where he can be seen as Presidential. We want him to be seen as a man who knows foreign policy and has good advisers, and also as a man of the farm and small town to whom family means a lot." And so Carter is engaged in several concurrent efforts: he is travelling around the country raising money to pay off his million-dollar campaign debt; in the course of these trips he is making a series of speeches on issues, in part to keep the press attention from the fact that he is going about raising money, and in part to establish himself as "Presidential"; he is making calls to people around the country soliciting opinions about his Vice-Presidential choice; he is planning for his fall campaign; and he is even taking a few steps toward getting ready to govern. But mainly he is busy raising money and getting himself seen as "Presidential." Yesterday, in New York, he gave a speech on foreign policy. Generally, it met what have become the conventional standards of the foreign-policy experts out of government, and, given Henry Kissinger's recent changes in direction, was not very far off from current policy. Carter espoused closer consultation with allies, and more attention to developing nations. He was critical of what he termed, without specifically referring to Kissinger, a "Lone Ranger" style of conducting foreign policy—almost everyone is by now. The determined candidate and his staff, meanwhile, are drawing up the organizational plans for the campaign. "What we do best is organize," Hamilton Jordan, his campaign manager, said to me recently, "and we'll have a well-organized campaign." Jordan, who in 1972 drew up the plan for Carter's nomination campaign, has now drawn up a plan for the fall campaign. Each state's importance has been assessed, along with Carter's assets and liabilities in that state. Carter's travel schedule is to be drawn up by the end of July. Plans are being made for an ambitious voter-registration drive by the Democratic Party, and for setting up training schools for gubernatorial, senatorial, and congressional candidates. "To the extent that they have well-managed campaigns, it will benefit us," Jordan said. With federal funding of the Presidential campaign, Carter will not have to raise money, and, moreover, he will be in a position to help local candidates raise money. That will both strengthen the Democratic Party in the election contests and put those candidates in Carter's debt.

In part, the emphasis on Carter's "image" in these next weeks grows out of a desire to correct for what his organization thinks went wrong toward the end of the campaign for the nomination. Carter did, after all, lose nine of the last sixteen primaries. A pattern had developed in which after he had been in a state for a while he went down in the polls. His campaign staff worried about the problem and concluded that he had become "overexposed." Jordan said, "In six months, Jimmy went from nobody knowing him, and then all people knew was that they saw him every Tuesday night winning another primary. So our appeal wasn't very deep. And his theme was non-ideological—'Trust in me,' 'Hope'—though his answers to questions were specific. And there were things that came along that added to the non-ideological idea and diverted people's minds from issues—'ethnic purity,' the attention to religion. People got tired of him. Then we got to the point where all these politicians were flocking to us, so the anti-establishment candidate wasn't anti-establishment anymore. And he wasn't a fresh face anymore. That's why we continued to do well against Udall and the others but not against Church and Brown. It worried me a little bit and scared me a little bit, but when you got back to the numbers it was there."

At first, some of Carter's staff worried that his emphasis on religion might be a problem, but then they decided that it might be an asset. "It may not go over well in the suburbs of Washington or in Manhattan or in Beverly Hills," said one of Carter's aides, "but it goes over well with the rest of the country." (Actually, Carter planned to write two books—a campaign biography and a book about his religious beliefs—but then decided to write just one, which combines the two.)

In retrospect, one can get a little more of a picture of what went on in Carter's final weeks of sewing up the nomination. There were several conversations with Thomas Eagleton, to work out a way for Eagleton to deliver the uncommitted Missouri delegates. There were only a few states where delegates were considered very much subject to influence by their political leaders: Missouri, Illinois, and New York. Birch Bayh made some calls to uncommitted labor delegates on Carter's behalf. Massachusetts delegates committed to Shriver were pursued by the Carter organization. Wallace's delegates were not pursued, so as not to give offense to Carter's principal adversary—a strategy that may have helped bring Wallace around in the end. There were calls to individual delegates even after the nomination was seemingly safe, to make sure that nothing went awry. There were weekly calls from Carter to Daley, which were usually followed by some public statement from Daley. The Carter organization was eager for various political figures—Wallace, Daley, Jackson—to see that the others were seeming to get ready to come around to him. These politicians would not want to be last aboard the train. And, as the cascade of endorsements just after the Ohio primary showed, this psychological strategy worked.

Someone here remarked the other day, "After Ohio, Carter seemed to grow four inches, and when he calls, the telephone rings a little louder." That mysterious mantle has fallen on him. And people want to get closer to him. Carter's effective nomination (and what many assume to be his inevitable election) has set off a scramble among Democrats—never quite accustomed to being out of power—to become part of his entourage. Some people had the foresight to join up this spring, not so much because they were enamored of Carter as because they assessed the situations of the other candidates and decided that Carter was, as several put it, "the only game in town." A rather unseemly competition for Secretary of State in the Carter Administration has been going on for months. The other evening at a cocktail party, a Washington lawyer and veteran of the New Frontier introduced himself to Peter Bourne, the Carter aide stationed in Washington, and said he would be calling him. "I've been in the woodwork," he remarked, smiling. People are getting in touch with people who they think have access to the inner circle. Most of this city's investors in power had failed to bet on Jimmy Carter, and now they are scurrying to make up for their lack of foresight. There is a feeling among some people here that those young men from Georgia may have had the political knowledge to get Carter nominated but now it is time for the pros —themselves—to move in to help him run the country. And the young men from Georgia are inclined to make disparaging remarks about "the Washington crowd," and to say that Carter doesn't want an Administration that will seem a "warmed-over New Frontier or Great Society." They are inevitably wary of letting outsiders in, inevitably protective of their own positions. One remarked recently, only half joking, "We have to make sure that when there is a transition we don't get transitioned out." So Carter is faced with some of the classic problems of a successful Presidential candidate, who must broaden his circle—problems that are exacerbated in his case by the fact that he has kept at least some distance from the traditional centers of power and influence, and by the fact that neither he nor his immediate entourage has had a great deal of experience working with people outside Georgia. So they now go around asking about people who have been in government, trying to sort them out. They do need some people with experience in government: people who can show them where the pitfalls are, advise them on the wisest use of their energies and political strength—not people who know too much, wise old heads who have seen too much, know all the reasons things can't be done, are now tired of mind and spirit, do not see the merit or the possibilities of trying to shake things up, of making new attempts.

Today, at the Sperling breakfast, Carter seems relaxed—more relaxed than he seemed during the campaign. "I don't feel ill at ease about the prospect of being President," he says. It is a typical Carter remark—like remarks he made during the campaign that seemed part uncommon confidence and part calculated effort to get people to take him more seriously. He seems to be smiling naturally today. It is not that stretched, pasted-on-looking smile we saw when he was campaigning. But there is still an edge to his manner. Three times, he refers to speeches he gave which he feels did not receive enough attention from the press. Asked about his position on the Vietnam war, about which there has been confusion, Carter says that he was "in the position of most Southern liberals—that we should not have got in in the first place, but that, having got in, we should have won as soon as possible." He says that whoever it is he chooses as Vice-President won't get lost in a Carter Administration.

"I can guarantee that won't happen," he says. "I don't believe I'll feel threatened by a Vice-President."

Carter points out that he is in a position to select his Vice-President without having to consider how that will help him with the delegates to the Convention, but, while that is true, there are other considerations. There is the consideration of the electoral votes in November. His aides also give attention to high-minded considerations such as the capacity of the Vice-Presidential nominee for serving as President in the event that anything happened to Carter, and the nominee's personal and professional integrity. This last consideration, of course, is essential to the success of the ticket. Another criterion listed by an aide was "acceptance"—the extent to which the media and Party leaders and the public would accept the choice as a good choice. A couple of weeks ago, the Carter camp let it be known that Patrick Caddell, Carter's pollster, was taking polls on the public reaction to fourteen possible Vice-Presidential candidates, but no one seriously thought that Carter was considering all fourteen. He seemed to be playing the old game of listing people whose constituencies would be pleased by their being listed, and even his aides concede that no more than about six were ever seriously considered. As of now, the list, from what one can gather, is down to Senators John Glenn, Walter Mondale, Adlai Stevenson, Frank Church, and Edmund Muskie. Some say that Henry Jackson is being considered. Charles Kirbo, an Atlanta lawyer, who is Carter's friend and adviser and the only associate, other than his wife, who has a peer relationship with him, and who is conservative, is checking around, eliciting various people's opinions. So is Hamilton Jordan, and so, even, is Carter. The indications now are that the favorite is Glenn: he rates highest in the polls; he comes from Ohio, which has a lot of electoral votes, and which the Democrats have carried in November only once since 1948; he has a nonpolitical, hero image; he is not too liberal; he does not have such a forceful personality or such an independent mind that he would cause problems for Carter. Mondale has the backing of labor groups and of blacks (including Andrew Young) and is known to be popular with the press, but he has liabilities in the eyes of some people in the Carter camp: he is too liberal for them (and too closely identified with busing, which he has defended in the Senate against attempts to overturn court orders); he may be too independent-minded; and—most interesting—he chose not to make the sort of race for the Presidency that Carter did. Carter and his aides have remarked to people that Mondale's withdrawal from the race toward the end of 1974, on the ground that he did not wish to spend a year and a half in the relentless and gruelling pursuit of the nomination, suggests that he is "lazy" and "a quitter." They apparently cannot understand—even though Carter has acknowledged that he had an advantage in not being employed as of January, 1975—that someone might walk away from that sort of life. Or perhaps it is that they cannot accept it, because it is a sort of reproach to Carter. Others chose not to make the race, but they did not talk about it; Mondale made the point out loud. Muskie is also said to be receiving serious consideration; he is a Catholic, and Carter is believed to have difficulty with Catholic voters.

Carter says that to change his campaign style "I would have to change my character," and he says that he will campaign "as aggressively as I did before." And he talks revealingly about how his campaign has succeeded with people of divergent ideologies. "I have had good relations with liberals on human rights," he says, and he goes on to say that he has had good relations with conservatives by emphasizing things like balancing the budget, which he has pledged to do in three years. (How, he does not explain.) "Most conservatives," he says, "are not averse to civil rights and human rights, would not be opposed to a revision of health-care programs as long as emphasis on the doctor-patient relationship is maintained, can be talked to about revision of welfare programs in a way that is appealing to them." He adds, "I've never been inclined to put voters in a box and say 'I'm in the same box, so vote for me.'" About the campaign for the Presidency, he says, "The problem of the incumbency may be the greatest unanticipated problem I might have. The President has the capacity to reach people—through crises, meetings."

On tonight's news, we saw pictures of Carter the conqueror on Capitol Hill. Congressional Democrats called him a "political genius," a reincarnation of Franklin Roosevelt. They had their pictures taken with him for their reëlection campaigns. The Senate Democratic Caucus gave him its unanimous endorsement; the motion was made by Hubert Humphrey.

The CBS–New York *Times* poll today says that voters preferred Carter to Ford by fifty percent to twenty-nine percent, and preferred Carter to Reagan by fifty-three percent to twenty-four percent.

State Department sources said yesterday that the United States was pulling its military advisers out of Quemoy and Matsu, two islands off the southeast coast of China which are controlled by the Chinese Nationalists based in Taiwan. Sixteen years ago, Quemoy and Matsu were a big issue in the Presidential campaign: they were being shelled then from the Chinese mainland, and Richard Nixon accused John Kennedy of advocating "surrender" when Kennedy argued that the islands weren't worth protecting.

JUNE 28

Over the weekend, Reagan picked up forty-six delegates—all the delegates in Montana and New Mexico, the four remaining uncommitted delegates in Idaho, and one delegate in Minnesota—and President Ford picked up seventeen, all of them in Minnesota. According to the Washington *Post*'s delegate count, this gives the President—out of the one thousand one hundred and thirty needed to nominate—one thousand and thirty-seven, and Reagan nine hundred and eighty-eight. The Republicans have four more state conventions left, and not even these are expected to settle the nomination. The real struggle will be for the votes of the uncommitted delegates. Several news organizations continually phone Republican delegates and bring the delegate counts up to date. No one can be sure if delegates are telling the truth. In Mississippi, a few days ago, Reagan said that there was "no way" he could accept the Vice-Presidential spot on a Ford ticket. He said that the Presidential and Vice-Presidential candidates should be philosophically compatible. He also said that there were "basic differences" between him and the "Washington establishment," and that, moreover, he had never believed that the Vice-Presidential nominee added measurably to the strength of the Presidential nominee. The Mississippi delegation, which has thirty votes, and which (against the Party's rules) votes at the Convention as a bloc, is believed to be favoring Reagan. But Douglas Shanks, Ford's leader in Mississippi, has announced that at the Convention he will cast his vote for Ford.

The President spent the weekend in Puerto Rico, where he met with the leaders of six other industrial nations on international economic questions. A principal matter on the agenda was the concern of the United States that as the industrial nations undergo their current recovery they are not taking sufficient steps to hold down inflation. Some economists think that our government's concern about this is premature.

June 29

Today, I had lunch with John Sears, Ronald Reagan's campaign manager. Sears, who is thirty-five, worked in the Nixon campaign in 1968 and in the Nixon White House for a while, but then fell afoul of John Mitchell and took up the practice of law in Washington. Not a particularly ideological man, he seems to have gone to work for Reagan because he wanted to run another campaign. "I would have to admit that the last Presidential experience I had was not all that rewarding, so I wanted to do it again," he told me last February. "I, among others, helped to get Richard Nixon elected, so I guess I felt I had to do better." Sears is somewhat stocky, has straight graying brown hair and dresses conservative Ivy League. He is pleasant and friendly and talkative, and is liked by the press for those reasons. Explaining to me on that earlier occasion why he had gone to work for Reagan, he said, "It isn't a matter of philosophy. This isn't a philosophical country. We act on a mode of practicality. We think it is better to act than not. We proceed on the theory that competition makes truth, but it doesn't." He said that defeating Ford was not his "motivating purpose," and that the fact that Ford was the incumbent President was "just incidental" to what he was doing. As for Reagan, Sears said, "You have to have men who are predictable about what they would do in office, but in individual cases would make all the exceptions necessary." He continued, "It's an interesting sociological thing to see what people want in a President. They want someone who would do the pragmatic thing under all circumstances."

I asked Sears to describe to me the process of trying to get the support of the uncommitted delegates.

"There's a lot of misconception about how you go about all this," he replied. "There's an idea that you go out and back a guy against the wall and try to sell him on Reagan, or that you make some overexpansive promise and he's for Reagan. But the people who can be sold on Reagan already are. While there are people who are interested in what you might do when you're elected, who are interested in jobs for themselves—that has its base in the spoils system—when you're talking about one guy or a few guys or uncommitted delegates from a county, they are interested in how the ticket would do there or whether you're going to campaign in the area, how you see the fall. So before they're interested in jobs they're interested in whether you can get nominated and elected. They're more interested in what they're trying to do politically—electorally or through Party advancement—and we have an advantage in not being tied to the Party structure. We tell someone we'll campaign in that area or we'll help him become Party chairman, because we don't have to consult with the congressman and Party chairman in the area, because they're against us."

Sears went on, "People talk about all these uncommitteds. There are no more than sixty or seventy truly uncommitted people—a lot of people who say they are uncommitted are just having fun. Anyway, the uncommitteds aren't the sum total of your flexibility. Some delegates indicate they are for Ford who may not be."

Tomorrow, Sears is going to Pennsylvania, and then he'll spend a day in New York. Almost all the delegates in those two states are technically uncommitted. A hundred and nineteen of New York's delegates out of a hundred and fifty-four have been "delivered" to Ford by Richard Rosenbaum, the Party's state chairman and Nelson Rockefeller's close ally. But Sears isn't settling. He plans to "talk to people who have to vote for Ford but can help Reagan," he said, explaining, "They have influence with other delegates, who can go either way." He said he has a good friend in Pennsylvania who has to vote for Ford but is not enthralled by him and can help Sears with people who are still undecided. He said he also has a good friend in Indiana who has helped. "If someone knows you well, he feels a certain predictability about how things would be handled," Sears said. "Your word is very important—the most important thing in politics. Politics is seen as a seamy business, yet your credibility is the highest virtue you could have."

Sears continued, "Politics works in a pragmatic fashion. But people work in givens: that you will never get support for Ronald Reagan in New York. That might be true if you went to New York and said 'Vote for Ronald Reagan but we don't expect to do well.' You don't have to do that. You go up there and say that if they're really interested in the Party ticket, one thing they have to grasp is that Jimmy Carter has a flaw in his ability to attract Catholic ethnic voters. They are not Republicans, but they are uncertain about Baptists from the South and candidates who are always talking about religion, which is a private matter. So you say, 'Who can do better—Gerald Ford or Ronald Reagan?' You show that in California Reagan did very well in attracting middle-to-low-income blue-collar workers. Usually, if the Republican candidate moves to the left he does well in a large state, attracts minority groups—Milliken in Michigan, Percy in Illinois, Taft in Ohio. Reagan did it with Italians in the San Francisco area. This is what you look at in New York, New Jersey, Pennsylvania, Connecticut. Also, Reagan has more flexibility getting votes than Gerald Ford does. Gerald Ford doesn't have a constituency and doesn't have the flexibility to create one. After the Convention, he could move, and change his stand on, say, race matters, and people would yell 'Politician.' Reagan doesn't have that problem. Reagan was able to be a more moderate governor than his rhetoric suggested. People feel they know what Reagan would do if he were President, and, most important, they feel he would make those exceptions to what he says he would do in order to govern."

I asked Sears to explain, then, what the advantage was in having Reagan sound so conservative in the nominating campaign.

"Since we lost the New Hampshire primary, there was no option but to try to get the nomination in a way that was predictable," he replied. "There was no option but to stress the things that would win the later primaries." He was talking about such issues as defense, the Panama Canal. He continued, "After the primaries, there will be an effort to moderate the image. We'll start repositioning for the fall. And we'll continue to work on the delegates. We've set up a program to deal with the people who are uncommitted, but we'll spend more time on people who are assumed to be for Ford."

JULY 1

Thursday. Statuary Hall, the United States Capitol. Today, the President of the United States is to participate in Congress's celebration of the Bicentennial by opening the inner door of the safe of which the outer doors were opened in January. Mrs. Charles F. Deihm, whose Centennial project the safe was, left instructions that it should be opened on July 4, 1976, "by the Chief Magistrate of the United States." Since Congress will not be here on Sunday, the Fourth of July, the safe-opening ceremony is taking place today. Bleachers have been set up for the press, and there are television lights. Members of the White House staff are here, and members of

Congress drift in slowly. The senators are taking time out from voting on the tax bill; the House is voting on the expense-account reforms. Later today, the President will meet with seven delegates from Pennsylvania, described as either uncommitted or "soft" in their support of Reagan, and seventeen delegates from Delaware. Later today, also, Congress will give its final approval to a bill authorizing new funds for military weapons, including a start on the B-1 bomber. Another fight will come on the bill to appropriate the money. House Speaker Albert, who made a little speech in January, makes another little speech. Albert, who has announced his retirement from Congress as of the end of this term, had, his legend goes, grown up in a tiny town in Oklahoma dreaming of being Speaker of the House. He had hoped to be a great Speaker, but his leadership was uncertain and at the end his Congress was tinged with scandal. Today, Albert is wearing a greenish suit and a sad face. He tells the history of the safe, and of the room we are in, which used to be the House Chamber. "Here Henry Clay and James K. Polk presided as Speakers," says Albert. "Here Daniel Webster and later Abraham Lincoln served as obscure representatives." Linking the present to the past just might lend more dignity to the present. Mike Mansfield, the Senate Majority Leader, who is also retiring, makes a little speech. The old order really is giving way on Capitol Hill. Mansfield tells how bad things were in 1876: crop prices were falling; the Reconstruction efforts "had come to nothing"; the Grant Administration was "shaken in its declining days by scandal and corruption," and "the Presidential contest of 1876, itself a model of corruption, was not finally decided until forty-eight hours prior to the 1877 inauguration ceremony'; there were pneumonia, malaria, typhoid. How will this year seem a hundred years from now? Mansfield mentions some of the notable inventions of that era: the telephone, the typewriter, the refrigerated freight car, and barbed wire. I shudder to think what will be seen as ours.

Then the President speaks, saying he is "deeply honored to have the opportunity" to open the safe. "As we look inside this safe," he says, "let us look inside ourself." He says, "On Sunday, we start a new century, a century of the individual." He pulls open the door of the big black-lacquered iron safe—it had been unlocked beforehand, so that the President would be sure not to have any trouble with it—and there is mild applause. Albert peeks around the President to see what is in the safe. Then, with the statues of Robert La

Follette, Brigham Young, and Kamehameha I (the first king of the Hawaiian Islands) looking on, the President pulls out some of the items in the safe, announcing what they are. A Tiffany inkstand. "This is a photo of an early statesman; I don't see his name." He pulls out another photograph and reads an attached card; it is President U. S. Grant. Then the President is able to explain that the first photograph was of W. F. Cooper, an employee of the Electoral Commission, and the President has the humor to laugh. There is a picture of a woman. The President doesn't know who she is, but "she looks mighty pretty." This situation lacks majesty, but the President is an amiable man and goes along. He pulls out a large brown-bound volume that contains autographs of citizens in 1876. "Here's a scroll," says the President, and he holds up a scroll bearing the autographs of the members of Congress in 1876. He pulls out another book and a few more photographs, and he sits down.

JULY 3

The Nuclear Regulatory Commission yesterday voted three to one to authorize the export of about nine tons of uranium fuel to India. It also delayed a larger shipment to India of such fuel pending a hearing on safeguards. In 1974, India became the sixth nation to develop a nuclear bomb. It was built out of nuclear equipment given to India for peaceful purposes.

JULY 4

The feeling of the day sort of crept up on many of us, took us by surprise. There was a spirit to it that could not have been anticipated. For those of us who had been in despair about this Bicentennial Fourth of July, who feared the worst, the surprise was a very pleasing one. Because of what the salesmen and the politicians and the media have done to so many things, a lot of us have become so jaded that it is hard to believe that anything is real. But the politicians and the salesmen did not destroy the day—they became almost irrelevant. The celebrating seemed genuine. There was a kind of inventiveness about what people were doing. Wagon trains and bicycle trips and improvised local festivities. There was the harmless nonsense: a man pushing a watermelon from Statesboro, Georgia, to Philadelphia; a forty-nine-thousand-pound birthday cake. But it was a people's day. The Tall Ships—the great sailing ships from around the world—captured the national imagination, and they seemed to do so simply because they did, not because we were told that they should. As the weekend approached, people appeared to be in a good mood, not feeling the dread that many people feel as they approach enforced holidays. In Washington, we kept being told that there were not so many tourists here as had been expected, but it turned out that a great many were here. The streets were busy, and the museums and parks were filled with people. This Fourth of July, a celebration of our independence, a day of national self-congratulation, was real. We had made it. We had experienced some terrible things, but we had come through. No doubt our having experienced them deepened the celebratory feeling of the day. One friend of mine suggested that we may be closer to the framers of the Constitution now than at earlier times in our history, because the framers were confident but realistic, and we forgot their realism almost immediately and came to believe that we could do anything, be anything. The events of the past forty years stripped us of that unthinking optimism, and may have brought us back closer to the state of mind of Jefferson and Madison. Despite our troubles, my friend pointed out, we haven't, up to now, turned cynical. Something seems to have broken in the last couple of days. That the country seems to be in a good mood is a big thing, may even be a historic turning. The deep Spenglerian gloom of the last few years appears to have lifted. Vietnam *is* behind us. We *did* survive Watergate.

No doubt the good feeling one observes today, even the patriotic feeling, comes out of confidence in our country, as distinguished from confidence in our government. There is a sense that we'll go on, that Congress and the President do not define everything. Some of us had emotional reactions today that we did not anticipate; the national event became a personal one, which all the hoopla could not stifle. Some of us felt things that orators for years had been instructing us to feel, but then the feelings came upon us when we least expected them.

This has been a nice summer weekend, when people have more or less relaxed and gone out, and done what they wanted to do. The Fourth is a peculiarly American sort of holiday anyway—a secular, uncomplicated day, observed with hamburgers and hot dogs and Cokes and beer. Yesterday, in Washington, there was a parade along Constitution Avenue. High-school bands from around the country played, and people in their various ethnic costumes danced. Other nations parade their weapons on their anniversaries, but we did not. On Friday night, the President participated in a ceremony in which the nation's official copies of the Declaration of Independence, the Constitution, and the Bill of Rights were put on continuous display at the National Archives for seventy-six hours. Yesterday and today, people were lined up to see them. Today, the Declaration was read on the steps of the Archives by an actor in costume, and when he came to various familiar lines the assembled crowd cheered. NBC and CBS are spending all day covering events of this Fourth, and are pleasantly showing us what is going on around the country. We saw the President at Valley Forge and later at Independence Hall, in Philadelphia, where he gave one of his better speeches. The coverage of his Bicentennial itinerary undoubtedly did not hurt his political situation, but that seemed all right, because Jerry Ford is a benign figure, who neither dwarfed nor visibly exploited the events. At two o'clock this afternoon, the President, on the flight deck of the U.S.S. Forrestal, rang a bell thirteen times, and bells rang out all over the country. The television showed the bells ringing at the National Cathedral, near where I live, and I could go out in my back yard and hear them.

This evening, some friends and their children and I went down to a Washington hotel to watch the fireworks. Hundreds of thousands of people were expected to watch the display from the Mall, and my friends drew the line when I suggested we go there. All around Washington, people were watching: from the Mall, from hotel rooms, from rooftops, from cars caught in the colossal traffic jam that clogged the area. We drank beer and ate hamburgers and chocolate cake until it grew dark. The children understood that this was a special evening. On television, Arthur Fiedler, in a white shirt, conducting an outdoor concert by the Charles River, led the Boston Pops in an all-out, let-'er-rip version of "The Stars and Stripes Forever," and people in his audience danced spontaneously and jubilantly. And then we stood outside on the balcony in the soft night air and watched as the fireworks exploded in great bursts of red, white, and blue around the Washington Monument.

18

NEW YORK. Saturday afternoon, the corner of Fifty-second Street and Seventh Avenue, just outside the Americana Hotel, shortly after four o'clock. Jimmy Carter, uncharacteristically late, was due here at four for his triumphal arrival in New York. The Democratic Convention, which begins Monday, is already his, and he will be free to spend his time in the coming week completing the process of selecting a running mate, and reaching out to those elements of the Party —and they are substantial—which are still dubious about him. The apparatus that was originally assembled to come here to obtain whatever number of additional delegates might be needed to guarantee Carter's nomination on the first ballot (all along, the assumption within the Carter campaign has been that he would be nominated on the first ballot or not at all) will now be used instead to batten down his support in the Party for the fall campaign for the Presidency. Hamilton Jordan figures that from seven hundred to a thousand of the three thousand and eight delegates assembled here remain emphatically opposed to Carter. "We'll work on them," he said recently. Moreover, Carter's strategists know that much of the support that Carter does have is what is known as "soft." So tomorrow evening Jimmy and Rosalynn Carter will throw a fried-chicken-and-beer party for all the delegates, and in the course of the coming week Carter will make occasional forays from his suite on the twenty-first floor of the Americana Hotel to greet some state delegations and Party officeholders. The trick, according to his staff, is to strike a balance between having him holed up in his suite, remote from the conventioneers, and causing him to be "overexposed." Gerald Rafshoon, Carter's forty-two-year-old media consultant, has prepared a handsome brochure about Carter for distribution to all the delegates. The actual managing of the Convention is ostensibly being left to Robert Strauss, the chairman of the Democratic National Committee, and Mark Siegel, the Party's executive director, able men with a proved capacity for threading their way among the conflicting and explosive subcultures of the Democratic Party. But

Strauss and Siegel do not make many moves these days without checking with the Carter camp. Earlier in the year, Party officials had prepared for a Convention that might require as many as five ballots for the Presidential nomination—even trying to figure what would be the psychological impact of adjourning overnight after which ballot.

Carter may have won the nomination, but he has not captured the Party. The principal concern within the Carter camp now is how to generate enough enthusiasm so that its candidate will win in November. The Carter people worry about the assumption that he has the election "wrapped up." Efforts will be made here this week to mollify the Party's liberal wing—the Carter forces have chosen some prominent liberals as floor leaders, who will be speaking both to delegations and to television microphones. The floor representatives and those who will speak for Carter from the rostrum are being instructed to strike the themes of Party unity and of Jimmy Carter as a hardworking person, and to stress the fact that the election is not sewed up. Some of his aides feel there has been too much talk out of Carter headquarters, including talk by the candidate himself, about planning for a transition to a Carter Administration—talk that, they feel, suggests arrogance on the part of the Carter camp and induces laxness among its workers. Last week, Morris Dees, Carter's fund-raiser, asked the Federal Election Commission for permission to accept private contributions for transition planning.

Patrick Caddell, Carter's twenty-six-year-old pollster, explained to me in a conversation yesterday that the very factors in our national political life which worked to Carter's advantage during his quest for the nomination could provide the greatest dangers to his election. Whether or not one agrees with what Caddell says—and my own feeling is that he is at times quite on point and at times too sweeping, seeming to overlook how much the factor of accident contributed to Carter's nomination—he is worth listening to, because much of what he says to reporters he also says to Carter. And Caddell is the one former outsider, not a longtime Carter associate, other than Greg Schneiders, Carter's personal aide, who has been brought into the small, tight inner circle of the Carter campaign. As Caddell sees it, there is a sort of vacuum in the country—a lack of clarity as to what is wanted of government policy—and also a high degree of volatility among the voters. The voters' uncertainty, he says, has been expressed in part in the low turnouts for the primaries this year. He argues that there are strong tendencies in the population: a desire for change; a feeling that things aren't working well; a desire for a restoration of basic values. These tendencies lead to a dichotomy, he argues: feelings of wanting to believe and feelings of having been burned. Caddell says, "You're dealing with a major psychological crisis in the country." According to this theory, the country is torn between its wish to hope and its feeling of cynicism, and, while a certain amount of cynicism is healthy, there is danger in a political system that people don't have confidence in—one in which, leaders having broken their contract with the people, the people no longer feel it worthwhile to follow their leaders. It is here that Caddell seems on point: the problem is how to grant our leaders not too much trust but enough trust to govern. "To have this kind of democracy function," says Caddell, "you have to have some belief that when the ballot is cast something will change. The public no longer believes that." The country's psychological crisis is brought about by the collapse of certain tenets: that we fought just wars, and won the wars we fought; that the Presidential office made the man. Jimmy Carter was the candidate of Watergate and Vietnam. He did not talk much about them explicitly, but he was constantly talking about what they did to us, touching the pain and offering himself as the soother, the healer, the one who would restore trust and virtue and belief and pride. But, as Caddell sees it, there will be disadvantages in having trust as major theme in a Ford-Carter race. According to Caddell's theory, if Ford is the Republican candidate, Carter is the issue, for he is new, Southern, different, complicated, while Ford is comfortable, known, safe. While Carter has been the best campaigner on the theme of values, Caddell's theory goes, the Carter campaign is asking people to take a risk—moreover, to take a risk on a candidate who is somewhat confusing to people, an enigma. While many argue that Carter should talk less now about themes and more about issues, Caddell believes that issues have been "devalued," because people do not believe that the government is capable of doing anything about the issues being discussed. "We still have not paid the price of Watergate and the war," he argues.

Carter's continuing search for a running mate is in some part a true process and in some part public relations, with no one, perhaps not even Carter himself, knowing how much of each. Nor, for all the speculation, can anyone be sure what is going on in Carter's mind. His friend and counsellor Charles Kirbo has now interviewed several possible running mates and given them a written question-naire about such things as medical records and tax forms, and has asked them about each other. In addition, Hamilton Jordan has asked questions around Washington. Carter summoned Senators Edmund Muskie, Walter Mondale, and John Glenn to his home in Plains, Georgia, last week. According to those who profess to know, he got along with Muskie less well than he had expected—found him stiff ("Muskie's reactions to people were the predictable behavior of a politician being watched by another politician and wanting to be Vice-President," said an aide afterward), his New England manners off-putting—and he got along with Mondale better than he expected. He will see Representative Peter Rodino and Senators Henry Jackson, Frank Church, and Adlai Stevenson III here in New York, but most of his aides believe that the choice will be among the senators who went to Plains. The interviews in New York seemed designed to soothe the subjects' patrons, follow-ers, and egos. Church, says one aide, would have been Carter's choice right after the June 8th primaries—Carter was impressed by Church's success as a candidate and by the way he opposed Carter without being hostile—but Church was eliminated after several of his Senate colleagues gave him poor marks for his handling of the C.I.A. investigation and for his general strength as a senator. Glenn, Carter's aides insist, received good reports from his fellow-senators, thus belying his reputation, particularly among the press, as a "lightweight." However, press reaction to Carter's decision on his running mate is important to the Carter camp, which sees it as the first major "executive" decision he will have to make—the biggest one of the campaign—and believes, too, that the Vice-Presidential candidate's reputation will be fixed firmly and quickly by the press. And Carter's aides know that Mondale is a favorite among the press. Carter's staff is surprisingly candid about its own preferences. Jordan, Jody Powell and Jerry Rafshoon tell people that they favor Mondale. They see him as a fresh face and as the candidate most likely to inspirit labor unions and liberals.

The scene outside the Americana resembles a street festival. A steel band is playing. A medium-sized crowd has gathered, drawn by announcements stencilled on the streets and by leaflets handed out by volunteers. It is a pleasant Saturday afternoon, and some people seem to be here because they are drawn by Carter and some because they are drawn by curiosity and some simply because they are trying to get down Seventh Avenue. There are pretzel vendors and Italian-ice vendors and people holding on to children, balloons, and dogs. A Frenchman carrying a tape recorder and a microphone asks for a bystander's impressions and remarks, "It's very folk-lorico, isn't it?" There are the inevitable components of any Convention crowd: people selling souvenirs (Carter buttons, Big Apple T-shirts, Bicentennial T-shirts, and Bicentennial Big Apple T-shirts), people handing out pamphlets (about amnesty, about abortion, about homosexuals' rights), and—it happens at every Convention—a person dressed as Uncle Sam. Yet the scene seems decidedly New York; the urban, jaded faces, the smart remarks to the pamphleteers, the women in the latest bloomerlike trousers and high-laced espadrilles. Some people, tired of waiting, drop into Nick's Deli for a cold beer. On the platform, awaiting the Southern conqueror, are, among others, Mayor Abe Beame and Averell Harriman. Harriman, now eighty-four, made a nearly forgotten race for the Democratic nomination himself in 1956, and later enjoyed a renaissance as a senior statesman of the Party. Earlier this spring, Harriman, who presides over one of Georgetown's more glittering salons, was quoted as saying of Carter, "How can he be nominated? I don't know him, and neither do any of my friends." Carter began to shoot back and then thought better of it and wooed Harriman, and now Harriman, like a proud father, is on the platform awaiting Carter.

Finally, Carter arrives. He is wearing a gray suit and is smiling—it looks like his more natural smile, as well it might be His wife and their eight-year-old daughter, Amy, are with him. These arrival scenes are set pieces for Conventions, providing morale for the candidate and his workers and a good scene for the television news programs. I remember Nixon arriving in Miami in 1968. The Nixon people, as was their wont, went all out, with "Nixonettes" wearing tall furry hats outside the Hilton Plaza Hotel. Carter makes a little speech in which he reassures New York that he will not, in the *News* paraphrase of Ford's initial reaction last year to New York's fiscal troubles, tell it to "drop dead." Carter needs New York in November. He teases the audience about his Vice-Presidential selection, hinting at first that he might reveal it on the spot—he does not often engage in such humor—and then strikes some familiar notes. He says that he will wage a campaign "of unity based on a common purpose . . . of correcting the problems that afflict our country." The country, he says, "has lived through the last few years of torment, a time of disappointment and disillusionment, a time of disappointment about the future of our country." The public-address system isn't very good, and his voice is faint. He continues, "But it's now time for us to approach some years of healing, pulling ourselves together, working to answer difficult questions and working to solve the problems that face our country." Then he asks, as campaigners often ask, "Will you help me do it?" And he closes, as he has closed many, many speeches this year, by telling the audience that we still live "in the greatest nation on earth."

In North Dakota on Thursday, President Ford won twelve of the state's eighteen delegates, and Ronald Reagan won four, with two remaining uncommitted. The Republican race is now so close that it has people keeping track as individual delegates make up their minds, and drawing grand conclusions from ordinarily minor events. North Dakota was generally viewed as a big victory for the President, who had not been expected to do so well. In Colorado today, Reagan won fifteen of the sixteen at-large delegates; the sixteenth went to Ford. And in Washington, D.C., the President Ford Committee announced that fourteen previously uncommitted delegates now supported the President. Some of these had already been counted as being for the President in the running tallies kept by news organizations. With eleven hundred and thirty delegates needed to win the Republican nomination, the Washington *Post* as of now gives the President a thousand and fifty-two and Reagan nine hundred and ninety-five, with a hundred and forty-one uncommitted, and the New York *Times* gives the President a thousand and sixty-seven and Reagan a thousand and forty-three. Yesterday, in a shift, the President said that he viewed Reagan as qualified to be President and had not ruled him out as a running mate. Of course, the possibility that Ford would select Reagan might make some delegates more favorable to Ford. The President said that earlier statements that Reagan was not qualified to be President were made with "political license."

JULY 12

Monday. The poor Democrats. When they are at each other's throats, as they usually are, over whom the Party should nominate and what its platform should say, the word among observers, particularly the press, is that they are "at it again," that they are "doing themselves in." The Party's fratricidal instincts elicit the kind of patronizing comments that might be made about someone who can't seem to do anything right. And now that the Party has, with some misgivings, settled the questions of this year's nominee and platform, it is being accused in the same quarters of being "dull." (Strauss, delighted with his party's new-found harmony, has said, "It can't get too dull for me.") Every Convention seems to have a buzzword that travels through the hotel corridors and across the Convention floor, carried mainly by cross-pollinators in the media, and the buzzword for this year's Democratic Convention is "dull." Whenever some five thousand political-minded beings and a thousand or two members of the press and perhaps another thousand or two lobbyists and pleaders for special interests are gathered, it is anything but dull. And when a political party gathers in a convention, whisking the old leaders offstage, even if temporarily, and bringing the new ones onstage, sending off the losers and accepting, with whatever degree of enthusiasm, the winner, it is anything but dull. Reporters may be hard pressed for a "story," and the television audience may be deprived of a suspenseful plot, but political conventions, by definition, are not dull.

Each day, the lobby of the Statler-Hilton, the Convention headquarters, across the street from Madison Square Garden, becomes more of a crush of people swirling about, trading rumors, heading for the black caucus or the women's caucus, for Frank Church's press conference, George McGovern's reception, the Americans for Democratic Action dinner, the bar. The coalition of nine liberal labor unions which had worked to get members elected as delegates in case there should be a brokered Convention—and succeeded in getting some four hundred delegates here—has been trying to keep its delegates interested and motivated to participate in the next nomination struggle. This morning, it held a rally for its delegates.

Each Convention is a thing unto itself. The delegates who are here are here as a result of accidents and strategies and primaries and state conventions, and there is also a scattering of governors and senators and local officials who managed to get here. To the extent that there is anything resembling a party, this is it. "The Party"—whichever party it is—is a skeleton fleshed out by the delegates of a given year. Interestingly, even some of the original Democratic reformers now think that reform has gone too far. They argue that Party participation should be among those who have some real identification with the Party. It is the same argument the former insiders—granted that they had rigged the rules to maintain power—made when the reformers, now insiders, were the outsiders. But it seems clear that the parties will never be what they once were. The welfare state and the Civil Service have removed some of the traditional functions of the parties. And lately something else has happened to them, as John Gardner pointed out to me earlier this year. They have become the captives of competing, sophisticated interest groups to the extent of being nearly paralyzed on many questions. At the same time, and probably in large part as a result, citizens have been finding other mechanisms, outside the parties, for seeking change—through the environmental movement, through organizations like Common Cause, through groups spawned by Ralph Nader, through local action groups. It is all these things that make the parties seem somewhat antiquated and sterile, and lamentations over "the decline of the parties" futile.

The statistics say that the percentages of women, blacks, and young people attending this Convention are down from what they were in 1972, when, as a result of stiff rules, they were at an all-time high, but, more important, the look of this Convention is different. That has to do, it seems, with changes in the country as well as within the Democratic Party. The California delegation looks as if it had turned in its thrift-shop costumes of 1972 and gone shopping at Bonwit Teller. A woman prominent in the New Jersey delegation who appeared in floor-length skirts and an Indian headdress in 1972 is tailored propriety this year. The war is over and passions are dead, and many of the delegates to this Convention look, as a friend of mine observed, like "modified Republicans." In 1972, the Massachusetts delegation was violently anti-war, culturally to the left, and barely controllable even by the George McGovern forces; this year, it is made up heavily of delegates who supported Henry Jackson, and it is tame. McGovern delegates represented a fairly coherent ideology in 1972; Carter delegates are conservative white Southerners, moderate Southern blacks, Northern liberals, Northern regulars. They are Mayor Daley and James Wall, the leader of the McGovern delegates from Illinois in 1972 who ran the Carter campaign there this year. And the statistics do not mean all that much. I met a black woman under forty who is a Cook County regular and, along with Mayor Daley, was thrown out of the 1972 Convention.

On Saturday, Morris Udall held a press conference. He seems to have calmed down since the immediate post-primary period, when he still talked of trying to affect the platform, or even the choice of the Vice-Presidential candidate, from the Convention floor. It is hard for candidates to stop running, to cut off the flow of adrenalin, to accept the fact that, after all that effort and all those dreams and fantasies, they have no role. Encouraged by their followers, they come to think of themselves as a cause. It is a natural reaction of people who have thrown everything into an effort and have built a following. Now Udall, who has become a national figure (for how long, no one can know), talks of remaining the spokesman for the liberal wing of the Party. Meanwhile, he has filed for reëlection to his House seat from Arizona and, unlike many Presidential candidates, seems—at least, as of now—to have concluded that he will make no more than one race for the Presidency. Looking relaxed and well, he told reporters gathered in the Gold Ballroom of the Statler-Hilton, "We had a great and interesting adventure in the last two years," and he said that they fought the good fight and talked about the issues and "now we're here to help Jimmy Carter celebrate his victory." Asked if he would run for the Presidential nomination again, Udall replied, "I think we had one good race. We ran it. I'm not looking forward to any more."

Jerry Brown, meeting today with his California delegation in the Trianon Ballroom of the New York Hilton, struck a very different note. Brown has not calmed down yet, and he sees himself, with reason, as having a future in Presidential politics. He did, after all, defeat the nominee every time he faced him but once, and that was in Oregon, where he won twenty-three percent of the vote on a write-in (Carter received twenty-five percent, and Church, who won the primary, received thirty-two percent). Had Brown entered the primary race earlier, anything might have happened. Brown is thirty-eight and has time, and he shows no inclination to curb his own ambitions on behalf of the nominee. This morning, Brown, wearing a gray suit and a blue shirt, looked, as usual, like a conservative banker. Brown continues to stress his unorthodoxy while behaving like a rather orthodox politician. He likes to describe his campaign as "unorthodox." I heard him do that in Oregon, and today, again referring to his campaign as "unorthodox," he said, "I said it would materialize in the West and if it was the will of the people it would spread East." And he added, "We're here." Then he recited his triumphs—"It was the will of the people in Maryland, it was the will of the people in New Jersey, it was the will of the people in Nevada," and so on—listing the states where he won, and tossing in Oregon, saying, "I count a write-in vote as one-point-five votes. On the basis of that, I won Oregon." He continued, "I've tried to raise issues in this campaign; I'm going to continue to raise them." Issuing a not very veiled warning to Jimmy Carter, he said, "I do not believe in a cult of personality," and added, "I'm not going to try to sugarcoat the problems." He talked of an "era of limits" and the growing claims on depleting resources, of unemployment, and of "bombed-out buildings"—vacant ghetto buildings he saw in the East have now become part of his repertoire. "That's what our nominee is going to have to address himself to," Brown continued. "And he can, with our help. We're here to have an impact." He was applauded. He started to say that he saw the Convention as a beginning, but then midway he stopped and said, "Actually, I see everything as a beginning."

Tonight, Jerry Brown's sister Kathleen Brown Rice is circling the Convention floor, gathering names and addresses of potential future Brown supporters. Hamilton Jordan is also circling the floor, greeting, he says, "old friends and old enemies." The instructions to the Carter floor managers are to "maximize" the number of votes for Carter, watch what's going on, and not make anybody mad. There are a few Oklahoma delegates holding out for Fred Harris, and to mollify them a last-minute arrangement has been made for Carl Albert, who also comes from Oklahoma, to address the Convention briefly. Now John Glenn is giving a keynote address, and only the Ohio delegation seems to be paying attention. Keynote addresses are supposed to light up Conventions and can help the speaker's political career, but Glenn's speech is falling flat. He looks small and lonely up there on the rostrum. The rostrum was deliberately decorated with picket fencing to give it an old-fashioned look. The bunting around the hall was designed to resemble the bunting at the 1924 Democratic Convention in an earlier Madison Square Garden. The hall is a bit small for such a sizable Convention ("Do you have to call it small?" a Democratic Party official asked me. "Can't you call it 'cozy'? 'Intimate'?"), and the aisles are hopelessly clogged. There must be thousands of still photographers on the floor, taking pictures of Warren Beatty and Jesse Jackson and of the new political celebrities—Hamilton Jordan and Gerald Rafshoon and Patrick Caddell. The large photographs of past Democratic Presidents are not here this year. Perhaps the reason is the size of the hall—but one wonders whether it is the increasing number of blemishes on past heroes. When a film to introduce Representative Barbara Jordan, the next keynote speaker, begins, showing a scene from the House Judiciary Committee's 1974 impeachment inquiry, the Convention audience cheers—its first demonstration of enthusiasm. That seems to be a period still deep in its consciousness, still a source of pride. And Barbara Jordan, the large black woman from Texas who imposed herself on the national consciousness then with her performance—her sharpness of mind, firmness of delivery, strength—wakes up the Convention now. Barbara Jordan, a black woman, a keynote speaker at the Democratic Convention. An important change has taken place. And as she stands there, in her green dress, delivering her speech in a forceful voice and clipping her words for emphasis, the delegates listen. A shrewd woman, she knows how to make the most of this opportunity. Yet the impact seems to come not from what she says—what she says is not very arresting—but from the way she says it, and from her symbolism. And she ends, quoting Lincoln, " 'As I would not be a slave, so I would not be a master. This expresses my idea of democracy. Whatever differs from this, to the extent of the difference is no democracy.' " The applause starts quietly and then, feeding on itself, grows. It seems that the delegates want to make this a moment, want an excuse to express emotion. Robert Strauss, standing by her side, smiles with satisfaction. He knows that it was a good stroke to have Barbara Jordan make a keynote address. The band plays "The Eyes of Texas," and Barbara Jordan and Robert Strauss, two outsiders who learned to make their way in Texas politics, happily clap in time.

JULY 14

Wednesday. The twenty-first floor of the Americana, early afternoon. Carter's top staff members are quartered here, as are the candidate and his family. His mother, Miss Lillian, who has captured the public's imagination with her direct talk, is giving an interview. His daughter, Amy, chases down the hall. Carter's younger brother, Billy, is dressed in a yellow double-knit suit, ready to go to lunch at "21." One is inclined to believe Billy Carter when he says he would rather be home in Plains, sitting around his filling station drinking beer. (He is also his brother's partner in the family's peanut-growing and peanut-warehousing business.) Yesterday, Jimmy Carter visited the New Jersey delegation; he had lost the

New Jersey primary to "Uncommitted," which really represented Brown and Hubert Humphrey. The delegation leader for Brown said he would now support Carter, and Jody Powell took pains to make sure the press found that out. Now Powell and Hamilton Jordan have just come from a meeting with Carter, along with Gerald Rafshoon, Charles Kirbo, and Greg Schneiders, to discuss the procedure for announcing Carter's choice of a running mate tomorrow. The candidate's secret has been well kept—even from his staff. At the end of the meeting, Jordan and Rafshoon made one last pitch for Mondale, Rafshoon arguing that the selection of Mondale would get the best press reaction. The staff has consulted with others who have been through the process of taking the final steps in selecting a Vice-Presidential candidate. Carter will telephone the man he has chosen between 8 and 8:30 A.M. tomorrow, to avoid a leak of his decision which could come from a call tonight (Jordan and Kirbo prevailed upon him to call the others, too, so that they would not have to do it), and will announce his choice at a press conference at about ten. (The Secret Service has asked for an hour's notice, to get to the Vice-Presidential candidate's side by the time his name is announced.) At that time, Carter will answer questions about how he arrived at his choice, and later in the day he and his aides will brief some members of the press to try to get across what a deliberative process it was. They think they have "a good story to tell," and want to make the most of it. The potential candidates' staffs are being called now and informed of these procedures.

Last night, the Convention paid its respects to some of its former leaders: George McGovern, Edmund Muskie, and Hubert Humphrey were all given a chance to speak to the Convention and then were bustled off. The stage was thus cleared for the nomination of Jimmy Carter, the newcomer, tonight. Because the Democrats are not at each other's throats, the word has got about, spread by the media, that this Convention is a "love-in." It's not. The Convention does have a sort of mellow feel—at least, compared with other Democratic Conventions—because the nomination is, as everyone knows, settled. Carter did not run the sort of campaign that gets people very excited. And Carter's followers are not particularly zealous. Delegates backing other candidates arrived here knowing that there was little they could do, so they are attending the Convention with varying degrees of resignation. But the surface tranquillity is misleading, as a tour of the floor indicates. A New York labor leader (a Jackson backer): "I don't like it, but we have no choice now. I think there's potential for a landslide, and potential for a disaster. No one knows what he's got in store, and he has only a few people around him. I guess that's a good strategy to get here, but we have to know now whether he'll broaden out." A governor, after saying that Carter had not been a bad governor and might be a good President: "My problem with him is that he is unnecessarily contradictory." The governor went on to explain the peculiar mood of this Convention: "Carter is bringing different elements within the Party together, but he does not appeal as strongly to any element as the candidate whose rapport is with that element in particular. We're getting back the old F.D.R. coalition, but for different reasons." Dina Beaumont, vice-president of District 11 of the Communications Workers of America, a California delegate and a Brown supporter: "This Convention is exactly what Strauss said he wanted—dull, dull, dull." I asked her if that bothered her. She replied, "In the sense that it means we'll come out of here united and put a Democrat in the White House, it doesn't. In the sense that it's taken some of the spice out of the Democratic Party, it does." She continued, "Carter has real problems in California. He is an unknown there, made no race there in the primary. Californians are very issue-oriented. There is that continuing, nagging question of where he is on the issues."

The methodical manner in which the Carter camp went about the selection of a running mate was intended not just to avoid disaster—as befell George McGovern when he chose Thomas Eagleton—but to give the desired picture of Carter. Characteristically, the process began with a memorandum written by Hamilton Jordan, in April. The memorandum stressed the importance of confidentiality and of drama at the Convention. Jordan suggested that three criteria be applied in making the actual choice of a running mate, with points assigned in each category: ability, fifteen points; integrity, fifteen points; acceptance, ten points. Next, he listed every Democratic senator and governor, several members of the House, and several Democratic mayors, and assigned them points in each category. The process was admittedly arbitrary, and Jordan was not familiar with many of the figures. (Despite all this methodology, the final list consists of the obvious names.) Next, he proposed that all those with a total of less than twenty-seven points out of the possible forty be eliminated, though exceptions could be made for a few, either because they had been particularly helpful to the Carter campaign or because it would be bad politics not to have them on the initial list. Then he added considerations of age, political philosophy, region, politics, and his own biases, and ended up with a list of twenty people to be considered—or apparently considered. Jordan and Patrick Caddell then decided that Caddell should conduct a poll on fourteen of those names. The poll, Carter aides said, showed that Carter would not be significantly helped or hurt by any one of them. Next came a period in which Carter received biographical material on the people being considered and made calls around the country to get reactions, while his staff and Kirbo also began asking around. Subsequently, Kirbo went to Washington to conduct his interviews with prospective nominees. About two weeks ago, Carter met in Plains with Powell, Jordan, and Kirbo. Afterward, Jordan wrote Carter a memo in which he said that the most important criterion was that the person chosen be seen by the public as honest and competent. The question, he said, was whether the Vice-Presidential candidate should shore up the South, which would probably support Carter in any event, or, while costing some support in the South, make up this loss in other regions of the country and create increased support and enthusiasm among liberals, independents, blacks, and unions. Then, reflecting the Carter campaign's propensity for thinking in terms of the words that convey impressions, Jordan listed the finalists and the words that he thought attached to their names. Jordan argued that the most important thing this year was that the voters were less interested in ideology than they were in a candidate's personal qualities.

A memorandum was also prepared on the role of the Vice-Presidential candidate in the campaign and, if elected, in the Administration. It emphasized the importance of giving that person independence. It remains to be seen how realistic the memo is. It argued that the Vice-Presidency had not been a very good job in the past because Presidents had not allowed it to be. Usually, it said, the President's staff caused friction, and a large number of staff people were allowed to give orders to the Vice-President, and it argued that things did not have to be that way. It made some suggestions about the Vice-President's role in the Administration and suggested that his office be moved into the White House proper from the Executive Office Building, across the way. At the beginning of the Nixon Administration, Spiro Agnew's office was in the White House. (Humphrey's had been in the Executive Office Building.) After a while, Agnew was moved across the street. Jordan was right, as far as he went, about the problem of the role of the Vice-President. But there is another problem, which defies the nice theories. The problem is that the Vice-President is a supernumerary, without any real power or machinery at his command, and supernumeraries are given short shrift by busy and powerful people who are playing for big stakes; the way to prevent this is to put real power and machinery at the Vice-President's command, but no President has wanted to do that. Still, potential Vice-Presidential nominees usually think that this time it will be different, and the men who select them usually talk as if they thought so, too.

The Americana is bedlam—even the twenty-first floor, Carter's own floor, which has been cut off by security guards one floor below. (The elevators have been wired so that they will not stop at the twenty-first floor.) Color-coded passes determine which Carter staff members have access to which floor, with green passes, the lowest rank, being liberally handed out, to make people feel good. In the vast Albert Hall, in the lower lobby, people sign up for passes, or to do volunteer work, or for jobs in the campaign. Promising organizers are sent up to the fifth floor to be interviewed by Timothy Kraft—the manager of Carter's efforts in Iowa, Pennsylvania, Michigan, and Ohio—who will be in charge of "field operations" for the November election. On the twenty-first floor, television camera crews file through, filming the candidate's top aides at work, and still photographers come to take pictures of them. Jody Powell gives briefings and fends off requests for interviews with the candidate, and even with Amy. Hamilton Jordan worries about everything from getting hold of additional tickets for tonight's and tomorrow night's Convention sessions to calls from Senator Eagleton, who is worried about restiveness within the Missouri delegation on the abortion issue. There was a time when these people might have been worrying about getting their candidate's nomination, but now that is secure, and other worries fill the space. During the brief time that Jordan spent in the Convention hall last evening, he was asked by the staff to soothe Pittsburgh's mayor, Peter Flaherty, who had come out for Carter early and now was feeling unloved (Jordan couldn't find him, so left him a note), and was stopped by a House member and asked if Carter would campaign in his district. Jordan is thirty-one, and has straight dark hair (which he gets out of his eyes by tossing his head), blue eyes, a pink complexion, and even, white teeth. He is heavyset, and he almost always wears a denim jacket and almost never wears a tie.

He is not without arrogance, but he hides it most of the time. He is solicitous of campaign workers, jollies them along, cheers them up, and tells all those who stop him to tell him what they did for the campaign, "You did a good job. . . . We've heard a lot about the good job you did for us. . . . We appreciate all your work." With people he knows better, he wisecracks.

Jordan does not profess to hold any particular philosophy or pretend to be very concerned about issues. His consuming purpose—which he has pursued since 1966, when Carter made an unsuccessful try for the Georgia governorship and Jordan, then twenty-one, was his director of youth activities—is to advance the political aims of Jimmy Carter. Jordan says he is convinced that Carter would "do good things" if he should be elected President. I once asked Jordan what it was about government that interested him, and he seemed mystified by the question. Carter's immediate staff remains a tight little group, suspicious of outsiders, protective of its power. This is not surprising, and it is also true that most men of great power and responsibility want a few close aides in whom they can place absolute trust. But these tendencies, if insufficiently resisted, can lead to trouble. Carter's aides do not as yet block the access or ideas of others, but they are possessive of their power. After all, they were there when it was only themselves and Carter. Their achievement is remarkable, but their range of experience is still limited. It remains to be seen how interested they are in branching out. These men clearly are not Haldeman and Ehrlichman, but it is clear that they would go to great lengths for their man. Still, every President I have observed has had people around him who would do some unattractive things for what they considered the greater good. The White House, like any seat of great power, is not a genteel place. There is no good way of assessing these people's sense of limits until great temptations—and serious challenges—confront them. The unpredictability of how people will behave in the White House grows out of the uniqueness of the place. There is no other place that produces this particular set of pressures, no other place that is so vanity-inducing, no other place that impels such pride and arrogance.

It is known by now that Carter has quite a temper, lashes out at the staff, and does not welcome bad news or criticism. (Powell is considered something of a hero for sitting with Carter on the plane when the campaign is running late.) But Powell and Jordan do not appear to be yes-men, and do seem to have fairly free exchanges with Carter—at least at times. They are not obsequious toward him—they still call him "Jimmy"—and they manage to talk about him and the campaign with loyal irreverence. They seem to understand the need for humor in the campaign, and they are fairly open with the press, as Carter surely knows by now, and relaxed about reporting to outsiders conflicting views within the entourage. But, unlike Rosalynn Carter and Charles Kirbo, they do not have peer relationships with Carter. Carter seems to have few friends. Kirbo, says an aide to Carter, "is the one who can straighten Jimmy out when he gets off balance." He cited as an example Carter's shaken reaction to coming in fourth in the Massachusetts primary and his public petulance in Florida in the ensuing days. Kirbo, the aide said, steadied Carter at that time.

This afternoon, Jordan is worrying about finding extra tickets for this evening for the Reverend Martin Luther King Sr.—Daddy King—who has arrived with fifteen members of his family; soothing a campaign worker who is handling the distribution of tickets for this evening (more Carter relatives have been arriving, reaching a total of seventy-four); talking with Gerald Rafshoon about a meeting Rafshoon will have later to work on the lighting and the sound system at the Garden; conferring with Powell and Kirbo (whom Jordan calls "Mr. Kirbo") about denying a report that Jerry Brown was offered ten minutes of time to speak at the Convention if he would refrain from having his name placed in nomination; going over with staff aides the question of who will sit on the rostrum tomorrow evening ("Let's get some of our friends up there. . . . Be sure half of them are women"), vetoing some names and adding others; teasing Miss Lillian about her social whirl (she is about to go to a reception); meeting with a columnist; and attending a meeting with officials of the A.F.L.–C.I.O.

The meeting with the labor officials, held in a suite on the thirtieth floor of the Americana, is attended by Lane Kirkland, the secretary-treasurer of the A.F.L.–C.I.O. and, many think, Meany's likely successor; Alexander Barkan, the director of the A.F.L.–C.I.O.'s Committee on Political Education (COPE), which distributes campaign funds and other help; Jesse Calhoon, the president of the Marine Engineer's Beneficial Association; Thomas Donahue, George Meany's executive assistant; and Landon Butler, the Carter campaign's political director, and Jordan. The meeting is being held because the Carter campaign has blundered into intramural union politics. The problem is that it has tentatively agreed to bring into the campaign as a representative of labor an official of the machinists union, which, while affiliated with the A.F.L.–C.I.O., is part of the liberal labor coalition, with several of whose members the A.F.L.–C.I.O. hierarchy is at odds. The coalition is essentially a rival force. Landon Butler looks nervous. Kirkland opens the meeting by saying to Jordan, "Do you want a unified labor effort or a factional one?" His blunt message is softened by a Southern accent and a gentle manner, but Jordan understands. He smiles and says, "That's not a hard question," and he goes on, "Being from the South, being from Georgia, we don't have the kinds of relationship with labor we would have if we were from Ohio, from the North. We've made mistakes along the way." The union leaders, who have been eying him intently, relax just slightly. Jordan goes on to say that he has talked with Barkan and wants to continue to, and he wants to work with COPE, and the union leaders slowly nod in assent. They are all elderly men, with gnarled, experienced faces, and they sit across the room watching this thirty-one-year-old man with the unlined face who sits in a big black leather chair. Jordan is wearing a suit and tie this afternoon, and he props his feet, in boots, on an ottoman. He is deferential but utterly poised, and the union leaders show a grudging respect for this young man who has made off with their Party.

Kirkland explains, as if instructing a son, that the problem is not just that the designated labor representative is from the wrong side of the street but that labor opposes having any designated staff spokesman. "We regard that as an impediment and as a source of trouble," he says. A designated labor representative, in a campaign or in the White House, he explains, could become fixed in the minds of those he works with as the channel to which labor officials should take their complaints and requests, and what he says could become discounted because, after all, he is the special pleader for labor. Moreover, Kirkland says, "if you take a specific fellow from any organization, what you're getting, by and large, is not a labor man—you're getting someone from one organization." He continues, "Our lines are open. George Meany will return Governor Carter's calls; you and I can talk. We have a regional office in Atlanta; we can strengthen that."

Jordan replies, "This would be another step in our educational process," and he smiles and laughs, and the union leaders, at last, smile.

Jordan asks their advice about how to work with the various unions.

Barkan explains that they do not mind what arrangements the campaign makes with other unions, but "when it comes to contact with the A.F.L.–C.I.O., what Lane is saying is you ought to deal with the appropriate structure." Barkan is something of a legend, because he has great power, which he does not hesitate to use, and because he has a close relationship with Meany. He has not hesitated to try to order the Democratic Party around, and though his wishes have carried less force in recent years—the reformers having reduced his power—people still want to know where Barkan stands. He is wearing a plaid suit, a red shirt, white shoes, and white socks; he is a large man and speaks with a strong New Jersey accent. The one thing that he and Jordan have in common is their understanding of the size of what is at stake. Carter got where he is without the help of the A.F.L.–C.I.O.—and with the help of the liberal labor unions—so now his aide must be convinced that he needs its help. The new campaign-spending law forbids contributions during the general-election campaigns to Presidential candidates who accept federal funding. Therefore, the unions cannot make contributions to the candidate, but there are other ways, as there have always been, in which they can be helpful. Barkan explains that Meany told him to tell Jordan that the A.F.L.–C.I.O. will endorse Carter and that Barkan should get together with Jordan to explain how the A.F.L.–C.I.O. can help. It has fourteen million members, he says, with computerized phone lists. "Nobody else has that," he adds. Its members are concentrated in sixteen states, which could produce forty-one percent of the popular vote, he says. Barkan says he is pleased that the Democratic National Committee will be raising and expending funds for voter registration. The A.F.L.–C.I.O. is always highly interested in the congressional races—sometimes more interested than it is in the Presidential race—because it wants to have in Congress as many supporters of its positions as possible.

One of the leaders tells Jordan that what labor will spend on getting out the vote will be worth twenty million dollars to the Carter campaign. "We can organize fourteen million members," says Barkan—there is some question as to how closely union members follow their leaders, but that subject does not come up today—and he continues, "We assume there is another voter in each family, so that makes twenty-eight million. We accept the responsibility for registering those people, educating them." He explains that in 1968 "we put out fifty-five million pieces of literature for Humphrey." Barkan and Jordan arrange to meet again soon, and Barkan offers to advise the campaign on which labor conventions Carter should speak before. Jordan thanks the leaders for their offers of help, says that the mistake about the labor representative will be corrected, and adds, "By just about the time the campaign is over, we'll finally have an understanding of the labor unions." He laughs and continues, "We'll probably make mistakes—we made one here—but the mistakes we make will be honest ones." The labor leaders smile.

Jordan, his wife, Nancy, and his remarkably calm secretary, Caroline Wellons, and I arrive at Madison Square Garden shortly after eight. Jordan, who has made no special arrangements to get in, docilely accepts the guards' instructions to go up several flights of escalators and then down again—the Garden is a maze—in order to reach the Carter camp's trailers, which are parked within the Garden, just off the Convention floor. It is a command post fit for a Convention struggle and seeming no less busy for the lack of one. There are three trailers, commanded by Rick Hutcheson, a serious, slim twenty-four-year-old man with straight sandy hair, a mustache, and wire-rimmed glasses. Hutcheson has served as the Carter campaign's delegate hunter. In the main trailer are fourteen phones connected to phones on the floor in each of the fourteen regions established by the Carter forces. A campaign worker mans each phone. There are other phone consoles, and a red phone that is a direct line to Carter. Jordan, Frank Mankiewicz (the former McGovern political coördinator, who is now helping the Carter forces), and some staff aides deal with a last-minute crisis concerning the arrangements under which, after the roll call is completed, Jerry Brown, who has offered to make the vote unanimous, will be called on to make the vote of his own state unanimous and, after several states have done this, George Busbee, the governor of Georgia, will move that the Convention make it unanimous. *"Acclamation,"* Mankiewicz tells Jordan. *"Acclamation.* If you move to make it unanimous, some bastard might hold out." Brown wanted to be the one to make the move about the Convention as a whole but the Carter aides—uninterested in giving him such a role—headed that off. Jordan talks with Powell and with Carter about the final arrangements. They need California in November, and they want to give Brown some role—but not too big a role.

The staff in the trailer reports the prospective vote to Hutcheson, who marks it on a large board. It is determined that the fifteen hundred and five votes necessary for Carter's nomination will be reached when the roll call gets to the "O"s—probably Ohio. One of the television sets in the trailer shows a replay of Carter on "What's My Line?" in 1973. "We'd do anything then," Jordan remarks. Then the television sets show Peter Rodino nominating Carter for the Presidency. Rodino, knowing that the consideration of him as the Vice-Presidential candidate was not serious, withdrew his name on the ground of health (he has glaucoma), and, according to an arrangement already worked out between Rodino's staff and Carter's, Carter asked Rodino to nominate him. In one person, Rodino is Italian, Catholic, and Watergate hero. "We may be living through the most difficult era since the first years of the Republic," Rodino is saying, and Jordan, on the phone to Powell is saying he's distressed that "I am missing my nominating speech." The challenge, Rodino says, is "to prove that a free people can make self-government endure." Jordan is going over last-minute details with Hutcheson. "I say to you his heart is honest and the people will follow him," Rodino says. "Through him we shall carry forward the great promise of our Founding Fathers." When Rodino finishes, Jordan lets out a great whoop, waves a beer can in the air, and whoops some more. When Margaret (Midge) Costanza, the vice-mayor of Rochester, begins her seconding speech, Jordan shouts, "Give 'em hell, Midge!" Andrew Young, the black House member from Georgia who has given Carter crucial support, then makes another seconding speech. He says, "When we have stumbled, it's been usually a stumbling over the burden of race," and he continues, "I don't know about you, but I'm ready to lay those burdens down." While Young speaks, Jordan talks on the phone with Strauss, who is on the rostrum. The demonstration for Carter at the end of the nominating speeches is strangely brief When Lindy Boggs, the chairperson, tells the demonstrators to sit down, they do. "What happened to my demonstration?" Jordan asks, and then he shrugs and says, "I'm not worried." Hutcheson's vote counters now have Carter's vote at two thousand and forty-five.

A Carter aide comes in from the floor and frets that the sound in the hall is bad and that there is no enthusiasm, but no one pays much attention to him. The television screens show Archibald Cox, another Watergate hero, nominating Udall: "He succeeded in the larger race. His defeat was a greater triumph than victory." And then Udall appears on the rostrum. His followers in the Convention audience react strongly—more strongly than Carter's did. It is the reaction of those who believe, who are really with their candidate. Udall stands with his arms folded, smiling, clearly enjoying his moment; it is his best moment since he and his followers thought he had won the Wisconsin primary, and it is his last such moment. "How proud I am of that army of Udall campaigners who gave us time and money and votes and dedication and saw us through the most second-place finishes in the history of politics," Udall says. Then he says, "We thought we had a special campaign. Old and young, we did our best. We hit hard but we hit fair, and we tried to talk issues and to talk about change and we weren't afraid to be gentle with each other and we tried to laugh a little bit at ourselves now and then. But it's all over now." Then Udall says that he wants the vote tonight "to be one of good will," and that he is releasing his delegates in order that they may vote for Carter.

Landon Butler, watching with Jordan in the trailer, says, "It takes a lot to get up and do that."

Jordan, reflecting the attitude of the Carter camp, had few kind words for Udall during the campaign for the nomination, but now he remarks, "He's a good man."

"As I leave this convention hall tonight," Udall concludes, "I'm going to have on one of those green buttons that dogged me all over America. And Jimmy, if you're listening tonight, if I can't put your buttons down I'm going to put 'em on, I guess. And tomorrow morning I'm enlisting as a soldier in the Carter campaign."

Jordan lets out a whoop. "Udall for Vice-President!" he shouts. "Let's send Kirbo out to interview him on the podium." He keeps talking. "It's a hell of a good speech, isn't it?" he says. "Udall is making a hell of a speech."

He is. Udall is making a graceful exit, and when he talks tonight about the questions that are important to him, he sounds better than he ever did in the campaign. Rafshoon, who has arrived at the trailer, remarks, "It seems like a Udall Convention."

On the television screens, Cesar Chavez is nominating Brown. It is a moving moment. He tells the Convention, "There is so much meaningful work to be done and so many people unemployed. Think of the thousands of people who are bedridden with sores on their backs because there's no one to turn them. Think of all the older people who are abandoned who need a glass of water, who need a warm meal but have no one to give them help."

A television crew arrives to shoot the scene at the trailers. Hutcheson tells those manning the phones that Carter wants to talk to Udall, Midge Costanza, Andrew Young, and Peter Rodino.

On the television screens, Edward Kennedy is being interviewed. He is asked his plans for 1976—a question that, in other contexts, he has been asked hundreds of times over the past four years. "Well, I'm obviously interested in being returned to the United States Senate," Kennedy replies. This time, no one can doubt him.

At ten minutes before eleven, Jordan decides that he wants to go out to the Convention floor, in order to be with the Georgia delegation for the balloting. He loosens his tie, pours some beer into a paper cup, thanks the workers in the trailer ("Great job, everybody. This is it"), and, with his wife and Caroline Wellons, heads for the floor. Two campaign helpers act, as best they can, as bodyguards, clearing the way: Evan Dobelle, the Democratic mayor of Pittsfield, and Jim King, who has been an advance man for Edward Kennedy and is said to be the best in the business. As Jordan passes the Ohio delegation, he gives them the thumbs-up sign. He is stopped for autographs, interviews, but eventually he makes his way to the Georgia delegation. Jerry Rafshoon has already arrived there. Jordan, chewing gum, standing with his arm around his wife, waits. Iowa. "That's where it all started," he says. In January, "Uncommitted" won the Iowa precinct caucuses, which represented ten percent of Iowa's Democrats, but the press made much of Carter's victory over the other candidates, as Carter and Jordan had expected it to. Jordan edges toward George Busbee, and his entourage becomes a knot of bodies. Michigan. Carter barely defeated Udall in Michigan. Jordan stands quietly as the states are called. New Hampshire. Carter edged out a crowded field in New Hampshire and became the established "front runner," his face on the cover of the following week's news magazines. His "winnerness" kept propelling him toward the nomination. Pat Caddell arrives. By the time the roll reaches New York, Carter has a thousand two hundred and thirteen and a half votes. New York, where Carter came in fourth, now gives him two hundred and nine and a half votes. "God, we're running thirty seconds behind," Jordan jokes. Ohio will do it. On June 8th, Ohio sent Jimmy Carter crashing through to the nomination (despite his poor showing in New Jersey and California that same day). "Here we go," says Jordan as the roll call gets to Ohio. He reaches his arms around his wife, then around Rafshoon, Caddell, Caroline Wellons, and Phil Wise, who ran the Carter campaign in Florida, Wisconsin, Maryland, and New Jersey, and, as Ohio casts its vote, his face dark red from the heat and the excitement, he lets out a series of great, loud whoops. He kisses his wife and his secretary, who are in tears from the emotion of it all, and the knot of people sways perilously beside the chairs of the Georgia delegation. It is a moment of unrestrained rejoicing for those who made the long march. Ben Brown, the black Georgia state senator, lifts Jordan onto a chair.

"Four long, wonderful years!" Jordan shouts into the microphone of Tom Pettit, of NBC. "People who took a chance and believed in someone."

"How do you feel?" Pettit asks him.

"More emotional than I expected," Jordan says.

Then Jordan heads back to the trailer. "That was a sweet moment," he says. "I'm glad we were on the floor. I didn't expect it to be that emotional." He says that several times. Back at the trailer, he says, "O.K., we're going to start the switches now. Back to work."

Greg Schneiders calls from Carter's suite: Carter wants to be sure of the final details of the balloting, and wants to talk to Brown after Brown moves to make California unanimous for Carter.

On television, Brown delivers a little speech as he announces the switch. "In the years ahead, we've got a lot of work to do," he says. He seems excited, and anxious to pack all he can into these few minutes in the limelight. "I don't think it's going to be done in a hundred days or a thousand days. It's a long, difficult struggle to live within our environment and work together and bring about justice. I think Jimmy Carter can do that; he's proved it to you, he's proved it to me, and I just want to be able to announce that the California delegation votes two hundred and seventy-eight votes for Mr. Carter and we're on our way to bring this country back into the Democratic column."

When Brown announces the switch, Jordan pounds his fist on a wall and lets out a rebel yell.

And then Busbee makes his motion.

The television screens show Carter, in shirtsleeves, smiling a broad smile.

"I wish Jimmy would frown for about five minutes," Jordan jokes.

The screens show the predictable picture of Carter hugging Amy.

Jordan stands in the doorway of the trailer, holding a beer, and talks to the campaign workers. "You all did great," he says, and as he goes on talking to them, quietly, Rafshoon joins him. Rafshoon, the street-wise media man, is blinking back tears. "It was just a more emotional thing than I thought it would be," Jordan says. "Try to stop and think what all this means. It's kind of hard to grasp." He pauses and then says, "O.K.?" He pauses again and then says, "On to November." And then he lets out a great, loud rebel *"Yahooooo!"*

JULY 15

Thursday Morning. The Georgian Ballroom of the Americana Hotel. In a few minutes, Carter will announce his choice of a running mate. The final vote last night was Carter, 2,468.5; Udall, 329.5; Brown, 70.5; Wallace, 57. In 1968, Richard Nixon came to the Jackie-of-Hearts Room in the Hilton Plaza after meetings that lasted all night, and announced that he had chosen Spiro Agnew; in 1972, in a room in the Doral Hotel, Frank Mankiewicz, after meetings that lasted all night, announced that McGovern had chosen Thomas Eagleton. Carter has at least had time. He has suggested that in the future the Convention recess for thirty days to give the candidate time to select a running mate—which seems, given what is involved in holding a party Convention, an impossible idea. He has made the alternative proposal that the National Committee meet thirty days later to ratify the nominee's choice. That doesn't seem to be a very good idea, either, since in effect it eliminates any possibility of an independent judgment on the part of the Party and removes at least some of the pressure on the candidate to make a good choice. It may be that there is no satisfactory solution. It may be that we shall have to rely on the sense of responsibility of the candidate, and hope that he takes some time and care with his decision.

Shortly after ten, Carter arrives with his wife and announces, "I've asked to serve as my running mate, if the delegates will approve, Senator Walter Mondale." Mondale will be a popular choice with the delegates and with the press, and many will think well of Carter for having selected a man who does not agree with him in all respects—one who is at least potentially an independent thinker. Mondale, in fact, backed Humphrey for the nomination, and was somewhat critical of Carter. Mondale is well liked by the press, because he is considered thoughtful, humane, and humorous. He not only talks about his concern for the poor, minorities, children, those who do not get a fair shake in life but, unlike some liberals, seems really to feel concern. He is popular among those who serve on Senate staffs—close observers of the place—because he seems to care about what he's doing and has not acquired the posturing airs so many senators do. People who have worked with him on issues have been struck by the amount of hard work he does himself. He is a believer in federal programs—more of them. He has done his share of shaving and playing it safe. He supported the war in Vietnam throughout the Johnson Administration, and explained later that that was because he did not want to embarrass his mentor, Hubert Humphrey. But he also said that that had been "the biggest mistake of my political career." He is thin-skinned about his press coverage.

Carter says he chose Mondale for his "comprehension and compassion for people who need services of government most," because he has shown "sound judgment in times of difficulty," because he has "the trust of a wide range of Democrats," and because he has a "clear concept of what the Presidency should be." Carter also says, "I feel completely compatible with Senator Mondale. . . . It's a very sure feeling that I have about that point." He says that he changed his mind three times about whom he would select. Perhaps he did; perhaps he does not know for sure.

There have been many odd turns of events over the past four years. Mondale came close to being asked by McGovern to run with him, and then, when Eagleton was dropped, he was felt out about joining the ticket (and turned down the chance). Mondale was up for reëlection to his Senate seat that year. In 1974, he made his abortive effort at running for the Presidency, found it frustrating and not to his taste, and, in November, dropped out, saying, "Basically, I found I did not have the overwhelming desire to be President which is essential for the kind of campaign that is required." His dropping out was one of the events that opened the way for a number of other candidates, and it helped Carter. Because many people took Mondale at his word, his dropping out also fanned questions about whether the long nominating process rewards the right qualities—a question that lingers concerning Carter.

After his announcement, Carter says a strange thing. He is asked by a reporter if his Presidency might differ from his campaign for the Presidency, just as his governorship of Georgia differed from his campaign for the governorship. Carter made big news, put himself on the national map, when, on the day of his inauguration, though he had campaigned for the Wallace vote, he said, "The time for racial discrimination is over." Today, Carter disputes the idea that the campaign he ran was different from his governorship, and says that "there was no ripple of surprise" when he made that statement at his inauguration. He adds, "I'm not ever going to be constrained by absolute consistency." Asked whether Mondale's having dropped out of the campaign bothered him, Carter replies that Mondale pointed out to him that he had conducted a spirited campaign but that "he knew that he could not win." That is not quite what Mondale and his staff said at the time he dropped out. Acknowledging that he was low in the polls, they argued, with validity, that it was too early for the polls to mean anything, and that he was dropping out because he did not want to live the life of a campaigner for two years.

The Mondales arrive in the Georgian Room and are met by Mrs. Carter, and the two couples stand, smiling, on the rostrum. We have seen such happy foursomes before—the Johnsons and the Humphreys, the McGoverns and the Eagletons. One is drawn to Mrs. Carter's face for what it might tell us; there are features of beauty, but she is not quite beautiful. It is a pleasant face, but it does not convey warmth, it is not expressive. It is as if it were molded, perhaps of metal. She is as unrevealing as Carter is, but Carter's face is relieved by wrinkles and creases. One is told by staff members that she is at least as ambitious as her husband, wants to be First Lady as badly as he wants to be President, and drove herself almost as hard as he drove himself during the long primary season. One also hears stories of times when he wanted to stop and rest and she pushed him to keep going. They clearly are close, and her face almost seems to have been molded by the life she has lived with him. Her mother-in-law, also a strong woman, has said, "I have never seen her let her hair down, never heard her tell a joke."

Mondale says, "No one could be honored more" at having been "selected by this remarkable and good man." Mondale barely knows Carter, and he can't really know yet whether he is a "good man." He then calls Carter a "great man." Mondale says he told Carter that "I was not interested in a ceremonial post." He says, "The Governor and I, I think, are very compatible." Asked how he had prepared himself for his interview with Carter, Mondale jokes, referring to Carter's book, in which Carter takes great pride (as I learned when I set out to interview him last March without having read it), "The first thing I did was to read the most remarkable book ever written, called *Why Not the Best?* I found every word absolutely brilliant." That is not like Carter's humor. Asked if he thinks he is competent to be President, Mondale replies, slowly, "I hope and pray that I could."

The Trianon Ballroom of the New York Hilton. Jimmy Carter and Jerry Brown are here together, smiling and waving at the California delegation. Jerry Brown presented the greatest threat to Carter this year, and could be his most dangerous rival in the future. Actually, Brown is only barely smiling, but he is not much of a smiler. Carter needs Brown, because he needs California, and Brown, as Carter knows, is unpredictable and unmanageable. Brown tells the audience, "I don't think I've seen this much unity in the Democratic Party in my whole life, and we may never see it again, either." He says that he will work hard "to elect our next President, Jimmy Carter." He introduces Carter, patting him on the back—they are both being conventional politicians now—but he does not introduce him with much enthusiasm.

"I want to thank the legislative leaders and the people of California for keeping Jerry Brown at home so long," Carter says. He is joking, but also speaking the truth. Carter continues, "He's a formidable man and a formidable opponent; he's going to be a formidable ally." He hopes. He says that he has known Governor Brown since 1974, and "we've grown to be close friends"—which is clearly not the case. He says, "I was talking with Governor Brown in his suite upstairs—excuse me, his room," and the audience, appreciating the joke about Brown's efforts to convey the idea that he prefers an austere way of life, laughs and applauds. Carter is looser today than I have ever seen him before, and the quick humor is new. His aides always insisted that he had it, but Carter never showed it on the campaign trail. It may be that his single-mindedness did not permit any diversion—not even humor. He said on *Meet the Press* last Sunday, "I have been a little bit hesitant during the campaign to tell jokes or to make light of things, because there might be one out of forty news people who will accept it as a very serious statement." He says that during the primaries he used to talk with his wife about Brown's campaign, and found that "there is a remarkable degree of mutuality of purpose." And then, working his own variation on a Brown theme, he says, "There's no limit on us. Material limits, yes. Governmental limits, yes. But I'm not ready to recognize that there's a limit to hope, to freedom, to individuality." Carter continues, "I said many times in the last nineteen months that I did not intend to lose the nomination, and I don't intend to lose the election, either." Now he must be taken more seriously than when he first started saying—and sounded so strange saying it—that he did not intend to lose the nomination. "I don't take the election for granted," he adds. "The greatest mistake would be overconfidence." And then, talking of millions of Americans in that peculiar Carter manner, he says, "If I ever take a state for granted, I would lose that state. If I ever take a voter for granted, I would lose that sense of the worth of that individual, and that person would feel it."

Thursday Evening. There is an upbeat feel to the Convention tonight. There usually is on the last evening, as on the last night of a college weekend. There are large photographs of Carter and Mondale in the Garden now, and delegates are armed with green-and-white Carter-Mondale posters. Gerald Rafshoon had arranged for the posters to be ready to be run off with the picture and name of any one of six of Carter's finalists, and this morning, when he got the word, he gave the printers the go-ahead. On each side of the rostrum, there are large banners that say "For America's Third Century, Why Not the Best?" Mondale has been nominated (Humphrey made the nominating speech), and now Peter Duchin's orchestra is playing, so that Mondale's and Carter's acceptance speeches will go out on television at just the right time. Perhaps I am mistaken—I will check at the Republican Convention—but Democrats and Republicans seem to have different songs. Peter Duchin's orchestra is playing "When the Saints Go Marching In," "Hey, Look Me Over," and "Hail, Hail, the Gang's All Here." The demonstration for Mondale when his nomination was affirmed seemed to be stronger than the one for Carter last night. A red-white-and-blue beach ball is being tossed among the Pennsylvania, New Mexico, and California delegations, with the crowd cheering or booing the finesse of each shot. The Convention has turned into a giant beach party. Nothing bad has happened; there have been no bitter fights, so the delegates are just having a good time now. Shortly before ten, Walter Mondale comes to the rostrum and waves his arms at the crowd, which cheers him lustily. It likes him, and he is clearly a happy man at this moment. Fate, having veered this way and that, has finally pulled him toward the upper reaches of power, where he wanted to be. He began to want the Vice-Presidential nomination badly, and he has got it. This may be the best moment of the campaign for him—the senior candidate has poured praise upon him, and the Convention is cheering him. It is one of those beginnings—unblemished and unrealistic, as beginnings usually are. No hard questions have been raised yet. No scars yet, no frustrations. The inevitable brutality of the fall campaign has not yet hit. The strains likely to arise between the two candidates have not yet developed. Now Mondale is seen as an asset to the ticket, but it is quite possible that if Carter's fortunes slide, Mondale, whatever his role, will be blamed. Will he be expected to campaign as relentlessly as Carter, and are there many men who could? Mondale turns from side to side, waving to the audience and accepting its cheers. His life is changed irrevocably now. "Tonight we stand together as a party," he says, and the crowd cheers. He talks of "a government that would restore honesty and decency and openness in American public life," and the crowd cheers. He has hit the political theme of this year. He attacks the Republican Administration's "values," saying, "they have tried to paralyze the momentum for human justice in America." Mondale believes this, has talked of it before, so it is not just acceptance-speech rhetoric. (Actually, he has been working on his speech for several days, worrying that it seemed presumptuous but figuring that if the right call came he had best be ready.) He talks about values and about real questions, about justice and compassion, but his delivery is uncharacteristically oratorical—he shouts and waves his arms more than he has done before. He seems—having often been told that he is too low-key—to be searching for a new style. "We solemnly pledge to restore government that tells the truth and obeys the law," he says, and he adds, "We have just lived through the worst political scandal in American history and are now led by a President who pardoned the person who did it," and gets the biggest applause of the evening. Watergate is anything but dead. He says that "the year of our two-hundredth birthday, the year of the election of Jimmy Carter, will go down as one of the greatest years of public reform in American history." Reform. Honesty. Openness. Those are the buzzwords of this year. Every good Democrat has to talk about jobs and health insurance, but the emotional response is to talk about restoration of a government in which people can believe and have pride. I think it is the first time that anything like this has been the principal campaign issue.

There is a fifteen-minute film, which shows Jimmy Carter in jeans in a peanut field and Jimmy Carter in a suit talking about his visions of America. It shows Jimmy Carter the obscure candidate, doggedly going about the country introducing himself to almost anyone he could find. The film cleverly includes cartoons of Carter, at once indicating how important he is and trying to demonstrate that the Carter campaign is capable of irreverence. Then Carter enters the Garden through the crowd on the floor. It is a new touch, a stagy way of showing he is a man of the people. Then, as the candidate stands on the rostrum acknowledging the cheers of the crowd, it almost seems that we are seeing another movie. The candidate and the cheering crowd—the faces are different, but the scene is familiar. Other Conventions have seemed more crazy about the candidate on the rostrum, but the crowd seems happy enough tonight: Carter gives them hope of victory, and he has kept them out of trouble. He smiles what appears to be his genuine smile. But there is a slight strangeness in this scene, and perhaps it has to do with the fact that Jimmy Carter and the Convention audience do not quite fit. He is still the outsider, who did it by determination, mechanics, good themes, and good luck.

"My name is Jimmy Carter and I'm running for President," he begins, and it is a nice stroke, reminding everyone of just how far he has come and how seriously he should be taken. The mannerisms are familiar by now: the hand extended in front of him, palm out, when he stresses a point; the shifting from one foot to the other. He is wearing a blue suit, a blue shirt, and a red tie. His family are on the platform, as are members of his staff, for several of whom this is the first national political convention. He says that 1976 "can be a year of inspiration and hope . . . the year when we give the government of this country back to the people of this country." And then he makes his own reference to the two periods of our past that still disturb people: "We have been shaken by a tragic war abroad and by scandals and broken promises at home." Carter has known how to tap these issues without upsetting people. He talks of being "a farm boy sitting outdoors with my family on the ground in the middle of the night, gathered close around a battery radio connected to the automobile battery, and listening to the Democratic Conventions in far-off cities," and one's mind inescapably turns to Richard Nixon, at the 1968 Republican Convention, talking of being a poor boy hearing the train whistles in the night. Carter pays his obeisance to past Democratic Presidents—mentioning that he never met one—and to the ethnic groups that "have shaped the character of our party." Some of the language is like what we heard throughout the primaries: "We've been hurt and we've been disillusioned" and "We've seen a wall go up that separates us from our own government." He employs his familiar technique of the repeated phrase; this time he lists the number of things that have gone on "too long." "There's a fear that our best years are behind us," he says, which is true, and he adds, "I say to you that our nation's best is still ahead," which would be good to believe. Aligning himself, as he has all year, with those who feel outside, disillusioned, he says, "We want to have faith again; we want to be proud again. We just want the truth again." He cannot talk of "ethnic purity" now, but he does say—once again touching base with the ethnic groups, which are said to still consider him alien—"It's time to honor and strengthen our families, and our neighborhoods, and our diverse cultures and customs." He strikes a populist note that is new; he talks of "a political and economic élite" and of an unnamed "they" who "never stand in line looking for a job . . . never do without food or clothing or a place to sleep." He says that "their children go to exclusive private schools," that "when the bureaucracy is bloated and confused, the powerful always manage to discover and occupy niches of special influence and privilege," and that they are served by an "unfair tax structure." It is easy rhetoric. He is ringing old and slightly tired chimes.

He talks of reform, and there is reason to think that he will try to effect government reform. In fact, we probably know a good deal about his program by now; to anyone who listened to him carefully during the primaries, for all his fogging his more liberal proposals in talk about a balanced budget and private enterprise, he often came across as a programmatic liberal. As a matter of fact, he has done the one thing he set out not to do. He has, like a conventional politician, "overpromised." He has endorsed a number of new programs—health insurance and jobs and education and aid to cities and welfare reform and more Social Security and so on—and he has also pledged to balance the budget by the end of his first term. But even if the programs were phased in slowly and given conservative price tags, there would not be enough money to pay for them and also to balance the budget. In his eagerness to please both liberal and conservative constituencies, he has set himself conflicting goals. What will happen if the public finds that once more it has been overpromised? And at times he said things that raised questions about how much he really understood. With Carter, it's his character, his impulses, that we don't know enough about. Those are what remain hidden. So much of his campaign was calculated and we have seen so little of him that is spontaneous that in important ways he is still a stranger. Jimmy—a familiar name, but he is still a remote figure. He was a manipulative campaigner. All politicians are manipulative; the question is what they manipulate for. All politicians are somewhat deceptive—Franklin Roosevelt was a charming deceiver—and doubtless must be deceptive, and lie at least a little. There are some things they simply cannot be candid about. Carter at least no longer goes around saying that he will never tell a lie or make a misleading statement. (He has been caught in deceptions this year. And I think of the governor at this Convention who said that Carter is "unnecessarily contradictory.") The question, again, is what purpose the deception serves and what keeps it in bounds. These questions get to deep things about a person, things we don't know about Carter. There seems little doubt that he would be as ambitious to be a good President as he is to be President—which is somewhat different from the idea of the office making the man. There also seems little doubt that he would be stubborn. Even his aides say that Carter's would be a very controversial Administration. We don't know how he would react when things went wrong. (There is that aide who said that Kirbo had to steady Carter after he came in fourth in Massachusetts.) He talks about doing some things that are very important, and he probably intends to do them. But the things he talks about are also popular. Where would he be if popular opinion took an ugly turn? He talks tonight, as he did during the campaign, about the poor and about compassion and about justice, and, as usual, he appears to mean what he is saying. He talks about "love," and, perhaps knowing that that has been caricatured, he says, "I have spoken a lot of times this year about love, but love must be aggressively translated into simple justice." He calls again for his programs—for a "complete overhaul of our income-tax system," referring to the current system, as he has done since New Hampshire, as "a disgrace to the human race." He calls for a "nationwide, comprehensive health program." He talks briefly and generally about foreign policy, saying that there must be "nothing less than a sustained architectural effort to shape an international framework of peace within which our own ideals gradually can become a global reality." He does not explain what he means. He talks of having a government that is "as decent and competent as our people"—he seems to have stopped giving the longer list, also caricatured, which included the phrase "as full of love." He talks of the need for a President "who's not isolated from the people but who feels your pain and shares your dreams and takes his strength and his wisdom and his courage from you." Carter sets much store by what he believes to be his ability to form an "intimate" relationship with the people. He says that they may go forward from this Convention "with some differences of opinion, perhaps, but nevertheless united in a calm determination to make our country large and driving and generous in spirit once again, ready to embark on great national deeds." He appeals to national pride, as he did in his effort to be nominated, when he closed many of his speeches by saying that this is "still the greatest nation on earth." Tonight, he closes by saying, "And once again, as brothers and sisters, our hearts will swell with pride to call ourselves Americans."

The hall has already begun to empty when Daddy King is called upon to give the benediction. Robert Strauss has summoned to the rostrum those whose faces filed past us during the primaries—Birch Bayh and Sargent Shriver and Milton Shapp and Morris Udall and Henry Jackson and Frank Church and Jerry Brown—and also runners-up in the Vice-Presidential contest and governors and mayors and Carter campaign officials, and even Strauss's wife. And then the stout old black preacher from the Deep South lets go with a benediction that thunders through the hall, and suddenly, at his direction, the hall is still. I have never before seen such attention paid to a benediction. He bends over almost double sometimes and raises his fist to the heavens sometimes, and the audience seems at first amused and then struck by his force. (Even Carter, who is familiar with this style, smiles a little.) Daddy King lost a son and a wife to murderers, and last week he buried his granddaughter. "Surely," says King, his voice booming, "surely the Lord sent Jimmy Carter to come on out and bring America back where she belongs." And then he commands, "If you have an unforgiving heart, get down on your knees." And when Daddy King finishes, the orchestra plays "We Shall Overcome," and the audience, spontaneously, sings it softly. Next to me, two white women delegates from the state of Washington, Jackson delegates, are in tears.

CHANCELLOR HELMUT SCHMIDT, of West Germany, visiting Washington, revealed yesterday that the United States, Great Britain, France, and West Germany have agreed that they will not take steps to help Italy out of its financial crisis—a loan to Italy was discussed at the Puerto Rico conference last month—if Communists are included in its new Cabinet.

The President won all thirty-five delegates in Connecticut yesterday, and Reagan won all twenty in Utah. According to the Washington *Post*'s tally, the President now has a thousand and ninety-three delegates and Reagan a thousand and thirty. This ended the delegate-selection process for the Republicans, and now the attention will be on the uncommitted and unpledged delegates. The two largest uncommitted delegations are Hawaii (eighteen votes) and Mississippi (thirty votes).

Our attention is on the Presidency, and little thought is given to the connections between that and another institution that has a profound effect on our national life—the Supreme Court. In 1968, in Miami Beach, Richard Nixon went about the Republican Convention telling state caucuses that he would appoint "strict constructionists" who would change the course of the liberal "Warren Court." And he did. Nixon appointed four of the current nine justices, and Ford named a fifth. While these appointees do not always vote in a bloc, the Court's direction has indeed been changed. On July 6th, the Court ended its latest term, having issued a series of rulings of great and enduring importance. The general effect of the rulings was to limit access to federal courts, strengthen the rights of states against the federal government, limit the rights of privacy, and cut back on the rights of criminal defendants. In one area, civil rights, the Court continued in the direction set by the Warren Court of affirming the statutory rights of minorities. It held that racial discrimination in private schools violated an 1866 civil-rights law, held that workers found to have been discriminated against and denied jobs were due retroactive seniority, and affirmed a lower-court decision that the courts can require public-housing construction in suburbs of cities whose public-housing policies are found to have promoted segregation. On the other hand, it held that the death penalty as applied to murder did not violate the Eighth Amendment ban on "cruel and unusual punishment." And it held that federal judges could no longer overturn convictions in state courts on the ground that evidence had been seized illegally. This ruling, which weakened the "exclusionary rule" that Chief Justice Warren Burger had opposed, had the effect of limiting the concept of habeas corpus. The Court upheld the right of states to prosecute homosexuals. Only two justices who were regularly in the majority on the Warren Court remain on the Burger Court. (Justice William O. Douglas, ill, retired last fall.) They are Justice Thurgood Marshall, sixty-eight and unwell, and Justice William Brennan, seventy.

JULY 19

This morning, I phoned Clarke Reed, the chairman of the Mississippi Republican Party. Reed, a Greenville rice grower and barge company owner, has managed over the years to accumulate power and get attention beyond what might be expected of the leader of the Republican Party in the state of Mississippi—representing all of a hundred and forty thousand Republicans. Reed, white-haired, fast-talking, and not without charm, likes the publicity and curries it with the press, and manages to get himself in positions where Republican Presidents and would-be Presidents have to pay considerable attention to him. Reed was chairman of the Southern Republican State Chairmen's Association in 1969, and was therefore in a position to make demands on Richard Nixon in Nixon's pursuit of a "Southern strategy." Now Reed is the leader of the largest uncommitted delegation to the Republican Convention and is being heavily courted by both sides. Two weeks ago, he was a guest at the White House dinner for Queen Elizabeth. But he is believed to be for Reagan.

"It's pretty hot and heavy, with both sides trying to put it over the top," Reed said on the phone this morning. "Close, close, close. I think the President has it, but I've been wrong before. The grand design, or realignment of the Republican Party with the South, is the only way to go over the top. As I told the President, picking Rockefeller was a mistake." Reed, like other conservative Republicans, was very much upset by the selection of Rockefeller to be Ford's Vice-President. Reed continued, "The South obviously is more in control of its own affairs than other parts of the country. We haven't spent ourselves broke; our institutions are intact. We're still fairly church-and-land-oriented. The Voting Rights Act should have been extended nationwide. Or take the common-situs-picketing bill: when labor fought for it, I knew it should be vetoed. Finally, Ford vetoed it, but weakly. Sometimes I wonder if they know where the future lies."

I asked Reed what he tells the President or his agents about how the Mississippi delegation will vote. By tradition, the Mississippi delegation, in order to enhance its importance, votes as a unit at Republican Conventions. The "unit rule" is contrary to Party law, but Party officials look the other way. Therefore, whichever candidate has a majority within the delegation could get all thirty votes. However, Douglas Shanks, the leader of the Ford forces, has already announced that he will not observe the unit rule this year.

Reed replied, "When they talk to me about delegates, I say we don't know what we're going to do, I say that the only way we could abandon our neutrality up until the Convention is if we had certain commitments. What Ford needs right now is to show that he's going to pick a running mate that will be compatible to his philosophy. The split ticket is a nightmare and a horror. With the so-called balanced ticket between a liberal and a conservative, you vote for a conservative and if he dies you get a liberal. Because of the campaign-finance law, ruling out private contributions, it's more important than ever that you know there will be a campaign in the South, an effort to win in the South. If they decide not to campaign in Mississippi, there's not a damn thing we can do about it."

I asked Reed what sorts of overtures had been made to him.

"I've been around so long, I know so many people all over the place. I'd say right now the delegation is leaning toward Reagan," he replied. "The Ford chairman down here is saying he may break the unit rule and go on his own. That's hardened the Reagan support. Both sides would like a solid declaration now. Well, they just won't get it."

Reed said he had received calls from Richard Cheney, the President's chief of staff; Harry Dent, a former Nixon aide, who is in charge of Southern delegates for Ford; William Timmons, another former Nixon aide, who is now a Washington lobbyist, and who is working on Convention strategy for Ford; Earl Butz, the Secretary of Agriculture; and William Simon, the Secretary of the Treasury. "Goldwater called the other day," Reed told me. "I wasn't in." (Barry Goldwater is backing Ford.) He went on, "They make the argument that the South has to deliver something, so why don't we do this?" Ronald Reagan also calls Clarke Reed, and so does John Sears, Reagan's campaign manager, and so does David Keene, Reagan's delegate hunter in the South. "I probably have more influence on the delegation than anyone," Reed said. "But the delegation's not deliverable. We're not kamikaze. If Ford's got it, we'll go for Ford. If he goes for the wrong Vice-President, I'll be ready to oppose it on the floor. I'm thinking about the long range, the culmination of the grand design. I've told them that. It's the first time in politics I've made any threat. I've thought the nomination was going back and forth. Now I guess Ford will get it."

John Sears, reacting to press reports that the Reagan campaign had about reached its end, held a press conference in Reagan's Washington headquarters, on K Street, today and announced that Reagan had enough delegates—ten more than necessary—to win the nomination on the first ballot. "I'm more confident today that we will be nominated on the first ballot in Kansas City," Sears said.

President Ford held a press conference on the north lawn of the White House, a few blocks away, and said, "We're getting very close right now to the magic number."

Last week, Reagan spent time foraging for delegates in New Jersey and Pennsylvania. Tonight, the New Jersey delegation will be President Ford's guests at the White House.

The State Department announced today that negotiations have been completed on the sales of nuclear reactors to Egypt and Israel. President Nixon promised these countries reactors when he visited them during the summer of 1974—his last summer in office.

JULY 20

President Ford's strategist claimed sixteen more delegates today and said that the President was now just eleven votes short of the nomination. Then the Reagan camp announced four more delegates, including Senator Strom Thurmond, of South Carolina.

Today the United States landed on Mars.

JULY 21

In what was supposed to be taken as a step toward reform, the Senate, by a vote of ninety-one to five, passed a bill today to establish a permanent Special Prosecutor's office to investigate allegations of criminal wrongdoing by the President, the Vice-President, the Cabinet, the director of the F.B.I., high White House officials, members of Congress, federal judges, or any federal official who is paid more than twenty-five thousand dollars a year. The Prosecutor is to be appointed by the President and confirmed by the Senate and is to serve for one three-year term only. The bill seems to be a fairly bad idea, on both Constitutional and practical grounds, but it was put forward in the name of preventing future "Watergates," and therefore right-thinking people felt they could not oppose it. The Ford Administration opposed it for a while, on valid grounds, but the President has enough Watergate problems and so, after a compromise was struck on the terms of the bill, he swung behind it. (At a press conference in Plains yesterday, Jimmy Carter said that he did not intend to criticize President Ford for pardoning Richard Nixon, but he added, "Had I been President, I would not have pardoned President Nixon until after the trial had been completed, in order to let all the facts relating to his crimes be known." He said he did not think that there was any "secret deal" between Ford and Nixon, but he thought that the pardon was "improper or ill-advised." The President, at his press conference the previous day, had said that whether the pardon should be a campaign issue was "up to the American people," and he added that he "would do it again.") The problem with the bill establishing a Special Prosecutor is that there are only three branches of government, and federal officials must be responsible to one of them. The idea is therefore an anomaly—one that was not quite faced when President Nixon, under duress, appointed a Special Prosecutor. The question is whether the Special Prosecutor is an employee of the

President, and that was the question running through a succession of incidents, including the firing of Archibald Cox and the Supreme Court argument over the tapes. The Court, while it ordered the President to surrender the tapes, did not quite settle the question. Moreover, if there is a Special Prosecutor in place, he might be tempted to justify his existence, or to get publicity, by pursuing questionable charges. Theoretically, instances of wrongdoing should be investigated and pursued by the Justice Department. That Nixon's Justice Department so spectacularly failed to make such investigations, and that a Justice Department in the future might, on not so grand a scale, be less than vigilant about the Administration of which it is a part, and that a President in bad trouble in the future might be less likely, in the light of what happened to Mr. Nixon, to appoint a Special Prosecutor—these are problems. But they are problems to which there may not be a good solution. Sometimes politicians, eager to strike a symbolic stance, overlook that possibility.

The Senate today overrode the President's veto of a public-works bill, with the President and some Republicans charging that the action was "political." Of course it was. Almost everything that happens now is. While the politicians seldom have the electorate out of their consciousness—which is as it should be—in an election year, and particularly a Presidential-election year, when fevers run even higher, they can think of little else. Once the Conventions begin, Congress becomes utterly distracted, and almost everything it does is done with an eye toward November. Thought takes a holiday. Senator Howard Baker, Republican of Tennessee, remarked today, "The sooner we adjourn, the better off we're going to be." He has a point.

The Reagan forces claimed two more delegates today, and the Ford forces said that they had known all along that those delegates were for Reagan.

JULY 22

One of the real questions before us is not whether or how quickly we might have an economic recovery but what sort of economy we have. One hears almost nothing in our political debate about that. We do not hear about our failing industries—held in place only by government subsidies—or about reconversion, or about whether or how we can set the stage for the kinds of economic growth that are neither damaging nor wasteful. I decided to talk with a business-man I know who thinks about questions of this sort. Victor Pal-mieri is a forty-six-year-old Californian who has been charged with much of the responsibility for straightening out the Penn Central Railroad, has several businesses of his own, and is a director of or adviser to a number of other companies. He is a lawyer and a Democrat, and has served in the government. Palmieri commutes between California and New York, and frequently stops in Wash-ington. We talked in Washington today. I began by asking him to outline for me what we ought to think about when we consider the nature of our economy. I knew from previous conversations that he felt we focus on the wrong questions, and tend to overlook the real trouble—beneath the statistics on unemployment and inflation and the gross national product—that the economy is in.

"One has to take account of the fact that the American economy is by any comparative standard enormously broad-based, and one that has great productive powers," he began. "As you generate activity, you get an enormous impact on real growth. You see this in the current recovery. We have achieved in this country the capacity for bringing about well-being for four-fifths of the popula-tion by maintaining a modest rate of growth. Once you've said that, you have to consider where we are in other ways. We have yet to learn how to include in the job structure a great mass of people— the people at the high end of the age scale and at the low end of the education scale. They make up a large percentage, and one we haven't done much about, and also one with the greatest claim on national policy from the standpoint of social justice. We have sought to buy off the problem through various forms of welfare support, and in the process a terrific burden has been borne both by the poor, as recipients of welfare, and by the middle class, who pay the freight. And there's underemployment, which is more difficult to trace—people who work for sub-scale pay in dead-end jobs."

He continued, "Recent developments offer a chance to reshape the economy in years ahead. The debate now is about economic growth: can we have it in terms of its environmental impact versus can we afford not to have it in terms of the standard of living. My own sense of the situation is that everything that is said about this is said in the context of an obsolete view of the economy—in Demo-cratic Party platforms, the slow-growth debate, the Jerry Brown formulation that we have to lower our expectations, and the

Humphrey view, embodied in the Humphrey-Hawkins bill, that says that government has to put everyone to work. All these formulations are politically and economically impractical, and overlook the real fundamentals of the problem and the opportunity that we have right now. Jerry Brown's make-do-with-less formulation has a superficial appeal, especially in middle-class-dominated southern California. But how just is it to talk about a lower standard of living when there is a large percentage of the population that is not adequately housed, clothed, fed, doesn't have adequate health care? It's a policy that either is foredoomed or will generate a tremendous amount of tension and social friction. As for Humphrey's idea of employing a significant number of people in government jobs, we don't have the infrastructure, we haven't figured out the purposes to be fulfilled. We have had enough trouble with the neighborhood youth programs—with kids disillusioned because there aren't satisfying jobs. Brown and Humphrey and the rest talk words, but the real point is that the world economy has changed. We now know that the entire energy base of the world economy is going to have to change within the next two decades. By anybody's measure, oil will be in very short supply by 1985—some say by 1980—and the petroleum-based economy will be in trouble. That's not reflected in policy or in rhetoric. Why? Because we have a short-term oil glut. But if you look at the rate of decline of those oil fields you see that between 1976 and 1982 it will be extreme. The fact that the Saudis are sitting on a virtual ocean of oil does not obscure the fact that in two decades they'll be the only ones with any left. What makes it so interesting from a policy standpoint is that it's pretty clear that there is no alternative to an environmentally sensitive energy economy. We can't go on the way we've been going. We know we have to go to an energy-efficient economy and also a clean-energy economy—in terms of the cost to health as well as the quality of life. If you put those two things together, you turn upside down the question of economic growth and employment and development. Pollution and energy conservation have always had a direct relationship to economic growth. And now we're saying the country is faced with bringing new people into the work force—people who have never been in it. Nobody in policy circles has quite recognized this set of connections. The politicians who talk about economic problems don't seem to understand that the question is not whether we have six- or seven-percent unemployment and how we balance that with inflation but how we convert to a clean-energy economy and at the same time employ more young people, poor people, old people, and even educated people who are now running into problems—particularly teachers. The debate is doing very little for the American people in terms of providing a vital and growing clean-energy economy."

I asked Palmieri how he would go about dealing with these questions.

"There are no simple answers," he said. "But what's implied in all this is a very difficult and long-term process—sponsoring clean-energy development, sponsoring a new industrial sector in terms of clean energy, and redirecting sectors such as the automobile industry over a long period—which has got to take place from a number of standpoints. There should be redirection of the petroleum-based power-generating industry. Most of our power plants are fired by oil. So the question is how, in an environmentally sensitive economy, we can create new directions of economic growth which will take up the employment slack. It won't be solved by decreeing that the government will employ every adult until we get to three- or four-percent unemployment, or by saying 'lower expectations.' It seems to me we have to raise our expectations. Nobody has the answers now, because we're just starting to ask the questions."

I asked Palmieri where he would begin.

"The first thing that has to be done in the democratic process is for people to understand what the problem is," he replied. "I would organize a procedure aimed at creating a national energy- and environmental-policy commitment. In the first year, I would sponsor legislation that would set up a series of regional groupings designed to pull in environmental and energy groups, and perhaps that would be combined with a Presidential commission. I know the limits of Presidential commissions—I served with one. But they can help with the analysis of the problem and the education of the public. So the first stage would be diagnostic, and designed to create some recognition by the public as to what the problems are as well as some agreement about the information—what the energy reserves are, what the needs are. Data on which there is disagreement. I tell you we are ripe for the first stage. Industry and the public are ripe for it. The energy issue has been dealt with in an adversary process. Very few of the cases are settled. We have litigation, and people throwing themselves on the wheels until something more satisfying comes along. We're having a great deal of difficulty getting new nuclear plants and oil refineries into operation. We're having trouble establishing a chemical capacity. The second year would be devoted to defining the national commitment—in terms of research funding, allocation to the private sector—to development of a 'plan.' That's a loaded word; it scares people. I use 'plan' in the sense of a set of directions and goals for an energy-efficient, environmentally sensitive economy—goals that would be debated, compromised. People say that public participation is impossible, or that Congress is obsolete. When you say that, you're giving up. Can the President and Congress move the country in this direction? Can you have something like a peace movement? Is this a way to move national policy? It seems that unless we get a new sense of direction we're going to move convulsively, let the Arabs move us, constantly courting double-digit inflation or economic stagnation. The problem is not lowering expectations or relying on the government as an employer of last resort. What the country needs now is some new goals."

I asked him about the point he had made earlier this year about the economy's being in worse trouble than is generally recognized.

"Until you have some goals, it's very difficult to start redirecting," he replied. "The fact is that in some of the major sectors of the economy we have potential for disruption and decline—which adds another reason for strongly seeking new patterns of development. The most obvious is in the aerospace field—in some sense the basis of the entire West Coast economy—which consists of four or five companies supported essentially in two ways; namely, by commercial aviation and by the military. Now, commercial aviation has shrunk, for a variety of reasons, or has failed to reach levels that can sustain the kind of structure we have in Lockheed, Boeing, McDonnell Douglas. They are producing jets the airlines can't absorb. And military-procurement programs can now be seen as welfare programs for the aircraft and electronic-missiles industries. That may be what the B-1 bomber is about. There is a sense that we have to keep this sector going, because we might want to call on it—we might not need the B-1 but we want to keep the manufacturing capability. The critics of the Pentagon and of weapons systems tend to overlook the fundamentals of industrial dynamics; these industries are not intent on blowing up the world but also don't want to give up their manufacturing capability. I have a theory that twenty-five percent of the cause of the Vietnam war was that it offered a tremendous theatre for testing and deploying weapons. The nuclear-power industry is already in serious trouble. The automobile industry has a built-in overcapacity. To some extent, that's been obscured by a surge in sales, spurred by a consumer psychology and a change in the view of the gasoline problem, but the automobile industry remains quite a soft area of employment and there is a real need to think about how that industry is to redirect itself. There's shipbuilding, and there are other areas that are noncompetitive in the world economy and are sustained by the taxpayer."

I asked Palmieri about the ideas put forward by some for getting more of a public voice, through government intervention, in business decisions—particularly for getting investment in what might be seen as public-interest ventures.

"In important respects, the current criticisms of corporations are healthy—legitimate reflections of changes in society and of a healthy capacity for examining institutions," he replied. "And corporations, like government, are offering a target for criticisms that are the result of great frustrations about the quality of our society, the lack of goals, abuses of power. There is great danger in the current situation, because the corporation is a vital—I would say indispensable—institution for organizing human and material resources. It is one very large part of our more or less uniquely successful economic system, and I think we ought to be careful about eroding the line between private responsibility and public responsibility. Where some critics go off the track of history is in failing to realize that the tension between the private sector and the public sector—even though we know they are mixed—is a key to our development, and that making over our corporate economy into a public bureaucracy would not be a very progressive change. That corporations need to change, that corporations have been irresponsible—these are facts of life and are not changed by making corporations public institutions. So has government been irresponsible. They say that public bureaucracy is more responsible and accountable than private bureaucracies, but the fact is that in many cases it isn't. Which is more responsible in the way it has run its business—Bell Telephone or the Pentagon? I know all the complaints about Bell—how it handles competitors, its power in Congress. But I'd rather see Bell handle that system than have the government run it. As I see it, the question is not how you get more government in the private sector but how you force more private responsibility. I see the answer to that not in government control but in government sanctions—criminal ones—when there is a lack of private responsibility. Rachel Carson and then the environmental movement, which came on like a summer storm, brought about one of the most drastic changes of government policy toward private industry. The new policy said you had to meet certain standards. There are a lot of problems involved, but the policy had the effect of forcing environmental responsibility into the industrial sector. If ten years ago you had said that industry has to make environmental investments, you would have been told that it was impossible, immoral—that it would break the back of the industrial economy. But you got a piece of legislation that simply said you have to do it, and it's being done, and the economy is making the adjustment. Anyone who doubts what can be accomplished if we have goals and standards ought to look at that."

He continued, "As for the redirection of investments, the utility of the corporation as an organizer of resources rests on its capacity for being compatible with the public interest. Without that capacity, it will become essentially a publicly managed bureaucracy and we will lose a vital element of American institutional pluralism. I believe that where some of the critics on the left are wrong is in overlooking the extent to which the American corporation is the strongest component of institutional pluralism that we have. Their ideal of substituting grass-roots organization overlooks organization on the scale that is mandated by the new world economy."

But, I asked him, what about the question of whether it is in the public interest to have investment made in plastic kazoos or in energy-efficient transportation?

"That's the question," he replied. "That's the point of institutional pluralism. Right now, those decisions are made where a lot of the critics don't want them to be made, and in some large part in ways they don't want. But where would they have them made? In the Department of Transportation? In the Defense Department? In H.E.W.? How would they change the special-interest nature of the American system? We're wasting breath talking about ideal decisions until we find the ideal decision-maker. To talk about dysfunctional, or even harmful, products is not to advance the argument very much until we find better ways of getting decisions. If you have a properly cynical view of human nature, you want a lot of different kinds of people in the decision process, with a lot of different motives and interests, in the hope—not the illusion—that out of it will come something reasonably in line with the public interest. To suggest that what is needed is a public bureaucracy imposing its values concerning allocation of resources against even the most distorted, market-oriented system is to me simply a naïve way of thinking about human processes. You have to step back and say that it's very dangerous to give anyone the power. However, it's essential to mobilize power to provide the public goods. Then, how do you do it with the least danger? You create as many power centers as possible. With all the corruption and abuses, you're most likely to get a mix, and avoid the danger of having the state be the originator of values rather than the steward of public welfare and of public values.

"That gets back to the idea of goals and new processes for decision-making. What you have to do is start moving the sights of business and the sights of government along congruent lines. Then G.M. might start to see its interests more in line with what its critics think they should be. It's hard for G.M. to know what its interests are now, except to produce more gas-efficient cars. The corporation has to clean up its methods. It has to say that its governance is in the hands of independent people who are responsible to the shareholders and the public, who are not cronies—that it is not a club. Then they can start to set standards: of consumer safety, minority employment, environmental quality, truth in advertising, compliance with antitrust laws—all the things that corporations as closed cultures with an eye on their short-term interest can ignore. Corporations could make themselves accountable to the public by publishing audits in those areas. Government could play a role in setting standards and sanctions. But I want to protect the corporation's role in our pluralism."

JULY 23

The President's chief delegate hunter, James Baker, a former under-secretary of Commerce, held a press conference today and announced that the President had won fifteen uncommitted delegates from Hawaii and one from Brooklyn, and that this gave him eleven hundred and thirty-five delegates and thus put him "over the top." But several counts had already given the President sixteen delegates in Hawaii. Between them, the Ford and Reagan camps now count more delegates than there will be at the Republican Convention.

Jimmy Carter's luncheon with business leaders at "21" yesterday, one week after he attacked the "political and economic élite" in his acceptance speech, was symptomatic of the puzzle about Carter. He told the businessmen that he would not come up with his tax-reform proposals until he had been in office a year—which he also had said during the primaries—and he was negative or opaque about changing certain existing tax benefits for business. Actually, Carter was consistent in detail, but more important was the fact that he had given off conflicting signals within one week. It is not a bad idea to appeal to different constituencies in order to govern, but we still don't know whether that is his purpose, or whether it is simply to please whatever audience he is standing before.

JULY 25

Eugene McCarthy is running as an independent for the Presidency, and no one is sure what effect his candidacy might have. Some believe that he could win enough votes to deny Carter a victory in certain states. Some think that McCarthy's Catholicism could be a factor in picking up support for him against Carter. A recent Harris poll showed McCarthy winning ten percent of the vote. McCarthy is now qualified for a place on the ballot in eleven states, and plans to enter in forty-five. He is a witty and irreverent man, and it is hard to know what he is about: what measures of idealism and sourness drive him. One often wonders whether he is serious and then he makes serious and interesting points. And he often has something to say that is just different enough to warrant attention. On the other hand, he is a skilled critic of his fellow men, and it is sometimes hard to know which of his statements are being made just for their effect. On *Meet the Press* today, McCarthy questioned Carter's "Constitutional conception" of the office of the Presidency. He used as an example Carter's declaration, made during the primaries, that he would take personal responsibility for the C.I.A. He also criticized Carter's use of language, and suggested that it was somewhat "demagogic." He used as examples a statement by Carter after the 1970 killings at Kent State that he would have called out the National Guard, with live ammunition and with orders to shoot to kill; the statement, in a speech about foreign policy, that the Soviet Union was using détente as a cover to carry out " 'world revolution' ' "; and the statement that the Vietnam war was " 'racist.' " McCarthy said, "I don't think you use words like 'racist,' for example, unless you are prepared to really historically and objectively demonstrate that it is true. I don't think that it was a racist war." McCarthy is the only public figure I can think of who would make a point of this use of language.

20

MONDAY. Ronald Reagan made the astonishing announcement today that he had selected Senator Richard Schweiker, of Pennsylvania, one of the most liberal Republican senators, to be his running mate. Perhaps the most striking thing about the announcement is that it came off as somewhat comical. It seemed to defy much of what Reagan stood for, and it mocked some of his own earlier statements. (Tonight's *CBS Evening News* quoted him as saying earlier this month, "I don't believe in the old tradition of picking someone at the opposite end of the political spectrum because he can get some votes that you can't get yourself.") It sent some of his supporters spinning. Last week, Reagan was deriding the selection of the liberal Mondale, but, whereas Mondale has a ninety-three-per-cent approval rating from the A.F.L.-C.I.O.'s dread (as Reagan backers see it) Committee on Political Education, Schweiker has a perfect score. And somehow Reagan has come to the conclusion that Schweiker is not part of that Washington "buddy system" he has been campaigning against all year. Schweiker was a target of the Nixon White House for having been too liberal in his voting in the Senate. He withstood that challenge with courage and dignity. What has happened to him? Perhaps he has been seized by the slight madness that seems to affect so many people when visions of great power dance before them. No one appeared to consider that Reagan was meeting the objections of earnest people who suggest that a Presidential candidate disclose his choice as running mate before the Convention. Whether the move was a brilliant stroke or a blunder remained in question at the end of the day, but there is no question that after a while we will all be very clear on which it was. The touch of comedy was reinforced by Schweiker's appearing, with his family, dressed in Sunday best, in the Senate Caucus Room—site of announcements of Presidential candidacies—and enthusiastically announcing his "acceptance" of the designation as Reagan's running mate. Schweiker had been planning to be a Ford delegate to the Republican Convention. Some counts indicate that there are as many as twenty-four uncommitted delegates in Pennsylvania. Actually, the move should not be all that stunning. Reagan was a more moderate governor of California than his rhetoric had suggested he would be. The problem is that his followers have believed his rhetoric as a candidate for the nomination. John Sears indicated when he talked with me last month that much of this rhetoric was designed for the purpose of winning certain Republican primaries, and that more pragmatic moves would have to be made to win the nomination and the election. But Reagan's problem now is that he appealed to those who thought Ford was "too pragmatic," who had never forgiven Ford for selecting Rockefeller and for taking other actions to cross the great divide within the Republican Party, and Reagan was believed. Now that he himself is trying to reach across the divide, no one seems to think he is guided by anything but opportunism. Reagan, you see, was not a "politician." He didn't compromise, the way Ford did. What will this do to his business career, not to mention his political career? Representative John Ashbrook, Republican of Ohio, a conservative who challenged Nixon in 1972 and supports Reagan, called the move "the dumbest thing I've ever heard of." He added, "You can't trust any of them."

A Harris poll taken shortly after the Democratic Convention showed Jimmy Carter leading President Ford by sixty-six to twenty-seven percent and Carter leading Reagan by sixty-eight to twenty-six percent. While the lead is said to be one of the greatest ever recorded, another interesting point is that there is so little difference in how Ford and Reagan do against him. Harris said that Carter has made "one of the most rapid ascendancies of a candidate to public popularity in the history of American politics."

JULY 27

Clarke Reed's telephone was very busy today. "He's on the line and has three others holding," his secretary said when I called him this morning. After a while, Reed returned my call. He spoke even more quickly than usual. (He also has a way of swallowing words, which makes him hard to follow.) "I've had it," he said. "I've said a thousand times a split ticket is a travesty on the system I'm ready to jump, but I'm trying to keep my people in mind. I'm on the phone with them."

* * *

With a pleased Gerald Ford standing by his side on the White House lawn, John Connally endorsed the President today. Somehow or other, John Connally has become, to many people, a moral force. The big, noisy Texan, former Democrat and intimate of Lyndon Johnson's, then Secretary of the Treasury under Richard Nixon, was acquitted of charges of bribery in connection with the milk-price-support issue that arose in the course of the Watergate investigation, but questions about the incident remain. Beyond that, there is something generally disturbing about Connally: he seems like a big missile out of control; one never knows where he will land. But it is commonly accepted that he is an effective campaigner—a reputation that recommends him to many people—and, moreover, he comes from a state with a large number of electoral votes. And so the President of the United States has been wooing him much of the year and now stands triumphantly while John Connally, who has been on speaking tours around the nation this year and who few think would not accept the Vice-Presidency, says that Mr. Ford "is unmistakably the better choice."

JULY 28

At the offices of the President Ford Committee, on L Street, almost back-to-back with the Reagan headquarters, they tell you that the Schweiker move was a disaster for Reagan. They say that by the end of the week several more delegates will announce that they are for Ford. At once, research was done on Schweiker's record, and the information went out to delegates. They were told of his liberal voting record, and word was also conveyed that he voted to break up the oil companies. James Baker told me, "The first thing we did Monday was get on the phone to our leadership in Pennsylvania and in the Pennsylvania congressional delegation. We polled all the state's delegates in twenty-four hours. Monday noon, we had a leadership meeting in Philadelphia. We see, at the outside, a loss of four Pennsylvania delegates out of a total of a hundred and three." The New Jersey, Delaware, and New York delegations were also polled. An official explained to me that while Schweiker may have political contacts in Pennsylvania, and will be the state's senior senator after Hugh Scott retires this year, in the other states he does not, as this man put it, "control their reward system." Moreover, they say at the Ford headquarters, a liberal Republican is not going to vote for Ronald Reagan because he selected a liberal as his running mate. They had been, in fact, quite worried about what is called "softness" in the President's support in some Northeastern delegations, but they feel that the Schweiker selection has taken care of that.

I asked Baker to tell me a bit about how the delegate hunting works.

He said that when a delegate is selected he receives a personal letter from the President, and, from the Ford Committee, a biographical form to fill out. He is also sent position papers and copies of newspaper stories that reflect well on the President or badly on Reagan. Then it is determined who ought to call that delegate, who ought to try to persuade him, which person he might most respect. Baker explained, "It might be a Cabinet officer, a congressman, his grocer." Sometimes it's the President. "He's called a bunch," Baker said.

In a room near Baker's office are kept large black notebooks for each state, containing biographical material on each delegate. In the front is a status report: C for Committed, L for Leaning, TU for Truly Uncommitted, SR for Soft Reagan, RR for Ronald Reagan. Next to the name of each delegate is a list of these initials, with a circle drawn around his status. As of Monday, Richard Schweiker was C. And, as of Monday, Pennsylvania had seventy-seven committed for Ford, thirteen leaning, nine truly uncommitted, two soft Reagan, and two for Reagan. The biographical sheets list the delegates' names, addresses, and occupations, and the form of address to be used in the letter from the President. For example, Charles N. Dodd was "Dear Chuck." Dodd was listed as uncommitted, and there was a notation that he had been talked to by Earl Butz on June 10th, and that he was upset about federal regulation of independent dairy producers.

The hearing room of the Joint Committee on Atomic Energy. This afternoon, the Joint Committee, which is supposed to oversee our government's policies on the development and export of nuclear materials, is holding a meeting on a bill to reorganize the procedures for making decisions on allowing the overseas sale of nuclear equipment by private companies, and to tighten safeguards against the use of nuclear reactors to develop bombs. The bill grew out of hearings held earlier this year by the Senate Government Operations Committee on the problem of nuclear proliferation. It was at those hearings that David Lilienthal, the first chairman of the Atomic Energy Commission, called for a halt by the United States, unilaterally, to the export of all nuclear devices and materials, saying, "The United States, our public agencies and our private manufacturers, have been and are the world's major proliferators." Lilienthal's was a lonely voice and his approach was dismissed, and our politicians are still struggling with the question of what to do about the facts that Lilienthal laid out. By now, the subject of nuclear proliferation has become somewhat fashionable among politicians. But it may be too late. There are pressures on and within our government to keep up the nuclear exports, and these pressures are increased by the fact that if the United States abstains, other nations step in. So the problem remains that no one knows how to call the whole thing off. Congress is still groping, and the executive branch remains confused and contradictory.

An assortment of government agencies have jurisdiction over questions of nuclear exports, with each, in the manner of government agencies—or any bureaucracy—reflecting its own exigencies and constituencies. The State Department, which perhaps has the principal role, reflects its own internal pressures, which come from the American ambassador in a given country and the desk officer for that country, to do something nice for that country. Higher policymakers absorb these pressures and also have their own interest in trading some United States beneficence for some favorable posture by the recipient country. People who have worked in the Pentagon have told me over the years that the greatest resistance to closing military bases overseas comes not from the Pentagon but from the State Department, anxious to keep our "presence" in a certain country rather than displease it by withdrawing something that country has come to value. The bases are supposed to give us what is called "leverage" over the countries concerned. Of course, State also often argues that we must not take this or that position because it might cause the host nation to throw out our military base—which says something about "leverage," but that is another story. The point is that the same turn of thought is often brought to bear on the question of exporting nuclear material. The Energy Research and Development Administration (ERDA) inherited from its predecessor, the A.E.C., the mission of developing the nuclear-energy technology of this country and so ends in promoting the industry. And ERDA makes the technical evaluations for the State Department of the uses to which an exported reactor would be put. The Nuclear Regulatory Commission, which inherited the regulatory function of the former A.E.C., and which licenses nuclear exports, deals with questions about complete plants. And the Arms Control and Disarmament Agency, which is supposed to advise the State Department on applications from American companies and foreign governments, has—perhaps inevitably, in light of the powers within the government against which it has had to stand—become rather weakened and demoralized. The Joint Committee itself is part of the picture, and its predilection, as is true of most Congressional committees, is to sympathize with the constituency over whose interests it has jurisdiction—in this case, the nuclear-power-and-weapons industry. This puts it in sympathy with ERDA (as it used to be with the A.E.C.) and, by extension, the State Department. These interconnections between the private interests and the public agencies that are supposed to superintend them—in the Congress and in the executive branch—are rather typical, whether the field is education or nuclear power. But in education the phenomenon is not so frightening. The nuclear-power industry itself is worth some hundred billion dollars and appears to be well organized. Like the educators, oil companies, and bread manufacturers, it has its own interest groups, or trade associations. The nuclear industry has the Atomic Industrial Forum, which is involved both in research and in public-relations programs, and the American Nuclear Energy Council, which is a trade association for the nuclear-equipment manufacturers, mining companies, utilities, and processors, such as General Electric, Westinghouse, and Allied Chemical. In addition, as in the case with many large businesses, the companies have their own representatives in Washington to keep in touch with the agencies and the appropriate members of Congress, and they also have numerous lawyers here to protect their interests.

Today's papers say that the General Accounting Office has reported that tens of tons of nuclear material cannot be accounted for by the thirty-four uranium- and plutonium-processing plants that it audits.

John Pastore, chairman of the Joint Committee, has called the meeting this afternoon to hear the reactions of the affected agencies to the bill that the Government Operations Committee has approved. Because of its involvement in the subject, the Joint Committee must also approve it before it is sent to the House and the Senate. As might be expected, and as Pastore clearly already knew, all the agencies are opposed to the bill. Agencies almost always are opposed to legislation that might curtail their powers or rearrange their jurisdictions or revise their customary procedures. Members of the Government Operations Committee are here to defend their work. Senator Abraham Ribicoff, of Connecticut, the chairman, referring to the witnesses from the various government agencies, says, "The only thing these gentlemen are coördinated on is they don't like the bill." Referring to the agencies they represent, Ribicoff says, "They don't tell the truth; the right hand doesn't know what the left is doing. . . . Everybody's got a piece of the action and consequently there is no action." Ribicoff and some other members of Congress are incensed by their recent discovery that the United States sent India some material (heavy water) that was used in the explosion of its nuclear device and then tried to prevent disclosure of this fact to Congress. They feel that the United States should put more pressure on its allies—Germany, France—that are selling reactors and reprocessing plants to other nations. Pastore himself mentions that in 1975 "we had an exchange" with West Germany in which we gave it nuclear material in return for its agreement to maintain our troops in Europe, and that "Congress had no knowledge of it." Pastore, however, also has other concerns. "We don't want to do anything to hurt American industry and international trade," he says. "There is no question at all about it that in the nuclear market ninety-two percent of the capacity is government controlled." And he sides with ERDA in its opposition to losing any jurisdiction. "Reorganization is not going to eliminate proliferation," he says, and he has a point. Senator Howard Baker, a member of the Joint Committee, cautions that proliferation is "a volatile and emotional issue," and adds, "We are not the only country in the world that has nuclear technology. . . . So there is an urgent need in my view to see that whatever legislation we report does nothing to diminish a single point of authority for the foreign policy of the United States in all respects, including the nuclear respect."

Myron Kratzer, the man most responsible for nuclear-export policy at the State Department, who is a former A.E.C. official, opposes the bill on the ground that the current government arrangements "are working satisfactorily." One of the problems that continually arise is that when, in the nineteen-fifties, the government initiated its drive to export nuclear technology, under the high-sounding program Atoms for Peace, it negotiated numerous agreements that did not take into account whether those countries to which it was exporting nuclear power plants could obtain reprocessing plants and thus the capacity for making the bomb. Some people think that those early nuclear agreements should be renegotiated to reflect the new realities, but Kratzer does not. His concern is that the United States remain a faithful supplier of nuclear material. The State Department apparently feels that such renegotiation might upset the nations to which we gave the nuclear reactors. This afternoon, Kratzer tells the Joint Committee that he thinks that the early agreements "carry a very strong presumption of supplies" regardless of changing circumstances, and that if our government's procedures were reorganized, the recipient countries might be concerned, and "it would discourage their coming to us" and might result in their turning to other sources of supply.

Pastore is worried about this, too. He says that "it seems to me that every time we step in and say 'no' " another country steps in and supplies. He points out that Brazil turned to West Germany, and that South Africa, after opposition developed in Congress to a sale of two nuclear reactors there, turned to France.

Last week, at a hearing by the N.R.C. on whether the United States should supply India with more enriched-uranium fuel, Kratzer took the position that it was important for us to continue to supply India so as to maintain influence over it. He argued that if we stop supplying fuel to India, India will say that our word is not good and that its contract with us, under which we sold it a nuclear reactor, is no longer valid. He also raised another argument, indicating another twist in this already strange situation whereby recipients of our nuclear largesse can use it to blackmail us: he pointed out that the current contract permits us to buy back India's spent fuel, which could otherwise be turned into bombs. India now has about a hundred bombs' worth of spent fuel. If we break the existing agreement, we lose the option—which we have not exercised—to buy this back.

Some experts think that the problem is that the politicians are looking at the wrong question. They say that the concern over the spread of the weapons and the attention to safeguards against their spread are too late. They argue that the reality is that the nuclear technology is out, and that our policy ought really to deal with the political and strategic reasons that countries want to develop nuclear power and the bomb, and should consider incentives to discourage them. They suggest that the United States and the Soviet Union stop nuclear testing and get serious about arms-limitation agreements, so as to stop emphasizing the disparities between the have and the have-not nations. They suggest setting up rewards for those nations which forsake nuclear weapons, and having the Soviet Union and the United States pledge not to use nuclear weapons against nations that don't have them. (But that runs afoul of NATO strategy.) Some say that we will have to be prepared to adjust certain policy goals to the overriding goal of stopping the nuclear spread. For example, in order to discourage South Korea from developing a bomb, they argue, we might have to promise to keep troops there, and overlook that government's unpleasantness toward political opponents. In fact, no one is quite sure what will work—or whether anything will work.

The Administration is sufficiently disturbed about the degree to which Congress is disturbed about the way nuclear-export policy is made so that it has resorted to the familiar approach of promising to study the matter. Yesterday, the President sent a letter to Representative John Anderson, Republican of Illinois, who is a member of the Joint Atomic Energy Committee, promising such a study, and, in what appears to be a henhouse strategy, placed a high official of ERDA in charge. The President also took the opportunity to praise the Administration bill called the Nuclear Fuel Assurance Act, which would allow private companies as well as the government to produce enriched uranium.

Today's committee meeting ends inconclusively. Pastore points out that there is not very much time left in the current Congress. (An official of one of the agencies who is sitting next to me during the hearing smiles and says, "In an election-year Congress, when you oppose something the best thing to do is delay.") But Pastore also utters the kind of dire statement one has come to expect from politicians when they address—however perplexedly—the subject of the spread of nuclear bombs. Talking of other countries that have developed nuclear capacities, Pastore says, "If we take ourselves out of the market, we lose our persuasiveness." He says, "We didn't like it, but what could we do about it? . . . They have sovereign rights. . . . I mean, that's the headache that faces humanity today."

Today, Clarke Reed announced his support of President Ford.

The Senate Caucus Room. The Pennsylvania delegation to the Republican Convention is meeting here this afternoon, and will be addressed by Richard Schweiker. Then the delegates will meet with the President at the White House. Before the meeting, I talk with some delegates. If there is a Reagan supporter in the room, I can't find him. I also look for Charles Dodd (the uncommitted Pennsylvania delegate who is upset about federal regulation of independent dairy producers) to see what he is thinking, but he is not here. He is now listed as a Reagan delegate. Charles Snelling, who tells me he is a good friend of Schweiker's, says, "He didn't talk to anybody. It was a disastrous move for him." Stanley Miller, an alternate, says, "I was absolutely stunned, if you want to know the truth." Senator Scott opens the meeting and reads Richard Schweiker's letter of resignation as a delegate. Then he tells the delegation, "We are in a position to decide the Presidential nomination today." That isn't quite true, but Scott is doing what he can to keep the delegates in line for Ford. Richard Frame, the state chairman, tells them to make their decision on whom to support "not on the personal basis of what may be best for you and for me and for our political careers." Schweiker comes in, wearing a bright-blue jacket. His curly hair is long now. He stands in a corner on the right, like a schoolboy who has been bad, and reads a statement. He begins by quoting his own Lincoln Day speech eleven years ago, in which he cautioned, "We Republicans should not look down our nose at other Republicans." He speaks of the "trials and tribulations" he went through during the eight days after Reagan asked him to join the ticket, of his discussions with his wife. This is more and more like a confession, or, at least, an apologia. He says that the idea of bringing together the elements of the Republican Party had been "exciting to me for many years." He says that the Republican Party is down to having the support of twenty-two percent of the voters, and that "if you divide that figure in half you start out with two warring factions of eleven percent each." He says that after "the shock and the tremors" had worn off, it was clear that this ticket was "probably about the only way that the Republican Party could be reunited, not become extinct." He points out that this is "the first time in modern history that a person from Pennsylvania has been asked to be on the ticket." Schweiker appears in shock himself. He undoubtedly did not anticipate the explosion that followed Reagan's announcement. Having justified the move to himself, he had to believe that others would see it that same way. Being accustomed to having a following, he assumed that the following would stay with him. But here he is, with his ostensible followers, and they are greeting him politely but silently. They have sent him to the Senate twice and they tend to like him, but they are baffled by what he did. They do not understand what seized him. "If Governor Reagan could cross the sound barrier [for Party unity] and ask me to join the ticket," he says, "I thought I could cross the sound barrier." He finishes, there is perfunctory applause, and he is out of the room.

JULY 30

Friday. The assumption all week has been that Sears may have more support for Reagan up his sleeve, but if he has, it is getting time for him to pull it out. The President's aides have been saying that the selection of Schweiker was a "disaster" for Reagan; perhaps they believe so, and certainly they want others to think so, in order to budge the remaining delegates they need. Some uncommitted delegates, of course, are trying to determine which way the wind is blowing.

This afternoon, I phoned John Sears. "We've survived the initial impact," he said. "We haven't lost any delegates at this point." Of course, this is what he wants the press to report. I asked him about Mississippi. He replied, "The way it was going for the last three weeks before we did this, it was seriously in doubt." There had been reports that the Ford forces were chipping away at Reagan's support there. The Reagan people would like it understood that the selection of Schweiker gave Reed an excuse to support the President, and my conversation with him before the selection was made does indicate that that was the way he wanted to go. Sears continued, "As another week goes by, there will be more pressure on Mr. Ford to say what he's going to do about a running mate. Whatever that is, I think it will be helpful to us." Sears has a frequent, somewhat nervous laugh. When he said that, he laughed. What Sears hopes to do now is pressure the President into naming his running mate before the nomination, figuring that, given the divisions within the Republican Party, anyone he selects will lose him some support. Sears said that the pickings are slim if the President wants someone from the Northeast. Several Republican figures from there are too old. "We've been over the list ourselves," Sears said. "If he wants to go that way, we've got the best guy." He continued, "We knew we'd have to take a lot of bitching. It is the absolute truth that we picked this guy and later decided it would make sense to announce it early, that he has credibility in areas where we need it. With Jewish voters, ethnics—he's worked on 'captive nations' issues —organized labor. And the fact that he doesn't look like he just stepped out of a boardroom helps. In places like New York, Pennsylvania, and New Jersey, there are people who, because of the addition of Schweiker, have changed their view of Reagan. There was an idea that if he was nominated he would pick a Bill Miller." William Miller is probably best known for his role in an American Express television ad that capitalizes on his obscurity. He was less well known as a member of the House from New York when Barry Goldwater selected him as his running mate in 1964. "There are two categories," Sears said. "Those who will switch from Ford to Reagan and those who before they vote for Ford want to know who his running mate will be." Schweiker has been phoning Pennsylvania delegates all week. Sears said, "We'll be announcing some names next week, and as we announce some names we'll be able to get more."

Today, Schweiker explained at a press conference that he would, as Reagan's running mate, drop his pro-labor position. Also today, the President flew to Mississippi, where he told the delegates he would conduct a poll among all the delegates to the Convention and among the Republican members of the House and Senate and among other Party officials on whom he should select as his running mate. The White House said the President would send out four thousand five hundred and eighteen letters asking for such advice. The President had polled Party leaders before selecting Nelson Rockefeller, and Richard Nixon polled the Congress before selecting Ford.

In one of those reports required by law to be submitted to Congress by the President but actually prepared and submitted by the appropriate agency—in all probability, the President does not read them—Mr. Ford reported that by 1985 nearly forty countries will have enough plutonium from their nuclear reactors to make atomic bombs and that twenty countries now have enough.

Now that the dust has temporarily settled, the big thing that has happened as a result of Ronald Reagan's selection of Richard Schweiker as his running mate is that very little has happened one way or the other. According to a story by James Dickenson in yesterday's Washington *Star,* President Ford picked up, in all, eight previously uncommitted Pennsylvania delegates, three uncommitted Louisiana delegates, and one delegate each from South Carolina, West Virginia, and Virginia, but all fourteen had already been counted as favoring him. Dickenson also reported that Reagan had suffered no real losses.

When I spoke with Clarke Reed on the phone this morning, he was uncharacteristically glum. He had jumped to Ford, but not many of his delegates had followed. "I'm not very happy with either candidate," Reed said this morning. "I think the thing is over. Reagan hasn't pulled out what he said he'd pull out."

I asked Reed why, then, he sounded so gloomy.

He replied, "Most people that think like me don't agree with me. So it's pretty uncomfortable. I'm not in a very optimistic mood. I usually am. The whole thing just took the wind out of people. Anyway, I've found that being with the winner is no big deal. We've been there before. You don't build a party from the White House. More Mississippi delegates accepted this Schweiker thing than I thought would. The people who normally agree with me are sticking by Reagan, and the people that approve of what I did are not the people I'm normally comfortable with. Maybe I jumped too quickly, but I'd been talking about this split-ticket business for years. So I'm kind of lonely."

The current issue of the conservative weekly *Human Events,* which arrived today, is headlined "The Schweiker Bombshell: Conservatives Should Stick With Reagan." It explains that conservatives should stick with Reagan because "there is not a scintilla of evidence" that he has "yielded to liberalism or relinquished any conservative principles." It asks, "Has Reagan now embraced

Kissinger's détente policies, Ford's unbalanced budgets, more regulation of the economy, a guaranteed annual income, busing, or
abortion on demand?" The answer: "Clearly not."

Over the weekend, it was reported that the Ford Administration
has decided to sell to Saudi Arabia fifteen hundred Maverick air-to-
ground missiles and an early version of "smart bombs"—bombs that
can be electronically guided to their targets—that were used in
Indochina and that the United States has supplied to Israel. The
Administration was already considering selling two thousand Sidewinder interceptor missiles and has sold sixteen Hawk ground-to-
air missile launchers to Saudi Arabia. The papers reported, too,
that Saudi Arabia has agreed to finance a Hawk missile system for
Jordan. Our government is reported to be much relieved. A proposal that we sell Hawk missiles to Jordan had been opposed by
Congress. Since 1975, Saudi Arabia has purchased over six billion
dollars' worth of arms from the United States. One reason given for
the arming of Saudi Arabia by the United States is that Iran has
been armed by the United States. And Iran, it's said, is being armed
to protect the area against the Soviet Union. Earlier this month, the
Washington *Post* reported that the United States is planning to arm
three black African nations—Ethiopia, Kenya, and Zaire—with
three hundred million dollars' worth of weapons. The announced
purpose of that, too, is to counter the influence of the Soviet Union.

AUGUST 3

Washingtonians are making their adjustments to Jimmy Carter.
Those who supported Hubert Humphrey—and they were many—
and saw him as a vehicle for a return to power, are hoping that their
misplaced loyalty will be overlooked. Many people here are volun-
teering for Carter task forces and calling around as if they were
now important members of the Carter team. They drop the names
of people they hadn't heard of six months ago. They talk about
"Jody" and "Hamilton," and about Jack Watson, a law partner of
Kirbo's, who is in charge of transition of administrations (should
that come to pass). At lunch today, someone who is only, at most,
on the fringes of the Carter campaign came up to the man with
whom I was seated and said, as if he were bestowing the Order of
the Cross, "I passed your name along to Jack Watson." (Someone
else I know who is serving on a task force received a mimeographed

letter from Carter, which began "Dear Task Force Member" and went on to say, "I want you to know how much I appreciate your willingness to provide advice on public policy. Your contributions will be increasingly important to this campaign and the nation in the months ahead. . . ." It continued in this vein, and it was signed "Jimmy.")

AUGUST 5

Two days ago, Jimmy Carter left Plains, where he has been spending most of his time since the Democratic Convention, and returned to New Hampshire, where, last February, he won his first primary. In Manchester, he made a speech. Many people seem to have been surprised by its sharp partisan tone, and by his complaints about attacks on him that are yet to come, but these were echoes of one facet of Carter's style during the primaries. The difference is that now he is the Democratic nominee, and people are paying more attention. Somehow, perhaps because it was so novel, the picture that many seemed to get of Carter during the primaries was that he went around speaking of love. He did use the word more than any other politician in memory, or perhaps ever, but he was also quite adept at slicing an opponent. I keep remembering that his mother called him "a beautiful cat with sharp claws." A number of politicians have felt those claws. Carter does not take well to opposition, so one of the big questions is what will happen when, if he is President, he meets with strong opposition to what he wants to do. Again the question is one of definition and of degree. Presidents have to be tough fighters for what they want to get done; otherwise, little will happen. The question is what the fighting is for, how it is conducted, and whether it is conducted in a way that makes further achievements less likely. In New Hampshire, Carter, in references to "the Nixon-Ford Administration," criticized it for governing with "vetoes and not vision . . . scandal and not stability . . . rhetoric and not reason . . . WIN buttons and empty promises instead of progress and prosperity." He spoke of "the almost unbelievable spectacle in Washington—the President of the United States deeply concerned about an ex-movie actor, travelling all over the nation to get a handful of delegates here, a handful of delegates there." He did not suggest how else the President could get the nomination. A friend of mine here has suggested that Carter is a master at establishing the political predicate—that he sets the terms: if Carter campaigns in thirty states for the nomination, that is what candidates should do; if Carter cannot get the support of established political leaders, "the bosses" are against him; if he is criticized, he is being subjected to vicious political attack. And thus in New Hampshire yesterday he established another political predicate: he said that the Republicans would mount an "almost unprecedented vicious personal attack" on him and on Senator Mondale, and that the Republican Party was "going to be desperate, and in desperation they will turn to personal attacks—mark my words."

Last week, in Plains, Carter received briefings from experts on defense, economy, and foreign policy, who travelled to Plains both to take the candidate information and, in many cases, to audition for jobs. Someone who was there said that the visitors tended to compensate for their reputations—doves became hawks, hawks become doves, and so on. In Carter's briefings for the press, he indicated some promising changes in policies: he said that the United States and the Soviet Union had a "rough equivalency" in strategic weapons, and he ruled out a first-strike strategy as one that would have disastrous consequences; he said he would make a greater effort to get labor and business to agree on curbing wage and price increases. But one wonders about these briefings. Even if one assumes that they are serious, not being held just for their public-relations value—and I think that is a fair assumption—one wonders how much Carter can learn from them. A one-day meeting with a collection of experts is far different from living with these questions for a long time. Carter is unquestionably an intelligent man who is what is known as a "quick study," and he seems to have great confidence in his capacity as a quick study, but his comprehension of what he is talking about sometimes seems not to run deep. And quick studies can get in trouble.

By now, the nation has become familiar with the tiny town where Carter lives, with its one main street and Billy Carter's gas station. We have read pieces documenting that the south Georgia he comes from is mean country, where race prejudice still runs strong; Carter's apartness from this was said to be one of the things that attracted Andrew Young to him. One wonders how—to the extent that he spent time there, when he was not in the Navy, not running for Georgia office—Carter filled his time. He reads, but he is not Thomas Jefferson. One begins to understand his restlessness. The other day, in its boredom, the press corps that is covering him there began a softball game. After a while, the candidate for the Presidency joined in. He plays as relentlessly as he ran for the nomination.

Today, Ronald Reagan and Richard Schweiker went to Mississippi. Schweiker explained to the press and then to the Mississippi delegates that he really was not all that liberal. He said that some of his votes had been "symbolic," and he said that he had supported such things as the Kennedy-Corman health bill and the Humphrey-Hawkins jobs bill because, faced with the alternatives of federal action and no action, he chose doing something. But now, he explained, Ronald Reagan had told him about this wonderful thing called private enterprise which could deal with those problems and he was all for that. The Mississippi delegates were said to be unimpressed.

Yesterday, the House approved the Administration's bill to allow private companies, with government guarantees, to join the government in the production of enriched uranium for nuclear power plants—a process that is still secret. The beneficiary of the measure is expected to be a consortium called Uranium Enrichment Associates, which is controlled by the Bechtel Corporation, a company that designs and constructs nuclear power plants. The current president of Bechtel is George Shultz, who was director of the Office of Management and Budget and also Secretary of the Treasury in the Nixon Administration. The bill was supported by the Energy Research and Development Administration. The Ford Administration said that it was important to get private enterprise into this field—albeit with no-lose guarantees. Former Representative Chet Holifield, a Democrat from California, who was once chairman of the Joint Committee on Atomic Energy, called it "the worst piece of legislation" ever to be approved by that committee.

AUGUST 6

Friday. Three separate items in today's papers have connections worth considering. One item is about Secretary of State Kissinger's current trip to Iran, where he will continue negotiations whereby Iran would pay in oil for more arms from the United States. Iran also wants to buy eight nuclear reactors from the United States. (Iran has already signed an agreement with West Germany to buy two nuclear power stations.) Earlier this week, the Senate Foreign Relations Committee issued a staff report saying that Iran had already bought ten billion dollars' worth of arms from the United States, under an agreement that President Nixon made permitting Iran to buy any weapons it wished. United States arms sales to Iran are the largest we make to any country. There are some questions about what Iran, which has internal unrest, and potential external foes other than the Soviet Union, plans to do with all that weaponry, and what we will do if it turns out that the Shah is not immortal, but such questions do not seem to come up much in public discussion. A second item points out that the world demand for oil is rising, and that OPEC, the Organization of Petroleum Exporting Countries, is moving into a stronger position vis-à-vis its customers. The impetus for the increased demand is said to be the recovery of the industrial countries from the recent recession, in which a major factor was OPEC's decision to raise the price of oil and then to shut off exports during the Middle East war in 1973. It was that cutoff which also produced what was referred to in the United States as "the energy crisis." The tax bill passed by the Senate today contains what remains of a once great effort to write legislation designed to reduce the consumption of energy, and what remains is almost nothing that would further that purpose. The third item—which appears on page D-9 of the Washington *Post* and not at all in the New York *Times*—concerns the announcement yesterday by Frank Zarb, head of the Federal Energy Administration, that this country's consumption of energy is rising, and so is its dependence on imported oil.

Many people will be going to Kansas City this weekend, where on Sunday—which happens to be the second anniversary of Richard Nixon's resignation speech—the opening rounds of the Republican Convention will begin. While the Convention itself does not officially begin until a week from Monday, the preliminaries may be crucial—may define the Convention itself. Earlier this week, I dropped in for one last conversation with John Sears before he left for Kansas City. He told me, "We have said that we are not planning to make fights at the Convention unless we feel we are being treated unfairly. That, of course, is saying something and saying nothing at the same time. It is never advisable under these circumstances, even if you have the votes, to win on a purely procedural issue, because it would cut up the Party. The whole game here is to try to win the Presidency. So you want to come out of the Convention with a Party emotionally united. If the press kicks you around for three or four weeks, the public stops listening to you. The press writes that you have no chance of winning, then the people won't listen to you, and you do lose. So it's a self-fulfilling prophecy. Therefore, you don't want to win on a purely technical procedure. If people feel you won it on chicanery, the Party is not united. So what you're looking for is something of substance or principle— and then people aren't upset that you won, and they're pulling for you." He stopped and laughed, and then he said, "I think there might be some issues of that kind." When I asked him what he had in mind, he said, "We could ask that the Convention require the other candidate to name his Vice-President before the nomination."

21

KANSAS CITY. Wednesday. At the Alameda Plaza, a southern-California-pseudo-Spanish-style hotel, which is to serve as the Reagan headquarters during the Republican Convention, John Sears is holding a press conference. The Convention itself does not begin until next week, but the preliminaries, dealing with the rules and the platform, started Sunday night, and have become part of the Convention itself: it is now clear that the crucial moment next week may well not be the roll-call vote on the nomination but a test that precedes that vote. As of now, Reagan is behind, and, as his strategists see it, the only way he can overtake President Ford is through some test on which delegates who are formally bound by their states' laws to vote for the President's nomination but are sentimentally for Reagan will vote for Reagan's position. The theory is that if a way is found to demonstrate, before the roll call on the nomination, that Reagan is in fact the real preference of the Convention, then enough delegates might consider Reagan to be in reality the stronger of the two candidates to give him the nomination. The Reagan forces figure that there are from fifty to sixty delegates who would be tempted to vote with Reagan if they thought he could win. In a close Convention, "winnerness" can be everything. Delegates to such a Convention oscillate and then move toward the center of gravity. The Ford forces figure that they have eleven hundred certain delegates, thirty-five who are committed but "soft," and twenty-five probable delegates. And they are very tense. They move about the corridors of the various Convention hotels with tight faces.

On Monday, Sears publicly proposed that the Convention adopt a rule requiring all Presidential candidates to announce their Vice-Presidential choices before the balloting for the Presidential nomination. The proposal fits Sears' prescription, as he spelled it out to me in the conversation we had in Washington last week, perfectly. It is a proposal that has some intrinsic merit—several reformers have been suggesting it for years—and therefore is a procedural move with substantive respectability. (Sears has thought all along that the Ford forces may not give him an opportunity to make a floor fight over the platform.) He believes that there must be a compelling reason—or an ostensibly compelling reason—for a nominal Ford supporter to support Reagan's position on a preliminary vote. Sears is full of political maxims. He has thought politics through more than most people who practice it, and this may account for his relative success. One Sears maxim: "You can never ask a man to do something in politics that is against his own self-interest. You have to find something of interest to him." That is what Sears' proposal about naming running mates is meant to do. The proposal is designed not only to put Ford on the spot, by forcing him to risk displeasing some faction within his following, but to attract the votes of those who will probably vote for his nomination but would be very much interested to know, or must appear interested to know, whom he would select as his running mate. It is probably the move with the greatest chance of carrying. And if it should carry, there is a chance—a chance—that Reagan could be nominated. The Ford people don't disagree. They have feared all along that the Reagan side might indicate, through tactical maneuvers, that Reagan has greater strength and might also set off emotions within the Convention in Reagan's direction—and they understand that Reagan stirs political emotions that Ford does not—which could block the Ford nomination. They know that their role is to defend the President's lead while the Reagan forces, being behind, go on the offensive. Reagan's selection of the liberal Senator Richard Schweiker, of Pennsylvania, as his running mate alerted them to the possibility of a succession of daring and surprising moves. They have tried to anticipate various moves that the Reagan forces might make here, but Sears' proposal on Monday appeared to take them utterly by surprise. On such maneuvers and countermaneuvers now hangs the nomination of one of the two major political parties, and perhaps even the Presidency.

Sears will hold a press conference every day—there won't be much time for talking to reporters individually, and, more important, press conferences are one instrument for keeping the other side off balance. Sears has a flat, round moon face and a slight, mysterious—sphinxlike—smile, and seems imperturbable. He moves slowly, talks slowly, and never appears rattled. His personal style, coupled with his political style, has the other side thoroughly spooked. When they talk about him, they nervously cite his maxim "Politics is motion." And they await his next move. At his press conference today, Sears says that he will pursue his Vice-Presidential proposal in the Convention's rules committee, which meets on Saturday, "and, if necessary, we will pursue that in the Convention." He is asked whether he has any other surprises in store. "I really don't know what surprises you," he says, smiling, and he adds, "There will be other things that we'll be doing that will be newsworthy." And he says, "It is our feeling here that this probably stands to be the most exciting Convention that our party has ever held." He may well be right.

Logically, it never should have got to this point. But then, if I have learned anything this year, it is that politics has little to do with logic. Logically, the President should have the nomination in hand by now. He is, after all, the President, and if he is not a brilliant one, neither is he generally considered a disastrous one. But he is only a fair campaigner, up against an accomplished one; his call had to be for preserving what is, while his opponent could call for dramatic change; he doesn't have any real following, and his opponent does; his forces relied on established Party machinery, while his opponent's went out and rallied the people; his campaign organization was sprawling and faction-ridden, while his opponent's was relatively small and tight. Both sides made mistakes, but it seems that the President's side made more.

"They have made it possible for us to be here," said Lyn Nofziger, who was once Reagan's press secretary and is now Reagan's Convention coördinator, this afternoon. "I don't know anyone on our side who thought we would win North Carolina," Nofziger said. That moment in the campaign turns out to have been more crucial, in several respects, than has generally been realized. About a week before the March 23rd North Carolina primary, Mike Deaver, Reagan's chief of staff, and Nofziger went to Washington to meet with Sears. Their assumption was that they would have to close out the Reagan campaign, because, for one thing, it was in debt. Sears had not drawn a paycheck since February. The money wasn't there to continue—not even to book hotel rooms in Wisconsin, where the next important primary would take place. Over dinner at an Italian restaurant, the Reagan men decided that, win or lose in North Carolina, Reagan would go on national television for a half hour afterward. At the least, they figured, the television broadcast would help raise money to pay off the debts. I recall thinking that the telecast, on March 31st, was rather poor. Reagan jumped from subject to subject, just as he had in his early speeches, when he shuffled his four-by-six cards; he talked too fast and about too many things, from energy to Social Security to the Panama Canal, but then he zeroed in on Henry Kissinger and defense and America's position in the world. "The evidence mounts that we're Number Two," he said, and he asked, though the connection was unclear, "Is this why Mr. Ford would not invite Alexander Solzhenitsyn" to the White House, and "Is this why he signed away the freedom of Eastern Europe in the Helsinki agreement?" Reagan said that the President's signing last summer of the Helsinki agreement—which, in exchange for Soviet pledges of freer immigration and expanded human rights, ratified the post–Second World War European borders—put an American "stamp of approval on Russia's enslavement of the captive nations." Every bit of evidence is that the speech was a huge success, raising money and reinvigorating the Reagan campaign. "You can't believe what it did for us to see that the little guy out there would respond," Deaver said to me today. "It also gave us the feeling that if we were down and out again, all we had to do was another TV show." But it may well have been that it was during this period that Reagan lost the nomination. For it was then that, strapped for money and stretched too thin, the Reagan campaign was unable, or failed, to field more than a few slates in states, such as Ohio and New Jersey, where Ford was expected to win but where Reagan had a chance to win in selected congressional districts and pick up delegates. (The Reagan campaign had already passed up an opportunity to file slates in Pennsylvania.) There were some districts in Wisconsin that, in hindsight, the Reagan forces think they could have won, but, lacking money, they had to cancel out Wisconsin, whose primary followed North Carolina's by two weeks. And it was during this period, as it happened, that the bill to reëstablish the fund-distributing functions of the Federal Election Commission was working its way through Congress. No federal campaign funds had been disbursed since March 22nd. (The Supreme Court's January 30th ruling that parts of the campaign funding law were unconstitutional was stayed through March 22nd in order to give Congress time to write a new law.) At the time of the North Carolina primary, in late March, the Reagan campaign was over a million dollars in debt, and was owed about a million dollars in federal funds. The President's campaign, however, had over a million dollars on hand as of March 31st and debts of only about two hundred and fifty thousand dollars. Congress took its time passing the bill, and after it reached the White

House the President delayed signing it for a week. In retrospect, the delay in providing federal funds may have been the decisive factor in the Ford-Reagan race. It certainly was a very important one. There were other financial advantages in being the President. The White House, being the White House, was not required, as the President's challenger was, to make a lot of its payments—for hotel rooms and so on—in advance. Most important, perhaps, the President could use staff members, offices, typewriters, and telephones in the White House to further his campaign.

We shall never know what would have happened if seven hundred votes had gone the other way in New Hampshire, giving Reagan instead of Ford the victory there. There are other "what-if"'s. Some Reagan strategists feel that if they had conducted more effective races in such states as West Virginia and Maryland, Reagan might have won there. Some think they should have made more of an effort in small states that selected delegates through conventions instead of primaries, such as Connecticut and Vermont. There will be a great deal of hindsighting and "what-iffing" about this campaign for the Republican nomination—the closest one in twenty-four years, and one that will turn on tantalizingly few votes. But it seems fairly clear that, while incumbency may not be all that it is considered to be, it has thus far saved Gerald Ford. Incumbency also, as Nofziger pointed out today, gave Ford the support of "the Establishment"—the Party machinery and members of Congress. John Sears has often said that Ford does not have a base, but to the extent that he does, that's it. That base was not enough to hand the nomination to him easily, but it was probably enough to keep him from losing it before he got here. "Moreover," Nofziger said, "a President can make appointments and promises. If you say, 'I, Ronald Reagan, will keep your shipyard open if I'm elected,' and Gerald Ford says he will keep your shipyard open, whom would you choose?"

And incumbency is helping Gerald Ford at this Convention. The officers of the Convention are all Ford's friends. The scheduled Convention speakers are Ford supporters. The Ford forces fear that a move will be made to have Reagan address the Convention before the balloting—a move that, at the very least, will make them look bad, unfair, when they oppose it, and that if it succeeds could end with Reagan, the captivating (as many think) speaker, "stampeding" the Convention. In a race this close, anything might make a difference. And so, while the world waits to see who will lead the

Republican Party into the election of our next President, aides on both sides are rushing around Kansas City worrying about such things as walkie-talkies, messengers, cars and drivers, odd-hours food for campaign workers, guest tickets (the Ford camp has more than twice as many as the Reagan camp does), telephone systems on the Convention floor.

This morning, at the Muehlebach Hotel, the Convention headquarters, I saw William Timmons, the President's Convention manager. Timmons, who is forty-five, was in charge of congressional relations for the Nixon White House and is now a Washington lobbyist. He worked for the nomination of Barry Goldwater in 1964 and of Richard Nixon in 1968, and managed the machinelike 1972 Republican Convention. Apparently at a loss for a competent Convention manager from within his own ranks, Ford reached for Timmons. When I saw Timmons in Washington last week, he told me that one of his prime goals was to present to the world the picture of a well-run Convention—both to impress the delegates and to help the President's "image" for the fall. "I would be very pleased if the impression were left that the President's operation was a smooth, tightly knit, well-functioning operation," he said. "God knows it isn't seen as that now." When I saw Timmons this morning, he was rushing from one meeting to another, but he stopped to talk for a few minutes. "We're trying to manage our people on the platform subcommittees," he said. "We have— God—wall-to-wall meetings. You're going to see a whole week of gimmicks on their part to try to get something going. We don't have the margin of votes on the platform committee that we do on the rules committee. The platform is particularly sensitive, because people feel so strongly. We're getting speakers for our positions lined up to go before the rules committee. That sort of thing. We'll meet some delegates at the airport and work with them on the way in on some of the issues." (Sears is not having delegates met at the airport. He doesn't think it's worth it. "We did that in 1968," he told me. "You find that you're meeting your own people.") Timmons has won a battle he has been waging with White House aides to get the President to come here on Sunday, rather than later in the week, and to go to some state caucuses—but not as many as Timmons and his group would like. "He'll spend two hours a day being Presidential," Timmons said to me today. "I see that as time I can steal." Timmons also is devoting a lot of time preparing the "caucus teams"—people who will go around to the caucuses and argue the

President's case. Briefing books, telephones, working space, kits to give delegates, a telephone directory—all these details are being looked after in an effort to win the nomination for Ford. Plans are being made for what is called "alternative programming"—which consists of making Ford spokesmen available for television interviews during lulls in the Convention, to keep the television interviewers from seeking out people who might not be so helpful to the cause. The President's strategists are trying to make sure that every politician of consequence receives appropriate attention. "Hell hath no fury like an overlooked politician," Timmons said. He was up half the night last night working on the official program—the order of the speakers. "We're very weak in the fluff part of it," he said today. And so time is being spent in finding people to lead the Pledge of Allegiance and the singing of "The Star-Spangled Banner." Because of the new campaign-finance law's limitations on spending, there is not the money there once was for bringing celebrities to town to lead the Convention in song. A proposal by the Republican National Committee to have Goldwater speak on Monday morning and Rockefeller on Monday evening—which Timmons thought especially terrible—has now been overruled by the President's Convention management, and both will speak Monday evening. "A bird needs two wings to fly," says Timmons.

Today, Ben Harbor, a black delegate from Baker, Louisiana, was flown out to California for an audience with Ronald Reagan.

Last night, I had dinner with Clarke Reed, who is the chairman of the Mississippi delegation here. The delegation arrived uncommitted, but as of now President Ford is believed to have at least half the state's thirty votes, and Reed has concluded that, what with the deep division within the delegation, the unit rule should be abandoned. Reed, who is forty-eight, is tall, white-haired, and somewhat handsome. He laughs a lot, and clearly thinks of politics as good sport. But it has become less fun for him now, since he got caught between two forces, both of which he wanted to please. He not only had supported Reagan but had told Reagan aides that he would deliver Mississippi for their candidate. Then he began to see that Ford was gaining ground in Mississippi, and he came under increasing pressure from Ford aides, and finally was courted by Ford himself—and he switched. One increasingly gets the impression that Reagan's selection of Schweiker was only an excuse for the switch. Reed appears to have wanted to move to where he thought the power was going to be. In playing games with both sides, he has been losing the respect of both. A John Sears maxim: "In politics, the most important thing is your word." Sometimes Sears puts it another way: "In politics, if you don't keep your bargains, it catches up with you rather quickly." The special hold that trust has in politics is a strange thing in a business that also puts such a premium on manipulativeness and looking out for one's own interests, but in fact trust is essential to make the thing work. Politicians deal in signals. When someone in politics gives a signal that he is going to go a certain way, others understand and are guided by it. They expect that he will not change course on them. They will accept someone who opposes them. What they cannot accept is someone who gives a certain signal and then, in a turnabout, does them in. Politicians are all playing their own games, and each understands that the others are doing that, but the smart ones figure out that they cannot be effective over any length of time without accruing to themselves a certain amount of trust—trust that they will keep the commitments they signal. This has nothing to do with idealism; it has to do with survival. Some of the most manipulative politicians understand the importance of a peculiar sort of honor in politics. Lyndon Johnson understood it, and so did Wilbur Mills, and so did Wayne Hays. Politicians have to have a code. Without it, the whole thing falls apart.

Last night, Reed was somewhat mellow, if unhappy, and he told the story of how he had become, for the moment, one of the prominent people in American politics—a role that he enjoys and cultivates—and a man who has been driving both sides crazy in this close nomination fight. Reed now has rivals for influence within the Mississippi Party, and his chairmanship is about to be passed on to a successor. He was still sad that his announcement of support for Ford had cost him some of his allies. Reed likes to keep everybody happy with him, even if it means telling them—as he told both the Reagan camp and the Ford camp—that they will have his support. "I'm not a Messiah man," Reed said last night. "A lot of my conservative colleagues are. Neither Ford nor Reagan is going to save the world. I've got my little act, they've got theirs."

I asked Reed how he had come to be a leader of the Mississippi Republican Party.

"I'd been pretty fortunate early in life. I thought the only thing I wanted to do was live a pretty good life and make a buck. But I woke up at age twenty-seven or eight and realized I was too comfortable to be comfortable. As Walker Percy said in *The Message in the Bottle,* the hostile environment is the only one where you're comfortable." Reed grew up in what is called the "boot heel" of Missouri—the southeast corner of the state. "It was more like Mississippi than a lot of Mississippi," he said. "The family tradition was to keep the river off the land and survive the Reconstruction." His family moved to Greenville, where his father brought in a soybean elevator. Reed himself, at twenty-two, went into the business of constructing grain-storage facilities. Then he went into the manufacture of grain-storage-and-handling equipment. "It was a great economic contribution to the area," Reed said. "I sold it six years ago and put the money back in the land." Reed has boasted that he is the largest rice grower in America, but, whatever the case, he has done very well. He is also in the barge-operating business. "All that time, I said things are so good for me, I got to keep them that way," he said. "And my part of the country had been sort of out of the mainstream politically since 1820. I didn't like the way things were going in the world. I was scared. I was very concerned about the South. I knew we were messed up. I had to figure out a way for us to get back in things. I saw that three-fourths of the country that thinks like us is in one party—the Republicans—and one fourth, in the South, is in another. So the only thing to do was to get together, to get with the three-fourths. And I saw the battle lines being drawn, and the question was who gets there first." It was apparent to Reed that the Republicans were going to need the South, and also that, given the established power in the Democratic Party of such men as John Stennis and James Eastland, a path to power and influence and attention might lie in getting there first as a Republican. Reed became county chairman in 1962 and state Party chairman in 1966.

I asked Reed to tell me something about the policies he wanted to see the federal government follow.

"We *are* the leaders of the free world," he replied. "The world is small. As free people, we owe it a game plan—at least, a goal—that the whole world is free."

And what did he want domestically?

Reed replied, "Adam Smith all the way. The system works beautifully. Small business is Adam Smith. Big business is an arm of government. The system is so good. We've got such an opportunity. Oh, man, we've got a whole continent. It's so great. We're the chosen people. Hell, I'm damn glad to be living in a place, in this country, where the whole act is going to be decided."

One striking thing about the group of strategists working here for the President's nomination is that so many of them worked for the nomination of Barry Goldwater, in 1964. Timmons was one. Others are Dean Burch, Goldwater's deputy campaign manager and Republican Party chairman, who was later named by Nixon as chairman of the Federal Communications Commission, then became a Nixon White House aide, and is now a Washington lawyer; Richard Herman, a member of the strategy committee at the Convention and an executive in the trucking business; and F. Clifton White, a Connecticut public-affairs consultant. In a way, the path of this group is symptomatic of what has happened to the Republican Party. The fight for control of the Party used to be between Richard Nixon and Nelson Rockefeller; then it was Nixon and Rockefeller and Ronald Reagan; now it's Reagan and Gerald Ford.

Tonight, at the Phillips House, a hotel across the street from the Muehlebach Hotel, subcommittees of the platform committee are holding drafting sessions. The Republicans have a little problem with drafting their platform this year: because of recent history, to which Republicans do not wish to draw attention, it cannot extoll the record of the past eight years. On the third floor, the foreign-policy subcommittee is meeting. Senators Scott, of Pennsylvania, and Roman Hruska, of Nebraska, are defending a draft of the foreign-policy section which largely represents the President's positions. It is odd to see Roman Hruska, a conservative of no particular distinction (except for his defense of the Supreme Court appointment of G. Harrold Carswell on the ground that even if he was mediocre, mediocre people "are entitled to a little representation, aren't they?"), playing a role of leadership, of moderation, but that, too, is symptomatic of what has happened to the Republican Party. Many say that the Party has clearly moved to the right. I am not so sure that that is how to explain it. There were two conservative candidates, one of them being the rallying point for the very conservative elements of the Party and winning almost as many delegates as the other. Therefore, this is a very conservative Convention. But whether that signifies an immutable trend I am not so sure. David Treen, who is a House member from Louisiana and is quite conservative, is also acting as a moderating force within this group. Two representatives of the Ford camp watch closely and from time to time speak into walkie-talkies. The subcommittee adopts a series of amendments that do such things as change the title of one subsection from "United States Relations with China" to "United States-Chinese Relations" and say that the United States is now in a position to "initiate dialogue" instead of "communicate" with the "leaders of a quarter of the earth's population." Then Yvonne Alford, a delegate from Alaska, offers an amendment to delete the section that refers to the restoration of communications with the People's Republic of China ("This extraordinary event, the culmination of a series of steps taken by President Nixon shortly after his inauguration in 1969, has allowed us to communicate with the leaders of a quarter of the earth's population"), the only reference to Nixon in the platform draft. Hruska suggests that "we should recognize outstanding events," but when the vote is taken the amendment is accepted.

AUGUST 12

Yesterday, Richard F. Trabert, of New Jersey, previously an uncommitted delegate, announced that he would support President Ford, and Gloria E. A. Toote, of New York, announced that she was switching from supporting the President to being uncommitted. These days, we read the names of people we have never heard of before and will never hear of again. If they play it right, they can have their names in the New York *Times* and the Washington *Post* and be on national television. For a moment.

This afternoon, I dropped in to see John Sears in his headquarters at the Alameda Plaza. It was late afternoon, and he had just come from a long staff meeting and was about to leave for his daily press conference. He had a sandwich and a Coke at his desk while we talked.

"We're going to have a floor fight," he said.

"On what?" I asked.

"Probably 16-C," he said. Rule 16-C incorporates Sears' proposal that Presidential candidates be required to name their running mates before the balloting for the nomination.

I asked Sears what the considerations were in selecting an issue to wage a floor fight on.

"What you do best on," he replied.

"What about the platform?" I asked him.

"I don't think this has been a very 'issues' year," he replied. "There isn't any particular point to having a fight over the platform. That's not to say we're not going to have one. The thing about this rule we proposed is that in one form and another there has been a lot of talk about reforming the Vice-Presidential process. It has a history to it. The reform itself stands up, so we can recommend it for the future, as well."

Sears talked about some of the things he has been doing: planning the visits to the delegations by Reagan and Schweiker; planning meetings of chairmen of Reagan delegations; planning for the meeting of the Convention's rules committee on Saturday, at which Rule 16-C will be proposed; organizing the ten regional field aides, who will handle about five states each in the coming week. Associates of Sears' are coping with a group headed by Senator Jesse Helms, of North Carolina, which is seeking to make the platform more conservative. Helms, a former radio and television broadcaster, is off on his own excursions here: backing, at the last minute, a Presidential candidacy by New York Senator James Buckley; working up his own platform group. Helms is the mirror image of what the left left wing of the Democratic Party often is at Democratic Conventions. Sears' own strategy for the platform was originally to give the Ford people their head and hope they would propose something that the Reagan forces could object to. But that strategy isn't panning out. For one thing, the drawing up of the platform draft by the Ford group was sufficiently behind schedule so that more than the usual amount is being drafted by the platform subcommittees themselves. For another, certain of the Reagan forces are out of control. Sears sought to put some of the ablest Reagan delegates on the credentials committee, which might have been a sensitive spot if there had been credentials challenges, and some on the rules committee. While he didn't exactly set out to put his worst delegates on the platform committee, neither did he assign to it his most dependable troops. And so certain Reagan supporters—some of them suspicious that Sears intends to "sell out" their most cherished beliefs (some even suspect that Sears, who is from New York, is actually a Rockefeller man)—are off on their own on the platform. A Sears maxim: "There are two ways to treat people you can't communicate with. You can try to stifle their efforts, which makes for difficulty. Or you can make use of them. The latter is usually the better thing to do." Sears said this afternoon, "Some of the people in North Carolina had fears we would bargain away the platform. So they started working on their own some time ago. We decided to see what they would propose. That's a better tactic: see what they are doing and then react to it, rather than the other way around. Now it's settled into a workable posture. Things that we may not particularly run on that might end up in there are the Helms group's planks, and anything we would like to claim credit for we can." He laughed.

Sears returned to the subject of Rule 16-C. "We think if we can force the issue on the Vice-Presidency we should be able to win the nomination," he said. "The actual name of the running mate the President chooses will help, because it will drive away some of his support, but also if you can force an incumbent President to do something he does not wish to do it's very helpful with people who are undecided or leaning the other way. If we won 16-C, a good maneuver then would be to have someone jump up and say, 'Let's let both tickets address the Convention.' I think you'd see it go through in no time. I would like to see the other side mount the podium in opposition. It's a more potent move even than asking for time for Reagan to address the Convention. It seems to be a patently reasonable proposal, and it's clear the President doesn't want to get on the same podium with Reagan." He smiled.

I asked Sears if he realized that he had the other side thoroughly off balance and tense, wondering what he would do next.

"Is that so?" he asked, and he smiled. "That's a good way to have people." He smiled again. "You can very often worry people into mistakes."

Today, Clarke Reed issued a statement in which he said that reports that President Ford was considering as his running mate such liberals as Senator Charles Percy, of Illinois; Senator Mark Hatfield, of Oregon; Senator Lowell Weicker, of Connecticut; and Senator Edward Brooke, of Massachusetts, "came as a shock" to him. Actually, none of these is a very likely choice—and Brooke and Weicker have already declined to run—but Reed's statement nevertheless has much of the press excited and writing stories about what he said. Which pleases Reed. Last night, he was fairly depressed, because now that he has committed his support to Ford he is not receiving much attention. He said, "I'll have to think something up." In the Muehlebach Hotel's bar at the end of the day today, Reed sips a gin and tonic and talks to reporters. The reporters now know that that bar is where to find him. (Some people at Conventions know how to station themselves so that reporters can seek them out for statements and they can make news.) "This all-spectrum stuff," says Reed. He is talking fast and, as usual, in half sentences and swallowed words. "That's Mickey Mouse. If Percy's part of that spectrum. And Hatfield's more liberal than Schweiker. My delegates are very unhappy. They want to know whether I led them down the primrose path." Reed is happy again.

AUGUST 13

Friday. The full platform committee is meeting in the Municipal Auditorium, just down the street from the Muehlebach. The committee, seated at long tables on the stage, is almost entirely middle-aged and older. I see only one black—a woman, Marjorie Parker, from the District of Columbia. Ford aides prowl the hall with walkie-talkies. They are staying in touch with Timmons, whose offices are elsewhere in the city. In reality, the platform fight is something of a pillow fight thus far: the Ford forces are so eager to avoid losing support for the President or provoking a fight over the platform at the Convention that they are acceding to most of the Reagan forces' demands. A plank on the Panama Canal, not included in the original draft, has been added, and subsequently compromised to the point where it closely resembles Reagan's position. Virtually every change that the Reagan forces wanted in the China plank has been accepted. Also as a result of the Reagan forces' efforts, the platform now calls for military "superiority" over the Soviet Union. The Ford forces—for all their consultation by walkie-talkie—are less concerned about what the platform says than they are about winning the nomination. So, while they are on guard against anything too embarrassing to run on, they are being flexible. Republicans really are different from Democrats—if not in their proclivity for appealing to interest groups, then in the interest groups to which they appeal. Yesterday afternoon, the platform committee adopted tax credits and write-offs amounting to an estimated fifty billion dollars. One platform drafter remarked, "This is our Humphrey-Hawkins." Joseph Coors, the brewer who supports right-wing causes and Ronald Reagan, proposed an amendment to eliminate all federal child-care programs; it was defeated by a vote of fifty-five to thirty-four. A proposal sponsored by David Treen to abolish federal aid to education and finance it instead through returning a portion of the federal tobacco tax to the states—a proposal that has been lying around Congress for years—was adopted yesterday, and now efforts are being made to reverse that decision. At today's session of the platform committee, Louise Leonard, a delegate from West Virginia, says that she supports the Treen amendment, and she denounces the "intrusion" of the federal government in our schools. Another woman, whose nameplate I cannot see, says, "That may be the biggest issue in the election: how to get the federal government out of our lives." After a while, the proposal is amended to suggest only that "a study should be authorized concerning funding of elementary and secondary education, coupled with a study regarding return to the states of equivalent revenue to compensate for any loss in present levels of federal funding."

Late this afternoon, Clarke Reed tells me that he spoke with Richard Cheney, the President's chief of staff, who is still in Washington, and that Cheney told him not to worry about the Vice-Presidential selection—that everything would be all right. Says Reed, "The only thing they understand is things public. It's a little insurance policy. Some of my delegates were concerned. You know, Jimmy Carter didn't submit James Eastland's name for so-called 'balance.' It's sort of late for that sort of foolishness. I castigated some of the other Southern Ford supporters for being patsies. I said, 'Look, the squeaking wheel gets attention. So why all this unquestioning loyalty?' "

August 14

At dinner, I ask Barber Conable, a moderate Republican House member from upstate New York, who is a friend of the President's and a member of the platform committee, what he thinks has happened to the Republican Party.

"You've got to understand," he replies, "that national Conventions are put together by activists. Most of the Reagan delegates are from areas that have never sent Republicans to Congress except by mistake. In New York, they're from Brooklyn. Most of the Reagan delegates—except those from California, where they have had time—are people who bear scant relationship to the political process. They are people who have been on the edges and feel frustrated and don't relate to it. They have never had a chance to be part of it.

They don't have to concern themselves with the political implications of what they feel. A woman serving on the platform committee came up to me and said, in effect, 'This is my first Convention and I'm so excited. Let's abolish federal aid to education.' As they see it, they are in a process that is going to be radicalized by disruption. Nineteen out of twenty Republican congressmen will support Ford, because he represents to them the real world.''

I ask Conable why the moderate wing of the Republican Party is so shrunken and beleaguered.

"The suburban middle-class people," he says, "who are humiliated by their support of Richard Nixon, are either going Democratic or going underground." He explains, "The Party is a middle-class party—made up of people who are not politically active, don't want anything from the government. Moderates think of politics as somewhat beneath them. They are more interested in paying off their mortgage and getting their kids to college than in politics. They are moderate people, and they want moderate representation. They felt betrayed by Richard Nixon and left the Party to the activists."

Why, I ask him, has Gerald Ford not been able to bring those people back?

Speaking very slowly, Conable answers, "Because he pardoned Nixon."

August 15

Sunday. A meeting of the Convention's rules committee in the Muehlebach Hotel. Dean Burch is walking around looking very tense. "This is it," he says to me dramatically before the meeting begins. "This is the big casino. We've been busting our ass, calling in all our I.O.U.s on this. *No more Mr. Nice Guy.* Sears is muddying the waters. He's throwing his cards in the air and hoping for a better hand." This isn't really "it," because even if Sears' proposal is defeated here, as he expects it to be, it will be taken to the Convention floor, where it might have a better chance. The Ford forces have a definite majority on the committee, which is made up of representatives from each state and territory, because they took care that they would. Reagan may have almost as many delegates to this Convention, but Ford won the primaries of more states and, moreover, was better connected with the Republican machinery of most states. Just after each primary the Ford forces went to work to see that as many members of the key Convention committees as possible were friendly to them. Burch will be acting as field commander for the Ford forces at this meeting. The speeches by those on Ford's side have been assigned and written. Again, Ford men with walkie-talkies are all over the place. There is a whip for every eight delegates on the committee. They are going about this as if it were World War III. If they were not working on behalf of the nomination of someone who comes across as a nice man who does not seem alarmingly competent, it would all strike us as more ominous than it does. I have tried to imagine how we would feel if all this monitoring and whipping into line and talking into walkie-talkies were taking place on behalf of Richard Nixon. As a matter of fact, a great many people who are carrying on in this way did work for Richard Nixon. But they seem nicer now—and, in fact, are more relaxed. People do take on the coloring of their environment. I can still remember the feeling of being in a combat zone at the 1972 Republican Convention, in Miami Beach. There was no doubt that Nixon would be nominated, but one would have thought that he was about to be dumped, and, moreover, that Cuba was about to invade. The Coast Guard patrolled the beach. This room is divided into quadrants, so that Ford aides can watch all the Ford people on the rules committee, to see that they vote the way they are supposed to. The Ford leaders on the rules committee conferred with their managers before this meeting. Gerald Ford does not go after legislation this way, and that may be just as well.

Clarke Reed is a member of this committee, and one Ford aide tells me, "We expect Reed to vote with us." That's odd, because, having made such a fuss over Vice-Presidential choices, and having based his switch from Reagan to Ford on Reagan's selection of Schweiker, Reed would seem to have to support Sears' proposal. Besides, that would be a way for him to make at least some amends to Mississippi Reagan supporters and to the Reagan camp. When I mention to another Ford aide the first aide's assumption that Reed would support their position, the man says, "If he thinks Clarke has made a commitment to us, he must have met him yesterday." The Reagan forces make earnest, political-sciency, good-government arguments in favor of Rule 16-C. They cite Common Cause. They say such things as "It is a very important political reform." It might be, but it has been offered in the context of this Convention's politics, and therefore that is how it is viewed. The Ford side makes the argument (which they hope will be effective with Reagan delegates) that this rule would prevent Ford from selecting Reagan as his running mate, notwithstanding the fact that Reagan has insisted he would not run for the Vice-Presidency. (Sometimes it seems that Reagan isn't even very eager to be President, so why should he seek the Vice-Presidency? Now sixty-five, he is unlikely to run for the Presidency four years from now, and he has a rather comfortable life back in California.) A Ford aide tells me that the President himself, who is to arrive in Kansas City later today, as is Reagan, will be working to persuade delegates to vote against the Sears proposal.

Sherry Martschink gets up to speak. She is an uncommitted delegate from South Carolina to whom both sides have paid quite a bit of attention. Some think that that is exactly what she wants. Mrs. Martschink, a striking platinum blonde, ran as a Reagan delegate and then switched to an uncommitted status, saying she was leaning toward Ford. Yesterday, Reagan strategists, in a meeting, conferred on what to do about Sherry Martschink. President Ford had called her four or five times, one said, and had invited her to the White House. One suggested that Reagan also call her. There was discussion of whether Sherry Martschink should be invited to be on the escort committee to take Reagan to the rostrum in the event that he was nominated, and some concern that if the Reagan forces did not extend such an invitation, the Ford forces might. There was a suggestion that Mrs. Martschink should be invited to join Mrs. Reagan in the special viewing box at the Kemper Arena, where the Convention will be held. But now Mrs. Martschink speaks on behalf of Ford's position on Rule 16-C. Others have used golf metaphors in their little speeches today. She talks of checkers, and says, "We decide how we're going to play before we start the game." When she finishes, she gets considerable applause.

The vote is taken on the rule, and it is defeated, fifty-nine to forty-four. Clarke Reed voted for it, though he had managed to take a Ford position on a preceding procedural question. It is shortly after noon, and soon he will go out to the Kemper Arena to be interviewed for a CBS special this evening. He tells me after the vote that he was talked to about the rule by Timmons, Cheney, and Harry Dent, who is in charge of Southern delegates for Ford, and also by David Keene, the Reagan delegate collector for the South. He goes on to tell me that the Ford camp wants the Mississippi delegation to vote tonight to break the unit rule and say how its members will vote at the Convention. The Ford people figure that their having votes in Mississippi, now listed as uncommitted, will help with their vote totals and with their effort to claim enough delegates for the nomination before the Convention opens. The only way Reagan can win is to hold Mississippi and have it vote as a unit. But Reed says he does not think that the Mississippi delegation will take a vote on breaking the unit rule until Wednesday. He looks distressed. He doesn't like the pressure, or his inability to please both sides. "I'm not very happy about that rule the Reagan people proposed," Reed says, "but right now I'm not happy about anything."

In a corner of the room, Robert Visser, the President Ford Committee's legal counsel, is talking into his walkie-talkie. "Tucker, Tucker, this is Visser. Need count of absentees. We're losing count of absentees."

Sunday afternoon. John Connally, who arrived here last night, is holding a jammed press conference at the Exhibition Hall. Connally is a large man of large ambition. The ambition took him from being a poor boy in Texas to being a lawyer accepted in wealthy Texas circles and a wealthy rancher himself, and then on to being Secretary of the Navy under John Kennedy, governor of Texas, Richard Nixon's Treasury Secretary, head of something called Democrats for Nixon (in 1972), and, finally, when he sensed that his political fortunes lay in the Republican Party, a Republican. Lyndon Johnson once said of him that the trouble with John Connally was that he forgot he had been poor. For some time now, Connally has been hovering about the Presidency, and one senses that he would settle for the Vice-Presidency only as a waiting room. There was talk of Connally's replacing Agnew on the Republican ticket in 1972, and Nixon came close to selecting Connally when Agnew left office. But Connally, a pugnacious man, has a knack for acquiring political enemies. There was a time in recent weeks when it appeared that he might well be Ford's choice as a running mate, but it now seems that Connally's milk problems—though he was acquitted—have ruled him out. Ford has enough trouble. Connally's following and his hold on people of influence are perhaps best explained by what a friend of mine calls Connally's peculiarly American persuasiveness. Connally is walking confidence, and he says things with such certainty, such an embargo on doubt, that he persuades others. Even his size is a factor. He is so large, and so certain, that people are impressed. But I have always found something slightly comic about him: he seems to give off something of the air of an impostor, almost as if he didn't expect one to take him seriously. John Connally seems to be always trying on different masks, darting on and off the stage, trying out against different backdrops.

This afternoon, he stands there in a blue suit with a blue shirt and a blue tie—all confidence and assurance, even though he must know, as everyone in this room does, that the Vice-Presidency has all but eluded him once more. The face is familiar—handsome, with the slight ski nose—but a bit older, the hair whiter and longer. Connally does have a certain animal charm. "I have come to this Convention in furtherance of the plan that I have held all spring: to better acquaint myself with congressmen and senators" running for reëlection, he says, "to see how my time might best be used this fall." Richard Nixon built his base in the Party by campaigning for representatives and senators. "I also came here, very frankly," he says, "to acquaint myself with the Party organization." When Connally speaks, his lower lip is out and his jaw seems to move from side to side. Connally doesn't just talk; he makes a case. Asked to discuss the pros and cons of his being on the ticket, he smiles, and replies jauntily, "I don't know whether I'll be on; I don't know whether I'll be off. I've not asked to be on; I've not asked to be off." Would he refuse to accept a place on the ticket? "I'm not going to say that I'd refuse to accept it. I think that reflects both a presumptuousness and an arrogance, and I don't want to be guilty of either." And then he says some things that make sense—that one doesn't hear from Gerald Ford or Ronald Reagan. "We're going to have to develop an energy policy, a food and fibre policy . . . a new policy with respect to economic expansion," he says. "The age of abundance for America is over and done with." The other countries of the world, he says, "are not going to let the United States consume a third of the food and fibre of the world." When Connally talks about these things, it seems that he has actually thought about them. And then the questions about the milk case come up. Have you ever been offered, accepted, or solicited a bribe? "Absolutely not." Questions about his finances. More questions about milk. Connally answers them with assurance. But if he ran for national office, these scenes would be on television often. Connally is trying to bluster his way into the future, but he is trapped in his past. He concludes his press conference by saying, "I haven't made any plans with respect to 1980."

The Hilton Airport Plaza Inn, about seventeen miles from downtown Kansas City. Ronald Reagan, who arrived at the airport a short while ago, and Richard Schweiker, who met his plane, have gone to see the Wyoming delegation and will be arriving shortly to meet with the Pennsylvania delegation, which is staying here. According to the Ford camp, Ford has eighty-four Pennsylvania delegates, Reagan has ten, and nine are uncommitted. On balance, the selection of Schweiker hasn't yet made any difference in the Pennsylvania delegation. Just before the meeting of the delegation with Reagan and Schweiker, Drew Lewis, the Ford campaign chairman in Pennsylvania, announces before a crush of reporters and television cameras and lights that four previously uncommitted delegates—David Wade, William Black, Edward Byrne, and George Stewart—are now supporting President Ford. Edward Byrne holds a little press conference. "I came to Kansas City to do what is right for my district," he says. After Reagan and Schweiker make their appearance here, representatives of the President will appear before the Pennsylvania delegates. At four-twenty-five, the Reagans and the Schweikers arrive. Reagan looks sporty in a beige jacket and brown trousers and a brown tie. Nancy Reagan, in blue and white today, always looks disconcertingly perfect. Reagan, on the rostrum, waves and smiles. It is that crinkly-eyed, openmouthed smile that has become so familiar. It is a nice-guy smile. Suddenly, one realizes that Reagan has been playing the role of the easygoing nice guy—in films, as a television salesman, as an after-dinner speaker, as a politician—for a very long time. Reagan has a kind of boyishness about him. It may be the boyishness that one notices in other movie actors, too—a kind of unformedness. A friend of mine once described another movie actor as a "boy-man," and the term seems to fit Reagan, as well.

Reagan's performance here is polished and professional, as well it might be. In brief remarks, he tells the Pennsylvania delegates that his choice of a running mate "was one that was born of a feeling that there may be a section of the country that felt it was being dealt out." He says that there was a lot of talk of unity, and that he felt "it was time that we implemented some of that talk." He speaks of the importance of building bridges "between the Northeast and the Sunbelt, the Plains states and the West." He says, echoing John Sears' line of argument, "The reason for the decision had nothing to do with this meeting in August. It had to do with November." He says, "I didn't run for the nomination. I ran for the election," and he adds, "I'm tired of Republicans going off the cliff with flags flying." I remember hearing Reagan tell an audience in Cincinnati in June, "Let's put up a banner . . . and let's promise that we won't compromise our principles for political expediency." He built his movement and solidified his candidacy saying things like that. But then he bowed to expediency, as he did when he was governor of California—and as politicians must—and now he is here, making his last moves in his effort to win the nomination. The effort has lasted a long time. When it began, there were many, including some close to him, who wondered whether he had the endurance to go through months of struggle. Of course, few thought that it would last this long; the assumption was that either Ford or Reagan—more likely Reagan—would be knocked out of the contest early. Now there are only three days left. Reagan is very forceful today, as if he had mustered all his energy for this last push. He looks healthy and rested. He has reason to be proud of having come this far, running not so much against Gerald Ford as against the powers, paraphernalia, and financial advantages of an incumbent President. He goes through the list of some of his issues: Congress, which is "the most irresponsible we've ever had . . . the increasing controls on the citizenry . . . the increasing burden of paperwork." He warns that we might "go down the path taken by our cousins in Great Britain, and from that path there is no return without upheaval."

Schweiker appears to be wearing the same electric-blue jacket he wore when I saw him address the Pennsylvania delegation in Washington in July. Today, he is forceful, too. In that earlier meeting, which took place in the midst of the uproar over his decision to join Reagan, he seemed almost embarrassed, and slunk into and out of the meeting as fast as he could. But now he has his arguments well rehearsed. If Schweiker can't persuade Pennsylvania, he will have real cause for embarrassment. He talks again about the fact that Republicans have only from eighteen to twenty-two percent of the voters, and he says that half of eighteen is nine, so the Republican Party cannot afford to be divided in half. "There's no way we can beat Jimmy Carter if we don't put the two wings together," he says. He complains about a "double standard" by which he and Reagan are criticized for joining forces, while Franklin D. Roosevelt picked

John Nance Garner, Adlai Stevenson picked John Sparkman, John Kennedy picked Lyndon Johnson, and, for that matter, "Grits picked Fritz." He goes on to say that he admires Governor Reagan's approach to government, his idea "of using outside task forces to solve problems," and also "the intriguing aspect of using a third approach"—private enterprise, rather than government action or doing nothing—to solve problems of government. He is arguing his case, doing the best he can. Schweiker has more than the nomination at stake here. He has reputation, and face, on the line. Reagan "has showed that 1976 is not 1964," says Schweiker "By picking Dick Schweiker, he's showed that he is pragmatic and realistic." Governor Reagan showed that, says Schweiker, "in one fell swoop." That's what has created the problem. Reagan switched signals too suddenly.

AUGUST 16

Monday. At ten o'clock this morning, the door of the Ford campaign's trailer, parked just outside the Kemper Arena, opens and about a dozen Ford aides and strategists wearing baseball caps, some red, some yellow, emerge. They stand around talking for a few moments, as if holding a pregame huddle, and then disappear into the Arena. In one's imagination, there were cleats on their shoes.

Once inside the Arena, the Ford aides appear extremely nervous. On the Convention floor, Tom Korologos, a business partner of Timmons and also a White House lobbyist during the Nixon Administration, explains to me that the red caps signify floor whips and the yellow caps signify "floaters, fire-fighters." Korologos, a beefy man with a broad face, is wearing a yellow cap. He looks pretty funny in it. He is carrying a walkie-talkie, as are the other yellow-caps. The Ford forces have the Convention floor divided into twelve regions, each supervised by a regional whip, and they also have ten floaters, fifty-four state whips, and a buddy system within each delegation. In one of the glass-fronted boxes high in the stands, which the Republicans are referring to as Sky Suites, Bryce Harlow, a former official in the Eisenhower and Nixon Administrations and now a lobbyist for Procter & Gamble, and Senator John Tower, of Texas, are watching the Convention floor carefully. (Timmons told me in Washington, "It may become necessary to move a delegate or two up to that Sky Suite to twist their arms half off.") Harry Dent is on the telephone in the Sky Suite. "At various places along the way, they may try something," Harlow says to me. "You never know." The Ford agents are still worried about Sears. Oddly, one hears not about Reagan but about Sears. Sears, not Reagan, is the opposition. Sears, who is operating from a trailer parked next to the Ford trailer, does not have a floor organization of this kind. He has people on the floor, but he thinks that floor organizations are a throwback to a time before managers could sit in trailers, watch television, and communicate with people on the floor by telephone. The Ford forces have white telephones spotted around the floor, and the Reagan forces have red ones. Most of the delegations have blue telephones, on which delegates can make calls to other delegations or to the outside world. The worry among the Ford group this morning is that some move will be made before the temporary rules are adopted, but none is. Sears has other targets.

A young black man addresses the Convention this morning (when, presumably, few are watching on television), saying, "This country was built on work, not welfare." The "Star-Spangled Banner" problem is solved for today by having it sung by John Ashcroft, candidate for attorney general of Missouri. On the Convention floor, a woman from the Ohio delegation tells Lyn Nofziger that there may be some "soft" Ford votes in Ohio, and Nofziger, in shirtsleeves and smoking a cigar, eagerly writes the information down. Actually, the Reagan strategists think they may have unannounced support in Ohio, Pennsylvania, New York, New Jersey, Illinois, Virginia, South Carolina (though they have given up on Sherry Martschink), and a few other states. Reagan delegates have been asked to talk with other delegates and with the press and to express optimism.

The Reagan forces are now preparing for a platform fight on foreign policy. Sears has concluded that if they can defeat Ford on 16-C, and then perhaps on a motion to permit both tickets to address the Convention and then on a platform plank, the "momentum" and emotion of the Convention will swing to Reagan, Reagan's strength will have been demonstrated, and Reagan will be nominated. The compass needle will swing in his direction. Much of Ford's support, Sears told reporters at a breakfast yesterday morning, comes from people who are not for him but do not want to oppose an incumbent President. "That is not what you would call an emotionally committed constituency," he said.

Just after this morning's session, I saw Dr. John East, a delegate from North Carolina who has been an advocate of a number of the changes in the platform which Jesse Helms proposed, and who has been working with the Reagan forces. Dr. East, partly bald, forty-five years old, confined to a wheelchair as a result of polio, is a professor of political science at East Carolina University, in Greenville, North Carolina. He was a candidate for Congress in 1966, and he is a Republican national committeeman. "I'm very pleased with the platform," he said to me this morning. "On a scale of one to ten, we came out with a nine." He told me he thought the foreign-policy plank should be strengthened, and why, and also about the way some of the conservatives here view things. "We will bring into focus a number of questions which raise the key question of whether we have a moral purpose in the world, as opposed to the realpolitik of Henry Kissinger, where you accommodate yourself to the realities of world power without any goals of your own," he said. "Is there an American foreign policy, and, if so, what is it? We will present an omnibus plank that will keep us from getting bogged down in particulars." And then he talked about the conservative movement. "I'm very sensitive to the point the critics raise," he said. "And I agree that if we turn it into a lot of ideological purity to cause political shock, rather than build a party, that's a problem. The American electorate is conservative. Americans certainly don't think of themselves as liberal; they certainly don't think of themselves as radical. I think they are uncomfortable with big government. I think they do believe in a strong defense. I think they are suspicious of the Russians. I think we are on the right track in building a good theoretical base. We have to be careful not to appear to be building for frivolous political shock waves, but I think we're on the right track."

Today, the Ford forces claimed to have a majority in Mississippi, and so they offered the Reagan forces a deal, in which the delegation would be divided evenly, fifteen votes for each side, but Sears and David Keene decided that the Ford forces were bluffing, and turned them down. This afternoon, Reagan met with four Mississippi delegates for about twenty-five minutes, and called some delegates from Pennsylvania, Louisiana, and New York. John Connally, on behalf of the Ford forces, met with seven Reagan delegates from Louisiana and asked them not to support Rule 16-C, because, since he was controversial with some Northern delegations, it would knock him out of consideration for the Vice-Presidency. (The Reagan forces thought that that was such a good story for their side—likely to make some Ford delegates unhappy—that they saw to it that it got on television.) Reagan suggested to Mississippi and Louisiana delegates that perhaps William Scranton would be Ford's choice; he told Pennsylvania and New Jersey delegates that perhaps it would be John Connally. As of now, the Reagan forces believe that they have a very good chance to win the fight on Rule 16-C.

While the delegates to this Convention appear older than the ones in 1972, the percentages are actually about the same: only twelve and a half percent under thirty and sixteen percent over sixty. It seems that more of them are white than before, and the statistics bear this out: in 1972, four percent of the delegates were black; this year, three percent are black. The Reagan delegates, on the whole, look different from the Ford delegates. They look more—well, country; more flashily dressed. They wear more funny hats and pins and baubles. There are only a few left of what used to be considered the stereotypical Republican, in pin-striped suit with vest. George Hinman, a New York national committeeman and close ally of Rockefeller's, who is so attired, looks almost like a museum piece. There is no connection between George Hinman and the young man in the Texas delegation, nearby on the Convention floor, who is wearing a red-white-and-blue vest and who from time to time excitedly jumps up and down on his chair to lead his delegation in cheers. And there is no connection between the Texans, on one side of the Convention floor, one hundred percent for Reagan, and the stolid Ohioans on the other, almost one hundred percent for Ford. The candidates may not be so far apart in ideology, but their delegates are temperamentally and culturally distinct.

Nixon—uninvited, unmentioned—is not here, but he is a presence. He is still the Banquo's ghost at this election. Everyone knows how Gerald Ford came to be the President. The pardon, intended to get a difficult problem out of the way, has lastingly bound Ford to Nixon. The shame of Watergate is in the atmosphere of this

Convention. At a breakfast with reporters this morning, Rogers Morton, the chairman of the President Ford Committee, confirmed that Senator Howard Baker, who is giving a keynote speech tonight, had been requested to reduce the number of his references to Watergate. When Morton—who has the liability of candor—was asked if the Party was trying to sweep Watergate under the rug, he replied, "You'd need a hell of a big broom."

Tonight, Rockefeller, as he stands on the rostrum about to give his speech, is applauded. Probably few here do not recall that in 1964, a startlingly long twelve years ago, he was booed at the Republican Convention. But he is no longer a threat, his days of seeking the Presidential nomination presumably past. Moreover, he was eased off the Ford ticket in the hope of placating the right—an effort that turned out to be in vain, as did all such efforts. So tonight the Convention seems to sense that it can be nice to him. The applause the delegates give him is warm but not emotional. Rockefeller, drinking it in, waves his arms in that two-armed wave that says, without meaning it, "Don't go on," and then he suspends his arms helplessly as if to say, "What can I do? They like me so much I can't stop them." As he speaks, the familiar gravel voice sounds more gravelly. And then he says some slightly embarrassing things. "Unaccustomed as I am to being a non-candidate," he says, and he also says, "I've tried to get your nomination for sixteen years." I remember Rockefeller being asked after the 1968 Convention why he had not received the nomination, and replying, "Have you ever seen a Republican Convention?" But he never gave up. Even this year, occasional bleeps out of the Rockefeller camp suggested that Rockefeller still considered it possible that he would be asked to join Ford's ticket, or even that, in the event of a deadlock between Ford and Reagan, the Convention would, of all things, turn to him. About two weeks ago, Rockefeller hosted a luncheon at his vacation place in Seal Harbor, Maine, for the Northeastern states Party chairmen, who were involved in an effort to head off John Connally's nomination as the Vice-Presidential candidate. Rockefeller told the chairmen, who favored him for the job, that he would be willing to run for Vice-President if he could also serve as the White House chief of staff. Ambition is a powerful source of fantasies. In his speech tonight, Rockefeller says, "I'm concerned about this Republican Party." That's undoubtedly true. And then, oddly, he makes a little joke about Ford. He says, "If it took a football player who played center without a helmet to pull us through, I say, thank God we've had him to lead the team." No doubt Rockefeller considers himself better qualified to be President than Ford. Something sad seems to have happened to him. He has been through too many battles, and he seems bitter and hardened. He tried to become President and that failed, and he finally became Vice-President and that failed, and then he decided to "free" himself and travel about the country giving speeches, but no one paid attention. Now Rockefeller makes the case for Ford. "My friends . . . the easiest thing a President can do with an appropriation bill is to sign it." It's all he can do now. He gives a dull speech. He has nothing to say. "We're going to win a great victory in November," he concludes. The band plays "The Sidewalks of New York," and he gets polite applause. He waves, he smiles, and he is gone.

Barry Goldwater, who started it all in 1964, looks like an old man tonight. He speaks more slowly and more softly than one remembers. After Goldwater's disastrous loss, the Republicans decided in 1968 to make a "sensible" choice, and selected Nixon over Rockefeller or Reagan. Had they gone with their hearts, they'd probably have selected Reagan. Tonight, Goldwater's words are fiery, but there is no fire in his voice. He seems old, and is obviously in pain, from arthritis. "Our enemies are deaf to the whining of weakness," he says. He warns against "a gallop toward nationalized economy," adding, "We must call it by its real name—Socialism." The applause is tepid.

On the Convention floor tonight, Clarke Reed tells me, "In this delegation, pressure works in reverse. The Ford people tried to get a caucus today—lower operatives, you know. I said I'm inclined to go along with the rules-committee, platform-committee stuff. They put out a statement I would go along with everything. I called Cheney. He denied it."

I ask him if he had talked any more with Cheney about the Vice-Presidential candidate.

He replies, "Cheney said today the Vice-Presidential candidate would be a good guy. Those are my words, not his. Dent suggested today we divide the delegation fifteen-fifteen. That kind of stuff is the sorriest stuff. They saw right away they'd screwed up."

After the Convention ends for the evening, I talk with John Sears in the Reagan trailer. It is more elegantly appointed than the Carter trailer was—the walls are panelled and the floor is carpeted. It is also surprisingly cool, considering the number of people who are here. It develops that the Reagan people are proud of the fact that through their foresight their trailer has six air conditioners, while the Ford trailer, a few feet away, has only three. The Reagan trailer has an extra room attached to one side at the back. The Ford forces, in retaliation, have added a Winnebago motor home. Sears sits at one end of the Reagan trailer, surrounded by four television sets—one for each of the networks and one that shows what the network-pool camera is picking up—and a large telephone console. Along the sides of the trailer are ten workers, each covering about five states, and each with a telephone console and a television set. Among those waiting to see Sears tonight are delegates from Georgia and Montana.

I ask Sears what he has been doing.

"Counting, counting, counting, all day," he replies. The counting has been on what will happen on Rule 16-C. "The count's up a little tonight," he says. "According to our count, we'd win it right now. That isn't worth much, because the vote isn't until tomorrow. The pressure comes on the last day. That's when your count goes down."

I ask him about the estimate by CBS that as of tonight Ford has enough delegates to win the nomination.

"Whatever happens tomorrow night establishes a new count," Sears replies.

He says that he has been talking with some individual delegates in the trailer, and to Reagan state chairmen on the floor by phone. He explains, "We discuss why we don't have somebody. Maybe I suggest some ideas. One of the problems you run into is that in those delegations where they are bound by law to support their candidates, you don't have much intermixing of the Ford and Reagan people. When you get off the subject of candidates and get to issues, your delegates haven't necessarily talked to Ford delegates. I talk to people about which delegations Reagan should go to see here. We canned Missouri for the purpose of rounding up votes on 16-C. We found it more important that he go to New Mexico. Even though New Mexico is for him, they're not so hot on the damn rule. All they have to do is hear that he wants it."

Tonight, Sears' face is pale and yellow, except for dark spaces under his eyes. He is finally showing fatigue, but he still talks imperturbably.

I ask him what he thinks the Reagan side's prospects are in the fight over the foreign-policy amendment to the platform.

"We don't need to take a count on that yet," he replies. "It was just announced today, and it will be a little time before it sinks in. We don't know what Ford's going to do about it—whether he will fight us."

Sears tells me that he had two hours' sleep last night. (Timmons, whom I encountered on the way to the trailer, told me that he had had two hours' sleep last night, too.) I ask Sears what he was working on through the night.

"Rules, rules," he replies. "A good lawyerly discussion about rules." He and his associates were talking about how, if 16-C carried, to bring up on the floor a proposal that all four candidates address the Convention.

A Ford aide had told me in Washington that the Ford camp would generally know what procedural options were available to the Reagan camp, because the two sides had an informal agreement to meet and discuss parliamentary questions and maneuvers with the Convention parliamentarian in advance. "There will be no surprises," this man had told me. I ask Sears how he went about trying to find out how to make his parliamentary move without tipping off the other side.

He replies, "What we did was ask the parliamentarian a hypothetical question about something else."

AUGUST 17

Tuesday. Last night, James E. Crockett, of Wytheville, Virginia, who is attending his first Convention, met with the President of the United States, and then, at ten o'clock, held a press conference at his hotel, the Sheraton Inn South, and announced that he would support Mr. Ford. This made Mr. Crockett, according to the New York *Times,* the one-thousand-one-hundred-and-thirtieth delegate —the last necessary for nominating a candidate—to announce his support of the President.

This morning, the President met with his key advisers and floor whips to plan the final strategy for the fight over 16-C, the pivotal vote of the Convention, and I joined the pool of reporters who were permitted a glimpse of this meeting. I wanted to see how Ford looked this morning. When we were shown into the President's suite, on the eighteenth floor of the Crown Center Hotel—part of a vast hotel-and-shopping complex—the President was seated at a long, marble-topped table with some of his lieutenants and allies: Senator Robert Griffin, of Michigan; Senator John Tower, of Texas; Representative Robert Michel, of Illinois, the House Republican whip. For an instant, the group seemed grim and tight-lipped, but as the photographers and reporters approached they rearranged their chairs and their mouths and posed for pictures of a smiling, confident team. But the President looked pale and tired. He was dressed in a brown suit and a brown-and-clay print tie, which seemed to contribute to a somewhat sallow look. "Who's winning?" a reporter asked the President, and he replied, with a slightly forced smile, "That was decided two or three weeks ago." In certain situations, politicians have to say certain things that they know no one believes—just as John Sears has been saying for some weeks now that Reagan would have eleven hundred and forty votes on the first ballot. Asked about the outlook for Rule 16-C, the President said, "I'm confident." One couldn't be sure.

The inevitable rumors about the President's choice of a Vice-President are travelling around Kansas City. In the lobby of the Crown Center Hotel, Ford aides will say with assurance things like "It's Baker," though in fact no one knows. There is said to be something called a final list, containing the names of Connally, Baker, Senator Robert Dole, of Kansas, William Ruckelshaus (the former deputy Attorney General who resigned on the night when Richard Nixon fired the Special Prosecutor, Archibald Cox, and when the Attorney General, Elliot Richardson, resigned), and William Simon, the Secretary of the Treasury. A brochure promoting Simon has been turning up at various points around the city. Today, John Tower went to talk to the Louisiana and Mississippi delegations on the President's behalf. The President himself made an appearance before the Illinois delegation, and so did Reagan. Reagan told the Illinois delegation that he was "sick and tired" of having people suggest—as the Ford people were suggesting, in their efforts to defeat Rule 16-C—that he might accept the Vice-Presidency. The Ford camp is also saying that to require the candidates to name their running mates before the balloting for the nomination might be a worthy reform for 1980. The Reagan camp responds that that argument is hypocritical. Ford told the Illinois delegation that he would choose a running mate who was "ideologically compatible" with him. Late this afternoon, word comes that the President's forces, having gone back and forth all day on the question, will not fight the Reagan foreign-policy amendment to the platform. Last night, Griffin was asked about the amendment by a reporter on the Convention floor, and he said, "We can live with that." One has the feeling of having heard the Ford forces say that quite often in the past few days. Ford's entourage is a problem; it includes a number of men who are somewhat limited and out of touch. But Ford clearly is comfortable with them and has sought out their counsel and companionship. Members of his White House staff spend a good bit of time sniping at each other, at his election-committee staff, and at his cronies, and the election-committee staff and the cronies return the fire. It is not a very inspiring picture.

At today's press conference, John Sears said that this evening would be "one of the most important in American political history." In the course of the day, the Reagan camp was quite tense. The people there knew, as Sears had indicated to me last night, that the Ford camp would put a lot of pressure on delegates today to support its position on 16-C. Both sides know that 16-C could be the ballgame. An idea that sprang from the brain of John Sears is now defining this Convention. Some in the Reagan camp were surprised to hear that the Ford camp might accept their foreign-policy amendment, which had been deliberately drafted so as to be humiliating to the President and unacceptable to his people. "If he accepts that, he'll accept anything," said one Reagan strategist. "We were hoping for a floor fight, but every time something came up they rolled over and accepted it." The Reagan camp heard this afternoon that Strom Thurmond, the very conservative Republican senator from South Carolina, who is supporting Reagan, might abandon them on the vote of 16-C, because Melvin Laird, Nixon's former Secretary of Defense and a former House crony of Ford's, told Thurmond that its adoption would rule out the possibility of a Ford-Reagan ticket.

Late today, word came that the Mississippi delegation voted to support, under the unit rule, President Ford's position on 16-C. That appears to end the Reagan camp's chances of carrying the vote. Clarke Reed had withheld his vote in the Mississippi caucus, and then, when it was clear that the delegation would not support 16-C—that he could vote with the Reagan camp without causing undue harm to the Ford camp—he voted for 16-C.

*   *   *

Over drinks before this evening's Convention session, John Anderson, a moderate Republican House member from Illinois, was depressed. He and some other Party moderates (Republicans, and some Democrats as well, will not use the term "iberal" anymore)—Senators Jacob Javits, from New York, and Charles Mathias, from Maryland, and William Coleman, the Secretary of Transportation—met for breakfast this morning. Anderson, chairman of the House Republican Conference, is a gentle man with white hair and big, round, deerlike eyes; he is one of the most thoughtful members of Congress, and is widely admired. "We feel it's important for Ford to get the message that once he gets the nomination the election will be won or lost depending on whether he moves toward a moderate position—that if he continues to capitulate to a vociferous minority it will be disastrous," Anderson said. "There are more of us in the Midwest and the Northeast. He should consider this in choosing his Vice-President and his campaign staff. They ask me to do things; yesterday I went to the Pennsylvania, Massachusetts, and Alaska delegations for them. I'm not going to be disposed to do that if I have to be semi-apologetic every time I turn around. The President's got to get that message. I don't think you can depend on filtering that message through a bureaucratic staff."

Then Anderson talked about the shape he thought the Republican Party was in. "The Southern strategy has come home to roost," he said. "And we haven't advanced young people to positions of leadership. We don't have very good leaders. And look at the platform committee here—one black, from the District of Columbia."

I asked him about the argument of some of his colleagues that there is a difference between the Convention Republican Party and the congressional Republican Party.

"Look at our percentages in Congress," Anderson replied. The Republicans have thirty-three percent of the House and thirty-eight percent of the Senate. He continued, "We believe in venture capital. We believe in the theory of risk in private enterprise, but when it comes to government we don't. We don't believe in an investment in education, we don't believe in an investment in the infrastructure of our society. We don't have any vision. We wear balance-sheet blinders: if it doesn't add up, it's bad. If any business thought that way, it wouldn't grow." Then Anderson said, "We have to stop appeasing the ultra-conservatives. We'll never convince them. They'll always say we weren't conservative enough."

I asked Anderson if he had heard that the Ford camp was planning to accept the Reagan foreign-policy amendment to the platform. He had not. Anderson was a member of the platform committee, and tonight he had no formal role.

"It makes you wonder," he said, "whether we'll come out of here with anything worth fighting for."

The moderates have a number of problems, and Barber Conable was correct on one key point: that the moderates somehow consider political organizing beneath them. They controlled the Party in the nineteen-forties and nineteen-fifties, but they did not dig in. And now they have a certain paleness. There are good moderates in the Congress but no compelling national moderate leaders. They seem to be suffering a certain fatigue from the battles on the right. And it is hard to say what, exactly, they stand for. It is easier to define them in terms of what they are not. They are not Democrats—though many of them do not vote so very differently or stand for such different things—and they are not conservative Republicans. They try to be "progressive" and "reasonable," offering "constructive alternatives" to what the Democrats propose. Their alternatives usually have to do with such undramatic points as how to finance a certain government venture. Estimable men and women, many of them, they end up sounding like mugwumps—not the sort of people great masses will follow into battle. "Reasonableness" in politics is not exciting.

At the Convention tonight, Mrs. Ford and three of the Ford children—Susan, Jack, and Steve—arrive a few minutes before eight o'clock, at a perfect moment, just after the credentials committee's report has been accepted and shortly before the debate on Rule 16-C begins. Their arrival, announced by the band's playing the University of Michigan's football song, "The Victors," sets off a demonstration. As it happens, the Ford strategists are very angry at Manny Harmon, the bandleader. The Ford strategists feel that Manny Harmon continued playing too long after Mrs. Reagan's arrival last night—announced by the band's playing "California, Here I Come"—thus helping Reagan partisans to prolong their demonstration. The demonstration lasted into the time that the Ford strategists had planned for the arrival of Mrs. Ford, who was "holding" in an anteroom at the Arena. And then, as Mrs. Ford made her entrance, the band was silent for three or four minutes. The Ford strategists spoke frantically into their walkie-talkies, and became very nearly apoplectic when the band struck up: it played "California, Here I Come." The Ford strategists are now suspicious of George Murphy, the former movie star and former senator from California and a friend of Reagan's, who is in charge of music for the Convention and who secured Manny Harmon, a Hollywood bandleader, and who from a position on the rostrum gives Harmon signals. These arrivals of the wives are maneuvers in the warfare here. The families are weapons. Betty Ford, dressed in yellow, waves to the crowd in a practiced way and smiles a broad, political smile. When Ford was the House Minority Leader and spent most of his time either on Capitol Hill or travelling on behalf of his colleagues, his wife was a rather retiring and tense woman. Now she has emerged as a poised, somewhat independent, and assertive figure. ("I graduated," she told a friend.) She clearly likes her new role and the attention, and has taken to them with zest and grace. She is immensely popular. She seems to have struck the proper balance, in the public view, between being the good wife and being an independent woman who speaks her mind. She is irreverent but not too irreverent.

On the Convention floor, Clarke Reed is speaking on the blue telephone. He finishes and smiles. "That was Cheney," he says. Reed shows me a copy of today's Birmingham *News,* which has a front-page story headlined FORD WOULD WRITE OFF "COTTON SOUTH"? The story is about Rogers Morton's breakfast with reporters yesterday, at which, it said, Morton indicated that Ford would "conduct a campaign based on a big-state strategy . . . virtually writing off the 'Cotton South' as the impenetrable private preserve of Democratic nominee Jimmy Carter of Georgia." (Actually, some of Reagan's aides have said that if their man is nominated, he has no intention of trying to beat Carter in much of the "Cotton South.") Reed says, "I told Cheney it's a losing strategy and dumb politics. He said the story wasn't true. Then he said, 'Would you change?' I said, 'In a minute.' " Tom Korologos, standing nearby, wearing his yellow cap, looks worried. He says into his walkie-talkie, "Volunteer, this is Socrates. What's your location?" Socrates, obviously, is Korologos's code name; surely "the enemy" could figure that out. A young man rushes up to Reed and says that the Reagan forces in the Mississippi delegation are saying that they might try to break the unit rule tonight. Reed says to me, "He's a very young man," and he laughs, and then he says, "He works for Ford," and he laughs again. "They're very nervous." John Tower materializes beside the Mississippi delegation. Tower, a diminutive man, looks worried. "We've talked to Cheney," Tower says to Reed. He is referring to the story in the Birmingham *News*. "This is not White House policy, Clarke. Cheney is going to make a call down here." Someone tells Tower that Cheney has already called. Now Tower starts waving his arms, and he says, "Morton shoots off his mouth. You know that as well as I do, Clarke." Korologos hovers close, and Tower continues, "Look at the question mark in that headline, Clarke. It's speculating. Morton isn't making campaign strategy. Let's not get all het up over that." Reed is smiling, enjoying the scene. It is Tower who is all het up.

On the rostrum, John Connally is making a speech. He asks, "Are you willing to place at the helm in these times a Commander-in-Chief who will not say—and may not know—where he intends to steer this ship of state?" The audience—the part of it that is listening—shouts "No!" Robert Michel, wearing a red baseball cap, gives reporters a projected count on the vote on Rule 16-C. The Ford camp says the rule will be defeated. John Connally says, "In the big leagues of world leadership, they rarely play softball."

After Connally's speech, Robert Dole, the temporary chairman, gavels the Convention to order and says, "This is the most important business to come before this Convention." The delegates quiet down. They know. Then Nancy Reagan arrives in the hall, and the Reagan supporters burst into a demonstration. As the music continues, Betty Ford draws attention from Mrs. Reagan by getting up and dancing with Tony Orlando, who has been sitting in the gallery with the Fords. Contrapuntally, the Ford partisans shout "We Want Ford!" and the Reagan partisans shout "Reagan, Reagan!" Both sides are worked up. The demonstration and counterdemonstration go on for about ten minutes, and Dole still can't get the Convention to come to order. At last, the band breaks into "God Bless America," and the delegates seem to feel they have no choice but to stand and sing.

On the Convention floor, an enormous crush has developed around the Mississippi delegation: David Keene is standing on a chair; the Reagan delegates want to leave the floor to caucus about breaking the unit rule. James Baker, Ford's chief delegate hunter, rushing across the floor, says to me, "We're all right on this if Mississippi holds," and then he says, "We're better off on the nomination than we are on this."

The speeches on Rule 16-C begin. Some people make the same

speeches they made in the rules-committee meeting on Sunday. Emotions are high, and the audience has flash-point reactions, cheering and booing the speakers. Everyone is aware that, as Dole said a few moments ago, what happens in the next hour or so "could decide the outcome" of this Convention. Whatever emotion has gone into either campaign, and has been fuelled by the excitable atmosphere of a Convention, seems to be compressed into these minutes. The cheers become roars, and come at you like a wave.

There is a scuffle in the New York delegation. Someone has torn out Republican state chairman Richard Rosenbaum's phone, and Rosenbaum has had him removed from the floor, and in an instant it seems that everyone in the Arena is looking over toward New York. There is a chemical reaction that links all those within the hall of a Convention. Suddenly, Nelson Rockefeller, standing at the New York delegation's standard, holds up Rosenbaum's white telephone with its cord severed. Part of the gallery starts shouting "We want Rocky!" and Rockefeller, obviously pleased with the thought, holds up the phone again. Television reporters rush to the scene, which takes over the Convention. Rockefeller goes on and on, standing on a chair and holding up the phone and talking to reporters. He is having another moment after all; he is reliving 1964. One has to force oneself to remember that that man cavorting there on the floor is the Vice-President of the United States. These scenes become uncontrollable, and even a little frightening. It turns out that before the phone was ripped out, Rockefeller grabbed a Reagan poster from a North Carolina delegate.

On the rostrum, Sherry Martschink, the formerly uncommitted delegate from South Carolina, now makes the same speech she made on Sunday against Rule 16-C—checkers and all. She seems to enjoy being on the rostrum, and speaks dramatically. Robert Griffin, the President's friend, addresses the Convention and says, "I don't know whether President Ford will ask Governor Reagan to be his running mate or not." Not a very subtle ploy. Alluding to the fact that Reagan has insisted that he would not run as Vice-President, Griffin says, "Governor Reagan should be in a position and be able to change his mind on Thursday morning." The Reagan people know what Griffin is up to, and boo. "I can also say with some authority," Griffin says, that "President Ford, if nominated, would like at least to consult with Governor Reagan" about his choice.

And then the Arena is still as the roll is called, ostensibly on the question of whether a Presidential candidate should be required to announce his choice of a running mate before the Presidential balloting. In reality, the vote will probably decide who is to be the Republican nominee. If Ford wins this vote, he wins the nominaton; if Reagan wins this vote, he *might* win the nomination. A big cheer goes up as Alabama, a Reagan state, casts all of its thirty-seven votes for Reagan's position. Many of us sit with tally sheets showing how many votes for the nomination Ford and Reagan are expected to get from each state, and will compare the vote on 16-C with that. A trend one way or the other will tell us who will carry this vote, and perhaps the nomination. Alaska's two uncommitted delegates go with Reagan. Ford picks up two in Arizona. A wash, so far. Ford picks up one in California, Reagan's state. Florida passes. It is having trouble counting its votes. Then Reagan loses ten in Georgia. On it goes. Ford picks up eighteen in Indiana, and that would seem to be that. But Indiana is a state where there are delegates—including Earl Butz—who are legally bound to vote for Reagan but actually support Ford. There are mirror situations in other states, the net result being that there are more Ford delegates who are actually for Reagan than the other way around. The Ford people had Indiana Governor Otis Bowen working on votes for them in his state. Mississippi. The hall grows quiet, and there is a shushing sound. The Mississippi Reagan delegates left the Convention floor to caucus on the question of breaking the unit rule and have now returned. But since the Ford supporters in the delegation would not join them, they couldn't take a vote. Mississippi, indecisive to the end, passes. As of Montana, Ford is fifteen votes ahead of his presumed nomination vote. New Jersey. Ford picks up one. The Reagan forces had expected to do better there. The New Jersey delegation is polled. Sears, in his trailer, asked for the poll. If people were going to betray him, they would have to do it publicly. Reagan picks up one in Ohio, where his aides had hoped for a few more. This morning, Sears himself made one last stab at Pennsylvania. At eight-thirty, he dropped in on a breakfast meeting of Schweiker and two Republican leaders from Philadelphia: William Meehan and William Devlin. They are not delegates, but Sears believes them to have influence in the Pennsylvania delegation, and Sears had been hoping for help from them since last spring (before he thought up the Schweiker selection). Meehan and Devlin were themselves committed to Ford, but they were believed to have—or said they had—a dozen or so votes at their disposal, and also influence over other delegates. They like Schweiker, and Meehan is an old friend of Sears'. (Devlin is one of the few people Sears consulted about Schweiker.) Their support of Ford is said to have been nailed down at a luncheon in Philadelphia on the Fourth of July. The President had visited Valley Forge and spoken at Independence Hall, and then, we were told at the time, when we watched the day's events on television, he lunched with "civic leaders." He did, but he was also working on delegates. I should have guessed. So Meehan and Devlin were no longer in much of a position to help Sears, but he made a try on 16-C. Sears figured that these experienced politicians knew as much as he did, so there was no point in arguing with them. What he tried to do was appeal to their political self-interest. He suggested that if Ford was forced to name his running mate before the vote on the nomination, he might choose someone from the Northeast, so as to keep people like Meehan and Devlin in line. By Thursday, Sears said, the President would feel free to name anyone. But it didn't work. If Meehan and Devlin had votes to throw to Reagan, they didn't do it. Ford picks up five votes in Pennsylvania. Sears has a plan, and an expectation, if he should win this vote. His plan is to work through the night rounding up votes for the nomination. "We have the votes," he would tell delegates he was trying to persuade. He would say, "We'll remember what you do for us tonight. You're one of a few that are getting a very good opportunity here." To certain Ford supporters he would say, "We know about Mr. So-and-So and Mrs. So-and-So. They'd be with us if you let them. You've been stopping them, so let them go." His expectation is that certain political leaders who are committed to Ford would send some delegates Reagan's way if Reagan won 16-C. He figures they wouldn't want to be known by the winner to have been on the other side. I see David Keene on the Convention floor. "It looks like we don't have it," he says.

So now it seems clear that Sears will not have to work through the night. He sort of thought he had lost when he heard the news this afternoon that Mississippi would support Ford tonight. But he did another quick count, called his aides to the trailer, and gave them each a quota. It seemed worth a try, and he thought it would be quite impressive if he could show that he could win without Mississippi. But he couldn't. It will never be entirely clear whether he could have won with Mississippi. News of Mississippi's decision to support Ford tonight undoubtedly cost the Reagan side some votes in other delegations—caused the compass needle to move. Now, knowing that the Reagan forces have lost on this vote, Keene has told the Mississippi Reagan delegates not to break the unit rule tonight. There is no point now in pressing them to do something that goes against their tradition. In spite of the way this vote is going, there is an explosion on the Convention floor when Texas casts all of its one hundred votes for Reagan's position. President Ford went to the Alamo, and spent five days and a million dollars in Texas, and he ended up with this. I remember the night of the White House correspondents' dinner last May, when the President stood there wearing a panama hat and making jokes while the dread news of his wipeout in that day's primary in Texas was coming in. Perhaps the Reagan troops on the Convention floor aren't yet aware that it's over. At the end of the first roll call, it's not formally over: the vote is a thousand and forty-one votes for Rule 16-C, eleven hundred and twelve against. But then Florida, having completed its count, votes, putting it over the top for Ford (even though Reagan picks up five votes). I recall travelling with Reagan in Florida in February. It was the next state after New Hampshire in which he challenged Ford. Had Reagan done better in Florida, as there was reason to think he would do, the story of this Convention might be quite different now. But Reagan was still finding his themes then—he was still explaining away his plan to reduce the federal budget by ninety billion dollars and was just beginning to talk about the Panama Canal—and his presumed lead in the state steadily shrank. Then Mississippi is called again. Mississippi is irrelevant now, and Clarke Reed says, "Mississippi, after much consternation and under the unit rule, casts thirty votes no." But Mississippi is too late to make the crucial difference. At the end, the vote is a thousand and sixty-nine for Reagan's position and eleven hundred and eighty for Ford's. The people in the hall are subdued, as if to absorb what has happened. The long fight for the nomination is at last over.

Ford strategists have been negotiating all day on the foreign-policy amendment to the platform, which will come up shortly. Entitled by the Reagan forces "Morality in Foreign Policy," it sounds chords designed to clash with the approach of Ford and Kissinger, but it is not so specific as to invite charges that it "ties the President's hands." It was aimed mainly at Kissinger, who has been a target of the Reagan forces all year. Secretaries of State are often controversial, but Kissinger has seemed to attract a special sort of hostility, which appears to be a blend of sheer opposition to his policies, reaction against his rather arrogant style, and, to be blunt about it, anti-Semitism. There are those who have felt the first two and have not felt a touch of the third, but anti-Semitism has been an unspoken factor. The Reagan foreign-policy plank commends "that great beacon of human courage and morality Alexander Solzhenitsyn, for his compelling message that we must face the world with no illusions about the nature of tyranny" (a slap at Kissinger for recommending that Ford not invite the new Russian émigré to the White House when Solzhenitsyn was in Washington last summer, on the ground that such a move might harm détente); it says that "in international negotiations we must make no undue concessions" (a slap at détente) and "must not grant unilateral favors with only the hope of getting future favors in return" (a slap at the Helsinki agreement); and it comes out against "secret agreements." The Panama Canal is not mentioned; Reagan aides said that they did not want to get so specific, and that anyway the platform had already largely incorporated Reagan's views on that subject. The plank is more emotional and symbolic than substantive, but so is much of the language in which foreign policy is usually discussed. Alexander Solzhenitsyn's becoming a symbol on the banner of the Republican right wing is an example of the strange things that can happen in a political atmosphere.

On the floor, I encounter Charles Mathias, the moderate-to-liberal Republican senator from Maryland. Mathias at one point considered running for President as leader of a "third force" that would draw on liberals and moderates of the two major parties. But, like almost all ideas for a major independent political movement thus far, this one fell through, for lack of a sufficient number of politicians willing to surrender their bases in the established parties, and for lack of resources. Tonight, surveying the Convention floor, Mathias says, "This party has lost its bearings."

"What's happened?" I ask him.

"Attrition," he replies. "Nineteen sixty-four, Vietnam, Watergate—all were costly to the progressive wing of the Party. Watergate caused a good many active Republicans either to leave the Party or to go dormant. They're not going to contribute. They're not going to vote. They're not going to lift a finger."

On the rostrum, the speeches go on. L. E. (Tommy) Thomas, Reagan's state chairman in Florida, says to me, "They can't find the 'off' button on these damn politicians."

It is now almost two o'clock in the morning, and the Republican Party, the party in power, is debating, in a manner of speaking, rather important questions about the foreign policy of our country. But few are paying attention. In the Florida delegation, where I am now standing, one delegate turns to another and says of Solzhenitsyn, "His name shouldn't be in the platform. What if he turns out to be a spy?"

Then Roman Hruska, on the rostrum, concludes a speech by recommending, "in the interest of Party unity"—in accordance with the Ford strategists' decision—that the Convention accept the foreign-policy amendment. And, by voice vote, it does. Timmons, on the Convention floor, shrugs and says to me, "We tried and tried to compromise." (The Ford forces had hoped to delete the references to Solzhenitsyn and Helsinki.) John Anderson, whom I encounter on the floor, says, "I'm mad," and he looks it. As the night's session ends, the minister giving the benediction prays that the Republican Party nominate "the man who can best serve this nation" and that we recognize "that there is no free lunch."

AUGUST 18

Wednesday. Today, the President's strategists have been meeting to get the latest count for tonight's nomination vote. One of the strategists said to me in a conversation that it was now clear that the President's team had finally got itself together into a smoothly functioning operation. When I looked at him skeptically, he paused, and then said, "Well, at least they've stopped shooting themselves in the foot." The President's side thought of employing various stratagems to defuse the 16-C issue. They considered having the President capitulate—they would have tried to make it appear otherwise—and name his running mate before the nomination. They considered offering an amendment to have the rule become applicable for the first time at the 1980 Convention. But then, one of the Ford strategists explained to me, they saw the 16-C fight in just the terms Sears saw it in: as a good test that, if they won it, would insure Ford's nomination. There have also been meetings here on questions about the fall campaign. Some observers think that the President can ill afford to spend much time in Vail, where he will go after the Convention, because there are only ten and a half weeks left until the November election. But in fact the President's strategists do not intend to have him campaign very much.

After much debate within the President's staff, the decision has essentially been reached to keep the President in the White House until late in the campaign. The idea is both to capitalize on his incumbency and to keep him out of trouble. One of the President's strategists shows visitors figures that demonstrate how during the primaries the President's percentage in the polls dropped after he began to campaign in a state. But it appears that there is something more to this fact than just the degree of Gerald Ford's competence as a campaigner. Jimmy Carter's polls went down after he began to campaign in a state, too. We may be reaching the point where the less the public sees of a candidate the better. What is the logical extension of that? Essentially, the President's strategy in the fall is to hope that Jimmy Carter makes a big mistake, or some big mistakes. One strategist said today, "Carter has got to be driven to the mat on the issues. Pat Caddell runs out and takes a poll, and Carter trots out a theme and talks around it. Everything about the President is known. We're going to get everything known about Carter. He's going to make some mistakes—he's going to drive some wedge in his soft coalition."

At the Convention this evening, some Reagan demonstration leaders are wearing *green* baseball caps, with earphones—one young man whom I asked about it insisted that this had been in the plans for weeks—and Reagan supporters are carrying long plastic horns. Tonight, the Republican Party will finally nominate its candidate for President, and, even though the process is a bit anticlimactic after last night, the rituals will be gone through. There seem to be a lot of young men with green baseball caps in the galleries. One of them, a pleasant young man who is carrying a walkie-talkie, tells me that he and his colleagues will "coördinate floor delegates with demonstrators in the galleries for emotional demonstrations at certain key moments." The Ford delegates are armed with posters bearing the campaign photograph of the President—deliberately chosen for its stern, "no more Mr. Nice Guy" look. One can feel that, despite last night, both sides are keyed up. The outcome may be clear, but the delegates, particularly the Reagan delegates, are not going to be deprived of their opportunity to let off steam and holler for their candidate.

Jacob Javits is speaking from the rostrum. Javits is one of the few moderates or liberals to address this Convention. It took an argument by Rockefeller and Rosenbaum against National Committee officials to get Javits onto the program. Some of the Reagan people, unable to wait, start blowing the horns. The long, low sound drowns out Javits and just about everything else. Even the playing of "God Bless America" doesn't work now. So the Ford family makes an entrance and the band plays "The Victors." One way to overcome noise is with more noise. The Ford forces, with their advantage in tickets, have packed the galleries even more thoroughly than the Reagan forces have. Both sides know how to do it. They are the same people. There will be a lot of noise tonight. It makes no sense—is a thing unto itself and, in fact, a little alarming, as mass emotions can be. The band plays another Sousa march and then reprises the University of Michigan song—Ford's "California, Here I Come." Political music and football music are very nearly the same thing: both serve the same purpose—both give a lift. This year has taught me that music is a far more important part of politics than I had ever thought. Nancy Reagan makes her entrance, and the band plays "California, Here I Come," but the Fords still, in effect, have the floor, so the Reagans don't really get their demonstration tonight. The Convention floor is all heat and signs and perspiration and horns. I see Earl Butz, in shirtsleeves, waving a Ford poster. After a while, the band tries "God Bless America" again, and the delegates stand and sing and then go right on with their demonstration and counterdemonstration—one can't tell which is which at this point. Jacob Javits is still trying to speak. Two more "God Bless America"s. The logical extension of this is simply noise. The Ford people wave their arms in the air and shout "Ford! Ford!" and we tend to think this is O.K., because we tend to think he is O.K., safe. But what are the real distinctions among political emotions? Some of the most menacing political figures in the history of the world have used stadiums and bands to whip up their followers.

At last, the nominations begin. First Reagan's. As Paul Laxalt, the Nevada senator, who has acted as chairman of Citizens for Reagan, finishes his speech, the band swings into "California, Here I Come" and "Dixie," and the Reagan supporters break into a loud, raucous demonstration. It is the emotion of people with something in their hearts. They are a movement. Reagan. The idea of Reagan stirs excitement in them. He spoke to their emotions. There are things they are after—and against. They won't win the nomination, but they came close enough to show 'em. I may have seen a more emotional demonstration somewhere, but I don't remember it. The

long, low sound of the horns goes on and on. The Reagan supporters are trying to make a point by the extended demonstration.
And some Reagan agents are trying to keep the Ford nomination
off of prime time. They must be under the illusion that Reagan will
be running against Ford in November. It's over, but that's something that people who have been caught up in a campaign often
have trouble recognizing. Now the Reagan "demonstration" has
become not a demonstration but a tactic, and it takes on a certain
ugly quality. Using force—in this case, the force of noise—to
disrupt.

At last, after some forty-five minutes, the demonstration ends
and the nominations of Ford begin, with a speech by William Milliken, governor of Michigan. At one point, before the Convention, it
had been rumored that the President would be nominated and
seconded by Rockefeller, Goldwater, and Connally. But that plan
was scratched when Ford aides realized that it might pave the way
for Reagan to address the Convention. Goldwater and Connally are
not delegates to the Convention, and, with the exception of those
speakers already announced in the official program, only delegates
may address the Convention unless there is a vote to suspend the
rules. The Ford people didn't want the Reagan people to get ideas.
These are the things that people think about when they prepare for
fights at national Conventions. The instant that Governor Milliken
finishes his nominating speech, the shouting for Ford begins and
balloons cascade from the galleries. They are large plastic balloons
that have been brought in and held under seats and then inflated.
The band goes into "The Stars and Stripes Forever." I now associate that with the Fourth of July this year, when, on television,
Arthur Fiedler led the Boston Pops in the most stirring rendition of
it I have ever heard. The song took on a special meaning then, and
I shall always hear it that way. The band plays "Great Day." It
can't play "Happy Days Are Here Again"—that's the Democrats'
song. Democrats and Republicans *do* have different songs. The
band plays its upbeat music, and as his partisans wave their posters,
thousands of stern-looking Gerald Fords bob up and down. The
music feeds their enthusiasm, keeps them going. "Hail, Hail, the
Gang's All Here." "Give My Regards to Broadway." "Seventy-six
Trombones." "The Yankee Doodle Boy."

The Ford side's seconding speeches are offered from the floor by
nineteen people, who speak for thirty seconds each. These speeches
were part of the Ford campaign's arsenal: the opportunity to sec-

ond the President's nomination was one of the plums offered to wavering delegates. ("We'd like you to second the President's nomination—if you're with us.") Sherry Martschink is a seconder. So is Thomas Evans, a delegate from Delaware, who is running for Congress and whom Sears was wooing. Late Monday night, Sears tried to persuade Evans to make a speech for Rule 16-C. He didn't, but now he is getting his exposure on national television after all. The seconders are male, female, black, white, from various parts of the country, and situated on various parts of the Convention floor. Arranging this was a major logistical problem, and much of today was devoted to it: making sure that all bands of the spectrum were represented; checking to see that television cameras were so positioned as to be able to show the seconders; making sure that each of the seconders was on the floor when it came time for his or her little part.

Then comes the roll call for the nomination. Hearing it is like reliving the history of the year. Alabama . . . Arizona . . . California . . . Colorado. The Southern and Western states are for Reagan. Florida. I recall travelling with Reagan in the northern cypress-and-moss country, and then chasing Ford and failing to catch him. Ford is being nominated for the Presidency. It would never be happening but for the most bizarre turns of events in American political history. Illinois. Charles Percy, who was pronounced a boy wonder in 1960, when, at forty, he was president and chief executive officer of Bell & Howell and head of the Party's platform committee, and who seems to have wanted to run for President ever since, announces Illinois's vote: eighty-six for Ford, fourteen for Reagan, one abstention. This is probably the end of Reagan's political career. Louisiana. Ben Harbor, the black delegate who was flown out to California last week for a personal audience with Reagan, votes for Reagan. Mississippi. Clarke Reed announces sixteen votes for Ford and fourteen for Reagan. This does not necessarily reflect the sentiment within the delegation. A deal was struck today: in exchange for agreeing to break the unit rule, so that Reagan could be given some votes, the Ford forces would be assigned a majority of Mississippi's votes. New Hampshire. "It all began in the snows of New Hampshire" has become a political cliché. Representative James Cleveland, Ford's New Hampshire chairman (I can recall how nervous he looked in New Hampshire last February) announces eighteen votes for Ford and three for Reagan, which doesn't seem quite fair, considering how close the primary vote was. Ohio, where I saw Ford and Reagan wind up the primary campaign in Cincinnati, my home town, and where Ford won overwhelmingly. Pennsylvania votes ninety-three for Ford and ten for Reagan, Ford picking up nine votes more than he was expected to. An embarrassment for Richard Schweiker. But this roll call is misleading: because people know how it is going to turn out, some are casting their votes with a view to what it means for themselves, not the candidates. And then West Virginia—one of the places where Reagan hurt himself by not campaigning. (We didn't pay much attention to the West Virginia primary results at the time; Nebraska, which Reagan won, was the same day.) To-night, West Virginia puts it over for the President.

AUGUST 19

Thursday morning. The Century Ballroom of the Crown Center Hotel, shortly before noon. Sometime soon, the President is to come here to announce to the press his choice of a running mate. For the first time in a long while, the Republican Party will have someone in the Vice-Presidential slot who has been put there by normal procedures. ABC has already announced that the President has selected Robert Dole, which is a surprise. Dole didn't appear on the final speculative lists. Yesterday, some papers speculated with certainty that it would be Ruckelshaus or Baker. So much for the lists. Dole is a scrappy politician and a funny man. I remember him saying to me in an interview in April, 1972, when he was chairman of the Republican National Committee—and when the Nixon White House was still terrorizing the Republican Party as well as a great many other groups of people—"I want to make it very clear, as the President does when he has some doubts . . ." Asked in 1974 whether he wanted Nixon to come to Kansas to campaign for his reëlection to the Senate, Dole said he'd settle for a flyover. Dole is generally labelled a conservative, but this year he fought along-side George McGovern to save the food-stamp program, and I also recall a conversation I had with him in May in which he expressed concern that the President was projecting too negative an image and should favor more "people" programs. So Dole is the second Vice-Presidential candidate this year who was previously critical of his leader. But Dole and Ford were, at least, political allies and friends.

Mr. and Mrs. Ford and Mr. and Mrs. Dole enter the room,

followed by Rockefeller and Laxalt. "I'm really thrilled with the opportunity of having Bob Dole as my running mate," the President says. This must be a strange moment for Rockefeller. He stands there smiling while the President announces his replacement. "Bob Dole has been a team player," the President says. That's very important to him. Last November, when he shook up his Cabinet (and also accepted Rockefeller's "resignation" from the ticket for 1976), he explained that he wanted "my guys," and emphasized the point by saying, "I wanted a team that was my team" in the important jobs. Ford, a club man in Congress, isn't much inclined to reach out. His selection of Rockefeller was one of the few instances in which he did. "Bob Dole will help to heal any divisiveness within the Party," the President says. The thought that he might do that was probably a big factor in his selection. The President looks very tired. I wonder when he made his decision. Dole is a partisan fighter with a sharp tongue and will run the kind of slashing campaign against Carter that some of the President's strategists desire. But there is some question as to how such a campaign will go over with the public. Now Dole says, "I did not expect to receive a phone call this morning, but I'm very pleased that we were in." Dole is safe— he won't be seen as too liberal. He will, despite his differences with the President, be seen as a crony. "I think America needs President Ford's leadership for four more years," he says. Then Laxalt makes some approving remarks ("I couldn't be more delighted than to hear the news"). And then they trot Rockefeller up to say something. This is really almost too much. Rockefeller seems hoarse, even for him, and he speaks slowly, in a low voice. "To me, this is a very important moment for every American and for the world," he says.

The Alameda Plaza, Reagan's headquarters, has a funereal air this afternoon. Some staff members are quietly packing boxes. One woman watches them, disconsolately fingering a Reagan T-shirt. Another woman, speaking into a pay telephone, asks, with some desperation in her voice, "Are you *sure* he wouldn't take the Vice-Presidency? Can't we draft him? Are you *sure?*" (During the night, Reagan supporters, unable to accept final defeat, tried to work up a Reagan-for-Vice-President movement, but the Reagan camp refused to go along.) Still another young woman says to a friend, "This has been my life since October. I'd have done anything for him." This morning, Reagan bade farewell to his staff, and he and his wife—the utterly controlled Nancy Reagan—allowed tears to show. Clarke Reed turned up for the event and, looking almost distraught, said to Reagan that he now felt he had made "the worst mistake I ever made in my life." Reagan replied, "That's all right, Clarke." Mike Deaver remarked later, "At least he's consistent. Clarke makes the same mistake every eight years."

The Reagan effort has left in place a movement, and a set of people—many of them young—who are trained in politics and have contacts. They know their way around the political system very well. Today, David Keene has time for a leisurely lunch, so there is an opportunity to ask him some of the questions that have been on my mind—what some of the serious young conservatives think about where the country ought to head, and what the future of their movement is. (Keene would never admit it, but Reagan was more their instrument than their leader.) Keene, who is thirty-one, has headed the Young Americans for Freedom and has worked for Spiro Agnew and James Buckley. He is a blue-eyed, somewhat chunky, and utterly pleasant young man. The serious conservatives have their own problems with the know-nothings, with those who have an unnerving look in their eyes. And they are trying to build a movement that will not be captured by those people "One of our problems is that we have a very weak bench," Keene says over lunch today. "Somebody has to develop as a new leader; there is a vacuum for somebody to fill. We don't know who it will be. The question is, Who shapes that leader?" And then he talks about the conservative movement. "It's a powerful and growing movement," he says. "Somebody will emerge."

I ask him why he thinks it is growing.

"Because the country is more conservative than it has been," he replies. "If we don't find a leader, we may get into conservatism without conservatives. Jerry Brown is not governing the way he is because he is conservative. He's governing the way he is because there is no choice. In many areas, we've reached the end of the string. The parameters within which leaders can function are much narrower than they used to be. We can't spend beyond our limits, but also you can slash only so much without getting thrown out on your ear."

I ask Keene what he thinks the most important questions before the country are.

"There are serious defense issues," he replies. "The liberal

Democrats are willing to make significant concessions in the area of defense. We have to keep pushing that the country has to be stronger than the Soviet Union, and it has to demonstrate that it will not tolerate incursions on its vital interests. I know the argument that we have enough megatonnage to destroy the Soviet Union several times over. But the issue is not the megatonnage. It's whether or not it can be delivered, and the Soviet Union's guess as to, one, whether you can and, two, whether you would be willing to if you had to deliver it. The question of war and peace depends on what they think your capability and intentions are. The only way to stop the arms race is through a mutual determination to stop. If we express unilateral interest in stopping, they'll question our determination and intention to resist. You have to keep them on guard. Khrushchev went into Hungary because he knew we would not resist. He withdrew the missiles from Cuba because he became convinced we might resist. When you get to domestic questions, the Schweiker thing was actually very instructive. There was an Alabama delegate who, when Schweiker stressed his agreement with Reagan on abortion and gun control, said, 'These are all window-dressing issues. What about the economy?' The relative importance to conservatives of economic questions is why there was more outrage at the Schweiker choice than people expected. The picture of hardhats taking to the streets over abortion and gun control is misleading. Those issues aren't what people care about. What it really comes down to is the economic system and the theory that the government is too big. The things that thinking conservatives think about involve questions of economics and questions of freedom. They draw on the frustration in the country from the increasing feeling that people can't do anything about anything. I resist any attempt to put anyone new in any government program now—because they become locked in and lose their freedom to act independently and rationally. People do vote their immediate interests if they are great enough. If you're getting a check every month, it's pretty immediate. There are so many groups in our society that get checks—it's not one of them, it's all of them. They logroll, and that's why the problem exists all over. A President can get up and single some of them out as long as the group receiving the help doesn't have majority status—like the group receiving Social Security. Some defense interests have majority status, too—like the B-1 interests. A political leader can chip away, cut out a few, hold the line. That's what Reagan did in California. He could get his message across over the heads of the special interests. Getting your message across is what politics is all about."

I ask Keene what he would do about that segment of our society which is down and out.

"I have mixed feelings about that," he replies. "Milton Friedman's idea of providing a negative income tax is administratively cheaper than other schemes and avoids the problem of telling people what they have to do. But it doesn't solve the real problem; in fact, it may worsen it. It locks people in cycles. I don't buy the idea of an environment making it impossible for people to get out. Why do some get out? My dilemma is that just giving money does not solve the problem. The trouble may be that there is no solution. We may have to accept that in any society there are people who aren't going to make it, and you have to make sure that the opportunities are open and be willing to pay the price to maintain them." He points out that when Reagan was governor of California he scaled back the number of people who received welfare but that he also raised the amount that they received. And Keene would maintain a federal education program. He continues, "I think the City of New York could have gotten national support for everything it wanted if it had been willing to say, 'We made mistakes. We really screwed up. We don't know how to keep books.' If you say, 'Here are people who need help,' I don't know a significant society that will say no. A lot of it is a matter of approach. It's saying that versus saying, 'Here is a group that needs more and you should work harder to give it to them.' In that case, people would say, 'Out, fella.' "

I ask him whether he thinks a moderate can ever again be nominated by the Republican Party.

"I don't think so," he says. "Moderates constitute only twenty percent of the Party. They would have to structure a special stance, and that would be difficult. Nixon tried to do that with the 1970 congressional elections"—when the Nixon White House tried to win what it called an "ideological majority" in the Senate, and the President himself campaigned on a "law-and-order" theme—"and the problem with that campaign was that it was a caricature of a conservative campaign. It was what people thought a conservative campaign would be. It would be like me trying to run a liberal campaign. I would structure it for what I thought a liberal campaign would be. One of the problems of the moderates is that they avoid any tough analysis of where they stand. And when they try to modify their stand and sound more conservative, it doesn't work. The main thing about politics is that people see people for what they are. I've read that Jerry Ford has almost as big a public-relations staff as Richard Nixon had. He has television advisers, and people writing jokes for him and telling him how to walk and talk, and he's still Jerry Ford."

Back at the Alameda Plaza, I see John Sears for a few moments. Another staff member has told me that late last night the imperturbable Sears, meeting with Reagan and other Reagan supporters, said, tears streaming down his face, "Governor, I wish I could have done more for you." Now Sears is composed but obviously tired. I put the question to him of whether a moderate can ever again win the Republican nomination. Sears, as usual, has his own way of seeing things. And what he sees may be quite ominous for our politics.

"It depends on what kind of person he is," he replies. "I don't think his philosophy matters that much. A man has to become popular enough. It doesn't much matter which philosophy he's tagged with. His constituency will follow. It does matter what sort of person he is. This country is devoid of heroes right now. If you have someone with the capacity for being one, he could take people with him."

Information is already coming to light about the way in which the President made his decision on his running mate, and much of it is troubling. In a briefing for the press on the subject this afternoon, White House aides explained that the President, after meeting with Reagan at 1:30 A.M., met with his own advisers from 3:15 to 5 A.M., and then, after sleeping about three hours, met with them again and selected Dole. That's no way to make such a decision, and it evokes unnerving memories. Meetings through the night. A principle: Leaders shouldn't make big decisions at all hours of the night. No one should, probably, but when political leaders do it, it can cause a good deal more trouble. Richard Nixon was up most of the night before he chose Spiro Agnew and, for that matter, George McGovern was up most of the night before he chose Thomas Eagleton. Richard Nixon chose Gerald Ford at dawn—his aides seemed to think it added drama to tell us that he had. Why didn't President Ford have a clearer idea about whom he would choose before he came to Kansas City? Why were he and his aides fumbling through the night? And why, to take a lesser point, did they not consider how it would look if they fumbled through the night. From other sources, it was learned this afternoon that by last night a tentative decision had been made to select Ruckelshaus, but that Reagan, in his meeting with the President, declined to say that he would support that selection (even though Sears had considered Ruckelshaus as Reagan's running mate). A stipulation that Reagan set on the meeting between him and Ford was that Ford not ask him to run as Vice-President. This afternoon, White House aides said that, of six names that Ford and Reagan discussed last night, Dole was the one that Reagan spoke most highly of. That may be because before the meeting Lyn Nofziger, a friend of Dole's, asked Reagan to put in a good word for Dole. In fact, I'm told by someone close to Reagan that Dole was the only one Reagan spoke highly of, saying that Dole had impressed him as a good, nondivisive Party man. The others the President is said to have mentioned to Reagan were Rockefeller (whose withdrawal was real, the President assured Reagan), Elliot Richardson, Connally, Baker, and Ruckelshaus. There are two possibilities: that Reagan's kind words for Dole actually influenced the President, or that, as some think, the President wanted to select Dole, and Reagan's kind words gave him a good reason to do so. There are also reports that some of the leaders of Southern delegations opposed the selection of either Ruckelshaus or Howard Baker. Baker, though a Southerner, was not considered *of* the South. Poor Baker. He has wanted to be Vice-President since 1968. I remember the "Baker" buttons that appeared at the 1968 convention in Miami Beach. Moreover, according to some Southerners, Baker's role in the Ervin committee hearings—the very role that was supposed to further Baker's career—caused some Southerners to hold him in low esteem. (During the hearings, Baker gave the appearance of opposing Nixon, though he did not oppose him as strenuously as it appeared to many.) It seems that as Ford went about choosing his Vice-President he was still playing Convention politics rather than considering the broader electorate to which he must appeal from here on out. This is a commentary not on Dole but on Ford. Moreover, it appears that he did not play Convention politics very skillfully. At least one Reagan aide was surprised that the President capitulated before apparent opposition to Ruckelshaus, which in reality, the Reagan aide said, was not very strong. And even some of the President's lieutenants—those who were most familiar with the situation on the Convention floor—were miffed that they were not consulted on the question of the supposed difficulties that some choices would encounter. Today, Howard Baker told reporters, "If I ever run for national office again, it won't be for Vice-President."

On the Convention floor tonight, I take my question about the future of the Republican Party to one other conservative. Weston Adams is a thirty-eight-year-old lawyer from Columbia, South Carolina, who is a former state legislator and a leader of the Republican Party in his state. I ask him about the future of the conservative movement. "We're not going to lose next time," he says. "Rockefeller and them have had their last fling. We've made contacts with conservatives in other delegations all week. We're going to create a network throughout the country, and we're going to use the Reagan organization as a conservative network. We're going to keep our lines of communication open. There are thousands of people who are activists, and millions who subscribe to the Reagan position. Next time, we'll control the Party. We made some mistakes this time, such as our failure to make more of a challenge in places like Ohio and Pennsylvania. We gave it away. Our goal will be to control a going party. The sentiment of this party is with Ronald Reagan. The professionals of this party were for Ford, but we're going to pull the conservative citizens into this movement. We're going to win next time. There is a conservative tide in this nation. We have not been able to find a handle on that yet. In the last three Republican Presidential nominations, the conservative position prevailed. Four years from now, the conservative position can prevail again, with a true conservative."

Ronald and Nancy Reagan enter the Convention hall, he in a dark-blue suit, she in white knit. It is like the entrance of royalty. Reagan is still a star, and suggests a dashing figure—at a distance—and his wife is a beautiful woman. As they stand up there in the gallery and wave, he looks very small—his head has always seemed sort of small, anyway. He looks good from where I am standing on the Convention floor—handsome, if Reagan is your idea of handsome, with that open-mouthed, jaunty smile, head slightly tilted. As the Reagans wave to the cheering crowd, he seems to take on a benevolence—probably because he lost. But then one also considers that, though he waged a tough campaign, it was not really a mean one. A few of his followers wanted to exploit the race issue in the South, but his lieutenants did not permit it—nor did Reagan himself exploit the issue, beyond being critical of busing and welfare, as most politicians are these days. And he has shown a certain grace: he could have been more divisive, and he certainly had grounds for complaining, as he has not done, about the tactical advantages the President has enjoyed here. The audience increases its cheers, the emotions feeding on themselves and growing. The Reagans stand on the ledge of their glass-walled booth, holding hands. The crowd starts chanting "We want Reagan!" and the chant, too, feeds on itself and grows, and then, after a while, the band plays "God Bless America," and Ronald Reagan (in the end one inescapably thinks of him as the Gipper—George Gipp, the all-American football player he portrayed in the movies) and his wife stand and join the audience in singing the song that is intended to silence the cheers for him.

Dole's acceptance speech falls flat. He has no particular following in the Party and had no real reason to get a speech ready before today. (Mondale, aware that he was a finalist, got ready.) Besides, Dole just made a speech on Monday. But he does say something that expresses a side of him which is not so familiar but which he expressed in our conversation in May. "Let us not," he says, "define ourselves in terms of what we stand against but in terms of what we stand for." In his flat Kansas voice, he also says, "We have to free the free-enterprise system," and he attacks "more federal spending, more federal control over our private lives." But he does not attack Carter and Mondale, and that is wise under the circumstances; if he did, it would only solidify his reputation as a slasher. When he finishes, it seems that almost everyone on the Convention floor is silent—except the Kansas delegation.

Some Florida delegates are holding up a sign that says, RON, WE ALMOST MADE IT.

Now Cary Grant is on the rostrum, making an embarrassing little speech in which he introduces Mrs. Ford. Cary Grant seems to have missed the point: he says that it would be good for women if there were "a further four years" of "pillow talk" in the White House between Betty Ford and her husband. The Ford strategists understand the impact of Mrs. Ford, and are using her tonight. "We've had a great Convention," she says. "And we are really going to go right down to November second and we're going to win this campaign." Then a Ford film is played. We are shown the President taking office just after Nixon departed; Ford did show good instincts and taste in those first days. Then we are shown the loneliness-of-the-Oval-Office shots—including a picture of the President leaning over a table, back to the camera, that is remarkably like the familiar picture of John Kennedy in the same pose. The narrator's voice, speaking about the Presidency, tells us, "Gerald Ford had been preparing for it for a lifetime." The voice tells us that he won an Eagle Scout badge and was captain of his high-school football team. This is a propaganda film—as was Carter's. Propaganda isn't new in our politics; it has just become more sophisticated. When Nixon used it, we were uncomfortable. Ford's benign quality excuses a lot. One of the photographs of President Ford and his staff was taken at the time of the Mayagüez incident, but the voice doesn't tell us that. Those celebratory pictures after that questionable venture always struck me as somewhat embarrassing. The film shows scenes intended to depict the President as a nice man: there is a scene from New Hampshire—I remember the occasion—in which the President engagingly responds to harsh questioning by a representative of the People's Bicentennial Commission. The film shows several scenes of the family. The Ford children are about the most attractive ones in public life in memory. Their healthy, wholesome, and natural appearance and obviously genuine affection for their parents do reflect well on the President—and his advisers are making political use of that. First families—an odd term in a democracy, now that one thinks about it—are fair game as instruments for political managers. And the Carters do not hesitate to use Amy. In the film, the President's children convey the idea that their father is a nice man whom we can trust. This is, in effect, Ford's "issue," more than what we usually think of as issues. Making that an issue is not a Ford invention; it was Eisenhower's issue, too. But because we have been through what we have been through, a President's character and even his personality have a particular cutting edge as issues this year. That's fortunate for Ford, because it is a more effective issue for him than his governance is.

The film ends, and the President comes to the rostrum, waving. He looks good. One can almost feel his position in the polls going up as he stands there. The band plays the Michigan song and then "Hallelujah." At last, Gerald Ford has been legitimatized. It is still an accident that he is standing there, but this Convention—though almost half of it preferred someone else—has now ratified his accession. The President looks like a Midwestern banker, in his dark three-piece suit—strangely old-fashioned. The lift of this moment will undoubtedly be washed away. It is one of the best kinds of moments a politician ever has. Ford also had a high moment when he was sworn in as Vice-President, and then again as President, and those were washed away. There was opposition to Ruckelshaus, and Ford caved. He does that too much. He is still the congressional leader, influenced, as congressional leaders tend to be, by colleagues they are ostensibly leading. "We concede not a single state," the President says in his speech. "We concede not a single vote." He has to rally his troops. "America is at peace," he says. Never mind the details. "This nation is sound; this nation is secure, this nation is on the march to full economic recovery and a better quality of life for *all* Americans." He says, "This year the issues are on our side," and he says that he will debate Jimmy Carter. Whether or not he should do this has been disputed among his staff. The crowd chants "We want Ford!" The political figure arousing crowds—that can be a neutral thing or a bad thing. He attacks Congress—always a useful target—and he gets applause. "After the scrimmages of the past few months," he says, "it really feels good to have Ron Reagan on the same side of the line." Reagan waves from his glass-enclosed aerie, and then clasps his hands over his head. "You are the people who pay the taxes and obey the laws," the President says, and he adds, "It is from your ranks that I come and on your side I stand." He allies himself with the plain people—politicians like to do that. Carter does it, too. "Something wonderful happened to this country of ours the past two years. . . . We all came to realize that on the Fourth of July," Ford says. He's right. The Fourth did feel like a turning point. Gerald Ford is a Fourth of July figure. Ford lists the troubles we have seen, including "wrongdoing in high places." He might as well recognize that. He even goes on to say, "I have been called an unelected President, an accidental President." He says that for him the Vice-Presidency and the Presidency "were not prizes to be won but a duty to be done." He is carrying the sacrifice point a little far. He recalls August 9, 1974, when he assumed the office of President. He quotes himself saying then, "Our long national nightmare is over." He is milking that successful moment. "On that dark day, I told my fellow-countrymen . . ." He is Winston Churchill. But then he says, "On balance, America and Americans have made an incredible comeback since August, 1974," which is undeniable. He says he has stood "against the big tax spender and for the little tax-payer." The speech is a bit circular. He talks about busing—can't avoid exploiting the subject. He becomes Harry Truman now, lambasting Congress again and again.

It's not really an inspiring speech, and it does not convey real thought; nor does he deal with very many of the hard questions. But his delivery is better than I have ever heard it before, and one starts almost unconsciously pulling for him—hoping he'll get through it without stumbling or committing some gaffe. He no longer engages in that exaggerated raising and dropping of the voice that I heard in New Hampshire. He and his aides knew that this would be an important speech, and have worked and worked on it. He practiced it three or four times on a videotape machine. His staff made sure that there were no convoluted sentences in it that would give him difficulty. An acceptance speech is only a speech, but all nominees consider it of monumental importance. The speech is to inspirit the audience at the Convention, and, more important, it is a rare opportunity to present oneself on one's own terms to a national television audience. It is one time that a candidate can give a speech on television without having to buy the time—and with a cheering audience as a prop.

"My record is one of specifics, not smiles," Ford says, to big cheers and applause. The Presidential seal is on the rostrum; the travelling Presidential seal that was in New Hampshire in February is now here. He promises a balanced budget by 1978. Unlikely. The current deficit is almost fifty billion dollars. "We will return control of our children's education to parents and local school authorities," he says. Big cheers. He got the message from Ronald Reagan—a line to that effect became Reagan's best applause line—and from what happened in the platform committee. He is a politician not leading but bending—bending to popular passions. Most do; Carter does. The question, again, is one of degree. Ford's benign presence provides a soothing cover for his policies, which are so hurtful to so many citizens—which leave them with little hope. He has purchased a reduction in inflation (which is still high) at a terrible cost in unemployment. Our current domestic tranquillity is probably deceptive. As it was under Eisenhower. Now, addressing himself to the farm vote, Ford says, "There will be no embargoes." He acknowledges that he trails Carter in the polls, and then he predicts that the American people are going to say, "Jerry, you've done a good job; keep right on doing it." He concludes, "My fellow-Americans, I like what I see. I have no fear for the future of this great country. . . . God helping me, I won't let you down." A pedestrian speech, but at least it wasn't hokey—no listening to Conventions on radios attached to car batteries, or to train whistles in the night. And his delivery put it across.

Then Jerry and Betty stand arm in arm, acknowledging the cheers of the crowd. Rockefeller and Dole join them. Again, the joint presence of the current Vice-President and his would-be replacement seems a bit awkward. Then just the Doles and the Fords stand there, and the band plays "Marching Along Together." Manny Harmon is literal. Now balloons rise from behind the rostrum. And then Ford crooks his arm and beckons Reagan to the rostrum. There has been a question all night as to whether Reagan would make some remarks to the Convention. The President's aides were reluctant to have him do so before the President spoke, in order to be sure that Reagan did not cause the President to suffer by contrast either in their styles of speaking or in their capacities for evoking passion from the crowd. As Reagan and his wife reach the rostrum, the cheers seem louder than they were for Ford. The President invites Reagan to say a few words. Reagan must, of course, return Ford's graciousness, and this will help Ford. But Reagan seems to rise to the occasion, just as the President has done. He, too, speaks more effectively than I have ever before heard him speak. Proceeding without notes, he moves unhesitatingly through what might be a little acceptance speech. He thanks the President for the grace with which Ford greeted Nancy Reagan at some point during the week (the papers reported an incident in which Mrs. Ford and Mrs. Reagan passed without speaking), and Reagan seems to be just as grateful for the courtesy to his wife as he says he is. "You . . . filled my heart with joy when you did that," he says. It is a very human moment. Then he talks about the platform. It is more his platform than Ford's, and he seems to be rubbing that in. "I believe the Republican Party has a platform that is a banner of bold, unmistakable colors with no pale, pastel shades," he says. Those are the same phrases he used when I heard him speak in Cincinnati in June, as he rallied the faithful and inveighed against compromise. Then he chose Schweiker. Now he is reclaiming his credentials as the conscience and spokesman of the conservatives. He needs those credentials. He has a career as a conservative columnist and commentator to resume. Then he talks, Reagan-like, about having been asked to write a letter for a time capsule that will be opened in Los Angeles a hundred years from now, during our Tricentennial. Reagan likes to speak in little anecdotes. This one brings to mind the Centennial safe that Ford opened in July; someone was bound to think of something like that for this year. And, Reagan-like, he warns of "the erosion of freedom that has taken place under Democrat rule in this country" and of the "horrible missiles of destruction" that the great powers have poised at each other, and he says, Reagan-like, "And suddenly it dawned on me: those who would read this letter a hundred years from now will know whether those missiles were fired." The Convention is utterly still as he speaks. And he concludes, quoting Douglas MacArthur, "There is no substitute for victory." He ought to know. And then Ron and Jerry—the nice guys—wave. They fought each other doggedly all year and, in the process, developed a strange sort of symbiosis: each needed the other tonight. Reagan backs off the stage, waving—the band plays "California, Here I Come"—and he is gone. Gerald Ford stands there, waving and smiling.

22

Labor Day. Today is the day when the fall Presidential campaigns, by tradition, begin, but in this, as in so many things about this year's election, there is a good bit of improvisation. The campaign of the Democratic candidate, Jimmy Carter, did not begin where the Democratic campaigns usually do, and the campaign of the Republican candidate, Gerald Ford, did not begin at all. It was perhaps symptomatic of this election that both candidates based their decisions on what they would do today in part on the fact that neither has generated a great deal of enthusiasm. This was one of a number of calculations that went into the decision to begin Carter's campaign in Warm Springs, Georgia, rather than in Cadillac Square in Detroit, where Democratic campaigns traditionally begin; there was concern that a sufficient crowd could not be drawn to see the candidate in Cadillac Square, whereas Warm Springs not only was in Carter's home state but did not require a large crowd to fill out, for the television cameras, the setting in front of Franklin Roosevelt's retreat. Carter's September schedule calls for him to begin and end each week's travels with a stop in the South, so as to clinch his support there, and to try to reach three media markets a day. And so he began today in Warm Springs, at once stopping in the South, assuring himself of a friendly audience, and identifying himself with one of the Democratic Party's most revered figures. In a long day of campaigning, he went on to the Southern 500 stock-car race, in Darlington, South Carolina (where the Republican Vice-Presidential candidate, Robert Dole, also turned up), and then to Norfolk, Virginia, and New York City. Before the week is out, he will be in Pennsylvania, New York again, Connecticut, Ohio, Illinois, Wisconsin, and Florida.

Ford, pursuant to his strategists' belief that he does better with the voters when he stays in the White House than when he goes out campaigning, remained in Washington today and will not officially begin his campaign until next week, when he will make a speech at the University of Michigan, in Ann Arbor. Tonight, on television, we saw Ford walking with the Ambassador to China, Thomas Gates, on the White House lawn and meeting with the Secretary of Transportation, William Coleman, on the problem of jet noise. Tomorrow, he will sign bills in ceremonies in the Rose Garden, and, again, the scenes will be televised.

Actually, neither candidate's election efforts ever really stopped. Even when, following their nominations, they were ostensibly resting, in Plains, Georgia, and Vail, Colorado, much of what they did was aimed at making a nice impression on our television screens each evening. So will much of what they do between now and the election. In Vail, the President and his allies made statements (John Connally said, "Frankly, everywhere I have gone throughout the country, in every strata of society, I have detected a note of fear about Governor Carter") and planned for the fall campaign. The President announced, as if he had suddenly had a vision, that he would now emphasize jobs ("meaningful jobs with an opportunity for advancement"), health ("quality health care that is affordable to the American people"), improved recreational facilities, and crime deterrence. He also made a passing reference to education. He did not explain how, given his fiscal conservatism and the projected budget deficit of nearly fifty billion dollars, he planned to achieve these goals. And the President's campaign organization was shaken up once again. This time, James Baker, who, beginning in May, was in charge of delegate-hunting for the President's nomination, was placed in charge. Baker had no other national-campaign experience, but his display of competence in the months just preceding the President's nomination made him seem to the President's associates a rare prize.

Carter has ventured out of Plains at least once almost every week since he was nominated, and some of his appearances, before special-interest groups, have subsequently caused him problems. And, oddly for people who pride themselves on proceeding methodically toward their goal, the Carter camp is still searching around for the appropriate tone, style, and themes for the fall campaign. In a meeting in Plains at the end of last week, Carter and his running mate, Walter Mondale, and their aides discussed these questions inconclusively. Carter told the group that he wanted to avoid further meetings with special-interest groups—such as his recent ones with the Catholic bishops and with the A.F.L.–C.I.O.

hierarchy; he said that his successful primary campaign had been based on his relationship with "the people," and he wanted to get back to that. He also wanted, he said, to avoid scenes in which he was onstage with "politicians." He cited as an example his recent trip to California, where he appeared frequently with Democratic Senator John Tunney, who is up for reëlection this year. Carter had, after all, premised his campaign for the nomination on the idea that he was an "outsider," not part of the "Washington crowd." He also expressed in the meeting some distaste for fund-raising for senatorial and other candidates—something that his aides once said he would do a fair amount of this fall, since helping to raise money for the Democratic Party in those candidates' states would in turn help him and would also obligate members of Congress to him if he is elected President. Carter's meeting with the Catholic bishops last week in Washington, designed to put to rest their misgivings about him—and emulating, in reverse, John Kennedy's famous meeting with the Protestant ministers in 1960—came a cropper, with the bishops pronouncing themselves "disappointed" in Carter's views on abortion. Carter also displeased those who favor liberal abortion laws and enhanced his image as a "flip-flopper" by telling the bishops that while he would not support a Constitutional amendment against abortion, neither would he oppose one. (Carter and Ford will be vying for the Catholic vote, which is apparently deemed to be monolithic and therefore the political determinant of the outcome in the key industrial states.)

As for the question of the campaign's themes, Patrick Caddell, Carter's pollster, has found indications that people consider the economic issue very important, that people are more concerned about inflation than about unemployment, and that the public's view of the Democratic Party is more positive than its view of the Republican Party. Caddell's polls also show that Carter's most serious, and ominous, problem is that the public thinks he "waffles" on the issues—a view that is rising among independent voters. Carter loves polls, devours them, and his recent actions and today's schedule show that he uses them as a guide. On Friday, he held a press conference in which he said that "there will be no programs implemented under my Administration unless we can be sure that the cost of those programs is compatible with my goal of having a balanced budget before the end of my term." His advisers, and particularly his friend and mentor Charles Kirbo, had become concerned that Carter was coming across as too liberal. They thought, in retrospect, that it had been a mistake for him to make a display of a visit to Plains this summer by Ralph Nader.

Predictably, once the question of the Republican nominee was settled, the national polls showed a narrowing gap between Carter and his Republican opponent. The latest Gallup poll showed Carter to be fifteen points ahead of Ford. (The Harris poll that had him thirty-nine points ahead shortly after the Democratic Convention was obviously affected by Carter's seemingly harmonious Convention and by the fact that Ford and Reagan were still slugging it out. Just after the Republican Convention, Carter was only about eight points ahead of Ford, according to the polls. But the polls cannot be taken altogether seriously, indicating, as they do, the mood of the moment—especially in a year in which moods change so rapidly and attachments to the candidates are not very deep. Still, their figures are solemnly cited.) The critical factor is, of course, the Electoral College—two hundred and seventy electoral votes are needed for victory—and election strategies are built around that. The Electoral College arithmetic will be defining our politics from here out, just as the need for primary victories in certain states defined our politics last winter and spring. As of now, the consensus—for what it's worth—is that Carter can count on winning thirteen Southern states, which will give him a hundred and forty-seven electoral votes (this count includes Texas, Virginia, Louisiana, and Florida, which some think are up for grabs), and can count on sixty-one votes in normally Democratic states elsewhere (Massachusetts, Connecticut, Hawaii, Missouri, Rhode Island, Minnesota, West Virginia, and the District of Columbia) for a total of two hundred and eight. Moreover, Carter is said to be leading in Pennsylvania, Ohio, New Jersey, New York, and California. If all this is true, and if he holds on to all these states, then he would be the victor by a comfortable margin. But this will be a long two months.

SEPTEMBER 14

Congress finally decided to postpone until next February 1st a decision on whether the B-1 bomber should be put into production, thus allowing the next President (with the concurrence of Congress) to decide whether to go ahead with the new weapon, which is now estimated to cost twenty-two billion dollars. Ford favors production of the bomber. Carter has indicated that he is opposed, but he has also said that he is for continuing research on the new weapon—which could, of course, lead to its production.

Sioux Falls, South Dakota. Wednesday morning. Jimmy Carter is making a tour of Hans Sieverding's farm. In this, the second week of his fall campaign, he has already been in Alabama, Oklahoma, Arizona, and Montana, and by the end of the first week he was already in trouble. Indications are that the race is indeed growing close. The President's aides happily point to polls showing that the President is narrowing the margin, or even leading, in some key states. Both sides, of course, are eager to put forward the most positive poll data, but still there are a number of signs that Carter really does have problems. However, the polls may be almost meaningless: there is an unusually high "undecided" vote, and both candidates' support is said to be quite "soft." This is a very strange election. The race is said to be growing very close in New York, and the President is said to be ahead in Michigan and Indiana and only slightly behind in Illinois, Ohio, and Wisconsin Moreover, there are some signs that Carter may not be holding the South as firmly as once anticipated. He is having trouble appealing to the varying constituencies he set out to knit together for a victory. And as he attempts to solve that problem, and as he flies about the country making statements on this and that, he seems to compound his difficulties. Carter approached this year with the theory that the principal issues would be not the traditional sorts of questions about government policy but questions about the personality and the character of the candidates. But now that set of issues is hitting—and hurting—Carter. He did not—undoubtedly he could not—see that there would be questions about his personality and his character. Like most human beings, particularly those who go into politics, he had to assume that he was a pretty pleasing person. And, anyway, what could he do? These issues have not been coming off so well for him, it seems, because many people have begun to see a rather cold, and even mean-spirited, side to him (as was evidenced in an exchange with the President about the F.B.I. director, Clarence Kelley); on the other hand, he sometimes comes across as a sort of medicine man, the "Music Man," sweet-talking and trying to please whatever audience he is before—and as just a bit too clever. The Kelley incident was a shimmering example of the absurd matters that can become campaign issues. Carter, responding to news reports that Kelley had accepted gifts—including two window valances worth all of three hundred and thirty-five dollars, a chair, and a lamp—from subordinates at the F.B.I., said that, on the basis of what he knew, the President ought to fire Kelley. Then, asked whether he would fire Kelley if he was elected President, Carter said, "I'll cross that bridge when I come to it." To compound the problem, when the President accused Carter of a "lack of compassion," because Kelley had accepted the gifts at a time when his wife was dying of cancer, Carter noted that Kelley, who is to be married this fall, had "found another loved one." The incident dominated the news for two days. There are serious issues about the F.B.I.: it still lacks a firm charter governing its activities, and there have been reports that it has been involved in illegal domestic burglaries during recent years, when such activities were supposed to have ceased; Kelley appears to lack the stature and the vision to lead the agency into the sorts of changes it needs. But the candidates were not talking about these issues.

The Carter camp was annoyed that the press concentrated on the Kelley exchange rather than on the candidate's set pieces. Candidates generally complain that the press focusses on something other than what they want it to focus on, but Carter helped bring his problem on himself, by yielding to the pressures to have an answer to everything, to respond to all the issues thrust upon him. In his appearances last week, Carter sought out "ethnic" audiences, and was photographed in Pittsburgh triumphantly wearing a T-shirt that said "Polish Hill." In Cleveland, he said, "I got in trouble one time using the word 'ethnic purity,' which I should not have used, but I do believe in ethnic neighborhoods, ethnic character, ethnic heritage." An unexceptional statement by itself, but one that in the context of his itinerary gave off clear signals. (He did not appear before a single predominantly black audience.) With his occasional propensity for simple candor, Carter, at the end of the week, told the reporters following him that his speeches had been conservative in tone because "when the Republican Convention was devoted to describing me as a spendthrift, irresponsible, ultra-liberal candidate, I thought it was good to reëmphasize my basic themes of balanced budget, strengthened local government, a maximum of personal privacy, and a minimum of governmental secrecy." It is not uncommon for political candidates to give a variety of signals in order to get elected. Franklin Roosevelt in 1932 did not at all prepare his public for the kind of activist government he conducted once he was in office. But the signals can get so confused that the audience starts to wonder what to believe, or whether it can believe anything at all. There is also the question of how far a candidate can go in pledging that he will do things that might prove impossible or unfeasible without inviting further disillusionment with our governmental system.

The conservative tone of Carter's campaign has been continued into this week. In campaign stops in Alabama (where he appeared with George Wallace), Oklahoma, Arizona, and Montana, he stressed his intention of balancing the budget, instituting zero-based budgeting, and keeping a strong national defense. In Oklahoma, he said that he favored the direction being set by the current Supreme Court, under Chief Justice Warren Burger and with the majority that was appointed by Richard Nixon and Gerald Ford, as opposed to the liberal stamp given the Court under the leadership of Earl Warren. Carter did say that he did not "want to undo" some of the Court's civil-rights decisions, but he added, "I do favor a shifting back toward the removal of technicalities which obviously prevent the conviction and punishment of those who are guilty. I believe the Burger Court is moving back in the proper direction." He said, "We went too far, and it got so that sincere, honest, dedicated, competent law-enforcement officers found it almost impossible to comply with all the technicalities that might be raised in court or on appeal and obviously guilty people were released unpunished."

There is actually an idea behind the Carter scheduling: each week his appearances will be designed around a certain theme and, within that, each day's appearances will stress a certain aspect of that theme. Last week's theme was that Jimmy Carter, the Southerner, comes to your neighborhood and listens to you. This week's theme is the economic plight that has befallen Americans, and, within that, he stressed small business on Monday (in Alabama) and the elderly on Tuesday (in Phoenix), and today the stress is on farmers. And so last night Carter flew into Sioux Falls, and at a rally near the motel where he was staying he inveighed against Earl Butz. Actually, the Democrats love Earl Butz—he makes a wonderful political target. Secretaries of Agriculture almost always do. ("What do you want Butz to do?" I asked a South Dakota Democratic politician last night. "Stay in office," he replied.) In any political year, no matter who is in office, it is a reasonable postulate that the farmers are angry. As a matter of fact, farm income has gone up by sixty percent under the ministration of Earl Butz, but it is also down from what it was last year, and that is what farmers remember best. Moreover, the farmers are said to be angry about the embargoes imposed on sales overseas in 1974 and 1975. And South Dakota has been suffering from a devastating drought—as bad in some parts as the great drought of the nineteen-thirties. But Earl Butz presumably can't make it rain. Still, South Dakota, its towns as well as its rural areas, is dependent upon the farm economy, and the farmers are said to turn out to vote in higher proportions than the city people. The polls show that Carter could carry South Dakota—though the state has an unusually high number of undecided voters. (The stop here, like those in the other states with few electoral votes, is designed to establish a presence, stir things up so that the Ford forces cannot ignore these states, and thereby gain some flexibility to concentrate on the large states as the election nears.) So today is farm day in the Carter campaign, and the Presidential candidate, in pursuit of the sort of "visual" that every Presidential candidate seeks, has come to Hans Sieverding's farm.

As the candidate for the Presidency of the United States tours the farm, a horde follows. Only a "pool" of reporters has been permitted to follow, including one television crew, but the pool and the retinue of Secret Service agents and Carter aides add up to about forty people. Sieverding is wearing a blue denim jacket and a red cap with "Vigortone" written on the front. Carter stops to admire some black-and-white hogs, and photographers record the scene. Then we go into a small building to observe a sow and its newborn piglets, and Carter holds up a pinkish-white piglet for the cameras. He commends it for not squealing. Then we stop to see some other sows, and Carter says, "That's beautiful," and watches the sows in silence for a while. A distinctly urban pool reporter asks Sieverding, "What is the economic function of those animals?" Carter asks Sieverding if he is raising Hampshires. (He isn't.) Carter at least knows a little bit about farming, though his is of a very different sort. Last night, he was introduced as the man who would be the first farmer in the White House since Thomas Jefferson. He asks Sieverding about crop insurance. "When we need it, we can't get it," Sieverding replies. We continue to troop about the farm, cameras, tape recorders, and notebooks catching the words and actions of the would-be President as he observes a feed machine and some cattle. Carter finally suggests that he and Sieverding walk down a cornfield by themselves, leaving the entourage behind. It is not so much that he wants to be alone with Sieverding as it is that he is aware that it makes a good scene for the cameras—the candidate and the farmer walking alone in a cornfield. The corn is stunted and brown. Carter, showing a sure sense of what makes a good picture, steps onto the running board of a tractor that is pulling a corn-cutting machine, and talks with the driver. Jim King, the former advance man for Edward Kennedy and now "trip director" for Carter, smiles with satisfaction.

Then Carter, standing on a hay wagon, addresses a group of farmers who have gathered outside a metal-walled storage shed. He makes a joke—something he rarely does. An auction has been taking place, and Carter, referring to Sieverding, says "He heard the auction going on and he thought they were selling his farm." He tells his audience, "I feel at home here." Perhaps he does, but he says that almost everywhere. He is still trying to establish what he used to call an "intimate relationship" with his audiences. (James Perry, of *The National Observer,* quotes him as telling a group of puzzled Slovenians in Columbus, Ohio, last week, "I want to be one of you, and I want you to be one of me.") This morning, he praises rural America for its "tight-knit families," its "stable communities," and its "pride in hard work." About two hundred people are here. Many of the farmers are wearing colored caps, similar to Sieverding's, provided by the supply companies. It is a cool, gray morning.

Down the road from where Carter is speaking is his motorcade—sheriffs' cars, private automobiles to carry him and a press pool and television crews, and three press buses. As soon as he finishes, we will all dash for the motorcade to take us to the Sioux Falls airport. The next stop is to be Mankato, Minnesota, which Carter will fly to in order to join Mondale and Hubert Humphrey at a farm fair in nearby Lake Crystal. Then he will fly to Minneapolis for a fund-raiser, and then to Dearborn, Michigan, for a speech at an A.F.L.–C.I.O. dinner, after which he will meet with some suburban mayors and then some Mexican-Americans before he retires for the night. Carter's schedule is somewhat reduced from what it was during the primaries, and his aides are trying to reduce it further, because at the end of last week the candidate was quite tired—to the point where he didn't make much sense when he spoke to members of Mayor Richard Daley's organization after a torchlight parade in Chicago. He is attempting to learn to curb his instinct for commenting on whatever little news item he is asked about, such as Clarence Kelley's valances.

Here on Sieverding's farm, Carter talks about the drought, and about farm problems. "You're now suffering your worst drought perhaps in history, certainly since the nineteen-thirties, and the closeness that ought to exist between South Dakota and North Dakota and Minnesota and Georgia and other farm states, with our central government to give us crop insurance and to take care of our needs and let us feel like we're part of the decision-making process, doesn't exist," he says. "And those families that are stricken now find that when you might go forward and say, 'I want to protect my family next year with crop insurance,' all of a sudden the right to buy crop insurance is cut off in areas that need it most." He tells them that he started out in the Future Farmers of America when he went to Plains High School. "My children will be the sixth generation to own the same land," he says. He tells city audiences this, too, stressing the values of roots, stability. This has been one of his campaign themes all year. "There's a lot of stability in our lives, as there is in your life," he tells the South Dakota farmers. He says, "I believe in what's called a work ethic—I think anybody that's able to work ought to work." He used to say that that covered only ten percent of the people on welfare and that the remaining ninety percent ought to be treated with "love" and "compassion," but he doesn't say that now. (He will not appear before a black audience this week, either.) He talks this morning, as he often does, about having grown up poor, but it seems that he wasn't as poor as he suggests. "We didn't have electricity or running water when I was growing up," he says. "We didn't have indoor plumbing." He says, "I think the best day of my life was when they turned the lights on in our house about 1937, when Roosevelt was President," and that leads him into a discussion of Franklin Roosevelt and how he began his fall campaign in Warm Springs. Carter now has a new little speech, which is unlike any that he used during the primaries. He establishes himself as a Democrat, and criticizes Republicans for opposing Social Security and the minimum wage in the nineteen-thirties. This New Deal rhetoric doesn't sound like him, isn't him. And he really isn't saying anything. In the primaries, he had a standard little talk that didn't say much, either, but at least it was distinctive. These days, he talks about Gerald Ford's lack of leadership, and then he asks his audiences if they know what the sign on Harry Truman's desk said. Usually, a few answer, "The Buck Stops

Here." Then he says, "Nowadays, the buck can run all over Washington looking for a place to stop." He talks of how he has campaigned throughout the country, "listening a lot." He says, "It is an amazing story." He says, "I owe the special interests [*pause*] nothing. I owe the people [*pause*] everything." The line nearly always gets applause. This morning, he seems mellow and in fairly good humor. The audience is polite, pleasant, but not very enthusiastic. He ends, as he often ends, by asking, "How many of you think it's time for a change in Washington?" And most of the audience says that it does.

When Carter travels now, it is with a personal and press entourage so sizable that it requires two leased 727s. Carter rides in the first plane, dubbed Peanut One, sitting in the curtained-off forward cabin, in a special high-backed green chair, which faces a table and two chairs. Along the opposite wall of the cabin is a couch that makes up into a bed, with tables and lamps on either side. Carter's personal assistant, Greg Schneiders, has acquired his own personal assistant, and not only does Jody Powell—who is ostensibly the press secretary, actually a close policy adviser—travel with Carter all the time now but so do five other members of the press staff, plus a secretary to Powell, and so does Carter's personal secretary. (Schneiders, who is twenty-nine, and who began as a bag carrier, has also become a policy adviser.) There are two speech writers and two members of the "issues" staff and a secretary for them and a man who provides local radio stations with "actualities" of things Carter has said and a man who gives television advice and a staff photographer and a man who handles the "mult box," into which television and radio crews plug their sound systems so that too many microphones do not have to be placed in front of the candidate when he makes a speech, and Hugh Carter, a second cousin, and two men who handle baggage and the manifests for the planes. This flying campaign organization is, of course, backed up by a staff of hundreds in Atlanta and the states. Anywhere from two to five advance men arrange each stop, and the whole trip is in the charge of Jim King, a large, wise, funny man with an innocent face and mellifluous voice, who carries his own portable bullhorn ("Carter press, this way. . . . Where have you been, Carter press?") and who understands the importance of keeping a candidate's press entourage happy and well fed—over the first of which he has limited power and over the second of which he is still losing to the airline. It is a long way from the time when Carter and Powell travelled about, usually without anyone else along, on what seemed, to some of those few who noticed, a quixotic venture. Such a rapid expansion inevitably brings problems. It was easier to operate with a few Carter staff members who knew each other well, and the smaller entourage seemed better suited to Carter's style of campaigning. Carter's schedule may have been reduced, but it still seems frantic. One theory behind the chasing around is that each appearance yields three days of coverage in the local press (he's coming, he's here, he was here yesterday). Moreover, Jody Powell said to me today, "The option of sitting on our rears isn't open to us. It would look a little funny for Jimmy to be sitting in Plains and walking in his peanut fields and issuing statements." Carter does have to get himself around and get himself known—he is still a stranger to much of the country—but does it have to be at this pace? There can't be much time for thinking now, or for learning. Speech writers. "Issues" staffs. Polls. Where is *he?*

King sits in the back cabin of Peanut One, where, like Carter, he has access to an air-to-ground telephone. The back of the plane looks more like a business office than like a campaign plane: a desk with two electric typewriters; a stencil cutter and a mimeograph machine; four telephones (three of them ground-based and one of them air-to-ground); a computer (which can send and receive messages when the plane is on the ground); and a telecopier (which takes down copy that comes over a telephone). When the plane is on the ground, the phones and machines are connected to special lines and, while Carter goes off on appearances, some staff members stay aboard to work in the office. The plane has become both the candidate's vehicle and his prison. He reads what newspapers are available, and relies on news summaries sent each day from Atlanta. (These tell him what the papers are saying and also what each television network focussed on in its political reports the night before.) Yet the candidate and his staff have to stay in touch with the outside world, to be prepared to respond and react. Questions come up about what is in the papers, on the wires—questions that the reporters get when they call their home offices. That's what campaigns seem to do a lot—react. On the way from Minneapolis to Dearborn, Jody Powell said, "We're going to try to run a Presidential campaign in which he has some direct contact with people instead of just floating around in this cocoon in the sky and then

being surrounded by Secret Service and television crews and reporters when he's on the ground. Otherwise, he'll always have
around him three network cameras, three local-television-station
cameras, the wire photographers, local newspaper photographers,
the news-magazine photographers, the poor writing press, four to
twelve Secret Service agents, and three or four staff members. And
there's one candidate trying to get through all that and perhaps find
and put his hands on a real live average American. It becomes a
tactical victory when he actually touches one."

Powell went on to talk about other problems in the campaign.
"We haven't been able to shake this thing of 'Jimmy Carter is
vague.' It's the single most frustrating thing we've had to deal with.
I think it's a bum rap, but whether it is or not is immaterial. We
haven't dealt with it successfully and don't know how to deal with it
successfully." Later in the conversation, he talked about another
difficulty that the campaign was facing. Powell is a very smart man,
but if he saw the connection between the aforementioned problem
and the one he subsequently discussed, he did not say so. I asked
him about the concern within the Carter camp that Carter had been
appearing too liberal. "That was a function of what it was necessary to do during the summer," Powell said. "We had to get the
Party back together. The liberals and the labor people needed the
most loving." Powell continued, "The ideological problem that re-
sulted was less severe than the style problem—having his picture
taken with big-shot establishment political types. It was a different
sort of picture than Jimmy had been appearing in. The polls right
after the Republican Convention showed, on agree/disagree questions, that only about sixteen percent agreed that Jimmy Carter was
a big spender. But one of our strongest areas has always been in
answer to the question 'Agree/disagree: Jimmy Carter cares about
people like me.' There was significant movement down on that. I
interpret that as a style problem. We still enjoy a tremendous margin
over Ford on that, but we just can't afford to run a traditional
Presidential campaign. The surest way to get beat is to go around
and appear in those traditional settings, where he can't be with
people, and people don't have access to him. He just can't be walled
off."

Dearborn, Michigan. Carter is here to address a dinner of the
Michigan A.F.L.–C.I.O. Convention, at the Hyatt Regency hotel.
Jody Powell has told the press that this date was accepted in June,

long before it was known that tonight President Ford would be
making the opening speech of his fall campaign at Ann Arbor,
thirty-five miles away. The Democrats are worried about Michigan,
know they could well lose it. Fewer than half of the union members
in some parts of the state are said to be registered to vote as of now.
This appearance in a Detroit suburb will be followed by a meeting
with about thirty suburban mayors at the hotel. His itinerary avoids
Detroit. (The city of Detroit now has an unemployment rate of
about seventeen percent; the rate for blacks is about twenty percent
and for black youths fifty-two percent. There has recently been a
wave of violence by gangs of black youths. The city is about forty
million dollars in debt.) The Carter campaign is counting heavily
on the unions to get out the vote. Alexander Barkan, the director of
the A.F.L.–C.I.O.'s Committee on Political Education, is on the
dais tonight. I remember observing a meeting of Barkan and other
A.F.L.–C.I.O. leaders with Hamilton Jordan, Carter's campaign
manager, last summer, during the Democratic Convention, in
which Barkan boasted that the labor federation could organize
fourteen million households to vote. (He and his allies were then
objecting to the placement on the Carter campaign staff of an official of a union that had been part of the liberal labor coalition
organized during the primaries, which was largely at odds with the
A.F.L.–C.I.O. leadership. At that meeting, Barkan and his allies
argued the principle that no representative of labor should be in the
campaign, because a labor representative in a campaign or in an
Administration tends to be discounted as a special pleader. But the
A.F.L.–C.I.O. hierarchy subsequently permitted this abstract principle to be overcome by the opportunity to have one of its own
employees placed within the Carter campaign.) Leonard Woodcock, who backed Carter in the Michigan primary, which Carter
barely won against Morris Udall, is also on the dais. The United
Auto Workers are on strike against the Ford Motor Company, but
Carter does not plan to make any reference to that; Henry Ford was
also a backer of Carter's in the Michigan primary. The key issue in
the strike is labor's demand for more paid time off, which many think
will lead to a shorter work week. On the wall behind the dais, there
is a large banner that says, "Registration . . . Voting . . . Political Action: KEYS TO PROGRESS." Bill Marshall, the state president of
the A.F.L.–C.I.O., gets the audience warmed up for Carter's speech.
Labor audiences are prone to get worked up, and this one breaks
into long, loud applause when Carter is introduced. He is still a

stranger to them, but they have, they feel, issues, and he is, after all, the Democratic candidate; they're angry, mainly at inflation, and they are partisan. In his opening remarks, Carter refers to Michigan as "Carter country," which is not quite the case, and tells the audience, "It's a tough job to defeat an incumbent President who is backed by a unified party." His speech is a partisan attack, in which he contrasts Republican Presidents (McKinley, Coolidge, Hoover, Nixon) with Democratic ones (Roosevelt, Truman, Kennedy, Johnson). He starts off with a slightly—very slightly—racy joke, which has to do with a man and a woman talking about spending the night together. It is not very funny, nor does he tell it very well; but he seems to feel that this labor audience would appreciate it (he told no such jokes to the farmers he spoke to today), and to want to show that he is one of the boys. The audience laughs politely. Then he reads his prepared speech. When Carter spoke to audiences during the primaries, he almost always spoke without a text, and he wove a spell; tonight, like other politicians, he is reading a speech. He lists what he says are the nine mistakes that Nixon and Ford made in managing the economy. It never really gets to what he would do to manage the economy; does not suggest the actions, such as wage and price controls, that might be necessary; does not even mention the trade-offs. The labor people listen attentively, but there is no real reaction. The speech is full of details and is lectury; and Carter, who does not seem comfortable with it, reads assertively but mechanically. It is as if a country preacher were suddenly asked to read an address prepared for someone else. But if he's President he's going to have to read speeches. He fluffs a number of words. He seems tired. From time to time, he departs from the text: he talks again about the Republicans who opposed the New Deal; he talks again about Harry Truman ("Harry Truman was a common man, like many of you and like myself") and asks if they remember what the sign on Harry Truman's desk said. They do. "Nowadays the buck can run all over Washington looking for a place to stop," he says, and he says that no one is willing to take responsiblity for Watergate, the C.I.A., and so on—thus slipping in some of his primary issues. His delivery is much better when he gets to these interpolations; he is much more himself. Carter aides say that he is still a bit uneasy speaking before large groups. They say that it helps him to get through a prepared speech if he interpolates every page or so—which makes him appear to be wandering. Now he talks about a theme he stressed in the primaries—the loss of faith in government.

He talks about "government by the people," and he lists what is possible "once the people rule again." He tells the A.F.L.–C.I.O., as he told the farmers, "I owe the special interests—nothing. I owe the people—everything." And they cheer. And then he ends, as he ended hundreds of speeches during the primaries, by saying that "we still live in the greatest nation on earth."

SEPTEMBER 16

Saginaw, Michigan. It was still dark when we left the motel in Dearborn this morning to board the press buses that took us to the planes that brought us here, so that Jimmy Carter could make an appearance observing Mexican Independence Day. Saginaw, Michigan, seems at first a strange place for a celebration of Mexican Independence Day, but it turns out that a fair number of Mexicans have come here to work in the automobile plants and in the beanfields. One of his staff members read about the Mexican-American community in Saginaw and added this stop. At the request of the Carter staff, we were all telephoned at five-forty-five this morning, and then, for good measure, someone came and knocked on our doors. Travelling with a candidate sometimes seems like nothing so much as being at camp, or in the Army. Here in Saginaw, in the cloudy, chilly morning, Carter addresses about four hundred people who have gathered in front of a low building that says on it "Union Civica Mexicana." Green-white-and-red bunting—the colors of Mexico—is strung about, and a mariachi band played as we arrived. This event has been staged for the sole purpose of providing a scene for television. Carter speaks Spanish —hesitantly and, of course, with a distinct Southern accent. Then he translates. "I was born and I live close to the land," he says, "and I understand the close ties to those who have to work each day to give our children better opportunities than we had." He talks about Roosevelt and about his own trips to Latin America. He tells them that Mexican-Americans have not had adequate representation on the White House staff, in top Administration jobs, and in judicial posts.

Indianapolis, Indiana. The candidate who ran for the nomination as the "outsider" is met at the airport here by members of the Retail Clerks Union, carrying printed signs, and by Vance Hartke, who is up for reëlection to his Senate seat. Hartke is not one of our more inspiring political figures; there are widespread jokes about his presumed attachments to various interests. But now when Carter lands at an airport he is likely to be met by the local politicians, particularly if they are seeking reëlection. (On the plane, I asked a Carter aide what today's theme was. He shrugged, and then he said, "It's episodic.") There are new questions about how long Carter's coattails may be—or whether he in fact has any—but when the Presidential candidate arrives, the local politicians are there to greet him. We are stopping here only long enough for Carter to make an airport appearance and to hold a press conference—less than two hours. (Ford is believed to be ahead in Indiana.) "I'm very proud to be here with this great senator, Vance Hartke," Carter tells the crowd gathered at the airport. And he tells them that he owes the special interests nothing. At the press conference, held at the nearby Hilton Inn, Carter reads a statement criticizing the President's speech last night. (In his speech, pursuant to his pledge at Vail, Ford promised to ease the purchase of homes. The President proposed something that appeared to have been hastily put together just so that he could actually pledge something in his speech. Presidents do that all the time.) Carter attacks the President's speech with all the outrage that politicians register over something supposedly outrageous that their opponent has done. He attacks "campaign rhetoric" as opposed to promises; he is trying to transfer to Ford the image of a "flip-flopper," catch him in his sudden effort to appear more "positive." Carter is wearing his familiar dark-blue hopsacking suit. He is asked about trust as an issue. "My assessment is that the people do trust me," he says. "The kind of campaign we've run is the best way to assure that the trust is equal to the trustworthiness of myself and my campaign." He is asked about a Harris survey that appeared in this morning's papers, which said that more voters than before felt "uneasy" about Carter because they didn't know "what kind of person he really is," felt that he was "a tough, cold-blooded politician underneath his soft talk," felt that he seemed less independent than he had earlier, and felt that he had "ducked taking stands on issues." He is prepared for this question, because some reporters on the plane had asked Jody Powell about the poll. It is an odd sort of question for a politician to be faced with. Carter says that he doesn't know what the comparative figures in the survey are, which might show how people feel about Ford on these questions. Powell nods; his candidate got it right. Carter is asked how he can say that he owes nothing to the special interests when labor is doing so much for him, and he replies, "I have never been asked by any labor leader to make any promise to them or even to their members that has not been revealed publicly." He is asked why, given the message of his campaign, he endorsed Senator Hartke. "I have no reticence at all about endorsing Senator Hartke," he says. "Senator Hartke and I are running on the same ticket; he's been nominated by the Democrats in Indiana, the same ones who voted for me in the primaries. . . . I think Indiana will be best served with Democratic U.S. senators, working with a Democratic President." He seems in command, but a bit tired. Greg Schneiders has sent a memo to the staff saying that from here out there will be few events after 7 P.M.; that is, too late for television coverage. And while Carter does not have a great many "events" now—at least, compared with the primaries—the pressures, according to his staff, are greater, because the stakes are so high and the focus on him is so intense. During the primaries, he could—and did—on occasion get facts wrong, lose his temper, but it all rolled past. People weren't paying that much attention. Now a misstep could be devastating, even fatal. Carter says in the press conference that "the issues are on our side, and there is an inclination for change in Washington."

Baltimore, Maryland. Midafternoon. The candidate is touring Highlandtown, a mixed Polish-German-Italian neighborhood in East Baltimore. Actually, he is not touring it; he is walking down two blocks, in an event designed to come over the television screens as a "walking tour" of an "ethnic neighborhood." (Tomorrow, in Washington, he will receive the endorsement of the National Education Association—a group representing nearly two million teachers—and then he will fly to Mississippi, accompanied by Senators John Stennis and James Eastland.) Walking with him now are Dominic (Mimi) DiPietro, a round man with a round face who is a city councilman from this neighborhood, and Representative Paul Sarbanes, who is running for the Senate, and Barbara Mikulski, who is running for Sarbanes' House seat. Sarbanes and Mikulski are very popular in Baltimore and can do Carter some good. They met him at the airport. Marvin Mandel, the Governor, could not meet him at the airport, because he is on trial for political corruption. Also surrounding Carter as he makes his way along South Conkling Street are Secret Service agents, a television crew, and a pool of reporters. "Neighborhood tours" have become practically impossible, given the requirements of security and the desire for coverage. Carter is, in fact, hard-pressed to find any citizens as he makes his way along past row houses and shops. He and his crowd of followers are penned in on a narrow sidewalk, which is roped off, with the rest of the reporters walking along out in the street, from which traffic has been blocked off; and most of the citizens who came out to see him on this cold, rainy afternoon are across the street, also behind a rope. They cannot possibly see him. There aren't very many people out anyway. A local organizer says he has never seen a Presidential campaign that stirred so little enthusiasm. From time to time, Carter, in search of hands to shake, ends up shaking hands with reporters in the street.

SEPTEMBER 20

Monday. Carter has bad new problems, which have raised more questions about him, or perhaps give new emphasis to some of the questions that came up during the primaries. There are questions in many people's minds about his judgment and his understanding and about how much he really knows. An interview that he gave to the Associated Press in which he talked about taxes (confusing the mean and the median income) conveyed the impression that he isn't very well informed. One begins to wonder again about those much-publicized briefings he had last summer, when groups of experts in various fields went down to Plains for meetings that lasted a few hours. It's impossible to absorb everything important about economics, or any other large subject, in a one-day meeting with several people. These things take years of absorbing—of becoming familiar with the information, the ramifications, the nuances. Then, this afternoon, the story broke about an interview that Carter gave to *Playboy,* in which, in an effort to show that he is not a prudish Baptist, he saw fit to discourse on the subject of lust and placed himself on both sides of the question. He said that he had only lusted in his heart ("I've looked on a lot of women with lust. I've committed adultery in my heart many times") but did not condemn those who lusted in other ways, and used some fairly earthy, if stilted, language, to make his point. It seemed that once more Carter was trying to please the audience he was addressing, to show that he was one of them—he has done it with blacks and workers and farmers and Slovenians, after all. The *Playboy* interview—word of it swept through Washington and across the country—is the kind

of unexpected event that whangs into a campaign and throws everything off balance. It has little to do with the important questions
before the country, but there it is, like a big rock that has rolled off
the hillside and onto the road. The question about the *Playboy*
interview is, again, judgment—the impression that Carter gives, not
about his attitudes toward sex but about his judgment. Also, it set
off jokes about Carter, the sort of ridicule that diminishes politicians. Ford has never really recovered from the ridicule that greeted
his falling down the plane ramp and bumping his head on the heli-
copter. This is the other side of our solemnity. We are terribly
solemn, it seems, about our politics. And so it becomes a very big
thing when our solemnity is disturbed.

SEPTEMBER 21

The *Wall Street Journal* reported today that the Special Prosecutor, Charles Ruff, was investigating campaign contributions that
may involve President Ford's campaigns when he was a member of
Congress from Michigan. This news flung itself across the campaign, and, while it is tempting to ignore it, we cannot, of course.
We can only wait. The funds in question appear to have come from
a maritime union that is currently supporting Carter. We are now
dependent upon the judgment and integrity of the Special Prosecutor, but then that is always true when it comes to a Special Prosecutor. Ruff is the fourth person to hold that job since Richard
Nixon acquiesced, in May of 1973 (it seems like at least a decade
ago), in the appointment of Archibald Cox to the new post. The
White House also confirmed today that Ford, while he was a member of Congress, accepted golfing weekends from his friend William
Whyte, a lobbyist for U.S. Steel. The subject of the Special Prosecutor's investigation and the matter of the golfing weekends are
entirely different, of course. The golfing weekends have stopped,
and, besides, we've always known that Ford, along with a number
of other politicians, enjoyed the company of successful businessmen
and the Burning Tree atmosphere, and that among his closest
friends have been lobbyists for major corporations. The issue is not
his choice of friends but his policies.

AUTUMN

23

BILLY GRAHAM was at the White House today. For good measure, John Connally was at the White House today, too, and tonight we see him on television saying of Carter, "I think he made a serious mistake both in content and judgment in the interview with *Playboy*." The indignity of what is being focussed on has lent indignity to the election. Carter is not the only candidate who took care to please those on both sides of the "affair" question. The President, presumably to neutralize the anti-affair vote (last year, his wife told a television interviewer that she "wouldn't be surprised" if their daughter, Susan, came to her and told her she was having an affair), has given an interview to *Ladies' Home Journal* saying, "I'd protest in a most vigorous way, and I'd counsel her. But I don't think that would happen—not the way Susan was brought up."

Yesterday, the Carter camp issued a plan to reorganize the federal agencies dealing with the subject of energy—an obvious move to defuse questions that could come up in the first Presidential debate, to be held tomorrow night, about his pledge to effect a vast, yet still unspecified, government reorganization. The plan would combine a number of agencies—something that has been suggested many times in the past—and contains some worthy and some quite bad ideas. The worst trouble with it is that it combines agencies that are to promote the development of energy sources with agencies that are to regulate the industries developing them. (It was this very combination that led to the breakup of the old Atomic Energy Commission.) The plan, like the housing proposals that the President put forward at the University of Michigan, has a sort of jerry-built, "let's-get-something-out-on-this" look. It reduces the number of agencies dealing with the energy question by consolidating the responsibilities of about twenty of them into a Cabinet department. From Carter's statement, it appears that only four agencies would actually be abolished. Carter has pledged to reduce the number of federal agencies from nineteen hundred (no one seems sure how many there are) to two hundred. He has a long way to go.

*   *   *

Today, a Senate subcommittee headed by Senator Edward Kennedy held a hearing on research involving genetic engineering. Now that scientists know how to recombine genetic material, a debate has been going on among scientists and laymen over what sorts of controls can and should be exercised over such research. The issue is the classic one of the constraints that can be placed on scientific "advances"—of who can impose such constraints, and whether they will work. The history of civilization indicates that such issues are rarely resolved.

SEPTEMBER 23

Thursday. Philadelphia. The first Presidential debate is to take place here tonight. I have had serious doubts about the idea of these debates—doubts that have been increased by the fact that they have received such a buildup. Moreover, they seem to be based on the concept—and this has increased the anticipation and the buildup—that the candidates for the Presidency of the United States should meet as two gladiators in the arena. The object of the exercise would appear to be to score points off one another. It seems that the debates have been anticipated more for their possible entertainment value than for their possibilities for showing us the differences between the two candidates on some of the important questions facing our country. The anticipation may well be based on what I think is a retrospectively distorted view of what happened in the debates between John Kennedy and Richard Nixon, in 1960. A number of people now see those debates as events in which a good guy in a white hat met and bested a bad guy in a black hat. I wonder how much enthusiasm there would be for debates this year if Kennedy were deemed to have "lost" in 1960? No doubt the debates did help Kennedy, but so narrow was his margin of victory that any number of things might have made the crucial difference. The debates place a high value on being glib of tongue, effective on television. The qualities that they reward have little to do with being President: memorizing a lot of data, being quick at repartee. They don't put any particular premium on wisdom, patience. Being quick on one's feet in the Oval Office can lead to trouble. There has been a lot of talk about who will "win" the debates. The idea that someone will "win" is what's wrong.

I have been asked to participate in the first debate as one of the panel of three questioners, and, despite misgivings about the whole enterprise, have decided to see what might be done with this opportunity to get some questions raised. So have dozens of interest groups, who have called and sent letters and telegrams suggesting questions dealing with subjects of concern to them. My colleagues and I took the 10 A.M. train from Washington, and our time was virtually filled this afternoon with two meetings to go over the logistics for tonight, at the Walnut Street Theatre, where the debate was to take place—the second meeting being necessary because of a faulty sound system, which would have made it almost impossible for us to hear what the candidates were saying.

Tonight, as the debate opens, Carter is obviously very tense—so much has been said to rest on tonight. I have never seen him so tense. Both candidates arrived here with large retinues of aides, who went over every conceivable detail on the set. "This is the big casino," Hamilton Jordan said this afternoon. (Between this afternoon and this evening, the water glasses, enclosed in little wooden rings, have been moved from the tops of the candidates' lecterns to a shelf inside the lecterns—presumably to protect the candidates from knocking the glasses over.) The first question, about jobs, is put to Carter, and as he answers, Ford watches him intently. This is probably as close to each other as they have ever been—at least, for this length of time. Carter says that we could get unemployment down to four or four and a half percent by the end of his first four years in office, with a "controlled inflation rate." He lists a number of particulars about how he would get there—clearly intent on dispelling the idea that he is "fuzzy." Asked if he thinks wage and price controls might be necessary, he says, "We have a long way to go in getting people to work before we have the inflationary pressures"—which begs the question. As Charles Schultze pointed out to me this spring, the whole problem with getting unemployment down is that at a certain point—probably when unemployment reaches about five and a half percent—unless there are controls on wages and prices, inflation takes off. Ford, in his rebuttal, eager to strengthen the idea that Carter is "fuzzy," says, "I don't believe that Mr. Carter has been any more specific in this case than he has been on many other instances." It is clearly a line that Ford had planned to say, no matter what Carter said. Ford observes that Carter did not mention the Humphrey-Hawkins jobs bill (Carter has been avoiding mention of it since last spring), and then he attacks it. Ford says that jobs should be created through cutting taxes and tax incentives.

Carter is asked how he would pay for all the programs that he has advocated or lent his support to (jobs, health insurance, child care, federal absorption of welfare costs, housing, aid to cities, a higher earnings limit on Social Security, federal aid to education), and, as he has pledged, balance the budget by the end of his first term. He does not really answer. He says that the Congressional Budget Committees estimate that if unemployment was reduced to four or four and a half percent, there would be an extra sixty billion dollars in federal revenues, but neither committee has made such an optimistic estimate. Moreover, even the lowest estimates of the costs of these programs put them above sixty billion dollars—anywhere from eighty-five to a hundred billion. In Ford's rebuttal to Carter, he exuberantly suggests that if there is a sixty-billion-dollar increase in revenues, "I think the American taxpayer ought to get . . . a tax reduction of that magnitude." It is the politician's reflex: the sort of thing he might have said, without thought, on the floor of the House of Representatives in order to make a point, or on the stump at a time when it didn't matter so much what he said. There is already a projected budget deficit of nearly fifty billion dollars, and the President has pledged (at Vail) to do new and still largely unspecified things in the areas of housing, health, recreation, and education, and also to reduce taxes. Both of them are talking about tax relief of the sort that cannot be wrung from tax reform—unless they are willing to advocate reductions in tax preferences of the sort that few politicians are willing to advocate. Tax reform is really a question of providing equity in the tax system, not of raising revenue. Moreover, in the face of the real national needs —which both candidates give some recognition to—why are they talking about lowered taxes?

Carter seems uncertain tonight, not in command. Sometimes he doodles on the notepad on his lectern as he talks. As the evening progresses, one can see the perspiration on his forehead and then on his face, and finally dropping from his neck. The President, it is clear, has been advised by his aides to look stern—as in his "No more Mr. Nice Guy" campaign photo—and it is the one expression he seems to have all evening. He is wearing a vest, which makes him look like a conservative banker. He is forceful in his way of speaking, but he doesn't say very much. Talking about jobs, he says we have to stimulate the economy and then he says we have to hold down spending. Carter, at last, injects a note of humanity when he talks about unemployment. But both of them seem overbriefed and overguarded, almost afraid of spontaneity. Even Ford's gestures—facing Carter and waving his arms—seem studied. Neither of them suggests that there are hard questions and real choices that have to be made. Ford recites bromides about the Democrats' controlling the Congress and about the size of its staff, and then he slips in that "there is some question about their morality." Asked if he thinks there should be new statutes governing the intelligence agencies, Ford doesn't seem to get the point.

And then, as Carter is giving his rebuttal (he doesn't seem to get the point, either), word comes that, unbelievably, the audio has gone off, and the two candidates for the Presidency stand there silently while we wait for it to go back on. Carter is one of the most impatient people I know of, and the President looks nóne too pleased. The President, having been programmed to stand during the entire debate and now being faced with this unforeseeable situation, remains standing. He cannot convene a meeting of his advisers now to consider the question of whether he should sit down. Carter, who, following the President's lead, had stood throughout the debate, at last elects to sit. Carter remarks, "Mr. Kelley may not have liked what I was saying," but, other than that, the two men are silent. Of course, the sound may come back on at any time, and at one point we thought that it had. Assured that the cameras are not on them, the two men glance at each other and then wipe their faces. Apart from that, they do not acknowledge each other's presence; they speak not a word to each other. Ford stares straight ahead, lips set; Carter, from time to time, manages a wan smile. I try to think of what other, more spontaneous politicians might have done in this situation. To my immense relief, the question period is over, so we don't have to keep anything more in mind, but those poor men have to keep the adrenaline going and concentrate on their closing statements. This has to be the greatest electronic foul-up of all time. The President and the would-be President are like prisoners behind their lecterns.

Finally, at eleven-seventeen, twenty-seven minutes after it went off, the sound comes back on. Carter, as if he were a wound-up doll, simply resumes where he left off, and says one sentence: "There has been too much government secrecy and not enough respect for the personal privacy of American citizens." In his closing statement, Carter reverts to the sort of sermonette he gave on the trail during the primaries, and he now seems more natural than he has all night. What he says has nothing to do with the debate subjects, but so be it. Hand moving up and down, palm out, in the familiar gesture, he says, "For a long time, our American citizens have been excluded." He says, "I owe the special interests nothing." He says that perhaps "we can once again have a government as good as our people," and, gazing at the camera intently, he affirms that we have "the best country on earth." Ford says that "one of the major issues in this campaign is trust," and, repeating a theme from his State of the Union Message, he says, "A President should never promise more than he can deliver and a President should always deliver everything that he has promised," and he says that "a President can't be all things to all people." He talks again, as he did in his acceptance speech at the Republican Convention—both men are using tested lines tonight—about what a nice day the Fourth of July was ("We had a wonderful two-hundredth birthday for our great country. It was a superb occasion. It was a glorious day"), and then, identifying himself with the working people, and also using his wife, who is generally considered quite popular, he says, "Betty and I have worked very hard to give our children a brighter future." He closes, and both he and Carter gaze at the camera sincerely.

SEPTEMBER 25

Yesterday, the Senate Foreign Relations Committee voted to block the sale of six hundred and fifty air-to-ground missiles to Saudi Arabia. Other pending arms sales, totalling about six billion dollars and involving fourteen countries, were not blocked (more than four billion dollars' worth of the arms are for Iran). Included in this were eight hundred and fifty Sidewinder interceptor missiles for Saudi Arabia, a reduction from the two thousand missiles the Administration originally proposed. The Saudis had already contracted to buy a thousand air-to-ground missiles, and the proposed sale of six hundred and fifty more air-to-ground weapons represented a scaling down of the original Administration proposal to sell them fifteen hundred. The Foreign Relations Committee's action was taken under the law designed to give Congress more voice in international arms transactions. Several senators complained that their role was hampered by the fact that the transactions were negotiated and signed before they were submitted to Congress, thus making Congress subject to charges —as it was in the case of the Saudi missiles—of disrupting foreign policy if it objects to the arrangement. Saudi Arabia is the largest supplier of foreign oil to the United States.

SEPTEMBER 26

Sunday. One can sense that a certain depression has set in about this election. Someone said to me today, "How did we end up with these two men?" That is something to be given more thought before the election is over. Neither candidate has given the public a lift, or offered any real vision, or even talked about reality. Moreover, the public dialogue, in which the press has complicity, is about the chaff—about such things as the *Playboy* interview. At the same time, the focus on the President has to do mainly with the degree to which he seems like a nice man. It is as if there were no hard questions, no real choices to be made. There appears to be a kind of flight from thought. If, after the difficulties of the last thirteen years, people were looking for something in public life to inspirit them again, they do not seem to feel that they have found it.

It is not necessarily a bad thing that so many people have come to expect less from politics. Some adjustment was necessary. We had become accustomed to the idea that Presidential contests should excite us, but in the process we were burned. And exciting politicians are not necessarily good for us. It is probably not a bad thing to recognize that there are limits on what our leaders can be and do. The question is where healthy adjustment ends and cynicism begins. Now the public seems to have practically no guidelines for figuring things out. There is no vision of the future now—no vision of America that is getting through to the voters. It is not the candidates alone who are causing this. The lack also has something to do with the mood of the American people. People may be tired—and also may be reappraising. The pet theories of the liberals have come up for reappraisal; the conservative nostrums aren't getting us anywhere. Maybe there is even a certain maturity in the absence of a vision of the future. Many of our most exciting visions of the future were understandable but not very profound— to win a war, to end a Depression—or were the adolescent dreams of onward and upward. Our vision of the future was more, better, richer, and happier. This country may be going through its own crisis of maturity. It is not clear now—won't be for some years—

whether the skepticism is a passing phase or whether the trust in the leaders by the led has been stretched almost to the snapping point. No doubt the character of the 1976 Presidential campaign is shaped in part by important aspects of the public mood. Obviously, the wound of Watergate is deep—not just that such things could happen but that for the first time in two hundred years we elected a truly evil man to our highest office. We have elected men of stunning mediocrity—*that* we can bear—but to think that we went so dangerously wrong cannot but undermine our confidence. Vietnam was a dreadful blow to the idea that America fights just wars and when it fights it wins. Only a lobotomized people would not be affected by thirteen years of assassinations, urban riots, a hated war, and the greatest scandal in our political history.

I continue to think that the candidates might do better if they slowed down, sat down, and thought. I wonder whether they wouldn't come over better to the public if they talked to us as though they were really trying to think through some of the problems we face. It would at least be interesting to see what would happen to a candidate who approached things this way. Of course the candidates should get about and see people, but there are limits. And, in any event, the essential purpose of all the travelling is not really to see people but to get on television. I wonder whether the impact of one true, honest, thoughtful speech about real questions might not be greater than that of thirty appearances, lasting about a minute, on the nightly news. But there don't seem to be any politicians around who are willing to take a chance on a different approach. The very process that the candidates put themselves through defeats any propensity toward a broad and worthy vision of the American future. The process sometimes seems to be not one that enlarges a man but one that diminishes him. The candidates come to see public policy in terms of winning over (or not alienating) myriad narrow interests. The people, their advisers and pollsters tell them, are not Americans but veterans, Polish factory workers, Jews, Catholic housewives, blacks, the elderly, young people, farmers, and on and on. If the candidates had a broad vision of the American future when they began, it will be badly battered by the time they finish. And if they have one it cannot be clearly communicated in such a process. What inspiring message can be conveyed by candidates who are scrambling, evading, overpromising, posturing—as they chase about seeking the support of

whatever group they are before, fashioning a line for sixty seconds
of exposure on television that night? It is no wonder that when a
red-eyed, bone-weary candidate drags himself to one more microphone and says "I have a vision . . ." or "I see an America . . ."
it sounds so empty.

The voters may not be able to follow all the intricacies of the
candidates' deceptions and evasions, and yet they know that they're
being had. (A steelworker in western Pennsylvania said to one of
my colleagues the other day, speaking of Carter, "He says he's for
all the programs to put people back to work but then he's going to
have a balanced budget. People aren't stupid; they don't buy
that.") Dostoevski's Grand Inquisitor said, in effect, that the people
should be treated like children, that to expect more of them is to do
them a great disservice. Several modern American politicians have
followed this formulation. Important political strategists in both
the President's and Carter's campaigns believed and propagated
the idea that the public wasn't interested in issues this time. Yet the
very fact that people are so discouraged and negative about the campaign suggests that they want something better. Moreover, the cynical formulation that the people are not interested in issues is, in
its essence, anti-democratic. Democracy rests on the idea that competing forces will put forward competing propositions and the citizens will make a choice. The choice is to be made, moreover, on the
assumption that there is some connection between what the candidates for their votes say that they will do and what they then do.
This is a rather simple proposition, which has almost been forgotten. To the extent that the assumption has been mocked in recent
years, faith in democracy has been shaken. Moreover, the logical
extension of the issueless, personality-based election is *person-
alismo*, which the history of the world has shown us can take a
dangerous turn.

Yesterday, Carter made a speech in which he said that if he
became President he would halt the sale of nuclear power plants
and fuel for them to any nation that did not promise to forgo
development of nuclear weapons, or that built its own reprocessing
plant. He proposed other policies that were more stringent than the
current ones regarding nuclear proliferation, and he also said that
he would seek agreement with the Soviet Union to halt further
nuclear testing for five years, including underground testing.

Nuclear proliferation is one important subject to which he has addressed himself from time to time. (His aides have said to me that it gives him an opportunity to stress his expertise as a "nuclear engineer" and also his competence at dealing with foreign affairs.) President Ford has been reported to be preparing to release the results of a study he ordered last summer on the question of nuclear sales abroad, and Carter's staff was eager to have Carter make another statement on the subject first.

The President travelled by steamboat, the S.S. *Natchez,* through Louisiana yesterday, and, from the top deck, shouted to people along the banks of the Mississippi, "Your President believes that the federal government spends much too much money!" There is, of course, no reason to travel by steamboat these days except to provide good scenes for television coverage. It was another stunt. Today and tomorrow, in an effort to steal some of the South from Carter, Ford will campaign in Alabama, Mississippi, and Florida. Carter, travelling in Texas a couple of days ago, tried to explain away that part of the *Playboy* interview in which he said that Lyndon Johnson had engaged in "lying" and "cheating" by suggesting that there had been an error in juxtaposition on the part of the magazine, but then he was constrained to withdraw that argument. Last week, Carter phoned Mrs. Johnson to apologize (just as earlier in the campaign he had called George Wallace to apologize for having said that Wallace might be the only person in public life who ranked lower in the polls than John Connally), but Mrs. Johnson, despite the call and despite pressure from Carter allies, declined to meet Carter at the airport or to make any campaign appearances with him, although she did greet Mrs. Carter and escort her through the Lyndon Baines Johnson Library.

Today, a Harris poll indicates that Ford "won" the first debate, forty percent to thirty-one.

Today's papers report that two and a half million more Americans were in poverty in 1975 than the year before. The percentage of the population considered to be in that condition is 10.7; the percentage of blacks is 29.3.

A big question that has come up about Carter is about his compass. The question of compass goes beyond matters of giving unfortunate or uninformed interviews. It has to do with one's general sense of direction. How did Carter, who started out casting himself as different from traditional politicians, end up overpromising? Even a number of liberals say that there have to be cutbacks in what the federal government tries to do. For all his talk about owing the special interests nothing, he has in fact allowed himself to become entangled in the special-interest politics of the Democratic Party. Dependent upon efforts by unions to get out the vote, he has endorsed legislation they favor, and he has happily accepted their endorsements. (He has been endorsed by the A.F.L.–C.I.O., the U.A.W., the American Federation of State, County and Municipal Employees, the National Education Association, and the maritime unions.) Even during the primaries, he welcomed the help of some of these groups, and, largely in exchange, lent his approval to some legislation they favored, such as an ambitious national-health-insurance scheme. (He had been talking about national health insurance since he campaigned in the New Hampshire primary, but the speech he gave on the subject in April was negotiated with the U.A.W., in anticipation of Leonard Woodcock's endorsement of him for the Michigan primary.) He lent his approval to the Humphrey-Hawkins jobs bill in order to assuage blacks for his having endorsed "ethnic purity." He has promised the maritime unions "a fair share" of cargo business. The vast array of federal programs —he has not actually specified which ones he would eliminate—has accrued a vast clientele, each clinging with determination to its share of the pie and working to increase it. About seventy-four percent of the federal budget now goes for various domestic, non-military purposes, and about sixty-three percent of this goes for "transfer payments" such as Social Security and Medicare, which bring in a wide number of interest groups. The growth of state and local government services has been even more rapid than that of federal government services. An immense government-oriented industry has grown up throughout the country—what one former member of Congress used to call "the educational/social-welfare/industrial complex"—and this has laid the foundation for social tensions. The growth of this force has led to an *upward* redistribution of income, with those whose income is below about fourteen thousand dollars being taxed to pay the salaries of those whose incomes are higher. Meanwhile, the service unions are gaining a stranglehold on our cities—can hold the cities hostage while they seek higher pay. It is perhaps understandable that pol ticians run-ning for national office don't want to talk about these thir.gs.

To be sure, Carter's commitments to some of the programs are vague, and he has not made a point of reaffirming them during the fall campaign. Still, he has left the impression that he will move forward in a number of domestic areas, the total cost of which will exceed the available resources. He does stress that he will try to bring competence and tough management to government, and, of course, it needs them. More competence is both a practical and a political necessity. While certain politicians and other people are wont to make broad statements to the effect that federal programs don't "work," they are actually referring to the social programs of the sixties, which have had mixed results. The problem, to be some-what general about it, was that there was excessive ambition, a sense of unreality, in regard to what could be accomplished; that there is now an overload and an underrelating of programs; and that in fact the experiment of the sixties was very short-lived. It did not really begin until after the middle of the decade, and soon ran into the competing claims of a war. By 1969, a new Administra-tion, headed by a man who had campaigned against the programs, was in office. Two things are needed, according to the most dispas-sionate thinkers: an unsentimental sorting out of what is efficacious and what is not, and more rational organization and management of the government's efforts.

While people expect politicians to be manipulative—take it for granted that manipulativeness is part of being a good politician, and of governing—they set unconscious limits. There is a large irony in at least one aspect of Carter's problem. When he made a big show of associating with Ralph Nader, he expected people to notice. And when he avoided further association with Nader, he expected people to notice that, too. They did, in both instances, but Carter did not seem to understand what the effect would be. The same was true of his "populist" acceptance speech and his meeting a week later with businessmen at "21." Perhaps he does not really understand the implications of being a national politi-cian, and still does not understand how his every act is magnified. There is a possibility, of course, that there would be differences between the way he has campaigned for the Presidency and the way he would govern if he was elected. It is possible that, once elected, he would be willing to take risks, to lose the support of certain constituencies—to offer a clearer vision of what he thinks is important. The problem for us is that there is no way now of knowing whether he will do these things. That is also the problem for him.

SEPTEMBER 27

In Miami Beach today, the President, appearing before the International Convention of Police Chiefs, issued an attack on "permissiveness toward crime." In his State of the Union Message, on the other hand, he had said, "Protecting the life and property of the citizen at home is the responsibility of all public officials, but is primarily the job of local and state law-enforcement authority." During his weekend campaigning in the South, he said that "the law-abiding citizens of this country should not be deprived of the right to have firearms in their possession." Ford is making headway in this campaign on the strength of the idea that he is "a nice man." It is understandable that, in the wake of the Nixon Presidency, Ford's personal decency should receive prominent notice. But it's almost as if we were choosing a neighbor instead of a President. A candidate may be kind to his cat, but what virtues are reflected in his public policies?

24

NEWARK, OHIO. Tuesday. The election is five weeks away, and the polls indicate that it's getting close.

Robert Dole is here in Newark—a town of forty-two thousand people, about thirty miles from Columbus, in central Ohio—as part of a tour designed to shore up the Ford ticket's support in small-town rural America, where the Ford strategists believe they should be doing better. Carter, the rural Southerner, has cut into this traditional Republican area of strength. And there is the fact that farm prices are down from a year ago. Moreover, Dole is promising that there will be no more grain embargoes—except, perhaps, in the case of an international crop failure. From what one can gather, most of the polls indicate that Carter is slightly ahead in Ohio, a state that Ford probably must win if he is to be elected. Today, Dole has already been in the Illinois towns of Quincy and Decatur ("the soybean capital of the world"), and in Marietta, Ohio, and this marks his third visit to this state. Mondale is in Ohio today, too, and the state will also get considerable attention from Ford and Carter before the election. A few days ago, the Ford organization received polling data indicating that Ford was not doing well in Ohio's farm areas (and also that he was doing surprisingly well in Cleveland), and it was decided that those areas would be given priority attention by Dole. Dole's main campaigning experience, after all, has been in the small-town rural areas of Kansas. Dole's campaign entourage is a mixed bag of Dole staff members, people on loan from the White House and from Rockefeller's staff, and veterans of the Reagan campaign. Lyn Nofziger, who was one of Reagan's top aides and is an old friend of Dole's, is helping the Dole campaign. I saw Nofziger on the plane from Washington to Columbus earlier today and talked with him for a while. He made it clear that the Reagan forces see this election as part of their continuing struggle for the Party. "We're in good shape," Nofziger said. "If Ford wins, we're in a position to put pressure on him. If he loses, we'll take over the Party. And, believe me, we're watching it closely. We're not going to let things go, the way Goldwater did after the '64 election." Dole's campaign has suffered from its own weak staffing and from lack of direction at the top of the Ford campaign apparatus. There remain questions of who is in charge.

It is a cool autumn evening; the leaves are beginning to turn. Dole is here for a rally in front of the Licking County Courthouse, a buff-colored American Gothic building. About four hundred people have gathered on the courthouse lawn, and a high-school band is playing an Ohio State song. Ohio seems to take its bands seriously, and has good ones, and this old-fashioned scene has the feel of a Midwestern football evening. Dole is tall, dark, and not quite handsome. He begins tonight by making a little joke that has become part of his standard routine. "Pineapple juice is a lot better for you than peanut butter," he says, "and, for one thing, it doesn't stick to the roof of your mouth." Dole has a true comic's sense of timing, and is capable of spontaneous humor. After he is cheered, as if on cue, following several statements, he remarks offhandedly, "Reminds me of those spontaneous demonstrations in 1972 in Miami," but the crowd does not catch his reference to Nixon. And then he swings into an attack on Carter: "I can't cover all of his positions on each issue, because you have a curfew here. I can say that so far Mr. Carter has yet to take a definite stand on anything." He talks against "big spending" and "programs." He pledges "fewer promises, and lower taxes, and fewer government programs, and less federal interference." This is not the Dole who told me last May that he was concerned that Ford was too negative in his approach and should favor more "people programs." Dole says that "Governor Carter will shade his discussions, he will tell you anything you want to hear." Dole's wife, Elizabeth, and his twenty-two-year-old daughter, Robin, are with him. He criticizes Carter for espousing a number of new programs and yet saying he will balance the budget. He cites different figures that he says are the varying amounts by which Carter has said he would cut the defense budget. He is making a negative speech, in his flat voice. He is tired, and his voice cracks from time to time. Continuing his attack on Carter, he says, "He won a few primaries here and there against scattered opposition," and he points out that Carter lost several of the last primaries. He goes into the interview that Carter gave to *Playboy* (he asks "what kind of a judgment a man has that would grant such an interview") and the one to the Associated Press about taxes ("He didn't know what the median income was"). "Does anybody here want their taxes raised?" Dole asks, and, of course, the crowd says "No." These people are undoubtedly already against Carter; the only point of this exercise is to inspirit them. And to get stories in the local papers for a couple of days. Dole continues, giving a slashing, negative speech. No smiles. No lift. No thought. Dole is capable of some thoughtfulness, but he has set that capacity aside. He asks the crowd whether it wants "the ultra-liberal ticket of Carter and Mondale" (it doesn't), whether it wants the candidate (Carter) who was endorsed by the Liberal Party of New York, and he says that if Carter is elected, he will have two hot lines—one to Moscow and one to George Meany. When he mentions the Americans for Democratic Action (which gave Mondale a voting score of ninety-four percent), it is booed. At last, he adds a light note, saying, "Oh, yes, we want to win. I figured it out: if Ford gets elected, I get elected."

In the press bus later, in Springfield, Ohio, to which Dole and his entourage flew from Columbus, Nofziger says to me, "It was essentially a negative speech, but it worked. In small-town America, they don't want to hear your 'vision of the future.' It's no place for 'I see an America.' That guy in that house we're passing—all he cares about are his taxes and keeping his kids from being bused."

SEPTEMBER 29

Wednesday morning. I have a talk with Dole in a motor home in which he is being driven from Springfield to Lebanon, Ohio. After a breakfast speech to Republicans in Springfield, he gave three interviews to reporters from Dayton television stations. Local-television interviews are considered very valuable to campaigns. They offer free local-television exposure, and it is assumed that the interviewers will not ask difficult questions. For the same reason, campaigners like airport press conferences with the local press, which have the added attraction that because of the noise almost no one can hear what the candidate says. Dole told one of his Dayton interviewers, speaking of the role of a Vice-Presidential candidate, "We're under some restraint. We can't go beyond what our leaders have said. We can't say what we'd do in the first hundred days. You don't do anything in the first hundred days if you're a normal Vice-President. I think some of the press just sort of trail us all day long looking for a negative. I think that's the role of the press, but it seems to me if you go into an area and have an enthusiastic crowd it's not improper to report that. There is a tendency to find some fault with the campaign, to try to find some contradiction between what I've said and what Ford said."

I ask him how much he has to say about his own schedule.

"They go over the schedules with me, hopefully in advance," he says. "I scratch out part of it, or, at least, demand to know why we're going somewhere. There's got to be some real input before you decide to go to a factory or a farmhouse, unless you're just looking for a media event. I think we need also to stir up the Republicans, the workers, where we can. You can't always do that with the chickens and the cows. We were on a farm last week, and as soon as I started talking the cows all turned around and walked off."

I ask him why he isn't talking about "people programs."

"Well, we did it a night or two ago," he replies. "We don't do it too often, but Carter has such a fuzzy record I don't have time to talk about our programs. I also think there's merit in standing up and saying you've had enough programs—give me a little quality in government, not so much quality of life. Maybe that's a tendency we all have in politics—do a job on the other ticket before they do a job on you, stay even. Anyway, I am out working for a President, and I'm not at liberty to lash out, advocate this program and that program. The President has his record; there's some constraint there. Mondale and Carter can say anything—they can promise anything."

I ask Dole if he thinks he would enjoy being Vice-President.

He replies, "I don't know. I talked to Hubert Humphrey about it the last time I was in the Senate. I said, 'Hubert, do you think you can really do something?' I've heard Hubert and Rockefeller indicate that it was rather a lonely job—nothing happened. Hubert said that if he had it to do over again he would do it. I'm certain Vice-President Rockefeller would say the same. Everybody says it's going to be a great opportunity. Mondale says that. Besides, you have a long time to plan for the next event."

When he says that, he gives Nofziger a knowing look, and the two of them laugh.

SEPTEMBER 30

Thursday. Philadelphia. Shortly after 7 A.M., Walter Mondale is standing under the Walt Whitman Bridge, talking to longshoremen at their morning shape-up. Last night, he complained to his staff about today's heavy schedule. On a plane from Cincinnati to Philadelphia, which we reached shortly before midnight, Mondale was tired—"I'm goddam tired," he said—but in good spirits. (Mondale's plane is just like Carter's.) After a shaky start, he has begun to find his own rhythms and themes. The economic issues are ones that Mondale is familiar with and, as a liberal Democrat, is comfortable talking about (as Carter is not). Like Dole, Mondale now has an entourage and an audience. "I'm getting a hearing," Mondale said on the plane last night as he relaxed in his forward cabin. He had his shoes off and his feet on the table in front of him, and he was smoking a cigar and drinking a couple of Scotches. (One could not imagine such a scene with Carter. Carter has forsworn alcoholic intake for the duration of the campaign, and, anyway, one could not imagine Carter allowing himself to unwind this way.) Mondale's entourage, reflecting the good spirits of the candidate, is a happy one now. Mondale, after all, tried running for the Presidency two years ago and couldn't stand the pace and the demands and the frustrations and the prospect of a candidate's life (such as Carter led) for two years, and he gave up. Now, having been chosen by Carter as his running mate, he has managed to leap-frog obscurity and get in position for another, and more promising, run for the Presidency. And it is probably the case that this is the only way Mondale could get in that position.

Mondale's appearance at the shape-up this morning is the equivalent of one at a plant gate. The dockworkers, most of them black, stand around in the gray morning outside a long, flat blue building. The briefing paper that Mondale's staff prepared for him tells him that longshoremen favor embargoes when domestic supplies are short (this puts them in opposition to farmers), and that they want more imports (this puts them in conflict with shoe manufacturers, cattlemen, and a variety of domestic manufacturers), and it counsels him to "stay away from a discussion of these issues." The longshoremen are underemployed, if not unemployed, and Mondale, his entourage nearly engulfing him, moves about talking with the workers about their difficulty in supporting their families. One of the workers tells me that last week he earned eighty-four dollars for fifteen and a half hours' work. "That's all I could get," he says. "I was here, but the work wasn't here." And then, nodding in Mondale's direction, he says, "Maybe he'll change my luck." I ask him what he thinks Mondale could do. "I think he could do something," he replies. "He could do more than I could. This year is the worst year on the waterfront. The worst year I can remember." Mondale's briefing paper does not tell him that this is a very rough area, that the union is run by labor toughs, and that the workers are said to have to pay off in order to get work. As he makes his rounds this morning, he is accompanied by Henry J. (Buddy) Cianfrani, the ward leader for this area, who came to my attention during the Pennsylvania primary. Cianfrani, an ally of Philadelphia Mayor Frank Rizzo, was part of the machine that helped to deliver Philadelphia to Henry Jackson then. Today, Buddy Cianfrani is wearing a tiny gold peanut pin. The backyard principle, which suffuses Pennsylvania politics—the principle whereby the actions that various people in politics take on behalf of the candidates have to do not so much with great questions about who should lead our nation as with how best to protect their own back yards—and which affected the primary, now promises to affect the general election. The question of whether or not a referendum on a proposed recall of Rizzo, the heavy-handed former police commissioner, will be on the November ballot is currently before the Pennsylvania Supreme Court. However, Rizzo's allies, Cianfrani among them, anticipating the possibility that it might be on the ballot, are said to have held down black registration. Mondale, talking with the dockworkers, looks humane and concerned. This is a good event for television. ("Almost everything we do is for television," says a Mondale aide, who is simply being more candid than aides to other politicians.) In addition, though, it is probably good for him to meet these people and hear some of their problems.

The next stop is the Melrose Diner, an eating place with a metallic façade, in the heart of an Italian district (also Cianfrani's), which is a frequent stop for politicians. This is to be another "visual." Shortly before eight o'clock, about fifty of us descend on the diner. We seem to outnumber the customers. Mondale makes his way along the counter, shaking hands. This might as well be the New Hampshire primary. Among those he greets are some waitresses who worked all night and got off at seven but waited to see him. It is not clear whether they are doing it voluntarily. Then Mondale sits down and has a cup of coffee, with Buddy Cianfrani on one side, and, on the other, Ozzie Myers, who is running for Congress from this district. Mondale's staff memo explains to him that the purposes of this visit are "(1) You will be seen with working people; (2) the location is well known to local people and will be good for the local press; (3) the event allows you to appeal to the Rizzo people."

Mondale is subject to the classic scheduling pressures: his schedulers in Atlanta absorb pressures from outside—from state organizers, from local politicians, and from representatives of interest groups who circumvent the state organizers—and tend to overschedule him. Someone is always saying, "You can't bring him in here without having him stop at . . ."

And so now, at eight-forty-five, at the Warwick Hotel, Mondale is meeting with his third group of the morning, a Jewish group, and is downing his third breakfast (this time, a bagel and cream cheese). Now Milton Shapp, the Governor and almost forgotten Presidential candidate, is with him. Mondale stands at a microphone and declares "my support for the State of Israe ." He says, "Both Governor Carter and I are completely committed to a permanent and secure Jewish state of Israel." He says that the Ford Administration has not really fought the boycott by Arab nations of companies that do business with Israel, or supported legislation to combat the boycott. (The Administration has been maneuvering to defeat the boycott legislation.) Mondale also denounces "the wanton and dangerous profligate sale of arms around the world— especially to Saudi Arabia." (The day before yesterday the Senate Foreign Relations Committee reversed its decision of a few days earlier to bar the sale of six hundred and fifty air-to-ground missiles to Saudi Arabia. Henry Kissinger, who had pleaded with the committee to change its position, said afterwards that a congressional veto of the missile sale "would have foreign policy consequences that are out of proportion to the technical military issues involved.")

Mondale holds a press conference in the Warwick Hotel, and opens with a statement calling on President Ford to hold a press conference. Like Carter, he wants to draw attention to the fact that the President has not been as accessible as they have, and to the fact that there are now some fairly embarrassing questions before the President—questions about the Special Prosecutor's investigation and about the golfing weekends in which he was the guest of a lobbyist for U.S. Steel. Mondale, under pressure from the Carter camp, raised the issue of the golfing trips on Tuesday. Mondale denounces "this policy of hiding behind that White House desk,

speaking through spokesmen." He is asked if he is likening Ford to
Nixon. "What I'm saying is, the tactic is the same," he replies.

The last stop of the day before Mondale returns to Washington is
in Oil City, in the western part of the state, about seventy-five miles
from Pittsburgh. It is a town of some fifteen thousand, with a heavy
Polish and Italian population, and is said to be highly conservative.
Mondale's briefing paper tells him that there are more registered
Republicans than Democrats here. There is some question as to
why we are here at all, and a good part of the answer may lie in the
fact that Oil City is within reach of three media markets—Erie,
Pittsburgh, and Youngstown, Ohio. Another reason Mondale has
come here is to help Joseph Ammerman, who is running for Congress from this area. The advance workers have got out a decent-
sized crowd for a rally on a slope overlooking the Allegheny River.
Before we got here, the Mondale staff released a statement in which
Mondale declared that "there will be tax cuts in a Carter-Mondale
Administration" and that "the great majority of taxpaying Americans will share in those cuts." The statement does not explain how
this will be brought about, but it does mention tax reform. So now
we're having promises of tax cuts, whether they can be paid for or
not, and without their being weighed against other needs, or even
against balancing the budget, which Carter himself promises. The
crowd here is cheerful. Little girls in blue-and-white cheerleader costumes with streamers across their chests declaring them to be "Minnesota Fritzers" do a little dance. As Mondale, standing in a metal
geodesic bandstand, begins to speak, they dance again. Mondale
smiles good-humoredly. He starts to speak again, and a high-school
band begins playing, and so he stands there and waits for it to finish,
alternately looking solemn and laughing. "Give me an M," the
cheerleaders cry, spelling out his name, and then, at last, Mondale
delivers his speech. "The issues are many," he says, but "I think
those at the very top of the concern of all Americans" are jobs,
inflation, taxes, needed programs, and how we pay for them.
"There is no answer for this nation's problems that does not include
full employment," he says. He does not talk about trade-offs. Still,
Mondale does give the impression that he believes what he says,
that he does have real feeling about injustice and inequity. "Please
help us elect a people's President, and we will change this country
on a course that will make you proud of your country," he says. He

has not mentioned Carter. He doesn't mention him very much; in part, he is still smarting from criticism early in this campaign that he was too effusive in his praise of Carter. Now he says, "Elect Jimmy Carter the next President of the United States" After the rally, he attends a reception in a nearby Holiday Inn. On the way, he obliges when a woman asks him to hold her baby whle she takes a picture of him with the baby. "She's a Bicentennial baby," she says. Mondale murmurs something about how his children were once that small, too. After the rally, we learn that the public-address system didn't work and about three-fourths of the audience couldn't hear what Mondale said. But, of course, the television equipment picked up the scene. We also learn that Ford met at the White House with the press.

On the plane back to Washington, I have a conversation with Mondale. Despite his fatigue, he clearly enjoys his nev role. "The days are hard and long, but it gives you a chance to be heard nationally on issues I feel deeply about," he says. "I have a feeling it's going well; I sense that when I'm with crowds, ard that's re-assuring. You know, I think I'm helping the ticket win, and I be-lieve that it's important to the country to win. I think I'm having some influence in shaping the issues. The interesting thing is I can see where a lifetime of involvement in politics and in government all comes to bear. Your research assistants are helpul, but the crucial thing is really whether you've got it all together yourself, in your own head. You can call and get a fact or a figure, or people can suggest things you should say, but it's really kind of your own instincts. Your own training and experience are on the line. You can't really hide whether you're ready or not; either you are or you aren't. Now I'm getting to say things I've wanted to say but felt frustrated about, because I couldn't get a large enough audience to move the country." Mondale does not mention Carter, but I won-der whether he has Carter's current problems in mind. Mondale has lived with many important national issues for years, anc Carter has not. The results do show in their respective campaigns.

I ask him if he thinks he is travelling just the right amount now.

"There is a constant fight between us and the schedlers in At-lanta," he says. "They always try to lay on more meetigs, because they're getting tremendous pressure. We're turning down probably a hundred events for every one we take. There are senators and congressmen and candidates who want help, and almos every state is really a battleground. The schedulers are pushing in one direction, and we constantly fight for some rest, some time to read and think. It's part of this job to get a night's sleep, you know. They were killing us at the beginning of the campaign—twenty-two-hour days, flying from one end of the country to the other. We couldn't get through to them, so finally we got a scheduler to ride with us for three days, and he was so tired we couldn't get him out of his seat. So then for about ten days we started getting civilized schedules. Now they're back at it. But we're doing all right—we're about to get two days off. It's not 'off'—we'll be working on issues, and so on—but it's not travelling. I've tried to set aside time—maybe twice a week if I'm lucky—to work on a serious speech. If you go for more than five days, it's really dangerous because you get so tired that you make a lot of mistakes, and the press gets tired, too. One of the good things about being on the road is that so many people can't pull at you—they can't get hold of you. When I go back to the Senate, everybody's got problems. Everybody's got calls they want you to make, appearances they want you to make. At least, when you're on the road that doesn't happen. Then, some days when you get too tired and you're shaking hands, you know your eyes are glassy, and you wonder if people don't get that feeling that you're not with it. When you're fresh, it's fun to look at people's faces, look them in the eye, kind of get a little communication. And that keeps you going. But when I'm too tired I find myself not even looking in people's eyes; it becomes mechanical and it's work for me, and I'm sure a lot of them feel kind of let down, because it isn't human, it's machinery."

When I talked with Mondale early this year, he said that liberals should talk more about the need to cut back on federal programs, to reduce waste. I ask him if he is talking about this in the campaign.

"Not really," he replies. "Not since the campaign started. During those early meetings in Plains, we talked about, for example, the welfare program, about program consolidation. We talked about that sort of thing, but we haven't had much chance since."

I ask if he thinks such subjects don't lend themselves to campaigns.

"It's hard to get specific," he says, "and if you get specific, people get glassy eyes. I don't think there's a lot of issues that you can talk about in a national campaign without getting spread so thin that themes don't come through. I think you have to decide what are the four or five themes that you want to emphasize almost constantly.

Usually, depending on the audience, it's things they're most interested in: senior citizens talk about their problems, educators about their problems, and so on."

Then Mondale talks with sophistication about economic policy, about wage and price controls—about the sorts of things, and in ways, that he says don't lend themselves to campaigns.

25

Sunday. Congress adjourned in the early hours of Saturday morning, amid the usual last-minute rush to pass a large number of bills. On the whole, the congressional year was one of housekeeping—passing routine measures, tidying up a bit here and there. This was what was largely to be expected under the circumstances: a divided government in an election year. The bill to limit nuclear proliferation by redistributing the responsibilities of the agencies that deal with it and imposing some curbs was gutted by the Joint Committee on Atomic Energy, which reflects the nuclear industry's interests, and then it died there. The bill, sponsored by the Administration (and the nuclear-power industry), that would have permitted and encouraged the private development of enriched uranium was also blocked in the final days of the congressional session. The "Watergate" legislation to make the office of Special Prosecutor a permanent one and to require financial disclosure by federal officials died. Such issues as the Humphrey-Hawkins jobs bill, national health insurance, and divestiture by the oil companies were put over until next year; a number of liberals had become increasingly leery of the Humphrey-Hawkins bill. Only a limited measure to provide new jobs was enacted. The Administration's attempt to reduce and combine a number of federal programs dealing with health and education got nowhere. The highest number of senators and representatives are retiring voluntarily, or choosing to run for other offices, in over thirty years.

Monday. The White House. Another rock has rolled down from the hillside. Now the attention of the press, which does much to decide the agenda, is on the issue of Earl Butz, who made some low remarks about blacks to, of all people, John Dean, who was covering the Republican Convention for *Rolling Stone*. On Friday, the President gave Butz what the White House termed a "severe reprimand," apparently hoping that that would take care of the matter, but there is considerable demand that Butz be fired. Butz, as it happens, is very popular with many farmers, especially the more conservative ones, and with agribusiness firms. Even many farmers who aren't happy about farm prices like Earl Butz— they think he speaks out for them, and they like his blurt style. The President does not seem to understand the symbolism of insults to whole segments of society by high officials. Butz has always been a limited and somewhat crude man, and his policies have bespoken insensitivity toward the poor. Carter, of course, is making the most of the Butz episode. It's that kind of campaign.

Today, shortly after noon, reporters are ushered into the Oval Office, where the President will hold a little ceremony in which he will sign the tax bill recently passed by Congress. The ceremony is, of course, part of his campaign. He couldn't hold it in the Rose Garden, because the weather is too uncertain today, and he couldn't hold it in the East Room, because there aren't enough members of Congress in town to fill out the setting. The photographers were let into the Oval Office first. The Ford Oval Office is decorated in yellows and cinnamons, with a beige carpet. The décor is in sharp contrast to the screaming blues of the Nixon Oval Office. (I still remember the bright-blue carpet encircled with stars.) Ford's desk is empty except for two microphones, a telephone, and a copy of the tax bill, which is five inches thick. A big globe is behind the desk. A couple of weeks ago, when Henry Kissinger went to Africa, the White House released a photograph of Kissinger and the President, who was pointing to the globe. (Today's papers have a photograph, released by the Carter campaign, of Carter meeting with James Schlesinger, whom Ford fired as Secretary of Defense for arguing that Ford's defense budget was too low. Carter is pointing to a globe. The foreign-policy-and-defense debate between Carter and Ford will be held Wednesday night.) Pipe racks are all over the place—on tables beside and behind the President's desk. A bust of Harry Truman, whom Ford selected as a role model early in his Presidency, is on a table on one side of the room. And off to the right-hand side of the desk is a ship's wheel with a brass plate on it that says "S. S. Mayaguez." Ford must consider it the trophy of a triumph. (In the attempt to rescue the thirty-nine crewmen of the merchant ship, the Marines attacked an island from which the crew had already been removed and the Navy bombed an airbase after the crew had been released, and forty-one American servicemen died in the effort. But for this loss of life, it would have been a comic affair, straight out of a Terry-Thomas movie. At the time, the President and his aides made much of this "success.") An American flag is behind one side of the desk, the Presidential flag behind the other. That nearly bare desk is strange. This looks more like a museum than an office. The President is late for the signing ceremony. A number of reporters are here to see what he may say about Earl Butz. Even if the President does fire him, he will appear to have been indecisive, to have based a moral judgment on the polls. We are in the President's office, and the President is some- where else: it's more as if he were dropping in on us than vice- versa. The President has a nerve to take credit for this tax bill and to make a big thing out of his signing of it. Essentially, it represents a congressional repudiation of his own tax proposals, which would have been substantially regressive. This bill also contains fewer new tax breaks than it did this summer, when the Senate, in particular, loaded it with new tax benefits, several of them in the name of conserving energy. The energy bill, which began as a conservation measure and developed into a set of tax breaks included in an overall tax bill, has now all but disappeared. The tax bill, in addi- tion to extending the tax cuts aimed at the recession which were passed last year, does impose slight curbs on some tax shelters, tightens up on some tax deductions (such as the one for vacation homes and the one for the use of one's home for business pur- poses), raises somewhat the taxes on capital gains, and makes a few other reforms. Given the form of the bill earlier this year, when it seemed to be open season on the Treasury, this bill is a minor miracle.

Finally, the President enters his office. He is wearing a gray pin- striped suit and vest. He sits at his desk and reads a statement to the television cameras: "Today I am signing the Tax Reform Act of 1976." He says that he supported some of the provisions and op- posed others, and he says that it "closes loopholes." He says he is "gratified that the Congress has adopted my program of estate-tax relief," which as proposed was not exactly a reform. The President offered this tax relief in his State of the Union Message and re- peated it during his campaign; as enacted, it does help estates of modest size, and, as a result of Congress's action, gradually raises taxes on large estates. The President reads carefully, looking into the cameras. The bill "fails to make many important and necessary changes," he says, and he adds that his own philosophy is that "the best kind of tax reform is tax reduction." He says that he will again ask Congress to enact his proposal to raise the personal exemption from seven hundred and fifty dollars to one thousand—which would benefit those with higher incomes more than those with lower incomes. But he has stressed this proposal so often as a tax reform that perhaps he has convinced people that it is one. "The bill that reached my desk is far from perfect," he says, thus having it both ways. Then he signs the bill, and he gets up to leave. A reporter says, "Mr. President, has Secretary Butz offered to resign?" If they get rid of him, they may well prefer to have it couched in terms suggesting that it was all the Secretary's idea to go. The President says that he is going to meet with Butz in a few minutes and that Ron Nessen, his press secretary, will have an announcement shortly. Nessen says, "We'll have something at about one." What they will have, clearly, is Butz's head. But they may have taken too long to get it.

OCTOBER 6

In the foreign-policy debate tonight, Carter answers the first question with a speech he has clearly planned to give, in which he says that "we can only be strong overseas if we're strong at home," that as President he would assure "a defense capability second to none," and that in détente "we've been out-traded in almost every instance." (He said this throughout the primaries.) The camera switches to Ford, whom we see glaring disapprovingly at Carter. I'm not sure it is just a pose. In foreign policy, Carter says, "Mr. Kissinger has been the President of this country. Mr. Ford has shown an absence of leadership and an absence of a grasp of what this country is and what it ought to be." Strong stuff. He said after the last debate that he had been awed by being in the presence of the President and "was a little too reticent in being aggressive against the President," and that he would be more "aggressive" this time. Ford, too, says something that he probably planned to say, and that echoes his beginning of the first debate. "Governor Carter again is talking in broad generalities," he says. Ford is wooden tonight, and looks sort of angry all the time. It is the same look he often had on the floor of the House when he was Minority Leader. The camera switches to Carter, whom we see smiling—or, rather, smirking. Probably planned—it undercuts what Ford is saying. In short order, Ford and Carter are into an argument over which one is for a stronger national defense. Ford accuses Carter of wanting to cut the defense budget by fifteen billion dollars, and Carter once did, but now he advocates a politically safe five- to seven-billion-dollar cut. He says he never advocated a fifteen-billion-dollar cut. Ford praises Kissinger's current efforts to ward off a racial war in southern Africa, and Carter argues that "we didn't go in until right before the election." He has something of a point. Kissinger's attention to Africa was belated, and seemed motivated by concern that the Russians were meddling there. Ford and Carter both express opposition to a Communist government in Italy, but what would they do about one? We are back to Cold War talk. It is as if nothing had happened since 1960. We are seeing a rerun. Carter refers to Ford's firing of James Schlesinger. Carter gives a little talk, like one he gave during the primaries, in which he says that there is a "deep hurt that's come to this country in the aftermath of Vietnam and Cambodia and Chile and Pakistan and Angola and Watergate, C.I.A. revelations," and says that "every time we've made a serious mistake in foreign affairs, it's been because the American people have been excluded from the process"; he says that he would end the "decision-making process in secret." No question, Kissinger got into some difficulties with his secretive ways, carrying out activities without informing Congress, much less consulting it, but I wonder if Carter would really make his foreign- and military-policy decisions in the open. There has to be some secrecy. Ford recites a list of things "we've done to avoid secrecy."

Actually, these men aren't very able debaters. Ford has his facts—which he recites in stentorian fashion—but he doesn't seem to have any idea how to use his facts, how to weave them into a fabric. He points out that the Pope signed the Helsinki Agreement. And then, talking about Eastern Europe, Ford says that "there is no Soviet domination of Eastern Europe, and there never will be under a Ford Administration," and in his follow-up answer he repeats the point. It's a slip, clearly—he obviously means to make one of those rhetorical assertions about how he will not acquiesce in this or that. Carter, sounding increasingly like Ronald Reagan, criticizes the Helsinki Agreement and Ford's refusal to invite Alexander Solzhenitsyn to the White House. Carter says that "we have become the arms merchant of the world," and that is an important issue, but it becomes lost in a welter of charges, as if he were reaching for every piece of crockery he could find. He's right when he says, "We still have no comprehensive energy policy in this country." If he could make a transition from these charges to thoughtful propositions of his own, he (and we) might get somewhere. Carter snidely says that "Mr. Ford acts like he is running for President for the first time," and that "he has learned the date of the expiration of SALT I, apparently." (No one expects the SALT talks to succeed before the end of the year. Like the negotiations over the Panama Canal, they fell victim to our election-year politics.) There is only a fleeting reference to nuclear proliferation: Carter criticizes the spread of nuclear technology, and Ford brags that he has recommended further development of the uranium-enrichment plant in Portsmouth, Ohio—which does not seem to get at the heart of the problem. The question in arms control is how to stop the nuclear-arms spiral, but they don't talk about that. Carter, arguing that our foreign policy is immoral, says that eighty-five percent of our Food for Peace aid to Latin America went to "the military dictatorship in Chile." But most of the large Latin-American countries are self-sufficient or even food exporters.

It goes on like that. It's very depressing. Then, Ford having said that the low unemployment rates during Democratic Administrations which Carter "brags about" were in times of war, Carter suggests that Ford is subscribing to the theories of Karl Marx. Is that the sort of thing Carter would say as President? Does that bespeak his impulses? Carter says, "I would never give up complete control or practical control of the Panama Canal Zone, but I would continue to negotiate with the Panamanians." Ford claims that last week his Administration tried to persuade Congress to enact legislation that "would take strong and effective action against those who participate or coöperate with the Arab boycott." On the contrary, his Administration fought such legislation. Both make heavy-handed appeals for the Jewish vote, the ethnic vote. In their styles, they are more forceful than before, but what does that have to do with anything?

There are a number of important questions they haven't talked about. The Third World has been barely mentioned. Nuclear proliferation has been skimmed over. There has been no mention of world hunger and diminishing resources. They have talked about obsolete formulations—about a bipolar world in which the United States and the Soviet Union are locked in struggle. They have busied themselves scoring points—any points, even if the Pope and Karl Marx had to be dragged in. Ronald Reagan must feel vindicated tonight. Sometimes it has seemed as if Ronald Reagan were debating

Ronald Reagan. There has been no indication of awareness of the need for new patterns of relationships among nations, or of the difficulties of changing old ones. The talk about a bipolar world is the ragged end of an old argument. Are they not aware, or do they think the public could not comprehend, that we now live in a multi-polar world with multiple dangers? Proliferation has happened. Of the two billion people in the roughly one hundred developing nations, about forty percent, or eight hundred million, are starving. We need new patterns of trade and economic development for the developing nations. The current world population of four billion is expected to reach six and a half billion by the year 2000. While problems and nations have become increasingly interrelated, foreign offices still play zero-sum games. We do in fact have to change the way we think. People who talk, as Harlan Cleveland, the former State Department official, does, of a "planetary bargain," or, as Buckminster Fuller does, of "planetary planning," or, as Jerry Brown does, of "planetary realism" are on to something. We have to face the fact that the developing nations, which are increasingly well armed, intend to demand a larger share of the world's wealth; that just as the United States has lost its military dominance of the world, it is going to lose its economic dominance. The Administration addresses the Third World in a Cold War context. A cleavage of opinion between the State and Treasury Departments has virtually paralyzed efforts to deal with the economic problems of the developing nations. We need new ways of thinking about, and handling, questions of world ecological balances and world resources, including those beneath the seas. The reality is that there is now an interdependence among nations which is of unprecedented complexity and scale. Certain things must be done—if not out of idealism, then to preserve world stability. Either the candidates do not understand these things or they do not think the public deserves discussion of them. Either possibility is disturbing.

OCTOBER 7

Already, the verdict in the press is that Carter "won" the second debate and that his campaign once again has "momentum." Very much is being made of the President's slip on Eastern Europe—as if Gerald Ford's anti-Communist credentials were questionable, or as if the United States might possibly liberate Eastern Europe—and it is now said to be a big problem. That's one trouble with the debates—a slip, which is highly possible under those circumstances, becomes magnified. But what does it have to do with governing? Today, Carter said, "I thought he disgraced our country." Ford campaigned at Rockwell International, the chief contractors for the B-1 bomber, and then at the University of Southern California, where he said, "We do not accept domination over any nation, period."

Today, it was announced that wholesale prices increased by nine-tenths of a percent in September. Bad news for Ford.

OCTOBER 10

Sunday. On Friday, Carter said that Ford had been "brainwashed" when he was in Poland, and called on him to explain his 1972 campaign finances, under investigation by the Special Prosecutor—to "tell the truth, the whole truth, and nothing but the truth." He said that Ford was a more secretive President than Nixon, and was less aware of the world around him. Ford, trying to explain his Eastern European slip, made another misstatement: "This Administration does not concede that there should be Soviet domination of the Eastern European countries. They [the people of Poland] don't believe that they are going to be forever dominated—if they are—by the Soviet Union." How did we get into this mess? How did we end up with a campaign in which so many people find either choice unsatisfying? It seems to go back to the process and, to some extent, to the role of the press in that process. Carter understood the rules, played by them, and won. That so many people are now unhappy with the result, that his victory still comes as such a surprise to so many, that he is still to so many a stranger, who takes getting used to, is not his fault. There is a time lag in the focussing on important questions about the candidates. It has happened before. Not that there were not, in the course of the primaries, analytical pieces of journalism about them. There were. But the major attention of the public as well as of a good portion of the press was on the horse-race aspects of the primary season, and there was particular fascination with the phenomenon of Carter, the "outsider," taking the early primaries. Carter *was* propelled to the nomination by his "winnerness," which, alone, some people find agreeable and attractive. And he established his "winnerness" in a system that rewards doggedness and time. He visited a hundred and fourteen towns in Iowa, beginning in 1975 (and his family made countless other visits), and, in precinct caucuses in which ten percent of Iowa's Democrats—or about fifty thousand people—voted, "Uncommitted" received the most votes, but Carter beat the other Democrats; and substantial segments of the press, as Carter and his aides had expected, ballyhooed a Carter "victory." Similarly, his victory in New Hampshire, over a crowded field, was a narrow one, and the credit given to it was disproportionate. The process by which we nominate candidates for the Presidency is brutal, and laden with distortions. Being driven may not be the only qualification for surviving it; someone of enormous political flair and drama—such as Edward Kennedy or Jerry Brown—can perhaps get through it, but it is a process that is enormously preselective. There were a number of accidents along the way this time. But there always are. One occurred just after the Pennsylvania primary: as one of Carter's aides explained to me last spring, the widespread assumption that he had the nomination "sewed up" after the Pennsylvania primary led a number of people to throw their support to him. (Among them: Thomas Eagleton, of Missouri.) Others got ready to move his way. The assumption got Carter past what an aide termed "the courtesies stage" with Mayor Daley, and it made it seemly for Carter to begin conversations with Senator Henry Jackson, a former candidate, and Senator Adlai Stevenson, each of whom was led to believe he was a Vice-Presidential possibility, and each of whom also held substantial blocs of votes. (Daley's were in Stevenson's name.) It persuaded Robert Strauss, the Democratic Party chairman, that Carter would be the nominee, and that it was time to consolidate the Party behind him. This gathering of support on the assumption that Carter had the nomination sewed up helped him survive a series of subsequent primary losses and was, as it turned out, one of the factors in helping him get the nomination sewed up. Moreover, each Tuesday night on which there were primaries—and there were many of them—was treated as if it were Election Night, and thus added to the distortions of the "victories." It is hard to see how to break these old habits. Some people argue that a number of men—Muskie, Humphrey, Udall—whatever their own liabilities, would have been better general-election candidates than primary candidates. Mondale, starting from where he had to, probably wouldn't have made it through the primaries. So something is off. This spring, Hamilton Jordan remarked to me that he knew Carter would beat Udall in the primaries when he read that in the course of long days of campaigning Udall took naps. (So does

Mondale now.) I still have my doubts that regional primaries would solve the problem; they might, in fact, simply reward the same qualities that the present system does, perhaps tipping the balance a bit toward prior well-knownness. Ford is the Republican candidate for more obvious reasons; if he were not the incumbent President, he would not be the candidate for President. The disappointment in Ford is the result of our having subjected him, as President, to the imputation process, by which we impute to public figures qualities we want to be there. When he was Minority Leader of the House, no one—not even he, probably—seriously considered him a Presidential possibility. But we have more of a monarchic streak than we care to think. His incumbency drove from the race all but the best-known, best-financed Republican candidate—a man who had already built a substantial constituency. So we have these candidates through a combination of process and accident.

Another consensus has arisen: that Ford has blown whatever gains he had been making against Carter and is now on the defensive, that he came across in the debate as clumsy and not very bright—two images he had been struggling to shed. The disproportionate focus on his Eastern European statement is another indicator of something else that goes on in our politics—the magnification process. Carter, of course, is making the most of the statement —as if somehow he were dedicated to the liberation of Eastern Europe. But the press also picked it up and made much of it. Such is the intensity of focus on what candidates say—after a certain point—that one misstatement can be devastating. It can become as important as all the other factors that go into our national decision as to who is best qualified to govern us. And it is easier to focus on. There are probably few people in this country remotely interested in politics who do not know (1) what Jimmy Carter said about lust in *Playboy,* (2) that President Ford appeared to suggest that the Soviet Union was not dominating Eastern Europe, (3) that Earl Butz said some obscene things about blacks. But how many citizens have any idea what the real questions are about the economic and social collapse of our major cities, or what the candidates propose to do about it? The furor over the Eastern European statement, of course, also has to do with the chase for what is known as the ethnic vote. By a coincidence, today and tomorrow mark the celebrations of Pulaski Day and Columbus Day, giving the candidates ample backdrops—dinners, parades—against which to campaign for the ethnic vote, just as they seek other backdrops for campaigning for the Jewish vote and—to the extent they wish—the black vote.

Perhaps people of taste and dignity and thought can get through the process with those qualities intact, but at the moment it would seem to be very difficult. Why doesn't a candidate, up against the kinds of pressures that now exist, just say (1) "I don't know," or (2) "That question does not deserve an answer." When candidates feel that they have to go around being answer men, pleasing everyone, the effect isn't really very pleasing. I frankly don't think that tinkering with the electoral process is going to help these things. And when we get done doing what we do to our candidates, we do not feel very good about them or about ourselves.

Yesterday (Saturday), en route from Oklahoma to Texas aboard Air Force One, the President signed a proclamation restricting the importation of beef. The day before, Carter had said that the President should do something about beef imports. In Texas, Ford said that "Lyndon Johnson never distorted the truth when discussing the tough issues." And today in Dallas, the Reverend W. A. Criswell, the pastor of the largest Baptist church in the country, endorsed President Ford. Tonight on television, we see the minister saying that he asked the President what he would do if *Playboy* sought an interview with him, and that the President replied, "I was asked by *Playboy* magazine for an interview, and I declined with an emphatic no."

OCTOBER 11

The White House has let it be known that the Administration will sell to Israel some sophisticated weapons that that nation has long sought. Tomorrow, the President goes to Brooklyn, where he will campaign for the Jewish vote.

Today, Carter was in Chicago, where he made an appearance with Mayor Daley. One of the things that are hurting Carter in Illinois is that a product of the Daley machine is expected to get badly beaten in his race for the governorship against the Republican candidate, James Thompson, who made his reputation as the United States Attorney who prosecuted several members of the

Daley organization. So there is the odd situation in which Carter is being damaged in Illinois by the Daley machine and is therefore all the more dependent upon the machine to get out the vote for him. In his appearance with Daley, Carter said, "I believe in tight, carefully organized political structures."

26

ATLANTA. Perhaps it is only my imagination, but Carter campaign aides, for all their confident talk, seemed tense and skittish when I talked with them today. They appeared a little down: the primaries were high adventure; this is grim business. It is clear that a decision has been made among Carter's top aides in Atlanta that he must cut out the strident tone that his campaign has taken on recently, and to make sure that he does so, they are sending in their ultimate persuader, Charles Kirbo, the Atlanta lawyer, who is perhaps Carter's closest friend and adviser. "When we need to make a point immediately and hard, we talk to Kirbo," Gerald Rafshoon, Carter's director of advertising, told me. I asked Rafshoon why Carter had developed such a tone recently. "He was down for a few weeks," he said. "He thought he could go for the kill. This is not a campaign where you go for the kill." Hamilton Jordan said, "He'd been down. People were kicking the hell out of us. He was down and he felt like kicking back."

Both Rafshoon and Jordan explained what they thought had gone wrong in the early weeks of the fall campaign. Rafshoon said, as Jody Powell had said earlier, that one of Carter's problems was that the former "outsider" had become entangled in the Democratic Party. One reason was the limit on campaign finance and spending. Each candidate can spend only twenty-one million eight hundred thousand dollars in federal funds, plus three million two hundred thousand raised by his party, so Carter was dependent upon Party people to organize and get out the vote. A subsidiary reason was that Carter decided it was time to make peace with Congress. Congress was a handy target during the primaries, but once Carter was nominated he realized that he would need the Democratic members of Congress to help him if he became President and also—backing up from that—to help him become President. Rafshoon said, "There was a feeling that he was such a maverick he would not be able to work with Congress and so they wouldn't work for his election." (Carter had rather famously bad relations with the

Georgia legislature, and during the primaries he said that he would not hesitate to take on Congress once he was in the White House, if it did not respond to his requests. But after he was nominated he began to talk about how coöperative he expected to be with Congress.) But Carter's aides say that his sudden display of affection for Congress hurt his image. Rafshoon said, "People were telling Jimmy that in the Northern industrial areas people weren't thinking of Jimmy Carter as a traditional Democrat, and that the Party label was important, especially in places like New York and Pennsylvania, where a Southern outsider might not be construed as a Democrat. So he started talking like one, and it was out of character. It's better for me to do it in the media—show faces of Roosevelt and Kennedy, and have E. G. Marshall saying, 'A good man can become a great President.' When he went against Ford with traditional Democratic rhetoric—Herbert Hoover, 'Remember what the Democratic Party did for you'—it hurt Jimmy. People didn't want to hear that from Jimmy Carter. He had whipped the Washington establishment."

Shortly before the first debate, when Carter was home in Plains, his aides showed him videotapes of the news broadcasts of his early appearances. When he is travelling, he can't see how he comes across on television—which is, of course, how most Americans are seeing him. What appeals to a partisan crowd, his aides felt, was not so attractive on television. "It comes across on TV as screaming and shouting," one said. "Politics has changed. Loud, booming oratory doesn't go over on television to a couple of people watching in their home. That's the undoing of the Humphreys." Another problem with Carter's early campaign was that it was run, as one aide put it, "with a primary mentality." It was as if Carter still had to work each state for all it was worth, doing all he could to beat his opponents out, to get on the evening television. He did not seem to understand that now that he was the candidate there was a slot reserved for him on the news broadcasts every night. Therefore, he went to great lengths to get himself covered, talked to reporters at airport stops—and got in trouble from talking so much. Inevitably, he grew testy from being asked the same question again and again, and, moreover, his answers to reporters' questions were more likely to be on the night's news programs than scenes of a well-planned rally. (One aide said today, "I was beginning to hope that Patty Hearst would escape.")

One of Carter's biggest problems now may be that he was a

better primary candidate than he is a general-election candidate. He had a style that worked—up to a point, but sufficiently—in the primaries, but it doesn't fit the general election, and he and his aides don't seem to know what to do about it. Therefore, the tone and the style keep changing. Carter did very well in living rooms and with small groups during the early primaries, and, given time, he could see enough small groups to make an impression. He stayed in people's homes and made his bed during the primaries—he probably made the beds of a fair proportion of the Democrats in Iowa—but he can't make the beds of the same proportion of the electorate. He cannot stand before a crowd at a large rally in Chicago and tell them, as he told primary audiences, that he wants them to be part of his family, that he wants to have an intimate relationship with them. He has long since stopped inviting his audiences to come visit him in the White House—an invitation that charmed them in New Hampshire. He and his aides were convinced that one of the things that worked in the primaries was that Carter stressed themes and style, not substance, but they don't seem to know how to construct such a campaign for the fall, so he doesn't seem to have very much to say. Carter wrote in his autobiography, *Why Not the Best?,* about how he shook the hands of six hundred thousand voters in Georgia in his second, and successful, race for the governorship. Patrick Caddell, Carter's pollster, said to me today, "Jimmy's style is not conducive to a general-election campaign. He's best with small numbers of people, in intimate and personal situations. The stump and the crowds—that's not how he succeeded in the primaries." Carter is still inclined to try to please and blend in with every audience he appears before—a technique that was largely successful in the primaries but is now catching up with him. He is weak at giving formal speeches. And this fall, instead of carving out some issues that people can identify him with, thereby enabling them to identify with him, he has presented the public with a confusing image. There is a truism among politicians that the country is essentially "centrist," and that a national candidate who veers too far from center will lose. Perhaps; but it takes real skill for a politician to blur ideology without appearing tricky.

One sign of the worry in Atlanta is that a decision has just been made to increase Rafshoon's advertising budget. The new funds will be concentrated in the South, which the Carter strategy counts on as the basis of his electoral-vote strength. Yet Caddell said today that "the South seems to be the area of greatest volatility and movement." Jordan said that the money was going into media in the South "to make sure." He said, "Once you start to slide, you can't stop—you can only slow it down." Caddell said that the Southern states were hard to gauge, because it was difficult to estimate how many blacks in those states would vote. Caddell, sitting in his office at the Carter campaign headquarters, his desk buried in papers, looked worried. "The volatility of this race is confusing," he said. "It bounces around too much. The turnout is really a concern. There have been so many tides in this election. The electorate does not appear very well anchored. A lot depends on who has the initiative and who is on the defensive. The changes are so large because the attachments to the candidates do not seem great. A lot of the small states where we have margins look as if they may break even. August was a month of decline for us—it had to be, because the margin was too wide. Then, in the first ten days of September, we started to see a rise in those who said they were concerned about Carter's changing positions so much and in those who saw a risk in electing Carter. That last one's the one we worry about. The percentage of those disagreeing that it was safe to keep Ford was going down. The percentage of those who said that Ford was a good man but was not in charge of the government was going down." Caddell's polls ask a variety of questions, which in themselves are reflective of this election. Among the things they ask people to say they agree or disagree with are: Jerry Ford is a good person but he is not able to take charge of the country (the same is asked about Carter); Jimmy Carter as President would have the vision to provide leadership for the country (the same is asked about Ford); Jimmy Carter (or Jerry Ford) cares about people like me; electing Jimmy Carter is too much of a risk (or Jerry Ford is a safe choice because we know what he'll do as President); Jerry Ford deserves a lot of credit for putting the country back on the road to prosperity; Jimmy Carter (or Jerry Ford) is trustworthy; Jimmy Carter is always changing his positions on the issues; Jimmy Carter is too much of a big-spending liberal; Jimmy Carter is too inexperienced to be President. And people are asked whether they feel that Carter or Ford "is closer to me on the issues." Caddell considers this last question highly important, because, he says, it is tied to whether voters feel that one or the other would be better at managing the economy, keeping inflation down, making government responsive. People are given a word or a phrase—competent, concerned about ordinary people, managing the economy, keeping taxes down, keeping inflation down—and asked which candidate they identify with it more. After the first debate, a question was added about whether people thought that Carter had overpromised. Many did. Caddell says that Carter's lead in the polls was rising in the period just before the first debate. "Then the *Playboy* incident was devastating," he said. "It had a major, major impact. The numbers just started diving. After the first debate, the Carter-is-a-risk numbers started to go down, and since the second debate we have seen some movement, but our numbers are not going up all that much. We've been pushing Jimmy harder and harder to find ways of going at economic themes and of stressing his anti-Washington theme. The problem is that the electorate can make a judgment on a number of grounds—whom they like best, whom they like least, the economy—and it hasn't decided what grounds to decide on. There are no cutting issues. We're having a thematic campaign without any themes, and we don't have any issues to substitute for that."

When I dropped in to see Hamilton Jordan, he was reading the day's campaign report. It said, in part:

1. Urban. Henry Maier (Milwaukee) distributing 5,000 C/M [Carter-Mondale] signs and activating phones on behalf of the ticket.
2. Seniors. Claude Pepper [Representative from Florida and a member of the House Select Committee on Aging] touring N.Y., Pa., and Oh. on behalf of C/M.
3. Greeks. National chairman of United Hellenic Congress endorsed C/M.
4. Indians. Excellent response from JC's meeting with Indians in Albuquerque.
10. New Jersey. Ford's impending visit getting good advance play in papers.
15. Michigan. McCarthy on the ballot, as expected.

Jordan, who directed the Carter campaign when it was a tiny guerrilla operation, now presides over a staff of fourteen hundred—about six hundred in Atlanta and eight hundred in the field—and a budget of about twenty-two million dollars. The Carter campaign organization now occupies three floors at One Hundred Colony Square, a modern high rise in a complex on the outskirts of downtown Atlanta. In what is called the Situation Room, on the twenty-fourth floor, charts and maps around the walls show where the various Carter campaigners are scheduled to go: Jimmy Carter, Walter Mondale, Rosalynn Carter, Joan Mondale, the Carter children (Jack and his wife, Chip and his wife, Jeff and his wife), Carter's Aunt Sissy, and "V.I.P.-Other"—mainly Andrew Young, Richard Hatcher, and Daddy King, all of them blacks. Jordan explained that the decisions on where all these people will campaign are based largely on polling data. One map has colored lines that show where Carter and Mondale and their wives and Carter's children are this week. Another map has colored pins in it showing where they have been. Most of the pins appear to be in Illinois, New Jersey, and Pennsylvania. In addition, plane-loads and busloads of Georgians are being sent to a number of states to campaign and get out the vote. These so-called Peanut Brigades are being concentrated in Maine, Vermont, and New Hampshire, where Jordan says the two candidates are very close. "If we take five or six small states from Ford," he said, "he can't win the election." The Situation Room is windowless and resembles a war room, which in a sense it is. There are files containing material that shows which groups are to get what sort of attention. A computer terminal that sends information to the Carter plane is there, and in an adjoining room, where Caddell's polling information comes in, wall maps display the most recent numbers for the various states (California: 51 for Carter, 43 for Ford, 3 undecided; Illinois: 45 to 45, and 6 undecided; Ohio, 49, 45, 5). Jordan maintains that Carter's strategy of running almost everywhere is the correct one, because it has forced Ford to spend resources on small states that he might otherwise have taken for granted. "The strength of the campaign continues to be that Carter and Mondale and their spouses have been all over," Jordan said. "The problems we had in September were counteracted by the fact that they were campaigning all over the place, since local coverage is ninety percent positive."

I asked Jordan why he thought people were so apathetic about the campaign.

He replied, "The sharp contrast between Jimmy and Ford has not been drawn. And most people don't feel they have a personal stake in who's President. That's the degree of frustration and personal alienation there is now."

I asked him about the effect of Carter's public embrace of Mayor Daley.

"It hurts," he said. "But we can't win Illinois without him pushing for us. Most people understand that he's a powerful political figure. If we go into the election with a margin of two points or so, just the turnout will make the difference. Besides, Jimmy really does like Mayor Daley."

I asked about Carter's approach in the foreign-policy debate.

He explained, "There's no way to win taking a more liberal approach than Gerald Ford on foreign policy. And people forget, Jimmy was a military officer." (When I asked Rafshoon about this, he said, "He went after Ford's strength in order to keep Ford on the defensive and away from Jimmy's vulnerability—his advocacy of cuts in defense spending.") "The mood of the country hasn't changed since the primaries," Jordan said. "I thought all along the danger would be in getting too far away from the things that won him the primaries. What turns people on is a message of hope—'We can do better.' "

When I saw Charles Kirbo this morning, it was in the offices of his firm, King & Spalding, one of the leading law firms in Atlanta. The offices are appointed with Chinese art and artifacts, thick rugs, and parquet floors. Kirbo himself is almost a caricature of the hooded-eyed, hidden, slow-talking Southern country lawyer who came to the big city and made good. His mannerisms—especially the slow talk—are those that are generally associated with shrewdness, but, of course, one never can be sure. (People thought at first that John Mitchell must be shrewd, because he puffed on a pipe and said little.) But Carter's associates say that Kirbo is truly shrewd, and no one questions his influence over Carter. The association between the two men began in 1962, when Kirbo was the "smart Atlanta lawyer" recommended to help Carter prove that the election for a seat in the state senate had been stolen from him. Kirbo won the case. (The story has an odd parallel with the one behind the relationship between Lyndon Johnson and Abe Fortas: Fortas helped Johnson in a legal battle over his election to the Senate.) While Kirbo is only seven years Carter's senior, he comes off very much the elder in the relationship. And he is the kind of loyal, trusted associate, always watching and listening, always looking out for one's interests, that people who lead risky lives—lives in which they put themselves on the line—come to value. I have seen Kirbo on a few occasions this year—at the Convention, at the first debate—and watched those hooded eyes taking in what was going on. I recall one of Carter's aides telling me last summer that Kirbo was the one who "can straighten Jimmy out when he gets off balance"; aides tell you that Kirbo is the one through whom they send delicate messages to Carter; one told me that it was Kirbo who persuaded Carter to go for broke in the Pennsylvania primary—to spend a lot more time and money in the state than he had planned to, in the hope that victory there would be decisive. Kirbo is said to be quite conservative, but some say that this shows up less in ideological arguments than in political ones. One Carter associate said, "Kirbo will say, 'It's better to be conservative on this.' " It is Kirbo who is consulted by other aides on whether or not to run rough television spots. And it is Kirbo who has been travelling around talking to other politicians, collecting their grievances about the Carter campaign and trying to calm them.

The word that comes to mind in the Kirbo offices is "affluence." Affluence and success. In Atlanta, the buildings seem to be going up before one's eyes. As Jack Watson, one of Kirbo's law partners and the man who has taken charge of the planning for the transition between Administrations, if there is one, put it, 'Washington works on power and reflections of power; Atlanta works on money." Though Kirbo, the careful lawyer, has developed the art of talking slowly and saying little, he said a few things this morning that I thought were revealing. He is a large man with wavy gray hair and blue eyes. This morning, he was wearing a plaid jacket and blue trousers. "After Jimmy got the nomination," Kirbo said, "there was a feeling that he had been overexposed and he needed to be low-key until after the Republican nomination." Other Carter aides had said something like this—that Carter's troubles during the last series of primaries, when he lost nine out of sixteen, stemmed from his having been "overexposed." This suggests either that, as Ford's managers also believe in his case, too much exposure of a politician to the public is not good for him, or that too much exposure of Carter in particular is not good for him—or both. "And he needed some rest," Kirbo continued. "It turned out he didn't get a hell of a lot of rest. There were so many people coming down to Plains. During that time, we had to let a lot of people go. We didn't have the money to start the campaign for the general election. There was a period of two to three weeks in there when we were putting together people for each state and figuring out how we were going to campaign for each state. Then we set out on a new type of campaign, which was somewhat frustrating for a while. We were campaigning against Ford and on a wide basis, loaded down with press and Secret Service, dealing with the establishment in each state. It took us a while to get going. As time went on, we developed information and recommendations about Ford, and Jimmy began to go after him. And Jimmy became more aggressive at times, which is his style. It's not a new style. But there's a time to be aggressive and a time to move softly. A month ago, people were saying, 'You're too soft, go back to the old style.' It's cramped his style to have to carry the press and the Secret Service with him. He likes to move fast and cover a lot of territory. If I had it to do over again, I'd take a good look at the possibility of moving the press in a different conveyance than they move in during the campaign. I don't think it's necessary that the press be right with you all the time. My feeling now is that he needs to make less frequent appearances. I think that the die is about cast." Less frequent appearances, of course, lessen the chances of mistakes.

I asked Kirbo some questions about the sort of Administration that Carter might have.

Kirbo made it clear that Carter thrives in an atmosphere of activism, but then said, "We won't be able to move quickly—the results won't be quick." Kirbo talks in terms of "we," as if he were Carter's partner. "I think he's going to be liberal in the so-called compassionate area," Kirbo said, "but he's going to be conservative and tight in all areas with money."

I asked Kirbo how much of a populist Carter really is.

His answer suggested an unsentimental approach. "That's hard to say," he replied. "I guess there's some populist in all of us. I think he believes, and I believe, that a lot of the so-called populist urges, properly managed, are consistent with good business and good government." Pause. Silence. One does not so much converse with Kirbo as wait for him to continue. "It gets back around to having confidence in government and confidence in business. Until some of those things that bother people a lot are eliminated, the country's going to have serious problems. It takes a populist approach to get some of those things straight. There's a limit on the power of government, a limit on the power of economics. You can't have a successful war in Vietnam. That was brought home to me. I never had seen a country that really was refusing to support the armed services and the government on a rather substantial scale. The same thing is true with respect to business. There's a vast majority of people who really feel like they are mistreated—and those things have to be reconciled. You take someone that knows his family isn't getting as good medical treatment—it'll make him bitter. The same thing is true with respect to our justice system. It's not only unfair and inefficient—it's so costly some people just can't afford it. You can call that populism, but they are factors that've just got to be dealt with. Until they are dealt with, you won't have a strong government that you can marshal a war or any other thing. I think that's the type of populism Jimmy's thinking of—correcting evils and inefficiencies, and developing a system of fairness among the various elements of this society."

I asked Kirbo about the conflicting signals Carter had given out in his acceptance speech and at the lunch at "21" a week later.

"You've got to establish yourself with all elements, and Jimmy's been seeing a lot of Republican businessmen, and I've had some input with that," he said. "He knows they're not going to vote for him. But he tells them he knows what their concerns are, and he wants to sit down with them after the election and get their input in the changes he wants to make. The biggest and the most direct criticism of the government is from business. He says—and I think it's true—that you can get these groups that appear to be competitive and separated, like environmentalists and businessmen, in a room and talking, and you can get ninety percent of it worked out, and he sees his job as handling that ten percent area."

I asked Kirbo about the Supreme Court. Some of Carter's associates attributed Carter's recent statement praising the Burger Court to Kirbo's influence.

Kirbo began by saying, "I think the Court will go in a conservative—" Then he stopped and corrected himself: "A moderate direction for the foreseeable future. It's going that way now. I think the Court recognized that some of the altruistic goals they had are just not working out. Rather than changing things more, they've been stopping and taking another look and seeing that they cannot be so broad in what they do."

Jack Watson, who is thirty-seven, is a pleasant man—he is apparently one of those who have developed the art of being pleasing. He is intelligent and ambitious, and people whom he has consulted in his work on the transition say that he asked good questions and seemed to learn fast. When I talked with Watson this morning, he explained that he wrote a memo to Carter after the Pennsylvania primary—when many people, mistakenly, thought that the question of the nomination was settled, and when Watson thought, as many people did, also mistakenly, that it would be far harder to win the nomination than the election. He explained in the memo that if

Carter was elected, he would be presented with an unusual situation: the timing of the new budget process would require his own budget proposals by February, and there were serious limitations in the fact that Carter was an outsider. After the final primaries, on June 8th, when Carter, in effect, won the nomination, he agreed to divert funds and people to a transitional planning effort. The transition group was staffed with people who were relatively unknown and fresh—for appearances' sake, it seems, as well as for the purpose of getting fresh ideas. (Some wise old heads are being consulted, but Watson plays that down. Moreover, only relatively young people were in a position to move to Atlanta for a few months.) A great many papers are being prepared. Watson told me that a hundred and thirty-five papers had been received on foreign-affairs issues, and had been synthesized into thirty-five. None of these will matter, of course, until the people with real responsibility are selected for the new Administration and choose—if they do—to read them. And the selection of those people has been studied, with Watson ascertaining the two hundred-odd jobs—out of approximately two thousand that a new Administration would fill—that are most important and deserve a President-elect's attention.

I asked Watson what the most difficult questions were that his operation faced.

He replied, "How in fact, not theory, does a small group of people really reach out and find formidable new talent that is outside the old-boy networks. You can make speech after speech saying that the American people are competent and compassionate—and mean it down to your toes—but the problem is, how do you find them? I don't mean 'old-boy networks' derogatorily. I really do not. I mean people whose recurring participation in government is endless. I began to find very soon that there are networks that not only self-circulate but interconnect with other networks. There will be people in the Carter Administration—if there is one—who have served in previous Administrations. There is no beauty in inexperience."

There is already, inevitably, some trench warfare in Atlanta between those who saw as the road to power in a new Administration the "issues" staff assembled for the campaign and those who have joined Watson's transition team. (Most people, of course, join campaigns not because they are mad about campaigns but because they see them as paths to future prominence and, to be blunt about it, because of the money that can be earned after one has gained the prominence and served in an Administration. The "sacrifice" of government service is often something quite different.) Watson's people are very critical, for example, of the energy-reorganization proposal that was rushed out just before the first debate—tried to stop it, in fact—on the ground that it was not thought through well. And they plan to lose it somewhere along the way. Hamilton Jordan, for his part, is eying the Watson operation suspiciously, and is clearly planning to move in on it. A member of the campaign staff remarked to me today, "Jack's got a lot of people over there showing off for Jimmy."

As I left Watson's office, I encountered a California Democrat who busies himself with candidates and causes and with assuring people that he is very important. "I'm here to have lunch with Jack Watson," he told me proudly. "I want to help some of my friends."

Today, the President increased price-support loans on wheat by fifty percent and those on corn by twenty percent. Carter had called for price-support-loan increases on Monday, and an Agriculture Department official had responded by saying that there was "no economic justification" for them. The President is to campaign in the Midwest tomorrow.

27

AT HIS TELEVISED PRESS CONFERENCE tonight, the President looks heavily made-up and tired. This morning, the Special Prosecutor announced that the investigation into Ford's finances had cleared him of any wrongdoing, and tonight the President crisply reads a statement saying that the action upheld "my personal reputation for integrity." He also says, having caught on to the public discontent with the campaign, that he hopes that the Special Prosecutor's action "will elevate the Presidential campaign to a level befitting the American people and the American political tradition." The campaign "has been mired in questions that have little bearing upon the future of this nation," he says. "The people of this country deserve better than that." A good move for him to say that. He adds that "Governor Carter and I have profound differences" on a number of issues. But there are other unwelcome questions. In an almost spooky resemblance to things we have gone through before, *John Dean* has just said that in the fall of 1972 Ford, as House Minority Leader, acted on instructions from White House aides to head off an investigation by the House Banking and Currency Committee into the Watergate break-in. He says that tapes not yet released prove this. Actually, the fact that the White House wanted Ford to head off the investigation is not news. Moreover, there were a number of people—no friends of Nixon's—who felt in the fall of 1972 that that was not the proper committee to conduct such an investigation. The problem for Ford is that during his confirmation hearings for the Vice-Presidency he told the congressional committees under oath that he had played a role in heading off the investigation, but he denied that he did it at the behest of the White House. Asked about this tonight, he says that "after full investigation," the Senate and House committees inquiring into his nomination "came to the conclusion that there was no substance to those allegations." He doesn't say he did not act to block the investigation. There are several questions tonight about his 1972 bank account and about his accepting free travel from lobbyists. But the President looks like a conservative banker and does not seem ruffled by these questions. One considers how Nixon would have reacted to them. Ford becomes more relaxed and genial as the press conference proceeds. (Two days ago, he dug himself out of a hole by admitting, finally, that he had made a mistake when he said that Eastern Europe was not dominated by the Soviet Union—saying that what he had meant to say was that he would not acquiesce in Soviet domination of the area.) He is asked about the cities, and he replies, "I would not embrace any spending program that is going to cost the federal treasury and the American taxpayers billions and billions and billions of dollars." I wish he would go to Detroit, where the unemployment rate for young blacks is fifty-two percent. Asked, in the last question, how he got along, as newspaper reports indicate he did when he was in the House, on five dollars a week in cash—the campaign for the Presidency has come to that—Ford replies good-humoredly, "I write checks."

OCTOBER 15

Tonight, on our television screens, we saw pictures of the President of the United States walking in a cornfield in Iowa. The scene looked just like one of Jimmy Carter on Hans Sieverding's farm in South Dakota. Carter went to Detroit and made a speech to the Economic Club attacking crime. That's all he did there.

Tonight, Dole and Mondale have their debate at the Alley Theatre, in Houston. Someone very wisely advised Dole to lean on his lectern, because this makes him look almost folksy. "I don't know much about Governor Carter," Dole says. "I know he's very ambitious. . . . He's been running three years." Mondale is obviously tired and very tense; he looks as if he would very much like to get out of there. Both talk of the "substantial" roles that their leaders have assured them they would play as Vice-President. Mondale slips in a couple of references to Watergate. (He recently made a speech on the subject.) Those lecterns look like corsets, holding them rigid. Dole refers to those "who lust for power." Dole tonight makes more of a case for the need to lower unemployment than Ford usually does, and, asked about his earlier comments that the President was vetoing too much and was too much on the wrong side of "people issues," Dole remarks, "Hindsight's very good, particularly when you're on the ticket." He adds that he can't defend every veto. Mondale, to get off the defensive about espousing federal programs, goes through a litany that begins "I'm unashamed" and lists things he has supported: programs to provide jobs, housing, education, health care. Dole cannot resist taking shots, and comments, "Senator Mondale is a little nervous," but he does mix in some humor, while Mondale, who clearly *is* nervous (as is Dole), plods on, talking substance. My guess is that Mondale's approach goes over better. Then, astonishingly, Dole equates Watergate with "Democrat wars." He says of the Second World War, referring to his own war injury, which left him with one arm useless and the other almost numb, "I think about that every day." With that, he undoes much of the heroism justly attributed to him. He says, "I figured up the other day: if we added up the killed and wounded in Democrat wars in this century, it would be about one-point-six million Americans—enough to fill the city of Detroit." Why does he do it? He can't seem to help himself. It is as if some low growl just could not be contained. Mondale, talking about how the various programs that the Democrats have proposed could be financed, comes up with a figure even higher than Carter's for the amount of revenue that could be generated by full employment and relatively fast growth of the economy: from seventy to eighty billion dollars—highly optimistic figures, to say the least. The thinking must be that one can simply throw these figures around and not be caught up with—which may well be correct. Mondale closes by saying that "Americans are not interested in partisan debating points." Perhaps he's right. He goes on to say, "What really counts is whether this country can begin to solve those problems that are overwhelming so many Americans." He says, "We've cared too little for people in this country that've gotten sick and can't afford decent health care. We've cared too little for the thousands and thousands of American families that cannot get or afford decent housing." His compassion comes through. He comes across as sincere, if stiff. Dole overdid it.

OCTOBER 16

Today, Jimmy Carter, at a news conference in Kansas City, announced that he had sent a telegram to President Ford complaining that Ford and Dole had misrepresented his positions on the amount by which he wants to cut the defense budget and on whether he would raise the taxes of middle-income people. Carter also said, "I think that Mr. Ford actually believed that Eastern Europe was not under the domination of the Soviet Union. But I have never thought that it was a slip of the tongue or that he misspoke himself. I think he stated what he actually thought." And tonight on television we see the President whistle-stopping through Illinois, shouting from the back of the train, "Jimmy Carter wants to divide America." He also says, "He wavers, he wanders, he wiggles, and he waffles, and he shouldn't be President of the United States." My impression, from watching these two men and talking with their aides, is that this is not just the usual campaign to-and-fro but that they have actually come to dislike each other. Perhaps candidates, for all their surface cordiality and attempts to appear sportsmanlike, almost always do. Perhaps they have to.

OCTOBER 17

Sunday. Eugene McCarthy is on *Issues and Answers*. In his way, McCarthy has proved a point about how difficult it is for minor-party candidates to conduct an effective campaign. Denied federal funds (unless their party's candidate received five percent of the popular vote in the last election), subject to the limitations on money (a thousand dollars per person and five thousand per committee) that can be received in private contributions, frozen out of the debates, and largely ignored by the press, they have a very difficult time breaking through. There are a number of dilemmas in this. McCarthy is correct when he says that the system is rigged to protect the two-party system. The Congress deliberately made it difficult for a candidate who is not a Democrat or a Republican to do well. On the other hand, do we want to risk paralysis by encouraging extra parties to the point where our elections could resemble European ones? (This year, there are a number of minor-party candidates in addition to McCarthy. They include Lester Maddox, who is running on the American Independent Party ticket.) Still, it is nowhere ordained that there should be only two major parties, supported by our governmental system. If the two parties become intellectually or morally bankrupt, why should we be denied another choice? My own guess is that if someone who could be taken more seriously than McCarthy were running as a third-party candidate this year, he would be receiving substantially more support than McCarthy is.

Today, on television, the pouches under his eyes are larger than they were when he was a more familiar figure, and the hair is longer and whiter. But still there is a certain handsomeness, and, in and around the biting and bitter comments, some fresh thinking and good sense. Asked about an ad that has been taken by some of his former followers disavowing support of his candidacy this year, he says, "They've made their own peace with the system and the Establishment; they have been elected to office and some of them are sort of on the make." He says, "I don't know what Carter's for." (Asked elsewhere whether he might not be "a spoiler," he remarked that he did not think there was anything to spoil.) He does have his own approaches, unencumbered by liberal dogma. He says that the Humphrey-Hawkins jobs bill is "about eighty-five percent fraud." He argues that "unless we redistribute work in this country, we're going to have six or seven percent chronically unemployed," and he points out that the recent contract agreed upon between the United Auto Workers and the Ford Motor Company, which guarantees more days off, moving toward a four-day week, goes in the direction of redistributing work. McCarthy is now on the ballot in thirty states: the Democratic Party is feverishly trying to keep him off any more, and is trying to get him off the ballot in New York. "A positive approach to politics . . . gets no attention," McCarthy says today. "I think the people have a right to hear an alternative position on unemployment, an alternative to the present poverty program, an alternative to the bipartisan militarism." He cites a report that says that our current destructive capacity is hundreds of thousands of times that of the Hiroshima bomb. He is asked what we should do about that. "You stop producing bombs," he says. "We don't have to have an agreement with the Russians to start being sensible." He says that when necessary the President should ask for statutes to clarify his powers, as in the management of the C.I.A. He says that in the domestic area Carter is "running on the old New Deal," and that "in the foreign-policy area I have more reservations about Carter every day."

OCTOBER 18

Carter, on television tonight, looks exhausted. He is back in Plains for two days of rest. We see him telling the press, "I'm going to bend over backwards the last two weeks not to make any sort of personal attacks on President Ford." He says, "I believe that the American people react adversely to that."

The election, eleven days away, is up for grabs. The polls of both camps show a surprising number of states that could go either way, and the pollsters also report that, in a most unusual development, the number of undecided voters is rising. While many analysts are giving the election to Carter, that outcome is by no means certain. The electoral arithmetic still works in Carter's favor—if he holds the South—and so does the particular structure of the Democratic Party. But in at least twenty states the polls are within what the pollsters call the "margin of error"—about three percentage points in either direction. Barring an especially dramatic turn of events in tonight's debate—the last of the three between Ford and Carter— the election will be decided in the course of the final days of campaigning. Stuart Spencer, deputy chairman for political organization of the President Ford Committee, says that it will be decided over the last weekend. The President will take off for non-stop campaigning following the debate. Carter, recognizing that even the South is not certain, campaigned this week in North Carolina and Florida, and, recognizing the limits of human flesh, will take a couple of days off in the period between the last debate and the long days of the final push.

Hamilton Jordan and Charles Kirbo were sufficiently concerned about the slide in their candidate's fortunes that they flew to Washington this week to counsel with Democratic Party leaders. One of the oddest turns of events in this odd year is that it just may be the machinery of the Party, which Carter used in 1974 (when he volunteered to head the Party's effort to help congressional and local candidates, and made a number of important contacts) to get in position to run, and then took the position of running against, that will save him in the end. The Party has machines in several highly populated areas—in Illinois, Indiana, New Jersey, Pennsylvania, New York. They are strong political organizations that are in place on a day-to-day basis and can frequently deliver the vote. Carter made a big point during the primaries of saying that he was not the candidate of "the bosses," but he is now relying heavily on Mayor Daley and on Philadelphia's Mayor Frank Rizzo, the heavy-handed ex-cop, to pull him through. Rizzo has promised the Carter organization that he will deliver more votes in Philadelphia than have been delivered for any previous Democratic Presidential candidate, and enough to assure that Carter carries Pennsylvania. Republicans have no such dependable base on which to build. Rural areas, where they are strong, are hard to organize. The suburbs, where they used to be strong, are becoming increasingly Democratic. Democrats can target their areas and "get out the vote." That's what they are concentrating on doing. The Carter campaign has set up what is called, in an era of television derivatives, the SWAT Squad, a team of four people which has organized get-out-the-vote efforts in key states—Florida, Illinois, Indiana, Maryland, Michigan, New Jersey, Ohio, Pennsylvania, California, New York, Texas, Virginia, and Connecticut. Labor groups have budgeted more than two million dollars to spend on getting out the vote, and plan to distribute about ninety million pieces of campaign literature in the last weeks before the election. The A. Philip Randolph Institute, which is funded largely by the A.F.L.–C.I.O, is working on black registration and voting, and it plans to send black members of Congress into black communities to encourage their political participation. Even the fact that Congress is so heavily Democratic helps Carter, since each Democrat working for reëlection is working to get out the Democratic vote. The Democratic National Committee is putting substantial get-out-the-vote money in key areas of key states. The Carter field organization is, of course, working on getting out the vote as well as on holding the hands and soothing the egos and trying to mediate the squabbles of local politicians. The Democratic National Committee is concentrating on registering blacks and Mexican-Americans and Puerto Ricans in Texas, California, and New York. In all, the Democratic National Committee has got more than three million voters registered for this election. The assumption is that of the nearly fifty million nonregistered potential voters in the United States a heavy proportion are either black or Spanish-speaking, and poor, and young—and so would tend to vote Democratic. "This program," a Democratic National Committee official said to me recently, "would have elected Humphrey in 1968."

This is a formidable backup for any candidate, but the Carter field organization has been hampered by difficulties—more than the usual number in a Presidential campaign—between the Atlanta staff and local politicians, and bedevilled by various states' backyard politics. Local politicians chronically complain that they are being ignored, congressmen that their potentially valuable service to the national ticket is being turned away, but there does seem to be a continuing tightness to the Carter circle, based on an understandable feeling that they did it, by God—a sense that they showed 'em in the primaries and they'll show 'em again—and this creates an atmosphere in which other politicians are, at best, tolerated. If these patterns are followed when the Carter group governs, if it does, there could be trouble. Morale within the Democratic camp is not good; a number of people are upset and wonder what has gone wrong. The downward turn in Carter's fortunes has intensified the criticism of him by former backers, who perhaps might have been critical in any event but seem less constrained now that things are going badly for him. They question everything from his convictions to his competence, and wonder if they succumbed to false charms. Undoubtedly, most of them will rediscover his virtues if he should succeed.

Perhaps this election was typified by the answers to the first question in tonight's debate, which was what sorts of sacrifices each candidate thought that the people might be called upon to make in the event he is elected. Ford, after citing the need for a strong defense, says that there would be tax cuts in his Administration, and Carter begins by saying that there would be even fewer sacrifices in his Administration. (Carter does go on to say that there might be a need for "voluntary price restraints.") In the course of the debate, Carter makes a little human-seeming apologia for giving the *Playboy* interview (while pointing out that Albert Schweitzer and Walter Cronkite had given interviews to the magazine). The Ford camp has been making much of this incident. It has published a tabloid called *Heartland* and mailed out two million copies of it, concentrating on rural areas. Its lead story is about a recent meeting that the President had with religious broadcasters, and the other front-page stories are about the *Playboy* interview (there are excerpts and a photograph of the magazine's cover inside) and the objections to it by the Reverend Dr. W. A. Criswell and other men of the cloth, and about the President's prayers. The front-page photograph is of the Ford family gathered around watching Mrs. Ford feed a fawn. The Ford campaign has been concentrating on what one strategist calls "the electric church"—radio and television gospel hours that are beamed to evangelicals, who make up heavy proportions of the population in Detroit, Cleveland, Chicago, some parts of Pennsylvania, and some Southern states. "It's driving the Carter people crazy," the Ford strategist says. Tonight, Ford refers to "alleged immorality" on Capitol Hill, and to the "new spirit born" on the Fourth of July. He referred to that in his acceptance speech, too, and seems to be trying to appropriate the Bicentennial celebration. Carter uses his selection of Mondale as an example of the care for quality which he would bring to selecting an Administration, and thereby forces Ford on the defensive about Dole. Polls have shown that people feel Mondale brings more strength to his ticket than Dole does to his, and Carter is making increasing use of Mondale in his advertising. It appears that, in this close election, and with our experience of the last thirteen years, people are paying more attention than before to the Vice-Presidential nominee. Carter says that if the Russians invade Yugoslavia, he would not send troops, and Ford, sensing an opening, delivers a little lecture on how Presidents shouldn't telegraph their intentions concerning such matters. Ford has been advised strongly by his aides to try to look relaxed tonight—they suggested that he look more at his questioners than at the camera, and try to relax his body, so that he would talk in a more relaxed fashion—but he is irretrievably stiff. The President has also been advised to stress taxes, spending, and peace, and he does. Carter is more quick-witted than the President, and better at handling this format. He makes a fairly strong case against the President's record, offering himself as willing to do more about cities, jobs, welfare costs, the environment. In a way, the debates have shown us true things about the candidates, and probably forced them to address themselves to real issues more than they would have otherwise. But still, both continue to avoid talking about trade-offs, about hard questions.

OCTOBER 24

Arms sales abroad by the United States for the twelve-month period ending in June have now been estimated by the Pentagon and other government agencies at twelve billion, seven hundred million dollars, or more than a billion dollars a month. This was the largest amount of arms ever sold in a single year.

The Washington *Post* has revealed that South Korea has distributed up to a million dollars in cash and gifts each year to U.S.

congressmen and other officials during the nineteen-seventies. The story appears to have the makings of a major scandal. But it is not clear that the South Korean government is doing anything very different from what our own government has done in foreign countries. Perhaps it even learned from us.

OCTOBER 25

Shortly before five-thirty, on one of the Washington television stations, we see Steve Ford, the President's youngest son, talking about what a good father his dad is, and then we see the President, in a sports shirt and sweater, talking about what a good son Steve is. We are shown pictures of the family cheering Ford at the Republican Convention, and then are shown Mike Ford, who is attending theological school, talking about how religious his father is. Then we see Susan Ford hugging her father—a picture that was in the film played at the Republican Convention—and Susan says, "My father and I have always been very close." Then the Voice—that resonant, anonymous, documentary Voice—intones, "The Fords: a close, loving American family." And then we see Jerry and Betty Ford, followed by a dog, walking arm in arm on the White House lawn, and Voice says, "Sometimes a man's family can say a lot about the man."

On the television news tonight, we see the President of the United States in Seattle at the helm of a hydrofoil, attacking Carter for wanting to cut defense spending, and saying that Carter's program would cost jobs in the Seattle area. The state of Washington has only nine electoral votes, but the President cannot afford to lose small states, and the polls there show the race to be close, with, as elsewhere, a high proportion of undecided voters.

The Ford campaign, having spent less than the Carter campaign at the outset (Ford campaigned from the White House while Carter was chasing about the country), has more money to spend in the final days. It has already spent eight million dollars on advertising and is planning to spend another four million—most if it on television advertising, but a good bit on radio, and even print, advertising. The Ford people figure that they are outspending the Carter people three to two on advertising in the last days of the campaign. (Most of the Ford spending is in Texas, Ohio, Illinois, Pennsylvania, Florida, California, and New York.) It is an article of faith that advertising is a crucial—some think *the* crucial—element in a campaign. There is, of course, no way of knowing whether this is so—of knowing how many people are affected, and to what degree, by advertising, as opposed to other things they see and hear about a candidate, especially a Presidential candidate, which provide so many grounds for making a judgment. But, whatever the facts, campaign organizations think that a great many people are affected by it, and put a lot of their resources into it.

Tonight, five minutes before the National Football League game begins on ABC, I see scenes of America—Mt. Rushmore, Indians, cowboys, early machinery, Presidents (Wilson, Roosevelt, Truman, Kennedy, Johnson), and then the White House and, again, Mt. Rushmore. Voice—sounding a lot like the other one—says, "If there's one thing that can bind our country together, that can make us have hope again, and faith in the future, it's a President who is in touch with the American people." Then we see Jimmy Carter saying, "We've seen walls built around Washington, and we feel like we can't quite get through." Then, as a song called "See the Dream, America" plays in the background, we see pictures of tall buildings, of citizens walking briskly and purposefully down the street, of children, and then Jimmy Carter says, "There's only one person in this nation who can speak with a clear voice to the American people . . . that can call on the American people to make a sacrifice and explain the purpose of the sacrifice." Then we see the Carter family walking together, and then photographs of flags, bridges, and a setting sun, and then photographs of Jimmy Carter, chin on hand.

The Ford campaign has ads in which unnamed people are asked their opinions of Carter. Some of them are from Georgia, and one of these says, "It would be good to have a President from Georgia, but not Carter." Ford aides say that this ad has been tested and is not seen by people as being "anti-Carter."

The Carter campaign has a collection of thirty- and sixty-second ads on the "issues." It has one on welfare, lasting sixty seconds, in which Carter talks about the ten percent on welfare who can work and should be given jobs and the ninety percent who can't work and should be treated with love and compassion. It also has one, lasting thirty seconds, in which he talks just about the ten percent who can and should work. The thirty-second ad is the one that is played in prime time.

Both sides tell you how the other is about to launch vicious, negative advertising.

At ten-fifty-five on the CBS network, Voice declares, "In troubled times, a distressed nation listened to a new and candid voice," and we see Gerald Ford being sworn in as President, on August 9, 1974, and then we see scenes of farms, a city skyline, the Statue of Liberty, and Gerald Ford taking the oath of office as President. (At the same time, the same Carter ad I saw earlier is being played on NBC.) In this ad, Voice says, "Honesty and moral integrity are essential: as Gerald Ford becomes the thirty-eighth President, he has undergone an exhaustive investigation by committees of both Houses. He has met the standards of Democrats and Republicans alike." We see a photograph of Ford, chin on hand, and the photograph of him with his back to the camera which was in the Convention film, and then other scenes from the Convention film. We are told that Ford earned an Eagle Scout badge, that his high-school football coach and college football teammates thought well of him, and (to the background music of "Gaudeamus Igitur") that there were a lot of bright people in his class at Yale Law School, in which he graduated in the top third. We are shown Second World War scenes of planes being shot down from an aircraft carrier. Captain John Cadwalader, who served in the Navy with Ford, explains that torpedoes from two Japanese torpedo bombers had missed the ship, "but Ford didn't miss; he fired and they both went down." Then we see worried faces of Americans, and Voice says, "He opens the Presidency to public view." Then we see a scene from Ford's acceptance speech at the Convention—which his aides consider a triumph—and the ad ends with a photograph of Jerry and Betty.

28

TUESDAY EVENING. The Howard Johnson's Motor Lodge in Palatine, Illinois, a suburb of Chicago. Tonight, the President will appear at a rally at a shopping center in the nearby suburb of Schaumburg, and before that, at six-thirty, he will appear with Joe Garagiola in a half-hour television show that is to be broadcast statewide. *The Joe and Jerry Show,* as it has come to be called, has already played in California, and after Illinois will play in Pennsylvania, Texas, and New York—all key states. The show is an invention of the President's strategists, who regard it as a way of solving a number of Ford's problems as a campaigner. All things considered, they would just as soon he did not take to the road at all, but the election is seen as so close now that everything has to be thrown into it. It was judged that, for all of Ford's liabilities as a campaigner, it still helped to have a picture of the President in motion, travelling, with his props—his personal entourage, the press corps, the limousine, and Air Force One. One of the President's advisers said to me last week, "That's how we won New Hampshire." The problem now is how to avoid having the President commit some embarrassing gaffe or become too shrill and strident, as he did in recent campaign appearances. (The Ford people are convinced that they would have the election sewed up by now if it weren't for the President's gaffe about Eastern Europe. They also tell of the efforts, beginning the next day, of some of his advisers to get him to admit that he had been in error. But, as they tell it, the President believed that he had done well in that debate, and was annoyed at all the comments that he had blundered, and stubbornly refused to admit error. Finally, six days later, he did.) One of the President's advisers said to me last week, "The more stump speeches he makes, the more the campaign deteriorates." The problem for Ford is, as it has been sometimes for Carter, that appearances before partisan audiences encourage the candidate to give the audiences what is called "red meat," stirring them to more fervent ovations and the candidate to more heated rhetoric, but while these scenes are satisfying to the candidate and the audience at hand, they do not go over so well in the living rooms of America, which is where the campaign is actually being waged. The President has another difficulty as a campaigner. "He doesn't really understand electronics," one of his advisers said to me last week. "He's the kind of guy who gets on the phone to California and starts yelling." This man added, "He gets on the stump and starts shouting at the microphone." And so a decision was made to have the President make a minimum of live appearances, and tape a television show, aimed at the state he was campaigning in, in what his aides call "a favorable mode." One of them said last week, "When we're on the road, we'll try to avoid the eight-speeches-a-day thing. He'll land, do a morning media thing, a thing in the afternoon, and then a TV thing that night—then get the hell out of town." Another adviser explained that the decision had been made to tape the half-hour shows because "when he's been campaigning all day, early evening is his worst time." Thus, the shows are taped just before airtime, to provide an opportunity to erase anything particularly disastrous. And the idea was to find an interviewer with whom the President would be comfortable. "We decide what the questions are," said an adviser. Joe Garagiola had volunteered to help the President earlier in the campaign, and John Deardourff, of the Washington political-consulting and advertising firm of Bailey, Deardourff & Eyre, which is in charge of the President's campaign advertising, conceived the idea of having Garagiola serve as the President's interrogator.

In these final days of this most unusual Presidential race—few elections get this far with so many states in doubt—the two candidates, proceeding on similar poll data, will be concentrating on essentially the same states. Both camps see the race as very close in some border states and in the largest states as well. Both see a possibility that Carter is slipping in some Southern states. While each will make a stop or two in smaller states that appear marginal, the consensus in both camps is that it comes down to the "big eight," the states with the most electoral votes—California, Texas, Illinois, Michigan, Ohio, New Jersey, New York, and Pennsylvania. It is generally expected now that of these Ford will carry California and Michigan, and Carter will carry Texas and New York, but the race is close enough in all of them to keep up the fight. Moreover, with Carter's presumed lead in the Southern states (some, such as Virginia, Mississippi, and Louisiana, are said to be shaky), Ford, if other states break as expected, must carry three of the big eight that are still considered undecided. His final schedule was being left somewhat open as late as last evening, attendant upon data from his pollster, Robert Teeter. Teeter's polls, like those of his opposite number, Patrick Caddell, guide not only the candidate's travels but the placing of advertising and the stressing of issues. Individual states are re-polled and re-polled, and certain questions are re-asked and certain new ones are added, to give the all-important "trend lines." Both camps now report that their polls show the number of those who feel that Jimmy Carter lacks sufficient experience, or would be a risk, to be increasing (but Caddell also says that the number who doubt that it is a safe choice to keep Ford on the job is also increasing), and both pollsters say that the number of those who see Carter as a "big spender" has gone up since the first debate. The poll in today's Chicago *Tribune* says that Ford is leading Carter in Illinois, forty-five to forty-four, with eleven percent undecided.

Joe Garagiola opens the television show tonight by introducing himself ("Hi, I'm Joe Garagiola, and for the next half hour you're in for a treat") and saying, "President Ford has been campaigning very hard today in Illinois, and it's been an exciting and it's been an interesting day, and I've been with him, and I can use one word to describe it: it's an *experience*." Then we are shown a videotape of Steve Ford on a horse in Kankakee and of Steve talking to a farmer about Carter and "all the federal programs he wants to introduce." The farmer is concerned, and says that if that happens we are "going to lose our freedom." Then we are shown pictures of Air Force One—the big blue-and-white plane with UNITED STATES OF AMERICA lettered on its side. Joe Garagiola says, "Imagine an old broken-down ex-Cub like me hitching a ride on Air Force One." Then we see pictures of Ford getting off Air Force One in Chicago and of Ford at a campaign appearance in Chicago this afternoon. Joe Garagiola remarks, "Not much question which candidate they were supporting for President." Then Garagiola turns to President Ford, seated with him in the studio, and says, "Mr. President, you really enjoy getting with the crowd and seeing the people one-on-one." The President says he does. The supporting cast tonight consists of James Thompson, the very popular Republican candidate for governor of Illinois; Charles Percy, the Republican senator from Illinois; and Edith Green, a former Democratic member of Congress from Oregon, who heads Citizens for Ford. Mrs. Green and Garagiola form Ford's travelling troupe. Garagiola asks Ford such questions as whether it makes any difference who is elected President, and says that he thought it was too bad that Ford couldn't always answer Carter during the debate, and that he wonders what Ford's response is to Carter's charge that he didn't do anything during his two years in office. On one hand, Garagiola plays a confused but awestruck Joe Sixpack to a President; on the other, he's a simple nice guy playing to a simple nice guy. A Presidential seal is on the wall behind where they are sitting. After observing that "Watergate really tore us up," Garagiola asks, "What is the difference between a Nixon Administration and a Ford Administration?" (Teeter's polls showed that while a certain unchanging percentage will not forgive Ford for Nixon, it is also true that one of Ford's greatest assets is that he contrasts well with Nixon.) The President responds, "Joe, there's one very, very fundamental difference. Under President Ford, there's not an imperial White House, which means there's no pomp, there's no ceremony, there's no dictatorial authority. We've tried to run the White House as the people's White House, where individuals have an opportunity to come in, individually or in groups, and express to me their views and recommendations." He gives the impression that any of us could drop around for a chat. Garagiola asks Charles Percy what he thinks of Ford, and Percy says that Ford is "a good man" who will "bring them prosperity, that will keep the peace.' Garagiola asks Ford to tell "the true story" about the economy, and Ford explains how he wants to reduce taxes. He talks again about his proposal to raise the personal exemption from seven hundred and fifty dollars to a thousand, and—having been urged by aides to be explicit about what this would do—explains that this means that a family with three children would have one thousand two hundred and fifty more dollars in personal exemptions. What he doesn't explain is that his proposal would mean a greater benefit for those with higher incomes. Edith Green, who reminds one of a Latin teacher one was afraid of, attests to Ford's character. Garagiola gets Ford to explain his proposal to provide insurance against catastrophic health costs, and observes how hard it is to buy a home, because the prices are "almost out of sight"—which prompts the President to mention his housing program. Jim Thompson says the President is a strong leader, and Ford looks stern. Garagiola asks the President if he has "a final thought," and the President makes a little speech about "the tough day in August of 1974—and, believe me, it was a tough one," when he "put the ship of state on an even keel," and he talks again about the Fourth of July, mentioning the Tall Ships, as if he had had something to do with them, and about peace, and about how "there's a swelling pride in the fact that we're all Americans" and "America is on the move again." The show ends with the campaign theme song, "There's a Change That's Come Over America" ("I'm feeling good about America, and I'm feeling good about me"), and a shot of the Presidential seal, then Ford smiling, then the seal.

A huge crowd has turned out, or been turned out, for the rally at the Schaumburg shopping center. If Ford is to carry Illinois, he must do well in Chicago's suburbs. Mayor Daley is working on Chicago itself for Carter. Thompson is running so well that his presence on the ticket is expected to help Ford. Enclosed shopping centers, such as this one, are among the preferred settings for political rallies (so are gymnasiums), because noise resonates so well in them, amplifying the shouts of enthusiasm for the candidate. This is said to be the largest indoor shopping center in the country, and I can believe it. People are packed in along three levels of ramps which define the modernistic interior—in front of Jarman Shoes and Shirt Tales and Marshall Field. At the President's approach, the Conant High School Cougars band plays "Hail to the Chief," a magisterial, martial tune that bounds back from the walls. The shouts of the crowd are nearly earsplitting. A lot of children are here, and there is a great deal of excitement. They are seeing a President, after all. The President waves and smiles and clasps his hands over his head. Ford looks happy at the reception he is getting, and why wouldn't he be? Percy and Thompson are with him. The President stands under a huge banner that says "Chicagoland Welcomes President Ford." That will be good for the television news programs later tonight and early tomorrow, which are essentially the purpose of the rally. The Presidential seal is on the lectern. Both candidates will be all over tonight's and tomorrow's local news programs. Carter is only a few miles away, making an appearance tonight in a North Shore suburb. Today, he toured the state with Michael Howlett, the machine politician whom Daley selected as candidate for governor, and whom Thompson is expected to trounce.

As the cheers continue, the President waves his right arm over his head in a circling motion, like a cheerleader, or a cowboy about to fling a lasso. He invites the audience to come to Washington for his Inauguration—a variation on an old Carter ploy. He tells them, "I want each and every one of you to know where I stand"—a dig at Carter. "I stand on your side for limited government, for fiscal responsibility, for rising prosperity, for lower taxes, for military strength, for peace in the world." The vision at Vail—his sudden embrace last August of new programs in a number of areas—has virtually disappeared. He does shout, just as his aides fear. "Not a single young American is fighting or dying on foreign soil tonight," he says. Cheers. The fact that his impulse was to send more military aid to collapsing Vietnam and to Angola seems to have got lost in this campaign. "As your President, we will keep it that way for the next four years," he says. He cites his sixty-six vetoes, and says that they "saved you, the hard-pressed American taxpayers, more than nine billion dollars." That sounds good, and the audience cheers. The real cost of it—in unemployment, lack of hope—does not intrude. To the people in this suburban shopping center, Detroit may be as remote as Vietnam. Ford adds that his vetoes "saved each American family two hundred dollars in federal spending," and then he says, "We will submit a balanced budget for the federal government in 1978, and we will have another tax reduction." This seems impossible. There is already a fifty-billion-dollar deficit. "My idea of tax reform is tax reduction," he says, and he talks about his proposal to raise the personal exemption from seven hundred and fifty dollars to a thousand, explaining, just as he did on the Joe Garagiola show, how much it would help a family of five. This seems to be another example of misleading statistics that politicians can throw around without the public's catching on. He comes across here as "fighting Jerry," and what he says he is fighting for sounds good. Of course, the economy is in bad shape: unemployment is almost eight percent, and the "recovery" that the Administration was bringing about is in what his economists call a "pause" —and growth has slowed to a mere four percent. Ford does say tonight that "too many people are still out of work." He also asserts his pride in the fact that "this week America made a clean sweep of Nobel Prizes." He'll use anything. It's a simple speech, appropriate for a pep rally, which this is. "We're going to win," he says. He seems to believe this might be possible, and that seems to inspirit him. He could be correct. The arithmetic is hard, but the polls tell him he can do it. He is the man in the conservative suit giving a conservative little talk—the consolidator. This is a pleasant occasion, a sort of classic political scene: the politician, the band, American families out in the shopping center. The crowd's enthusiasm helps him. He is trying, he is giving it his all, and he seems to enjoy doing it. Watching Ford, I wonder what this campaign would be like if his looks were different. He has a healthy, uncomplicated look. His face, a plain face, but pleasant when he is relaxed, serves him well. Oddly, it is *his* smile that pays off; it seems more natural than Carter's. In fact, it is one of the ironies of this campaign that several of the qualities that Carter is seeking to establish as his are widely attributed to Ford: honesty, decency, trustworthiness. And Ford has even made off with the smile. He looks solid. Even his size is reassuring. The analogies with Eisenhower are startling. "I have no fear for the future of America," he says forcefully. "The future is our friend." He says something that it never used to occur to us that Presidents needed to say: "I promise you once more, as I promised you before, to uphold the Constitution."

OCTOBER 27

Wednesday. Station WPVI-TV, Philadelphia. This is the President's second stop in Pennsylvania in two days. Pennsylvania is one of the small group of states that the President needs to win, and the race here is, by all accounts, close. One of the President's tacticians calls this *the* key swing state in the election. The two candidates are fighting hard over it. The President got here today via New Jersey, which he is given a good chance of carrying, thanks in large part to back-yard political squabbles that are rending the Democratic Party there. (The Carter campaign's SWAT Squad was asked to leave by the Carter coördinator for the state.) The picture one gets is that this is not so much a person as a windup doll—a Presidential windup doll—who goes through his set routine as his managers watch anxiously. Of course, the President travels with an impressive entourage. There is the equipment—the airplane, the limousine. (There are two limousines, which are transported about the country on C-141s.) Among the staff members who travel on Air Force One with this candidate are his press secretary, Ron Nessen, and four press aides, plus four women who get out the schedules and the instantly reproduced transcripts of the President's public utterances, plus a man who handles advance work for the press; his military aide; his physician; two speech writers; Don Penny, a former comedy writer, who has been advising the President on his public appearances this year; Richard Cheney, his chief of staff; Terry O'Donnell, an aide who keeps track of the President's schedule and leads him to and from platforms; his photographer, David Kennerly; his secretary; several Secret Service agents; Ray Zook and Robert Manning, who have been handling White House press travel arrangements for as long as anyone can remember; and a National Security Council aide. A press aide was at pains to explain that the President Ford Committee pays for all these people's travel expenses, and that their salaries are covered by the overtime work they do in Washington. Two planeloads of reporters and camera crews fly ahead of Air Force One as it chases back and forth across the country carrying a President in search of votes.

Today's schedule for the President is actually more crowded than his managers had planned, reflecting, as it does, pressures by local officials to add just this one more stop, and then another one, and the receptivity on the part of the candidate to trying one more thing, and then another, that might make the difference. The extra efforts will be bent toward strengthening support for the President in Philadelphia's suburbs, to offset the vote for Carter that Mayor Rizzo is expected to produce in the city. Drew Lewis, the chairman of the Pennsylvania President Ford Committee, has explained to me that the suburbs all have their own small papers, which will feature a visit by the President on their front pages. Therefore, Ford made a speech at Villanova University, on the Main Line, this afternoon; and tonight he will tape another show with Joe Garagiola (I'm being allowed to sit in on the taping of this one). The speech at Villanova combined several campaign goals: a stop in a Philadelphia suburb; a speech to cheering students in a field house (resonant, like enclosed shopping centers); and a Catholic audience. ("We need suburbs and we need Catholics," said one of the President's advisers. "I look at those kids and I see rows and rows of Catholics.") In his speech, the President attacked Carter for suggesting—in an interview with *Liberty* magazine, a publication of the Seventh-day Adventist Church—that there should be taxes on church properties (other than the church buildings themselves), a suggestion that Carter later backed away from, and said that we must find a way to ease the tax burden on parents who send their children to non-public schools. He also said: "It is not enough for anyone to say 'Trust me.' Trust must be earned. . . . Trust is not

being all things to all people but being the same thing to all people
. . . not cleverly shading words so that each separate audience
can hear what it wants to hear." After Villanova, a visit to the
residence of John Cardinal Krol, of Philadelphia, past president of
the United States Catholic Conference, was added to the schedule.
The Cardinal obligingly escorted the President to his limousine
after a twelve-minute visit, and the scene was duly recorded by the
television cameras. (Today, in New York, Jimmy Carter paid a call
on Terence Cardinal Cooke.)

At six-twenty-five, the President, as he did last evening in Chicago, drops in on the local news broadcast and takes a seat at the
anchor table. (Larry, the anchorman, announces, "Our guest, live
on Channel 6 tonight, is President Ford.") The President chats
with Larry for a few minutes, and then goes down the hall to the
studio where he is to tape the Joe Garagiola show. Garagiola, wearing glasses and reading a script, is practicing his running commentary and supposedly spontaneous remarks as a videotape of the
President's day is shown on a monitor. What appeared last night on
television to be a majestic Presidential seal on the wall turns out to
be a piece of cardboard suspended by two wires. The President puts
on a pair of glasses and watches. Edith Green is here, and so are
former Pennsylvania Governor William Scranton, now Ambassador to the United Nations, and the President's son Jack. As Garagiola rehearses, John Deardourff shuffles cue cards the size of large
posters on an easel near the center camera. One card says, HI, I'M
JOE GARAGIOLA. FOR THE NEXT HALF HOUR YOU'RE IN FOR A REAL
TREAT, etc. The videotape for today shows the President in Atlantic
City and at Villanova. Deardourff removes a poster that says AGRI-
CULTURE. LOTS OF FARMERS IN ILLINOIS—WHAT IS YOUR ADMINIS-
TRATION DOING FOR THEM? As they wait for the taping to begin,
Garagiola relaxes the President by making little jokes. Then the show
starts, and Garagiola, smiling, says, "Hi, I'm Joe Garagiola. For
the next half hour I think you're in for a real treat." He talks about
campaigning with the President, and remarks, just as he remarked
last night in Illinois, "It is an *experience.*" As the videotape of the
President's campaigning in Pennsylvania is shown, Garagiola reads
his script. We see Jack Ford visiting the Italian Market in Philadelphia. "My kind of neighborhood," Garagiola reads. Then we see the
scene in Atlantic City earlier today where, at a rally on the Board-
walk, Miss America, Dorothy Benham, dressed in a prim, navy-blue

coat, kissed the President. (The President was also presented with an honorary lifeguard certificate by the mayor of Atlantic City.) Garagiola reads, "I think Dorothy Benham, Miss America, loves Jerry, too." Villanova. "I mean, these young people at Villanova this afternoon are something else," Garagiola reads. "Not much question which candidate they're supporting." We hear the band there playing "Hail to the Chief." Then Garagiola, turning to the President and taking his cue from a card, says, "One-on-one really turns you on, doesn't it?" The President responds, "Politics is a one-on-one relationship, because if you don't feel some warmth and friendship with people, then you ought not to be in politics." The program continues in much the same vein that it did last night. Tonight, Ford takes a little more time stressing the difference between him and Nixon. It is almost as if he were running against Nixon. Maybe he should have thought of that before. Jack Ford says what a good fellow his father is. The card for Garagiola's question to Jack Ford reads, WHEN YOU'RE ASKED ABOUT YOUR FATHER, WHAT DO YOU TELL 'EM?

The Valley Forge Music Fair, Devon, on the Main Line. The President will have done a good bit of travelling back and forth on the Schuylkill Expressway before this evening is over. By appearing—for about fifteen minutes—at a Party fund-raising dinner in Philadelphia, Ford repaid a favor from the two men in charge of the affair, William Meehan and William Devlin, who run what there is of the Philadelphia Republican organization, and who last summer resisted the importuning of John Sears, Reagan's campaign manager, to help him out. Richard Schweiker, Ronald Reagan's running mate, has been making the rounds with the President today and tonight. Schweiker says that he has not spoken with Reagan since the Convention. As the President travelled about today, he sometimes stood up, through an opening in the roof of his limousine, and talked into a microphone to the crowds who have come out to see him in the brisk fall weather. A rally at the Plymouth Meeting shopping mall, where he appeared just before this stop, will also give him a scene for tomorrow morning's news programs. "We have just six days left," the President told his audience, in what he called "this Bicentennial election." He's doing all he can, and he's beginning to look very tired. This would have been a gruelling day even for a young man. Tomorrow, he goes to Indiana and Ohio, and on Friday to Wisconsin, Missouri, and Texas. This may not be a brilliant campaign, but there is something reassuring about it. Our elections are open, free. We can make our own mistakes. The President of the United States has a lot of advantages, but still he has to go to shopping centers and campuses. *The Stars of the Lawrence Welk Show* are playing at the Valley Forge Music Fair, a theatre-in-the-round, where another fund-raiser is being held. (On the way out here, I heard Lillian Carter, who is in Philadelphia, being interviewed on the radio.) The orchestra plays "Hail to the Chief," and the President comes down an aisle and goes to the stage. For once, there is no lectern. No politicians stand beside him. He is all alone there, holding a hand microphone, like an entertainer. He starts turning in a little circle as he talks, and I am worried that he will get dizzy, or that he will trip over the microphone cord, which from time to time he has to remove from underfoot. "I've never been to a political meeting where I occupied this kind of podium before," he says, and he suggests an "experiment." He suggests that the audience remain silent—not cheer—while he talks. And then he launches into the most astonishing performance I have ever seen him give. He delivers essentially the same talk he has been delivering the last two days, but tonight he delivers it quietly and naturally. He gets the hang of turning and of handling the microphone cord, and delivers his talk to the hushed theatre as if he were a polished actor. The theatre is dark and a spotlight is on him—the solid-looking man with the athletic build in the dark-blue suit, holding the microphone. The talk sounds a great deal better when he delivers it this way. "So then we started to move," he says, "and you could feel the new spirit that was generating in America." I can't help thinking how much better off he would be right now if he had talked this way during the debates. He says, "Wasn't that a wonderful experience for all Americans that we could celebrate our two-hundredth birthday with a rejuvenation, a rebirth, the spirit that our forefathers developed when they put this country together two hundred years ago?" As he talks, a perplexed-looking White House aide is off to one side holding the Presidential seal—seeming to be trying to figure out where to put it. "I want the kind of a society where the free-enterprise system makes it possible for any American who wants to work to get a job," Ford says. He's a man of some grace when he relaxes. Why hasn't he had the sense to talk this way before? He's doing the best he can in his job. He has some personal humanity, but he lacks vision—and sensitivity. He talks of the importance of military strength. He says, "Pennsylvania is a key state in this election." He closes by saying—almost pleading with them—"What you do between now and November 2nd when the polls close will make a significant difference in the third century of America's future. I know you won't let America down and, as the next President, I won't let you down." As he leaves the stage and goes back up the aisle, the orchestra plays "America, the Beautiful."

29

FRIDAY. The Philadelphia airport. Jimmy Carter will be arriving shortly, and Mayor Rizzo is here to greet him. On the latter fact could rest how Pennsylvania goes next Tuesday and who our next President will be. A crisis of some magnitude was set off with an announcement in yesterday's Philadelphia papers that Rizzo would not attend a rally that had been scheduled for Carter at noon here today. The rally actually was to be Carter's way of making up for declining to attend the Philadelphia Democratic City Committee dinner, starring Rizzo, on Wednesday night. When I was in Atlanta earlier this month, I was told that Rizzo was bringing pressure on Carter to appear but that the Carter people did not feel that Carter could afford to be seen in that sort of display with the controversial mayor. Mondale was sent instead. Among other things, Rizzo had been found to have a squad of thirty-three policemen operating out of City Hall, spying on his rivals, and his allies had shut down for six hours the Philadelphia *Inquirer,* with which Rizzo was in a court fight. Despite the efforts of the Carter camp to keep everyone happy, Pennsylvania's back-yard politics have tripped up the Carter campaign. (The Rizzo problem is not the only one. Rivals for future power in state politics are causing problems for the ticket in the western part of the state.) A few days ago, former Democratic Senator Joseph Clark and two other Philadelphians who, with Clark, had been leaders in the attempt to force the recall of Rizzo—the State Supreme Court ruled the recall off the ballot—held a press conference to announce that they had been invited to share the platform at today's rally. Rizzo, the authoritarian former police chief, would not hear of such a thing, and cancelled out. ("I wouldn't sit on a platform with their mother," one of Rizzo's allies said to me yesterday.) The trouble is that Carter needs to have Rizzo get out the vote for him on Tuesday, cannot afford for the Mayor to be miffed, and cannot afford for the Mayor's followers to think that he is miffed. Pennsylvania was crucial to Carter's winning the nomination, and now it is one of the states he needs in order to become President.

By spending yesterday in Philadelphia, I received some illuminating instruction in just why it is so important that the Mayor not be offended, and I learned some things I had never been taught in political-science courses in college. I recall vividly that when I was here in April, before the Pennsylvania primary, I attended a Carter press conference at which he held up a newspaper with a headline about a "stop-Carter" bloc that was being formed here—Rizzo and labor leaders were rallying around the candidacy of Henry Jackson—and said, proudly, that he was not the candidate of "the political bosses." It was one of many times when he said he was not predicating his campaign on political endorsements—which he was having trouble getting—and that evening he attended a dinner of the Americans for Democratic Action, where he was endorsed by Joseph Clark. Rizzo did deliver for Jackson, giving him the one county he carried in Pennsylvania. Rizzo, everyone agrees, can deliver. If he delivers two hundred and fifty thousand votes in Philadelphia to the Democratic ticket, it can carry the state. Not only is he popular in the white ethnic neighborhoods but he also controls most of the city's Democratic organization. That organization takes money raised at the annual dinner and passes it out to the ward leaders, who give it to the committeemen (there are two per "division," or precinct), who give it to "street workers" as "walking-around money" to get out the vote in each division. Some of the money gets pocketed along the way; some ward leaders raise and toss in extra money, to assure their successful delivery of the vote. My tutors in the niceties of Philadelphia politics tell me that about a hundred dollars goes to each division, with about two hundred dollars going to black divisions. (I am also told that such money can go, if need be, to *hold down* the vote.) Yesterday, I called on Buddy Cianfrani, the ward leader who came to my attention during the primary, and whom I saw campaigning with Mondale. We talked at the offices of the Democratic County Executive Committee, the headquarters of the Philadelphia machine. Cianfrani, a friendly, partly bald man who talks like a tough guy right out of the movies, explained to me, "The two committee people are charged with responsibility under the direction of the ward leader to give people service and get close to them, so that when the election comes around the voter will show him some courtesy in what he thinks about what person would be best for the needs of the community. If he's done a good job, they won't be undecided." Cianfrani added, "We've *always* delivered. It won't matter if there's a storm." He and one of his aides, who came into the room while we were talking, expressed some annoyance that Mayor Daley's organization gets more publicity than theirs. Cianfrani told me that the organization would continue to support the Democratic ticket but that the news that the Mayor would not attend the rally "confuses a lot of people." He said, "The Mayor enjoys a tremendous amount of popularity here. This laundry should have been washed a long time ago." A number of people are blaming the Carter campaign's outside coördinator for Pennsylvania, Joseph Timilty, of Boston, for the mixup over today's event. I asked Cianfrani what sort of job he thought Timilty had done. He replied, "I think it would be hard for Albert Einstein to come to Philadelphia and know what he's doing in a situation like ours." When I left, Buddy Cianfrani gave me a button. It has an American flag on a blue background, and the inscription RIZZO FOREVER.

And so yesterday, as Jimmy Carter was trying to become President of the United States, as the American people were trying to decide which leader was best suited to begin our third century with, the big question was whether Frank Rizzo would meet Carter at the airport. ("I'm going out of my mind," said a Carter advance man, whom I called to see what was happening.) Carter himself phoned Rizzo. And now Rizzo is here, as we await Carter's plane. He is a big, beefy man with slicked-down black hair parted just off center. His narrow eyes—they remind me of Spiro Agnew's eyes—look out over heavy jowls and a rounded, strangely soft-looking face. He strikes me as the sort of politician who should not be taken seriously but who builds a certain constituency and retains power by instilling fear. (Agnew was a similar type. Some have ruled nations.) Reporters ask Rizzo about the dispute. He says, "He's coming, I'm here, I'm supporting the entire ticket." Actually, I think this is working out rather well for Carter. Rizzo is making it clear he is still for Carter, and Carter doesn't have to be seen in public with him. Rizzo adds, "I wouldn't be found dead on the same platform with the people that led that recall." And he says, in his fashion, "They've had their way for a long time. Frank Rizzo is going to stop them dead in their tracks. After this election, I'm going to move the moves to disenfranchise them." He does not elaborate. Shortly before eleven-thirty, Carter's plane arrives. Rizzo gets on the plane, spends about ten minutes talking with Carter, leaves the plane, and disappears.

It's no trick to get a crowd for a noontime rally at Fifteenth and Chestnut, one of the busiest intersections in Philadelphia. Moreover, Chestnut is a fairly narrow street, so in the scenes of this on television the crowd will look all the more packed in. Notices of this rally were stencilled on the streets, leaflets were passed out, and sound trucks went through Philadelphia announcing an opportunity to see "the next President of the United States." The tall buildings surrounding this intersection house the First Pennsylvania Bank and Brooks Brothers. A few blocks away are garment factories. To assure a crowd, the garment-workers' union made a deal with employers that the workers would be given time off to come to the rally. Milton Shapp, the long-forgotten candidate for President this year, introduces Carter. Carter tells the crowd he wants to talk to it in "a very quiet, a very sober, and a very important way." He says that this morning the Commerce Department released indicators showing that "the economic news is bad." He cites the indicators—a rise in the layoff rate, rising unemployment. His voice is loud and clear over the loudspeakers, but the crowd is largely silent. He says that he will "put Americans back to work if you help me next Tuesday." Finally, the crowd cheers. "It's not going to be easy," he says. He has been urged to say this, to avoid giving the impression that he is overpromising. "The problem has been," Carter tells the crowd, "that too often government officials who get in office forget who put them there." He tells them, "When I began my campaign, not many people thought I had a chance," which is true enough. He points out that he comes from a small town, didn't have political support. "I ran for President just like you would have if you had decided to," he says, which is an improbable thought. He talks about how he and his wife and family campaigned all over America. "Now we have a tough fight," he says, and his tone changes a bit, becomes harder. He is speaking the truth. "The polls that are coming in now are up and down. . . . That means that every vote counts." He points out how close it was in 1960, when Kennedy barely beat Nixon. He says that if one more person in every precinct had voted for Hubert Humphrey in 1968, Humphrey would have been elected over Nixon. He says, as he said way back in New Hampshire, "I don't claim to know all the answers. I'm just an average human being, just like you are." (Some time ago he stopped saying, as he said there, that he will never tell a lie.) He says, "We have a spirit that began here in Philadelphia two hundred years ago, and it says, when the going gets tough, Americans get tough and get going"—thus wrapping together the Founding Fathers, Vince Lombardi, and Richard Nixon. He says, "I see a nation with a new vision," and he lists the visions of hope, unity, good education, families owning their own homes. "I see a government with balanced budgets," he says. He talks very fast now. It's sometimes hard to understand what he is saying. He says, as he has been saying all year, that "our system of government is the best on earth," that Watergate and other unpleasantnesses (C.I.A. activities, Chile, Vietnam, Bangladesh) haven't hurt it. He is still separating these problems from the people and even the government. It is as if they just happened. The crowd is not at all worked up. "I've been running for President for a long time," he says. "I don't intend to lose." He has been saying that all along, and people have long since ceased doubting him. He has simply been candid. He asks for the crowd's help in the next four days. That's all the time that's left. He, too, must give it his all.

St. Louis. The Northwest Plaza Shopping Center. 7 P.M. Carter's second shopping-center rally today—the first was in Toledo, en route here from Philadelphia. (As Carter left Philadelphia, he was presented by a Rizzo supporter with a six-foot pizza shaped like a peanut.) Ford was at this same shopping center thirteen days ago, and he was in St. Louis today. Yesterday, both candidates were in Cleveland. The two men, now strangely interdependent, following the same poll data, are hopscotching the country, often landing in the same place. In Cincinnati yesterday, the President made a statement about nuclear proliferation—an issue on which Carter had grabbed the initiative. The President's proposals did not go as far as Carter's but did go further than might have been expected, given the Administration's prior positions and the resistance within the bureaucracy to changes in nuclear policy. The final report had undergone many drafts, and did represent some intra-governmental compromises. Whether either candidate's proposals would actually prevent nations from fulfilling their desire to acquire nuclear weapons remains to be seen. Ohio is said to be extremely close. Logically, the election should not be this close, but one of the things that make politics interesting is that it is not logical. A President who is presiding over eight-percent unemployment, six-percent inflation, a slow economy; who was handpicked by Richard Nixon and who then pardoned Nixon suddenly one Sunday morning; a once dim figure who, as far as can be told, never crossed anyone's mind, including his own, as a Presidential possibility—this man appears to be within an eyelash of election. The essential problem for Carter seems to be that he has become the issue—just as his pollster, Patrick Caddell, predicted to me last summer that he would. Caddell said then that if Ford was the candidate, Carter would be the issue, because Ford would be seen as familiar, safe, while Carter would be seen as complicated, different, a risk. Carter's fumbling campaign has not helped him, and now, at long last, Ford has begun to hit his stride. On the other hand, Americans tend to vote for change from time to time—seem to consider that that's what the option to vote is about: the option to change. Carter has been advised, according to aides in Atlanta, to be very "positive" this week, to talk about the need for change ("We can do better"), and also to stress that there are limits on what he can do. The approach, one aide said, is to be "a modified 1960." He said, "Kennedy was blatantly idealistic. Jimmy has to tone it down, because people are skeptical now." It seems that for Carter the election can't come too soon.

As Carter travels about, his campaign is, of course, proceeding on several levels. The field organization is at work. Phone banks have been established in the swing states. Labor and other groups are making their efforts to get out the vote. Caddell is studying his poll data and forwarding them to the plane. (Atlanta s said to be very tense about how close the polls are growing.) Carter himself must get on the phone and assuage egos. He was informed, for example, that Muhammad Ali might endorse President Ford today but that Ali would be willing to receive a call from Carter. There are the back-yard politics: a stop in New Jersey this morning was cancelled because of the intramural squabbles there, and because Governor Brendan Byrne is so unpopular, largely as a result of the recent enactment of a state income tax, that it was deemed the wiser course to avoid sharing the platform with him. (Still, Carter reached three media markets today, and New Jersey was reached from Philadelphia.) Both candidates give local-television interviews at most stops. When Carter landed at St. Louis today, he had a brief meeting with some black ministers. The members of Carter's issues staff who fly around with him make suggestions on how to handle certain questions: he is being advised on ways to make his talk about the economic indicators more dramatic; he was advised (the advice was ignored) to avoid praising his choice of Mondale as his running mate in the presence of John Glenn during stops in Ohio. (The possibility that I saw last summer of tensions between Carter and Mondale in the course of the campaign has not come to pass. Mondale has done well, and Carter seems to recognize and appreciate that. Carter's ads now emphasize Mondale. But if Carter is elected and if his Administration proves as controversial as many people expect, Mondale could still find himself in some difficult spots.) The issues staff also works up releases for the press, hoping to provide it with fresh leads while the candidate gives speeches that vary little. This evening's release is about Carter's pledge to reform the postal service. Carter received a big break today when Eugene McCarthy was ruled off the New York ballot for good. The Democratic National Committee raised more than thirty thousand dollars to bring that about, on the theory that if McCarthy was on the ballot, it might tip the state to Ford. And, aboard the plane, Jody Powell puts out favorable poll data.

Tonight, Carter delivers his talk—essentially the same talk he has made all day—with a bit more feeling. Carter, like Ford, is moving cautiously, almost by rote, being careful not to make a mistake. Both candidates have learned that one ill-considered statement, one slip of the tongue can be devastating. Two years of work could go crashing if one of them should trip in the next three days. Carter has to hold on tight now. Ford is gaining on him. It is an odd thought that what Lyndon Johnson used to refer to as "the leadership of the free world" could ride on a single gaffe this weekend. It is a difficult thought that our choice may be made that irrationally. Watching these men go through what they are going through, one thinks about the effects on them: the incredible pressures they are absorbing, the enormous stakes for which they are striving. They are aspiring to ultimate temporal power. The process is both gruelling and exhilarating. Crowds cheer them and aides flatter them and all manner of advisers give them contradictory advice. One is President, and the other may be, and people treat them accordingly. Carter talks tonight, as he has talked all day, of how he and his family campaigned in homes, labor halls, shopping centers, barbershops, beauty parlors, restaurants, stores, factory-shift lines, farmers' markets, livestock-sale barns, county courthouses. All year, he has offered his dogged campaigning as a qualification for the Presidency. Both Presidential candidates, as they jet around the country, surrounded by retinues, are endeavoring to convince the voters they are men "of the people." Carter does a little variation tonight on a theme he has been stressing since early fall—that "it doesn't matter when we came to this country, what matters is why we came to this country." In an effort to be graphic, he says, "It's more like a mosaic, a beautiful painting with different kinds of colored spots on it." He is drawing respectable crowds now—that took some time—which is a tribute as much to the advance work and the fact that the election is near as it is to excitement about him. His speeches are an assortment of themes he developed during the primaries and this fall, with no driving theme or memorable point coming through. He is applauded—it is as if the audience knew that it should applaud after certain lines—but his listeners do not get particularly worked up. (The one time they do, invariably, is when Carter says, "It's not right for the average American who makes a mistake to go to jail and the big-shot crooks go free.") Carter talks to his audiences, but he doesn't really connect with them. There are two approaches to political audiences: the thoughtful speech and the pep rally. Carter doesn't really accomplish either. His rhythms are off. And he seems lonely. He appears on the platform with other politicians, but he doesn't seem to connect with them, either. He rides in the front of the plane, curtained off, talking with almost no one except Jody Powell and Greg Schneiders— young personal aides. The Carter group really does seem to feel that it has done all this on its own—and may well behave that way if he takes office. When I asked one top Carter aide earlier this fall about all the help they were getting from labor, he replied, "We don't owe anybody anything." The political leaders who endorsed Carter in June, he said, "came in in the last of the ninth." Labor, for its part, seems to be going into this on a wing and a prayer. Ford's policies and his inaccessibility to labor could no longer be stomached, and so labor is giving Carter help and hoping that this means some commitments to it, and is also prepared to fight him if necessary. ("If he tries to merge the Commerce and Labor Departments," a labor official said recently—a frequently proposed reorganization—"we'll destroy him.") Anyway, labor's real strength is in the Congress. There is a line between being so bogged down in political obligations as to be paralyzed and feeling so free of them as not to be able to get anything done, either. Or feeling so free as to assume one can pretty much do as one likes. Governing does require collective action. It remains to be seen how good Carter—a loner—is at that.

Jim King, the Carter campaign-trip director—planner of events, guru to advance men, shepherd to the press, campaign humorist, and wise political head—has prepared a manual for advance men which shows how little of what we in the press entourage observe, and how little of what comes over our television screens, is left to chance. It combines some of the classic advancing wisdom, distilled over the years, with King's particular insights. It includes such time-honored principles as "Never select an auditorium or meeting room larger than you can fill" and "Be wary of any hall seating more than two thousand." As a rule, it says, there should never be more than ten dignitaries on the platform with the candidate. Other strictures: Be careful to schedule filing time for the press. Arrange the candidate's TV tapings at the beginning of his stops, when he is "freshest." Allow time for the candidate to shake hands at the airport, thus giving the press time to board its buses; the Secret Service requires that the motorcade take off as soon as the candidate is in his car (a vulnerable spot). Don't organize a welcoming crowd at the airport: "You need those fans elsewhere." The candidate is to travel via a largely unpublished route (for security) and to be visible only for a few blocks (to build a crowd at the designated spot). The science of crowd-building is spelled out: leafleting (use high-school students), including where to leaflet and how to leaflet ("SMILE"); literature drops; telephone campaigns; posters; sound trucks; media (radio spots are recommended during certain times —prime or drive or housework—on country-music stations, and in the late evening "on the teenybopper stations"); how to call in to a talk show and ask when the candidate is coming and then call in and answer; and so on. Further instructions include: Organize car caravans to bring people to the event. "Bend every effort in advance to assure a 'base crowd' through clubs and groups, groups making good cheering sections." Cook up stunts to catch the eye of the public and the local press (hold press conferences to introduce the entertainers who will precede the candidate; run pretty girls around town on an old fire engine). There are instructions for the bands ("School or union bands, please!"), which should play "bright, happy music" before the candidate arrives. Signs: "Home-made signs are best." Arrange at least one large "Welcome to . . ." sign in front of the crowd "to remind the candidate where he is." Decorations. Ticker tape. Even the applause and the cheering. The instructions on "organizing 'spontaneous' cheering" are: "Don't leave enthusiasm to chance. Plan in advance to sprinkle your crowd with cheerleaders and claques. They must start clapping, chants, cheers, and even songs when the candidate arrives and after appropriate lines during his moving through a crowd and/or during his speech. . . . Scatter your core supporters in clusters throughout the audience. Instruct them to cheer loudly and often; this will warm the rest of the audience to the occasion."

OCTOBER 30

Saturday. Today, the Carter campaign has been to Tulsa, Oklahoma (where Carter landed, addressed an airport rally, held a brief meeting with a newspaper editor and a state politician, and took off again); New Orleans (where he rode through the French Quarter in a parade, complete with jazz bands and doubloons struck specially for the occasion); and McAllen, Texas, near the Mexican border (where he addressed a rally of Mexican-Americans). The day's campaigning will finish tonight in front of the Alamo—seemingly as obligatory a stop for politicians as the Liberty Bell—and after this he will fly to Dallas. (Ford was in Houston today, where John Connally appeared with him. Connally seems to be giving Ford more help than is Ronald Reagan. Both appear to have their eye on the Republican Party, and odds are that neither would be heartbroken if Ford lost.) Carter should be able to carry Texas, but it is very close here. The turnout of Mexican-Americans could make the difference. As we left St. Louis this morning, Carter's staff issued a release that said that in 1973 Ford, in a letter to a historian, described the Truman Administration as "one which smacked of scandal and extreme partisanship." In New Orleans, the staff released a statement attacking Ford's tax proposals. In Tulsa, Carter gave a bit more stress than usual to his thought that "I believe the United States ought to be a working country, and not a welfare country." And, for what seemed like the first time, he made a fairly persuasive argument about the cost of unemployment to the middle class. I wonder why he doesn't do that more. He told his Tulsa audience (which was got out to the airport in the chill early morning with the help of the teachers', oil workers', and machinists' unions) that "we need to deregulate the price of natural gas." Elsewhere, he has said that only five percent of it should be deregulated. In New Orleans, he said, "I got my education at the U.S. Naval Academy," and said, "I know the first responsibility of the United States President is to guarantee the security of our nation." He continued, "The Number One thing I am going to insist on is a strong defense. The South has always believed in strong patriotism."

In his efforts to cope with the pressure to avoid offending any particular constituency—to win one constituency but do it in a way that does not lose another—he has painted himself opaque. There is nothing wrong with a politician's shading what he says so that audiences in different parts of the country or representing different constituencies know that he understands what is on their minds. It is something else for a politician to say contradictory things (is Carter's Number One priority jobs, inflation, or defense?) or to drop little promises better left unheard elsewhere. In retrospect, one of the earliest stories we heard about Carter this year—about how he led different groups in Iowa, where he was to undergo his first political test, to believe that he had different views on abortion—is significant. At the time, it was hard to tell. The real question is, as it has been all along, what Carter's campaign means in terms of governing. Clearly, he intends to try to do some fresh things, and he has led us to believe that his policies would be more compassionate than those of his predecessor. There is every indication that he means it when he expresses his determination to try to reorganize government, to bring more openness to it, to try to break up the "sweetheart arrangements" and "revolving doors" between the regulatory agencies and the regulated, to pardon draft resisters. What we still don't know about—and won't until (if he is elected) he has tried to govern for a while—are his vision, his impulses, his sense of proportion, and his reaction to frustration and opposition, of which there will be quite a bit. The indications are that he is a stubborn man and does not take opposition very well.

Carter reminded his New Orleans audience—gathered in Andrew Jackson Square, near the St. Louis Cathedral, and standing on wrought-iron balustrades along the surrounding streets, on a pleasant, sunny Saturday afternoon—that he would be the first Southerner elected President since Zachary Taylor, in 1848. He talked about his determination to have a balanced budget by the end of his first term. (He said that his family and business budgets were balanced, which makes him sound quite Republican.) In New Orleans, he was introduced by his wife, an obviously strong, determined woman, who made the case for him. Formerly a very shy woman, she has worked up an effective little speech about her husband—praising his virtues ("He is a good, honest human being capable of leading our country"), decrying waste in government ("simply unbelievable"), and saying why we need him ("Our country is leaderless, we need a leader")—which she delivers with spunk and polish. Carter does try to reach for idealism, saying, "I see ahead of us a nation with a new spirit," and talking of "a country with your help that can live up to the dignity of the Constitution." (Other times, he talks about "the majesty of our Constitution and the simple decency of the American people.") Afterward, Carter was presented with a pumpkin on which a likeness of his face was carved.

I talked with Jody Powell on the plane between Tulsa and New Orleans. (Carter, as is now his wont, had slipped on a gray cardigan sweater and was taking a nap on the couch, around which a curtain was drawn.) Carter often seems tense and tightly coiled; the appearance of relaxation seems an act of will. What human being would not be tense in the situation he is in? He has bent his all for years now toward one prize; whether or not he wins it will be decided very shortly. The policy of no appearances after 7 P.M., which Greg Schneiders tried to establish earlier this fall, never went into effect, but its enunciation did have the effect of cutting down Carter's schedule. Now Carter gets more sleep than he used to, and keeps to a more closely controlled schedule. When he gets to his hotel room, he makes phone calls (invariably, one is to his wife), eats lightly, reads the memorandums that have been given him. According to his aides, he still reads a chapter of the Bible, in Spanish, every night. My guess is that he really does; that it is a way of finding peace and continuity amid all the tension and chaos of a campaign—a process in which serenity is almost impossible. A certain tension remains between Carter and the press—beyond that of a candidate who must be on guard and a press corps that must watch carefully. He has never really worked out relations with the press, though this was something that could have been done. The press is wooable and winnable (Mondale has wooed and won it), especially by a candidate who may well succeed. Carter and Powell have complained about the press coverage, saying that it tends to stress the *faux pas* rather than the substance, and they have a point, but they had better get accustomed to a certain amount of that. If

Carter is elected, will he and his aides understand that the magnification process is certain to continue, and that churlishness on their part could be very damaging? What the press sees as its role is to be on the lookout for inconsistencies and misleading statements, and why shouldn't it be? Carter's circle is critical of reporters who criticize the candidate, and this suggests that it may not really understand the role of the press—suggests something beyond the normal paranoia of politicians.

I asked Powell why he thought the election had got so close—what he thought Carter's essential problem was. He was fairly candid in his response.

"The problem all the way through the general election is that we never really did and still haven't set up a unifying theme for the general election," he said. "Without that, everything we did seemed to be a discrete event. It contributed to the diffuse nature of this campaign."

I asked him how that had happened.

"Partly because I didn't do my job right," he replied. "We thought we had a unifying theme in this leadership thing—that Ford is not a leader. In fact, we should have seen ahead of time that that was too narrow. It didn't cut. Also, we missed a lesson we should have learned from Jerry Brown—the thing about overpromising and skepticism. We've started to deal with that, but it's so late it might not have an effect on the election. We're including it in our final television spots." (Another aide says, "The partisan theme is one that has to be used subtly, and we didn't use it subtly. We beat people over the head with it. Saying 'Vote for me because I belong to the same party as Roosevelt' was unsalable." Some aides think one problem is that the summer months were not used sufficiently to plan for the fall. "We fumbled the national presentation," one says. "What you saw was one of the most elegant primary campaigns and one of the most inept fall ones.")

I asked Powell how Carter had got himself in the position of overpromising.

"I don't know," he said. "Part of it was responding to the cries to be specific and programmatic. Part of it was some things we said in the primaries—reorganization, welfare reform, and all that. It helped us in the primaries that people thought Jackson overpromised and Jimmy didn't."

Powell continued, "It's taken us a long time to figure out how to handle Ford—how Jimmy Carter should handle Ford, which is more complex. We kicked him a little bit, we patted him a little bit—none of it seemed to work. Maybe the way to do it was humor, but Jimmy has a tendency to deliver a line that should be funny in a way that sounds serious."

Then Powell talked about another problem that candidates encounter: a lot of conflicting advice from well-meaning aides and advisers. "He was getting political advice from the issues people; issues advice from the political people; press advice from the organizing people; organizing advice from the press people. Everyone thinks he's an expert on press relations. Jimmy sort of got overloaded."

Hubert Humphrey's last trip to Texas in 1968 included a stop in McAllen, and Democrats felt that that turned Texas around for him. Robert Strauss had urged Humphrey to make that stop, and he urged a similar one on Carter this year. And so Jimmy Carter went there today. A record number of Mexican-Americans are registered in Texas this year, and their votes could determine the outcome in the state. A long line of mayors of the little towns of the Rio Grande Valley were at the airport to greet him, as were Robert Strauss and his wife, and Luci Johnson Nugent. Carter hugged Mrs. Nugent, who stood stiffly. About fifty people were on the platform at the rally in McAllen's Archer Park, Jim King's strictures notwithstanding, and State Senator Raul Longoria went through an interminable list of introductions while, in front of the stand, the advance man for the event was in agony and kept motioning for Longoria to get on with it. All sorts of Texas V.I.P.s were there, several having arrived in their own planes. Strauss, who worked hard to get the Johnson family to show forgiveness to Carter for his insult to Lyndon Johnson, read a telegram from Lady Bird Johnson, who managed to be out of the state. Then Luci Johnson Nugent made a pointed and moving little speech, in which she endorsed the Democratic ticket headed by a man who, in the *Playboy* interview, had called her father a liar and a cheater. (She said that her father, "despite disappointments, stood steadfast to the Party to the day that he died," and that "my husband and I are voting, as Daddy did, Democratic.") She didn't endorse Carter, but he seemed grateful for what he could get—that she had permitted herself to be used even to that extent. As the other speeches went on, Mrs. Nugent seemed to be fighting tears. Strauss, for his part, was mopping his brow in the midday south Texas sun. The advance man muttered, "I'm not sure I can take three more days." Carter managed a look of amusement. What else could he do? He was stuck. He does not seem to smile the broad smile as much as before—it's as if he were trying to contain it, knowing it has been caricatured. Carter has one big smile and two little ones. There is the little one that appears and then gets turned off suddenly. It does not seem real. Real smiles fade. Carter has another little smile, a sort of half smile, that suggests genuine amusement or pleasure. One does not see it very often.

Finally, Carter got a chance to talk. He said many of the things he had been saying elsewhere, and when he talked about a balanced budget the Mexican-Americans cheered, as if on cue. I wonder how important a balanced budget is to them. Carter also said, "Lyndon Johnson was a man with a big heart. He gave our people human rights, he gave our people civil rights. He gave our people good Medicare, good Medicaid; he gave our people better education." (Asked at the San Antonio airport by the waiting press what he thought was the most serious mistake of his campaign, Carter replied without hesitation, "I think the most serious mistake was making a statement that distorted completely my feeling about President Johnson.") It appeared that to that particular audience Carter was a Kennedyesque sort of figure, and they cheered him with more emotion than I'd heard any other crowd cheer him. At the end of his speech, he was given a great black-and-silver Mexican hat and a colorful serape. I went with the pool reporters, who stayed close to Carter this afternoon, and as he worked the crowd I watched people grab at him, pushing, shoving, eager to touch him, and Carter and the Secret Service working to free his arms and enable him to keep moving. In the plane on the way to San Antonio, Luci Johnson Nugent was seated with Carter, who talked to her animatedly.

Today, the Harris poll puts the race at forty-five percent Carter and forty-four percent Ford.

The Alamo, San Antonio, Texas, Saturday evening. To my astonishment, the Alamo is smack in downtown San Antonio, hard by the National Shirt Shop. (One of my closest friends is from San Antonio, and I can't imagine why she never told me this.) I had always pictured it as out in a field, with plenty of room for people on horses to gallop around. It's a rather odd national shrine, actually, symbolizing one of the more imperial streaks in our history. Tonight, Carter waited to go onstage ("held," in political jargon) in "the long barrack"—the low outer building of the Alamo, where most of the fortress's defenders died. It was dark by the time we reached here; the sun set in the big Texas sky as our motorcade came in from the airport. (The advance man told me he was up till two this morning lighting the Alamo.) A mariachi band is playing. Again, people grab at the candidate as he makes his way among the crowd and up to the platform. Again, Luci Johnson Nugent makes her speech, not seeming quite so defiant this time, and Robert Strauss looks pleased with his work. It is a cool evening. A half-moon has risen over the Alamo. It is a rather small stone building, with a crescent-shaped façade. Still, Carter looks small as he stands in front of it to make his speech. "As we stand here tonight in front of this historic shrine, which demonstrates bravery," he begins, and then he says much of what he has said before. About how it doesn't matter when we came to this country. About how our system of government is the best on earth. There was some thought given to his making a special speech tonight, but Carter is sticking to what he has tested and is used to. He doesn't seem to like to make formal speeches. He talks fast again, and the response is rather flat. He talks about Lyndon Johnson again. "It's time for a change in the White House," he says. Maybe we've run out of new rhetoric. Again, he adapts to where he is. "There is no reason for our nation to be mediocre or weak," he says. "There is no reason for us to have a defense capability second to any on earth." (Ford, in April, running then against Reagan, came here and said much the same thing.) In following the campaign for the Presidency, I don't think I have heard anything about reconversion of parts of the economy from military to civilian purposes. A paper from the Carter campaign on the subject came across my desk, but I have never heard the candidate mention it, or read that he had mentioned it. I have even less indication that Ford has gone near the subject. Neither man has talked about those young blacks in Detroit—or anywhere. That would have been impolitic. Neither has talked about the Third World (at least, that I heard). That would have been impolitic, too. Both candidates have ultimately engaged in majoritarian politics, the goal being to win. One candidate may have been submerging these subjects in order to win; the other hasn't seemed to have any thoughts on them to submerge. These people are asking for enormous power. It is fashionable now to say that Presidents can't do much, because of the checks on them and because of the conflicting interest groups. They may be limited in what they can accomplish on the hard questions—social issues, changing the economy, urban organization—and on cutting through the selfish nature of just about all of us, on getting beyond immediate interests and their own political futures. But still they have enormous power. They can affect the civility of our discourse, our domestic harmony. They can start a war. I think that people are getting a little hesitant to entrust this power to Presidents. It has been—in recent, vivid memory—abused, internationally and domestically. We were lied into a war, which it was all too hard to get out of, and our Constitutional system was treated as a mere plaything. The terms—"Vietnam" and "Watergate"—don't get across the depth and impact of that experience. People are correct to be skeptical about conferring great power. They are supposed to be skeptical. That's what the framers of the Constitution had in mind. We may, indeed, as a result of recent history, be getting closer to what they had in mind.

The candidates are virtually automatic men now, somnambulistic, going through rituals. What they see must be a blur and what they say is largely programmed. Two fallible mortals—very fallible—at the end of a long, long process that seems to be somewhat beyond them. It is beyond almost anyone. No one is prepared for it. Trying to stay afloat amid conflicting constituencies, a staff that is full of contradictory advice, the confusions of local politics, a press corps that is ready to fall on a single slip—I doubt if they could stand it much longer.

Carter does his "I see a nation" litany, and talks, as he has lately, about how the results of the 1960 and 1968 elections might have been different. "If just one person in every precinct had voted who didn't go to the polls for Hubert Humphrey, we would never have had Richard Nixon as President," he says, "we would have had a good President to carry on the tradition of Lyndon Johnson." He says, "The next three days—Sunday and Monday and Tuesday— might be the most important days in your life." They are in his. "I love every one of you," he concludes.

At the Dallas airport tonight, Carter stands—as is his wont— holding his own suit bag (a common touch), and talks to a minicam that is reporting live. Another chance at television exposure. His face looks thin and tired. He is asked what he thinks has brought him this far. He replies, "I think I have a natural and accurate sense of the hopes and aspirations of the American people. I think I understand their deepest concerns, and I have a closeness with them, I think, that will stand me in good stead Tuesday and make me a good President if I'm elected." He is asked if he is tired. "No, not much," he replies. "I feel better now than I did when I began the campaign. It's become a routine for me. I've been campaigning every day for twenty-two months."

30

Washington. The election, at long last, is tomorrow. Good weather is predicted around the country, which is good news for Carter. The Gallup poll puts the percentage at forty-seven for Ford, forty-six for Carter and, like the Harris poll, says that the election is "too close to call." But pollsters also say that most of the undecideds are Democrats. Tonight, Carter appeared in Flint, Michigan, with Mondale, and Ford appeared in Grand Rapids, without Dole.

In Detroit, General Motors posted a notice on a bulletin board that some jobs might become available, and more than five thousand people showed up. Not nearly that many jobs were available.

The New York *Times* reports today from Paris that at least a third of the world's industrialized nations are in financial trouble, and that "an air of gloom is spreading over prospects for the world economy." It says that the poor nations of the developing world are also in bad financial shape, with some hundred and thirty-five billion in debts. The dialogue between the rich and poor nations is still going on in Paris after ten months, with little progress. Britain, like Italy, is facing a severe economic crisis. "Virtually everyone is living on credit, " the *Times* reports, and it adds that "some bankers, businessmen and government officials in Europe are worried that the whole system may crack."

Similarly, little progress has been made since the World Food Conference meeting in Rome in 1974 set the goal of abolishing hunger within a decade. Lester Brown, president of Worldwatch Institute and an expert on food problems, recently wrote, "A moderately successful grain harvest this fall may lull world leaders into a false sense of security over the world food situation." A goal of the conference, the establishment of world food reserves in case of famine, has not been carried out. The recent world harvest is about what it was in 1974, but at the same time the world population has increased by about a quarter of a billion people. Our Department of Agriculture has resisted setting up the food reserves.

The Carter campaign made a number of last-minute moves to try to nail down a victory. Yesterday, Carter himself called Rizzo, Daley, and New York's Mayor Abraham Beame. (Last week, he called a number of other political leaders around the country.) Hamilton Jordan had called some of the political leaders over the weekend, and also some of his own troops. There was a morale problem building, what with the narrow, and even negative, polls coming in. But while the people in Atlanta were busy bucking people up, they were themselves getting very nervous, having that sinking feeling that the election might indeed be slipping from them. They asked whether Hubert Humphrey, just out of the hospital after a cancer operation, could make appearances for them in Pennsylvania. He was unable to, but before leaving the hospital he had made some radio tapes, which were rushed into the state. Tapes were made by black leaders to counteract the church incident. (A squabble had arisen over an attempt to integrate Carter's church in Plains, and several blacks rallied to Carter's aid, as they had at crucial points all year.) Carter did reach Muhammad Ali, who even offered to fly to California on Carter's behalf. The news about the Gallup poll was broken to Carter carefully. Jordan reached Powell just as Carter and his entourage arrived at their Sacramento hotel Sunday night, after an appearance in San Francisco with Jerry Brown, and suggested that Carter not be told about it until the morning. Campaign aides were sent from West Virginia to western Pennsylvania, and from Tennessee to southern Illinois. Labor is hard at work—especially in Ohio, Pennsylvania, and Connecticut. It may be working harder for Carter this year than it did for its friend Humphrey in 1968. The Democratic National Committee sent "street money" into Maryland, and money into Florida, Virginia, Louisiana, Ohio, New Jersey, and California.

Tonight, the campaign struggle was transferred to a contest between the two camps' image-makers, in half-hour shows presented back to back on all three networks, at staggered hours. Carter's is called *Ask Jimmy Carter*. Carter looks very Presidential sitting in a gray suit behind a desk in his book-lined study in Plains, and he gets at the heart of what he thinks has been his problem by explaining, in his characteristic manner, that during the primaries "I had a close, personal, individual, direct relationship with the people of this country" but that during the fall campaign "that's the kind of relationship that was disturbed"—by the crowds, the press, the Secret Service. What does he think it's going to be like if he's President? And so, he says, the show tonight—he calls it a "show"—will demonstrate individual people "in a direct person-to-person relationship with me." After a little talk—effectively presented—in which he says some of the things he has been saying in his campaign ("The problem is not that people have lost confidence in the government, the problem is that public officials, once they got in office, lost confidence and trust in the people who put them there"), we see what are supposed to be just folks stopped in the street, asking Carter questions. The footage is edited in a way to suggest that Carter is answering them from his book-lined study. One of the questioners is the girlfriend of one of Carter's television advisers. Some of the questioners look down as they talk, as if they were reading. Carter is asked about jobs, about welfare, about taxes. It's very slick. He addresses his questioners by name, and looks folksy and accessible and responsive; and, of course, his answers can't be challenged. He is asked by an elderly person what he would do for the elderly (appoint "a full-time counsellor just speaking up for elderly people"); what he would do about foreign aid (he says, as he said in New Hampshire living rooms, "I'm tired of seeing the poor people in this rich country taxed and the money sent to the rich people in the poor countries"); by a man in Houston how much he would cut the defense budget ("I'm trying to cut out waste and he's [Ford's] defending waste"). A farmer asks about farm policy, and a woman asks what he would do if his wife were offered a job (he talks about how much his wife and family have campaigned, and says that it has made them closer and that "in bringing our family together with a mutual understanding of what our country is, I hope we can bring the country together in the next four years"). And then he gets up and walks around to the front of his desk and leans against it and reiterates some more of his campaign themes: about how the American people have been "turned off" in recent years (he offers himself as the healer); about the need for "tough, competent management of government" (he seems to understand that if he was to get anything done as President, people would need to believe that competence was being applied to government, and that some reorganization is necessary, but he may have underestimated how resistant the problems, the bureaucracy, and the interest groups would be); about how "we need to have someone going to Washington who is not a part of that establishment, who hasn't been there for the last twenty-five or thirty years, to root out unnecessary programs." He says, "The promises that I've made have been very cautious"—he knows this is not true, but it is part of the last campaign thrust—"and I'm going to keep them." We'll see. And he ends as he has ended countless times all year—by saying that we can "prove once again that we still live in the most wonderful country on earth."

The President Ford show begins with Joe Garagiola and pictures of Air Force One. This might be the first election that was won by an airplane. Then Pearl Bailey endorses Ford ("Oh, he's made some mistakes, honey, you better believe he has"). Then we see another shot of Air Force One, and see Ford accepting the Party nomination ("Hail to the Chief" plays in the background), followed by scenes from the Fourth of July, including the Tall Ships, and the President ringing the bell on the flight deck of the U.S.S. *Forrestal*. The President has tried to appropriate the Fourth of July after all. Why couldn't he have left well enough alone? There are other scenes that have been appearing in the ads—the childhood pictures, the Eagle Scout badge, the football team, Yale ("Gaudeamus Igitur" playing in the background). The Voice out of "March of Time" tells us about these things. It gives the documentary—the commercial—a strangely old-fashioned flavor. The Second World War scenes. Vietnam-war scenes, and scenes of anti-war demonstrators—as if we were to think he opposed the war. Pictures of the Ervin hearings! Voice: "In those troubled times, a distressed nation was stirred by a new and candid voice." The President being sworn in and saying, "Our long national nightmare is over." The aides telling us how nice he is. Pictures of him working hard. Voice: "America started back to work." Unemployment is substantially higher than it was when Ford took office. Scenes of plenty: potatoes bouncing, grain being poured from an elevator. This is very slick propaganda indeed. Pictures of Air Force One banking into a turn. The President meeting foreign leaders. *Kissinger* getting off a plane after the Mideast settlement. Films of weapons firing. Voice: "The America of Gerald Ford is secure, idealistic, and mature." The America of Gerald Ford? Family scenes. Voice: "Gerald and Betty Ford are a love story." There is even material about Betty Ford's mastectomy. Anything goes. The

White House heralds, blowing their horns, on the White House veranda. I somehow thought they had disappeared with Richard Nixon. Edith Green vouches for Ford, and then his son Jack does. Brass bands. Marines marching. A lot of militarism in this ad. The theme song: "There's a Change That's Come Over America." Voice: "Gerald Ford—a man of strength, a decent man, a man America can trust." Ford, for the second time in this film, telling the Convention, "You are the people who pay the taxes and obey the laws." More Air Force One. And then the President, dressed in shirt and vest, sitting on Air Force One—the new throne, the flying throne—gives a little talk. "Tonight, America's strong, America's free, America's on the move," he says. He seems a bit hoarse, and it's hard to hear him over the sound of the plane. "I pledge to you that the United States will remain Number One," he says. "The best tax reform is tax reduction," he says. Air Force One is shown banking again. The chorus swells: "I'm feeling good about America." Pictures of fields, rivers, mountains.

NOVEMBER 2

Election day. A beautiful, clear day. There seems to be an unexpected upbeat feel to it, and it invites unexpected thoughts. We *are* free. We did get rid of a crooked, dangerous President, and we ended a wrong-headed war. Both took all too long to do, but, acting as a free people, we did it. Election Day is something we share—it's the one communal act we have. All over the nation tonight, people, many of them gathered in parties, will watch the same television reports. And, as this election ends, it is anything but dull. Even now, it is not clear who will be our next President. (Four years ago, at noon, an ashen-faced Washington lawyer stood in the doorway of the Federal City Club and said, to no one in particular, "Is everyone ready for the disaster?") And this year, as we look back on it, was anything but dull: the unknown political figure emerging from Georgia; the down-to-the-wire race for the Republican nomination, capped by a tumultuous Convention; a horse-race finish to the final election. We have become accustomed in recent years to living, in our civic lives, at high intensity. Any time we choose a President, it isn't boring. The campaign wasn't uplifting, but I have a feeling that that is a more relative statement than our memories tell us, or than we care to admit.

There are predictions that it will be a long night. Four years ago,

John Chancellor called Nixon the winner a few minutes after seven. The networks have become cautious as a result of the experience with the Wisconsin primary this year, when ABC and NBC called Udall the winner of a primary that Carter won. Whoever wins tonight won't have much of a mandate—not just because the victory may be narrow (Kennedy's was narrow, and so was Jerry Brown's in California) but because the public does not seem to be in a mandate mood. It is more skeptical and questioning. I think either President—and especially Carter—will be watched carefully. Too many people—including politicians—have been burned by giving loyalty and credence to Presidents. Carter has no deep ties with many of those with whom he will have to work if he is to govern. Whoever wins will be facing very hard—almost intractable—problems. The sorts of problems they didn't talk about much. And, inevitably, as the final decision neared, those problems receded further and further from our consciousness. What was right in front of us became reality. But the problems—the collapsing cities, the continuing racial tensions, the increasing claims on diminishing resources, the rising demands of the developing nations, the spread of arms and nuclear capabilities—are all there, and are getting harder.

By six-thirty tonight, CBS, NBC, and ABC have all awarded Kentucky to Carter and Indiana to Ford. No surprises there. When I travelled with Carter earlier this fall, he stood at the Indianapolis airport with Vance Hartke. Hartke is losing badly and is already counted out. There were reports today that the turnout may have been very large after all. There is nothing that the candidates can do now. They have to sit there, like the rest of us, and wait. A lot of other people have a great deal at stake tonight—especially the investors in power, whose careers and fortunes ride on whether their candidate wins. James Thompson is winning big in Illinois, and is already being set up as a Presidential candidate. So was his predecessor, Daniel Walker, a Democrat who didn't even survive this year's primary. About eight-thirty, John Chancellor gives Florida to Carter. Carter has also won West Virginia and South Carolina. So far, the South is sticking. Florida is where Carter, in accordance with long-nurtured plans, scored his first big win over George Wallace. At eight-thirty-three, Walter Cronkite gives Texas to Carter. His trip there was worthwhile. Now, at eight-fifty on ABC, Lou

Harris says that the turnout wasn't much higher today than it was in 1972 (when it was fifty-five percent, the lowest since 1948). Paul Sarbanes has won the Senate seat in Maryland. Ford has won Kansas and Connecticut. Edward M. Kennedy wins reëlection to the Senate from Massachusetts, of course. He might have been elected President—and he knows it. Even if Carter wins, other power centers within the Democratic Party will remain intact. The interest groups that made their contributions to Carter will ask for their due—and if they don't get it, they will fight him, and they will have very strong allies in Congress. Edmund Muskie is reëlected to the Senate. He actually thought the nomination might come to him this year. Within a few hours, Carter could be the President-elect.

Nine-thirty. The big states are coming in. Ford is ahead in New York and New Jersey; Carter is ahead in Pennsylvania, Illinois, Michigan. It's too early to call them. We aren't told what parts of the states these returns are from. At ten-thirty, Carter gets Missouri. Both candidates were there last Friday. Carter has also won Louisiana. It now appears that this election will indeed be very close. Murray Chotiner, an adviser to Nixon from the early days of his career, used to say that if you lose an election, you should lose big—that that's far preferable to sitting around afterward thinking of all the things you should have done differently. The TV analysts say Carter isn't doing as well as he should—as a Democrat should—with Catholics or Jews, but that he is way ahead with blacks. Ford has won Oklahoma; Carter's stop in Tulsa on Saturday morning didn't win it for him.

Midnight: The calculations are becoming complicated. If Ford wins New York and California, and two out of three of Michigan, Illinois, and Ohio, he wins the election. But then if he loses Iowa he loses—unless, that is, he wins Oregon. And then, again, if he wins Texas and Ohio and loses New York, he still wins. A telephone report from Atlanta: The Carter camp is very tense. A few minutes later, the networks are saying that New York is fifty-fifty. (Daniel Patrick Moynihan has won election to the Senate as a Democrat from New York.) Hubert Humphrey, Henry Jackson, and Lloyd Bentsen—all of whom wanted to be elected President this year— have been reëlected to the Senate. Marilyn Berger, of NBC, reports from the White House that the President has lost his voice completely. At twelve-fourteen, NBC gives New Jersey to Ford. Carter did not survive the state's back-yard politics. It is very odd to sit here still not knowing who our next President is going to be. Jody Powell is on television, looking subdued. "We feel cautiously optimistic at this point," he says.

At twelve-thirty, NBC gives New York to Carter. That would seem to do it. Still, according to NBC, Carter has only two hundred and eight of the necessary two hundred and seventy electoral votes. NBC gives Michigan to Ford, and Illinois is 50–49 Ford-Carter. Ohio is 49–49. Maine is 49–49. The Democratic-Republican ratio in the House will be virtually unchanged, and the Senate ratio is not changing—both will be heavily Democratic. Ford is clearly carrying the Western states, and he and Carter are battling over the industrial states and some Southern ones. Ford gets Virginia. Rizzo delivered a margin of two hundred and fifty thousand votes for Carter in Philadelphia. The money to the ward leaders did go out. According to a telephone report, Daley has told Robert Strauss and Atlanta not to worry—Carter will carry Illinois. It's nearly 2 A.M., and in state after state the vote is either tied or within one point. It's not absolutely out of the question that the candidates will be tied at two hundred and sixty-nine and it will go to the House of Representatives. Ohio and Illinois, stubborn Midwestern states, are still out. NBC says that in the twenty-two months of his overt race for the Presidency Carter made 1,495 speeches in 1,029 cities, that he travelled 461,240 miles. Ford has won Iowa—where Carter, coming in second, after "Uncommitted," with the vote of ten percent of the state's Democrats, began it all. South Dakota, where Carter toured Hans Sieverding's farm, is still up in the air. So is Oregon. Oregon just doesn't seem to be Carter's state.

At 3 A.M., Walter Cronkite says that U.P.I. has put Carter over the top. But the networks are holding out. NBC gives Hawaii to Carter. That gives him two hundred and sixty-five electoral votes. Ford is ahead in Illinois by one point, Ohio is dead even, and Carter is ahead in Mississippi by one point. Mississippi—over which Ford fought Reagan and then Carter. Ford campaigned there in September, and Carter arranged to get James Eastland and John Stennis and Aaron Henry together on a platform there. Now only Mississippi, Illinois, Ohio, or California has enough electoral votes to end it. At three-thirty, John Chancellor gives Mississippi to Carter and says that he has been elected. All that campaigning in Ohio and Illinois is now moot. One minute later, ABC elects Carter. At three-forty-six, CBS joins in. At the World Congress

Center, an exhibition hall in Atlanta next door to Carter's hotel, a country band plays "Happy Days Are Here Again." Carter did it. He'll be our thirty-ninth President.

Robert Schieffer, of CBS, reports that Ford has gone to bed—that he did so before the last projections. That gives him time. And then Jimmy Carter, the President-elect, makes his way to the stage. He is wearing the familiar navy-blue suit. There are lines under his eyes. His family and his campaign aides are on the platform with him. At shortly after 4 A.M., he starts talking to the crowd and those of us who are still awake. He calls Ford, as he did toward the end of the campaign, "a good and decent man." He says, "I pray that I can live up to your confidence and never disappoint you." The shift from foot to foot. The slight drawing in of breath. "Sometimes in the past we've been disappointed in our government," he says. "But I think it's time to tap the tremendous strength and vitality and idealism and hope and patriotism and a sense of brotherhood and sisterhood in this country to unify our nation, to make it great once again." He says, as he has said all year, "I don't claim to know all the answers," and he adds, "I'm not afraid to take on the responsibilities of President." He looks genuinely happy, as well he might. He had said that he wanted the Presidency more than he had ever wanted anything else in his life, and there was no reason to doubt that. He drove himself without mercy. And then he got it—barely. He said countless times that he did not intend to lose, and he did not, but he had to have had some very anxious moments. And he concludes, "I love everybody here." And then, after a moment, he returns to the microphone with an afterthought. "It's been a good campaign," he says. "It's going to be a good Administration."

NOVEMBER 3

I awoke (late morning) to hear over the radio that the President is in his office discussing with his aides what to do, and that there is some thought that he should not yet concede. We waited for Nixon, too, in 1960. I also remember that when, on that morning after, one of Nixon's aides was asked what Nixon was doing, we were told that he was upstairs explaining the Constitution to his daughters. Carter has won Ohio, by only a few hundred votes thus far. Ohio went Democratic, after all. Ford has carried Illinois, California,

Oregon. Daley didn't deliver. (Rizzo did.) Carter is leading in New York by two hundred thousand votes. It appears that Eugene McCarthy cost Carter Oklahoma, Maine, Iowa, and Oregon. If he had been a little stronger, he might have cost Carter the election.

Shortly after noon, on television, the President comes into the pressroom to concede. His family, who, like Carter's, were an important part of the campaign, are with him. The familiar Presidential seal, which travelled all over the country with him, is on the lectern. The President, barely able to speak, says that he has called Carter, and then asks his wife to read a telegram he has sent him. And so Betty Ford reads slowly, with what seems to be a gritted-teeth smile; this is obviously hard on her. The telegram says, "Dear Jimmy: It is apparent now that you have won our long and intense struggle for the Presidency." All those people standing there tried so hard. Ford's face seems to show his own struggle now to hold back tears. The long strain, the fatigue, capped by the disappointment, are almost too much. One can't help feeling for him. It's a graceful telegram. "As one who has been honored to serve the people of this great land . . . I believe that we must now put the divisions of the campaign behind us and unite the country once again in the common pursuit of peace and prosperity." Then Ford goes down from the platform to shake the hands of the press. His daughter, Susan, is in tears. It ends for Ford where it began—in the White House. I remember his doing the same thing—going down to shake hands with the press in the pressroom—after he was sworn into office under those very bizarre circumstances. It can be said for him that he tried—that he did the best he could within his limits. Incumbency almost saved him. But now Ford is suddenly a two-year interim President.

On returning to Plains early this morning, Jimmy Carter, also exhausted, and overcome by the sight of his loyal townsfolk waiting for him, broke down in tears, as did his equally disciplined wife. Tonight, the scene is on television, and they look more human than we have ever before seen them. At last, they could let go. Carter says, "I came all the way through, through twenty-two months, and I didn't get choked up, until I . . ." And then he bites his lip and reaches for his wife. "Until I turned the corner and saw you standing here, and I said, people that are that foolish— we couldn't get beat." And then we see a second scene in Plains, where Carter responds to Ford's concession. We're very good at transferring power. "I deeply appreciate the President's call and his gracious expression of congratulations and coöperation," he says. "I look forward to working with President Ford and others like him, who, even though divided by partisan affiliation, are united by common devotion to this country and the well-being of our people."

INDEX

ABOUT THE AUTHOR

ELIZABETH DREW, who has been a journalist in Washington for seventeen years, has won the Award for Excellence from the Society of Magazine Writers and the Dupont-Columbia Award for Broadcast Journalism. In 1976 she was selected for the first panel of questioners in the Presidential debates. A regular contributor to *The New Yorker,* her articles have also appeared in *The New York Times* and *The Atlantic,* for whom she was the Washington editor for six years. Her pieces have been published in some thirty anthologies. Her book on Watergate and the impeachment process, *Washington Journal,* published by Random House in 1975, has been called "a brilliant evocation" of the period, and "unquestionably the best book yet on Watergate, and conceivably the best we will ever get."

In addition to her work as a writer, Ms. Drew is a commentator for the Washington Post–Newsweek stations, and often appears on nationally televised public-affairs shows. From 1971–73, she hosted her own television interview program on the Public Broadcasting Service. Born in Cincinnati and a graduate of Wellesley College, she has been awarded honorary degrees from Yale and Hood College. In 1977 she received the *Ladies' Home Journal* award as Woman of the Year in Communications.